PERSEPHONE

GÜNTHER ZUNTZ

PERSEPHONE

*Three Essays on
Religion and Thought in
Magna Graecia*

OXFORD
AT THE CLARENDON PRESS
1971

Oxford University Press, Ely House, London W. 1

GLASGOW NEW YORK TORONTO MELBOURNE WELLINGTON
CAPE TOWN SALISBURY IBADAN NAIROBI DAR ES SALAAM LUSAKA ADDIS ABABA
BOMBAY CALCUTTA MADRAS KARACHI LAHORE DACCA
KUALA LUMPUR SINGAPORE HONG KONG TOKYO

PRINTED IN GREAT BRITAIN
AT THE UNIVERSITY PRESS, OXFORD
BY VIVIAN RIDLER
PRINTER TO THE UNIVERSITY

PER TE CHE SAI

CONTENTS

BOOK TWO: EMPEDOKLES' KATHARMOI

BOOK THREE: THE GOLD LEAVES

DETACHED NOTES

LIST OF PLATES

Note. The Plates do not represent an atlas of the objects discussed in the text. A few basic items apart, they aim to illustrate what is not easily found depicted elsewhere. For an intelligent reading of the first part of Book One, J. D. Evans and Bernabò Brea are indispensable, and likewise Langlotz-Hirmer and von Matt for the second— as a minimum; see also p. 71 n. 6, p. 90 n. 1–4, p. 91 n. 3, and the Bibliography.

Figs. 1 and 2 on pages 8 and 24 are reproduced from J. D. Evans, *Malta* (Thames and Hudson) and Fig. 3 on page 172 from *Notizie degli Scavi di Antichità*, 1913, *Supplemento*.

BOOK ONE

THE GODDESS OF SICILY

ϹΠΕΙΡΕ ΝΥΝ ΑΓΛΑΙΑΝ ΤΙΝΑ ΝΑϹΩΙ
ΤΑΝ ΟΛΥΜΠΟΥ ΔΕϹΠΟΤΑϹ
ΖΕΥϹ ΕΔΩΚΕ ΦΕΡϹΕΦΟΝΑΙ

PART I

THE ANCIENT GODDESS

I. INTRODUCTION

THE prehistoric section of the Museo Archeologico in Syracuse is alive
to this day with the spirit of the great Paolo Orsi, who arranged its contents—the fruits, to a large extent, of his own immense labours—in
a manner which makes the silent past of Sicily rise before the mind of the
visitor. In the 'Sala 4' he may find his attention held by the crude but
powerful carvings on two stone-slabs[1] (these, too, discovered by Orsi)
which, for more than three thousand years, guarded the entrances of
graves cut into a steep rock at Castelluccio, some twenty miles inland.
The visitor will at once observe that these slabs are decorated, in the
main, by two pairs of large spirals placed near their corners and connected
by a central bar, and he will feel that their arrangement does not suggest
a merely decorative purpose. This pattern in its crudeness and irregularity, on the battered, heavy, ancient stone, seems agog to speak; its
silent appeal holds you like the eyes of an animal behind the bars of its
cage. You look again, and you notice that, on one of the slabs, the lower
pair of spirals is not elaborated, its place being taken by two solid discs,
which are connected by upward bars merging into a pointed tip, while
the central bar is vertically split and continues out-and downward, like
a pair of legs bent at the knees.

These are symbolic representations of the ancient goddess of Sicily. Her
essence is conveyed by the four-spiral-slab; the other intimates her
agency: the representation on it is of a phallus penetrating the vulva.[2]

The act of begetting depicted on the door of the grave! To grasp the
meaning of this symbolism we turn, first, to the neighbouring islands of

II. MALTA AND GOZO

(a) THE TEMPLES

For there may indeed be one or two Sicilian relics of similar relevance—
we shall return to them—and there is a further vast set expressive of the
same ideology, but it is in Malta that this ideology became explicit.

[1] See Plate 1.

[2] Mrs. D. Burr Thompson told me that, on seeing the slab, the same interpretation had
forced itself upon her.

I believe that Malta was, throughout a millennium, an *isola sacra*[1]—allowed to remain inviolate so that its people might devote themselves to the cult of a godhead which was worshipped far and wide, and particularly also by the inhabitants of nearby Sicily.

He that visits Malta in our days will find—as long as the vanity of the age has not finally swamped also this rock—that the life, thought, and effort of its inhabitants are centred on religion as radically as hardly anywhere else within the orbit of our civilization. They are poor; their houses are of the skimpiest, their fare meagre. But every village boasts a church—and most of them more than one—which in size, splendour, and attendance would easily be a match for a cathedral in our parts. These churches, whether old or new, retain the fixed style of past centuries; they are the prime concern and the pride of the people, and especially the women.

It must have been so four thousand and more years ago, when the islanders built, with the most primitive tools, those monumental places of devotion whose ruins now stud both Malta and Gozo. It is unlikely that the sites of all of them have been identified; the very fact that fair numbers of them remain close to each other—Tarxien and Kordin; Ħaġar Qim and Mnajdra; Ghain Tuffieha, Mġarr and Skorba; Ġgantija and Santa Verna, etc.—makes it unlikely that other districts could have been without them. Moreover, at all of the places mentioned there stood, not one but two, three, or even more of these structures. In many instances it is evident that they were built at different times; it is no less evident, though, that as a rule they were in use simultaneously, for there are connections from one building to the next and alterations designed to fit them together; moreover, many of them have been repeatedly refashioned and modernized, and often (Ġgantija, Kordin, Tarxien) one large façade gives access to more than one building. There must then have been large crowds both to build these places and to worship at them—a fact underlined by the vast elliptic piazzas preserved in front (e.g. Ġgantija and Tarxien) and also between some of them (Ħaġar Qim, Tarxien).

The islands are likely to have been more fertile in those days than now;[2]

---

[1] T. Zammit, *Prehistoric Malta* (1930), p. 132 ('the holy island of neolithic faith'); similarly C. F. C. Hawkes, *The Prehistoric Foundations of Europe* (1940), p. 154; cf. J. D. Evans, *Malta* (1959), p. 158.

[2] It stands to reason that soil-erosion had not had its pernicious effects in the early days of man's presence on these islands. To the arguments adduced by Evans (p. 37) I would add one drawn from the much-discussed 'cart-tracks' found in the rocks all over Malta and Gozo (Evans, p. 189). Their profusion as well as the frequency of parallel and neighbouring ruts seems to exclude the assumption that they could have been designedly cut (even if traces of the pick-axe should really have been discerned at some few points); it becomes understandable if, at the time of their origin, the rocks were generally covered by five or ten inches of soil. The first 'slide-car' dragged over it would impress its trace into the soil; others following would naturally and conveniently use these traces; by and by, they would penetrate to the rock underneath and cut into it.

they could thus have supported a comparatively large population. Even so, the erection and maintenance of these numerous, stupendous constructions could only have been possible, if the whole energy and productivity of the people were centred on it. Their individual persons, so one would infer, counted for little or nothing—apart from their contribution to this service. This inference would be in agreement with the fact that very few traces of their habitations have been found; presumably they lived in light huts or also in caves (as was customary until recent times and persists, in a few places, to this day); a few such have been discovered.[1] And even with this assumption the achievement of these islanders seems to border on the impossible. One would therefore like to assume that their resources, limited on any count, were augmented by contributions from neighbouring lands; as Delos was supported by dedications from many sides, and as was Malta itself in those later days when the bulk of its classical churches were built. This latter assumption, it is true, is poorly supported by the fact that very few relics from this period testify to connections with other countries. There are however a few such; we may be able to suggest one or two more, and in any case these contributions, if any, could have been of a kind which would leave no traces; for example by active help, or contributions of victuals and woven materials.[2]

Throughout many centuries, then, and perhaps for a thousand years, the islanders devoted all their efforts to the erection of ever more, and ever more perfect, 'temples'. This designation is not unreasonably applied to these monuments; they were not graves like most of the megalithic structures throughout Europe, for no burial has ever been found in any of them, nor, obviously, could they have been designed for human habitation, like the Sardinian *nuraghi*. But this designation must not prejudice our concept of their meaning and purpose—which may emerge with the attempt at visualizing them in their original shape.

This shape is, strangely enough, the same throughout—and it is unique; structures like these exist nowhere else on earth. These unknown people seem to have been dominated by one supreme vision which they strove to express in stone, and they appear to have achieved it after a comparatively short time of determined quest and trial. Once the intended form had been attained, it was elaborated with ever greater precision and refinement, but it was never changed.[3]

The prime characteristic of this architecture is the absence of straight lines (excepting passages and the trilithon-framing of doorways and

---

[1] Cf. Evans, pp. 156 f. 'Irregularly' shaped traces of buildings at Kordin and Tarxien have been suspected, on uncertain grounds, to have been habitations, perhaps of priests (cf. *BSR*, vi (1913), 35 and Zammit, p. 39).

[2] Evans, pp. 63 ff., 73 f.   [3] See Pl. 2 and p. 8, Fig. 1.

shrines). Nor, on the other hand, is it based on the circle, as are so many megalithic structures, from Mycenae to Los Millares and Stonehenge. It is essentially curvilinear. The shapes effected by the curves are customarily described as 'bays', or 'apses', extending from a central court, but this description inverts the true balance of these buildings; for the 'bays' are their dominant feature and the 'courts' little more than their joins and connections.[1] Moreover, this description tends to obscure the evident interrelation between the earlier and the final forms—the so-called 'trefoil' or 'clover-leaf' plan (as at Skorba, Kordin and, probably, also at Mġarr and, once, Mnajdra[2]) and the 'standard type' consisting of 'two pairs of lateral chambers and a rear recess issuing from a central court'.[3] Anyone who has walked through these ruins will, I expect, agree that their essential feature is the large oblong, whose shape might be likened to that of a broad bean or a kidney, with an apse issuing from its long side opposite the entrance; in the developed type a second, and larger, transversal oblong is placed in front of the first and connected with it by a short and narrow passage, while the apse opposite tends to shrink until, finally, its place is taken by an elaborate shrine (e.g. Ġgantija-North and Tarxien middle temple).[4]

He who walks through these ruins, overgrown with flowers, gleaming under the southern sun, may conceive a very deceptive idea of their original character. Wherever their outer walls survive to an appreciable height, the stones of the upper layers progressively overhang inward in the manner used for corbelled vaulting. A complete corbelled dome is out of the question on foundations of the shape and size of, at any rate, the larger Maltese temples; even so, this feature is proof that they were roofed, and the preserved models as well as the extant imitations of this kind of hall in the Hal Saflieni hypogeum show that, above a certain height, the remaining, narrowed opening was covered with long beams.[5]

They also show that, in proportion to their size, these halls were not high.[6] And they were dark: there is no hint and no possibility of a window

---

[1] This fact, though, stands out correctly in the descriptions by earlier students, such as A. Mayr (e.g. in *Reallexikon der Vorgeschichte*, vii. 358) and T. Ashby (e.g. *BSR*, iv (1913), 6).

[2] If, that is, the trefoil temples there have been correctly and completely reconstructed.

[3] Thus e.g. Evans, pp. 96, 110, 115 and, earlier, Hawkes, p. 153.

[4] Only at Ġgantija-South is the first oblong smaller than the second; Evans is very likely right in suggesting (p. 98, after *Proc. Prehist. Soc.* xix (1953), 57) that it was added to an original 'trefoil' plan. The impression that the middle temple at Tarxien had a third oblong in front of the other two is deceptive, for the third is actually an elaborate 'forecourt' between this and the neighbouring Western temple (cf. Evans, pp. 124, 134).

[5] Cf. Evans, pp. 126 ff. and Pls. 15, 20, 29, 30, 77.—I cannot suppress some doubts with regard to the carving (ib., Pl. 76) of a façade very like that of Mnajdra incised on an inner wall at Mnajdra. What motive could make a worshipper reproduce the façade inside the temple? Could it be, rather, the work of some modern enthusiast? Many visitors, alas, have left their marks on the temptingly soft stones of the Maltese monuments.

[6] If the reconstruction (Evans, pp. 114 f., Fig. 19 f., after Ceschi) of the Tarxien façade

anywhere, and very little light could penetrate through the long and narrow entrance passages—which, besides, were closed by heavy doors. Moreover, I take it that all these 'temples' were covered with earth mounds[1] (excepting, of course, the façades)[2]—as is the rule with megalithic structures; even though most of them have been laid bare in the course of time. To some extent, most of the Maltese ones are thus covered to this day, the space between their outer walls and the surrounding wall being filled in. These fillings are, I suppose, the remainder of the original, complete covering; above the actual buildings it has been carried away by wind and rain—and by the excavators.[3]

These must then have been very considerable artificial hills; though nothing like the enormous tumuli at e.g. Sardis or St. Michel (Morbihan) or New Grange (Ireland). Technically, these mounds (resting against the outer walls surrounding the temples) served to fortify and contain the buildings underneath;[4] but their significance is not merely technical. It has to be considered in connection with the fact that the buildings themselves—all of them, as far as I can see—are strenuously, purposely sunk into the ground. Ġgantija, Ħaġar Qim, Mnajdra are dug into sloping hillsides which, at their rear, rise considerably above their floor-level; Tarxien, on level ground, has been cut into the rock.[5]

These mighty and elaborate buildings, then, were kinds of caves; artificial caves in artificial hills, deeply united with the Mother Earth. And these carefully planned and laboriously executed structures; this masterful interplay of curves and vaults achieving, in the final stages— Mnajdra—a *raffinement* which calls to mind late-baroque designs; the blood-red hue of most of the walls and ceilings and the bright white plaster on others;[6] the abundance of décor enhanced, no doubt, by strong colouring; the bewildering profusion of chapels and altars, images and

is taken for the basis of a tentative argument, the interior would have been less than 20 feet high (I assume the roof-beams to have rested on the widest course of horizontal blocks). The width of the first oblong hall is 65 feet. By contrast, the height of the 'Treasury of Atreus' is 40 feet: nearly as much as its diameter (for this calculation, I have deducted the three courses which Ceschi added to the model of the Tarxien façade on which his reconstruction is based).

[1] This was mentioned as a possibility already by T. Zammit and T. Singer, 'Neolithic Representations of the Human Form', *Journal of the Royal Anthropological Society*, liv (1924), 68.

[2] The courses of blocks above the widest one of the Tarxien façade (Evans, Fig. 19) were designed, I assume, to retain the mound on this side; as did the surrounding wall on the other sides.

[3] Cf. below, p. 395, Detached Note II.

[4] The same purpose has been discerned e.g. in the stone-rings surrounding Etruscan tumuli and the graves at Murgia Timone near Matera (M. Mayer, *Molfetta und Matera* (1924), p. 248), and also at New Grange.

[5] The level was raised again by repeated reflooring (Evans, p. 122; Pl. 27); the essential fact, to the builders, apparently was in the foundations being inside the natural ground.

[6] Pieces of red wall-plastering have been found in several places; white is mentioned, from Tarxien, by Zammit, p. 30.

dedications, doorways, barriers, passages and recesses: all this became visible only in the uncertain flicker of candles and torches![1]

A kind of cave . . . a very particular kind. He who entered them entered, in the most precise sense, into 'the bowels of the earth'. These buildings reproduce, in a fixed symbolic form, the body of the Great

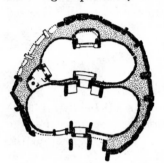

Mother; as medieval churches reproduce the cross of Christ (with infinite symbolism in every detail), and the Mesopotamian zikkurat, the successive storeys of the universe up to the abode of the gods. The reader whom this fact does not strike as immediately obvious is invited to glance at the ground plan of any one of them (see Figure 1). This, I expect, will easily convince him that the so-called 'trefoil' signifies the womb of the Mother (its rear-bay—no doubt the cultic sanctum sanctorum—intimating the rest of her body, per-

FIG. 1: Mnajdra, the middle temple

haps the head), and that in the final type the womb is represented by the larger, first hall; the nurturing breasts, by the second. Everyone recalls 'idols'—Aegean, Trojan and others—which, on a small scale, express a similar concept by a similar symbolism.[2]

These are, so far, assertions and suggestions; they call for elaboration and confirmation.

(b) ANALOGIES AND ORIGINS

The Maltese 'temples' are currently designated as megalithic structures and it is today almost commonplace to regard all megalithic monuments (all, at any rate, from Northern Europe to Spain and, again, from the Canaries to Syria and Palestine) as testifying to this very concept: the devotion to the Great Mother, the Earth, as the giver and preserver of life. This view is not lacking some basis of facts. For one thing, symbolic representations of a female deity are found in, or in front of, monuments

---

[1] Lamps had been invented in late palaeolithic times (cf. H. Kühn, *Ipek*, xx (1960–3), 89), but since none has been found in the Maltese temples, they appear not to have been used there.

[2] See e.g. A. Evans, *The Palace of Minos*, i (1921) 48, Fig. 13; V. Müller, *Frühe Plastik in Griechenland und Vorderasien* (1929), esp. Figs. 19 (Crete), 29, 44–8 (Cycladic), 142, 153, 155 (Troy); B. Goldmann, in *Ipek*, xx (1963), Pls. 5. 6, 6. 10–18, 7. 19–28, 8. 34 (Ras Shamra); in particular, the outline of the neolithic figurine, in greenstone, of a seated goddess found at Malthi in Messenia (N. Valmin, *The Swedish Messenia Expedition*, i (1938), Pl. I) and, closely similar to it, that of the 'goddess of Philippopel' (below, p. 29, n. 5) could almost represent the ground-plan of a Maltese temple. The analogy of the typical Maltese statues is—for good reasons (below, pp. 49 f.)—far less close. For earlier views, similar to those here suggested, concerning the Maltese temples see G. von Kaschnitz-Weinberg, *Grundlagen*, i. 74 f. and the literature quoted there.

of this kind, at least in Spain and France. Such representations, though, are frequent also in parts where no 'megaliths' exist, e.g. in Hungary, the Balkans, and neolithic Greece; while, on the other hand, 'megalithic' structures occur with shapes so various as to suggest wide varieties of ideology and purpose. What indeed could be more different than are, for example, the shapes of Stonehenge and the Maltese temples![1] And yet, these two have this at least in common: they are not graves, as are almost all other megalithic structures. This negative feature does not establish more than a vague and superficial analogy between them (and some few others such as Avebury and Carnac); on the contrary, their radical difference serves to stress the need to look elsewhere for positive and significant analogies to illumine the Maltese monuments.

Perhaps one ought not to classify them as 'megalithic' at all.[2] It is, of course, true that they—nearly all of them[3]—are built of 'large stones'; that at least the outer, surrounding walls of e.g. the Ġgantija and Ħaġar Qim consist of enormous irregular blocks, and that settings, side by side, of upright slabs (such as line many passage- and gallery-graves) occur at Kordin, Ħaġar Qim, and Mnajdra. But already the Ġgantija façade consists largely of fairly regular layers of large, horizontal ashlar blocks, and this regularity increases in the subsequent buildings, culminating in the beautiful precision of the stonework at Mnajdra and Tarxien. This, surely, is not megalithic art in the sense of the word which applies to

[1] An attempt at demonstrating a 'near relation' and 'close resemblance' between these has actually been made by G. Sieveking (in *Vanished Civilisations*, ed. E. Bacon (1963), p. 321 and *ad* 'plates' 23–4); which, to me, seems plain perversion. It is true that the so-called 'trilithon' occurs in both; unavoidably so, one may hold, where a doorway had to be built of large blocks; at Stonehenge, though, their structure and use are quite different. The 'horseshoe' there is not comparable, in shape or function, with the Maltese entrances, nor with the 'bays' (which anyhow are not formed by 'trilithons'); and there is less than no 'resemblance' between the English circular place of assembly, open to the sky, and the wholly differently shaped and mystery-laden caverns in Malta.—G. von Kaschnitz-Weinberg (*Grundlagen*, i. 40 with Figs. 36 and 37) offered a more impressive analogy by confronting a plan of the Ġgantija with that of one of the tombs at Carrowkeel Mountain in NW. Ireland; the similarity, however, seems to me accidental and insignificant. Not only is the Irish monument rectilinear throughout; it is, moreover, only one of many varieties of the 'gallery grave' (for instances of 'bays' jutting out from their 'passages' see e.g. Glyn Daniel, *The Prehistoric Chamber Tombs of France* (1960), pp. 118 and 156: a type non-existent in Malta and Sicily). If the Maltese 'temples' are to be compared with, or even derived from, tombs—on this point see below, pp. 47 f.—the reference surely ought to be to typical local tombs and not to an untypical one in a distant country.

[2] It is sometimes asserted that 'megalithic graves' exist in Sicily and Malta, and this assertion has to serve as a connecting link in theories aiming to account for the spread of a 'megalithic religion' from Egypt, or elsewhere in the Near East, to Western and Northern Europe. It should therefore be stressed that no graves of this type exist in either Sicily or Malta and indeed no megalithic structures at all in Sicily (for one would do too much honour to the very recent habitation of a Sicul chieftain at Pantalica, to the modest so-called 'Temple of Diana' at Cefalù, or to the still more recent, tholos-like, rock-cut tombs at Sant'Angelo Muxaro, if one were to class them as 'megalithic').

[3] For exceptions (especially at Mġarr) see Evans, pp. 85 f.

monuments in Western and Northern Europe.[1] It is a telling fact that the
most characteristic of megalith structures, the 'dolmen', is absent from
the Maltese 'temple-culture'; it is, in fact, the outstanding mark of the
later, 'Borg-in-Nadur' immigrants. The achievement of the 'temple-
builders' finds its counterpart around the Aegean—five centuries, and
more, later: in Troy VI, Boghazköi, Knossos, and Mycenae. For contemporary, and older, work of the kind one has to look to Egypt.

This (and very much else) follows when the indications of Carbon 14
tests, however upsetting, are duly accepted: they make the Malta temples
five centuries, and more, older than J. D. Evans had taught us, relegating
them to the third millennium.[2] Any dependence, however suggestive,
upon Minoan and, especially, Mycenaean models is thus excluded,[3] but
the Maltese monuments are not thereby thrown back into a haze of
primeval primitiveness. They now stand out as nearly contemporaneous
with the great civilizations (anything but primitive) of Sumer and the Old
Kingdom in Egypt; and the recent, breathtaking discoveries of Near
Eastern archaeology—Jericho, Çatal Hüyük, Haçilar, to mention only
a few household names—have opened up vistas, chronological and
material, which play havoc with the accepted prehistorical terms of 'neolithic', 'chalcolithic', and 'bronze-age'[4] and show Sumer and Egypt as
the summit, rather than the beginning, of a millennial effort.

The repercussions of this effort stand out to the east (Mohenjo-daro,
Harappa) and west (Sahara, Spain, Balkan) of its Near Eastern centres.
On the vexed question of the origins of the 'megalithic movement' I hesitate to pronounce. They have been sought in Egypt by, among others,
O. Menghin and W. J. Perry. However this may be, if any outside
inspiration for the Maltese masons' work is sought, I see no other conceivable model than the Egyptian. Besides, one marked feature of Maltese
art could well be traced to the same origin: namely, the characteristic
posture of all of the standing idols, with the right arm hanging down while
the left, from the elbow, lies across the chest; this posture is typical of
female Egyptian statues of all ages. It is not quite unknown, though, in

---

[1] Glyn Daniel, *The Megalith Builders of Western Europe* (1958), p. 18, reasonably seeks to dif-
ferentiate between 'megalith' structures proper, consisting of upright slabs, and 'cyclopean',
with horizontal courses. The difficulty remains that often, as in Malta, both forms occur
together and, in addition, the use of both rough and shaped blocks.—G. von Kaschnitz-
Weinberg, *Grundlagen*, i. 12 ff. considers the tendency towards the upright monumental and
phallic as the primary megalith characteristic, to which the expression of the horizontal and
motherly, of Eastern origin, joined itself (ib., pp. 35 ff.) towards the end of neolithic times—
an analysis which may meet with chronological difficulties. On this basis anyhow the Maltese
monuments ought not to be called 'megalithic' at all.

[2] D. Trump, *Antiquity*, xxxv (1961), 300; ib. xxxvii (1963), 302. Oddly enough, we are thus
brought back to the view which was current thirty or fifty years ago (on the vague assumption
that they were 'stone-age monuments').

[3] Certain features which are widely held to presuppose Cretan prototypes will be considered
in due course.   [4] J. Mellaart in *Anatolian Studies* (hereafter *AS*) xiv (1964), 114.

the Mesopotamian orbit;[1] and if the Maltese masons and sculptors really benefited from Egyptian achievements, their dependence would seem to have been confined to the technical sphere; for the fundamentally geometric and rectilinear character of all Egyptian art is the strict opposite of the Maltese, nor are the religions by which either was inspired in any way comparable.

Analogies with Sumer, on the other hand, are not confined to technical features but apply to a whole set of interrelated and essential characteristics. 'Man was created for one purpose only: to serve the gods'; accordingly, the greatest effort of the communities, physically, economically and artistically, is spent in their service. Enormous temples are erected; temples with recesses containing altars and a sanctum sanctorum with image, altar, and a (lower) offering table at one of its small sides, and with statues of priests and worshippers 'in eternal attendance'. This summary applies to Sumer[2] as to Malta—and where else in the third millennium? Add that, as opposed to the Egyptian, the Sumerian style of statuary is essentially sphaeroid—reducible to curves, that is, and not to planes.

The most striking single illustration of this set of analogies is given with the figure of a priest which T. Zammit found when excavating, in 1916, the middle temple at Tarxien.[3] There were in fact two, and possibly three or even four of them, but since they were made of very lightly baked clay, only fragments of them could be preserved. One figure, though, could be almost completely reconstructed[4] and we have the excavator's word that they all were of one and the same type. This type Zammit (using the terminology of his day) described as 'Chaldaean'; since then, we have been given the evidence which entitles us to say that it is strikingly similar to Sumerian representations of worshippers—and, so far at least, to no other type. With his flounced skirt from the waist down—the typical attire of the Sumerians[5]—and with his hands clasped on his chest, in the Sumerian attitude of reverence, he specifically reminds one of the 'shaven priest' found by H. Frankfort in the temple of Anu at Tel Asmar[6] and

[1] For examples see V. Müller, pp. 90, 93, 100, 204, and Figs. 175, 327 and 365 (these two, though, are late), 357–9 (Elam).

[2] This much, I suppose, may still legitimately be asserted, even after the previously current, exaggerated notion of a Sumerian 'theocracy' has been incisively criticized by I. M. Diakonoff (as reported by S. N. Kramer, *The Sumerians* (1963), pp. 75 ff.).

[3] Zammit–Singer, pp. 76 and 94 f. (nos. 38–41) and Pls. XII f.; Zammit, p. 96 and Pls. XXVI. 9, XXVII; Evans, p. 145 and Pl. 60. [4] See Plate 3a.

[5] S. Langdon, *Archaeologia*, lxx (1918–20), p. 146 with Fig. 4 shows that the Sumerian skirt ('kaunakes') was worn also in neighbouring Elam.

[6] H. Frankfort, in *The Oriental Institute of the University of Chicago, Communications*, xix (1935), Figs. 63 (centre) and 66; id., *The Art and Architecture of the Ancient Orient*, Pls. 13 and 17; the same, plain kind of kilt (with no indication of sheepskin fringes) also e.g. in A. Parrot, *Tello* (1948), p. 57, Fig. 14 and p. 96, Pl. VII, and in many figures on the Ur 'standard'.—One of the other Maltese figures wore 'a plain skirt, with the line along which the garment overlaps

of the 'worshipper' now in the museum at Istanbul.[1] We may add two minor parallels of detail; namely, the animal friezes on, or near, the altar in the left-hand apse of the first temple at Tarxien,[2] and the ground-plans and models, in clay, of buildings.[3] Animal friezes, of course, are a most typical feature of Mesopotamian art (for the oldest times, reference may be made to the lowest register of the alabaster vase found at Uruk[4] and to the friezes of bulls (in copper) and cattle (inlay work) on the temple of the Mother Goddess at El Ubaid);[5] architectural plans in baked clay, too, have been found in Sumer,[6] and one may recall the one on the lap of one of the many statues of Gudea of Lagash.[7]

These agreements in matters fundamental and incidental can, to an extent, justify the description of Malta, with C. F. C. Hawkes,[8] as 'an early outpost of Eastern religious culture'; but it would be rash, in this context, to equate 'Eastern' and Sumerian, for the similarities just noted are countered by fundamental differences. The facial types represented by Maltese statuettes are entirely different from the Sumerian: these were not (and how could they have been) Sumerian immigrants. The very existence of large temples, with all that is implied by it, does indeed constitute a striking analogy between places so distant; but we have to note also that the Sumerian temples are recti- not curvilinear,[9] and that they are not dug into the ground but erected on artificial mounds symbolizing mountains approaching the abode of the gods. And while the fixed, symbolical shape of the Maltese buildings and the sameness of the surviving images proclaim an exclusive devotion to one, female deity, the extant Sumerian literature[10] (reaching back to c. 2500 B.C.) tells of numberless, and different, gods and goddesses; the mother-goddess Ninhursag is one of the four, or seven, greatest among them but by no means uniquely outstanding. In fact, all the Sumerian evidence bears the marks of highly rationalized theological speculation and literary invention; perfectly in accordance with their refined and diversified patriarchal civilization but worlds apart from the profound and unified devotion

indicated by a deep incision' (Zammit, p. 96); this feature recurs on one of the mother-of-pearl inlays from the Square Temple at Tel Asmar (H. Frankfort, *Or. Inst. . . . Chicago, Discoveries in Iraq, 1933–4* (1935), p. 25, Fig. 25, left). See our Plate 3*b*.

[1] A. Parrot, *Tello* (1948), p. 80 and Pl. IV; our Plate 3*c*.

[2] Zammit, p. 16, Pl. III, Evans, p. 151 and Fig. 23. It may be not irrelevant that, according to one authority, 'The animals appear to represent the red Asiatic moufflon' (Zammit, p. 17).

[3] Zammit, p. 87, Pls. XXIV f.; cf. Evans, pp. 87 f. and 127, Pls. 3 and 76 f.

[4] H. Frankfort, *Art and Architecture* . . . , Pl. 3; A. Parrot, *Sumer* (1960), Pl. 89.

[5] Hall and Woolley, *Ur Excavations,* i (1927), Pls. 32 and 38; Woolley, *Development of Sumerian Art* (1935), Pl. 30; id., *Excavations at Ur* (1954), Pl. 14a.

[6] H. Frankfort, *Or. Inst. . . . Chicago, Discoveries in Iraq, 1933–4* (1935), p. 2, Fig. 2.

[7] A. Parrot, *Tello* (1948), Pl. XIV.   [8] p. 155.

[9] The temple-ovals at Khafaje, Al Uqair, and Al Ubaid (P. Delougaz, *Or. Inst. . . . Chicago, Publications,* liii (1940) can hardly affect this general impression, since the temples within them, as far as known, were rectangular.

[10] I follow the authoritative outline given by S. N. Kramer, pp. 112 ff.

to which the Maltese monuments testify. They witness to an earlier stage structurally, if not chronologically, of religious perception.

Substantially akin and nearer in space, but far removed in time, they have a counterpart in the amazing discoveries of J. Mellaart at Çatal Hüyük in the Konya plain, which have been profoundly interpreted by the excavator.[1] The inhabitants of this closely-built early townlet—the site in question is now dated c. 6500–5650 B.C.[2]—were devoted to one concept of deity; there was a shrine to every four or five houses, and every one dedicated to the 'Mother Goddess'.[3]

The cult of the Mother Goddess is nowadays widely regarded as a concomitant of man's transition from hunting and food-gathering to agriculture; the dependence upon the fertility of the soil (so it is said) and the vital importance of sowing, growing, and harvesting are reflected in the concept of the Earth as the 'Great Mother' and the mythology centring on her. It cannot indeed be denied that the new mode of life was bound to foment an awareness of this aspect of the divine and that the evidence for it seems largely to coincide with that for the spread of agriculture (which—to say it again—is far from covering the regions and periods in which megalithic monuments were erected). Not everywhere, though, did early agriculture find its religious image in a Mother Goddess (Osiris, the giver of fruit and lord of the Netherworld, is the obvious counter-instance) nor was she first recognized in this comparatively recent age. To be gripped by the realization of deity in woman, the spring and harbour of life, mankind did not have to wait for the invention of agriculture. Everywhere, from Spain to Siberia, so many palaeolithic documents of this devotion have emerged,[4] and with traits so specific recurring in neolithic relics, as to forbid the facile inference that this change, however epochal, in man's living habits could by itself account for what is loosely called 'the cult of the Mother Goddess'; and indeed I am at a loss to quote, from this orbit, any striking evidence for its specific connection with agriculture—apart from Eleusis, many thousand years later. What evidence there is—and it is not a little—points to concerns more comprehensive and profound. This is the oldest godhead perceived by mankind. What reality was severally grasped through it (beyond what is superficially and generically obvious) may to some extent be discerned where the attempt at a specific interpretation can rest on a documentation sufficiently variegated and suggestive.

---

[1] AS, xii (1962), 41 ff.; xiii (1963), 49 ff.; xiv (1964), 44 ff. To these reports can now be added the recent summary in J. Mellaart, Earliest Civilisations of the Near East (1965), pp. 77 ff.

[2] Mellaart, p. 81.

[3] Even if, as the excavator now assumes, the part so far excavated contained the 'priestly quarters', the forty sanctuaries are evidence of an overwhelming and unified devotion.

[4] H. Kühn, Kunst und Kultur der Vorzeit Europas, i (1929), p. 308 and Pl. 53–7; id., Vorgeschichtliche Kunst Deutschlands (1935), pp. 47 f.

At Çatal Hüyük it is starkly, and even brutally, explicit. The divine reality which dominated the minds of these people and which they worshipped in their small shrines was—the very fact of life and death; these felt as the deeds of ruthless and unaccountable powers; death pictured in the shape of enormous vultures over headless (that is, dead) human bodies; opposing them, the goddess appears in one, ever-recurring shape, namely, in the act of giving birth.[1] Her progeny is the bull, the essential begetter. His emblem, large actual bucrania, is everywhere, in astounding numbers, asserting his power to overcome death; in two of the shrines, moreover, his large image, cut out of the plaster, dominates one of the walls.[2] The begetter and the parturient: these two are constantly undoing the work of the vultures—whose prey is the perishable flesh, and no more. When they have done their part, the lasting bones are gathered and buried under the floors of the houses; the males under the bed of the father, women and children underneath the mother's.

This custom[3] bespeaks an intimate communion between the living and the dead. The dead underneath are ever present with the living; the living have risen from there, for a time; soon to rejoin them. The horror of dying remains unabated, but the power of life constantly regenerated embraces even this terror. A sentiment of the unity of life and death stands out in a crude but powerful symbolism. From many walls protrude models of the female breast moulded over the heads of beasts which signify death; such as boar's tusks, the beaks of vultures, the snouts of weasels and foxes. 'Media vita in morte sumus' or, rather: death encompassed by the nurturing vis vitalis. In one of the shrines human bones, significantly, were found scattered underneath this symbol.

Our interpretation cannot entirely divest itself of terms more or less abstract; in fact, though, the very power of these representations bespeaks the concreteness of this ancient experience. There is not really any thought of vis vitalis, but breasts and beak; no 'concept of fertility', but the act and fact of birth; no 'symbol of death', but horrid vultures feeding on bodies. The miracle of life, unending with eruption and destruction, stands out as the content and boundary of this religion. Its intensity is evident from the great number of shrines, the labour lavished on their construction and equipment, and the incessant care evident in their maintenance (the excavators have been at pains to distinguish, on

[1] See Plate 4a, b, d. I find it difficult, with J. Mellaart (AS, xiv (1964), 64), to find 'the Great Goddess, qua death, preparatory to resurrection' in the vulture frescoes. Is not the possibility of this profound monism negated by the general, strict opposition of the pictures representing 'Life' and 'Death' respectively?

[2] AS, xii (1962), 62 and Pl. XVa; ib. xiii (1963), 62 and Fig. 9; ib. xiv (1964), 57 and Fig. 18; our Plate 4c.

[3] Already Neanderthal Man buried his dead beneath the floor of his cave homes; burial underneath houses was practised in pre-pottery Jericho and at Natufian Eynan in N. Palestine as well as in neolithic Persia and at Khirokitia in Cyprus; it recurs, later on, at Boghazköi.

walls of the shrines, as many as fifty, or even a hundred, layers of plaster; every one of them involving the renewal of the whole plastic and painted decoration). The sum of this religious experience was comprised in devotion to the Goddess. Ever parturient, she is the perennial source of life. Its begetter is seen as her offspring; subordinate to her also in that his force is incorporate in the mightiest of animals, the bull;[1] it does not, like the mother, attain to the dignity of the human form; nor does her perennial antagonist, Death.[2]

Thus the whole of the power that originates and preserves life tends to be found in the female deity (and one would incline, as its counterpart, to infer a matriarchal order of society). One striking illustration of this tendency is in a small stone figure, found in one of the shrines:[3] it represents the goddess, yet has the shape of a phallus; a symbolism of the 'two-in-one' which has analogies near and far and from periods older as well as later.[4] Various palaeolithic representations expressive of the bi-sexual

[1] This import of the bull-symbol seems self-evident. While the giver of birth is revered as the primary and superior divinity, the power of fecundation, subservient to her, is perceived as the second, indispensable, and comforting divine reality. The very absence (or nearly so: see below) of the symbol of the phallus at Çatal Hüyük is a confirmation of this meaning of the countless representations of the mightiest male animal. One would not, in this context, refer to certain primitive tribes which are reported to be unaware of the connection between copulation and birth; the carving, on a slate plaque, of a concubitus, combined with a group of mother and child (*AS*, xiii (1963), p. 90, Fig. 27 and Pl. XXId; Mellaart, Fig. 76 and on cover) is proof to the contrary (I trust that this, and not 'mother with daughter', is the subject of the representation, both in view of the actual posture of the figures and of the recurrence of the theme, in a more naturalistic style, at Hacilar (*AS*, xi (1961), Pl. Xa = Schachermeyr, *Die minoische Kultur des alten Kreta* (1964), T. 43a)—not to mention those many representations in palaeolithic, neolithic, and later times, e.g. on rock-carvings in the Sahara, the Val Camonica, Sweden, and, nearer our field, on a neolithic vase from Alyabad in Persia, pictured by G. Wilke, *Die Religion der Indogermanen* (1923), p. 16, Fig. 23). One may infer a rite of 'hieros gamos' enacted or prefer to assume a symbolical import; in any case, this representation confirms the significance which was seen in the act of generation.

[2] The present discussion is based upon the monumental decor of the shrines, which may be supposed to attest the central concepts of this religion; its mythical elaboration, as suggested by figurines, will come up later.

[3] *AS*, xiii (1963), 83, Fig. 19 (I do not presume to decide whether or no the roughly carved limestone figure Pl. XIXd represents a phallus—a possibility tentatively mentioned by J. Mellaart.)

[4] The figure as a whole reminds one of the typical neolithic idols in Spain and France such as the Boulhosa stele (e.g. *apud* O. G. S. Crawford, *The Eye Goddess* (1957), p. 65, Fig. 22c and Pl. 18) or the statue at St. Sernin (e.g. Hérault, in *Vanished Civilisations*, ed. E. Bacon (1963), p. 303); though flat, these two share the phallic outline. At Arpachija, a whole set of clay female figurines has been found, ingeniously so shaped that they might as well be called phalli (*Iraq*, ii (1933), Fig. 47. 5–13); in others (ib. 2 and 3), the rather naturalistic rendering of the thighs of the goddess continues upwards in phallus-shape; the more abstract form of the same (ib., Fig. 46. 5) is important, because it bears out the same, male–female interpretation of a frequent type of Cycladic idol. The latter was suggested first, to the best of my knowledge, by R. Reitler (*Ipek*, xx (1963), 27; cf. ib., Pls. 6, 10–12) in an article in which he interpreted the Cyprian 'cross-idols', convincingly to my mind, as another instance of the bi-sexual representation of the creating deity. This latter type has, in fact, antecedents at Arpachija: that same 'Maltese cross' is once (*Iraq*, ii (1933) Fig. 45. 10) painted on the

concept of the primary creative force have been collected and discussed by S. Giedion;[1] among them are some which are comparable to the figure under discussion (one of these, from the Jordan valley, is in fact neolithic and thus not very much more ancient). The dominant deity at Çatal Hüyük, though (as indeed also in palaeolithic ages), is not a bisexual concept but 'the Mother'.

Is she 'Mother Earth'? This is, to say the least, not obvious. There are, it is true, certain features which seem to hint towards this identification. The bones of the dead are buried in the earth; but is not the fact more significant that they are placed under the floor of the habitations, and some (perhaps, as J. Mellaart suspects, the priests or, rather, priestesses) under the shrines—as though nearness to the living and their goddess were the primary concern? No traces of sacrifices have been found in the shrines but offerings of burnt grain: this indeed suggests that the goddess was regarded as fostering the fruits of the fields, and this much is confirmed by the fact that one specific image of hers was found in a grain-bin.[2] Finally, two 'deep caverns' on either side of the main image in one of the shrines have been suspected perhaps to indicate a chthonic cult.[3] These hints combined do not seem sufficient to seriously qualify the impression so powerfully conveyed by the bulk of the evidence, which proclaims the goddess, in the palaeolithic tradition, as the spring of all life. As such, the fertility of the fields—as well as of man and beast—will naturally be felt to be of her province; but there is no special feature that could identify her with the pregnant depth of the earth.[4] Another special aspect of hers actually contradicts such identification, for a number of representations show her as the 'mistress of animals' (πότνια θηρῶν);[5] a concept which, in itself and in view of its later occurrences, appears distinctly different from that of the 'Mother Earth'.[6]

Çatal Hüyük thus yields a significant analogy to illustrate the religion of ancient Malta. The inspiration and its expression are not by any means identical at the two places; but there is the same fervent devotion to

shoulder of a mother goddess figure; it occurs as amulet (Fig. 51. 3) and may be recognized also in a 'winged bead' (ib., p. 95, Pl. VIb, no. 860).

[1] S. Giedion, *The Eternal Present*, i (1957), pp. 223 ff.; esp. p. 236, Figs. 166 f.—The palaeolithic 'staff' (ib. 231, Fig. 159) is closely similar to a bronze-age clay symbol from Tarxien cemetery, Malta: another instance of the persistence of palaeolithic concepts (Zammit, Pl. XVI, centre; the other two figures, ib., are analogous to those from the Cyclades instanced in the preceding note, though independent).

[2] *AS*, xiv (1964), 95.   [3] Ib., xiii (1963), 73.

[4] The semi-iconic figures which show her head at the top of stalactites, as well as the natural, strangely shaped stones and concretions found together with statues could, as Mellaart holds (pp. 92 f.), indicate this aspect; alternatively they may express her quality as the giver and guarantor of life—of which stone is the lasting essence and symbol (cf. below, p. 51).   [5] *AS*, xiii (1963), 83 ff. and xiv (1964), 76 ff. and Pl. XVII.

[6] Cf. A. Dieterich, *Mutter Erde*[3] (1925), pp. 82 ff. distinguishing between the Asianic 'Great Mother' and the Greek 'Mother Earth'.

a single deity, this deity being the superior antagonist of death and mother of all life. It could seem preposterous to consider the possibility of an actual connection between places separated by about a thousand miles and three or four thousand years; but Çatal Hüyük, of course, is no more nor less than a specific representative—uniquely instructive and early— of a religion widely spread and amazingly persistent, even in significant detail, throughout Anatolia, and beyond. Of this, some illustrations:

Apart from the ever-recurring bucranium representing the male deity, the excavators found alabaster figurines of a male god—once young, once older and bearded—on a bull.[1] Even though it is, probably, a matter of mythology rather than of the cult, one may well wonder at so early an instance of the typical development from an animal-god to the animal-attribute of a god in human shape; anyhow, here is a precursor of the type that was to persist through the ages, finally to penetrate, as Jupiter Dolichenus, to the far corners of the Roman Empire.

Like the vultures, the boar also is a symbol of death: his huge head appears on the wall of one of the shrines.[2] It is impossible not to think of Attis and Adonis killed by the boar.[3]

The most striking illustration of the persistence, in Asia Minor, of religious concepts is a figure of the Goddess seated between lions:[4] the very type of the Asianic 'Mater' or Kybele, which was to be adopted in Greece in late archaic times and to penetrate, like Jupiter Dolichenus, the Roman Empire.

The Magna Mater, goddess of many names, the perennial deity of Asia Minor from early neolithic to late Roman times: she could indeed be assumed to be related, in one way or other, to the Maltese goddess. If, however, we want to go beyond vague generalities, we have to try and identify specific features of this goddess and her cult—a task to be approached with the utmost reserve and caution, for it is only too evident that, in the course of several thousand years, and at different places, she was perceived and worshipped in widely different ways, and most of the extant evidence comes from, comparatively, quite recent times. Even so, there are three facts in the light of which the task does not appear entirely hopeless: namely, the persistence, just mentioned, of certain significant and specific features; the evidence, mainly from figurines, of the wide spread and persistence of the devotion to the 'Mother Goddess', and the correspondence of this devotion with a basic and perennial human disposition.[5]

---

[1] AS, xiv (1964), 78, Fig. 32 and Pl. XVII; Mellaart, p. 96, Fig. 78.

[2] Mellaart, p. 45, Fig. 6; Pl. IIIb.

[3] The name Adon(-is) is not originally Semitic but 'Asianic'; see Mus. Helv. viii (1951), 34; add Nossis, Anth. Pal. vi. 275, Theocrit. xv. 149 (with Gow's note, quoting Alcman, fr. 112 Diehl = 109 Page and Hesych. s.v.). [4] AS, xiii (1963), 95; Mellaart, Fig. 73.

[5] It will, I trust, be realized that I am at pains to escape the fascination of A. Dieterich's

In historical times we meet with individualizations as different among themselves as the war-like Mā of Komana, the bisexual Agdistis, the semitized Atargatis, the Ephesian Artemis. Primitive names like Mā and Nana ('mother') confirm their ancient origin, but very little can be inferred concerning the specific character of each and all of them in pre-historic times. We may however make bold briefly to consider Kybele, whose ancient prototype has just emerged. It would be hypercritical not to acknowledge the alternative form of her name, Κυβήβη, anticipated in the Kubabat of the Kültepe texts and the Hittite Kubaba;[1] continued by the Phrygian Ματαρ Κυβιλε. As 'the Mother' she was received into the Athenian state-cult; Pindar (who worshipped her), Euripides, and later poets describe her ecstatic rites; from the Roman period we have some evidence for her myths and her mysteries.[2]

The Mountain-Mother: her seated image, flanked by her lions, is found in caves high-up in the rocky wilds or in artificial niches imitating the caves;[3] her very name is reported to imply 'mountains (in Phrygia), caves and bowers',[4] and the names of many mountains are combined with her general designation as 'the Mother' (Mater Dindymene, Idaea, etc.). But—strange though it may seem—this mother has no offspring; the beautiful young Attis whom she loves with a chaste and tragic love is not, in the extant myths, her son.[5] He dies, and Kybele is not able to revive him;[6] his fate is symbolized by the ritual of the pine-tree cut off, decorated, lamented, and finally burnt. This myth, then (like the Sumerian Dumuzi–Tammuz parallel[7]), fails to fit the widely-favoured 'pattern of dying and reviving fertility-deities'.

Kybele is 'the Mother' absolute; the eternal *vis vitalis* persisting *vis-à-vis* the irrevocable transientness of her creature. Hence Greeks could find in her the 'Mother Earth' as well as the 'Mother of the Gods' and she could, in the end, be felt to further the yield of fields and groves and to protect cities (*Mater turrita*); but her essential character remained as it

classic book *Mutter Erde* (3. Aufl., 1925), whose teachings have been generalized by a host of successors far beyond the intentions of its author. The effect has been a dogmatism which frequently tends by a hackneyed pattern ('fertility cult') to obscure the live variety and specific inspiration of the documents of ancient religions.

[1] A. Goetze, *Kleinasien*[2] (1957), pp. 80 and 133.

[2] The present sketch may be supplemented from the relevant articles in *PW*, Roscher, and other current handbooks; also A. Graillot, *Cybèle* (1912), and especially H. Hepding, *Attis* (1903).   [3] See e.g. Perrot–Chipiez, *Hist. de l'art*, v, Figs. 109 ff.

[4] Hesych., s.v. Κύβελα· ὄρη Φρυγίας καὶ ἄντρα καὶ θάλαμοι.

[5] It is possible to analyse the reports about the ancestry of Attis (Timotheus *apud* Pausanias vii. 17 and Arnobius, *Adv. Nat.* v. 5) back to a primitive form with Attis the son of the 'Mother' (Agdistis = Kybele); the very fact, though, that the different, canonical story came into being shows that the point of the myth lies elsewhere.

[6] M. P. Nilsson (*Gesch. der griech. Religion*, ii (1950), p. 623) has disposed of the one, late, and speculative source (Firmicus Maternus, *De errore* 3) which asserts that Attis 'lived up again'.

[7] As recovered by S. N. Kramer.

had been perceived by her early worshippers. They met her in the soli-
tude of the wilds, in the seclusion of rock and mountain and in the awful
yawning of crevasse and cave; in the rigour of frost and heat, of storm
and thunder, and in the independent and indomitable life of beast and
plant in glade, forest, and glen. To this revelation of the divine life-force
in the violent and extreme nature of the Anatolian highland the worshippers responded with an extremism which is unlikely to be within the
range of experience of many, if any, of us. There is no need to rehearse the
graphic Greek and Latin descriptions of this frenzied cult; of the devotees
rushing through forests and mountains with torches, drums, and pipes;
an ecstasy closely akin to the eruption of the profoundest, hidden emotions
awakened by Dionysos. But Greeks forever rejected the culmination of
such frenzy in self-mutilation; in the surrender, that is, of the worshipper's
manhood, by which the Anatolian devotees of Kybele likened themselves
to her mythical favourite or even to the goddess herself.[1]

The act of castration stands out, in myth and factual reports, as the
culmination of this devotion; it is the extreme response, conceivable only
in a state of paroxysm, of man overpowered by the apprehension of
a deity in whom he perceives the power and sanctity of life unending;[2] the
life, all life, on earth, from stone and plant to animal and human; maintained against ineluctable death by the miracle of unceasing procreation.
It is on this basis very understandable that the mysteries of Kybele could
in the Roman period convey an assurance of personal immortality; their
ritual traditions being reinterpreted in accordance with the thought of the
age. But the rites themselves, whose original import we are striving to
discern, go back thousands of years beyond this reinterpretation. Evidence
to this fact is their general unrestrainedness and expressiveness—that kind
was not devised under the rule of Greek custom and restraint—and,
in addition, one specific feature: the ritual castration had to be carried
out *silice acuto*; it must then go back to 'The Stone-Age'.[3] Can this age

---

[1] Photius, s.v. Κύβηβος· ὁ κατεχόμενος τῆι Μητρὶ τῶν θεῶν.

[2] I can only regard as naïve certain theories which would explain this extreme act as
designed to 'fertilize the Earth' or, alternatively, to assure permanent sexual purity. An act
like this does not originate from considered purpose but from emotional frenzy. Origen's self-
mutilation had better not be mentioned in this context; it was the very opposite of the culmination of an ecstatic cult. The ecstatic experience of the all-overwhelming force of life and
procreation, culminating in the sacrifice of the very organs of procreation: this irrational
response is not explicable on a rational plane; one has to know what ecstasy means. The
facts anyhow are there, and Catullus 63 (that is, Kallimachos) can help us to fathom them.

[3] To judge from M. P. Nilsson, *Gesch. der griech. Religion*, ii. 616, the view (originated by
Rapp in Roscher, *Lexikon . . .*, ii, Pt. 1, 1657) seems current that the act of castration was not
an original feature of the cult but added to it 'under Semitic influence' during the Hellenistic
period, in consequence of the 'Syrian' (i.e. Seleucid) 'conquest of Asia Minor' (and this,
although Timotheus, who reported the relevant myth, was a contemporary of the first
Ptolemy). The reason given for this, to my mind, untenable view is the fact that no Greek
earlier than Timotheus mentions the myth, nor the rite either—an argument which requires
no refutation. The allegedly older version—Attis killed by a boar—is an evident replica of the

be more precisely defined? Could it be possible to trace this complex of rites and concepts back to Çatal Hüyük?

The ecstatic cult of the Great Mother is quite generally, in the Greek and Latin sources, called 'Phrygian' and 'Lydian'; modern scholarship tends to trace it to the Phrygian immigrants (about 1200 B.C.) in Asia Minor who, so it is said,[1] added to the native cult the ecstatic element with which they are not unreasonably credited in view of the similar tendencies among their former neighbours and (*qua* race) cousins, the Thracians. This plausible theory though meets with forbidding obstacles. Thracian orgiastic rites never led to castration, and the further suggestion that this feature was added under Semitic influence will not bear scrutiny. The alleged prototype, the Dea Syria, is herself no more nor less than one of the forms of the Asiatic goddess; whose cult is not a compound of various influences but one, in all the details of its orgiastic abandon, from music and dance to its gruesome consummation. Phrygians and Lydians —who anyhow were not 'Stone-Age-people'—must have adopted it from the people among whom they settled; as did, later on, the Celtic Galatians.[2]

Having traced the name as well as the typical representation of Kybele back far beyond the age of Phrygians and Lydians,[3] we now find that her orgiastic cult too reaches back, in Asia Minor, into prehistoric times. One easily imagines that it could have been carried on, in popular worship, separate from the state-cults of the Hittite conquerors, who term Kubaba a Hurrian goddess; we may thus confidently trace it to, at least, the beginning of the second millennium B.C. It persisted, from thence onward, changing superficially but essentially the same, for more than two millennia (and may be held, after this, to have lived on, or re-emerged, in disguise with Montanists and Katharans and 'Dancing Dervishes'); dare one assume its essence to have been present, and persisted, throughout the enormous span of three or four millennia before this early date?

Adonis-story; whether ancient or not, it does not prove the alternative version recent. This version—the cult-legend of Pessinus, the centre of the Kybele cult—is anything but Hellenistic in character. Its closest analogy, in general and in significant detail, is in the Hittite Kumarbi-myths, and even so, it is itself far from primitive; older forms, more direct and less involved, must lie behind it.

[1] e.g. by H. Hepding, *Attis*, pp. 213 ff.

[2] The striking phenomenon of orgiastic prophetism in Israel, described 1 Sam. 10: 5 ff., 19: 19–24, and 1 Kgs. 18: 18 ff., was traced to an 'Asiatic' substratum of the population by G. Hölscher (*Die Profeten* (1914), 140 ff.; cf. *Class. et Mediaev.* viii (1947), 218 f.). This—to my mind persuasive—hypothesis would be very hard to maintain if there was no 'orgiasm' in Anatolia prior to the immigration of the Phrygians.—I would not shrink from the opposite assumption that the orgiastic cults of the Thracians derived from the same Anatolian source; this would agree with the general trends evidenced by archaeology.

[3] M. C. Astour, *Hellenosemitica* (1965), p. 64, n. 3 quotes Kubaba from Sumerian texts; I do not presume to judge whether this is an instance of accidental homophony or could help in tracing the Asiatic goddess back into the prehistory of the 'Fertile Crescent'.

It would be wrong to overstress isolated points of coincidence. When the whole of the evidence from Çatal Hüyük is compared with the general pattern of the cult of Kybele, important differences stand out as well as striking analogies. The 'Kybele-type' figurine at Çatal Hüyük is, so far at least, an isolated instance and comes from the (comparatively) recent, second level; the standard representation, which shows the goddess in the act of giving birth, has no parallel in the later representations of Kybele. The same is true of the bull-symbol: outstanding as it is at Çatal Hüyük as well as in many of the later cults of Anatolia and beyond, it does not enter into her cult. Likewise, the vulture-imagery remains peculiar to Çatal Hüyük, whereas in the orbit of Kybele the idea of death finds expression in the figure of Attis and his fate.

Moreover, it goes without saying that the religious experience to which the archaeological finds testify must have been reflected in a mythology; even though this is almost completely beyond our grasp (who could have inferred, from the archaeological evidence, anything like the ample and variegated mythology attested by the Sumerian, Akkadian, Hittite, and Ras Shamra tablets?). And indeed some tantalizing finds at Çatal Hüyük seem to hint at accepted myths. J. Mellaart may well be right in suggesting[1] that the statuettes of the male god young and old, and those of the goddess young, parturient, and old, may represent various aspects of the same two deities; moreover, these aspects, as well as the connection of the deities with animals (bull and leopard), imply corresponding myths. Whatever these may have been like, they can hardly have fitted the frame of the Kybele myth. The observation that the figure of the male god is absent from the décor of the shrines underlines the absolute prerogative, in the religion of Çatal Hüyük, of the *dea parturiens* and, again, it is hard to imagine how any mythical expression of this fact could be squared with what was told, thousands of years later, at Pessinus.

These are marked differences indeed; no more so, though, than the enormous distance in time would have led one to expect. The points of convergence, on the other hand, go far beyond the mere recurrence, at that earliest and again at a comparatively recent date, of a 'cult of the Mother Goddess'. The reader will have noticed that the endeavour to discern the basic experience attested by the two cults led to almost identical definitions. Both realize the divinity of life eternal in the form of the 'Mother of all'; they acknowledge the ineluctable lot of death awaiting every one of the Mother's creatures; they sense and lament its irretrievable horror yet are passionately certain of the Mother's—of Life's superiority and permanence. The question of course is of this life on earth—there is

---

[1] Mellaart, p. 92; cf. *AS*, xiii (1963), 82 ff.; ib., xiv (1964), 73 ff.—Could the Hellenistic Athenian reliefs with the 'Mother' represented twice (Svoronos, nos. 1540 and 1921) be in any way related to the representation of the 'twin goddess' at Çatal?

no other—and the means for its permanence is in the miracle of sexual reproduction; which, accordingly, is with both, though in different ways, in the centre of awful devotion.

When, in addition, the central fact is duly stressed that, as distinct from the 'hundreds' or 'thousands' of gods acknowledged by Sumerians, Akkadians, and Hittites, this devotion is centred on the one, female deity, the giver, protector, and mistress of all life in man, beast, and plant; then it will have to be admitted that this is basically the same religion. The question remains if the form in which it was experienced and realized was the same at Çatal Hüyük as it was, so much later, in Pessinus; in short, if the early cult, too, was of the 'orgiastic' kind.

One would hardly have expected it. If the believers found their goddess in rapturous processions in the wilds, why should they have built those numerous shrines which, quite obviously, were cult-places? There is no hint of cave and rock and mountain . . . or could, in fact, that amazing little fresco (in shrine vii. 14) with the representation of volcanoes erupting[1] be meant to represent her haunts? There are, moreover, the puzzling pictures of the 'running goddess' with whirling hair.[2] This primitive yet striking device: could it be intended to convey the rapture of 'maenadism'?

I dare not here go beyond these questions. It is clear, at any rate—from the great number of shrines, the endless care spent on their elaboration, and the number and power of the representations in them—that the people of Çatal Hüyük worshipped their goddess with a devotion no less fervent, exclusive, and even fanatical, than was offered, thousands of years later, to Kybele.

After all, one had perhaps best conclude that this earliest religion on earth of which more than the faintest and most general features can be discerned, was an answer to the same experience which, thousands of years later, found expression in the cult and myth of Kybele; that certain constituent traits of the latter appear to have been anticipated in that earliest religion, while other features faded away to be replaced by different symbols and devotions. Maybe Anatolian archaeology, which has of late achieved results so fantastic and significant, will one day succeed in illumining intermediate stages. Meantime, the fact appears to be established, and is confirmed by the uninterrupted series, from many and widely distant places, of the fixed symbols representing 'The Mother', that her religion existed and persisted throughout the Near East, beginning at an age in relation to which the Sumerian is, to us, almost a recent past, and continuing down into the Graeco-Roman period.

The Çatal Hüyük 'Kybele' figurine represents the goddess, in strict

---

[1] *AS*, xiv (1964), 55 with Pls. Vb and VIa.
[2] Shrine B vi. V 31 (*AS*, xiv (1964), 48 with Pl. IIIc and Fig. 8. Was she holding a snake? It would support the interpretation tentatively proposed).

contrast with her later images, as *parturiens*. In this figurine, as J. Mellaart observes,[1] 'neolithic man has summed up his creed in a Great Goddess, Mistress of all life and death'. This creed persisted, although its object was perceived and worshipped in varying forms; which offer themselves for comparison, illustration and, perhaps, correlation in the study of the Goddess of Malta and Sicily.

(c) BACK TO MALTA: TEMPLES AND GRAVES

We return from our excursion into distant ages and regions attuned, it is hoped, to approach the religion which expresses itself in the Maltese monuments. These indeed remain as unique as they appeared to us from the first; they proclaim an original and compelling vision of deity. It was a new vision of the goddess whose earlier manifestations we have tried to interpret. The goddess of Malta is, again, the 'Mistress of Life and Death'; but she is seen anew: Death is not the enemy, constantly overcome yet never finally vanquished; Death is part of her self. For she is the Mother Earth; all life returns to her, to be received in her womb to grow again and to live from there. All begetting is a begetting on her, helping the dead committed to her to grow into life, as the seed grows out of her furrows and as the child grows in the mother's womb and into the light.

The unique shape of the Maltese temples has been accounted for by earlier students as a reproduction, above ground and in large size, of older rock-graves such as have been found, in particular, at Xemxija in the North-West of the main island:[2] the 'kidney-shape' of these graves was held to be the model in particular of a small and primitive 'trefoil' temple at Mġarr not very far from Xemxija, and hence of all of them. An inference concerning the rites carried out in the temples was based upon this premiss: if they had the shape of graves, the cult there must have been a cult of the dead; they were, then, places of ancestor worship.

This was a mistake. If the inference is correct, why is there no trace of burial in or near the temples? If the cult of ancestors had been an eminent concern, would it not have been celebrated at their graves? Would not these—rather than sanctuaries carefully kept apart from contact with the dead—have grown into gigantic structures, with ample space for worship, as at Mycenae and in Sardinia? Moreover, the assumed direct evidence for the supposed imitation, in the temples, of the rock-graves has been eliminated since the small 'trefoil' at Mġarr has proved to be a comparatively recent structure.[3] In fact, graves remained modest throughout the 'temple-period'; although—this is important—a new type of grave was

---

[1] *AS*, xiii (1963), 95.

[2] G. Childe, *The Dawn of European Civilisation*[4], (1947), p. 246 (quoting some earlier statements to the same effect); Hawkes, p. 153; Evans, pp. 88 ff.

[3] D. H. Trump, *Antiquity* (1961), 302.

adopted at its beginning and persisted throughout it; namely, the communal rock-grave (instead of the earlier simple, and single, pit).[1] And when finally, in the great catacomb at Hal Saflieni, spaces for religious celebrations were carved out of the rock, these were elaborated in imitation, on a small scale, of the fully developed norm of the temples—and not vice versa!

And yet the observation on which this hypothesis had been based

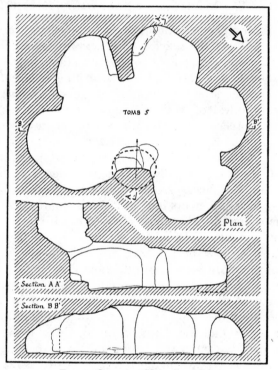

TOMB 5

Plan

Section A A'

Section B B'

FIG. 2: Graves at Xemxija, Malta

was correct and essential. It is perfectly true that the predominant formal feature of the temples—that large, 'kidney-shaped' oblong—and the normal form of the contemporary rock-graves are the same. Not because either of them was an imitation of the other, but because both repeat one and the same ideal model. The shape of these graves provides an analogy to, and confirmation of, our previous assertion concerning the symbolical meaning of the temples. The 'ideal model' of either, obviously, was—not the kidney.

What it was, will be felt by everyone who penetrates into one of these rock-cut graves (see Figure 2).[2] This small, curved room, deep in the cool

[1] Trump, loc. cit.   [2] Cf. Evans, Pls. 32 and 33.

earth, not circular, nor properly oval or elliptic, with its roof sloping towards the gently bending edge, is shaped in the likeness of the womb. It *is* the womb of the earth; the dead are laid into it for new birth. The temples reproduce the same model on a large scale. The living who enter them enter the body of the goddess. Here is the clue to the faith which built these stupendous monuments. If we understand them aright, they were the places of a mystery-cult in the exact sense of the word.

These assertions, to carry conviction, require some detailed demonstration. If it is accepted that the standard shape of the Maltese temple repeats the life-bearing body of the goddess—or, to speak concretely, *is* that body (for the symbol *is* the idea realized), it follows that he who enters this temple is passing through the vulva of the goddess. This symbolism may shock our sensibility; it certainly calls for an elucidation of its meaning. First, however, it has to be confirmed, if possible, by further evidence. Such we expect to find in considering

(d) THE SYMBOLISM OF THE SPIRAL

Ornamentation was applied to the masonry of the temples only during the more recent period (Hal Saflieni and Tarxien);[1] then, however, in profusion. Apart from pitting, almost the only, ever-recurring motif is the spiral,[2] in greatly varying shapes and combinations. The ornamentation has of course in many places vanished under the impact of time and weather (thus in the Ġgantija),[3] but well-preserved pieces survive from Tarxien and Hal Saflieni, Ħaġar Qim and Bugibba. One is bound to ask why this particular motif was given almost exclusive preference.

The history of the spiral motif has been thoroughly and variously discussed for a very long time.[4] One result which has met with almost universal acceptance is that it originated in neolithic cultures ('Bandkeramik') around the middle and lower Danube, whence it spread Southward into Greece (Dimini), the Cyclades and, finally, to Crete and thence to Mari on the Euphrates and to Egypt[5] as well as, later on, to Northern

---

[1] Where it is found in older buildings, as in the Ġgantija, it is reasonably supposed—in view of the parallel development in the decoration of pottery—to have been added later.

[2] The place of interconnected spirals is occasionally (Ġgantija) taken by connected circles, and this motif may result in the form ⟨ccc⟩ (Tarxien i, first bay right; T. Zammit, *Archaeologia* lxviii (1916–17), Pl. 37); but these are rare exceptions. For once, a totally different ornament occurs on the basis of the huge goddess figure (same place; 'egg-and-tongue pattern' *sec.* T. Zammit, *Prehist. Malta*, p. 13).

[3] See the old painting reproduced by Evans, Pl. 7.

[4] I recall G. von Kaschnitz-Weinberg, *Praehist. Zeitschr.* xxxiv–xxxv (1949), 193 ff., as an excellent treatment of the subject but could not at the time of writing lay hands on it.

[5] This argument was pursued in detail by F. Schachermeyr, *Die ältesten Kulturen Griechenlands* (1955), pp. 94 ff.; summarized in *Die minoische Kultur* . . . (1964), pp. 18 f.; cf. e.g. H. Frankfort, *Studies in Early Pottery*, ii (1927), pp. 49 ff., 116, 151, *et passim*; J. Hawkes, *Prehistory* . . . (1963), p. 332, and below, pp. 56 f.

Europe. Even this plausible result will have to be qualified in the light of certain recent finds in the Near East. We may for a moment consider the implications of an inquiry, however limited, into the tradition and meaning of this motif.

It cannot here be the question of the mere, mechanical repetition of a shape once devised, as with a letter-type put on to paper, *ad infinitum*, by a printing press. Anyone drawing or carving a line—any line; but particularly one as specific and expressive as is the spiral—therewith gives expression to some motive within himself; it may be superficial and momentary (especially if he is mechanically copying a model) or significantly expressive (especially if he is decorating a temple). Again, the motive force that seeks expression through this line may be peculiar to the draughtsman's isolated person (especially if he is a modern artist) or it may be of the pulse quickening a closely knit community (especially if he is sharing in a common religious devotion). Moreover, a pattern as characteristic as the spiral, once devised, will tend to retain the meaning which was first embodied in it; it tends to become a symbol and to be taken over as such. This fixation, however, is by no means absolute. A new impulse may invest the symbol with a new meaning (and thoughtless copying reduce it to an almost meaningless scrawl); and, finally, there are different shapes and combinations of spirals, products of, and witnesses to, different impulses.[1]

With these reflections in mind we proceed to consider the most outstanding special form of spirals in the Maltese temples. The entrance, from the open central forecourt,[2] into the middle temple at Tarxien is reduced (as also in the other temples) to a narrow and longish passage, five feet wide, by two mighty, upright slabs; the remaining actual entry is blocked by a slab two feet high which has to be stepped over on entering the temple. The ornament in question, covering the whole slab, faces outward; it consists of two large spirals back to back, so to speak, and developing down- and outward; with a small triangle, point downward,

[1] Cf. K. Kerényi, *Labyrinth-Studien* (2. Ausg., 1950), a thoughtful and suggestive study, but impaired—to my mind—by one-sided dogmatism. Not every spiral (I submit) is a labyrinth, nor is every labyrinth a spiral. One might go further and assert a marked difference between the two symbols (even though occasionally they occur together; as in the Val Camonica); for the spiral develops sideways from its starting point while the labyrinth is entered at the centre of its periphery and offers two alternative routes into its interior, with a different shape (and, presumably, a different meaning) resulting. And it strikes me as the final triumph of dogma over fact when, in the end, even the mausoleum of Hadrian is presented as a labyrinth. —D. A. Mackenzie, *The Migration of Symbols* (1926), has much about the spiral; his recital of past arguments about its interpretation may be found interesting; likewise his evidence for its connection with birth in Indian myths and ritual. For the rest, his argument is unrelated to the one here pursued.

[2] This forecourt, intermediate between the western and middle temples, has often, but wrongly, been considered to be a first, large set of 'apses', (and hence the feature under consideration as the entrance to 'the Holy of Holies'); but see above, p. 6, n. 4.

between them at the top and a larger but less marked one pointing up-ward from below.[1] An almost identical slab from the temple at Bugibba may be seen in the museum at Valetta; likewise a third, from Hagar Qim[2] (this one lacks the lower triangle). The precise, original place of these two is not known; a fourth is said to have been in the Ġgantija.[3]

'Almost certainly the pattern is intended as a stylized representation of eyes, conceived of as guarding the place behind'; 'a formalized expres-sion of the eyes and nose of the ancestor goddess': such are recent com-ments by specialists, who apply to this representation the technical term 'oculus-spirals'.[4] But the Maltese temples were (if the argument above is accepted) not destined for a cult of ancestors, and the pattern under discussion symbolizes (so we are now going to argue) what its position, at least at Tarxien, demands; namely, the entrance into the womb of the goddess.

The interpretation of this symbol concerns us very much, for, as the reader no doubt has realized, it is closely related to the reliefs on the two tomb-slabs from Castelluccio which occasioned the present inquiry. We shall accordingly combine the consideration of the Sicilian and the Maltese instances. Their relationship has repeatedly been noted.[5] J. D. Evans, commenting on their 'close similarity', adds that on the Castel-luccio slabs 'a very stylized representation of the rest of the figure is added, making the interpretation more certain'.[6] This is plausible; but one is bound to ask: which interpretation? The Maltese spirals, develop-ing from the centre downward and standing on the ground, obviously correspond with the lower pair on the Sicilian four-spiral slab. If these really represented eyes, what is represented by the upper pair? To put this question is to refute its premiss. If a representation of eyes was intended, it goes without saying that this is conveyed by the spirals at the top of the Sicilian slabs. I do indeed suspect that these may convey a dif-ferent meaning, but the view that eyes are meant is undoubtedly arguable. It was proposed by O. G. S. Crawford,[7] who thereupon found himself faced with the question of the meaning of the two lower spirals (or discs).

[1] The triangle at the top stands out high like the spirals; the one below is part of the (less high) surface remaining after the pattern had been carved out. See Plate 5a and Zammit, p. 26 and Pl. IX. i; also *Antiquity* (1930), Pl. I; Evans, p. 118 and Pl. 26; S. von Cles-Reden, *The Realm of the Great Goddess* (1961), Pls. 28 f.

[2] Evans, Pl. 78.

[3] According to A. Mayr, *Abhandl. d. Bayer. Akad.* xxi (1901), 666 (I have not seen this: could the spirals—comparable but not identical—on the 'altar' in the old painting (above, p. 25, n. 3) be meant?).

[4] Evans, pp. 119 and 122; G. Sieveking, in *Vanished Civilisations* (1963), ch. xiii, on Pl. 22.

[5] After P. Orsi (*Bull. di paletnol. ital.* xviii (1892), 70, n. 37) and T. E. Peet (*The Stone and Bronze Ages in Italy* (1909), p. 285), e.g. by Hawkes, p. 154; L. Bernabò Brea, *La Sicilia* (1958), p. 105 ('una vaga analogia'); Crawford, *The Eye Goddess* (1957), pp. 44 and 49.

[6] Evans, p. 119.

[7] Ib., p. 44.

His answer was: they represent the breasts of the 'funerary goddess'.[1] One glance at the monuments will convince of the inadmissibility of this answer. The distance between the pairs of spirals, their position, the shape and size of the part between them: all this leaves no room for doubt about the real purport of the lower half of the Sicilian representations—and, by implication, of the Maltese pattern which has to be equated with it.

The interpretation here suggested is borne out by evidence from many parts and ages. The latter fact does not militate against the relevance of the evidence to be cited,[2] for these symbols, as will presently appear, correspond to a basic and perennial human experience and accordingly persist throughout the ages. Specific variations apart, the spiral appears to be, throughout the vast region here considered, pre-eminently a symbol of the female, with all that is implied by this term, and this from the earliest times onward. H. Kühn has published and interpreted[3] a late palaeolithic 'bâton de commande'[4], on which the female component of this androgynous symbol is expressed by a network of spirals and not merely —as is the rule—by a perforation; from much later, historical times may be cited one of the 'snake-goddesses' (or 'priestesses') from the temple repositories of Knossos[5] or an archaic Carthaginian figurine from Ibiza[6] whose garments are significantly decorated with a profusion of spirals. The aptitude of the circular spiral for this connotation may be found in its symbolizing an urge and invitation to find a way to a final centre; perhaps also to return from it and infinitely to repeat the same experience. The latter component becomes indubitable where several of these spirals are joined into a pattern of endlessness, and even in the single S-spiral: with these, at any rate, the symbol becomes expressive of the experience of the *coniunctio oppositorum*: the up-and-down; the forward-and-back; the in-and-outward—and therewith of birth and death. These implications, so it would seem, constitute the aptitude of the spiral for symbolizing the experience of the female principle.

We turn to analogies fit to illustrate the Maltese instances. A single, circular spiral is drawn in the lap of the Kurotrophos statuette from Sesklo and also on the seat of the mother as well as of the child in this astonishing

---

[1] The odd latter term was apparently suggested to him by G. Childe (*The Dawn . . .* (1947), p. 230).

[2] I shall however refrain from adducing instances very far from, and almost certainly unconnected with, our field of study; such as ancient Mexico and Peru as well as the New Hebrides, because I feel entirely incompetent to evaluate them. They can be found in the books of Kerenyi (above, p. 26, n. 1), E. Neumann, and G. Wilke (above, p. 15, n. 1).

[3] *Symbolon*, ii (1961), 167 f. with Fig. 3.

[4] On these cf. lately S. Giedion, i. 160 ff.

[5] A. Evans, *The Palace of Minos*, vol. i, title plate; F. Matz, *Kreta, Mykene, Troja* (1960), Pl. 60; *BSA*, ix (1902/3), p. 76, Fig. 55 (for view of back).

[6] *Handbuch der Archaeologie*, ii (1954), Pl. 57, 4.

neolithic composition.[1] This threefold occurrence tends to throw some doubt on G. Wilke's downright explanation of the symbolism of spiral = snail = vulva; the fact, though, is undeniable, and suggestive, that snail and phallus occur together on Roman amulets and lamps,[2] and that fossilized snails were worn as amulets in palaeolithic times and later on, right to the present day.[3]

The so-called 'Venus of Sălcuţa' belongs to a group of Roumanian bronze-age figurines 'à robe cloche' which will presently concern us. Here we may note that into the lap of this, rather crude, 'Venus' a spiral is drawn in the same manner as on the Sesklo Kurotrophos.[4]

A single 'S-spiral' is incised, inside the 'lozenge' marking, as usual, the genital zone, on the grim but powerful, late neolithic clay-figure of the seated goddess found in a tumulus near Philippopel (Plovdiv) in Bulgaria.[5] The symbol here clearly is not intended simply to picture the vulva but indicates it as the place of the eternal 'up-and-down', of life and death.

The S-spiral has only to be continued with one or more windings at either end to turn into an interconnected pair of circular spirals; the meaning contained in this figure would presumably be the same and, if anything, even more explicit. Rightly, therefore, G. Wilke joined to the instance just quoted the developed S-spiral on a Portuguese tomb-slab and the rich double spiral on one of the outer kerb-stones ('b') of the megalithic chamber tomb, called New Grange, in North Eastern Eire.[6] The former designates the grave as the place where life, after coming to an end, will begin anew; the analogy of the Bulgarian statuette makes one infer that this 'end-and-beginning' was understood as entering the body of the Great Mother, the Earth, to be reborn by her. New Grange provides support for the inference. This grandiose monument forms the central subject of a recent, illuminating study by S. P. ÓRíordáin and G. Daniel,[7] in which the stone in question is pictured and discussed on

---

[1] C. Tsountas, *Dimini and Sesklo* (1908), Pl. 31. 2 and hence often reproduced; e.g. by Müller, Figs. 70 f. and F. Schachermeyr, *Die ältesten Kulturen* . . . , Pl. VII. 1. The excavator reports (p. 285) that the figure was found a mere 20 cm. below the surface; Schachermeyr therefore was justified in ascribing it (p. 120) to the Dimini period.—A new photograph is in P. Demargne, *Aegean Art* (1964), Pls. 35 and 36. See our Plate 6a.

[2] See Wilke, pp. 13 f. with Figs. 14–18.

[3] Cf. K. Oakley, in *Antiquity*, xxxix (1965), 13.

[4] V. Dumitrescu, *L'Art préhistorique en Roumanie* (1937), Pl. x.

[5] See Plate 6b; Hoernes–Menghin, *Urgeschichte der bildenden Kunst in Europa*[3] (1925), p. 319, Abb. 1; hence Wilke, p. 216, Abb. 268 and V. Müller, Fig. 104; E. Neumann, *The Great Mother* (1955), Pl. 6 (the best photograph; see also the valuable comment ib., p. 106). The 'statuette' is actually a vessel. This fact underlines its symbolic import: woman is the 'vessel'— of life. In illustration of this concept it is enough to point to the 'face-urns' from Troy (cf. Neumann, pp. 42 ff.).

[6] Wilke, p. 181, Figs. 232 and 233; Hoernes–Menghin, p. 229; our Plate 6c.

[7] *New Grange and the Bend of the Boyne* (1964).

p. 63 with Fig. 12b and Pl. 35. It will be seen there that two 'lozenges' are placed above and below the curve connecting the two spirals. Exactly the same combination occurs on a unique potsherd found at that amazing neolithic settlement uncovered by G. Childe at Skara Brae in the Orkneys (except that there the two spirals, instead of being interconnected, grow out separately of the lower ends of the upper lozenge: this, as we shall see, is the original form of this design).[1] We know the import of the 'lozenge'; it is stressed at Skara Brae by hatching and at New Grange by a thin wavy line along its diameter.[2] Lozenges and triangles are, together with spirals in various combinations, the main elements of the decoration which, in profusion, overlies many of the stones at New Grange. It is by no means given that every spiral must have the meaning which we discern in the one under discussion, but the very combination of the two elements mentioned suggests that in fact the spiral was there felt to be expressive of the divine female, the source of life and harbour of death.[3]

What is a matter of inference for these neolithic monuments from Northwest Europe is demonstrable with regard to another typical combination of two spirals, which archaeologists describe by the graphic, if inappropriate, term 'spectacle spirals'. This shape, ∞, could easily be effected by rolling up a piece of metal (e.g. copper or gold) wire, and indeed it is in these materials that many of the earliest samples—for use as trinkets—were wrought. Notwithstanding the ease of production (which could as well have led to many other shapes), the persistence and wide spread of this particular one suggests that it represents more than the chance product of a craftsman's fancy; and indeed its significance has been discovered. We have every reason briefly to consider this particular

[1] G. Childe, *Skara Brae* (1931), Pl. xlv and p. 132 ('the only example of an elaborate spiral pattern incised on native pottery from North or Western Europe'). A reconstruction of this pattern may be found in G. Bibby, *The Testimony of the Spade* (1957), p. 322 (the drawing, though, ought to be looked at upside down).

[2] This is to say that I cannot find an 'oculi motif' on the New Grange kerbstone; I am glad, however, to agree with the learned authors (above, p. 29, n. 7) in so far as we find 'the goddess' represented by this symbol. A representation of eyes is evident on the back stone of the chamber tomb at Knockmany (their Plate 61, in the centre, underneath the large spiral; add the second stone, pictured by Crawford, p. 91, Figs. 31, top right, and 32, top left); possibly also on the cap stone of the North side chamber at New Grange (their Plates 28 and 30). All these, however, are not spirals at all (nor are any of the 'eye-symbols' adduced by Crawford from all over the world—with the sole exception of the very ones, in Malta and Sicily, which are our special concern). Rather, these are variations on the typical 'owl-face' known from e.g. the Trojan face-urns or the Sicul bronze plate from Mendolito (Crawford, Pl. 12a, L. Bernabò Brea, Pl. 75), which can be traced back right to pre-Sargonid Sumer (A. Parrot, *Sumer* (1960), Fig. 200; cf. G. Childe, *The Dawn*...[4], p. 43, who refers to analogous representations on Sumerian funerary jars). For a representation of eyes by actual spirals one may compare a Gothic bronze fibula from South Russia published by H. Kühn (*Ipek*, xix (1954), Pl. 21. 2): the comparison will further discourage this interpretation of the New Grange spiral.

[3] The vulva character of the lozenges is particularly evident on Pls. 17 and 18 of the book by ÓRíordáin and Daniel.

pattern, for it is almost identical with the Maltese motif with which we are concerned—except that, in Malta, its very top has, so to speak, been cut off, leaving the pair of spirals unconnected.

As a trinket, it was frequently worn in Central Europe from the late neolithic period onward. G. Childe quotes[1] one sample from Jordansmühl in Silesia and an identical one from Poland, and particularly rich, though more recent, evidence is provided by a series of 'goddess figures' which V. Dumitrescu unearthed in a Bronze Age ('Urnfield') necropolis at Cîrna on the lower Danube and published with a full and instructive commentary.[2] These elaborate clay figurines belong to a fairly wide-spread group ('Vattina'), specimens of which have been known for a long time.[3] They will shortly interest us further; here it suffices to say that most of them are wearing the symbol in question attached to a necklace. In two instances[4] there are even two such shown, the one below the other; the result is a four-spiral pattern which perhaps may be compared with the first Castelluccio slab. The same symbol is frequent on the bronze-age (and later) rock carvings in the Val Camonica in the Italian Alps; as E. Anati in his exciting recent book shows[5] (he calls it, sans plus, a 'fertility symbol'). There again it occurs doubled, and not only as an independent symbol but also, as a meaningful décor, on menhirs. The women of the Veneti—as their graves at St. Lucia, east of the Isonzo, have shown— wore this together with many other apotropaic symbols on necklaces;[6] it also occurs, large and expressive, on a grave at Nesactium in Istria, east of Pola.[7]

The same motif is found on pottery. It decorates, in relief, the rims of four pithoi discovered in the 'double megaron' at Sesklo[8] and is painted underneath the rim of a 'Palace style' pithos from Knossos[9] and on a Late

[1] *The Danube in Prehistory* (1929), p. 87, Fig. 57; *The Dawn . . .*[4], p. 104, Fig. 49; cf. pp. 114 f. Childe (*The Dawn . . .*[4], p. 229), moreover, mentions one from Sicily; this I have been unable to trace. I have little doubt that the 'curious, anchor-shaped ornaments' which he reports from Bavaria (*The Danube . . .*, p. 191; Bell-beaker period) and Macedonia (*The Dawn . . .*[4], p. 84; Early Bronze-Age) represent the same symbol.

[2] *Ipek*, xix (1954–9), 16 ff., esp. 35, and Pls. 14 ff. I have been unable to see the large work by the same author about the same subject (*Necropola . . . de la Cîrna* (1961)). From the brief report about it in *Ipek*, xx (1963), 103 the important fact may be quoted that the large funerary urns of Cîrna are decorated with symbolic patterns similar to those on the statuettes, which are examined below, pp. 33 ff.

[3] See Hoernes–Menghin, p. 409, Fig. 1 and p. 411, Figs. 1–7; cf. G. Childe, *The Danube . . .*, pp. 268 ff., esp. p. 286. The 'Venus of Sălcuţa', quoted above, p. 29, belongs to this group.

[4] *Ipek*, Pl. 18 (top); our Plate 6.

[5] E. Anati, *Camonica Valley* (1964), pp. 67 ff. and 198.

[6] Duhn–Messerschmidt, *Italische Gräberkunde*, ii (1939), p. 118 and Pl. 19a; cf. ib., p. 87 and, for the same usage in Picenum, p. 182 (Novilara).

[7] Ib., p. 148 and Pl. 23d.   [8] Tsountas, pp. 229 f. with Figs. 123–6.

[9] H. T. Bossert, *Alt Kreta* (1921), fig. 73 (after *BSA*, ix. 139, Fig. 88); Schachermeyr, *Die minoische Kultur*, Pl. 62 (bottom right); Demargne, Pls. 203 f.

Minoan jug from a grave at Katsabas nearby.[1] All the rest of this vessel is covered with short protrusions, no doubt suggesting breasts; the meaning of this combination of symbols—in a grave—requires no comment. And, finally, it is a frequent element of Mycenaean jewellery.[2]

Leaving aside more recent, or distant, European instances (e.g. from Scandinavia where, in the service of a different religion, spiral motifs are likely to have been expressive of totally different ideas), we turn to Asia; for the symbol under discussion originated in the Near East; as was brilliantly shown by H. Frankfort.[3] It is used to this day by Egyptian women as an amulet to ensure safe and easy childbirth; it is the sign of Ninhursag, the Sumerian goddess of birth, whose name is, in at least one list, translated as 'uterus'. Among many striking instances of the persistence of symbols, this surely is one of the most amazing; Frankfort, who elsewhere[4] published a Syrian statuette of 'the Goddess' wearing the symbol as a trinket just as do those from Cîrna, summarized its occurrence from Ur to Anatolia.[5] Its transmission to Europe may well have been through Troy, for it occurs in profusion on several well-known pieces of jewellery from the 'treasures' found in Troy II g,[6] and also—this fact will presently prove particularly interesting—on the middle of some of the 'face-urns' from Troy II and III.[7]

What material model—if any—caused this particular pattern to be chosen for a symbol of the goddess Ninhursag has not so far been convincingly established. The suggestion that it represents swaddling bands will hardly convince; but it may be squeamishness to baulk at the alternative of acknowledging the resemblance to a cow's uterus. Perhaps, though, the origin has to be sought in the field of psychology rather than in any material substratum. At any rate this type of spiral pattern, too, has

[1] C. Zervos, *L'Art de la Crète* (1956), Pl. 701; Demargne, Pls. 206 and 209 (I would acknowledge it also on the Middle Minoan jug from Phaistos pictured ib., Pl. 127). The Late Minoan golden necklace from Phaistos, pictured by H. T. Bossert, *Alt Kreta* (1921), Fig. 228c (cf. *Mon. Ant.* xiv. 59 and Zervos, Pl. 786) appears to be entirely made up of the same symbol, even though the spirals are reduced to discs.

[2] *Brit. Mus. Catal. of Greek and Roman Jewellery*, nos. 138 and 179; R. A. Higgins, *Greek and Roman Jewellery* (1961), Pls. 9 and also 8d and 10h.

[3] *Journ. of Near Eastern Studies*, iii (1944), 198 (with indication of literature; esp. Douglas van Buren in *Archiv für Orientforschung*, ix. 167, who presents the Sumerian evidence in full).

[4] *The Art and Architecture* . . . , Pl. 144; our Plate 7a.

[5] It has been found e.g. at Tepe Hissar (in N. Persia); see *Iraq*, ix (1947), 173, Fig. 15; at Assur, *Iraq*, xxii (1960), 108, Fig. 1; at Nimrud even a mould for casting it: ib., Pl. XIII. 1. The meaning is made unambiguously, even painfully, plain on one of the Luristan bronze pins (R. Ghirshman, *Iran* (Penguin, 1954, reprint 1965), Pl. 8a).

[6] e.g. in G. Childe, *The Dawn* . . .⁴, Fig. 22, 3 and 4; Winter, *Kunstgeschichte in Bildern*, i. 82, Figs. 18 and 21; F. Matz, *Kreta, Mykene, Troja* (1956), pp. 19f. and Pl. 6 top, (left); our Plate 7b.

[7] H. Schliemann, *Ilios* (1880), no. 233 (= Hoernes–Menghin, p. 361, no. 8 = Neumann, p. 122, Fig. 17); H. Schmidt, *Schliemanns Sammlung* (1902), no. 433 (= H. T. Bossert, *Altanatolien* (1942), Fig. 56); C. W. Blegen, *Troy*, I part ii (1950), Pl. 390 (no. 35. 490); cf. ib., Pls. 389 and 370b, type C 31; id., *Troy and the Trojans* (1963), p. 80, Fig. 19 (left) and p. 96, Fig. 22 (left); our Plate 7c.

proved to symbolize the female; again with particular reference to the fact, and act, of birth. We noted its similarity—close but not perfect— with our specific object; we proceed to move even closer to it.

The ten figures (not counting the fragments) of 'the Goddess' found at Cîrna combine abstract stylization, in a remarkable manner, with a realistic rendering of detail. The over-all shape is the same in all of them; it consists of a disc ending in a small prism (the head) at the top and joined, by a narrower part (the waist), to the larger, bell-shaped bottom.[1] This abstract shape is made, by incised lines, to suggest the costume (and, as we saw, also the necklaces) worn by the women of that time and region. Dumitrescu's painstaking interpretation shows that it consists of skirt, blouse, belt, a long wide skirt and an apron—the traditional costume worn in those parts to this day. It was (as it is to this day) richly decorated with embroidery; which is likewise indicated on the statuettes. This décor largely consists—as we are about to show—of sexual symbols (to use modern parlance); symbols which interpret the body encased in the shapeless dress. This fact, though possibly shocking to the reader, is not really surprising. The sexual symbolism underlying much of the most lovely folk-art, in the Balkans and elsewhere, is well known; we met with a precedent when interpreting the pendant worn by the Cîrna figures. This again is but one instance confirming a general rule. Beads were, from the first, worn not merely for decoration but as amulets, and as such sexual symbols have from of old been considered to be uniquely efficient. Such were worn by the queens of Troy (as Schliemann's finds showed); and should they not become the woman-goddess?

Seven of the ten Cîrna figurines[2] exhibit, immediately below the middle of the belt, one and the same ornament.[3] It is made up, with slight variations in detail, of two elements. Its upper, hatched part is either a diamond-shaped lozenge, longways downward (thus in no. 4 only) or the lower half of the same, i.e. a triangle (thus in the other six). The

---

[1] The shape is basically identical with that of countless abstract 'idols', and this fact weakens the case for the derivation of the 'figurines à robe cloche' from Minoan Crete. The dress indicated on this abstract foundation does indeed show great similarity with that of Cretan women; moreover, there is a notable similarity in the indication of pigtails as worn by Cîrna women (Dumitrescu, Pl. 16. 6b) and on a Late Minoan male statuette (H. T. Bossert, *Alt Kreta* (1921), Fig. 149a). Primarily, though, this was the attire of the persons for whom the statuettes were made, and similar skirts were worn in Sumer and in Malta. Hence the Minoan derivation of the Rumanian figurines and of the Maltese dress does not seem to impose itself. Cf. below, p. 38, note 6, and Dumitrescu, p. 48, note 74.

[2] The reader who cares to check the following will with advantage compare the excellent photographs in Dumitrescu's publication (*Ipek*, xix (1958–9), pp. 16 ff., some of which (nos. 1, 2, 5, 10) are reproduced on our Plates 8 and 9). In the text above I am referring to the front views (marked 'a' by Dumitrescu) of the statuettes. The three divergent figures are nos. 1, 5, and 6; they will be considered presently.

[3] For late-neolithic antecedents of the same see J. Dombay, *Zenovarkony* (1960), Plates C, CI. 3, CIII.

pointed lower end of this part develops downward into the second element; namely a pair of spirals back to back, curling down- and outward.[1] There can be no doubt about the meaning of this compound pattern, in this place. Its upper part depicts the pubic region;[2] the spirals are identical with those worn as trinkets, on necklaces, by the same figures. They are 'the symbol of Ninhursag', identical also with the Maltese relief slabs (for their tops are not here joined, as they are in the usual 'spectacle pattern'); they thus confirm decisively the interpretation of these.

Certain details of the ornamentation of the Cîrna figurines have a particular bearing on our subject. For one thing, two of them (nos. 8 and 9) exhibit a second pair of spirals, curling in the opposite sense, at the upper, outer ends of the pubic triangle. The effect is a pattern comparable with that on the first Castelluccio slab.[3] We shall revert to this point, to which there are further important analogies in other details of the statuettes. Secondly, in two instances a straight (no. 4) or wavy (no. 3) line extends from below, between the spirals and towards the triangle above. The impression that it may stand for a phallus is confirmed by many further details. The 'spectacle pendant' (or, more properly, the 'symbol of Ninhursag') similarly has, in three instances (nos. 2, 6, 7) a line, resolved into dots, ascending towards its centre; in three others (nos. 5, 8, 10) the same line is continuous and has at its lower end a motif which Dumitrescu calls 'papillon'; I suppose it signifies testicles. In one, final instance, otherwise identical (no. 3), its place is filled by two cross-bars.

Of particular relevance to the present investigation is the large pattern, underneath the one just discussed, on statuette no. 10. Although it is crossed by the usual horizontal strip which Dumitrescu interprets as the lower end of the apron, the upper and lower halves are evidently intended to be continuous (and we shall presently confirm this impression by parallels). The cut-off lower part is, once more, the now familiar 'Maltese' two-spiral-pattern; the upper part is, so to speak, its mirrored reflection. The effect is a four-spiral-pattern practically identical with that on the first Castelluccio slab; except that the lines connecting the upper and lower spiral, on the left and right respectively, are almost straight. The same pattern recurs on statuette no. 1; there, however, it is placed in its entirety above the horizontal strip (which, on this figure, is significantly decorated with ∽-spirals); this four-spiral-pattern thus here fills the place in which all the figures so far quoted, including no. 10, have the compound design whose meaning has just become clear; the conclusion

---

[1] The slight variation in no. 9 will presently be described.

[2] For a striking parallel—one among a thousand—see the cult figure found in a cemetery at Dechsel near Landsberg/Warthe ('Lausitzer Kultur', c. 800–600 B.C.), pictured by H. Kühn, *Vorgeschichtliche Kunst Deutschlands* (1935), p. 354, and by E. Neumann, Pl. 31a.

[3] This applies strictly to no. 8 only; on no. 9 (which, besides, is damaged) the direction of the spirals is inverted.

regarding the pattern under discussion is self-evident. Differently from no. 10, the lines connecting the upper and lower spirals are, in no. 1, strongly bent so as to form almost half-circles, back to back; accordingly, the distance between the spirals right and left is greater and the similarity with the Sicilian slab even closer.

On both figures a strong vertical line penetrates the space between the lines connecting the spirals. Here again the phallus appears to be symbolized, testicles being suggested by a fairly elaborate ornament at the bottom of the staff in no. 1.

It is not easy to say whether this spiral pattern was felt to be an essentially symbolic expression or whether, in addition, it was intended as an—extremely stylized—representation of a concrete bodily substratum. If an indication of the phallus has rightly been acknowledged, the latter alternative becomes almost inescapable; the four-spiral-pattern would then represent the vulva; and its place on the figure as well as the analogy of the pattern which the other statuettes have in this place strongly commend this interpretation. In distinction from the plain lozenge or triangle motif, this spiral pattern would appear to convey the notion of the divine vulva as the mysterious place of eternal birth and re-birth.[1]

And yet it seems possible that the spiral motif was capable, in addition, of suggesting other, and larger, concrete parts of the body. Statuette no. 1 has, underneath the horizontal strip, a decorative pattern similar in size and general shape to the one just discussed but different in significant details. For one thing, the direction of the phallus (if that is what the central straight line means) is inverted: this may or may not be a matter merely of decorative distribution.[2] Secondly, the lines analogous to the curves which, in the pattern above the dividing strip, connect the upper and lower spirals descend, in the pattern below, in an almost straight line from the upper spirals. Near the bottom they bend outward at a sharp angle and, instead of terminating in spirals, continue horizontally and end in a figure like two fingers stretched apart. The whole of these lines fairly definitely suggests legs and feet, and this accords well with the place on the statuette filled by this pattern. The two spirals at its top could, in this combination, quite easily be taken to represent eyes, but their position as well as the analogy of the figure above suggests that the pattern as a whole is intended, rather, to symbolize the lower half of the body.

[1] It may be worth observing that the shape, in statuette no. 1, of the left and the corresponding right part of the pattern is fairly similar to that other well-known symbol, the cowrie shell.

[2] I see no convincing explanation for the differentiation in a subordinate motif in the pattern above and below, namely, two angles pointing at the central line in the former, but two pairs of parallel dashes in the latter—and yet this differentiation may conceivably yield the clue of the whole problem. Nor should I venture to interpret the whole of the lower pattern as a male symbolism: this would seem contrary to the ideology of all the representations on all the figurines.

A variant of it occurs, in the same position, on the statuette no. 5. While the space above the dividing strip is, for once, filled by an X-shaped figure,[1] the one below it is as in no. 1; except that the 'phallus' is reduced to a single, undecorated line and that the lines at the bottom do not end in 'feet' but continue upward, until right above the spirals, in a wide circular sweep. Even so, the general impression conveyed is as in no. 1.

At this point—or even earlier—some readers may perhaps feel, or have felt, inclined to protest: what justification is there for interpreting these renderings of bronze-age embroideries partly as indications, and partly as symbolizations, of intimate parts of the body covered by a rich costume—rather than as products of the playful imagination of painstaking needle-women? Apart from the theoretical considerations sketched at the beginning of this section and the fact that the same ornaments recur on funerary urns (not an indifferent kind of vessel), the following facts may be urged against an approach of this kind. The makers were evidently concerned also in other parts of these abstract figurines to indicate concrete parts of the body; as throughout, by abstract motifs. Details of the face are intimated by an ornament which looks somewhat like a lyre; the breasts by small spirals which realistically would represent the upper ends of skirts (no. 1) or of arms (no. 8) or even the 'spectacle pendant' (no. 7). I could enter into further detail, but these will, I trust, suffice to confirm the implications discerned in the—remarkably standardized—details on which we have been concentrating.

It has not been—from the point of view here adopted—a wasted effort. As the 'spectacle pendants' and their like could serve to illuminate the Maltese relief, and the 'four-spiral-motif' the first of the Castelluccio slabs, so the motif considered last, with its intimation of legs issuing from spirals at the top, affords a welcome and close parallel to the second of the Sicilian slabs which occasioned the present investigation. Another parallel to it may be quoted from an age immensely far remote; namely, one of the pebbles with symbols painted on it found in the cave of Maze d'Azil in the Pyrenees and dating from the mesolithic age, perhaps 8000 B.C. This often-depicted stone[2] intimates the 'goddess' with 'spidery legs' bent at right angles and is thus comparable to the second Castelluccio slab as well as to the Cîrna motif discussed last.

The 'four-spiral-motif' has been shown, like the 'spectacle pendant', to have originated in the most ancient Near East. I am not aware that its

---

[1] The same symbol is the centre of a 'magical dance' in a comparatively late rock-engraving in the Val Camonica (Anati, p. 218). Its formal relation to, and identity of meaning with, the four-spiral-sign are easily seen (ꟓꟅ, ꓛC and X: cf. below, p. 41). The cross—so J. Mellaart observes (p. 124)—'is still the symbol of fertility in Anatolia'.

[2] e.g. *Ipek*, xx (1960–3), Pl. 5. 3; *The Dawn* ... , ed. S. Piggott (1961), chapter 1, Pl. 20.

symbolic meaning, as it has just emerged, has been traced to the same region, but the one appears to be given with the other.

Reporting his excavations at Tell Brak in the upper Khabur valley, M. E. L. Mallowan used the emergence of this motif in the Sargonid layer of this site to illustrate its occurrence, as a small bead made of silver or gold, in the Near East and beyond,[1] and Maxwell Hyslop, resuming the topic, stressed the primary religious purpose of this ancient jewellery.[2] Four-spiral trinkets, then, of this type have been found, apart from Tell Brak, at Mari, Alaça Hüyük,[3] Troy II and III,[4] and also in the shaft graves at Mycenae and even in the Caucasus. Its transmission from the Orient to the Danubian regions will readily be granted in view of the manifold impact of Troy upon the neighbouring Balkans.[5] An important confirmation of the suggested, 'female' meaning of the four-spiral pattern is given by the fact that it covers the back of a Late Minoan clay model, found at Ialysos (Rhodes), of a *Götterthron*,[6] for wherever the figure seated on these 'thrones' is preserved, it is a female one.[7] Here, then, this pattern—strikingly similar to the one on the Castelluccio door—proclaims the goddess the owner of the throne.

The symbolism conveyed by the set of decorative motifs which we have been studying has emerged with increasing definiteness. This set of ancient motifs—specific patterns of two or four spirals, separate or in combination with triangle or lozenge—has had an amazingly long history; in those Danubian parts where we found it most fully developed it has survived to this day. A brief glance at its later history may serve to confirm our interpretation and to support its application to the monuments in Malta and Sicily which are our primary concern.

[1] *Iraq*, ix (1947), 171 ff. [2] *Iraq*, xxii (1960), 105 ff.

[3] Illustrated also by H. T. Bossert, *Altanatolien*, Figs. 309–12.

[4] Schliemann, *Ilios*, pp. 489, 490, 501; cf. Blegen, *Troy and the Trojans*, p. 76.

[5] A closely similar motif from the inside of a dish from chalcolithic Hacilar I is to be found reproduced in *AS*, ix (1959), 61, Fig. 5. 1 (now also in Mellaart, p. 109, top left). The excavator states (*AS*, ix (1959), p. 60) that the variety of geometric patterns used for decoration of the 'truly enormous' amount of pottery from this site is 'extremely rich and varied, so that no two vessels are ornamented exactly alike'; hence this similarity might be regarded as the chance product of a purely abstract imagination (if indeed such can be assumed to have existed). Yet there are, among the samples depicted, several which forcibly recall those motifs on which we are concentrating (see ib., Pl. IXb2 and XIIIa and Fig. 4. 1) and the frequency, among the standard motifs, of triangle, lozenge, and spiral suggests the possibility that, as Dumitrescu said of the Danubians, 'ces artistes géometrisaient toujours leurs images, même lorsqu'ils voulaient représenter la nature'. If, similarly, a symbolic meaning were to be attributed to the geometric patterns from Hacilar, the probability of an Anatolian derivation of the Danubian symbolism would be enhanced.

[6] Pictured by H.-G. Buchholz, *Zur Herkunft der kretischen Doppelaxt* (1959), p. 17, Fig. 4 (Buchholz oddly finds the double-axe in this pattern, although it has not the faintest similarity with any of the many specimens of this cultic implement which he himself has so carefully collected).

[7] Id., p. 17, after M. P. Nilsson, *The Minoan-Mycenaean Religion*[2] (1950), p. 350; cf. Schachermeyr, *Die minoische Kultur*, p. 166.

We may start by supplementing the earliest evidence. Some of the Trojan face-urns have been cited above because they exhibit the 'symbol of Ninhursag' on the centre of their bodies. In its place, another one[1] has a 'two-spiral-motif'. It is indeed somewhat drawn apart, because the artist wanted to join its outward ends to the handles (shaped so as to suggest raised arms); even so, the meaning of the pattern is indubitable in view of its position; and this all the more so since breasts are indicated above it.—In contrast to neolithic Crete, the refined eroticism of the Minoan civilisation shunned any direct representation of sex;[2] none the less we noted[3] some instances of the 'symbol of Ninhursag' on Late Minoan vases. Nor are our other motifs absent from this art. Among Pendlebury's[4] drawings of patterns on Middle Minoan I pottery we may note the four-spiral figure with lozenge (Fig. 17. 19); a variant of the 'spectacle pattern' (ib., 22) and the triangle, divided along its middle and decorated with small spiral hooks (Fig. 18. 5): these, and perhaps others,[5] may have conveyed the same symbolism in Crete as elsewhere.[6]

The large span of time separating the folk art of our own age from these and the other ancient instances previously quoted may be bridged by reference to a few selected instances. The Cîrna figurines were fashioned in the Late Bronze Age; the decorative motifs on them, which we have studied, recur on pottery of the same age and region.[7] From the subsequent Early Iron Age—more than a thousand years, that is, after the Minoan instances just cited and perhaps half a millennium after Cîrna—

---

[1] *Handbuch der Archaeologie*, ii, Tafel 18. 4 = Winter, *Kunstgeschichte in Bildern*, iii. 82 = Schachermeyr, *Die ältesten Kulturen* . . . , Pl. X. 3.

[2] G. Childe, *The Dawn* . . .⁴, p. 25 lists as 'phalli' the strange, pipe-shaped objects found in sanctuaries at Koumasa and Gournia (pictured e.g. in Nilsson, *Geschichte d. gr. Relig.* i, Pls. 1 and 2). This interpretation, however, is anything but obvious; see, for a full discussion, Nilsson, *The Minoan-Mycenaean Religion*² (1950), pp. 315 ff.

[3] Above, pp. 31 f.

[4] *The Archaeology of Crete*, pp. 108 ff. (some also in R. W. Hutchinson, *Prehistoric Crete* (1962), p. 168, Fig. 30).

[5] Perhaps also Fig. 16. 1 (triangle), 9 and 10 (lozenges); Fig. 17. 6 and 18 (the cross, in X-shape as in Cîrna no. 5 and upright as in Hacilar, *AS*, ix (1959), Fig. 6. 5); Fig. 17. 24 the 'whorl shell' (cf. Pendlebury, p. 110)—which, like other shells, may have conveyed specific associations. Cf. also the Linear A mark on a potsherd from Phylakopi (Brice, Pl. XXV, no. ii. 22. iii).

[6] Even if the instances quoted are accepted as analogous to the Danubian (I regret that, owing to lack of material, I cannot go beyond the suggestions proffered in the text), I should hesitate to quote them in support of the derivation of the Vattina figurines from Crete—where no figurines of this type and with this décor exist (cf. above, p. 33, n. 1, and Müller, p. 56, n. 55). Analogies between M.M. I. and prehistoric Rumania, far more significant than these, do in fact exist; but I have no wish to dogmatize where an authority like F. Schachermeyr (*Die minoische Kultur*, pp. 58 ff.) finds reason for hesitation. The primitive forms of the Balkanic 'figurines à robe cloche' instanced by V. Dumitrescu (*Ipek*, viii (1932–3), 49 ff.; see esp. Pl. 11. 6) to my mind rather militate against his thesis of their Minoan inspiration. To say this is not, of course, to deny the oriental ancestry of the Balkanic figurines in general.

[7] Some samples may be seen in Hoernes–Menghin, pp. 405 and 407; cf. above, p. 31, n. 2. The South Russian pot, Childe, *The Dawn* . . .⁴, p. 155, Fig. 77. 1, may be compared.

two Danubian samples may be quoted (using the word 'Danubian' in its widest connotation). First, a two-storey funerary vase ('Hallstadt C') found North of Vienna.[1] The broad rim of the lower part of this elaborate vessel is decorated on each of its four sides with a large V made up of small circles, the lowest of which has a cross inscribed in it. The symbolism is obvious. Along the sides of the V, and extending below it, are double spirals; the whole resulting in the pattern of e.g. Cîrna no. 8. Further spirals develop downward from the top of each of the upper ones, effecting, together with these and the neighbouring pairs, the familiar upright 'four-spiral-pattern'.

Somewhat more recent ('Hallstadt D') is a funerary vase from Brauchitschdorf in Middle Silesia, decorated with a design which, again, is a variation on the central Cîrna theme.[2] This design, which covers the whole body of the vessel, consists of an upright lozenge, subdivided into triangles; single lines run downward along its left and right sides which, below its lowest point, bend outward into incipient spirals—the now familiar symbolism: the vessel of Death is the vessel of Life, through the unending miracle of Birth.

We move on another thousand years. Among the relics of Germanic tribes from the age of migrations are the characteristic 'arched brooches' ('Bügelfibeln'). The same scholar to whom we are indebted for our last sample, H. Kühn, has presented a thoughtful, richly illustrated study of them.[3] He pictures one from the neighbourhood of Kiev, now in the British Museum,[4] on which the place of the symbols which normally occur on these fibulae is filled by a representation of the Magna Mater, identified as Πότνια θηρῶν by the addition of five animal heads. Apart from the naturalistic rendering of her head, the representation is thoroughly

---

[1] Hoernes–Menghin, p. 483. 2; reproduced in R. Pittioni, *Die urgeschichtlichen Grundlagen der Europäischen Kultur* (1949), p. 242, Fig. 101. 4.—Hoernes–Menghin on the same page (no. 1) picture a vase from NW. Hungary with, in principle, the same décor as the Trojan face-urns referred to above, pp. 32 and 38. Its handles are shaped as raised arms; the centre of the vessel is filled by a lozenge (or 'rhombus', to vary the terminology), right and left of which are spirals; not rounded though but rectangular, in accordance with the style of the whole; the rest of the ornamentation consists of triangles. Pittioni likewise, on the page quoted, reproduces another vase (no. 1) whose spiral décor, right and left of a central circle, bears on our present subject, and so do the two vases illustrated in Hoernes–Menghin, p. 485. I refrain from labouring the point, but it is worth mentioning in order to show that the instances quoted in the text above are not isolated. See our Plate 10.

[2] H. Kühn, *Vorgeschichtliche Kunst Deutschlands*, p. 360, Pl. X, no. 2.—For an instance of the same design from Celtic France see R. Joffroy, *L'Oppidum de Vix* (1960), Pl. 63, and for its frequency in Etruscan jewellery, *Brit. Mus. Cat.*, p. 129.

[3] *Ipek*, xix (1954–7), 49 ff.; cf. Cîrna, nos. 2, 4, 10.

[4] Ib., Pl. XXV. 2 (*BM. Guide to Anglo-Saxon Antiquities* (1923), p. 172, Fig. 227). I fail to see how this piece could be called 'Gothic' underneath the picture, while on p. 55 it is ascribed to the 7th century; nor does the description of it at the latter place quite tally with that given on p. 59, nor indeed with the photograph.—One may note, in the same place (no. 4), the 'four-spiral-motif' on a Christianized, Anglo-Saxon fibula.

symbolical; with spirals and triangles and also with branches—'signs of fertility', which I suppose to signify phalli like the, almost identical, 'feathers' in palaeolithic carvings.[1] The spirals are not, on this fibula, arranged in exactly the same manner as in our other samples; even so, the analogy is striking.

Once again we move on by a millennium and more (for I lack the knowledge of medieval handicrafts which could serve to illustrate the continuity of the tradition which is demonstrated by its survivals in our own times). A richly carved and painted dowry-chest (*Brauttruhe*) made in Upper Austria in the eighteenth century and destined to hold the linen of a peasant bride is covered, not unfittingly, with the symbols in which we are interested.[2] Its heavy lock is set in the centre of a huge V surrounded by running spirals; underneath and on both sides are squares filled with the four-spiral motif which we have traced from Tell Brak to Castelluccio. Another chest of the same type, from Carinthia,[3] has an S-spiral on its centre (recalling the goddess from Philippopel); on the right and left is the familiar hatched lozenge (henceforth 'rhombus'), divided into two triangles by a horizontal line and emitting small pairs of spirals from its upper and lower ends. A facing pair of S-spirals hangs down from the middle of this familiar pattern and the corners of the chest are decorated with chains of the same motif.

Easter eggs are much-favoured carriers of the same symbolism; a fact which will not surprise those conversant with the pagan roots of this piece of traditional lore. Various shapes of the four-spiral-pattern—the double spiral beneath a triangle or rhombus (exactly as at Cîrna), with or without 'branch' and 'spectacle pattern'—the whole set can be found, in the Hungarian-Rumanian region,[4] painted on these modest tokens of immortality.

The main field for it, however, is in the products of women's handiwork, weaving and embroidery, especially on clothes and bed linen. From Rumanian folk-art may be mentioned · the four-spiral-pattern, doubled, on a girl's cap;[5] on smocks, the rhombus, either with small spiral hooks on all sides (the Minoan pattern), or as the centre of pairs of spirals;[6] on apron belts, S-spirals, alternating with branches, above a row of triangles and rhombi; and in particular the lower border of an

---

[1] S. Giedion, i. 200 ff.; cf. the combination of spirals, upright branches, and snakes on a Late Minoan sarcophagus pictured by G. Wilke, p. 105, Fig. 112 (for this type see lately E. T. Vermeule, *JHS*, lxxxv (1965), 123 ff., esp. 134 f.).

[2] *Peasant Art in Austria*, ed. C. Holme (1911; special number of *The Studio*), Fig. 5; our Plate 11*a*.

[3] Ib., p. 459; our Plate 11*b*.

[4] C. Viski and others (edd.), *L'Art populaire hongrois* (1928), pp. 227 f.; G. Oprescu, *Peasant Art in Roumania* (1929; special number of *The Studio*), p. 36.

[5] G. Oprescu, loc. laud. p. 63.

[6] Ib., pp. 77 and 93.

apron from the province of Olten (the very region of Cîrna),[1] which
centres, once more, on the rhombus, with spirals issuing from its upper
and lower ends—the whole being practically identical with the pattern
on a bronze-age plate from Vattina[2]—except that, in the embroidery, the
spirals are made rectangular.[3] Analogous, and telling, is the lace-pattern
on a pillow-slip.[4] It consists basically of the ancient four-spiral-pattern
(circular), but its meaning has here been made explicit in a simple and significant manner. The straight line connecting the upper and lower pair
of spirals continues upwards and ends in the semblance of a head;
at the lower end is a small circle inscribed with a cross.[5] In this context, the
spirals clearly mean arms and legs, and the whole pattern means—woman.

Significant though these survivals are, they must not be supposed to
dominate Rumanian folk-art (in H. T. Bossert's vast collection of patterns I found only one bearing on the present subject).[6] The same applies
to Greek embroidery, so fully and authoritatively presented by A. J. B.
Wace:[7] it too continues a very old tradition, but this is so thoroughly
affected by the motifs and methods of Turkish tapestry that survivals
of the kind here sought are not easily and convincingly shown. It may
still be observed that the most frequent of traditional patterns fits our
frame. It is called the 'Queen's pattern' and centres on the (Minoan)
'rhombus' surrounded by diminutive spirals ('hooks').[8] The same,
ancient and meaningful motif provides the décor of the front of Bosnian
women's dresses;[9] rows of alternating rhombi and lying crosses (XXX)
encircle the centre of Serbian women's costumes,[10] and the 'sign of
Ninhursag' minus the line connecting its two halves—as at Tarxien—
decorates a Croatian kerchief.[11] Finally, a glorious woman's costume from

---

[1] Ib., p. 112.—From the neighbourhood of Sofia comes a peasant woman's surcoat
richly decorated with the 'symbol of Ninhursag', closely similar to the Cîrna figurines,
especially no. 8: see M. Tilke, The Costumes of Eastern Europe (1926), Pl. 26; cf. Pl. 43.

[2] Hoernes–Menghin, p. 405. 2.

[3] Cf. above, p. 39, n. 1.—The same pattern is illustrated from a woman's dress from
Monastir and from a woman's embroidered boot from near Skutari by L. E. Start, The
Durham Collection, Halifax Museum (1939), Pls. IX.A and X.E. The boot, moreover, has
a large 'Ninhursag symbol'.

[4] Viski, p. 106; cf. ib., pp. 104 f.; also Holme, p. 752.

[5] The pattern is crossed, in its middle, by a vertical line suggesting the belt; like Cîrna,
no. 10.—The transformation of the four-spiral-pattern into a human figure may be seen also
in embroideries in the study-case 9 in the Department of Peasant Art in the Victoria and
Albert Museum, London.

[6] Folk Art of Europe (1954), Pl. 27. 10.

[7] Mediterranean and Near Eastern Embroideries (1935).

[8] Cf. the definition and illustration given by P. Johnstone, Greek Island Embroidery (1961),
pp. 27 ff.

[9] Victoria and Albert Museum, London, Department of Peasant Art, study-case 28.

[10] National costumes of Serbia, ed. M. S. Vlahovic (1954), title picture.

[11] Victoria and Albert Museum, ib. 26. The same motif, inverted, is on a medieval tomb-
stone from Lipenovići; see M. S. Vlahovic, Peasant tombstones in Serbia (1956), p. 4.

Herzegovina, exhibited in a show-case in the Victoria and Albert Museum, London,[1] is held together by a belt: its round buckle has in its centre the 'four-spiral-pattern', surrounded by a circle made up of the same, repeated motif.

(e) THE MALTESE GODDESS

We know now what the pair of spirals at the entrance of the middle Tarxien temple, and in other Maltese temples, meant: we also know that the small triangles between them are not mere decorative space-fillings but intimations of a specific motif which we have followed through the ages. These then are sexual symbols—if, once more, we may use the current, all-too-narrow term; misleading though it tends to be. Such symbols abounded in the Maltese sanctuaries; they are primary evidence illustrating the religion which was realized in them.

The rich and various ornamentation applied—at least in the more recent periods—to their interiors is largely based on the spiral. On the sides of altars, on the edges of platforms, on upright slabs and also on ceilings (preserved only at Hal Saflieni) there are running spirals of various types as well as other developments of the same basic motif; some of them suggesting plants and branches. Are they quite generally to be understood as symbols of the female deity, like the special forms which we have studied?

It is (to say it again) by no means given that every spiral must be expressive of the same, female principle; one would not, for example, assert this with regard to the Babylonian reduction to spirals of the entrails of sacrificial animals, nor of the profuse ornamentation of Scandinavian Bronze Age armour; but in Malta as well as in the Balkans the very combination of specific and unambiguously female motifs with many other forms likewise based upon the spiral makes it *a priori* probable that the same sentiment, or at least related sentiments are at the root of all of them. This probability increases when one examines a striking pair of patterns in the middle temple at Tarxien which is intermediate between the specific symbols and the freely flowing spiral ornaments.

On stepping over the symbolic pair of spirals at the entrance and walking through the narrow passage behind it one meets these patterns immediately on emerging into the first hall. There, two slabs, five feet high and almost as wide, stand at the back of low stone benches, or altars, partly screening the bays on the right and left. Their expressive ornaments (originally standing out white from the red colouring of their pitted background) seem to intimate specific aspects under which the goddess was worshipped in the bays behind them.[2] The patterns on both

[1] In the Department of Peasant Art.
[2] Cf. Zammit, p. 28 and Pl. IX. 3 (this really represents the left and not, as alleged, the

these screens consist of four large spirals and small triangles; not, though, in the particular form which we have traced from and to Castelluccio, for the spirals develop from each of the four corners towards a disc in the centre. Alternating triangles and pairs of)(-shaped spurs jut from the rim into the interstices between the spirals. So far, the description fits both slabs, and yet they are significantly different. Technically this difference can to a large extent be accounted for by simply stating that one of the slabs is turned by 90° compared with the other:[1] that is, the basis of the one forms one of the sides of its counterpart. As a result, the effect made by each is strikingly different in spite of their basic identity, and that, surely, is not due to chance or mistake. In fact the left slab has, in addition to its position, a feature peculiar to itself: namely, a triangle in the space between the root and the first winding of each spiral. On this slab, the upper and lower pairs of spirals appear to be moving towards each other and to the central disc, and the spur-like connection between rim and spirals suggests passages from below and above towards the centre. On the right slab, triangles take the place of the 'passages', and vice versa; the additional four triangles of the left slab are lacking; the upper and lower pairs of spirals seem to be moving away from each other and, instead, to be turning upon themselves.

It seems incredible, after all that we have seen, that these elaborate patterns, set up, as they are, in those two corresponding and important places, could be no more than pleasing figments of a decorator's fancy. They are certainly symbolic, and the analogy (in principle though not in detail) of the Castelluccio slab and so many related four-spiral-patterns confirms that, like the two spirals at the entrance a few yards away, they too intimate the goddess of the place. I regard it as possible that the left slab conveys her basic female quality; the right, the same in conjunction with the male principle which would thus be shown as an integral part of her all-comprehensive divinity. We shall soon meet with other indications of the same idea.

The last inference is, of course, no more than a guess; but the symbolic character also of this pair of freer spiral compositions may, I trust, be taken for granted. From here an inference regarding the remaining spiral motifs seems permissible. Running spirals in significant places—for example on the magnificent block facing the raised floor of the inner-most bay of the western Tarxien temple,[2] on altars,[3] and also on the ceiling at Hal Saflieni—may proclaim the deity in a more general way;

right slab; hence read 'Apse B' for 'Apse A'); Evans, p. 119, Pl. 28; von Cles-Reden, Pl. 30; our Plate 5*b*.

[1] Not, as Zammit avers, 'upside down'.

[2] Zammit, p. 20, Pl. VI. 1., cf. Pl. II; Evans, p. 117, Pl. 25, cf. Pls. 23 f.; von Cles-Reden, Pl. 25 (left).

[3] Zammit, p. 14, Fig. 1; Evans, Pls. 7 and 23 (right); von Cles-Reden, Pl. 25 (right).

spirals developing into floral patterns[1] may intimate the same deity as the giver and protector of fruitfulness, and so on.

In this wide application the spiral more or less loses the specific quality of a sexual symbol which it has in the specific form of the 'sign of Ninhursag'. Probably though—as we shall see,—there are other intimations of the female sex; veiled ones.[2] On the other hand, the male potency is represented by a great number of phalli. Many such of small size, in stone and clay, have been found at Tarxien, and it stands to reason that many more votive offerings of this type existed in that majority of temples which were excavated, long ago, without care for, or reports of, details. There are single phalli and groups of two or three, with bases and without; free standing and also within frames shaped as small shrines.[3] The latter are evidence that larger representations of the same kind stood on the raised bases in some of the actual shrines; moreover, huge phalli as well as smaller ones (coyly termed 'baetyls'[4] or 'conic stones' or, at best, 'fertility symbols') stood free in various parts of the temples.[5] Besides, there are the 'winged' or 'phallic' beads,[6] large counterparts of which, in stone, have been found in the temples and may be seen in the museums in Valetta and Gozo.

We have to consider what concept of the part played, in Maltese religion, by the male element may be indicated by this profusion of male symbols. One of them, striking by its very peculiar form, conveys a notable first hint. It is a quadrangular phallic cone, 17 cm. high, found in the first right bay of the first (i.e. Western) temple at Tarxien. It was carefully pressed into the soil beneath a stone behind the large idol the lower half of which still remains.[7] Apart from this significant location, a

---

[1] Zammit, p. 15, Pl. III. 1; von Cles-Reden, Pl. 22.

[2] Explicit indications of it are very rare in Malta, or even non-existent, apart from the *ex votos* representing diseased bodies (on these below, p. 47). The torso pictured by Zammit–Singer, Pl. VIII, no. 54 (cf. Zammit, Pl. XXVI. 3), should belong to this class. Besides, a fairly realistic delineation of the vulva may perhaps be recognized in the 'deep incision representing something like the horns of a bull' on a fragmentary soft stone from Hagar Qim (*BSR*, vi (1913), 88 and Pl. XIX, Figs. 1 and 2). It seems strikingly similar to many unambiguous palaeolithic representations (for these see Giedion, i. 190; cf. a figurine from Alishar in Bossert, *Altanatolien*, Fig. 293); in Malta it is, to the best of my knowledge, unique.

[3] See Zammit, Pl. XXIV; also *BSR*, vi (1913), Pl. IX. 4 (Kordin); Pl. XVIII. 3 and 4 (Hagar Qim); Pls. XXVI. 1, 14, and XXVII. 10 (Mnajdra).

[4] The misuse of this term persists, in spite of my efforts, long ago, to reassert its original connotation (*Class. et Mediaev.*, viii (1947), 169 ff.; esp. 180 ff. and 213).

[5] Zammit, pp. 17 f. and Pl. V. 1 (Tarxien); cf. id., *Archaeologia*, lxvii (1916), 143; Evans, p. 99 (the ' "baetyl" shaped rather like a high-explosive shell' from the Ġgantija is apparently identical with the huge 'fertility symbol' on view in the Gozo Museum and with the 'bétyle de Malta' discussed and pictured by E. de Manneville in *Études Syriennes . . . R. Dussaud*, ii (1939), p. 895 (although alleged to be in the Museum at Valetta)); for Kordin see *BSR*, vi (1913), p. 44 ('a column (no doubt a *baetylus*) similar to that discovered in the entrance passage'); for Hagar Qim, ib., pp. 65 and 67; for Mnajdra, ib., p. 98 ('one of the familiar megalithic pillars').   [6] Evans, p. 161.

[7] Zammit, in *Archaeologia*, lxvii (1916), 142; a photograph is in Giedion, i. 195.

particular feature of this symbol calls for attention: it is covered, all over, with drilled circular holes, resembling—not only in this respect—an early 'Danubian' clay-torso found at Birmenitz near Meissen (Saxony);[1] the latter figure, though, is pronouncedly female. S. Giedion has shown at length[2] that, from the Old Stone Age onward, holes, circles, 'cupules', and perforations were frequently (though not exclusively) used as female symbols and that as such, strange though it may seem, they occur 'time and again' on phalli. The Maltese object under consideration, then, like others previously mentioned,[3] is an instance of the idea of the 'two in one'. Nor is it, in Malta, the only one of its kind. Zammit pictures two more and mentions a third.[4] The male potency, so these symbols seem to suggest, is taken up in the female; and this suggestion agrees with our previous, tentative interpretation of one of the pair of symbolic slabs in the Middle Temple at Tarxien.

In one instance,[5] the basis of a miniature shrine, and not the phalli in it, is decorated with small drilled holes. Is the same meaning intended? The fact that the base of a statue, found at Ḥaġar Qim, of 'the Goddess'[6] is decorated in the same manner may support this assumption. If so, one would be led on to the conclusion that the 'pitting' of slabs—so frequent a means of decoration in the more recent buildings—likewise served to intimate the female principle. The fact that this appears to hold good for the only other decorative motif used, namely the spiral, would lend some plausibility to this assumption; and yet one may hesitate to entertain it on considering that the same might in consequence be claimed for the vast amount of pottery similarly decorated. There are, however, other, and perhaps more cogent, instances of the same symbolism.

One of those miniature shrines[7] contains, in addition to two of the male symbols, a round disc with a hole through its centre. There can be no doubt about its meaning in this context, and it is possible that the 'perforated flat stone discs with rounded edges' mentioned by Zammit and others[8] are symbols of the same kind. We are thus led to consider the import of the many, and various, artificial holes which puzzle the visitor of the Maltese sanctuaries.[9]

---

[1] H. Kühn, *Vorgeschichtl. Kunst Deutschlands*, p. 241; also Wilke, p. 121, Fig. 130; cf. also two figurines from Butmir in Hoernes–Menghin, p. 287, and two from Alishar in Bossert, *Altanatolien*, Figs. 287–8.

[2] i. 132 ff., especially 194 ff.   [3] Above, p. 15, n. 4.

[4] Pl. XXIV. 2 (centre) and 3 (right), and p. 86.   [5] Ib., Pl. XXIV. 1 (left).

[6] Evans, Pl. 49; the similar decoration of the garment of a seated 'priestess', from Tarxien (Zammit–Singer, Pl. XV, no. 61), may in this context be considered.

[7] Zammit, Pl. XXIV. 3; also, clearer, in Evans, Pl. 87.

[8] Zammit, p. 82; cf. *BSR*, vi (1913), Pl. XIX, Fig. 1, 3.

[9] Cf. Zammit–Singer, p. 77. Zammit shows that even some female statues have 'biconical holes' drilled into them; some of these in places where they cannot possibly have served for fitting-on a head; e.g. his nos. 7 (Pl. 54 Evans) and 20.

Some of them evidently served straightforward practical purposes. Heavy bars by which passages could be shut off rested in some of them; others were destined for leather thongs which served as door hinges. On the other hand there are the many holes drilled into the floors and closed by removable lids: they served to receive libations and sacrificial ashes; offerings which thus reached the chthonic deity in the most direct manner.[1] Next, there are holes cut into large upright slabs and serving as doorways; one (Mnajdra North) as main entrance; [2]others leading to 'chapels' in 'apses'. Since the easier method of achieving the same end, by means of a lintel resting on walls or uprights ('trilithon'), was used in many places, the adoption, in others, of this laborious procedure calls for an explanation. Where a large oblong opening (as a rule with rounded edges) has been effected in this way—as, for example, in the first chamber on the right at Haġar Qim—the resulting shape is strikingly similar to that of many 'doors' at Çatal Hüyük.[3] And indeed in a mud building this was a natural procedure, for in this material it was as easy to cut out a passage when the material had to an extent hardened, as it was difficult, or even impossible, to lay a beam across an opening. One might therefore consider the possibility that (as in the case of Greek triglyphs and metopes) a form conditioned by the use of primitive building materials was retained in stone-buildings. This technical explanation, however, cannot apply to other Maltese forms of cut-out passages. Some of them are so narrow as to make climbing through them a moderately acrobatic task.[4] Comparable so-called 'port-holes' are frequent in megalithic graves, where they are alternatively described as 'Seelenlöcher'. I need not here enter into the theory behind this designation: it could in any case not apply to the Maltese temples which were not places of burial; hence no 'souls' could be expected to make their way out, or in, by means of these holes. We shall presently return to the question of their purpose; but may first recall those numerous perforations in slabs and walls for which no credible practical purpose can be devised. They actually recall many similar palaeolithic features, which have been collected and discussed by S. Giedion.[5] His contention that, like the 'cupulae', they are symbols of the female has convinced me; once it is accepted, this whole set of Maltese features falls into line with the various other intimations of the deity of the place.

To the details which we have examined in order to approach the core of Maltese and, therewith, Sicilian prehistoric religion we have to add

---

[1] Zammit, p. 12; Evans, p. 136 f. [2] Evans, p. 113.
[3] Cf. e.g. Evans, Pl. 14 (or *BSR*, vi (1913), Pl. XIII. 2: Haġar Qim) with *AS*, xiv (1964), 44, Fig. 5; or also Evans, Pl. 20 (or *BSR*, ib., Pl. XXIII. 1: Mnajdra) with *AS*, ib., p. 65, Fig. 20. Very similar also are doors cut out of the entrance slabs of megalithic graves; e.g. at Los Millares (von Cles-Reden, Pl. 67). [4] e.g. Evans, Pl. 15. [5] i. 156 ff.

others that have long since been observed. They add up to the suggestion of a highly developed and diversified cult.[1] There were priests—with more than a suspicion of eunuchism—and priestesses, and accordingly, so one would infer, a theology. The rich and varied equipment of the temples, with apses, chapels, shrines, images, altars, offering tables, etc., is evidence of abundant established rites. Special installations indicate that the illusion of hearing a supernatural voice was created, and the two well-known terracotta statuettes from Hal Saflieni[2] testify to the practice of incubation as a means for obtaining divine guidance and, quite probably, also relief from various diseases (as at Epidauros). At any rate it is clear that sufferers sought healing in the sanctuaries; for reproductions of diseased bodies and of various limbs have been found in them, and the meaning of these *ex votos* is clear from countless analogies pagan and Christian.[3] Sacrifices of all kinds played a great part in the rites; as is evident from the reliefs showing sacrificial animals, from their ashes kept inside some altars and in holes in the floors, and from the installations, already mentioned, for the pouring of libations.

These, then, are vestiges of an abundant cult observed, in the temples, throughout many centuries.[4] Its object and motives may be considered after a glance at the hypogeum at Hal Saflieni.[5] This is, apart from the ancient graves at Xemxija,[6] the only notable burial place known, so far, from the temple-period. It is impressively large because it contains a large number of collective graves; this, however, is the result of a gradual growth owing to the addition, throughout a long time, of ever more burial chambers. The chambers themselves are all of the type of those at Xemxija, and small. In consequence, the complex as a whole is not comparable to any of the large temples which are realizations of one grandiose design and reach back much farther in time than even the earliest burials at Hal Saflieni. None the less, inferences about the purpose and meaning of the temples have been based upon assumptions, uncertain enough in themselves, concerning the ideas connected with

---

[1] Cf. Evans, pp. 135 ff.

[2] Pictured e.g. by Hoernes–Menghin, p. 211; cf. Evans, Pl. 57.

[3] Evans, p. 152, Pl. 64. The well-shaped bodies, Pls. 61 and 65 (also Zammit–Singer no. 24), may represent thanks-offerings; the deformed body, Pl. 62, with numerous sharp pieces of shell stuck into it, suggests that *Schadenzauber*, too, was practised at the holy places (the *Defixionum tabellae* attest the same for Greek 'chthonic' sanctuaries). For a full documentation of this topic see Zammit–Singer, p. 76.

[4] I leave aside the question of a cult of 'pillars' other than phalli. This question is bedevilled by the ambiguous use of the term by Sir Arthur Evans (*JHS*, xxi (1901), 99 ff. and in *The Palace of Minos*, passim; cf. the criticism by M. P. Nilsson, *Gesch. d. gr. Rel.* i², pp. 278 ff.). In Malta I know of no instances which are not naturally understood as either phallic or as ordinary supports of tables, altars, or cross-beams (cf. Zammit, p. 19).

[5] Cf. Evans, pp. 129 ff.

[6] Cf. above, pp. 23 f.; for a very few and small other burials see Evans, p. 129, and T. E. Peet, vi (1913), 11 f.

these burials. The 'Hypogeum'—one ought to rather speak of 'catacombs'
—doubtless was the place of a cult; whose nature is sufficiently clear from
the places for worship with which the 'Hypogeum' was gradually equipped.
These were reproductions in miniature[1] of typical parts of the temples;
with 'trilithons', shrines, altars, oracle chambers, and doors cut out of slabs
quite as in the temples. Here then is one more instance of the tendency,
widely characteristic of popular religion, towards the identity of rites for
birth and death[2] . . . But I am anticipating. For the moment it must
suffice to note the identity of rites in temple and catacomb: the dead
were laid to rest—in family graves, so it seems—with the same deity
whom the living served in the temples, and the same cult was celebrated
at both places. But, as already observed, it by no means follows that this
cult consisted in 'the worship of deified ancestors'. On the contrary: there
is no trace of such in the temples, but every indication of a worship
entirely differently orientated. The catacombs, likewise, have failed to
yield any of the characteristics by which an ancestor-cult is recognized
everywhere from Rome to Japan; the cult celebrated in them was the
same as that offered in the temples.

The primary feature of this worship, in temple and catacomb, is that
it is rendered to one deity. The variety of rites is evidence that the worshippers recognized its might in many different provinces; but there
is the one, typical image of this one deity, numerous samples of which
survive, and no other. In particular, there are indeed, as we saw, many
symbolic intimations of the male force, but no hint at the existence of
a male god; if there had been any, his image would surely have emerged.
Instead, everything proclaims the all-comprehensive might of the one
godhead whose essence centred on begetting and birth, on procreation
and fruitfulness; from the symbolic shape of the temples as a whole to the
symbols facing the worshippers at their entrance and, in varying forms,
throughout their interior. The most telling of these—at least to our mode
of seeing—are the images big and small, invariably repeating one and the
same type or, rather, two variants of one type: namely, a standing and
a squatting one.[3]

[1] The besetting sin of many photographers, the endeavour to make their objects appear
larger—and thus more 'effective'—than they really are, stands out in many current pictures
of Maltese objects and particularly of views from the 'Hypogeum'. Evans, p. 131, rightly
describes the so-called 'Holy of Holies' there as 'a small chamber'; this one would hardly
believe on contemplating e.g. Pl. 19 in S. von Cles-Reden's *The Realm of the Great Goddess*. The
tendency to over-dramatization in the pictures is the weakness of this otherwise engaging
(though badly translated) book. The small clay figurines of the 'Venus of Malta' and the
'Sleeping Lady', of actually 5 and 4½ inches, appear colossal on Pls. 13 f. and 20 f.; three
even tinier clay phalli tower like rocks or factory chimneys on Pl. 27; and so on.

[2] Dieterich, p. 57, quoting H. Diels.

[3] Zammit, pp. 80 ff., Pl. XXII, and Fig. 14; Evans, pp. 141 ff., Pls. 49–53. The fullest
presentation of the material is in Zammit–Singer, pp. 67 ff.; many good photographs
accompany an article by R. Battaglia in *Ipek*, iii (1927), 131 ff. See our Plate 12.

Symbols indeed they are. Everyone beholding them will spontaneously, and very properly, take them to represent 'the Mother Goddess'. This is indeed what they do; but they do it with a rather perplexing symbolism. The Maltese artists proved themselves capable, in some realistic figurines designed no doubt as *ex votos*, of rendering the human form competently and even impressively;[1] but far from developing and idealizing it to represent their godhead, they chose, with a complete disregard for any consideration of beauty, to do violence to it in order to express the superhuman.

Midway between the typical idols and the realistic representations of human persons are a number of female figures—the two sleeping women and five seated ones in long skirts[2]—which are near the idols in the obesity of arms and thighs, but differ from them in that they are dressed—for the idols are naked—and in that they are unambiguously characterized as female. They may confidently be taken to represent priestesses. Fatness is likely, in Malta as elsewhere, to have been an actual and valued feature of women[3]; its exaggeration in these seven figures appears designed to approximate them to their divine model. In the idols, the same feature is exaggerated still further, and varied, in a manner which defies and transcends reality. These enormously, even revoltingly, inflated forms; the colossal arms and thighs; the very disregard for natural proportions: all this conveys immediately the notion of boundless and inexhaustible fecundity. Palaeolithic sculptors had striven to give expression to a similar concept, and by similar means; they exaggerated particularly the progenitive parts of the female body, womb, breast, and vulva. It is significant indeed that in the Maltese idols these very parts are reduced—in fact, non-existent. They have a chest but no breast and not even nipples; a short flat belly but no womb; the part underneath, finally—the region of the thighs, if indeed anatomical notions are applicable—is excessively wide and bulging and divided, all through its middle, by a single vertical line.[4]

Zammit classified all these idols as 'male' in view of the absence of female sexual characteristics. This opinion could hardly convince any unbiased beholder of these statues; it becomes quite unacceptable when one compares the essentially similar priestess-figures. And yet the observation which led to this untenable view was correct and important.

[1] Especially in the so-called 'Venus of Malta', Evans, Pl. 65; also Evans, Pl. 61 and Zammit–Singer, no. 24 = Battaglia, loc. laud., Pl. 47, Fig. 13.

[2] Zammit–Singer, nos. 22 (Evans, Pl. 57) and 23 and nos. 6 (Evans, Pl. 63), 7 (Evans, Pl. 54), 58, 59, 61.

[3] Battaglia, loc. laud., pursued this aspect, giving ample illustrations of the wide-spread preference for female obesity but failing (p. 143) to grasp the significance of the specific features of the Maltese idols.

[4] The latter feature is wanting in the figure no. 8, Zammit–Singer ('of crude workmanship'); with the squatting type the same line naturally is bent, not straight.

Evans then was right, and realistic, in stressing that the idols 'lack all sexual characteristics';[1] a fact remarkable indeed with figures expressing the quintessence of a religion which we found dominated by sexual concepts. For this very reason it is incredible that this 'highest being came to be regarded as a-sexual'; rather, it seems to be represented as transcending sexual differentiation in order to intimate the all-comprehensiveness of the one deity. This is not to disavow its essential, female and motherly character. As it is stressed throughout the sanctuaries by symbols small and great, so it is conveyed by the general impact of these figures and in particular by that long, median incision; symbolically again and not representationally. The absence of specific sexual indications entails a widening, and not a reduction, of that basic character; these figures are not really 'a-sexual', but 'supra-sexual'.

We seemed previously to notice analogous indications in the phallus with 'female' cupulae and, perhaps, in the differentiation between the two corresponding screens, decorated with spirals, at Tarxien; nor are traces of a similar ideology rare in the remaining documents of prehistoric religion from other regions. We recall the symbolism of the 'two in one' in the palaeolithic 'bâtons de commande'[2] and in neolithic figurines variously combining male and female symbolism.[3] Compared with these, the distinctive achievement of the Maltese artists is in the creation of an image which does not, in one way or other, combine the opposing features but conveys the unity of both without actually rendering either. There are analogies also for this. V. Dumitrescu published and discussed numerous figurines from the Lower Danube.[4] There, too, male figures are almost— and in some regions (Gumelniţa) entirely—lacking, but phalli frequent.[5] The majority of the figurines are explicitly female, but a proportion lack sexual characteristics. This fact had led some students to regard these as male; against them, Dumitrescu stressed that the absence of female marks does not make male representations. He interpreted the 'a-sexual' ones as, likewise, rendering the one, female goddess, the 'divinité de la fécondité'; the male is conceived as 'un simple agent de création et nullement une divinité à part'[6]—hence its representation by phalli only. He was thus led, by observations analogous to those pursued above in relation to Malta, to acknowledge in neolithic and chalcolithic civilizations around the lower Danube, and generally in South-Eastern Europe, a monotheism centred on the worship of a deity essentially female but comprising, in its all-embracing essence, the qualities of both sexes and

---

[1] p. 142.   [2] Above, p. 28.
[3] Above, p. 15; add e.g. the bisexual idols from Bosnia depicted in Hoernes–Menghin, p. 53, or the well-known menhirs with breasts in Sardinia and Corsica.
[4] *Dacia*, ii (1925), 80 ff.; *Ipek*, viii (1932–3), 49 ff.
[5] *Dacia*, loc. laud., 89 with Fig. 67 and note 1 (list).
[6] *Ipek*, loc. laud., 66.

hence represented, at times though not always, without any indication of sex.[1]

Such then seems to have been the notion of the Great Mother in whose service the early Maltese lived and died. She is the deep Earth receiving in her womb the bodies of the dead; she is the power of birth which renews all life; she is the force of sex through which, miraculously and unceasingly, this renewal is brought about and, therewith, the eternity of all life, in plant, animal, and man.[2] The dead entering her womb are themselves the seed of renewed life; and the living . . . We may perhaps venture, at this point, to try and guess at the substance and meaning of the cult for which her servants, with endless toil and devotion, erected their grandiose and elaborate temples.

Imagine the worshipper on the piazza in front of one of the temples. Before him, the huge mound covering the 'body of the goddess' but presenting bare the mighty façade gently curving towards the entrance in its centre; that façade of gigantic stones, exposed only here but suggestive of their continuation inward, to sustain the mysterious caverns there. They are not mere 'building materials', these stones; the vital powers pulsating throughout the animate earth are contained and concentrated in them as in impervious and inexhaustible repositories (we may recall, in order to overcome our mechanistic preconceptions, ancient myths of living stones such as the Hittite Ullikummis epic).[3] That solemn and vital façade, then—commanding, even minatory, in its massiveness; inviting, even alluring, by its shape—impels the worshipper to enter. It was no small matter to follow this impulse: he who stepped over the divine symbol at the entrance, went under the sombre trilithon and penetrated through the following, low and narrow passage into the interior, had gone 'the way of all flesh' and had mystically experienced death; at the same time, having passed through the divine vulva, he had, in a realistic

---

[1] A similar sentiment may account for the paradoxical concept of Cybele: the goddess stirring the profoundest sexual emotions yet herself chaste.

[2] The elegantly carved rendering, on the pitted side of an offering table from Ħaġar Qim (Evans, Pl. 79), of a 'potted plant pattern'—no doubt a variant of the oriental 'tree of life'—and the pictures of fishes (from Bugibba and the Hypogeum, Evans, pp. 152 and 157) and birds (ib., Pls. 73 f.)—both traditional 'fertility symbols' and often connected with representations of the oriental goddess—are indicative of her power beyond the human sphere. See Detached Note XIII, p. 412.

[3] Cf. the sensitive delineation of early concepts of 'the stone' by M. Éliade, *Traité d'histoire des religions* (1949), p. 191; also von Kaschnitz-Weinberg, *Grundlagen* . . . , i. 13 f., with literature, p. 68 (I could not, though, make all of his theories my own). This notion of the sanctity of the stone may have led to the avoidance of copper and bronze in Malta, as also in French megalith graves (Glyn E. Daniel, *The Megalith Builders* . . . (1958), p. 95); an archaism retained for religious reasons, like the *silex acutus* in the cult of Cybele (above, p. 19). The impression that the elaborate perfection of the Maltese stone ornaments must have involved the use of metal tools has been experimentally refuted; see Ó Ríordáin and Daniel, *New Grange*, Plate 55.

symbolism, become the mate of the goddess.[1] It must have been a ritual act of profound solemnity and an experience of deep emotion and significance. He that so entered died, and begat—himself; when, after going through the further rites for which the elaborate interior was designed, he went out where he had entered, he had become the newly-born child of the goddess.

The temples, then, seem to have served the celebrations of a mystery of rebirth.[2] It is well here to recall the associations given with the notion of 'entering'; particularly in its sexual aspect (so well known from the Old Testament) and to ponder the meaning of the word 'initiation'. The 'entering' of any sacred place is fraught with danger as well as with promise; it must have been eminently so on entering the very body of the world-goddess. 'Pénétrer dans un labyrinthe et en revenir', says M. Éliade,[3] 'voilà bien le rite initiatique par excellence' (I here take the concept of the 'labyrinth' in the wider sense of a region fraught with obscurity and peril).[4]

Following the rite of 'entering', other ceremonies must have been performed in the interior of the sanctuaries. In the dark, or dimly lit, halls the neophyte must have been guided by a knowing priest, and it is likely that successive stages of initiation were attained through various rites in different parts of the temples; but the details remain unknowable. One guess, though, may be hazarded in pursuance of previous observations.[5] The survival, in contemporary superstition, of extremely ancient religious ideas is well known; among these is the belief in the fertilizing power of upright stones (i.e. phalli) and so-called 'ringstones' (symbolizing the vulva). I borrow some illustrations from M. Éliade's summary.[6] In Greece (Paphos) as well as in certain parts of England sterile women, to secure offspring, climb through holes in certain rocks; elsewhere, they merely pass an arm through the opening; newly-born babes, too, are invigorated by the same procedure; Sir John Marshall[7] reports similar usages from India. These analogies may clarify the purpose of the various 'puzzling holes and perforations' in the Maltese temples. Part of the rites, intimating fertilization and birth, may have consisted in 'entering' through the

---

[1] On the statuette, discussed above, p. 15, from Çatal Hüyük (*AS*, xiii (1963), p. 83, Fig. 19), the vulva is indicated by the figure of a trilithon; for further parallels see Neumann, p. 158.

[2] We have thus been led to acknowledge an ideology and procedure for Malta, such as was alleged for Eleusis by Clement of Alexandria (followed by A. Dieterich), but refuted by modern criticism. The Asianic ('Phrygian') mysteries of Attis and Cybele, on the other hand, seem to afford a valid analogy.

[3] p. 327.

[4] The closely similar ideology of the 'labyrinth' in Malekula (New Hebrides) may here be compared (J. W. Layard, *Stone Men of Malekula* (1942), p. 652, cited by E. Neumann, p. 176).

[5] Above, p. 47.   [6] pp. 197 ff.

[7] *Mohenjo Daro and the Indus Civilisations*, i (1934), p. 62.

larger openings and in creeping through, or manipulating, the smaller ones; and where male devotees experienced rebirth, the female may have gained trust and strength in the fulfilment of their paramount task of motherhood. In the catacombs, the same rites conveyed the assurance of the revival, presumably through the permanence of the family, of the dead.

The myth in which this religion became explicit is unknown to us in its entirety;[1] of the rites by which it was realized we discern in dim outline, at best, a small part; the fullness of its meaning is beyond our range of experience. But the sincerity and profundity of a millennial devotion stand out in the ruins of the Maltese sanctuaries. These men of an age from which not one word reaches to us perceived and worshipped in their goddess the wonder of life unending, embracing death as a stage and a step to its eternity.

(f) ANTECEDENTS AND ORIGIN OF THE MALTESE RELIGION

By way of a supplement, we may briefly consider what origins and antecedents may have culminated in this religion and its outward expressions. And we may well find that essentially there were no origins and no development—but a revelation.

Contacts and analogies, at any rate, there were; many of which have already been noted. Some of them point back right to palaeolithic antiquity: the sacred cave (artificially erected in Malta) with cultic

---

[1] An uncertain hint at a myth might be sought from the badly damaged small reliefs carved on the right and left sides of a seated figure of the standard type, found at Tarxien (Zammit–Singer, pp. 75 and 99 f., Pl. XVI [here again the captions 'right' and 'left' appear to have been inverted]; also *Archaeologia* (1918–20), pp. 197 f., and Pl. XV; a better photograph of the main relief in *Ipek* (1927), Pl. 45. 5). Each of these reliefs shows two standing female figures of the usual fat kind facing each other across a pillar half their height. Underneath one of these groups (the corresponding place on the other side is broken off) there is 'a depression of about 2 cm., in which a group of three or four figures is cut in bold relief'. The interpretation of this unique, composite representation is precarious. Ought one to recognize two goddesses—a Mother and Daughter, as possibly at Çatal Hüyük, or even like Demeter and Kore? No other Maltese monument could be cited in support of this guess, and all our previous observations are against it (the 'two gigantic statues', traces of which have been found, side by side, at Ħaġar Qim [Zammit–Singer, p. 85, no. 14] must have represented priestesses not deities, if the distinction drawn above, p. 49, is correct. This would equally apply to the other statues of the same type [nos. 42, 43, 55]). More likely the two main groups show priestesses making an offering at an altar (the 'pillars' in fact show indications of a level plate at their top and the two figures are not properly in 'heraldic' correspondence; there is thus no suggestion, in these compositions, of a 'pillar-cult'). The small figures underneath may stand for the community attending the sacred action. Thus understood the two representations in their entirety would be fitting for their place, for the statue on which they are engraved—only its lower half is preserved—no doubt represented a priestess and the reliefs on her garment would thus be illustrating her task.

representations emerging out of the darkness for short, solemn occasions;[1] sexual symbols; the devotion to a supreme, female deity represented, in token of fecundity, with unnatural obesity: these are, obviously, reflections of a persisting, or reviving, mentality rather than indications of an immediate connection. Such connections, however, appeared to stand out in significant details pointing to Egypt,[2] Mesopotamia,[3] Asia Minor,[4] and the Balkans[5]; pre-eminently in the concept of 'the Goddess', her image, and the intimation of her might by symbols based upon various forms of the spiral. The spread of figurines representing her, from Mesopotamia right to Central Europe, is too well established to require more than a passing mention.[6] Among many varieties of these, there are some, from neolithic Crete, Sparta, and other Greek sites, comparable to the Maltese 'idol' in so far as they are generally obese without particular stressing of breast and womb, while the extremities (hands and feet) are more or less disregarded.[7] The same features occur in Asia Minor (Hacilar and Iflatun Bunar);[8] but none of all these statuettes shows the characteristic, Egyptian position of the arms, nor are any of them, like the Maltese, 'a-sexual': which striking feature we found recurring only in the Balkans. Also the un-typical small bead of bone, found in the Hypogeum,[9] looks Balkanic; its shape is actually the same as that of the Cîrna figures. But though these may be regarded as analogies, or *Vorstufen*, there is nothing anywhere that could be called really similar to the typical Maltese idols; they remain unique and original in the same way as the temples[10].

Important relations of Malta with Minoan Crete, and even with Mycenae, have been asserted by Sir Arthur Evans and—perhaps owing to his outstanding authority—continue to be asserted. As initially noted: if the new C-14 dates are accepted, this becomes impossible—unless the accepted date of the Mycenaean shaft-graves is likewise moved back by at least half a millennium; which seems inconceivable. For the same

---

[1] On this point the sensitive comment by S. Giedion deserves to be pondered (i. 528).

[2] Above, p. 10.   [3] Above, p. 11 ff.   [4] Above, p. 13 ff.   [5] Above, p. 33 ff.

[6] A competent and useful survey was given by W. Franz, 'Die Muttergöttin im Vorderen Orient und in Europa', in *Der Alte Orient*, xxxv. 3 (1937); cf. also B. Goldman, 'Typology of the Mother Goddess figurines', *Ipek*, xx (1960–3), 8 ff. (with excellent plates and full indications of literature); a staggering illustration of the spread of the figurines is presented in the same volume, pp. 16 ff., by H. Schoppa: an idol, made in Mesopotamia (Tel Asmar) and found in Hessen!

[7] V. Müller, Pls. I. 5 and 19, III. 49 and 56; S. Weinberg, *Am. Journ. of Arch.*, lv (1951), 121 ff.; L. Franz, *Ipek*, viii (1932–3), 39 ff., and Pl. 9. 1; Schachermeyr, *Älteste Kulturen* . . . , Pl. II; *Ipek*, xx, Pl. 5. 4; J. D. Evans, in the *Festschrift* for Bosch–Gimpera (1963), 161 ff. An extreme realization of this principle (and actually similar to the ground-plan of the Maltese temples rather than to the idols) is the neolithic marble figure recently found at Azmak in Bulgaria (*Antiquity*, xxxix (1965), Pl. VIId–e; cf. below, p. 58).

[8] *AS*, xi (1961), 57, Fig. 17 and Pl. XI; Childe, *The Dawn* . . . , pp. 48 and 50; A. Evans, *The Palace* . . . , i. 48, Fig. 13. 6–7; Müller, Pl. VI, pp. 118 f.

[9] Evans, Pl. 80 (top, centre).

[10] Above, p. 5.

reason, any relation between Late Minoan Crete and Malta may be ruled out, and even the Middle Minoan (barring any drastic revision of its date) would appear only just to overlap the end of the Maltese 'Temple-period'; and yet it is there, if anywhere, that the possibility of contacts might still be considered. Hence it seems worth while briefly to set out the mutually exclusive features of the two.

The origins of the Maltese civilization are a riddle indeed; but dependence upon Minoan Crete is—so it seems to me—the least attractive among many possibilities. There are no temples in Crete and no palaces in Malta; neither the minute domestic shrines, with room for two or three persons only, nor the little open-air sanctuaries attested by Minoan gems and paintings bear comparison with the Maltese places of worship. Large cult-images, like the Maltese, are unknown in Crete and out of the question in these tiny chapels;[1] and the actual representations of the Cretan goddess are totally different. There are no double-axes in Malta[2] and no 'horns of consecration'; of the unambiguous sexual representations which abound in Malta there is no trace in Minoan Crete, and of the specific Cretan 'pillars' and columns (as distinct from phalli and table-legs)[3] there is no certain instance in Malta; the altars resting on curved bases as represented on Minoan gems and paintings are thoroughly different from the Maltese 'mushroom altars';[4] the so-called 'libation-tables' have counterparts, not only in Crete but also in neolithic Italy.[5] On the other hand, the 'tholoi' in the Cretan Mesará have no counterpart in Malta, nor have the careless M.M. graves, nor the princely Mycenaean tombs (and who, anyhow, would now maintain any relation with monuments as late as these?).

This set of differences is symptomatic of the incompatible basic qualities of the bright and mundane, rich and elegant Minoan civilization with its accomplished and manifold art and the Maltese which, with its single devotion, could be characterized as its strict opposite in almost every respect; it is a different world and a different age, and that not only chronologically.[6] But there is the motif of the spiral; this has, almost generally, been taken for an evident piece of borrowing by Malta from

[1] The recent evidence for large-size clay statues and 'temples' at Keos (*Archaeology*, xv (1962), 223; xvi (1963), 285; *Hesperia* xxxi (1962), 221 ff.; xxxiii (1964), 328 ff.) suggests similar features at other Late Mycenaean places but not in Minoan Crete.

[2] See Detached Note I, p. 394.

[3] As in *JHS*, xxi (1901), p. 170, Fig. 48.—The pillar standing as an abbreviation for the (sacred) palace (Schachermeyr, *Die minoische Kultur*, pp. 160 and 164), as on the Lion Gate at Mycenae, could not, in the nature of things, have any analogy in Malta—where there are neither palaces nor pillars (cf. above, p. 47, n. 4).

[4] The latter can be paralleled from Ur; see J. Pritchard, *The Ancient Near East in Pictures* (1954), Fig. 606.

[5] According to Peet, p. 57, reporting on finds in the cave Il Tamaccio, north of Pisa.

[6] Neolithic Crete and neolithic (Ghar Dalam) Malta do show indubitable similarities in the decoration of pottery; but this type occurs, in this age, *un peu partout*.

Minoan Crete or even from Mycenae, where a well-known relief on one of the shaft-graves has often been quoted as affording the obvious model.

The spiral is not, in Crete, autochthonous; it emerges suddenly, and becomes dominant, in M.M. I, that is, from about 2000 B.C. onward; earlier instances are doubtful and in any case scarce.[1] Since the end of the 'temple-culture' in Malta is now put around 2000 B.C., no Mycenaean influence can come into question,[2] and the Minoans must hurriedly—if at all—have communicated their new fashion (starting at about the same date) to the Maltese; who must with equal hurry have applied it to their previously unornamented, sanctuaries immediately before their own extinction. It seems unrealistic. Add that the specific symbols at the entrance of the middle Tarxien temple and in its first bay have no parallel in Crete and that the development of the spiral into vegetative patterns is different at each place.

And yet the spiral is not an easy and obvious pattern, no *Allerwelts-produkt* which could legitimately be assumed to have arisen spontaneously in sundry places: there are vast regions without it, while its spread throughout others can be followed step by step; it is therefore legitimate to seek for a place from which it could have reached Malta. The Minoans —this seems to be fairly generally agreed—took it over from the Cyclades, where it had been *en vogue* for many centuries; it is therefore a possibility well worth pondering that the widely-roaming Cycladic traders could have brought it to Malta.[3] In that case, though, it would seem strange that there are no other indications of their influence in Malta; no 'frying pans', for example (to use the current crude misnomer), nor—as in Sardinia—any idols of the characteristic 'Cycladic' type. The outstanding and basic significance, far beyond merely decorative purposes, which (if the preceding argument is accepted) the spiral had in Malta, leads one to seek its origin, rather, in a region where it was embedded in a similar general context. It is, after all that has been said, evident that therewith we are directed to the Balkan and the Danubian regions: the true centre and home, at least in Europe,[4] of this motif—and of a devotion to a female deity similar to the Maltese. Anyone who has seen reproductions of the

---

[1] I am here following Schachermeyr and S. Hood, *Gnomon* (1961), 828; for an earlier instance (?import) see Marinatos–Hirmer, *Kreta und mykenisches Hellas*, 1959, Fig. 7.

[2] 'At shortly [why 'shortly'?] before 2000 B.C. the correlation of the spirals with Mycenaean shaft-grave stelae immediately falls to the ground': thus D. Trump, *Antiquity*, xxxvii (1963), 303, who, however, would still maintain their derivation from Minoan Crete (on which presently).

[3] L. Bernabò Brea, *Antiquity*, xxxiv (1960), 135 suggested the Melian pyxides, instead of the Mycenaean shaft-graves, as models for the spirals in Malta.

[4] Although some further, oriental instances of the spiral have been found since his day, H. Frankfort (*Studies in the Early Pottery* . . . , ii. 116, reasserted in *The Art and Architecture* . . . , pp. 249, 25) seems to me right against G. Childe (*The Danube* . . . , pp. 66 f. and 94) and A. Furumark (*Opusc. Archaeol.* vi (1950), pp. 215 ff.) in denying the Babylonian origin of the Danubian spirals (apart from the two special motifs discussed at length above, pp. 25 ff.).

outstanding spiral decoration on pottery from the neolithic site at Butmir[1] (near Sarajevo, in Bosnia) will easily feel tempted to trace the inspiration of the Maltese spirals to this region; especially since it has of late become known that pottery like the Butmir ware was made also on the Dalmatian islands and, so it appears, exported from there (perhaps also to the Cyclades).[2] It is an easy distance from Lesina to the Isole Tremiti and Monte Gargano and thence to the centre and to the heel of Italy; accordingly, the shores of Apulia have, from early prehistoric times onward, received traders, invaders, and settlers from across the Adriatic. It is a widely accepted view that the spiral motif of decoration, which is so frequently found on neolithic pottery in Apulia ('Serra d'Alto') and which travelled, through Central Italy ('Capri style') even to the Aeolian Islands[3] and Sicily,[4] had its origin in the Western Balkans.[5] It remains characteristic of Italian pottery throughout the Bronze Age (Pertosa: 'Apennine style');[6] quite possibly under renewed inspiration from the Balkans; hence it seems perfectly possible that from about the heel of Italy, say Taranto, the spiral might have reached Malta.[7]

[1] It should suffice to look at Hoernes–Menghin, pp. 281 and 283; cf. our Plate 13; more impressive, though, are Pl. V in vol. i and Pl. VIII in vol. ii of the original publication: W. Radimsky, H. Fiala, und M. Hoernes, Die neolithische Station von Butmir . . . , i (1895); ii (1897). See especially the interlaced spirals—as in Hal Saflieni—in vol. ii, Pl. VIII. nos. 6 and 9; also the zigzag décor as in Malta (Zammit, p. 117, Fig. 32, centre); the studded ware in vol. i, p. 24, Fig. 42 and 43 (as Zammit, p. 115, Fig. 30 and Pl. XXXIA; Evans, p. 77 and Pl. 42) and the 'chequer-board pattern' Pl. VI. 12 and 15 (as Evans, p. 70 and Fig. 10). Although none of these patterns is confined to Malta and Butmir, these coincidences seem significant. And could it be irrelevant that, together with all this, the characteristic ribbon- and zigzag-patterns, with white dots inside or outside, as in Malta, recur in this and other Balkanic and Danubian cultures? A glance at H. Frankfort, The Art and Architecture . . . , Pls. ii and iii suggests the opposite conclusion, and M. Mayer, Molfetta und Mafera (1924), Pls. XXI. 5 and 11 and XXIII. 11 and 12, the way of transmission.

[2] Hoernes–Menghin, p. 339, Figs. 1, 4, 5 picture some sherds with Butmir spirals from the northern and north-eastern coast of the Adriatic; Schachermeyr, Die ältesten Kulturen . . . , pp. 144 ff. reports about finds of the same type on the island of Huar (Lesina) and gives some illustrations of it (Figs. 37 and 38).

[3] L. Bernabò Brea, pp. 50, 52 ff.

[4] Ib., p. 53 and Pl. 20; cf. also the pintadera pictured by Griffo–von Matt, Gela (1964), p. 35.

[5] The derivation of the South Italian neolithic spiral décor from the Balkans, and especially Butmir, was impressively argued by Peet (pp. 414 ff.; cf. 108 f.), hampered only by uncertainties of chronology, which since have been cleared up by R. B. K. Stevenson (Proc. Prehist. Soc., xiii (1947), 85 ff.) and particularly by L. Bernabò Brea's excavations in and around Lipari. Peet's thesis was accepted e.g. by G. Childe (The Danube . . . , p. 74) and Hawkes (p. 151); cf. Duhn–Messerschmidt, ii. 163 ff.; Mayer, pp. 100 f. and 117; H. Frankfort, Studies . . . , ii. 49.

[6] Hoernes–Menghin, p. 397, reproduce sherds with spiral decoration from the Pertosa (near Salerno; cf. Peet, p. 404), including one with the typical four-spiral-pattern with a lozenge in its centre (similar to the Lengyel pattern quoted above p. 39, n. 1 and its many counterparts); L. Bernabò Brea, p. 124, Fig. 23c shows 'Apennine ware', decorated with spirals, from Milazzo; cf. also Mayer, pp. 274 ff.

[7] This possibility was suggested by A. Mayr (Reallexikon der Vorgeschichte, vii. 357).

And, perhaps, not the spiral only. This was the route which, according to Evans,[1] was taken, at a later date, by the 'Destroyers' of the Maltese 'Temple civilization'. The spiral was, as we have seen, with the Maltese, not merely a pleasant decorative motif but a means for expressing their dominant religious concern. This concern has its analogy, as has the motif in question, in the 'monotheism' of the Danubians. If the 'temple-people' had themselves immigrated from those regions—presumably via South Italy—and retained some contact with them, their predisposition both for this religion and for its symbolical expression would be seen as elements of one historical context.

An indication supporting this suggestion may perhaps be afforded by a sherd recently found by G. Georgiev in a neolithic mound at Azmak in South Bulgaria.[2] It is decorated with a small figure, in relief, of a man (and not merely a face). A strikingly similar counterpart was found in the cave north of the Ġgantija and can be seen in the Gozo Museum.[3] Nobody would posit a direct connection between Malta and Bulgaria. Closely similar figures, however, have been found not only in Iran (Luristan) and Mesopotamia,[4] but also on Chios[5]—and in the Middle Danube region.[6] Hence it seems conceivable that they were adopted also by the related cultures in the Western Balkans; whence they could have reached Malta by the same way as the spiral.[7]

The Balkanic origin of the Maltese temple-builders could thus account (in so far as origins can account for anything) for some basic features of their mentality—though certainly not for all; not, in particular, for the practice of collective burial nor for the Sumerian analogies previously

[1] p. 179.   [2] *Antiquity*, xxxix (1965), Pl. VId.
[3] I know of no reproduction of it. Pieces possibly comparable from Haġar Qim and Mnajdra are pictured in *BSR*, vi (1913), Pl. XI, Fig. 1. 5 and Pl. XXVI, Fig. 1. 15; these however are so schematized that they could be described as 'stars' (ib., p. 105; a third is said to have been found at Kordin).
[4] Tepe Giyan, reproduced by Schachermeyr, *Die ältesten Kulturen* . . . , p. 90, Fig. 16. 3, after Contenau–Ghirshman, *Fouilles du Tépé-Giyan* (1935), Pl. 63; this, though, is painted, not relief (ib., p. 65); for a similar one at Samarra see Herzfeld, Abb. 1.
[5] At Agio Gala; see A. Furness, *Proc. Prehist. Soc.*, xxii (1956), Pl. XXI, no. 11 (I owe the reference to J. Mellaart, *AS*, viii (1958), p. 154, n. 46; the other instances quoted by him, *Saeculum*, v. 3, p. 291, nos. 12 and 14, are beyond my reach).
[6] Schachermeyr, loc. laud., Fig. 16. 2 (Körös); cf. ib., 16. 5; Hoernes–Menghin, p. 305 (Tordos; both in Siebenbürgen, i.e. now Rumania); G. Childe, *The Danube* . . . , p. 28, with Fig 12 (Vinca near Belgrade and Csoka on the Tisza). The Bulgarian and Maltese instances, however, are more closely interrelated than all the rest in that the little figure has both arms bent downward and not raised as in the others.
[7] The same derivation may perhaps be considered for the early Maltese 'terracotta figurines with characteristic tilted faces' (D. Trump, *Antiquity* (1964), 303; cf. Evans, pp. 140 f.), in preference to their derivation from Cycladic models, which is problematical in view of their early date ('before 3200 B.C.'). Compare, rather, e.g., Hoernes–Menghin, p. 287 (top), 291. 1 (right), 305 (centre) and the impressive figurines recently found at Cernavoda (D. Berciu, *Antiquity*, xxiv (1960), 283 and Pl. XXXVIII; M. Gimbutas, *Archaeology*, xvi (1963), 54).

noted. The Danubian peasants, as far as we know, built no temples and fashioned no large-size idols.[1]

In the present upheaval of all prehistoric chronology it would be hazardous, particularly for a non-specialist, to go beyond mentioning this possibility; perhaps some expert in this field may care to consider it.[2] There are obviously alternatives equally deserving of consideration; the oriental analogies mentioned could suggest, for example, a connection with Northern Syria or Southern Asia Minor[3] (but had not these regions, at the time in question, reached a very different stage of style and religion?). This much, however, seems certain: no single region can be described as the fountain head of all of the essential features of the Maltese achievement,[4] and even if its various aspects were traced to various, definite points of origin,[5] no more would thereby be established than, at best, plausible sources of disposition and means of expression. The Maltese phenomenon as a meaningful whole—meaningful in the reference of every detail to the one, dominating religious concept— stands out as the human response to a vision of the divine. Whatever help there may have been from precedents and promptings, these people were able to create their unique and grandiose form and frame of life, primarily, because they obeyed no impulse, and allowed no purpose, other than this: to receive, and respond to, the revelation of the godhead of the place.

III. THE ANCIENT GODDESS OF SICILY

(a) THE EVIDENCE

We had to turn to Malta in the endeavour to descry her essence; but the goddess of whom the Maltese monuments tell held sway also over

[1] On this point we may be in for surprises: see the outline report, by S. Piggott, in *Antiquity*, xxxiv (1960), 289, about the discovery of 'fragments of huge cult figures in baked clay' and 'an "altar" over a yard high', with elaborate décor, at Truseşti in Eastern Roumania, with C⁻¹⁴ dates around 3000 B.C.

[2] G. Childe (*The Danube* . . . , p. 213) notes the identity of 'tunnel handles' in Slovenia and Bosnia with Maltese ones (on which J. D. Evans, *Proc. Prehist. Soc.* (1953), 55 f.; *Malta*, pp. 81 f.). I seem myself to have noticed analogies between 'Danubian' and Maltese pottery (cf. above, p. 57, n. 1), and while I have every reason to distrust my judgement in this field, I feel encouraged by a hint to the same effect given twenty-five years ago by Hawkes, p. 154.

[3] The primitive clay-head from Haġar Qim (Zammit–Singer, Pl. VIII, no. 15) seems to point in the same direction; it may be compared with the 'mother goddess figures with turtle-like face' from Mesopotamia (e.g. Ur, Tel Brak; cf. Neumann, Pls. 10 f.) and Cyprus.

[4] Dependence upon Libyan North Africa, which Sir Arthur Evans asserted both for Minoan Crete and for Malta (*The Palace of Minos*, ii. 37 ff.; similarly even now Schachermeyr, *Die minoische Kultur* . . . , pp. 17, 55, 167) appears poorly supported by the indications in O. Bates, *The Eastern Libyans*, 1914, to whom they refer; the circular Libyan structures— anyhow apparently recent—have no similarity with the Maltese. Nor do the recently discovered rock-paintings in the Sahara, as far as published, show any significant analogies.

[5] For the suggestive similarity of Maltese (Xemxija) and Sicilian tombs see below, p. 61.

Sicily—through thousands of years, from the earliest metal age down to
the coming of the Greeks; much longer, that is, than in Malta, where her
temples were destroyed, and her worshippers exterminated by newcomers,
at the beginning of the Bronze Age, about 2000 B.C.[1] Sicily, too, experienced several waves of immigrants, but archaeology shows that, so far
from abolishing her cult, they were drawn into her service.[2] The peaceful
inhabitants of the two small islands devoted to her were unable to offer
resistance once the spell of their inviolability was set aside; the large
island to the north, by no means sacrosanct, was sufficiently populous to
absorb immigrants and invaders; to continue and develop the native
traditions and to give new and lasting witness to her might.

No temple indeed gives such witness in Sicily, no altar nor image; for
these—if the guess be allowed—the worshippers sailed across to the *isole
sacre*. The actual surviving witnesses are: the thousands of collective rock-
graves analogous to Xemxija and Hal Saflieni; the decorated tomb-doors
from Castelluccio analogous to Tarxien; the 'bossed bone plaques' found
at Castelluccio and analogous, likewise, to those from Tarxien, which
were recognized, by J. D. Evans, to be in fact highly abstract idols.[3]

(b) THE ROCK GRAVES

Collective burial is a practice which, together with 'the' cult of 'the'
Goddess, was widely adopted, during the third millennium and later,
around the Mediterranean and in Western and Northern Europe. We
have seen that in fact this cult, and 'the' Goddess, were realized in widely
different ways; the same is true of collective burial. Natural caves may
be used for it, or tombs built above ground; megalithic 'dolmen',
passage-, or gallery-graves; structures circular or rectangular, with or
without side-chambers; grandiose domes or tiny chambers; or graves

[1] On the end of the 'temple folk' see Detached Note II, below, p. 395.

[2] It is one of Bernabò Brea's many outstanding accomplishments in the field of Sicilian
archaeology to have freed us from the notion that every change of style must indicate
a change of population and, vice versa, that a change of population must involve a thorough
change of style and mentality. *In casu*, the immigration of the Siculi is not indicated by the
emergence of the style which Orsi termed 'Sicul i' (now 'Castelluccio'); it coincided with
'Sicul iii' (now 'Pantalica'), which largely continues the preceding developments (see
Bernabò Brea, pp. 147 ff. and 169 ff.). For the comparable persistence of religious features
in Asia Minor see above, pp. 17 ff.

[3] The characteristic small horns of clay which recur so frequently on Sicilian sites, from
the Castelluccio-period right down to the age of the Greek colonization, are one more indication of one persisting religion. They are undoubtedly symbols of the life-giving male potency,
like the big horns at Çatal Hüyük and the phalli in Malta. I cannot, however, see any similarity
between them and the Minoan 'horns of consecration'; nor can I confirm that the like of
them has been found in Malta, as R. N. Bradley (*Malta and the Mediterranean Race* (1912),
p. 99; cf. 130) asserts. Professor J. D. Evans kindly informed me that he found no trace of them
in Malta.

under ground, again in greatly varying shapes. In Sicily one particular form comes into use in the San Cono period[1] (at the very beginning, that is, of the Copper Age and contemporary with the earliest relics of the 'temple folk' in Malta); it develops, from somewhat freer beginnings (burial in natural caves and shaft-graves), into a standard form and thus persists into historical times, witnessing to a persistent and dominant religion: the so-called *tombe a forno*.[2]

They are small artificial caves which have been cut laboriously into rocks with stone tools[3] (for, possible ritual considerations apart,[4] bronze was rare and precious except in the most recent period, and anyhow too soft, and iron became available only towards the end of the indigenous civilization). They are approached through a short, low, and narrow corridor which is often expanded so as to form a small antechamber, but often is no larger than required to fit in the closing slab; for the graves were of course always closed—either by a slab or a built-up wall (even though, for obvious reasons, these have survived only in a few instances). Not rarely, several intercommunicating graves are approached by one entrance. The grave-chambers themselves are normally small and low; their shape is round; rarely they are circular, most often oval or 'kidney-shaped'; only in the most recent period are they predominantly rectangular. And they are normally—that is, wherever the terrain permitted—cut into steep or even vertical rock-faces, often bafflingly difficult of access. Where no such were available, the same effect was as far as possible achieved by cutting short sloping tunnels or shafts into rocky ground until a depth sufficient for the excavation of chambers of the same kind was reached (thus e.g. at Tranchina di Sciacca and, much later, at Thapsus, north of Syracuse). Differently from the graves of the preceding age, which by comparison are few and of no fixed type, the *tombe a forno* lie together in large necropoleis, often comprising hundreds and even thousands of chambers; an indication of an increased population settled in villages large and small, but also of a new and overmastering concept of life and death which prompted the prodigious labours spent in placing the dead in the very heart of the enduring element.[5] This concept stands out, with classical finality, in the grandest of these 'cities of the dead', Pantalica, twenty miles west of Syracuse.

---

[1] Bernabò Brea, p. 76 and *Antiquity*, xxxiv (1960), 136; S. Tinè, *Bull. paletnol. ital.*, lxix–lxx (1960–1), 130 ff.

[2] The oldest *tombe a forno* known, at Tranchina di Sciacca (Agrigento; S. Tinè, loc. laud. and *Kokalos*, ix (1963), 77 ff.) are astonishingly like those at Xemxija (Malta); they were destined, still in the neolithic manner, for single burials.

[3] According to Orsi, e.g. *Bull. paletnol. ital.* xxi (1895), 152.   [4] Cf. above, p. 51, n. 3.

[5] As far as possible the graves seem to be so placed as to face the rising sun; a meaningful custom which has been observed elsewhere; see e.g., for Italy, D. Mackenzie, *BSR*, v (1910), 108 and Peet, p. 120; for Spain, G. and V. Leisner, *Antas lo concelho de Reguengos de Monsaraz* (1951), p. 44.

This enormous rock, three-quarters of a mile long and about a third of a mile broad, an unassailable fortress, rises nearly a thousand feet between the upper Anapo and a tributary, the Calcinara, like a gigantic petrified ship; the graves are cut into its steep flanks.[1] There are more than five thousand of them. They have often been said to make the cliffs appear 'like huge honeycombs', and photographs may indeed convey this impression; but this comparison is untrue; it is refuted by the sheer size and the dignity of the place. The inestimable labour with which each and all of the thousands of graves were cut; the devotion which, through hundreds of years, was spent in providing the dead with durable abodes such as the living denied themselves; the severe beauty and power of the rock: invest the scene with an aura of sublime solemnity. Death resides in this immense stone; at the same time, it is vibrating with the potency of unquenchable life. Enter any one of the graves; you feel, as nowhere else, that you are in the womb of the Great Mother, from which the dead will be reborn, mysteriously, for another span in the light above. Above were the huts of the living, so lightly built that only the scantiest traces of a few of them can now be faintly discerned;[2] underneath, and far below, the animate rock[3] guarded the perennial resting-places of the dead.

With this simple and grandiose symbolism the people of Sicily, in the Copper and Bronze Ages, built their settlements wherever the formation of the ground permitted it; for example, apart from Pantalica, at Castelluccio, Finocchito, Noto Vecchio, and Priolo. More often, though, not even the slightest traces remain of the villages whose inhabitants were laid, for rest and rebirth, in those chambers of stone. These were abodes in the precise meaning of the word; as can be seen from the fact that, in the older graves, the dead were often found crouching around the walls and equipped with flint-knives, food-bowls, and beakers as though they had assembled for a family feast; in more recent ones they are 'laid to rest' literally, on beds of stone; but even so the equipment for the 'banquet of the dead' continued to be provided. Moreover, the entrances were increasingly elaborated like the porches of houses,[4] and when finally rectangular houses came into use by the living—this custom seems to have been brought by the Siculi—the abodes also of the dead were increasingly given this shape. These facts are not inconsistent with the fundamental meaning, as suggested, of these burials. We recalled previously that, in the language of myth and poetry as well as psychology, 'house', 'womb', and 'woman' are interchangeable terms.[5]

---

[1] I am trying to describe this great phenomenon because no picture can give an adequate notion of it and because it is bound shortly to disappear from sight under the waves of—*il turismo*.

[2] So at least it seemed to me on examining, in 1963, the plateau towards its eastern end.

[3] Cf. above, p. 51, n. 3.   [4] Bernabò Brea, pp. 110 ff.; Pls. 36 f.

[5] Above, p. 29, n. 5.—G. von Kaschnitz-Weinberg, *Grundlagen* . . . , i. 44, mentions a ceme-

Collective burial—as we said—was a custom widely adopted during this long period. Smallish graves used for it, as in Sicily—suggesting their designation for families, in contrast with huge tombs for kings (Mycenae) or whole settlements (as in the Cretan Mesará)—may be instanced, for example, from Early Helladic Greece (Hagios Kosmas; Zygouries) and the Iberian Peninsula; the specific form of the *tomba a forno* occurs around Matera in Apulia[1] and, among many other forms, occasionally in Early Bronze Age Sardinia.[2] Nowhere, however, is there anything like the rigorous adherence, through so long a period, to this one form; for the equally abounding rock-graves in Lycia and, to a less extent, in other parts of Asia Minor (Phrygia; Paphlagonia) are suggestive indeed but far more recent and different in shape. It is this persistence in the toilsome elaboration of one and the same type of grave which, quite as much as the similar adherence to one type of temple-building in Malta, evinces the persistence, here as there, of a definite and authoritative religion. And it is, here and there, the same religion. The analogies will have struck the reader beyond any need for further elaboration; the identity is confirmed by the carvings on the Castelluccio slabs from which the present study started.

(c) THE CASTELLUCCIO SLABS

They were discovered, in 1891, by P. Orsi, whose assessment of 'questo primissimo tentativo di scoltura' in Sicily appears to be widely accepted.[3] According to him, they are primitive, and indeed 'quasi infantile' attempts at reproducing Mycenaean spiral ornaments. Orsi found their prototypes on stelae on the fifth shaft-grave at Mycenae[4] and suggested that 'oggetti d'arte micenea, introdotti per commercio di scambio' had served as models; adding that the Sicilian imitations had 'un compito puramente decorativo, non simbolico'.

tery at Cerveteri with the graves of men marked by phalli and those of women by models of houses.

[1] Mayer, pp. 182 ff. and 246 ff.—With regard to the instances from the Cyclades, which S. Tinè (*Kokalos*, ix (1963), 84 ff.) offers as prototypes of the Sicilian—they include (tav. xxxii. 4) even one of the tiny, built-up cupola-graves at Chalandriani but not one really cogent analogy—I must confess myself sceptical, and quite unconvinced by their final derivation from Egypt. The similarity of some rock-graves near Chalkis (Euboea) has repeatedly been remarked upon (e.g. by Mayer, p. 182); a few others, though probably more recent, may be compared (such as Mavro Spilio near Knossos; Cyprus); but these are, so far, hardly sufficient to establish the source of the new inspiration, at the end of the neolithic period, in Apulia, Sicily, and Malta.

[2] Taramelli, *Mon. Ant.*, xi (1901), 38 ff.; especially Figs. 24, 27–9, 33, 36–9.

[3] Orsi, in *Bull. di paletnol. ital.*, xviii (1892), 68 ff. (graves nos. 31 and 34); cf. Bernabò Brea, p. 110, with Figs. 19 (which, on comparison with Orsi's plans, seems a trifle fanciful) and 20, and Pl. 33.

[4] See e.g. *BSA*, xxv (1921–3), Pls. XIX–XXI and pp. 126 ff.; A. B. Wace, *Mycenae* (1949), Pl. 79; Lord W. Taylour, *The Mycenaeans* (1964), Pl. 20.

After all that has been said above in connection with the Maltese spiral motifs the reader will be prepared, I trust, on this point to disagree with the supreme master of Sicilian archaeology.[1] For one thing, the Mycenaean and the Sicilian patterns are strictly not comparable, since the former make a potentially endless border, while the latter, in their combination with other lines curved and straight, effect definite, closed figures. Besides, the indubitable dependence of the Sicilian upon Maltese prototypes[2] precludes any relation with Mycenae; for chronological, apart from all other reasons. Once the spiral ornaments at Tarxien and other Maltese sites lay buried under silt and ashes they could not possibly stimulate the Sicilian 'rozze scolture'. For this very reason (and others, to be mentioned later)[3] the initial date for the Castelluccio period has to be moved back from the second well into the third millennium.[4]

About the definite 'compito simbolico' of the two slabs we need waste no further words. They convey Death as the begetter of Life and the dead received in the 'house' of the Goddess. L. Bernabò Brea more recently observed[5] that they 'peuvent être interprétés comme l'extrême schématisation de la figure humaine' and O. G. S. Crawford, in a particularly unfortunate passage of his stimulating but erratic book, found his ubiquitous 'Eye-goddess', 'mixed up with death and resurrection', represented on them.[6] It is indeed always possible for an abstract symbol to turn into a more or less concrete representation, and vice versa; the triangular bucks on Samarran pottery are a stock example and we have noted several instances in following the development of particular spiral symbols.[7] The same happened very clearly on the second Castelluccio slab with its indication of phallus and legs. Even so, it is extremely difficult to say—and perhaps even meaningless—how far those for whom these carvings were made conceived of them as abstract, or realistic, representations of their goddess. Do the two upper spirals merely complete the traditional symbol? Or were they perceived as rendering breasts, or eyes? The alternative mentioned last may be felt to be commended by the spontaneous impression made by, at least, the second slab, which is comparable to that of some Trojan face-urns; a very strong counter-

---

[1] Lord W. Taylour, *Mycenaean Pottery in Italy* (1958), p. 67 with n. 2, echoes Orsi with, so it seems, a note of doubt ('. . . which in a manner recall the sculptured stelae from the Shaft Graves at Mycenae').

[2] Their similarity was noted at once by Orsi (*Bull. di paletnol. ital.*, xviii (1892), p. 70, n. 37). Cf. above, p. 27, n. 5.

[3] Detached Notes II and III, pp. 395.

[4] T. J. Dunbabin (*The Western Greeks* (1948), p. 2, n. 1), following Hawkes, dated it '*c.* 2400–1400 B.C.'; more recently, though, S. Tinè proposed 1900–1400 (*Bull. paletnol. ital.*, n.s. xiii (1960–1), 151).

[5] *Musées et Monuments de Sicile* (1960), 22.

[6] p. 48.

[7] Above, pp. 35 f.; cf. below, p. 67.

argument, however, is in the fact that, as far as I know, there is no pre-historic parallel for the representation of eyes by spirals. On the other hand, there are parallels for spirals indicating breasts,[1] and such would form the more obvious complement to the meaning conveyed by the lower half of both slabs.

There is in fact more of the kind from Castelluccio and, though still cruder, it supports the interpretation of the more elaborate slabs from the graves nos. 31 and 34. Orsi himself considered the possibility that the two parts of the door of no. 22 (now likewise on view in Syracuse) combined might be 'tentativi di una rozza ed elementare rappresentazione sim-bolica';[2] namely, of breasts and head, and G. Childe unequivocally took them for a representation of 'the funerary goddess',[3] comparing 'the carvings on many megalithic tombs in France' (presumably the St. Sernin type) and a stele from Troy I[4]—neither of which look really very similar. Orsi himself in the end preferred to assume that the relevant protuberances were no more than handles for the moving of the heavy slabs. He made the same assumption also with regard to the still plainer door of the neighbouring grave 23 and the mason work on no. 32.[5] The labour involved seems out of proportion to this modest purpose, and the representational effect too marked to be due to chance; finally, the simi-larity of the two 'protuberances' with the 'sporgenze mammillari' which mark out the 'female menhirs' in Sardinia[6] seems decisive; these crude carvings, like the two spiral ones, intimate the Goddess. Even so, the subordinate question to what extent the carvings were conceived of as realistically representational is not finally settled; perhaps to some of the ancient beholders the upper spirals suggested breasts, to others eyes, while still others appreciated the unity of the pattern as a whole. Any-how, while a certain amount of 'realism' is indubitable, at any rate in slab 34, as well as in the three inferior ones, their main impact comes from their symbolism.

Our interpretation of this symbolism is borne out by the fact that

---

[1] A volute pattern very similar to the 'sign of Ninhursag' indicates breasts on a pre-Etruscan grave-stela at the Fondo Arnoaldi near Bologna (Neumann, p. 127, after Hoernes–Menghin, p. 461. 3, after Montelius, La Civilisation primitive en Italie, i, Text, p. 365). A characteristic type of so-called 'amphorae', widespread during the Bronze Age in Central Europe and particularly in Hungary, has the body of the vessel shaped into a suggestion of breasts (e.g. Childe, The Danube . . . , Figs. 162 and 180; Hoernes–Menghin, p. 413, v and vi) and these elevations, by turns, are sometimes covered with spirals such as, made of bronze-wire, were actually worn as breast-ornaments (Childe, ib. Figs. 182, 183, 215; Hoernes–Menghin, p. 415); cf. also the statuette from Beirut (above, p. 32, after H. Frankfort, The Art and Architecture . . . , Pl. 144 (our Plate 7a) ; with 'Ninhursag' underneath the breasts and single spiral on the lap) and what was said above, especially p. 35, about the Cîrna figurines.

[2] Orsi, Bull. paletnol. ital. xviii (1892), p. 29 and Pl. V, Figs. 1a and 2.

[3] G. Childe, The Dawn . . .⁴, p. 230, with Fig. 113.

[4] Blegen, Troy and the Trojans, Pl. 17.   [5] Orsi, loc. laud. p. 73, with photo.

[6] Taramelli, Not. Scav. (1915), p. 110.

representations of 'the Goddess'—schematized but unambiguous—guard many late-neolithic and bronze-age graves in Spain, France, and Corsica.[1] On the other hand, the entrance of an early rock-grave recently discovered at Pimentel near Cagliari[2] is decorated with two-spiral-patterns which are not indeed identical with those from Castelluccio, or Malta, but doubtless convey the same idea. A close and instructive analogy to the Sicilian necropoleis, indicative of the spread of a similar faith, is found in the heart of France. In the Vallée du Petit-Morin, in the Départment Seine-et-Oise, about 150 graves have been hollowed out in steep rocks in late-neolithic times.[3] Their shapes indeed are different from the Sicilian type, for they are, approximately—but far from uniformly—square; but they, too, were closed by monolithic slabs, and representations of 'the Goddess', on the walls of the 'antechambers' of seven of them, placed the burials under her authority. The variety of shapes within this set of graves and, even more so, the fact that completely different forms of burial were used in the other, neighbouring provinces of the same 'Seine–Oise–Marne culture' illustrate, by contrast, the rigid adherence in Sicily to one established type of burial, and the permanence of the religion which enjoined it.

Still further north, two analogies with Castelluccio may be noted. A very crude little idol, found in a megalithic grave on Alderney (Channel Islands)[4] and made of local stone, looks like a debased offspring of the spiral patterns on the Sicilian slabs. Its uppermost part, with two circles possibly suggesting eyes (or, rather, breasts?) can indeed justify comparison with the type of Spanish and French idols just referred to, but the remainder, with its vertical median elevation issuing in two spirals (legs?) recalls Castelluccio, even though the direction of the spirals is inverted in the manner which we observed in other, more recent derivations of the traditional pattern. Here again the dead appear to have been committed to 'the Goddess'. And, finally, the large stone, covered with spirals, which served to close the entrance to the grandiose tomb of New Grange north of Dublin[5] appears to indicate the same idea as the Castelluccio slabs, even though the patterns on it are quite different in detail.

[1] See e.g. Hoernes–Menghin, p. 217; von Cles-Reden, pp. 212 ff.; *Vanished Civilisations*, ed. E. Bacon, p. 299.

[2] M. Guido, *Sardinia* (1963), pp. 57 f. and Pl. 18.

[3] J. Dechelette, *Manuel d'archéologie*, i (1912), pp. 455 ff. and 583 ff.; von Cles-Reden, pp. 229 ff.; G. Bailloud et P. Mieg de Bofzheim, *Les Civilisations néolithiques de la France* (1955), p. 194 (with recent literature); G. Daniel, *The Megalith Builders . . .* , p. 100 and Pl. VI; id., *The Prehistoric Chamber Tombs of France* (1960), i. 46.

[4] Now in the Guernsey Museum. See D. T. Kendrick in *The Antiquaries Journal* (1924), pp. 407 ff.; id. *The Archaeology of the Channel Islands* (1928), 33 ff.; H. Breuil, *Les Peintures rupestres schématiques*, iv (1930), p. 128, Fig. 107; G. von Kaschnitz-Weinberg, *Die Grundlagen . . .* , i. 23 and Fig. 19.

[5] Above, p. 29 f.

(d) BOSSED BONE PLAQUES

The much-discussed 'bossed bone plaques' finally confirm the worship of one and the same goddess in Sicily and Malta. Orsi secured six of these from graves, and one from a hut, at Castelluccio;[1] since then, several more have been found at other Sicilian sites of the same period and one at Tarxien.[2] They have been discussed by J. D. Evans in an exhaustive and penetrating article[3] showing that these curious objects were not destined for some practical use but are abstract idols comparable to (though very different from) the Spanish 'phalanges'.[4] They are made of a long bone of some animal (sheep or goat?); their characteristic feature being a row of round or oval bosses, every other of which bears, in most instances (although not so on the Maltese sample),[5] some incised decoration. Evans interpreted these, highly stylized, patterns as representing, from the broader, upper end downward: eyes—or rather, a face—breasts, navel, and the female organ. The first patterns are sometimes repeated; the last— a cross with a hole in its centre—is always at the bottom end (wherever this is preserved; for many of the pieces are fragmentary). This interpretation carries conviction on the whole,[6] and in particular with regard to the feature mentioned last.[7] By putting these idols into their graves the Castelluccio people expressed the same idea as by the carvings on the entrances to them, and they may have left abstract idols of this

---

[1] *Bull. paletnol. ital.* xviii (1892), 155 f. and 170 f.; ib. xix (1893), 215.

[2] T. Zammit, *Archaeologia*, lxx (1918–20), 195; *Prehist. Malta*, p. 93.

[3] *Antiquity*, xxx (1956), 80 ff.—Bernabò Brea (Pl. 41) contributes three excellent photographs and (p. 114) the information that some further pieces have been found in Sicily in addition to the ten described by Evans.

[4] Pictured e.g. by von Cles-Reden, Fig. 38 (p. 201) and Pls. 71 f.; Hoernes–Menghin, p. 213.

[5] Also Evans's nos. 6 and 10 are undecorated; so are all of the, otherwise comparable, samples from Lerna and Troy. The latter are different from the Western ones also in that they are not hollowed out; hence the connection between the Eastern and Western groups is, as Evans stresses, loose, and chronological conclusions based on it are accordingly uncertain.

[6] Evans may be going too far in terming the whole series 'a variant of the ubiquitous Mediterranean oculus idol'. Here, as previously in the interpretation of the Castelluccio door, the question arises whether a certain pattern means eyes or breasts. Eyes are probably to be acknowledged at the top of Evans's no. 1 (Fig. 1; Bernabò Brea Pl. 41, right), since the different volute-pattern underneath is reasonably taken to suggest breasts—and yet this same 'star-figure' indicates the breasts on the Kličevac figurine (Hoernes–Menghin, p. 409. 2; Neumann, Pl. 20), and what is reasonably taken to indicate eyes elsewhere, may represent breasts on the 'phalanges' *apud* von Cles-Reden, Fig. 38 (p. 201) and Pl. 72 (cf. above, p. 30, n. 2). This alternative seems preferable where an ambiguous pattern of the kind appears repeatedly, either underneath one which is reasonably taken as eyes or right above the unambiguous symbol at the bottom (Bernabò Brea, Pl. 71, left).

[7] Confirmation of this interpretation may perhaps be sought from the Sicilian clay 'piramidette', which I. Bovio Marconi published in *Bull. paletnol. ital.* n.s. (1938), 74 ff. (cf. B. Pace, iii. 458, Fig. 105). They are probably far more recent than the bone plaques and quite different in shape; even so, they may be amenable to an interpretation on similar lines, for the incised ornamentation, consisting of 'lozenges' and triangles with circles in the centre may be expressive of the same idea in the same abstract manner.

type as thank-offerings when visiting the temples of their goddess in Malta.[1]

(e) HYBLA

They and their successors remained devoted to her, for a thousand years and more, after her temples in Malta had been laid waste. The attempt at defining her identity may be concluded by a guess at her name. We have endeavoured to show both the fact that, and the reason why, Pantalica was pre-eminently her haunt, and it appears that the place bore her name (as Athens by its name proclaimed itself the ward of its goddess), and that this name was Hybla.

Stephanus of Byzantium, s.v., states that 'many cities in Sicily were called Hybla': he himself specifies four and Pausanias (v. 23. 6), two.[2] The inscription[3] VENERI VICTRICI HYBLENSI found at Paternò (south of Mt. Etna), combined with Thuc. vi. 62. 5 and 94. 3, proves this place to have been the site of 'Lesser Hybla',[4] with a sanctuary of the goddess Hybla or Hyblaia, whose priests, the Galeotai, were famed as expounders of portents and dreams.[5] Another Hybla, identified with Styella, lay near Megara (Steph. Byz.); a third, the 'smallest', in the Heraean mountains (probably = modern Ragusa). 'Hybla the Great' finally may be found in Pantalica.[6] Hyblon, 'King of the Sikels' according to Thuc. vi. 4. 1, 'of Hybla' according to Steph. Byz., handed over[7] to the Megarians the land

[1] Cf. below, p. 396, the Detached Note III on the date of these plaques.

[2] For this much-and-fruitfully-discussed problem I am using, and condensing, what has gradually been established by J. Schubring (*Umwanderung des megarischen Busens*, pp. 450 ff. —for this work I have used an off-print, and have been unable to trace the original journal from which it is taken), A. Holm (*Geschichte Siziliens*, i (1870), pp. 68 and 362 f.), E. A. Freeman (*History of Sicily*, i (1891), pp. 512 ff.), and Dunbabin (pp. 144 f.). Like everybody, I accept Schubart's and Schubring's corrections of the corrupt passages in Pausanias and Steph. Byz.

[3] *CIL* x. 2, 7013; pictured in B. Pace, iii. 509, Fig. 137.

[4] It does not by any means prove the local goddess to have been equated with Venus or, indeed, Aphrodite, although this paralogism is being repeated *ad infinitum*. The tutelary deity of Caesar and Augustus could be, and was, worshipped in countless places, without any reference to local cults.

[5] The much-discussed evidence for the Galeotai is well summarized and assessed in *P.W.* vii. 1, 592 ff. (Kjellberg). The cult of the pre-Greek goddess (Paus. v. 23. 6) could not have been instituted by Delphi; Greek assertions to this effect (Clem. Al., *Strom.* i. 21 and Steph. Byz., *s.v.*) are evidence of Delphic propaganda, and indeed what is reported about this cult strikes one as anything but Apollonian. The name of the Galeotai is evidently one with the epithet of their city, Hybla Gereatis, as Holm and Freeman noted; its association with Greek γαλεός 'dog-fish' and γαλεώτης 'lizard' are irrelevant Greek puns—there is no such thing as a divination by lizards or sharks—and the assumption of a cult of Apollo at Hybla rests on nothing but a corruption in the text of Athenaeus (672 e: pre-historic Karians could not have been alleged, *sans plus*, to have turned for guidance to an—otherwise unattested— oracle of Apollo in pre-historic Sicily).

[6] The identification struck me on the spot. From Bernabò Brea, p. 164, I learned that it had previously been proposed by F. Villard—I cannot tell where; it is also approved by A. von Stauffenberg, *Trinakria* (1963), p. 128.

[7] The correction, in Thuc., of the transmitted προδόντος to παραδόντος is necessary for stylistic as well as material reasons.

where they founded Hyblaean Megara. Only at Pantalica is there a royal palace; it is far and away the mightiest Sicul fortress and, at the same time, 'the nearest to the strip of coast where Megara Hyblaea lay';[1] it is thus the obvious, and indeed the only possible, residence of 'Hyblon of Hybla, King of the Sikels'.

If then Pantalica was called Hybla, it bore the name of the Goddess. No other explanation could account for the profusion of places (and persons) thus called, and we have found the goddess actually attested at one of the places of the same name. A rapid survey of the other pre-Greek deities of Sicily will show how uniquely this one agrees with what we have inferred about 'the ancient goddess of Sicily', while the others— and quite a few of them are known—all are significantly different: they are particular in function and place, while Hybla is universal, and their names seem Indo-European, as Hybla is not. The Palici are domiciled at, or in, their fiery lake and their name recalls the Latin Pales; the fire-god (H)adranos resides in his temple, guarded by fierce dogs, at Adernò on the slopes of Mt. Etna, and the similarity of his name and (H)adria is at least suggestive. Both these recall features of Italic religion by their relation to violent and exceptional natural phenomena.[2] Anna with her παῖδες has been found at Buscemi only and has convincingly been compared with the Roman Anna Perenna; the 'Mothers' of Engyon finally may be likened to the Thracian 'Nymphae'[3]—so different from Greek nymphs—and Celtic and Germanic matronae. By contrast, Hybla is found —as the places called after her show—far and wide in Sicily, and if the identification of Pantalica with 'Hybla the Great' is accepted, she must be the Great Goddess whose traces we have been concerned to follow. A specific concern with dreams is in keeping with what we seem to have found, for these rise from the depths of the earth.

The pre-Greek population of Sicily was the product of a fusion of 'Mediterranean' and 'Nordic' races, just as were the Greeks who came to settle there. The traditional distinction of Sicani and Siculi may or may not be authentic evidence to this fact; at any rate, the particular deities just surveyed seem to have been primarily worshipped by the Siculi. But long before their arrival, and down through the ages, Hybla— the live rock sustaining the city of Pantalica; the pregnant force of the abiding Earth; the womb of all life—had been, and remained, the universal goddess of the land; her priests retained their authority down, at least, to the times of the tyrant Dionysios, who himself consulted them.

And could the similarity of her name and that of Asianic Cybele possibly be more than a mere freak of chance?

---

[1] Bernabò Brea, p. 164.
[2] See A. Evans as quoted by Freeman, i. 528.
[3] For these see Dobrusky in *Bull. Corr. Hell.* xxi (1897), 119 ff.

PART II

THE GREEK GODDESS

I. THE GODDESSES IN SICILY

To Sicily under the sway of that silent goddess of Life and Death the Greeks came with their own and unique vision of the divine. The powers of the deep which, from of old, had been felt and worshipped but not seen or represented except by symbols, they grasped in definite, human form and dignity. For they were granted the revelation of another realm of divine reality; of gods and goddesses abiding in light and beauty, at home in the brightness of the ether yet haunting the world of men and directing their destinies. Their light irradiated and transformed the perennial powers of earth and fecundity, of darkness and death; who now gained form and individuality like them.

Wherever Greeks landed, altars in sacred precincts betokened their lasting devotion and gratitude to the gods who had guided them; where they settled, sanctuaries and temples arose to honour and propitiate the divine protectors of the new cities. So in Sicily, where to this day the remains of these temples are the most imposing monuments of the island's Greek past. Where, during that great age, was its ancient goddess?

'Insulam Siciliam totam esse Cereri et Liberae consecratam': thus Cicero.[1] Diodorus says the same: ἱερὰν ὑπάρχειν τὴν νῆσον Δήμητρος καὶ Κόρης;[2] Timoleon made good use of this tenet;[3] the oldest coins of Enna (about 450 B.C.) show Demeter on her chariot in search of her daughter;[4] Gelon, after his victory over the Carthaginians in 480 B.C., dedicated temples to the two goddesses in Syracuse.[5] This is commonplace; and so is

---

[1] *In Verrem* II. iv. 48, 106.   [2] Diod. v. 2. 3.
[3] Diod. xvi. 66; Plut. *Timol.* 8; cf. E. Sjøquist, *Kokalos*, iv (1958), 107 ff.
[4] *Brit. Mus. Catal. of Coins, Sicily*, p. 58. This coin by itself—so it seems to me—is sufficient to disprove the widely held but improbable view that the rape of Persephone was not localized in Sicily until Timaios published his *History*; more likely, he recorded a tradition current in his homeland. Demeter represented with torches, on her chariot, is seeking her daughter (cf. H. *H. Dem.* 48), and the people of Enna clearly put this scene on their coin because—then as later—it was connected with their city. Cf. below, p. 157, n. 3.
[5] Diod. xi. 26. 7.

the relation—stressed ever since the two authors just cited—between this cult and the fertility of the island, which, for centuries, made it the 'granary of Rome'. It was necessary to repeat the commonplace; be it only as a starting-point for our special subject, be it because the oldest written evidence is slightly but markedly different. Pindar asserted (*Nem.* i. 13)— with the words prefixed to this Book—that Zeus gave Sicily to Persephone (and not to Demeter, nor to both goddesses together). The poet is quoting (in 476 B.C., so it appears) a current tradition.[1] His following words justify the scholiast's comment that the island was Zeus' wedding gift when his daughter married the Lord of the Netherworld; given εἰc ἀνακαλυπτήρια, as the scholiast says. This technical term implies a festival of this name; and indeed Κόρης Θεογάμια (which comes to the same) are attested in Sicily;[2] Pindar, then, was indeed quoting a Sicilian tradi- tion. Fourteen years earlier he had called Akragas a 'seat of Persephone' (*Pyth.* xii. 2), hardly, as the scholiast annotates, because the gift of the whole island implied that of the particular city, or vice versa; the two versions could have been current together. Akragas, however, must have had an eminent cult of the goddess and a tradition that it particularly had been that gift τῆι Περσεφόνηι εἰc τὰ ἀνακαλυπτήρια—as indeed schol. *Ol.* ii. 15 d states. Two other Greek cities claimed the same for themselves: Thebes[3] and Kyzikos;[4] the latter eminently devoted to the cult of the Σώτειρα, the former worshipping the Mother no less than the Daughter. And, finally, there is the outstanding and ancient cult of Persephone in Italian Lokri, which in due course will engage our attention.

The indications of a particular devotion to Persephone in Sicily are confirmed by the historian Timaios who, according to Plutarch,[5] described Kore as the specific protectress of Syracuse, and they are carried back beyond the age of Pindar by a century with the oldest extant relic of great Sikeliote art, the Laganello head.[6] The remains of a statue, twice lifesize, this grandiose sculpture retains—notwithstanding the injuries of time and wilful mutilation—an aura of divine solemnity tempered with a hint of gentleness and maidenly charm. P. Orsi devoted to it an essay[7] fully

---

[1] Echoed (from the Pindar scholia) in schol. Theocr. xv. 14 and, again, by Cicero and Diodorus, ll. ll. (they follow a common source; probably Timaios); similarly Plut. *Timol.* 8 (end).

[2] Pollux, i. 37.

[3] According to Euphorion in schol. Eur. *Phoen.* 682 (cf. Paus. ix. 23. 3; Pindar, fr. 37 Sn.); but according to Euripides, ib. the city was founded by Persephone and Demeter; cf. Paus. ix. 16. 5 and Xenoph. *Hell.* v. 2. 29.

[4] Appian, *Mithrid.* 75 (ὑπὸ Διὸc τῆι Κόρηι ἐμπροίκιον δοθῆναι, κτλ.).

[5] Plutarch, *Nicias* I. 2; Jacoby, *Fragm. der griech. Historiker*, 566 Timaios, fr. 102.

[6] E. Langlotz and M. Hirmer, *Die Kunst der Westgriechen* (1963), Pl. 3 (wherever I could refer to this outstanding work, I have cancelled my references to earlier publications, unless these seemed to retain a special value for the present discussion).

[7] *Daedalica Siciliae*, in *Monuments Piot*, xxii (1916), 131 ff.; cf. B. Pace, *Arte e civiltà della Sicilia antica*, ii (1938), p. 4, n. 2.

worthy of its great subject. With penetrating scholarship, archaeological and topographical mastery, and artistic sensitivity he demonstrated that this late-dedalic head, a local work,[1] belonged to the cult statue of Kore from her sanctuary (which has not so far been exactly located) at the spring Kyane. This was, according to Sicilian tradition, the spot where the earth split open to receive the chariot of the Lord of the Netherworld with his prey, the 'Maiden'; the place, according to Diodorus[2] (that is, Timaios), of annual celebrations by the people and state of Syracuse. The recovered cult-statue is proof of the very early origin of these celebrations, which were said to have been instituted, long before the founding of the city, by Herakles.[3] The crude rites observed at them likewise proclaim their antiquity: bulls were dropped into the depths (the Kyane is a small and deep circular lake) as a sacrifice to the infernal deity.

The evidence so far adduced for the early cult of Persephone in Sicily is important for the following disquisition; it entails, besides, a qualification of a theory proposed by E. Ciaceri which has had some considerable repercussions. In his learned and useful book on the *Culti e miti nella storia dell'antica Sicilia* (1911), p. 191, he stated that 'devesi sopratutto alla politica del grande Gelone, se il culto di Demetra e Cora si diffuse nel interno dell'isola'.[4] The basis of this theory is in Herodotus' report (vii. 153) about Gelon's ancestor Telines settling a civic dispute in Gela by using the sacred symbols (ἱρά) of the 'chthonic deities'; whence their priesthood—publicly recognized, so it appears—remained in his family; and indeed Hieron of Syracuse, his descendant, held the priesthood of Demeter and Kore.[5] It is indeed conceivable that the Deinomenids, founders of temples to the two goddesses in Syracuse and nearby, used their cult 'as a political instrument',[6] but they cannot be credited with 'bringing it to Syracuse'; still less, with causing its spread all over the island. It had older and deeper roots.

These roots must not be sought in assuming that the Greek immigrants simply adopted, and renamed, the cult of the great local goddess whose traces we have striven to discern.[7] Not one of the Greek sanctuaries so far

---

[1] Its material is the local limestone (from Plemmyrion). Originally it was covered, like so many products of Sicilian sculpture and architecture, with a fine stucco slip, and painted; it cannot therefore be 'purely Korinthian', as E. Langlotz once asserted (in *Antike und Abendland*, ii (1946), p. 116, n. 6; but 'Korintho-Syracusan' in *Die Kunst der Westgriechen*, p. 55) and may confidently be taken as expressing a Sicilian concept of the goddess.

[2] Diod. iv. 23. 4 and v. 4. 2.

[3] Diod. v. 4. 2.

[4] Ciaceri is here summarizing an earlier book of his entitled *Il culto di Demetra e Cora nell'antica Sicilia* (1895). His thesis, as quoted, was repeated in Pace, iii (1945), p. 464; cf. recently D. White in *Greek, Roman and Byzantine Studies*, v (1964), 263 (note his important *caveat*, p. 261, n. 1 and 264, n. 12).

[5] Pindar, *Ol.* vi. 95/160 c. schol.; Jacoby, 566 Timaios fr. 96.

[6] This phrase is part of the title of the article of D. White quoted above, n. 4.

[7] 'È ammesso quasi generalmente che Demetra e Kore si siano sovrapposte nei vari luoghi

discovered has its foundations in a native cult-locality. Even the one instance which T. J. Dunbabin[1] would allow, namely the 'Santuario Rupestre' below San Biagio at Akragas, has meantime lost its credentials,[2] and the abominable sculptured stelae in the precinct of Meilichios outside Selinus, 'precious evidence of the capacity of the natives for a rough but sincere expression' according to B. Pace,[3] have recently been found to be Punic and therefore late;[4] not one pre-Greek sherd has been found in the whole of this ancient precinct. Occasional Sicul sherds in some other early Greek sanctuaries can suggest that natives joined in the cult but not that the cult was 'pre-Hellenic'.

On the contrary: the Greeks of course came, as we recalled, with their gods,[5] and the natives learned to see and understand their own deities largely in Greek forms, as nymphs, 'mothers', and—perhaps—even Demeter. Here the Great Goddess of Enna continues to pose the problem 'Greek or native', often argued *in utramque partem* but insoluble for lack of pre-Greek evidence; when she first comes into view, she is Demeter.[6] And Hybla—as we saw—remained Hybla (though Adranos became Hephaistos). At Grammichele, on the other hand, where Greeks and Siculs are seen living together for a long time,[7] the latter are found endeavouring to fashion their goddess in the Greek manner; the outcome was that 'bruttissima statua', now in the museum in Syracuse, on which Orsi, its finder, heaped adjectives of abuse, not undeserved and yet unjust.[8]

For this crude statue is a symptom of the progressive and rapid Hellenization of the Sicilian natives. As the archaeological exploration of the

---

ad un culto indigeno affine di divinità della natura feconda': thus Pace, iii. 469—a valiant overstatement.

[1] *The Western Greeks* (1948), p. 181. I can be brief because I can refer to this authoritative discussion; even though I would take exception to some of D.'s statements. The assertion (p. 180) that the rape of Persephone was placed not in Sicily but in Crete by Bacchylides (fr. 64 Bergk = 47 Snell) in a poem 'written in Sicily' is unfounded and hence cannot demonstrate that this localization of the myth originated later (cf. above, p. 70, n. 4). Pindar was under no constraint to quote this detail; in fact, though, it is implied by his words as quoted at the head of this Book. The gift, by Zeus, of Sicily implies the rape in Sicily; and so does the ancient cult at the Kyane.

[2] *Klearchos*, xx (1963), 114 ff.   [3] ii. 157.

[4] A. Di Vita, in *Accademia Etrusca di Cortona, Annuario*, v (1961–4), 235 ff.

[5] For Syracuse (as D. White reminds me) the recently discovered 'chthonic' sanctuary on the slope of Akrokorinth may represent one of the points of origin for the early cult of the two goddesses.

[6] Wilamowitz repeatedly maintained that the Demeter of Enna must have been the successor of a native goddess. He was anything but alone in holding this view (cf. Pace, iii. 470), which may well be correct; but there is no concrete evidence to support it.

[7] Dunbabin, pp. 122 ff. and 174.

[8] *Mon. Ant.* vii (1897), Pl. 3, with Orsi's comment; Pace, ii. 153 f., Fig. 142 f. The noble *dea seduta*, now in the same room, and from the same site (Pace, ib., pp. 41 f., Figs. 39–41; Langlotz–Hirmer, Pl. 39), represents the kind of model which the native sculptor strove to emulate; cf. below, p. 150.

hinterland of Leontinoi, Gela, and Akragas proceeds,[1] the large amount of contact between them and the Greeks is becoming increasingly clear. The ground had been prepared in pre-colonization and even in My-cenaean times; the final result was the Hellenization of the Siculi. The crisis and outcome of this historic process are personified in the tragic figure of Duketios, the contemporary of Empedokles, the heroic pro-tagonist of the native cause, finally finding refuge with his Greek adver-saries. Henceforth there is one populace of 'Sikeliotae', essentially Greek but with characteristics markedly their own and due, no doubt, to an essential strain of native blood and tradition as well as to the impact of earth and sky and the extremes of affluence and of mortal danger in this outpost of the Greek world.[2]

In a manner calling for elucidation, the worship—so evidently out-standing with the Sikeliotae—of female deities seems to assign to these the place formerly held by the pre-Greek Great Goddess. We saw that, beside its more normal form—furthered though not created by the Deino-menids of Gela and Syracuse—of a devotion to the divine pair of Demeter and Kore, a particular worship of Persephone by herself is attested by the earliest literary evidence.[3] My intention is not, after Cia-

---

[1] The lessons from the highly successful work in this field by Italian archaeologists have been utilized by Dunbabin and, more recently, von Stauffenberg. Lists of important recent literature are in *Not. Scav.* (1960), 68 and in Griffo–von Matt, *Gela* (1963), pp. 216 ff.

[2] I cannot believe in a noteworthy Punic element in the classical Sikeliote mentality (which has sometimes been asserted). One or two Punic names occur, together with Sicul ones, on *defixionum tabellae* of *c.* 475–450 B.C., which have more recently been found in the Gaggera outside Selinus (S. Ferri, in *Not. Scav.* (1944–5), 168 ff.; L. H. Jeffery, in *BSA* (1955), 72 f. and 81); viz., Magon and (probably) Nannelaios: slaves, presumably, and prisoners from the battle at Himera. Trade relations between Carthage and Selinus and, no doubt, other Greek cities must have existed during the fifth century as before, and personal relations, and even some intermarriage, between leading Sikeliote and Punic families are attested. Even so, it would seem preposterous—to me, at least—to assume any Punic impact upon life, art, and religion in Selinus, and still more so to assume it for the rest of Greek Sicily, prior to 409 B.C. Matters become very different after the catastrophes at the end of the fifth century; it is the merit, in particular, of A. Di Vita (see also *Kokalos*, iv (1958), 98 f.) and D. White (*Amer. Journ. Arch.*, lxxi (1967), 335 ff.) to have demonstrated by concrete instances the Phoenician impact in this later period.

[3] Evidence quite as old as Pindar's for a unique authority in Sicily, not of Persephone but of Demeter, may be sought from Simonides. According to schol. Theocr. i. 65–6 he said (fr. 200 Bergk; 47 Page) that Aitna—presumably conceived as a nymph (cf. *Anthol. Pal.* vi. 203. 6 and Servius, *Aen.* ix. 581)—was the arbiter in a dispute about Sicily between Hephaistos and Demeter, and one will legitimately infer that Demeter won. This however is a poetic invention rather than an authoritative tradition. Simonides, I submit, devised it on the classic model of Athena's and Poseidon's litigation about Athens (the Argive version of the same motif, Paus. ii. 15. 5, may have helped); devised it for that great occasion to which Pindar and Aischylos likewise contributed, namely, the inauguration of the city of Aitna founded by Hieron. Pindar depicting Hephaistos' fiery rivers flowing down from Aitna; Aischylos in his Aitna-play presenting the Sicul Palikes as the offspring of Hephaistos' daughter, and Simonides making Aitna arbitrate between Hephaistos and Demeter: the analogy is striking enough (cf. Paus. i. 2. 3). If our inference is correct, the primacy allotted to Demeter must have

ceri[1] and Pace,[2] once more to enumerate the evidence for these Sicilian cults but rather to try and gain some insight into their significance.

II. THE GODDESSES IN THE MOTHERLAND

With this end in view we may, first, briefly consider the traditions which the new settlers brought with them. The literary and archaeological evidence concerning the cult of Demeter and Persephone in the motherland is very rich; it has been collected, examined, and discussed for more than a century by scholars from whom we gratefully learn[3] while endeavouring for ourselves to reach a point from which to view Magna Graecia.

There are two singular features about these goddesses. First, there are indeed, in Greek mythology, many other pairs of deities; they are husband and wife, or lovers, or brother and sister; but this pair of Mother and Daughter is unique. And, secondly, this unique pair actually comprises three persons, for the younger goddess is also Persephone, and this is not merely the name of the—otherwise unnamed—'Maiden'. This designation, 'Maiden' or 'Daughter', Kore, is itself her name; on the other hand it has long since been acknowledged that by its widely varying forms (Pherephatta, Pēriphonā, Persephoneia, etc.)[4] this alternative name is proved non-Greek, that is, non-Indo-European. The opposite is evidently true of Demeter, the 'Mother' and, with her, the 'Daughter', Δήμητρος Κόρη.[5] The non-'Greek' Phersephassa could not originally have been the daughter of the 'Greek' Demeter. The question arises how and why she became it.

pleased Hieron; nor does it exclude, to say the least, a cult long-established in Sicily of the goddess; but it does not demonstrate an accepted prerogative of hers in the way implied, for Persephone, by Pindar's Φερσεφόνας ἕδος.

[1] pp. 187 ff.

[2] iii. 463 ff. On looking at the actual evidence from writers, coins, and inscriptions one may well feel struck by its scantiness, especially for the pre-Roman period. The validity of the generalizing statements in Diodorus and Cicero has to be tested by the archaeological material, and in particular the terracottas; and this material stands in need of careful interpretation.

[3] From L. Preller, *Demeter und Persephone* (1837) down to G. E. Mylonas, *Eleusis and the Eleusinian Mysteries* (1961). My debt is particularly great to Wilamowitz (esp. the relevant sections of *Der Glaube der Hellenen*); also to M. P. Nilsson (esp. in *Opuscula*, ii) and W. F. Otto (in *Eranos Jahrbuch* (1939), 83 ff.; reprinted in *Die Gestalt und das Sein* (1955), pp. 313 ff.).

[4] Listed in Roscher, *Lexikon der . . . Mythologie*, ii. i, 1286 f.; Preller–Robert, *Griech. Mythol.* i (1894), p. 800, nn. 3 f.

[5] The failure to acknowledge this is one of the weaknesses impairing W. F. Otto's impressive article (p. 86).

The Nordic (*sit venia verbo*) immigrants brought with them, so one may infer,[1] this divine pair; deities of a people of peasants and worshipped mainly by their womenfolk. In their devotion to them—the Daughter-goddess disappearing and returning and the Mother ever remaining, in sorrow and again joyful—they experienced as divine the basic emotions of woman's life and the essence of all life, its transience enfolded in eternity. What surrounded them; what made and unmade their lives; trust and anxiety about the seasons and their gifts, and primarily the grain, on which they depended: all this lived for them in the persons of the divine Corn-Mother,[2] who is the lasting earth,[3] and her daughter, whose return causes all seeds to sprout and buds to open which lay as dead while she was away. The whole: a symbol and surety of the eternity of Life.

The immigrants entered Greece gradually, in several waves, in the course of many centuries, but the cult of the two goddesses appears to have been common to all of them, even though those who came first conceived of them somewhat differently from their successors—hence the peculiarities of some ancient Demeter cults, especially in Arkadia, as reported by Pausanias.[4]

In Greece, the immigrants found a goddess Persephone–Phersephatta worshipped by the native population which they gradually subjected, and with which they mingled; to become, through this fusion, in the end one people of many tribes: the Greeks. And this new Greek people came to worship the pre-Greek Persephone as one with the 'Maiden', and therewith Persephone became the daughter of Demeter.

How could it have been possible to conceive of the two as one? Wilamowitz says:[5] 'What kind of a goddess she (the pre-Greek Persephone) was it is impossible to say; presumably, though, she was *eine Unterirdische*.' Indeed: she could not have been felt to be one with the 'Maiden', had she not been what she is in the oldest Greek testimonies (in Homer, that is; cf. Hesiod, *Th.* 914) and for ever remained—the Queen of the Netherworld. Too great a goddess to be forgotten, she must in some essential aspects have been so like the Nordic 'Maiden' that the two could be felt to be one and the same. The 'Maiden' who every year brings fruitfulness and life on earth cannot have been conceived of as the queen of the unchanging infernal realm of death. Could her periodic absence, which caused life on earth to languish, have been thought of as

---

[1] Cf. Wilamowitz, i. 203 ff.

[2] The writer expects the reader to be as impressed by W. Mannhardt's *Antike Feld- und Waldkulte* (1877) as he is himself.

[3] The (often advocated) etymology of Δη-μήτηρ as 'Earth'-mother seems highly probable to me; see Wilamowitz, i. 198.

[4] Cf. M. P. Nilsson, *Geschichte der griech. Religion*, i² (1955), pp. 477 ff.

[5] ii. 107.

her stay in the Netherworld, perhaps with some Hel (to use the Germanic name) or a similar godhead? Or, alternatively, could the pre-Greek Phersephassa, beyond her rule over the dead, have been worshipped also as a bringer of fruitfulness? Both of these possibilities—which are not mutually exclusive—have to be borne in mind; but some pre-existing similarity of this kind has to be assumed to account for the identification of Kore and Persephone.

Thereafter, the periodic absence of the 'Corn-maiden' was understood as her stay in the place of Persephone. The 'Nordic' goddess and the Mediterranean one were unified through the myth of Kore's abduction by Aidoneus. Ever present in cult, poetry, and art, this myth impressed their identity all the time and there could be no identification more pro-foundly meaningful;[1] even so, it was never complete.[2] The realm below could never really be without its queen, and she who returned to be with the Mother was the Maiden, the Daughter: this was τὰ τῆς Κόρης μυστήρια. No farmer prayed for corn to Persephone;[3] no mourner thought of the dead as being with Kore.[4]

In the Greek homeland the cult of the two (or three) goddesses, united or singly, is attested in countless places.[5] To those already quoted (Akra-gas, Lokri, Thebes, and Kyzikos) for a specific cult of the younger goddess —this is by far the least frequent kind—Erythrai, Sparta, and Arkadian Megalopolis may be added,[6] and also the Athenian Φερεφάττιον.[7] Demeter alone is found often, as the specific giver of grain, in places where this abounded;[8] but most frequently Mother and Daughter are worshipped

---

[1] For this consider the suggestive pages of W. F. Otto, *Eranos-Jahrbuch* (1939), 93 f.

[2] In Homer, the orbits of Demeter and Persephone never touch, and Kore is not men-tioned.

[3] *Hymn. Orph.* 29 (to Persephone) v. 17 καρποὺς δ' ἀνάπεμπε is not a counter-instance which one would take seriously.

[4] Euripides, though—no doubt for stylistic variation—repeatedly speaks of Kore as the goddess of the Netherworld (e.g. *Alc.* 852, *H.F.* 608; 804).

[5] See Roscher, ii. 1, 1288–1307 for a list of their attested cult-places.

[6] The Σώτειρα on the coins of Kyzikos is expressly named Κόρη in the Roman period only; but the lovely youthful head, crowned with ears of barley, which appears on them from the end of the fifth century onward, evidently means the same (apart from the *Brit. Mus. Catal. of Coins, Mysia* (1892), Pls. VIII ff. see especially H. von Fritze in *Nomisma*, ix (1914), 34 ff.). Accordingly, the city celebrated Κόρεια (but also Φερεφάττια) and τὰ μέγαλα μυστήρια τῆς Σωτείρας Κόρης; even so, the inscription ...]ΠΗ ΔΕΣΠΟΝΗΣΙΝ[... on the fragment of an archaic marble bowl from Kyzikos (H. Roehl, *I.G.A.²* (1882), no. 501, after Chandler), the terracotta Louvre C165 and a few inscriptions (F. W. Hasluck, *Cyzicus* (1910), pp. 210 f. and 270) are evidence of some cult also of Demeter. It thus appears that, albeit with a par-ticular predominance of the 'Maiden', a cult and mythology analogous to the Eleusinian prevailed at Kyzikos. Soteira was worshipped also at Erythrai (here, too, not to the ex-clusion of Demeter; see Preller–Robert, p. 754, n. 5); for her cult at Megalopolis see Pausanias viii. 31. 2; for her Spartan temple, allegedly built by Orpheus or Abaris, id. 3. 13. 12; for Athens, Aristoph. *Ran.* 378.

[7] Demosth. *c. Con.* 8.

[8] Many instances are quoted in Preller–Robert, pp. 749 ff.

together. And perhaps it ought here to be stressed that this is not a 'mother-and-child-group'—where Demeter is represented as Kouro-trophos, the babe in her arms is not Persephone—but a pair of mature women often hardly distinguishable in age, or even identical, as in the most ancient (seventh century) types, from Kamiros and Korinth, of terra-cotta figurines representing the two goddesses wrapped in one cloak,[1] or seated on a chariot,[2] and in many later examples.

We are concerned to visualize what these goddesses meant to their worshippers, and rather than try to summarize what may be read in sundry authoritative books we may here urge that—short of immediate revelation—it is the words of poets and the works of artists which preserve live what once was felt live and would, but for them, elude us: a thousand reported facts become meaningful through the inspired word and image. Ἐπαινὴ Περσεφόνεια, the queen of the dead, ἀγανή, ἀγνή: she remains for ever in Homer's verses. Demeter, the solace and refuge of women, the divine paradigm of their sorrows and joys: if all reports about her were lost, her Knidian image would still convey all this; Theokritos can still soothe you in the aura of the good Corn-mother, and Kallimachos make you perceive her bounty and her might. And, finally, it is Aristophanes[3] who enables you to share the trust in a better life beyond the grave, and the happiness arising from this trust, with those who, through the Eleusinian mysteries, had partaken in Demeter's sorrow at the loss of her daughter, turned into joy at her return from the Realm of Death. These initiates were the same people who experienced, in tragedy, the fated limitation of human existence and its root and summit in inescapable suffering. What a range of realistic perception! And it is they, again, who, for all the consolation flowing from Kore's return would not forget the absolute and final reality of death and its queen.

It is likely, and indeed certain, that not every facet of this religion remains, crystallized into a lasting form through art. At those countless places of worship believers must have perceived other aspects of the god-desses, reflected in specific myths; some of which may be brought within our grasp by reports, significant symptoms, and reasonable inference. The Homeric Hymn admits of such inference both by its actual contents and by certain inconcinnities of its narrative. It centres on Eleusis and no doubt gives the myth in a form acceptable there; it contains the mythical

---

[1] The ivory group, from Mycenae, of two women, likewise with one cloak, can be taken to represent the same; in which case the child on their knees would be a predecessor of the Plutos-babe on later, Eleusinian representations.

[2] *Brit. Mus. Cat. of the Terracottas* . . . , by R. Higgins, i (1954), nos. 231 and 897; S. Mollard-Besques, *Cat. . . . des figurines et reliefs* (Musée nat. du Louvre) (1954), nos. B197 and B207; C138 and C165.

[3] Need I add that the reference is to Theocr. vii, Callim. *Hymn.* vi, and Aristophanes, *Ranae*?

aitia for several of the specific Eleusinian rites; even so, it has no room for what at all times was the chief pride of Eleusis: namely, the tradition that Demeter had there first bestowed on mankind the gift of corn. This tradition was incompatible with the version which places at Eleusis the myth that the goddess, by stopping the growth of corn, enforced the return of her daughter—the myth which was at the centre of the Eleusinian mysteries. This incompatibility did not trouble the worshippers, nor does it prove the wording of the hymn to be incomplete; it is, however, evidence that this central myth was not originally localized at Eleusis. A second observation points to the same conclusion. Demeter has roamed the earth 'for nine days' in search of her daughter (vv. 48 ff.); thereafter she learns from the sun-god that Persephone has been abducted, with the consent of Zeus, by the Lord of the Netherworld (v. 77). This knowledge must be the end of her search, and since in the Netherworld her daughter is beyond her reach, this is the point for the angered goddess to force the issue by withholding her gift. The rhapsode, however, makes her resume her wanderings—so as to be able to bring her to Eleusis;[1] after he has narrated her doings there the situation is exactly as before (v. 91 ∼ 304) and the action now takes the expected course.

These literary observations serve to confirm that the story of the wrath of the Earth-mother enforcing the return of her daughter was not originally localized at Eleusis (the rape is not, in the hymn, placed there anyhow).[2] Presumably the whole myth was not originally attached to any specific locality, and hence believers in many places would tend to locate and celebrate it in their own neighbourhood;[3] Sicilians, for example, in Sicily. It would therefore be wrong to infer 'Eleusinian influence' wherever that form of the myth recurs which, in consequence of the cultural and political predominance of Athens, became primarily associated with Eleusis. Even where the goddess, or goddesses, are called 'Eleusinian' this inference does not by any means impose itself; for it has long since been observed that this is a 'pre-Greek' word (as is the name Persephone) recurring in the name of the goddess Eleithyia–Eleutho[4] and, moreover, in places—particularly in Arkadia—where any 'influence' from (Attic) Eleusis is out of the question. On the contrary, the occurrence of this epithet suggests the early and independent origin of the respective cult,[5] which therefore could easily have centred upon

---

[1] Cf. Wilamowitz, ii. 49.

[2] If the tradition mentioned by Pausanias i. 38. 5 had existed at his time, the rhapsode would have found his task greatly lightened.

[3] See e.g. Preller–Robert, pp. 758 f.

[4] Roscher, ii. 1, 1337; Preller–Robert (see Index, iii, p. 949, s.v.); Nilsson, i. 312 ff. and 475. The basic suggestion, much discussed and developed by successive generations of scholars, was made by K. O. Müller (1825).

[5] Thus even where, in the course of time, dependence on (Attic) Eleusis was alleged, as in the case of Demeter Kidaria–Eleusinia at Pheneos; see Pausanias viii. 15. 1–4.

a divergent concept of the goddesses and their myth. This variety of local concepts in the motherland will have to be borne in mind in considering the cults of the Western Greeks.

Persephone stayed before the Greek mind as Homer had depicted her—the Queen of the Dead. A symbol of ultimate power and expressiveness representing her are those 'aniconic stelae' which the people of Cyrene placed on their graves.[1] On these busts without face: the dead have no face; the rich hair around that shapeless void, and the crowning polos, indicate the queen of those who are not, and thus are with her.[2] She is the total negation of life; to think of her as a giver of life would be preposterous. Accordingly, her marriage with Aidoneus must be without issue; as indeed it is in Homer and all authoritative tradition; the goddess of death is barren.[3]

The 'Orphic' tradition, which makes her the mother of Dionysos-Zagreus, does not invalidate this axiomatic statement.[4] This tradition resulted, here as elsewhere, from the combination and systematization of variants of popular myths current in different regions. Dionysos is, essentially, the offspring of Zeus and a goddess of the Earth. Semele has long since been recognized as being, originally, just this; in other versions

---

[1] S. Ferri published and discussed them in *Divinità ignote* (1929). Quite apart from the competent presentation of the archaeological material, this book is rich in original observations and suggestive ideas. All the more do I regret my inability to accept the author's interpretation (pp. 39 ff.; esp. 75) of the stelae; which strikes me as an odd combination of sensitivity, wide knowledge—and barren speculation. A photograph of one of the stelae is in Nilsson, Pl. 52. 5. Since then, some more have been found; see A. Rowe, *The Cyrenaican Expeditions of Manchester University, 1955, 1956, 1957,* (1959), Pls. 27 ff.—P. Marconi (*Agrigento arcaica* (1933), pp. 45 ff. and Pl. XV. 3) found in the Santuario Ctonico at Agrigento a terracotta tube, damaged at its lower end and roughly 40 cm. high (and, in addition, two fragments of another one). Near its upper end, a pair of ears is crudely added, interconnected by the indication of a strand of hair. Marconi interpreted it as a ritual object, destined to conduct libations into the ground, comparing it with the well-known vases without bottom placed on graves and with two similar tubes, decorated with rings, which had been found at Lokri and Monticchio in Calabria. This seems convincing. He compared it, moreover, with the 'face-less goddess' in Cyrene and declared it to be a similar, aniconic representation of Persephone. On inspection, the Akragantine object proves to be far less impressive than photographs (such as in von Matt–Pareti-Griffo, *Das antike Sizilien* (n.d., c. 1960, cited hence as von Matt[1]), Pl. 106) would lead one to expect. It is indeed possible that the odd and sketchy indications on it are meant to denote the goddess into whose realm the libations were to flow; but the whole thing lacks the symbolic power of the Cyrenian stelae; it cannot be related to them ideologically, nor genetically either, for the stelae are not tubes.

[2] On the latest of these stelae (of Roman times), the original, profound symbolism is spoiled by the addition of dress, arms, and even a face.—S. Ferri, in 1959 (see his *Opuscula* (1962), p. 65) presented 'aniconic' figurines from Tepe Gawra of c. 1500 B.C., as analogies and indeed ancestors of the Cyrenian. To me, the similarity seems slight (see *Excav. at Tepe Gawra*, Pl. XLVa) and any relation incredible; the Hurrian figurines are small, not from graves, and represent, I feel, one more variety of the traditional symbol of the 'Mother goddess'.

[3] Late sources quote Hades and Persephone as the parents of various infernal potencies (e.g. the Eumenides: thus the Orphic Hymns and Proclus, but no earlier witness; see Orph. fr. 197 Kern). These however are rationalistic platitudes rather than true myths.

[4] Cf. Detached Note XI, below, p. 407, on the Chthonian Dionysos.

her place is taken by Demeter,[1] Rhea[2]—or Persephone.[3] It is clear from the parallel versions that this 'Persephone' is not the goddess of Death but Demeter's innocent daughter.[4] This indeed is what the myth tells wherever it is given in any detail, and never is Hades said to be the begetter of this (or any other form of) Dionysos.[5] On the contrary, the myth goes on to tell that, afterwards, Zeus ceded the Maiden to Hades. Therewith she became, in this form of the story, the queen of the Netherworld; the fact that in many relevant reports she is called Persephone from the first— which is, as we saw, in agreement with poetical convention—does not affect the point at issue: the goddess of Death is barren.

There is, however, some other evidence, now to be surveyed, which may suggest a different concept of Persephone. The identification of the queen of the Netherworld with Demeter's daughter is so ancient that one would expect to find characteristic features of the 'Corn-maiden' to recur with the former. There are indeed some instances of this; but they are scanty. It is significant that the triad Demeter, Kore and Pluto is worshipped in several places,[6] but—to the best of my knowledge—the second deity in this triad is never Persephone; it is the 'Daughter' that shares in both realms, not she. In the cult the title Καρποφόροι is, naturally enough, sometimes attributed to Mother and Daughter together[7] but not, as far as I can see, to Persephone alone; if (according to Hesychius) she was

---

[1] Diodor. iii. 62. 6 and 64. 1; Lucret. iv. 1168.

[2] Eur. fr. 586 N².

[3] The oldest testimonies come from the gatherer of mythographical eccentricities, Kallimachos (fr. 43. 117 Pfeiffer = 171 Schneider) and Diodoros (v. 75. 4), who locates the story in Crete, adding that it agreed with Orphic poems and rites (cf. iii. 62. 8). For further evidence see Lobeck, *Aglaophamus* i. 547 ff.; Kern, *Orph. Fragm.*, fr. 58, pp. 139 f. and 230; O. Gruppe, *Griech. Mythol.*, p. 1436, note 0 (also, for irrelevant reports about other offspring of Zeus and Persephone, ib., p. 1272, note 6). Anyone surveying this abundant hotch-potch of mythological curiosities (Cicero, *De nat. deor.* iii. 53 ff. affords a sample) will see that it is the late and shapeless sediment of Hellenistic scholarship; of collections, that is, of local mythical traditions, some of which were adopted by 'theologoi' writing under the name of Orpheus; collections which were quarried by commentators on classical poets as well as by Epikurean and Skeptic critics of the traditional religion and thus benefited their successors, the Christian apologists.

[4] Explicitly so e.g. Ovid, *Metam.* vi. 114 (*Deoida*).—A Selinuntine coin-type (on which see Detached Note IV, below, p. 397) may represent Zeus, in the shape of a snake, approaching Demeter's daughter. If it is correctly interpreted thus, it could be evidence that, at the time when these coins were struck, this particular myth was known at Selinus. It is not a certain conclusion, and still less would it follow that the Orphic theological system, into which this myth was incorporated, did at the time exist.

[5] According to Aischylos, fr. 228 Nauck = 377 Mette (brilliantly restored by G. Hermann, *Aeschyli Tragoediae*, i (1859), p. 331) Zagreus is son of Hades; but is he Dionysos? And is Persephone his mother? I hesitate to base conclusions on this fragment and, with J. Harrison (*Prolegomena* . . . , pp. 479 ff.), to combine it with Euripides, fr. 472 N. and the one line from the *Alkmaionis* (fr. 4 Kinkel); for this scanty old evidence about Zagreus, the 'great huntsman', is insufficient to clarify the notions connected with him. He may have been one more popular impersonation of Death, like Admetos and Agesilaos (on these see below, p. 402).

[6] E. Rohde, *Psyche*⁵, i (1910), pp. 208, n. 2, and 210, n. 1.

[7] Preller–Robert, i. 749, n. 1, 766.

worshipped as *Φλοιά* by the Lakonians, this by-word, pointing to fruitful growth, was transferred from the Corn-mother to her daughter; when Persephone was invoked as *Μελιτώδης*,[1] this was a euphemism. But it is notable that, on a few black-figure vase-paintings,[2] Persephone is shown, in Hades, holding ears of corn. Is this to be understood merely as a reminder that she is Demeter's daughter? Or does it intimate a genuine trait found in the goddess of the Netherworld as such? Was she, the Queen of the Dead, felt to be also the dispenser of life? Could it be that this polarity was her true and original character, remembered through the ages? Was the pre-Greek Phersephassa in fact one with the great Goddess whom our previous investigation sought to approach? Of her dominion the Homeric Persephoneia, in all her unapproachable grandeur, embraces only one province; she lacks the very aspect of the great Mother, the giver of life and fruitfulness. Could it be that the notion of her was thus confined because that other, positive aspect was embodied in the 'Mother and Daughter' brought by the new folk? Are the few features just adduced survivals of an older, all-comprehensive notion of the goddess?

This really is a 'meta-historical' problem, involving axioms which call for very serious consideration. And even if the questions just formulated were answered in the positive, the fact would remain that she was perceived overwhelmingly in the character of the deity of Death alone. And indeed this notion of Persephone, the Queen of Death, is in itself a revelation final and absolute, and profoundly different from that of the 'Great Mother'; nothing short of a fresh revelation could have made her devotees conceive of her so differently. The way to so different a concept indeed was open. The poets from Hesiod onward called Persephone the 'daughter of Demeter', urging her identity with Kore which was inculcated also by cult-legends like the Eleusinian; but the awareness of their distinctness remained. *Μελαντειχέα νῦν δόμον Φερσεφόνας ἔλθ', Ἀχοῖ*: Pindar (*Ol.* xiv. 20) could not have thus sung of Kore. Against this background, the few traces just mentioned of a different concept of Persephone would appear to indicate a transference of names rather than the effect of a revelation reasserting, in Persephone, the ancient and universal form of the 'Great Mother'. The same may be suggested with regard to two often quoted vase-paintings. The Vlasto krater shows ΠΕΡΣΩΦΑΤΑ rising through the earth and returning to ΔΕΜΕΤΕΡ,[3] and φΕΡΟφΑΤΤΑ

---

[1] See the commentators on Theocr. xv. 94.—The alleged cognomen *Μελίβοια* rests on a false reading in the fragment of Lasos' hymn *apud* Athenaeus 624 f (p. 365, no. 702 Page).

[2] One of them is reproduced in Roscher, ii. 1, p. 1343; cf. ib. 1345.

[3] See M. P. Nilsson's instructive list (*Opuscula*, ii. 611 ff.) of the numerous and various representations of that much-discussed scene of a goddess emerging from the earth; add the vase found at Kameiros (*Clara Rhodos*, iv (1930), 103 ff.), on which the goddess is named ΑφΡΟΔΙΤΕ: the bold invention, no doubt, of the writer of some satyr-play (to be added to

is similarly depicted on a krater now (?) in Dresden;[1] none the less this scene is, in popular parlance, ἡ ἄνοδος τῆς Κόρης. And the Eleusinian procession approaching the sanctuary called out, while crossing the river Kephissos,

Πάριθι, Κόρη, γεφύραν·
ὅσον οὔπω τριπολεῖν δεῖ:[2]

the daughter of Demeter came to bless the new seed; but Persephone remained below, the inexorable Queen of the Dead.[3]

I am deeply conscious of the imperfections of this typological sketch, in which what were considered by the writer to be the essential elements have been over-stressed in the interest of clarity—with a corresponding neglect of that detail in which religion becomes real. For its reality is in the communion, at a particular place and time, of the individual worshipper, or community, with his, or their, godhead. Only in attending to such detail could it really have been ascertained if, or in how far, the asserted identity of Kore and Persephone had led, in the motherland, to the recognition of a giver of life in the ancient goddess of death.[4] The evidence here mustered at any rate did not suggest a wide-spread realization of this kind.

If it has reminded the reader of some main features, in the homeland, of this part of Greek religion, the preceding sketch, however imperfect, has served its purpose of providing the background against which we may view Magna Graecia and in particular Sicily.

III. PINDAR

The temples whose ruins remain as the grandest monuments of the island's Greek past are evidence—like the medieval cathedrals towering over their modest cities—of the devotion of the communities; they found the most worthy use for their resources in erecting buildings ever grander,

---

F. Brommer, *Satyrspiele*[2] (1959), p. 54); for a satyr, as well as Hermes, is standing by.—The Vlasto vase was reproduced e.g. in Overbeck, *Atlas zur Kunstmythologie* (1872 ff.), T. xviii. 15; see now G. M. A. Richter, *Red-figured Attic Vases in the Metropolitan Museum* (1958) Pl. 124 and text p. 156.

[1] Nilsson, i, Pl. 39. 1; Harrison, p. 277, Fig. 68.

[2] Plutarch (quoted by Proclus) on Hes. *Op.* 389; see Wilamowitz, *Verskunst* (1921), p. 286 and *Der Glaube* ... ii[2]. 51, n. 1 (but are not these clearly two Ionic dimeters, the first catalectic? Cf. Ar. *Ran.* 323 ff.).

[3] Persephone—and not Demeter; see Detached Note VI, below, p. 399.

[4] It may be observed, in passing, that the distinction is maintained even in the reproduction, in the *Frogs*, of Eleusinian eschatology (to which the identification is, after all, basic): inside the 'house of Pluton' is Φερρέφαττα (v. 671); outside, Δημητρὸς Κόρη (337). Cώτειρα (379), ἡ θεά (445).

richer, and nobler for the worship of their gods. It is today often impossible to say which god or goddess was the owner of a particular temple, but drawing on all the evidence it is clear that, generally speaking, these temples were dedicated to the great Olympians, whose cult the immigrants had brought with them and who were alive in their minds, primarily, as they are in the Homeric poems.[1] Their cult and their festivals were the heart and summit of civic life; the unity, strength, and confidence of the communities were rooted in the hold of each and all of its members upon these divine protectors and paradigms.

Since the Greeks of the age with which we are concerned lived, and felt themselves, as members of their civic—and this meant, with them, religious—communities to an extent which we can hardly imagine, the religious significance, to them, of the communal cults has to be rated highly indeed; at the same time, these cults were far from engaging the whole of their devotion. Every Athenian no doubt walked in the procession for his city goddess and attended also the Dionysiac festivals; almost everyone also appears to have been initiated in the Eleusinian Mysteries, however different their appeal and reward. Beyond all this there were the specific cults of each house and each tribe, of deceased members of each family, and many others of which we get some glimpses through Aristophanes and other writers as well as from inscriptions and other archaeological finds. And where individual Athenians, thus surrounded by deities, found the centre of their devotion it would be bold to guess without much evidence.

No doubt there was a similar wealth of religious experience with the Greeks overseas—of which we know even less. With one outstanding exception. Pindar's Second Olympian Ode reveals the devotion and eschatological persuasion of one of the greatest Sikeliotes, Theron of Akragas; a persuasion at which otherwise nobody could have guessed. It is a reminder how distant we are bound to remain from a concrete understanding of the religion of individuals and communities; a warning that any attempt at discerning and outlining an aspect of Greek religion in Sicily is bound to remain on the surface and can result only in a typological picture which, at best, may define the region within which lay, beyond our grasp, the reality and variety of cult, belief, and devotion.

In this very personal ode[2] Pindar puts into words of unfading lustre

[1] This is what Herodotus says (ii. 53); not that they were invented by Homer and Hesiod. The power of the poet's word conveyed images of the gods so definite and myths so impressive and lucid as to determine men's notion of them.

[2] *Ol.* ii, and in particular the sections here relevant, have been the subject of many incisive studies; see the exhaustive bibliography in J. van Leeuwen, *Pindarus' tweede Olympische Ode* (1964), pp. 339 ff. (This book was not available to me until after the completion of the present chapter, nor did the opinions presented in it (esp. p. 170) cause me to abandon mine. The interpretations of an E. Rohde and Wilamowitz—whom I largely follow—are not invalidated by disregarding them).

the essence of a religion which had its roots in the conviction of the divinity of the soul; its divinity and not merely its immortality—of which, as far as I can see, no Greek down to his time had ever doubted. Here indeed was a fresh revelation resulting in new concepts of deity and of man and his destiny, widening but not abandoning the traditional foundations of Greek humanity. We may still, in this context, use the term 'soul', although the peculiarity and variety of Greek concepts of man's non-corporeal component has often, and rightly, been stressed and discussed; and even though Pindar avoids the word ψυχή in the ode under discussion and uses it with various nuances of meaning elsewhere.[1] Reflecting a momentous development of thought and experience, the word had by his time become fit to denote the totality of mental and emotional features which constitute, beyond the changeable and perishable body, the persisting unity of the individual.[2] This Pindar calls αἰῶνος εἴδωλον (fr. 131b)[3] and he adds the essential assertion: 'it alone is from the gods'. It is this insight which is realized in the eschatological myth of *Ol.* ii, the fragments of a threnos (fr. 129–31a),[4] and the verses quoted by Plato (*Meno* 81b; fr. 133), and while it can neither be proved nor disproved that all these poems[5] were addressed to Theron and his circle, they may all be taken to convey essentials of the same religion reflected in the mind of the poet.

In this religion the Greek belief in the after-life of great men, the heroes, is understood in a new context and dimension. An existence in a realm of timeless bliss, like the Homeric Elysium, awaits the perfected, and perfection is achieved in the fulfilment of the most noble potentialities of life on earth. This fulfilment is within reach of those who have attained the highest forms in the scale of human existences, as kings, wise men, and athletes;[6] it involves for them the observance of religious as well as ethical obligations. The blessed ones, so we are told, have shared in the 'rites which free from suffering',[7] and the aged Theron may trust to join them: the ruler of a great city, he is just and generous in his dealings with

---

[1] See Rhode, ii. 207 (*N.B.* ἀνδιδοῖ ψυχάς, fr. 133).

[2] We shall have to return to this point in discussing Empedokles (below, p. 270).

[3] Developing Homeric usage (as *Il.* 23. 72, *Od.* 11. 476).

[4] The constitution of this essential text by B. Snell, based upon Wilamowitz's (*Pindaros*, 497) has put all earlier editions out of court (I suspect that in fr. 129, after the lacuna at the end of v. 5, the particle καί may be Plutarch's, introducing a new extract, as before fr. 131b).

[5] Fr. 143 may come from the same orbit, cf. below, p. 268.

[6] Pindar no doubt gives (in fr. 133) only a selection of those highest types (cf. on Empedokles, below); besides, its rendering in a modern tongue is misleading: σοφία would apply primarily to poets like Hesiod or Pindar himself and, no doubt, also to 'sages' like Thales or Solon—and Pythagoras. And to appreciate the inclusion, in this selection, of the 'swift-footed' one has to be alive to the revelation of human perfection which an aristocratic society hailed in the persons victorious at the national games and festivals.

[7] Fr. 131a, restored by Wilamowitz (the conclusions drawn from this fragment remain whatever attitude to its corrupt wording be taken).

inhabitants and strangers, a 'benefactor' (εὐεργέτας) like no other, and a worshipper of the gods; he has thus reached the threshold which gives entrance to Elysium.[1] Such consummation is not reached at one step, but by stages, in the course of repeated lives on earth; each of them followed by a judgement and a period of either reward or punishment. The 'long year' ('ennaeteris') of punishment—a penance like that undergone by gods who violated the supreme oath (Hesiod, *Theog.* 793 ff.) or were guilty of murder (like Apollon serving Admetos)[2]—is exacted by Persephone as amends in retaliation for 'ancient grief' (ποινὰν παλαιοῦ πένθεος). The reference of the latter, much-discussed phrase remains obscure;[3] it must be to a myth which accounted, in a manner unknown to us, for the fact that the soul, which is 'from the gods', ever lost its divine status. It is Persephone, again, who sends the souls, after purgatory (if the medieval term be allowed), to a new life on earth or alternatively—this corollary seems self-evident—to final bliss (*Ol.* ii. 68 ff.). May one infer that she is herself the judge at whom Pindar (*Ol.* ii. 63 ff.) hints with cryptic words; that 'someone' who, 'under the earth', judges 'with inimical duress' the fault committed in the Upper-world? This cannot be cogently demonstrated, but it seems possible.[4] Rhadamanthys who, in Plato's time and henceforth, was believed to judge the dead, is in Pindar's poem on the Isles of the Blessed, as in the *Odyssey* (4. 564). Aischylos[5] speaks of 'another Zeus', or Hades, as the judge, and Pindar may indeed be hinting at him; with the same restraint as a speaker in a fourth-century comedy.[6] The pronoun τις, followed by the participle φράσαις, naturally

---

[1] *Ol.* ii. 6 ff. and 92 ff. Theron was free to take in the same sense the words with which Pindar concluded the hymn for the public celebration of his Olympic victory (*Ol.* iii. 43 ff.). His expectation was fulfilled: after his death, four years later, Theron was accorded worship as a hero by his grateful citizens (Diodor. xi. 53. 2; cf. xiii. 86. 2).

[2] Rohde, ii. 211, n. 2.

[3] I cannot bring myself to believe in the ingenious suggestion of Reinach and Rose, who would find in these words an allusion to the Orphic myth, which makes all men share in the guilt of causing the death of Dionysos, the son of Persephone—because men's bodies contain some of the ashes of the Titanes who murdered and devoured the god. Quite apart from the fact that I cannot visualize Pindar, or Theron, indulging in theological abstrusities of this kind, there is in ancient Akragas, and most of Sicily, a marked scarcity of evidence for any cult of Dionysos (on this point later)—and without Dionysos this whole 'Orphism' becomes non-existent.—I may at once confess my disbelief also in a second trace of 'Orphism' which some students would find in the same poem. Why is it stated (v. 29) that Semele, received on Olympos, is loved by Pallas Athena as well as by Zeus and Dionysos? Perhaps it is reason enough that Pallas is Zeus' daughter; I could not, in any case, believe that it was because she —according to 'Orpheus', i.e. Clem. Alex. (fr. 35 Kern) and Firmicus Maternus (fr. 214 Kern)—had brought the heart of the slaughtered god to Olympus. This act could not establish an intimacy between her and Semele, for the Dionysos in question was not Semele's son but his namesake, in an earlier age. The son of Semele escaped a different disaster by a different and well-known device. In short, arid speculations of this 'Orphic' type seem to me unlikely to have been an element of the religion of Pindar, Theron, and their circle. Cf. however, Detached Note IV, below, p. 397.

[4] The suggestion is not entirely new; see Schroeder's *ed. mai.* (1923), p. 511.

[5] Aeschylus, *Suppl.* 230, *Eum.* 270.   [6] Philemon, fr. 246 Kock.

suggests this interpretation but does not enforce it. Against it is the pre-dominant part played in this context by Persephone, while there is no reference at all to Hades; it is she who finally 'accepts the amends' (ποινάν) of the sinners; it would therefore seem at least plausible that it was she who, 'immediately' after death, passed sentence on them to 'pay amends' (ποινὰς ἔτεισαν).

I do not wish to press this detail; the dominating part, in this religion, of Persephone is anyhow evident,[1] and this fact is, to us, of particular interest. Before pursuing it we may for a moment turn to those points by which historians of religion tend to be exclusively fascinated. Here is, undeniably, a doctrine of rebirth; of the transmigration of souls; of a judgement of the dead; of final redemption: where did all this originate? How is it to be classified? As Orphic? Pythagorean? Derived from Egypt? From India? And in the flurry of rash definitions, questions, and answers the object loses its individual shape and concreteness. It is indeed evident that a central concept of the religion expressed in these poems recurs in the teaching of Pythagoras.[2] It is the one and only tenet which, thanks to Xenophanes, is ascribed to him with certainty;[3] namely, the doctrine, so-called, of 'transmigration'. As long, however, as its place and context in Pythagorean teaching remains obscure, the recurrence in Akragas of this doctrine constitutes a problem rather than an insight. There is still less reason for harking back to India; seeing that the belief in 'transmigration' is no more, nor less, than a restatement, dictated by a fresh realization of man's essential nature, of the age-old and world-wide realization of the unending interconnection of life and death. And, finally, one ought not to talk of 'Orphism' where there is no trace of, nor room for, Dionysos.

To these questions of history and nomenclature we shall return after assembling further evidence (which is by no means lacking); meantime, we may strive further to exploit Pindar's testimony. The poet praises and comforts the king, picturing for him, in glowing hues, the other world where he expects soon to dwell, and the way to it. We may say, on examining this picture, that it is a composite one. The blessed state of the heroes is painted in Homeric colours; the expectation to achieve this state through sacred rites (τελεταί) and noble conduct is a non-Homeric element which, in turn, did not necessarily imply the reincarnation of

---

[1] This assertion rests of course on fr. 133, the reference of which to Akragas is not attested; but its contents fit perfectly into the indications of *Ol.* ii, supplying an essential and indispensable detail, which one would have to infer if it were not attested; some infernal deity must have dispensed what is described in *Ol.* ii, and Persephone was a, or even the, chief godhead of Akragas. Hence fr. 133 is legitimately used to complete the evidence of *Ol.* ii.

[2] Schol. *Ol.* ii. 123 (p. 93. 10 Dr; cf. p. 88. 1) plainly states that 'Pindar here follows Pythagoras'; Clement of Alexandria (*Strom.* v. 103, p. 710 Potter) says the same.

[3] Also, still in the fifth century, by Ion of Chios (fr. 4 DK); see F. H. Sandbach in *Proceed. Cambr. Philol. Soc.*, n.s. v (1958–9), 36.

souls (as in fact it did not in the theology of Eleusis). It makes none the less a meaningful whole—from the cult and conduct demanded in life through judgement and reincarnation to final exaltation. That divine light which, through Homer's genius, brightened everything and every person in his world of heroes and gods now shone beyond the grave.

This was the religion of Theron of Akragas; but obviously not his alone. Pindar—who could not, I feel sure, have so profoundly and fully put it into words if it had not corresponded with his own deepest convictions— speaks of it in an outstandingly personal and intimate poem: these are not topics for the market-place, and not even for the public celebration of a victory; for all that, it is not a private matter. A cult is involved, and there is no such thing as a cult for and by one individual. The goddess of this cult is Persephone, and one is bound here to recall that she was outstandingly the goddess of Akragas. It is not indeed certain that she was worshipped as the main godhead of the city, as at Kyzikos, or like Athena at Athens; the greatest temple of Akragas—and of all Greek cities outside Asia Minor—was dedicated to the Olympian Zeus, and Athena resided, as in Athens, on the Akropolis. This much, however, may be inferred: that the people of the city which Zeus had given to Persephone paid her as universal a devotion as the Athenians paid to the goddesses of Eleusis. And one may allow one's imagination to visualize them at the 'Santuario Ctonico' (by the 'Temple of the Dioscuri', wrongly named and wrongly reconstructed); for Pirro Marconi's excavations and L. Leporini's brilliant reconstruction-drawings[1] allow us to envisage the people in this walled precinct, sacrificing at many altars, pouring libations and the blood of victims, offerings for the powers of the deep, into hollow bothroi; carrying out secret rites in the seclusion of small buildings, and worshipping in common in a larger temple (it is telling that the first larger temple—a forerunner of the grandiose buildings of the fifth century—appears to have been built in this precinct).

Such imagining however is bound to be vague and to touch, if anything, only the surface of the cult; what precise rites were carried out in this precinct we shall never know. But we learn through Pindar what is far more essential: namely, the ideas and expectations attached to this cult—certainly by Theron and his circle, and probably by others. The rites 'freed from suffering'—in the other world; ensuring, like the Eleusinian, 'the better lot' yonder. These τελεταί may, then, justly be called a mystery-cult. They are, however, essentially different from the Eleusinian. Here is no Demeter anxiously awaiting her lost daughter; no Kore whose return from the realm of death conveys to the believers the joyous cer-

---

[1] P. Marconi, *Agr. arc.*, esp. pp. 13 ff. and Figs. 5 ff. (partly reproduced by Pace, iii. 500 ff., Figs. 131 f.)—brilliant though not in every detail final; see lately P. Griffo, *Nuovissima guida . . . di Agrigento* (1961), pp. 134 ff.

tainty of a blissful after-life. Here is Persephone, the dread Queen of Death; man's task is to propitiate the inexorable; a task demanding the activation of his highest potentialities and, even so, impossible but for the efficacy of rite and faith.

Such then seems to have been the concept and cult of Persephone at Akragas—or, rather, a concept and a cult. As Zeus was worshipped, in the same city, under three aspects—as Olympios, Atabyrios, and Polieus —thus the goddess of the Netherworld could very well have shown herself in different forms. We shall presently turn to the archaeological evidence which evinces that such was indeed the case; here we may quote an isolated scrap of literary evidence because it points back to the earliest period in the city's history. Phalaris, according to Polyaenus v. 1, made himself master of Akragas by exploiting the celebration of the Thesmophoria. Therewith the early cult of Demeter, most probably together with her daughter, is suggested.[1]

The cult of Persephone, and its theology, left marked traces in the thought of Empedokles (who, as a young man, may well have listened to Pindar). Of this later. Pindar gives us evidence, profound and explicit as no other, of one facet of Greek religion in Sicily; others become discernible, though far less distinctly, through a vast body of silent witnesses. They have been known for a long time, yet no one has cared to interrogate them. I am speaking of the terracottas.

IV. SICILIAN TERRACOTTAS AND RELATED OBJECTS

(a) INTRODUCTION

They stand, small figurines of baked clay, in every antiquarium; in London, Paris, Copenhagen . . . and especially in the museums of Sicily— Syracuse and Gela, Agrigento, Palermo, Trapani. Vitrines and vitrines containing these inconspicuous representations of, mostly, women standing or sitting: the lover of classical art is likely to pass them by; if he cares for *Kleinkunst* at all, he will hurry on to the products of a later age; to those lovely 'Tanagras' with the immediate appeal of their elegance and variety. To him, however, who is willing to bide and contemplate them, the archaic and early-classical terracottas will appeal—in a different but

---

[1] If the recent view (P. Griffo, ib., pp. 134 f.) is correct, according to which two neighbouring temples in the Santuario Ctonico, presumably dedicated to Demeter and Kore, were built shortly after 480 B.C., the place of the specific cult of Persephone would have to be sought elsewhere. It could still have been in the same precinct or, perhaps, at San Biagio, or even at Theron's residence "ἀν' ἄκρα πόλεος".

compelling manner; for in their very monotony and primitiveness they emanate a strange power and dignity, telling of a persisting and profound devotion such as is scarcely felt in the richer offerings of the later times. If, following this appeal, you study them with some attention, you will soon observe that no two of them are quite alike, even though they all belong to a few easily defined types. On further comparison, the expressiveness of their features and gestures will stand out more strikingly; all the more so when you realize that it was emphasized by rich and lively colouring; and the devotion which created them is felt overwhelmingly in the fact that, for every sample exhibited, many others, and maybe hundreds, are stored away in the vaults of the museums—and all this is no more than a tiny fraction of what was once dedicated in sanctuaries and piously committed to graves! These figurines, then, may suitably be compared with the cheap pictures of the Virgin and of Saints which nowadays are traded and dedicated at Southern churches and cemeteries; they are mass-ware like them; but how superior in expression and taste! And while it remains true that after, roughly, the middle of the fourth century the variety and elaborateness of the terracottas increase immensely, the gain for the lover of pretty things and for the student of art and manners is paid for by the eclipse of that simple and profound inspiration.

We are concerned with that earlier kind, and we are not, of course, the first to be so concerned. They have been discussed, more or less fully, in many excavation reports[1] and museum catalogues;[2] a comprehensive corpus was published before the turn of the century,[3] and the studies in this field have been summarized and pursued by L. Quarles van Ufford.[4] As a result of these studies, the mass of Sicilian terracottas has been arranged by types; stylistic analysis has served, in combination with data gained from excavations, to establish the approximate dates and the development of each type, and their origins have been illuminated by

[1] Outstanding are P. Orsi's reports on Gela (*Mon. Ant.* xvii (1906), cited 'Orsi, *Gela*') and Grammichele (ib., vii (1897), 212 ff. and xviii (1907), 121 ff.), and E. Gàbrici's on Selinus ('Gaggera', ib., xxxii (1927), cited 'Gàbrici'); among the more recent ones are those of P. Orlandini on Predio Sola at Gela (*Mon. Ant.* xlvi (1963)), and D. Adamasteanu and P. Orlandini on various sites at Gela (*Not. Scav.* lxxxi (1956), 203 ff.). See also P. Marconi, *Agrigento* (1929), and *Agr. arc.* (1933). Further reports are quoted by van Ufford (see below, note 4), p. 14.

[2] Outstanding is R. A. Higgins's recent *Catalogue of the Terracottas in the British Museum* (1954); most valuable also the catalogues of the Louvre by S. Mollard-Besques, i (1954), and of the Danish National Museum by N. Breitenstein (1941).

[3] R. Kekulé von Stradonitz, *Die Terracotten von Sicilien* (1884); most useful also F. Winter, *Die Typen der figürlichen Terrakotten* (1903). The drawings in these standard works, though admirable, are not as a rule sufficient for details of style and expression.

[4] *Les Terres-cuites siciliennes* (1941). In quoting this valuable study I do not wish to imply agreement with every statement contained in it.

Addendum: After the final revision of the present book the masterly and richly illustrated handbook *Greek Terracottas* by R. A. Higgins (1967) appeared, references to which have been added where possible.

comparison with material from outside Sicily. The majority of these types has been found to have originated in the Greek East, particularly in Rhodes, Samos and, perhaps, Miletus; some few in the Peloponnesus and particularly in Corinth; and every one of these was imitated and variously developed in Sicily.[1]

Valuable and indispensable though these studies are, they tend to put the terracottas—most of them small and unpretentious—in an inappropriate light; for they are primarily religious not artistic objects. They are indeed *agalmata*; things, that is, in which the deity of a sanctuary and the dead in his grave were meant to delight;[2] if a donor could afford a large and well-worked piece, such he would present; much more often, though, the recipients were expected graciously to accept what modest gift a poor dedicant could offer. Whether costly or cheap, these were primarily tokens of devotion; of this devotion, and of its divine objects, they may tell us if we make bold to ask after this, their essence.

It has not been done so far; not systematically, at any rate; even though some students have, on occasion, given precious hints.[3] And indeed, the attempt at an interpretation on these lines, even when it is restricted to the limited province here under review, is beset with all but forbidding difficulties. It ought to be undertaken, if at all, in daily communion with the originals and their milieu; this the present writer is denied; he has to rely on impressions and notes gathered years ago and on the testimony of photographs and the printed word, the precariousness of which he has himself previously emphasized.[4] Quite apart from these personal shortcomings—enhanced by the difficulty of securing even the most essential literature—an interpretation which goes beyond the registration of formal features involves at every step decisions of a personal

[1] A scholar whom I hold in particular respect, C. Blinkenberg, after examining the exhibits in the Syracuse museum, expressed the view (*Lindos*, i (1931), p. 509) that all Sicilian terracottas are imports just as are the Attic vases found there. This view, if correct, would make the following investigation largely illusory; but it cannot be correct. All of the archaeologists who have devoted a prolonged study to them—such as Orsi, Gàbrici, Marconi, Orlandini—distinguish imported and Sicilian ware; so do van Ufford (*passim*), Dunbabin (p. 265), and Higgins (*B.M. Cat.* pp. 8 f. and 297). And indeed the differences both of style and material strike the eye even of the non-specialist; besides, the relics of a workshop have been found near the temple-terrace at Agrigento, with no less than forty moulds for figures still surviving (Marconi, *Agr. arc.* p. 50) and moulds have been found also at Selinus and Morgantina (*Am. Journ. Arch.* lxv (1961), 280).

[2] Terracottas are found also in houses (Higgins, ib., p. 7 with note 8), even though I know of no Sicilian instances; in any case, the fact of their main, religious quality would apply there too.

[3] Here again I would quote, first and foremost, P. Orsi; his sensitive and penetrating characterization (*Gela*, pp. 686 f.), esp. concerning the expression of 'ò morte ò profonda concentrazione mistica' in certain of his finds at Bitalemi, remains fundamental. Very helpful, besides, is the comment which E. Langlotz has contributed to those statuettes included among Hirmer's masterly photographs (in *Die Kunst der Westgriechen*); reference to which will in the following pages be made wherever possible.

[4] *Proceed. Brit. Acad.* xlix (1963), 177.

nature with which other students may disagree. Does this or that standing figure represent a mortal devotee or a goddess?[1] Must a seated figurine represent a goddess[2]—seeing that this does not apply to the Branchidai at Miletos nor to Phileia on the Geneleos monument in Samos?[3] Can the wearer of a 'Polos, die griechische Götterkrone'[4] confidently be held to be a deity—seeing that the polos may be worn also by humans engaged on cultic activities?[5] And if some figure is confidently held to represent a deity: how is it to be identified? Could not one and the same type have been dedicated to different deities at different places? And, finally, when beyond these questions of identification, one proceeds to define the character, expression, and spirit of a figure, he risks taking for specific what is the common mark of some type, and for intended characteristics what may be technical shortcomings; moreover, the loss of the colours may have altered the original effect, and in identifying some particular expression we are liable to substitute our own for the archaic mentality. In the face of so great a risk of error I shall confine myself to a sketch of observations reasonably obvious (and accordingly superficial), which others more competent may correct and develop.

The difficulties just summarized are not in fact entirely intractable;

[1] This question arises constantly; one has only to compare the observations of various excavators, or in different catalogues, regarding types frequently recurring. Is a woman carrying a piglet Persephone or a devotee? Do the Samian figurines (often transformed, by the addition of a spout, into scent-bottles) of a maiden carrying a dove represent Aphrodite, or the prospective owner, or her maid-servant? R. A. Higgins found Aphrodite in them in his booklet *Greek Terracotta Figures*, 1963, *ad* Pl. 4: not explicitly so in the B.M. catalogue, p. 48; in *Greek Terracottas*, pp. 30 ff. he speaks of the 'Aphrodite Group' but states (35): 'It is by no means certain that Aphrodite herself, and not a votary, is represented.'

[2] Blinkenberg—with whom I regret once more to disagree—would regard practically all female figurines, the seated ones included, as representations of humans (i, pp. 28, 34, 509), in opposition to 'l'ancienne manière de voir, selon laquelle la plupart représenteraient des divinités', for which he quotes the authors of the older catalogues of the Louvre (Heuzey) and the British Museum (Walters). The only exceptions which Blinkenberg actually admits are the two types which he claimed to be reproductions of the first and second cult-image of Athena Lindia.

[3] E. Buschor, *Alt-Samische Standbilder* (1934), pp. 26 ff. Admittedly, though, what Eastern grandees emulating oriental royalty permitted themselves is unlikely to have affected the standards observed by dedicants in the West.

[4] This is the title of the instructive monograph by V. K. Müller (1915).

[5] Müller, ib., pp. 81 ff. Iphigeneia, the priestess, wears a richly decorated polos on South Italian vase-paintings (L. Séchan, *Études sur la tragédie grecque* (1926), p. 384, Fig. 112); similarly the statuette of a priestess (4th cent.) found at Morgantina (E. Sjøquist, *Kokalos*, iv (1958), 118, Pl. 44); one may compare Philostratos' (*Apollon. Tyan.* iv. 28) lucid description and interpretation of a statue at Olympia representing Milon of Kroton in the guise of a priest of Hera and, as such, wearing a 'mitra'. The odd Boeotian figures—male as well as female—with huge poloi on top of enormous hairdresses cannot represent divinities (B.M. nos. 846 ff. and 870 ff.; Louvre C59 ff.; see the text, with literature, p. 93). One will therefore agree with Müller that typical figures with gifts—victims or fruits—represent human dedicants even when wearing the polos. An illustration of the type may be found in *Not. Scav.* (1956), p. 247, Fig. 5b ('un tipo di offerente molto comune a Gela') and in von Matt[1], Pl. 92.

they can, to some extent, be met by combining conclusions from a general survey with the interpretation of individual figures rendered dependable either where these belong to an amply attested type or, with luck, where a well-worked and clearly definable sample happens to survive.

Of the older Sicilian terracottas, a small minority were found in graves.[1] Most of them come from sanctuaries or their *favissae*;[2] repositories, that is, to which the overflow of less precious votive offerings was from time to time relegated (unfortunately, as a rule, broken up, to prevent re-use). Outstanding sites are:[3] just outside Selinus, the Malophoros precinct at the Gaggera; at Akragas, the so-called 'Santuario Ctonico', and the one at San Biagio with its *favissa* below, the so-called 'Santuario Rupestre'[4] (which, in the fourth century, became the place of a nymphaeum);[5] at Gela, the precinct at Bitalemi just across the river, and a whole series of sanctuaries small and great both inside the town and outside; at Grammichele (?Echetla) a sanctuary and *favissa*, again 'fuori le mura' (and above a necropolis).[6]

The terracottas found at all these places are, in their overwhelming majority, representations of women; other subjects, and particularly male figurines, are completely absent from some sites and rare exceptions in others;[7] in particular, I am not aware of one single figure which could

---

[1] This is in marked contrast with e.g. Kamiros (Rhodes; I am referring to the diggings by Salzmann and Biliotti) and Elaious, where practically every grave contained one or more statuettes. In Sicily, many were found in the cemetery del Fusco at Syracuse, but most of them are more recent than those with which we are concerned. At Gela, on the other hand, where almost every grave contained pottery, much of it of the highest quality, statuettes are extremely rare (cf. Orsi, *Gela*, pp. 265 ff.; he found only one 'bustino' in the earth above a sarcophagus, ib., p. 425, Fig. 307. Recent excavations similarly yielded only one figurine, of the so-called 'Lindia' type, in a child's burial; *Not. Scav.* (1956), 366). Graves at Monte Bubbonia north of Gela yielded a fine seated figure with babe (Siracusa, Mus. Naz. 24905) and several others; about the same holds good for Monte Saraceno, inland from Akragas (*Not. Scav.* (1928), 500 ff.; ib. (1930), 412; I know nothing about graves at Akragas itself). Graves at Kamarina, on the other hand, contained very many terracottas (some of which will concern us later); see Orsi, *Mon. Ant.* xiv (1904), esp. pp. 869 and 948 ff. It seems therefore quite possible that, Gela apart, the comparative scarcity of terracottas from graves in Sicily is due to the fact that many necropoleis have either not yet been found or have been plundered long ago.

[2] The term comes from A. Gellius, *N.A.* ii. 10.

[3] For essential literature see above, p. 90, n. 1.

[4] This now seems to me the satisfactory way of accounting for the relation between the two sites. They would thus correspond exactly with the sanctuary at Grammichele and its 'depositi di anathemata di rifiuto' in 'ingrottamenti artificiali nel fianco della collina' (Orsi, *Mon. Ant.* vii (1897), 216). At Lokri (Mannella) the situation, I suppose, was the same: what Orsi discovered at the bottom of the valley was a thesauros; the famed temple stood high above it.

[5] *Klearchos*, xx (1963), 114.

[6] Other, less outstanding sites, will be mentioned in due course; cf. note 1 above.

[7] P. Marconi (*Agr. arc.* p. 48) speaks of the 'eccezionale scarsità di rappresentazioni virili di fronte alla grande copia di quelle femminili'. From the Gaggera, Gàbrici mentions (p. 219) and pictures (Pl. XLI) the following 'rarissime figure maschili': a few Ionian scent bottles; two figures of kouroi; a fine little bearded head—an excellent piece in relief—probably the attachment of a vase; a tiny Silenos mask; a 'Bes', and some other grotesques; I saw in

be claimed to represent a god; specifically Dionysos.[1] The female element
is predominant also in the rest of the Greek world, yet not so absolutely
as in Sicily;[2] moreover, the Sicilian figurines everywhere repeat and vary
a fairly small number of types.[3] These, however, recur in vast or even
fantastic numbers. Orsi found them 'by the hundred' in the small
excavated part of the modest sanctuary at Bitalemi;[4] P. Marconi[5] refers
with the same words to his finds at the Santuario Ctonico at Akragas
(which unfortunately he failed to catalogue); at and below San Biagio,
their number must have gone into the thousands (for, prior to excavation
proper, the site had been ravaged for decades); at the Gaggera (Selinus),
part of the subsoil was practically made up of (mostly fragmented)
figurines; Gàbrici estimated their number at about 12,000.[6] This, then,
is powerful evidence of a perennial and dominant devotion, common to
all Greeks but outstandingly prevalent in Sicily.

Palermo Mus. Naz., moreover, the archaic figure, almost entirely animalic, of a Pan. These
symbols of the generative forces occur also on other sites in Sicily, though far less frequently
than elsewhere. And there is the strange mask, Gàbrici, ib., Pl. XLVII. 6; could it be the
portrait of a non-Greek worshipper? (According to R. J. H. Jenkins, *BSA*, xxxii (1932), 29,
it is the local reproduction of an Argive statuette. It is presumably due to my lack of expert
knowledge that I am not struck by the similarity of the Argive specimens; I felt confirmed,
though, when noticing the objections raised by van Ufford, p. 74, Dunbabin, p. 277, n. 4 and
now D. White, *AJA*, lxxi (1967), 348, n. 115: 'Punic'). The situation in Akragas is similar
(Marconi, *Agrigento*, pp. 187 f.; id., *Agr. arc.*, pp. 51 ff.): a few kouroi and banqueters, some
insignificant heads and tiny figurines, and an admirable head of a negro.—Besides, many
Sicilian sanctuaries yielded terracotta reproductions of animals—mainly sacrificial ones, but
also occasionally lions—and of fruits.

[1] There is less than no reason for finding Dionysos in one or other of the Agrigentine
banqueters (Marconi, *Agrigento*, pp. 188 f., Fig. 122 f.). The marvellous satyr heads from
a temple at Gela (*Not. Scav.* (1956), 229; von Matt, Pl. 95; Langlotz–Hirmer, Pl. 33) are not
evidence of a cult of Dionysos. As with Medusa and lion-head antefixes, their purpose was
apotropaic. In Aischylos' *Theoroi* (*Pap. Ox.* 2162; fr. 17 Mette) satyrs affix their own effigies to
a temple of Poseidon. Generally speaking, representations indicative of a cult of Dionysos
become increasingly frequent in Sicily—as also in Lipari—from the fourth century onward,
but are almost non-existent earlier (for vase-pictures see below, p. 106, n. 3). The main exception to this statement are the coins of Naxos—and there was an obvious inducement for putting representations of Dionysos and his train on the coins of this very city; as H. Cahn (*Die
Münzen der sizilischen Stadt Naxos* (1944), 1 ff.) has reasserted in detail. They no doubt indicate
a local cult of Dionysos, and so does the image of Dionysos on small fifth-century coins from
an unidentified small inland place, Galaria (Holm, *Geschichte Siziliens*, iii, Pl. II. 3; Hill, *Coins
of Ancient Sicily* (1903), p. 90, Fig. 12), and so does, probably, also the Silenos of Katane. On the
slopes of Mt. Etna, then, Dionysos was worshipped in the classical period. The coins very
clearly show the prevailing concept of the god as the giver of the vine; their earthy vigour
precludes all 'mystic' or 'Orphic' associations.

[2] This has been stated e.g. by Marconi, *Agrigento*, p. 187.

[3] We are primarily concerned with the older period, down to about the middle of the fifth
century. After that, the variety, ever increasing through the Hellenistic period, includes some
different types also of goddesses; such as the Hellenistic representations of Aphrodite and,
somewhat earlier, those of Artemis which Orsi found in her rustic sanctuary at Scala Greca
outside Syracuse (*Not. Scav.* (1900), 363 ff.; for their date see A. DiVita, *Kokalos*, iv (1958),
99, n. 59).   [4] *Gela*, pp. 683 ff.   [5] Marconi, *Agr. arc.*, p. 47.

[6] pp. 119 f. This number includes those many scent-bottles, alabastra, most of which are
all but identical with figurines.

(b) THE DEVOTEES

What devotion, to what deities, the terracottas shall tell; it is immediately clear, though, that the deities are female ones and that they were worshipped by women. This is a matter for surprise which is not allayed by the evidence from the rest of Greece being similar. It is in fact less extreme there, and shows greater variety. One may recall that, on the Athenian Akropolis, statues of korai as well as of kouroi were dedicated, by men, to Athena and also to Poseidon, and one may think of the votive statuettes of comic actors in classical Athens;[1] of Boeotian and Corinthian dancers and genre-scenes; of the masks of Artemis Orthia; of the mythological 'Melian reliefs'; of the long series of male worshippers from Halikarnassos ('in all probability from a shrine of Demeter and Persephone')[2] and Kos; of the sanctuary of Apollo Hylatas at Kourion (Cyprus) with its 10,000 terracottas—all of them representing male worshippers.[3]

In considering the Sicilian ones we aim to play safe. In view of a paramount problem of interpretation, previously mentioned,[4] we shall take every statuette to represent a human person unless there is some definite indication that a deity is meant. The seated posture of a statuette entails such an indication, for rarely—if ever—is there any reason for assuming that some devotee had herself represented in this attitude of authority. On the other hand, the vast majority of standing figures may be taken to represent human women (as is the view prevailing today). They were dedicated in sanctuaries; those dedicating them must have felt some relation established, by their gifts, between themselves and the goddess of the sanctuary. Primarily, all and every kind of *agalma* would be expected to delight her and to secure her favour, particularly such pretty things as Ionian alabastra or, exceptionally, the imported statuette of a kouros. Images of the goddess herself, dedicated to her, would in addition witness to the givers' devotion to her, and the figures of human women must have been intended to stand in lieu of the givers themselves (though not, of course, as individual portraits). They were thus reminders, for the deity, of the donors' attendance or even, as in the Ancient Orient, stood in their place in 'perpetual attendance'. Thus the frequent representations of sacrificial animals and other offerings could be a reminder of sacrifices brought, or even take their place.

[1] A few Sicilian parallels belong to the later period.

[2] *B.M. Cat.* pp. 102 ff.

[3] See the instructive study of these by J. H. and S. H. Young, *Terracotta Figurines from Kourion in Cyprus* (Philadelphia, 1955).

[4] Above, p. 92 with note 1.—The profound reason for this old puzzle (which can be summarized by the formula 'Apollon or kouros?' or indeed 'Kore or kore?') will be touched upon later (below, p. 272).

The manner of this 'attendance' is worth pondering. It is so different from analogous representations in our Middle Ages or the Baroque. No kneeling, no wringing of hands; no contrition, no tearful glances, no mystic raptures: the devotees just *are*, and are there; in the shape, most pleasing to the goddess, of young women in their prime. Rarely, if ever, are they represented in an attitude of prayer.[1] Their presence is enough.[2] Many, though, carry a flower,[3] a chaplet[4] or a fruit,[5] a bird[6] (usually a dove) or a piglet;[7] offerings for the goddess of the place. Some others carry a child—a babe in their arms[8] or an older one on their left shoulder.[9] Not every woman with a child has to be taken for a θεὰ κουροτρόφος; a woman may well, by a figure of this kind, commend her child to a divine protectress of children. This interpretation is particularly probable where the child is seen to be weak, presumably sick; as on a touching little group from Gela with the child sitting on the mother's shoulder and leaning its head on hers.[10] The women carrying some offering finally often wear a high diadem[11] or even the polos;[12] sometimes, in addition, also a large shawl.[13] This attire, as will presently be seen, distinguishes some typical divine images; in the case of *donne offerenti* it has to be understood as a priestly guise.[14] There is no reason why figures of women thus attired

---

[1] One may consider whether the gesture of arms stretched out sideways, which is seen in a few figures from the Gaggera (Gàbrici, Pl. LXIII. 2; cf. ib., p. 265 with Fig. 125), is an (unusual) attitude of prayer. Perhaps B.M. no. 33 may be compared. Van Ufford (p. 68) registers it and quotes Gàbrici, Pl. LXI. 4 as a (doubtful) parallel but, as usual, offers no word of explanation. Could it be taken to illustrate the Homeric phrase χεῖρε πετάccαc (for which see C. Sittl, *Die Gebärden der Griechen* . . . (1890), pp. 147, n. 6, 148, n. 8, 174, n. 5)? J. Boardman recently (*Tocra*, i (1966), 152) suggested that, rather, a dancing posture may be intended. Cf. Gàbrici, Pls. LVII. 6 and LX. 2.

[2] See e.g. Gàbrici, Pls. XXXVIII. 2, 8, 9; LV. 5; LXII. 2, etc.

[3] e.g. von Matt[1], Pl. 165 (from Grammichele); Gàbrici, Pl. LII. 1; Brit. Mus. 1089 (?Gela).　　　　　　　　　　　　　　[4] e.g. Gàbrici, p. 228, Fig. 117; Pl. L. 3.

[5] e.g. von Matt[1], Pl. 92 (from Gela; a good illustration of various types).

[6] e.g. Gàbrici, p. 230, Fig. 120; Pl. XXXVIII. 1 and 3; Pl. LVI. 7.

[7] e.g. Orsi, *Gela*, pp. 700 f. Figs. 523 f.; von Matt[1], ib.　　　[8] Orsi, *Gela*, p. 705, Fig. 529.

[9] Ib., Fig. 530; (*Not. Scav.* (1956), 134 with Fig. 13a (from Siracusa): a Rhodian type: B.M. no. 229 f.; cf. Blinkenberg, no. 2256.　　　　[10] Orsi, *Gela*, p. 706, Fig. 531.

[11] e.g. Gàbrici, Pl. LI; LXIII. 1, etc.; *Not. Scav.* (1956), 245, Fig. 3 (Gela); B.M. 1091 (Kamarina).

[12] e.g. Gàbrici, Pl. LV. 2; LVII. 2; LXI. 4, etc.; *Not. Scav.* (1956), p. 247, Fig. 5b (Gela); B.M. 1139 f.

[13] e.g. Gàbrici, Pl. LVII 4; Marconi, *Agr. arc.*, p. 63, Fig. 36; von Matt[1], Pl. 92.

[14] At least one Agrigentine statuette (Marconi, ib., Pl. XV. 1) appears to show, in the hand of a standing woman, the characteristic attribute of priestesses, a large key.—To obviate certain assumptions it ought perhaps to be stressed that the similarity of dress by no means implies the identification of deity and priest (or priestess). The Greek priest is and remains the official charged with the due performance of the cult. Even if the Athenian archon basileus were known, at the Anthesteria, to have taken the place of Dionysos at the 'sacred marriage', no Greek supposed him, and his wife, to have been transmuted into deities; the priest who, at Pheneos, put on the mask of Demeter Kidaria—if indeed the rite reported by Pausanias viii. 15. 3 is ancient—was not himself thereby deified, and when the Iobacchoi performed the mummery of which their inscription tells, Greek religion was dead.

and not carrying offerings should not, likewise, represent human devotees. Many figurines of this kind have come to light in the Gaggera,[1] but the act that one such was found standing inside an *aedicula*[2] (and therefore must represent a goddess)[3] shows that in 'playing safe' we are liable to miss the tenuous line separating representations human and divine.

These devotees, then, stood thus before their goddesses: not abject, not in any frenzied emotion, but trusting them as they trusted themselves; performing rites and sacrifices, and readily and continually offering their gifts; secure in a communion which gave meaning and fulfilment to their existence without impairing their liberty and responsibility. This, however, is the common Greek attitude to the gods; it cannot, therefore, tell us who the goddesses worshipped by these Sicilian women were and which particular power and character their devotees perceived in them. The statuettes, though, give one suggestive hint. The piglet which so many of the *offerenti* are seen carrying is pre-eminently—though not exclusively—offered in sacrifice to Demeter and Kore (remember Xanthias at the entrance to Hades![4]); moreover, many cults of these goddesses are known to have been the preserve of women. Hence these terracottas are currently regarded as evidence for the cult of 'chthonic' deities and the sanctuaries where they are found, as places destined for it. A rapid survey of the main sites will serve to clarify this point. Archaic sculpture is restricted in individualization, and this the more so the older the specimen; in this uncertainty, our attempt at interpretation will benefit from a definite notion of the milieu in which the figurines under review had their original place.

(c) SURVEY OF SITES

Most instructive, thanks to Gàbrici's monumental work, is the sanctuary in the Gaggera, below the akropolis of Selinus and across the river of the same name (its situation thus is exactly analogous to that of Bitalemi outside Gela).[5] There was, right from the beginning of the city, an open temenos with an altar; a small megaron was built early in the sixth century and replaced by a larger one before its end, when the precinct was surrounded by a wall and furnished with a conduit carrying,

---

[1] e.g. Gàbrici, Pl. LV. 6; LVII. 2, etc.   [2] Gàbrici, Pl. LVII. 7.

[3] It is in fact the same goddess—the head perhaps from the same mould—as the seated one on the same plate (no. 5) on which we shall comment later: namely, Persephone.

[4] Arist. *Ran.* 338 c. schol.; cf. Preller–Robert, i. 796, n. 4.

[5] After writing this chapter I was finally enabled to read G. Charles-Picard's article 'Sanctuaires et symboles de Zeus Meilichios' (*Rev. Hist. Rel.* cxxvi (1943) 97 ff.), which centres on a reconsideration of the Gaggera and its monuments. I was delighted to find (Demeter) Malophoros described as 'déesse agreste' and agreement also in other observations; but certain shortcomings (such they seem to me), on which my respect for a justly renowned scholar prevents me from enlarging, have caused me to refrain from adding further references to it.

H

from a nearby spring, water into and through it, which feeds a small pool in front of the megaron; at the same time the altar was greatly enlarged. Outside but adjoining one corner of the surrounding wall lies a small additional precinct. The latter is tentatively assigned to Hekate, because the base of a dedication to this goddess was found nearby.[1] Since no other dedication to or image of her has come to light, Hekate is unlikely to have played any considerable part in this sanctuary; and since the dedication implies that she played some part in it, Gàbrici suggested that she may have been the 'guardian of the gate', προθυραία, a suggestion which tallies perfectly with the location of this small precinct.[2] The main precinct is held to have belonged to the goddess Malophoros on the evidence of an inscription on stone[3] and a fragmentary one on a potsherd[4] (the site proved amazingly rich in dedications, almost all of small size, but strikingly poor in inscriptions; perhaps the Carthaginians removed them together with the valuable dedications of which they formed part). Very close to the large precinct and quite as ancient, but outside it, is a small one within its own surrounding wall,[5] with a strange 'field of stelae', of the Punic kind, adjoining.[6] Of these tufa-stelae—there were hundreds of them—a proportion is now known to be Punic:[7] namely, those 'decorated' (if this be the word) with two crude heads, one male one female (some have only the male, bearded head),[8] and probably many more. Some of them, though, must be Greek and ancient, for they bear, in archaic Greek letters, those much-discussed inscriptions[9] in which the stele describes itself as the 'Me(i)lichios' of some noble man or family or, once, as belonging to Zeus Meilichios (το(ῦ) Διὸς το(ῦ) Με(ι)λιχίο(υ) ε(ἰ)μὶ Πρωτᾶ το(ῦ) κτλ.).[10] Sacrificial remains have been found underneath some of them;

---

[1] Gàbrici, p. 379 and Pl. XCVI. 4; cf. M. Guarducci, *La Parola del Passato*, viii (1953), 209 and again *Kokalos*, xii (1966), 187.

[2] Gàbrici, pp. 75 and 406; cf. Aristoph. *Vesp.* 804 attesting Hekateia, in Athens, 'before every door' and, generally, Wilamowitz, i. 165 ff. (esp. p. 167: Hekate at the gates of Miletus and of the Eleusinian sanctuary; p. 168: Selinus as evidence for Megara Nisaia, itself under Attic influence, in assigning this role to Hekate).

[3] Gàbrici, p. 380.—Wilamowitz (*Hermes*, xlv (1930), 258) supplemented the problematical last word of this inscription to read ἐμπέλα[vον. If this is correct, the dedicant recorded, by some sculpture in bronze or stone, that he had fulfilled his vow to present Malophoros with—a sacrificial cake! M. Guarducci (*Kokalos*, xii (1966), 190) achieves greater probability by reasserting the old reading ἐν πελάγει.

[4] Gàbrici, p. 340.

[5] It is difficult, from Gàbrici's indications (pp. 95 ff. and Pl. 2), to deduce a clear notion of the original date of this peribolos—and indeed of the stratigraphy of the whole site.

[6] Ib., p. 103, Fig. 61.   [7] Above, p. 73.

[8] Gàbrici, Pls. XXVII–XXIX; also Pace, iii. 476 ff.

[9] Gàbrici, pp. 381 ff.; cf. pp. 155 f. and 174 ff.; L. H. Jeffery, *The Local Scripts* . . . (1961), p. 270. Difficult problems of stratigraphy and interpretation here remain to be solved.

[10] Cf. Nilsson, i. 413, n. 10.—Pausanias ii. 9. 6 mentions an 'artless image', at Sikyon, of Zeus Meilichios 'like a pyramid'. This may have been a 'stele' like those at Selinus. A roughly contemporary and similar 'aniconic pillar', set up by the famous athlete Phayllos (Hdt. viii. 47), has recently been found at Kroton (*Not. Scav.* (1952), 167; Jeffery, ib., p. 257 and Pl.

one will therefore assume that they were erected on the occasion of sacrifices by the members of local noble families, each of which worshipped its Meilichios.[1] Inside this precinct stands a very small temple (naiskos),[2] some later buildings even smaller, and some altars. Its ground contained much ash and other remains from sacrifices but practically no dedications, except a few from the Punic period. On the evidence of the inscribed stelae, this precinct is held to have belonged to (Zeus) Meilichios, who is assumed to have been associated with a female paredros. The latter assumption is not quite certain in so far as it rests upon the evidence of the figured stelae; these being Punic they must represent Punic deities (Baal Hammon and Tanit?). It is, however, perfectly possible that the Punic was adapted from an antecedent Greek pair of deities, and this possibility gains probability from the fact that in front of the naiskos stand two altars, one larger and higher than the other; another altar, at the back of the naiskos and outside the wall of this precinct, is divided by a slab into two uneven parts.[3] This indeed suggests that Meilichios was worshipped together with some paredros (of, so it appears, inferior dignity).[4]

The three precincts just described were, about the end of the sixth century, enclosed by a common wall. We proceed to consider the identity of the deities thus associated. As for Hekate, it may be added that, apart from her function as προθυραία,[5] her relation to Persephone may be relevant; both as the witness to her abduction (in the Eleusinian hymn and with late authors)[6] and in view of the occasional assimilation of the two goddesses.[7] The fact remains that there is no further evidence of her cult at Selinus or anywhere else in Sicily (except that Sophron is practically certain, in one or other of his mimes, to have introduced her as the causer of spooks and terror:[8] this aspect of hers can hardly here be

50. 22), with the inscription ΤΟ ΔΙΟΣ ΤΟ ΜΕΙΛΙΧΙΟ· ΦΑΓΛΛΟΣ ΗΕΖΑΤΟ; for later instances see Nilsson, p. 412, nn. 2–4 and M. J. Jannoray, *Bull. Corr. Hell.* lxiii–lxv (1940–1), 49 ff.

[1] Cf. Gàbrici, pp. 403 ff.

[2] Of the fourth century, if I understand Gàbrici aright (p. 101 and tav. ii), and Punic, as D. White has now shown (*Am. Journ. Arch.* lxxi (1967), 349 ff.).

[3] Gàbrici, p. 105, Figs. 62 and 63.—I fail to see why C. G. Yavis (*Greek Altars* (1949), p. 134) dates it in the fourth century (but cf. above, p. 98, nn. 5 and 9), in which case it would probably be Punic. I find however in Gàbrici's text nothing to contradict the indication 'vi. cent.' on his map, Pl. II.

[4] Gàbrici, p. 104, reasonably refers to the six δίδυμοι βωμοί dedicated to the Twelve Gods at Olympia (Pind. *Ol.* v. 5(10); x. 25(31) and 49(58), with the scholia).

[5] This may be confirmed by her place beside Persephone and Pluto on South-Italian 'Hades vases' such as *Mon. Ant.* xvi (1906), 517 and Pl. III.

[6] Cf. the Attic-Eleusinian vase pictures showing Hekate present at the departure of Triptolemos and, most probably, also at the abduction and return of Kore; see H. Metzger, *Recherches sur l'imagerie athénienne* (1965), pp. 11 (nos. 6 and 7), 16 (no. 29), and 25.

[7] Cf. Wilamowitz, i. 169 f.

[8] *Pap. gr. e lat.* xi (1935), no. 1214; cf. Sophron, fr. 27 Kaibel.

relevant). Her presence in the Gaggera then—if indeed it has been rightly inferred—entails a hint at the character of the deities worshipped there, but no more.

As for Malophoros, matters are very different, for she is mentioned, in the most famous inscription from temple G,[1] as one of the deities 'through whom the people of Selinus are victorious'; on the other hand, Pausanias (i. 44. 3) mentions a sanctuary of Demeter Malophoros at, or rather outside, Megara Nisaia—the 'pre-ancestor' town of Selinus.[2] The early immigrants must then have brought her cult with them,[3] and the consistent usage at Selinus shows that her original name was Malophoros; subsequently she was understood to be one with the great panhellenic goddess. In opposition to Pausanias it is now agreed that she has her name from μᾶλον, 'apple' and not from μῆλον, 'sheep'. It is perhaps possible, as Wilamowitz held, that her ancient cult-image, at Megara, held an apple,[4] but this assumption cannot account for her name: it shows her to have been worshipped as the giver of fruits—a goddess easily at home ἐν πολυμάλωι Cικελίαι.[5]

Demeter is of course primarily known as the giver of corn, and according to the authorities quoted before,[6] it was as such that she was worshipped in Sicily. The fact however is worth noting that, to the best of my knowledge, not one of the thousands of figurines shows her, or any goddess, with ears of corn; nor do any coins prior to the fourth century;[7] this type of representation—traditional in the Attic-Eleusinian sphere—seems to have been originated in Sicily, or at least powerfully stimulated,

---

[1] IG. xiv. 268.　　　　[2] K. Hanell, Megarische Studien (1934), pp. 178 f.

[3] Their fellow citizens took her to Byzantium, where a month named after her is attested. And therewith the evidence for Malophoros is exhausted.

[4] i. 106, n. 1. Many goddesses, of course, were represented holding some fruit, but an image of this type older than the foundation of Megara Hyblaia (traditionally 728 B.C.) is not easily visualized.

[5] Pind. Ol. i. 12 (cf. O. Schröder ad loc. in his editio maior (1923); cf. Eur. H.F. 396 and Wilamowitz ad loc.). Many clay imitations of apples and pomegranates have been found in the Malophoros precinct (Gàbrici, p. 374, Figs. 166 f.) as well as in sanctuaries elsewhere: e.g. at Lindos and Samos (Athen. Mitt. lxxiv (1959), Pl. 22); cf. generally P. Jacobsthal, Greek Pins (1956), pp. 188 ff.

[6] Above, p. 71.

[7] The head of Demeter on a coin of Enna, of the later fourth century, has on the reverse ears of corn together with other symbols (Holm, iii. 674, no. 399; Hill, p. 178). Grains or ears of corn appear on many older coins (Leontinoi, Himera, Akragas, Selinus, Segesta, Morgantina, Eryx), but never in combination with Demeter. The one exception is the 'head of Demeter, facing and crowned with barley leaves' on small Geloan bronze coins from the end of the 5th century (Hill, p. 125, Fig. 30). I should call it Kore rather than Demeter. Kore indeed is represented, crowned with ears, also on Syracusan coins from about 400 B.C. onward. This fact will interest us later but it does not affect the present issue. Demeter or, rather, Ceres as the Sicilian giver of corn appears to be mainly a Roman symbolism; witness the coins and Roman poets. L. Lacroix who (Monnaies et Colonisation dans l'Occident grec (1965), pp. 108 ff.) illustrates from Greek coins the fertility of καλλίκαρποc Cικελία, does not quote any instance of Demeter represented as the giver of corn.

by Timoleon; it becomes increasingly frequent after him, particularly in Roman times. It is not thereby implied that in Sicily the gift of corn was not, in older times, attributed to Demeter;[1] but the name Malophoros suggests that her bounty was felt in all the gifts of the fruitful earth[2]—

φέρβε βόας, φέρε μᾶλα, φέρε στάχυν, οἶσε θερισμόν,
φέρβε καὶ εἰράναν[3]—

and this we shall presently find confirmed.[4]

The name Μειλίχιος raises intricate and far-reaching problems. They have been thoroughly and fruitfully investigated by a succession of scholars, whose results we shall here utilize in so far as the present context demands.[5] From archaic down to Hellenistic and Roman times[6] there is ample evidence for the cult of Meilichios and Zeus Meilichios from Athens, Boeotia, Thessaly, the Peloponnesus, Cyrene, and some Aegean Islands; the great inscription from Halaesa[7] attests his cult persisting in Sicily in Roman times; but the inscriptions from Selinus are indicative of a particularly archaic and instructive stage. They show that families or even individuals, could worship their own Meilichios (as Romans their *genius* or *lar familiaris*), and that, at the same time, this deity could be regarded as a 'Zeus'; surely not, though, as one with the Homeric Lord of the Gods but comparable to Zeus Chthonios. This peculiar concept recurs at Cyrene, where Meilichios and Zeus Meilichios are commemorated, by inscriptions of the same type, in a particular sanctuary which is shared by the Eumenides. This fact illustrates what had anyhow been inferred long ago: the name Meilichios is a euphemism,[8] denoting a deity which one desires to be 'benign' but which essentially is feared;[9]

[1] Demeter Σιτώ had a sanctuary in Syracuse according to the testimony of Polemon the Periegete (*apud* Athen. 109 a and 416 b; Aelian, *V.H.* i. 27).

[2] I am anxious to avoid the term 'fertility-cult', which is loaded with the burden of modern fancy rather than indicative of the reality of ancient religion.

[3] Kallimachos, *H.* vi. 136.—The implication of the frequent epithets καρποφόρος and εὔκαρπος thus need not be confined to the καρπὸς ἀρούρης.

[4] It is, I am afraid, strictly the opposite of the teaching of Nilsson, i. 472. Against the narrow concept of the goddess, her gift of the fig to Phytalos (Paus. i. 37. 2) may be quoted.

[5] Rohde, i. 217, n. 1; Wilamowitz, i. 222, n. 3 and 398; id., *Hermes*, lxv (1930), 258; Nilsson, i. 411 ff. (with ample indication of sources and literature).

[6] An instance from the Imperial Age are the Διὸς Μιλιχιασταί on the inscription *IG*, xii. 3. 104 from Nisyros.

[7] *IG*, xiv. 352, i. 16 παρὰ τὸ Μειλιχιεῖον.—For Kroton see above, p. 98, n. 10.

[8] This obviously does not hold good when the same adjective is applied to Aphrodite (Plut. *De Is.* 48, 370 d) or Dionysos (Athenaeus 78 c; cf. Plut. *Antonius* 244 and *Quaest. Conv.* i. 3, 613 d; of wine, ib., vi. 2, 692 e). The assertion however (which Nilsson, i. 411 adopts from J. W. Hewitt) that μειλίχιος does not mean 'benign' but denotes one who 'has been propitiated' cannot convince; how about Homer's μειλίχια ἔπεα? Μείλιχος and μειλίχιος are related as are φίλος and φίλιος.

[9] The implied antithesis is ἀμείλιχος (of Hades, *Il.* 9. 158) and μαιμάκτης; cf. Wilamowitz, i. 222, n. 3.

like the Eumenides, then, and like Melitodes–Persephone, Meilichios was a power of Darkness and Death (to become, gradually, truly 'benign' and Philios, like the Erinyes who became Eumenides); and after what has been seen of him previously he must have been the deity into whom the dead of each family were absorbed (one may compare the notion of heroes, but that these retained an individuality). Even as such, he could be regarded as Zeus Meilichios. Therewith the concept of a more universal deity, no longer confined within the cult of individual families, offered itself; a deity of a similar range as Hades yet never identified with him (there is no Hades Meilichios) because, so it appears, the difference of the original concepts continued to be felt—Hades impersonating the vast dark expanse below the domain of light and life; Meilichios, an embodiment of the life-force of those who have left the sphere of life—and hence sacrifice is brought to him but not to Hades;[1] μόνος γὰρ Θάνατος οὐ δώρων ἐρᾶι. This interpretation is confirmed by two facts. Zeus Meilichios is a god to whom kathartic rites are addressed[2]—these are notoriously offered to the deities of the Netherworld—and he appears in the shape of a giant snake;[3] he is then indeed an 'infernal' deity.[4] It is in accordance with this character that, at the Gaggera, the double-altar just mentioned is of the low kind, an eschara sunk into the ground, such as is usual in the cult of chthonic deities,[5] and that bothroi have been found inside the precinct.[6]

The concept of (Zeus) Meilichios which we have outlined is difficult to grasp in its combination of universality and particularity, and yet this feature is not attested at Selinus and Cyrene only. It recurs in Thera, the mother-city of Cyrene, in the same form as, though later than, at Selinus,[7] and with this recurrence suggesting the wide spread of this primitive feature, its emergence at Selinus is accounted for by the inscription Διὸς Μιλιχίου Πανφύλο(υ) at Megara Nisaia.[8]

[1] The (insignificant) exceptions are quoted by Nilsson, i. 452.

[2] The mythical prototype is Theseus purified by the Phytalidae at their altar of Zeus Meilichios, Paus. i. 37. 4 and Plut. *Thes.* 12. 1.

[3] The well-known reliefs from the Piraeus have often been pictured; e.g. by Nilsson, i, Pl. 27. 2; Harrison, pp. 14 ff.; A. Rumpf, *Die Religion der Griechen* (H. Haas, *Bilderatlas* . . . xiii/xiv (1928)), nos. 23 and 24; for the stelae from Lebadeia see Nilsson, i. 412, nn. 2 and 3; ib., n. 1 for the bronze-snake with the inscription ἱαρός ἐμι τô Μελλιχίο τô Πελ(λ)άναι.

[4] The analogies with Zeus Chthonios and with Hades–Pluton may account for his fusion, especially in Attica, with the benign Zeus Philios. With this aspect of Meilichios we are not here concerned.

[5] Cf. F. Robert, *Thymélè* (1939), pp. 167 ff. and C. G. Yavis, *Greek Altars* (immensely useful but perhaps somewhat pedantic in its conclusions), pp. 91 f. and 134 f.

[6] Accordingly, a number of ancient *defixiones* were found buried in the ground where the stelae stood (so one may conclude from Gàbrici, pp. 388 and 396).

[7] *IG*, xiii. 3, Suppl.,1 316 Ζεὺς Μηλίχιος τῶν περὶ Πολύξενον (mentioned by Hanell, p. 178, n. 4): here, as at Nisyros and Halaesa (above, p. 101, n. 6), an association has taken the place of the *gentes* in the older inscriptions.

[8] This inscription is mentioned in *JHS*, xviii (1898), 332; it is not in the supplements to

If such was the deity residing in the smaller part of the combined precinct, one would look for the resting places of those over whom he held sway. No graves have been found in it;[1] and the same holds good for the sanctuary of Meilichios and the Eumenides at Cyrene. Greeks did not, to the best of my knowledge, bury their dead inside sanctuaries. A vast necropolis (Manicalunga), however, extends beyond the sanctuary inland and towards the sea, and notwithstanding certain chronological problems,[2] one may abide by the assumption that in the precinct of Meilichios rites were performed, sacrifices offered and a stele erected for each of the noblemen whose remains were thereafter buried in the necropolis (cf. the similar situation at Grammichele).

Who was the deity associated with Meilichios? Gàbrici[3] suggested, though not with complete assurance, Pasikrateia, whose name appears, after Athena and Malophoros, at the end of the list of deities on the inscription from Temple G—and nowhere else in Selinus nor anywhere else in Sicily nor, in pre-Roman times, anywhere else in the Greek world. Gàbrici assumed her to be a kind of Persephone, and this interpretation of the name derives some corroboration from its only further occurrence, which is in the great Magical Papyrus Parisinus (l. 2774); moreover, these two names, Meilichios and Pasikrateia, variously euphemistic, could seem suitably to denote a couple of infernal deities. K. Hanell[4] objected that the synonymous name Pasikrata is used of Artemis at Ambrakia,[5] and refers to a goddess similar, perhaps, to Aphrodite or possibly to Artemis, and anyhow not to Persephone, in dedications from

---

IG, vii published in *SEG*, nor have I found a full publication anywhere else. According to its discoverer, S. Lambros (cf. *Athen. Mitt.* xxiii (1898), 168) it was a boundary stone; which seems incredible. Was it not, rather, a small stele like those at Selinus?

[1] Nilsson, i. 413 is mistaken in describing the temenos as a 'Begräbnisplatz'.

[2] Cf. Gàbrici, p. 7.—In 1874, F. S. Cavallari, the discoverer of the sanctuary (we shall hear more about him later), found some graves in the neighbourhood, none of them older than the second half of the sixth century; less old, that is, than the beginnings of the sanctuary itself; while graves quite as old as the foundation of the city have been found, far away, at its northern edge. Since then, no systematic search has been made—except no doubt, by local treasure hunters . . . Under these circumstances it would seem an excess of scepticism to deny the original interconnection of the sanctuary and the necropolis. Fairly recently, a fifth-century grave has been found 800 m. NNW. of the precinct (J. Bovio Marconi, *Kokalos*, vii (1961), 109 ff.) with an inscription, on which cf. W. M. Calder III, *AJA*, lxix (1965), 262 (I could not accept the assertion that it is written in verse; as little as with regard to the great inscription from Temple G). The hope, which Gàbrici expressed in 1927, that further excavations would settle this question, may still be fulfilled, but the chances are bound to dwindle from year to year. G. Cultrera, who (*Mon. Ant.* xxxix (1956), 625) elaborated this problem, concluded that the purpose of the sanctuary and the dedications found in it must not be sought exclusively in 'cerimoni funebri'; he pointed particularly at the near-by spring whose water was led into it, in evidence of the cult being also of the living forces of nature. Our results are in agreement with his conclusion; the running water, though, is likely, as at Morgantina, to have served for purification.

[3] p. 103.

[4] *Megar. Studien*, pp. 179 f.

[5] *Arch. Ephem.* (1910), 397.

a sanctuary at Pagasai-Demetrias.[1] This is not a very strong point, for a name like this could evidently be given to various goddesses;[2] but a further observation militates decisively against Gàbrici's suggestion. Both the Punic images and the shape of the altars are evidence that the synedros was considered inferior to Meilichios himself; nor is she mentioned on the stelae dedicated to him. Such inferiority seems inconceivable of a goddess named 'The Almighty one', who, if anything, ought to have filled a place similar to that taken by Persephone beside Hades.[3] But Meilichios, as we saw, is a deity quite different from Hades; he is not, like Pasikrateia, mentioned on the inscription as one of the main deities of Selinus, and Persephone—if indeed she is Pasikrateia—would not be for him a suitable partner. It ought to be remembered, rather, that a plurality of Meilichioi is widely and variously attested and is perfectly in keeping with the basic concept of this deity. We mentioned the Meilichioi of families and individuals; moreover, Pausanias[4] describes the rites in a sanctuary of Meilichioi in Lokris; another such is attested by an inscription from Thessalian Thebes. The Punic stelae represent a female paredros; a Cretan altar, of Roman date, is dedicated to Hera Μηλιχία together with Zeus Μηλίχιος, and Miliché is attested by an inscription from Thespiae.[5] The companion, then, of Meilichios at Selinus is likely to have been Meilichia.[6]

[1] *Praktika* (1920), p. 22 (*SEG*, iii. 481 ff.); cf. F. Stählin, *Das hellenistische Thessalien* (1923), pp. 71 f.; id. (with others) *Pagasae und Demetrias* (1934), p. 188, n. 2 (literature).

[2] Thus Sosipolis is the name of a nymph, or Tyche, on Geloan coins; in Elis, of a daemon in the shape of a babe or a snake; in Magnesia, a cognomen of Zeus.

[3] The combination of Enodia (not Hekate) with Zeus Meilichios in a dedication at Larisa in Thessaly (cf. Wilamowitz, i. 171) is not sufficient to support the tempting assumption that, at Selinus, Hekate could have been the consort of Meilichios; add that the dedication to her was found far from his precinct.

[4] x. 38. 8.

[5] *IG*, vii. 1814; cf. P. Foucart, *BCH*, ix (1885), 404, n. 15; Rohde, i. 273, n. 1; Nilsson, i. 412, nn. 11 and 12.

[6] Could this divine couple have been represented by the very ancient terracotta fragment, Gàbrici, Pl. XXX. 4, cf. p. 200 (very similar to an ivory group from the sanctuary of Orthia at Sparta, *BSA*, xiii (1906/7), 98, Fig. 28; R. M. Dawkins, *The Sanctuary of Artemis Orthia*, 1929, Pls. CXXIV f.; cf. Mollard–Besques on Louvre B168)?—An archaic terracotta group of a bearded man seated to the right of a smaller woman has been found at Bitalemi (fragmentary: Orsi, p. 713, Fig. 540) and elsewhere (Rhodes: B.M., no. 80; Samos: J. Boehlau, *Aus ionischen . . . Nekropolen* (1898), p. 159 and Pl. XIV. 6 and 8, repeated by Buschor, iii, Abb. 178; cf. Louvre, *Catal.*, no. B90; Delos: *Exploration . . .*, xi (1928), 163; ib. xxiii (1956), 81; Tocra: J. Boardman, *Tocra*, i (1966), no. 44): evidently an Eastern type, imported to Gela. It is traditionally held to represent Hades and Persephone, and reasonably so, seeing that it has been found in graves and 'chthonic' sanctuaries. Regarding this interpretation, however, some doubt may be stirred by the marked predominance, in this group, of the male partner. It could thus very well have served, at Selinus, to represent Meilichios with Meilichia; but no sample of this group is recorded from there. The male figure alone though has been found there (Gàbrici, Pl. XLI. 10), shaped into a vase (as are other samples of it, and also of the group); it too is evidently of Eastern origin (cf. B.M., no. 79). At Selinus, it could have represented Meilichios.

Pasikrateia may still have resided at the Gaggera—if, as is probable, she was a local realization of Persephone. Being mentioned, on the great inscription, together with Malophoros she need not, but may well, have been 'the Daughter'—who, under whatever name, must have been worshipped together with Malophoros–Demeter.[1] For the cult at this sanctuary was, as has been seen, centred on the dead and the Netherworld no less than on fruitfulness on earth. The goddess 'Giver of Fruits' is not a deity of the Netherworld.[2] Meilichios and Meilichia are, but the terracottas found in Malophoros' section of the sanctuary are evidence, as we shall see, that together with her a younger goddess was worshipped there, and the obvious implication is borne out by the find, in the latest stratum (post-fifth-century), of figurines which, in the later manner, represent Persephone unequivocally with polos, torch, and piglet.[3] Beside Malophoros, the giver of the fruitfulness which vouchsafes the perpetuation of Life, Pasikrateia—if that was her name—wielded the ineluctable power of Death. Perhaps the triad of main deities worshipped at this sanctuary— Malophoros, (?)Pasikrateia, and Meilichios—was represented on a very ancient terracotta relief decorating one of its sacrificial tables, striking fragments of which are exhibited in the Museo Nazionale at Palermo.[4]

Much combination, inference, and even guess-work has been needed to attain an approximate notion of the deities worshipped at the Gaggera and of their cult. It is incomplete, hazy, and superficial; even so, nothing like it is attainable for the other sites at which terracottas have been found. At Agrigento, P. Marconi's excavation of the 'Santuario Ctonico' has brought to light the suggestive framework of a variegated cult. The effort of the imagination at visualizing this cult and recovering the ideas connected with it may perhaps draw on Pindar[5]—to a certain extent; for the profound persuasion which the poet adumbrates in communion with his royal friend cannot be supposed to have been generally held by the plain folk who, here as everywhere, dedicated the identical tokens of their

[1] The tentative suggestion (Gàbrici, p. 170, on Pl. XXIV) that an early tufa relief, found in the temenos, represented the abduction of Kore by Hades does not, to my mind, correspond with the (dance-like) character of the representation (Pace, ii. 34, Fig. 32).

[2] Cf. Detached Note VI, below, p. 399.

[3] Gàbrici, pp. 295 f., Pl. LXXVII. 4. I prefer to describe as torches also the objects held by ib., nos. 2 and 7, for a 'thyrsos' in the hands of a hieratic figure with polos and piglet is inconceivable.

[4] It is more complete there than apud Gàbrici, Pl. XXX. 1 (cf. p. 188); it consists of a male head en face and, facing away from it, two female figures. The analogy of the 'metopa arcaissima' (Pace, ii. 12, Fig. 11) could indeed suggest that it, likewise, represented the 'Delian triad'; but a more direct reference to the place where it was dedicated may be preferable. It is true, though, that mythical scenes exhibited in the sanctuary need not always refer to its deities; there is no such reference, for example, in the elegant relief which shows Eos pursuing Kephalos (Gàbrici, Pl. XXXVI and p. 196; Pace, ii. 30, Fig. 28 strangely describes it as a 'gigantomachia').

[5] Above, p. 88.

simple devotion.[1] In tracing this popular devotion, the imagination is not helped, as at the Gaggera, by even a minimum of concrete information. Within narrower limits, the situation is the same at San Biagio; and at Grammichele, Kamarina, Bitalemi, and many smaller sites there is nothing but the masses of small finds—mainly pottery and terracottas— to tell that the *favissa* of a sanctuary, or even the actual site of some sanctuary, has been found.

P. Orsi has shown, in the concluding section of his report on Bitalemi,[2] what vision of the past life at one of these sanctuaries may be attained through the study of its silent and broken relics. His profound interpretation of the εὐϲέβεια attested by the mass and variety of the votive offerings and his evocation of the goings-on at the feasts celebrated within the temenos are a model of 'wissenschaftlich gelenkter Phantasie'; these classic few pages can serve as basis and background for any attempt at discerning the religion which expressed itself in these votive offerings. I do not indeed believe that the remains of pottery can contribute much towards this endeavour; their endless variety is an indication that decorated vases, beakers, and vessels of all kinds were meant, generally speaking, as *agalmata* for the dead or for the local deities (and perhaps, at least in the earlier times, for their actual use); but they cannot, as a rule, enlighten us about the religious notions of those who dedicated them.[3] Matters are significantly different with regard to the terracottas, for their very monotony bespeaks a devotion consistent in form and content. The same types recur, with slight differences of local workmanship, everywhere throughout Greek Sicily, and since at least two outstanding sites have been recognized to have been places of a 'chthonic' cult (to adopt, in spite of its problematical implications, the term preferred by our Italian colleagues),[4] it is legitimate to assume the same for all of them; and indeed they are currently described as 'chthonic sanctuaries' or, synonymously, as sanctuaries of Demeter and Persephone (or Kore).[5]

---

[1] It is significant that Pindar dwells on this persuasion in the personal and esoteric ode *Ol.* ii, but not in *Ol.* iii, which was destined for the public celebration of Theron's victory.

[2] *Gela*, pp. 726 f.

[3] If, for example, the frequent representations, on vases found in graves, of symposia and of Dionysos and his train were held to presage a blessed afterlife in the dominion of this god, how should one interpret the equally frequent representations of numberless myths or, in earlier times, the endless processions of cocks and other animals, mythical and real, on Corinthian pottery? There is, surely, a more obvious reason for the occurrence of scenes more or less Dionysiac on vessels designed for the enjoyment of the wine-god's gift. This is not to deny that the addition to the funeral gifts of special types of pottery, such as Attic white lekythoi, could witness to a particular attitude to death and after-life; as E. Buschor has shown in his beautiful pamphlet entitled *Grab eines attischen Mädchens*; similarly, a specific vase-painting dedicated in a sanctuary may occasionally be relevant to the cult practised there; as we shall ourselves have occasion to observe (below, p. 165, n. 3).

[4] For the connotation of χθών see below, pp. 153 and 400.

[5] *Addendum*: This has of late been proved correct for Bitalemi (Gela), which was completely excavated in 1964 by P. Orlandini. His preliminary report in *Kokalos*, xii (1966), 8 ff.

The preceding excursus on the sanctuary in the Gaggera has shown the limitations of this description. At this one site for which at least a few indications beyond the silent votives exist there is no Demeter—but Malophoros; Persephone is not attested and in her place there may have been Pasikrateia, or a goddess whose name is not known; in addition there were, so it seems, Hekate, Meilichios, and Meilichia. Most of these deities indeed deserve to be called 'chthonic', but not so the most outstanding among them, Malophoros herself. In a manner similar to the previously quoted passages from Pindar, though far less incisively, this very modest evidence has served to intimate the wide and thorough variety of nomenclature, cult and, presumably, myth which may underly these generalizations. We have no means of estimating its extent and guessing at the names and peculiarities of other individualizations of the later, panhellenic deities.[1]

And yet individualizations they are: particular forms—whether consciously so or not—of the great goddesses in whom, in the course of time, they were all absorbed. The uniformity of their presentation shows it; the one exception—the representations of Artemis Limnaia at the Fontana Calda near Butera—confirms it; and even there, representations of the standard type prevail. From, at any rate, the second half of the sixth century onward, different deities could be recognizably characterized; why then was it hardly ever done? Why does the spade, time and again, uncover sanctuaries whose deities were adequately rendered by those

makes exciting reading. Orsi's findings are basically confirmed, and among the *c.* 20,000 pieces of votives found there are very few which have no counterpart from the earlier excavation. Orlandini, however, discovered the foundations of a built-up sanctuary and was able to elucidate the history of the place and, on the basis of a refined stratigraphy, to establish precise datings. There was a mere temenos from about the middle of the seventh to the middle of the sixth century ('o poco dopo'). The beginning of the next phase coincided with the foundation of the buildings just mentioned; its lower limit is given with the destruction of Gela by the Carthaginians in 405 B.C.; a marked division stands out about the middle of the fifth century. A chronological framework for the various types of terracottas is thus provided, and I have been happy to find that the datings which I had accepted are nowhere controverted by it.

The post-550 stratum yielded the lid of an Attic pyxis with the graffito ἱαρὸν Θεσμοφόρō (p. 20; Pl. X. 4). The goddess of the place then was worshipped under the name Thesmophoros. Like Malophoros at Selinus, she was Demeter and, here as there, the terracottas confirm that, as normally, she was joined by her daughter: the two are τὼ Θεσμοφόρω (Aristoph. *Thesm.* 83, etc.) and there was a month Thesmophorios in Krete and Rhodes, whence the earliest settlers of Gela originated. (The vase besides has a second inscription scratched around the centre of the lid, indicating where it had been bought: it came 'from the shop of Dikaios' ἐκ τᾶς Δικαίō ϲϲκανᾶϲ).

In the lowest stratum, finally, was found a tell-tale set of votive offerings; namely, an iron hoe, a sickle, and two ploughshares—a precious hint at the character of the local cult.

[1] Who, for example, could have guessed at the existence of a Πολυϲτέφανοϲ Ϲώτειρα, of whom the inscription on an *arula* at Agrigento (*IG*, xiv. 262) gives unexpected but trustworthy evidence (even though the genuineness of the actual writing may be doubted)? And who would make bold to identify her? (And yet the scanty evidence quoted in L–S–J, s.v. shows that she is not the figment of a forger's imagination).

ever-recurring types? Why have, so far at least, no corresponding finds been made at the great temples at Syracuse, Akragas, Selinus, and Himera? And why, among the many small sanctuaries which are being uncovered all the time, are so few dedicated to the Olympian gods?[1] Even if, one day, deposits should emerge to demonstrate a comparable devotion to them, the fact remains that an outstanding and general devotion was given, by Greeks all over Sicily (and, to say it by way of anticipation, in neighbouring Calabria) to the non-Olympian, female deities. These appear to have been worshipped predominantly by women; who were, as they are to this day, the chief guardians of religious tradition.[2] The Greeks had brought the cult of these deities from their home-country and enriched and varied it in their new land. It was, in a manner, a fresh impulse of the age-old devotion to the Mother which we have studied, but we desire now to perceive it in its Greek and Sicilian peculiarity. We cannot hope to penetrate its full reality in local cult and personal devotion, but we may aspire to discern, beyond the multitude of their individualizations, the features of the great goddesses in whom these found their ideal unity. The terracottas aim, in their restricted typology, to give ever more adequate expression to their image as it was alive in the minds of the devotees. Our attempt to recover it from these renderings should derive some guidance from the preceding sketch of the localities at which they had been dedicated; its hazardousness will be reduced whenever some carefully worked piece offers itself for interpretation; in the main, though, we shall have to consider the less distinct features of pieces produced in the mass. Even these were intended to convey the worshippers' dominant concern, and their very primitiveness may prove to express it in an elementary but unambiguous manner. They may be ever so crude; even so, there is about them a compelling dignity and power, conveying that numinous impact which the worshipper felt in his godhead. It is this numinous dignity which primarily distinguishes the ancient images of deity; even though a reflection of it often adds a similar dignity to the representations of its devotees.[3]

---

[1] The Artemis sanctuary at Scala Graeca (Syracuse) post-dates our period and was any-how of a rustic character; Fontana Calda (Butera) naturally yielded many statuettes of Artemis Limnaia but far more of a 'Demeter' type (*Mon. Ant.* xliv (1958), 589 ff.; esp. 631 and 637 ff.); only at the small Athena temple at Molino a Vento (Gela) Orsi was able, from among its extremely damaged statuettes, to salvage one helmeted Athena head (*Not. Scav.* (1907), 38); cf., for the last-named, below, p. 126, n. 2.

[2] P. Orlandini tells (*Kokalos*, xii (1966), 33) that to this day the May processions at S. Maria di Bitalemi are attended only by women with their children.

[3] This applies e.g. to B.M. 1091 (from Kamarina), which used to be described as representing a goddess but is now, rightly no doubt, held to represent a worshipper.

(d) THE TWO GODDESSES

Our primary interest is in Persephone, and we shall indeed find evidence of that pre-eminence of hers which Pindar's words led us to expect; even so, Demeter owed her later reputation as the representative goddess of Sicily not merely to the policy of the Deinomenids and Timoleon. As Malophoros we have already found her, with, perhaps, Pasikrateia–Persephone, in the early popular cult at Selinus, and in search of her lost daughter on the earliest coins from Enna. Explicit archaeological evidence for the cult of 'Mother' and 'Daughter' combined is, however, very scanty in ancient Sicily.

Various typical and ancient representations of the two goddesses together are known from the Mainland and the Greek East; standing or sitting side by side;[1] seated on a chariot[2] or wrapped into one cloak;[3] or one of them standing beside the other seated.[4] None of these groups has, to the best of my knowledge, come to light in Sicily; and there may be some significance in this fact. However, P. Orsi unearthed at Terravecchia di Grammichele the upper end of a small fragmentary terracotta plaque[5] carrying side by side two frontal female heads, one older one younger, both with polos, and with the faintest, if any, indication of the body below; most of the lower part being lost anyhow. It was natural to interpret it as representing Demeter and Kore, and this all the more so, since it came from a spot abounding with relics attesting a 'chthonic' cult.[6] It must, however, be admitted that, as a representation of these two goddesses, the plaque would be unique. The only analogies known to me are the upright plaques, decorated at the top with three heads of nymphs, which have been found in a spring-grotto at Lokri in Calabria.[7] They come from the Hellenistic period, while the plaque from Grammichele

---

[1] From Rhodes (Louvre, B197: two heads on one body; *Clara Rhodos*, vi–vii (1932–3), Fig. 101; both from graves at Kamiros); from Melos (B.M. 610).

[2] From Corinth (B.M. 897; cf. colour-plate A in Higgins, *Greek Terracotta Figures*, p. 16).

[3] From Rhodes (frequent: Blinkenberg, nos. 2232–5); from Kamiros (Louvre, B207; B.M. 230–2); from Kyzikos (Louvre, C165); for geometric antecedents see Winter, p. 5, no. 2. M. Guarducci, *Athen. Mitt.* liii (1928), 52 ff. (I owe the reference to Prof. T. B. L. Webster) compared (pp. 59 f.) these terracottas with the representations, on vases, of two or more women wrapped in one cloak; against her, P. Demargne, *Bull. Corr. Hell.* (1930), 195 ff. maintained that not all of these two-women groups represent Demeter and Kore. This is probably true with regard e.g. to figured vases with two heads, such as have been found also in Sicily (Orsi, *Gela*, p. 314, Figs. 230 f.; Gàbrici, Pl. XXXVIII. 5), but for the instances here quoted the traditional interpretation seems safe.

[4] From Athens (Winter, p. 48. 6).

[5] Siracusa, Museo Naz., inv. 18942; *Not. Scav.* (1902), p. 224 (the drawing in Pace, iii. 490, Fig. 124 is extremely inaccurate); our Plate 14a.

[6] Cf. above, p. 73.

[7] P. Arias in *Not. Scav.* (1946), 141 ff. One of them is pictured in Pace, iii, 489, Fig. 123, who noted the similarity.

seems to date from the fifth century; even so, the latter may be an—
earlier—instance of this representation of nymphs: for it seems possible
that a piece of it with a third head has broken off.[1]

The only extant representation, from Sicily, of Demeter and Kore
together which almost certainly antedates the fourth century thus becomes
problematical. What significance are we to attribute to this fact? From
the later period, evidence of the cult of the two goddesses in close connection does exist—we shall return to it[2]—but this later evidence gives
uncertain help in defining the religion of the earlier period. Concerning
it, we have had evidence of the pre-eminence of Persephone but also of the
cult and myth of both goddesses, particularly at Enna; we know of
temples for both built by the Deinomenids, and the survey of archaeological sites has yielded some general hints. The terracottas must help further.

(e) 'LA DEA RODIA SEDUTA'

An outstandingly frequent type, found by the hundreds throughout
Sicily and occurring on almost every site, may for convenience be termed
(as is done in Sicilian museums) the 'dea Rodia seduta'.[3] The goddess,
with round face and heavily built, is sitting in hieratic, frontal posture,
with both hands resting flat on her knees. A distinctive feature is the large
shawl covering her head and most of the body; or, more precisely, the
himation is worn in the manner of a large shawl. With many of these
statuettes, a very high polos, still under the shawl, covers her head;
beside this most characteristic variety, and equally frequent, is one with
a diadem instead of the polos; rarely, the shawl lies immediately upon
the hair. Terracottas of this kind have been found in great numbers in
Rhodes, both on the akropolis of Lindos[4] and in graves in the necropoleis
around Kamiros and Ialysos;[5] they were exported to Syria and Palestine[6]

---

[1] The three Graces with high poloi, as represented by Boeotian terracottas (Louvre C35)
may be compared and, for the origin and shape of these pinakes, the triple herm dedicated
to the Nymphs from the region of Tegea (Nilsson, i 206 with note 4 and Pl. 33. 2).

[2] Below, p. 155.

[3] Van Ufford, pp. 44 and 71. Samples from Syracuse (necropolis del Fusco, *Not. Scav.*
(1893), 480), and from another grave, *Not. Scav.* (1943), 88), Buscemi (Monte Casale,
unpublished; cf. Dunbabin, pp. 100 ff.), Megara Hyblaia (necropolis, *Mon. Ant.* i (1890) 246,
797 ff. and 861 ff.; 'very frequent', van Ufford, p. 110), Kamarina, Akrai, Grammichele, Monte
Bubbonia, Naxos, and Lipari are on view in the Museo Nazionale at Syracuse. The literature
on these not being to hand at the time of writing, my illustrations will largely be drawn from
the publications on Selinus, Agrigento, and Gela (beside Orsi, also *Not. Scav.*, 1956 and 1960)
and from the catalogues of the British Museum and the Louvre, whose Sicilian terracottas,
almost all of them, come from Gela; the result, unavoidably, will be a certain slant in the
selection of the evidence.

[4] Blinkenberg, i, nos. 2119–42; Pls. 96 f. and (more recent) 2191–2219.

[5] B.M., nos. 68–73 and (more recent) 121–30; Louvre, nos. 202–6; *Clara Rhodos*, iii (1930),
230; ib, iv (1931), 292 and 297; etc.

[6] One found at Amrith is pictured in L. Heuzey, *Les Figurines antiques ... du Louvre* (1883),
Pl. XI.

and occur also on Samos, Kos, Thera, and Aigina, at Elaious (on the Dardanelles), Olynthos, Perachora, Cumae, and even at Punic Solus and Carthage.[1] The type is very likely to have originated in Rhodes and may have been modelled upon some outstanding cult-image there. The name of the goddess whom originally it rendered is not known—it might quite well have been Athena Lindia; this, though, is by no means the current view;[2] her character, at any rate, is unambiguously clear from these representations. In Sicily, the type was undoubtedly derived from Rhodes. Imported pieces—of which many have been identified—were dedicated first; soon, however, they were locally copied, imitated, and modified.

The persistent character of the goddess which these figurines convey is that of a benign dignity. This dignity may appear rather severe in some few instances,[3] more affable in others;[4] most often it is tempered by a gentle kindness which in some particularly charming and somewhat later figures breaks forth in a friendly smile.[5] Sometimes she holds the bud of a flower in her hand, or a little bird;[6] once even a lion.[7] She is not thereby identified as Kybele, the goddess of the Asianic wilds; but always the same friendly protectress of all life is meant. One thus understands why her image has been found in graves; very frequently so in Rhodes, sometimes also in Sicily.[8] She is not a ruler over the Land of Death; but even after death her devotees remain in her protection.

So they had been from the beginning of their lives; for the goddess is repeatedly represented nursing a small child.[9] She is represented as kourotrophos also at Rhodes,[10] but the Sicilian instances are local

[1] R. A. Higgins *ad* B.M., no. 68 (i, p. 51) quotes the evidence; add Perachora, nos. 283 ff. (Payne and others, *Perachora*, i (1940), 191 ff.), and Hiller von Gaertringen, *Thera*, ii (1903), pp. 25 f., 123 f., and 219.

[2] One may feel some surprise that C. Blinkenberg, in view of what he had inferred concerning the character of the *dea Lindia* and the appearance of her ancient image (*L'Image d'Athana Lindia* (1917), 6 ff.) did not trace to it this outstanding Rhodian type but another one of very doubtful relevance. We shall return to this question.

[3] Gàbrici, Pls. LV. 7, LVI. 1; and particularly in the very early figure Pl. XXXVII. 11.

[4] Ib. Pls. LV. 9, LVII. 3; Orsi, *Gela*, p. 710, Fig. 535 (one of more than twenty-two samples).   [5] Gàbrici, Pl. LVIII. 8.

[6] Gàbrici, p. 213; Pls. XXXIX. 9 and LVIII. 8.

[7] Ib., Pl. XXXIX. 8. It is a piece imported from the East (cf. Gàbrici, pp. 214 f.; van Ufford, p. 72, B.M. 132; Louvre B86; Buschor, ii. 39). Small figures of lions have been found at the Gaggera (Gàbrici, Pl. XLII. 11) as well as at Syracuse (von Matt[1], Pl. 14). Recently, though, several Kybele statuettes 'of the middle of the sixth century' are said to have emerged at renewed excavations at Bitalemi, Gela (*Arch. Anz.* (1964), 739; see now *Kokalos*, xii (1966), Pl. XIX. 1 and pp. 24 f.: dated 550–540 B.C.). This would not, I think, evidence the acceptance, at this early date, of an Asianic cult in Sicily (the Hellenistic 'Santoni' at Akrai, Pace, ii. 122 f., are a different matter); but these images could be dedicated there, as at Athens and Thebes (Pindar, *Pyth.* iii. 78) as another impersonation of the 'Great Mother'.

[8] e.g. at Monte Bubbonia, and cf. above, p. 93, n. 1.

[9] Seeing that van Ufford (p. 48) declares that she has not found this type of kourotrophos in Sicily, I shall quote the evidence known to me in full.

[10] Blinkenberg, no. 2125.

creations. One of them found its way from Selinus to the Louvre.[1] It is a delightful composition, with the babe sitting frontally between the guarding arms of the motherly goddess, its hands resting on hers, while her plain round head—the head of a good peasant woman—rises like a friendly moon straight above that of her little ward; the characteristic shawl finally emphasizes the symmetrical unity of the monumental little group. Similar in quality and character though different in structure is a votive terracotta found near Caltanissetta (now in Gela)[2] which, like the preceding one, may have been fashioned towards the end of the sixth century. This time, the babe—in very long swaddling clothes—rests in the bend of the goddess's left arm; her right supports a dove; maybe for the babe's delight or, perhaps, as on other similar figurines,[3] in further evidence of her care for all life. The friendly round face, with a rather thick nose and the hint of a smile, is slightly inclined to the left; its contour within the shawl—like the preceding one, also this figure lacks the polos—combines with the outline of the thick-set body to convey a rustic homeliness. Even so, this is no human mother; this statuette, whether repeating some local cult-image or due to the artist's ingenuous imagination, represents a divine kourotrophos.

There are, moreover, two specimens from Bitalemi,[4] of poor workmanship, on which the goddess is actually suckling the babe, and an uncertain number of very small ones from the Gaggera[5] on which she is holding it with both arms[6].

Kourotrophos: the good mother; giver and guardian of all life, from earliest childhood until and beyond death, in human beings and all creatures; the inexhaustible source of help and bounty, ever alike and ever accessible to men's needs: the rustic goddess so consistently repre-

---

[1] B560; our Plate 14b. The parallels quoted by Mme Mollard-Besques ad loc. are not very impressive, and two of the three may anyhow be Sicilian.

[2] Langlotz–Hirmer, Pl. 21 (left). Here, as always, the comment by the first-named editor deserves every attention; I must confess, though, that some of his datings have failed to convince me. In the present instance, the individual expression of the traditional round face (contrast Blinkenberg, 2129) and the variation of the traditional posture, together with the indication of the chiton by fine waving lines, combine (or so it seems to me) to make Langlotz's dating 'about 530 B.C.' appear too early. Nor can I see much reason for positing, as the model of this statuette, a 'cult image of about 540 B.C. somewhere near Miletus'. The posture of the Branchidae is not peculiar to them and anyhow was and remained traditional with the type of terracottas here under review.

[3] Above, p. 111.   [4] Orsi, Gela, p. 709 with Fig. 538.

[5] Represented by Gàbrici, Pl. LXX. 9, cf. p. 293; some of them can be seen in the Palermo Museum.

[6] From a grave at Monte Bubbonia (north of Gela) comes a small figure ad asse (on this type presently) worked into a charming kourotrophos, and from Megara Hyblaia two very primitive ones (Inv. nos. 1082 and 1830; all on view in the museum at Syracuse). There is little 'numinous power' about them; but the figures ad asse, I suppose, always represent divinities.

sented by these statuettes may indeed have been invoked by various names at various places; at Selinus she was Malophoros; but she is Demeter. The statuettes, from all parts of Sicily, are evidence of a general, uniform concept underlying the varieties of local cult; they convey the image of the goddess as it was alive in men's minds and the sentiments of trust, love and devotion with which they approached her. Once more, though, we may note with some surprise that there is no hint, in these representations, at Demeter's most outstanding gift—at least according to the Attic tradition—that is, the gift of grain; nor, indeed, at any fruit of field or orchard which the name Malophoros, in particular, would have led one to expect. This expectation indeed will be met by other monuments. Before turning to them, we have to consider a significant special variety of the *dea seduta*.

One of the divergent statuettes is pictured both in Gàbrici's book (Pl. LX. 4) and by Langlotz–Hirmer (Pl. 68). The freedom in the adaptation of the traditional type—independent of any Eastern model[1]—and the individual expression of the face suggest a comparatively recent date; say, early in the fifth century.[2] The goddess is seated in the same, solemn posture as the other *sedute* and, like many of them, she wears the high polos with, on top of it, the large shawl (himation) which covers her shoulders and arms and reaches down to her feet. And yet, this is not the goddess whom we know. The body is slim, not plump as with the Demeter images; it is the body of a maiden or a young woman. The face, again, is not the round and friendly one of the good Mother; it is youngish, narrow and almost lean-cheeked; its expression, without the hint of a smile, is austere and withdrawn. She holds a large pomegranate in her right hand and some grains—the fatal seeds, no doubt[3]—in her outstretched left. She is the Queen of the Dead.

This noble and even majestic statuette may well be modelled on some cult-image; it has, on any count, the unity of form and expression of a great work of religious art. The same holds good for a cognate figure, two copies of which were found, likewise, at the Gaggera.[4] This figure, too, retains the traditional hieratic posture with the hands resting on the knees; instead of the polos, a low diadem covers the head; the shawl is so

---

[1] A youthful variety of the veiled *seduta* exists at Rhodes (Blinkenberg, nos. 2142, 2191, 2196–2203); it may represent Persephone, and one figurine of this type at least has been found in Sicily (Orsi, *Gela*, p. 710, Fig. 535, left); but the images about to be discussed are independent of it.

[2] This is Gàbrici's view. Langlotz's reasons for putting it as late as '*ca.* 460 B.C.' do not seem compelling to me.

[3] Gàbrici (p. 274) guessed at peas or lentils.

[4] Gàbrici, Pl. LXXI. 8; Langlotz–Hirmer, Pl. 34; evidently from the same mould, though the former is seated on a more elaborate throne. I fail to see why Langlotz would ascribe to this figure a date fully fifty years earlier than to the preceding one; I suspect that it might even be slightly later.

thin as to make visible the parts of the body covered by it. The body is, again, a youthful one; 'il corpo slanciato traspare con la sporgenza delle mamelle di sotto alle vesti liscie'.[1] The face of this goddess, too, has that expression of withdrawn dignity; its regular features are, at the same time, of an unearthly loveliness. She is the bride of the Lord of the Netherworld.

Gàbrici shows, next to this statuette, two other seated goddesses,[2] without polos and himation and, consequently, with bodies more definitely modelled. Their left hands only rest on the knee; the right supports a dove. Is this the same bride? Or Aphrodite? These figurines in fact belong to a very numerous group which has its origin, not in Sicily but in Epizephyrian Lokri; it can contribute decisively to that theology (if the term be allowed) which we are endeavouring to trace, but will have to be considered together with the other evidence from that centre of the cult of Persephone. In concluding the present section it may be noted that representations of the *dea seduta*, which were so frequent, and remarkably uniform, throughout the half century from about 530 to 480 B.C., cease after this (approximate) date; the date, roughly, of the representations of Persephone just discussed. There must be some significance in this fact.

(f) THE *FIGURINE AD ASSE*: THE 'ATHANA LINDIA' OR 'TELINES' TYPE

1. *AD ASSE* : GENERAL REMARKS

The term 'figurine con corpo ad asse', or 'Brettidole', denotes representations which repeat, or continue, the shape of primitive, and more or less aniconic, cult images; namely, of xoana consisting of an upright wooden board, or plank (*cavíc*); the body could be indicated in painting and a head fixed on its top. To imitate this shape (best known from the Nikandre statue) in terracotta was easy enough; one had only to cut out and bake a rectangular strip of clay. If it was to stand, it had to be broadened into a base at one end; a head, either fashioned by hand or cast in a mould, was joined to the other. To suggest a seated image, the *cavíc* was slightly bent, twice, about its centre; if, for a more realistic effect, the figure was more definitely bent, it had to be supported at the back by one or two struts which could intimate the legs of a stool. Thus originated statuettes which may leave one uncertain whether a seated or a standing image is intended, and others, whose body is one with the chair and its arms, if any, with the armrests.

It must have been the traditional sanctity of this shape, and perhaps the authority of some particular images, which caused figurines of this kind

[1] Gàbrici, p. 289. [2] Gàbrici, Pl. LXXI. 7 and 9.

to be produced long after the representations of gods and humans had advanced beyond this primitive form;[1] after, that is, the age of 'dedalic' sculpture in the accepted sense of the term.[2] It was not done generally throughout the Greek world; not, in particular, in the sphere of Ionic art (including Rhodes); but in parts of the Peloponnesus—Sparta,[3] Argos[4] (with Tegea), Corinth[5]—and, in different ways, in Attica[6] and Boeotia.[7] Some of these archaizing types recur in Hellenic Italy,[8] and in Sicily.

The type of the seated goddess combined with her chair—we just referred to its occurrence in Italy—was found by Orsi in a fair number of samples at Bitalemi;[9] he mentions others from Gela, Agrigento, Kamarina, and Grammichele and suggests that the type was developed 'in un centro artistico delle coste di mezzogiorno';[10] and indeed the mainland instances just quoted are not similar enough to be regarded as the direct model of these very characteristic figures, even though they too were exported to Sicily.[11] This type, spread over the whole of Magna Graecia, thus seems to have originated there after the middle of the sixth century; it was retained for rather more than fifty years.[12]

Another variant of the *ad asse* was evidently imported to Sicily from Corinth, even though some of the samples may have been made in Argos. With this kind of figure the head (with shoulders) being moulded separately easily breaks off; but a few of those found in Sicily are luckily complete; standing ones as well as 'almost' or 'completely' sitting ones.[13] They are, compared with the mass of Sicilian terracottas, extremely rare;

[1] Thus the Lokrians in Calabria retained the excessively elongated neck of the archaizing Boeotian 'pappades', putting a contemporary head above and a modelled body below it (that is, I see no 'native influence' in these odd shapes; differing with Langlotz's comment on his Pl. 18).

[2] As established by R. J. H. Jenkins in his *Dedalica* (1936). Some truly 'dedalic' figurines (from Gela) will have to be mentioned later (below, p. 116).

[3] Dawkins, Pl. XXXIV. 1–3.

[4] Discussed, illustrated, and arranged by R. J. H. Jenkins, *BSA*, xxxii (1934), 23 ff.

[5] R. J. H. Jenkins *apud* H. Payne and others, *Perachora*, i (1940), pp. 191 ff.; *Archaeology*, xv (1962), 191; Higgins, *Greek Terracottas*, Pls. 20D and F (Corinth) and 21F (Argos).

[6] B.M. 647, 652.

[7] For illustrations see e.g. B.M. 761–7 ('pappades') and 768 f.; Louvre B55–61; B63–75. Of these, B.M. 768 and 769 (= T. B. L. Webster, *Greek Terracottas*, Pl. 13), and Louvre B72 can show the life and brightness imparted to these crude figures by colourful and richly-patterned paint.

[8] See e.g. Langlotz–Hirmer, Pl. 16 (Paestum) and von Matt–Zanotti-Bianco, *Großgriechenland* (1961, cited von Matt[2]), Pls. 30 (Foce del Sele), 53 f. (Paestum), 117 (Lokri) for the type of the seated goddess combined with her chair.

[9] *Gela*, p. 709, referring to Winter, p. 125.

[10] Later on, Orsi thought that Lokri might have been that centre (*Not. Scav.*, Supplem. 1913, 84; cf. von Matt[2], Pl. 117).

[11] Orsi found a Corinthian one in the necropolis del Fusco at Syracuse (*Not. Scav.* (1895), 178, Fig. 76).

[12] For still another type of Sicilian figurines *ad asse*, which seems not relevant to the present subject, see van Ufford, pp. 55 f. and 87.

[13] Cf. Gàbrici, p. 206.

among them are, at least at Selinus, a few local imitations of the imported
pieces. Gàbrici illustrates some complete ones (one of them without
indication of arms)[1] and two busts.[2] The latter two are very closely similar
to three others found by Orsi at Bitalemi;[3] two more have recently been
recovered on the akropolis of ancient Gela.[4] The thorough analysis of the
Corinthian material by R. J. H. Jenkins has shown that the term 'dedalic'
ought no longer to be applied to these figurines; for they are to be dated
about the middle of the sixth century. Three at least of the Sicilian pieces[5]
wear ornaments; not mere bands attached to large discs on the shoulders
but discs, or globules, on the uppermost of the two, or three, bands.

It is not proposed to attempt a thorough interpretation of these figures,
for I do not have sufficient pictures of the Sicilian 'goddess with chair',[6]
and the standardized Corinthian import cannot tell us much about
Sicilian religion. The preceding summary was none the less indispensable
as a background for the consideration of the outstanding type which has
come to be called—'miscalled', as will be argued—'Athana Lindia'. In
this context, two particular *figurine ad asse*, not previously mentioned, are
of particular importance.

One of them is pictured by Gàbrici, p. 239, Fig. 121. It is the body,
almost complete but minus head, of a standing 'Brettidol',[7] covered all
over with painted ornamentation—no doubt representing embroidery—
which H. Payne[8] identified as Corinthian and dated 575–550 B.C. The
body is somewhat broader at the top, slightly narrowed about the waist
and again broader at the base; the arms appear to have been symbolized
by mere stumps.[9]

This figure compares with one now lost but known from an ancient
drawing.[10] Found at Agrigento, it had the same shape as the preceding;
the head was preserved and—if the drawing is to be trusted—was of

---

[1] Pl. XXXVII, nos. 1, 4, 5, and (armless) 2; the latter, as well as no. 5, definitely standing; no. 2 seems a local product. Cf. *Perachora*, no. 75.

[2] Pl. XLIII, nos. 1 and 7; cf. *Perachora*, nos. 69 and 85; cf. p. 211.

[3] *Gela*, pp. 706 f. with Fig. 532.

[4] *Not. Scav.* (1956), 211 f. with Fig. 9b and c. Add Winter, no. i. 29. 2 (Megara) and *Not.
Scav.* (1895), 178, Fig. 76 (cf. *Perachora*, no. 112).

[5] Gàbrici, Pl. XLIII. 1 and 3 (cf. also 9 and the carefully worked fragment Pl. XXXVII.
7); *Not. Scav.* (1956), p. 212, Fig. 9b.

[6] Gàbrici, Pl. LXXV. 1 and 8 and LXXVI. 8 will come up later.

[7] Gàbrici (p. 238) indeed compares it with two seated figures; but if the picture is anything
to go by, the body consisted of a straight strip. At best, the figure may have been 'almost
seated'. This point does not in fact affect the argument. Van Ufford (p. 38) lists the figure
as the only standing one of this type found in Sicily.

[8] *Necrocorinthia* (1931), 340.

[9] To visualize the figure as a whole, one may compare *Perachora*, Pl. 88 nos. 5 and 15—
which are about a century older—or the almost contemporary Boeotian, B.M. 768 (now in
Higgins, *Greek Terracottas*, Pl. 18G).

[10] Kekulé von Stradonitz, p. 17, Fig. 22; Winter, p. 127, n. 1; Blinkenberg, *L'Image* . . . ,
p. 27, Fig. 3 (our Plate 15a).

a kind which one would date near the end of the sixth century, if not later. Instead of the arm-stumps, the region of the shoulders seems to have been covered by large ornaments representing huge pins, and instead of the painted embroidery (or in addition to it; for the figure must originally have been painted somehow, even though the drawing does not indicate it), two rows of pendants, round ones and longish ones respectively, cover the chest. They hang on two parallel chains, or strings, which, one below the other, issue from, and below, the shoulders; between them is a gorgoneion (hanging from the upper string; or perhaps a brooch is meant). This last detail seemed to Blinkenberg[1] to clinch the argument by which he aimed to demonstrate that a frequent and characteristic type of Sicilian terracotta reproduced the ancient image of the city-goddess of Lindos, Athana. This hypothesis, presented with wide learning and impressive acumen,[2] seems to be generally accepted.[3] If it were correct, this would not indeed be fatal to our purpose of interpreting these figurines as representations of Persephone and Demeter; for the aptness of any figurine for dedication to one deity or the other depends on the aptness of the representation, not on the original destination of its archetype.[4] It would still be surprising if images of the city-goddess of Gela (as well as of its Rhodian ancestor) had been so generally adopted as offerings to, and representations of, a pair of different goddesses, while none such, as far as I know, has been found in any Athena sanctuary.[5]

In fact, Blinkenberg's theory is wrong—or so it seems to me. Its detailed discussion has to be deferred until the figurines themselves have been examined; here it will suffice to mention one crucial point. Of this representation, supposedly, of the city-goddess of Rhodian Lindos, not one instance has been found at its alleged place of origin; not on the akropolis dedicated to her, nor anywhere else in Rhodes[6] (which yielded other terracottas by the thousand; nor anywhere in Ionia, on the Islands, the Greek mainland, and not even in Italy; the type occurs only in Sicily,

---

[1] Ib., p. 33.   [2] In the pamphlet quoted in the two preceding notes.

[3] See e.g. Higgins, *B.M. Cat.* i, p. 301 (on no. 1099); Mollard-Besques, *Catal. Louvre*, i, p. 79 (B549); p. 114 (C182); p. 160 (C604); van Ufford, p. 55; Marconi, *Agr. arc.*, p. 56 ('tipo . . . frequentissimo a Rodi nel santuario di Athena Lindia'; not one single sample has been found at Lindos, or anywhere on Rhodes! See the text above).

[4] Professor Webster allows me to quote a formulation which he threw out once in a different context: 'The terracottas are on sale, whether imported, copied from imports, or local originals: the shop probably gave them relevant local names, but the purchaser can alter these for his particular purpose as he likes.' One may add that the importers, sellers, and makers of terracottas are likely to have been the same people; that coroplasts were imbued with the same religious tendencies as their local customers; and that some among them were capable of giving fresh and specific expression to these tendencies. Cf. on the same problem K. Schefold in *Antidoron J. Wackernagel* (1923), p. 169.

[5] *Postscript*: This statement is now liable to qualification, though only in a marginal way: see Detached Note V, below, p. 399.

[6] I have in vain searched excavation reports, museum catalogues, and the whole set of *Clara Rhodos.*

whence a few pieces have been exported to Cyrenaica and to Punic terri-
tory (where they were even imitated).[1] By contrast, types which really
were derived from Rhodes—namely, the 'seduta' and the 'maschere' (our
next topic) abound in their homeland and are found, exported, all over
the Greek world. The 'Lindia', so-called, must be a Sicilian creation;
we may proceed to study it, unhampered by a brilliant but misleading
theory.

2. The so-called 'Athana Lindia'

The alleged 'Lindia' is almost as frequent a type in Sicily as is the 'dea
seduta'. It has been found in great quantity at Gela, Akragas, and Selinus,
and also at the smaller sites of Megara Hyblaia, Akrai, and Grammichele.[2] There is a considerable range of variation about it; even so, it is
capable of a comprehensive definition. The body is rigidly *ad asse*;
a plank, with no indication of the arms and sometimes slightly narrowing
from the shoulders downward. The head is almost always covered by
a high polos;[3] its features and expression vary greatly. A most characteristic detail, which seems as much *de rigueur* with this type as it is unknown with any other, is the indication of a peculiar garment by, at least,
a distinct line along the four sides of the *cavíc*,[4] but normally by the
rectangle inside these lines being slightly higher (or, rarely, lower) than
the edges outside them.[5] The garment thus indicated is a straight, broad,
and heavy strip of material hanging from the shoulders down almost to the

---

[1] e.g. B.M. 1118 comes from Tharros, Sardinia. In Barcelona are some pieces from Ibiza
with a notable Punic twist. Cf. below, p. 135, n. 2.

[2] Van Ufford, pp. 96 and 101 f.

[3] Exceptions are Gàbrici, Pl. LIX. 4, and Louvre, B551–4. All these are heads of young
maidens; so are B.M. 1113–15, with untypical, Attic heads and diadems in lieu of the polos
(against Mr. Higgins, I would plead for a considerably later date for these than the end of the
sixth century. To me they seem to range among the very latest of the type, also in view of their
peculiar attire, with the himation flung over the shoulder).

[4] e.g. Louvre B550.

[5] e.g. Louvre B551 and 548.—Van Ufford, p. 81, posits a primitive form without any
indication of this feature, basing herself upon a figurine from Selinus (her Fig. 32) from which
it appears to be absent. I submit that the figurine is imperfect; either from negligence of the
coroplast or owing to modern restoration. Gàbrici, Pl. LXVII. 2 (cf. p. 280), shows that, in
this particular type, the same garment was indicated by a broad stripe at the top and raised
edges along the sides. The former is present in van Ufford's figure, while the latter are lacking.
—The garment is not visibly indicated either on two figurines on Fig. 33 in P. Marconi's *Agrigento
arcaica*, p. 57 (where a third one looks unfinished). The small drawings may be incomplete in
this detail; besides, one may always reckon with some slip by the makers of these 'prodotti
dozzinali' (Gàbrici, ib.). Finally, on some of the more careless specimens of this mass-
production (as also e.g. on Gàbrici, Pl. LXXVI. 6) the décor could have been given in paint
only; cf. below, p. 119, n. 5 ff. For all this, I do not wish to deny the possibility that some
figurines without any indication of these paraphernalia may have been produced, for van
Ufford has seen many more of them than I myself; if so, there may be a better reason for this
than mere 'primitiveness'—as we shall see.

feet; it remains completely flat also on developed figurines which indicate the rich folds of a chiton underneath it.[1] Even though with these figurines the back is never elaborated, a similar piece of material has apparently to be imagined hanging down the back. This follows from the fact that all of them—excepting a very few of the plainest ones—show a pair of huge pins, or clasps, in front of and above the shoulders. Most often they are rendered by large discs; alternatively, by box-like rectangles,[2] which are often covered with elaborate ornaments; e.g. palmettes or rosettes.[3] These must have served to hold this raiment in position; either by pinning it to the shoulder of the chiton underneath—but there are obvious practical difficulties in this assumption—or by joining it to a counterpart at the back; and indeed some figurines seem to indicate a strap, or continuation, from the corners of the front-piece to the shoulder-clasps.[4]

Another outstanding, and indeed unique, feature is the rich décor which, more or less completely, covers the chest of most of the figurines of this class; on the minority from which it is absent[5] it could conceivably have been rendered in paint, as on Rhodian 'masks'[6] and on the Boeotian 'pappades'.[7] It consists of pendants hanging from two or three ribbons, or chains, which stretch across the chest (rarely, there is only one such;[8] once[9] there are even four) either in parallel, horizontally, or—with more naturalistic versions—in parallel arcs. An observation which will prove decisive in the (later) attempt at tracing the origin and meaning of this décor is that these ribbons, or strings, are not attached to the shoulder

---

[1] e.g. Louvre B549 and B554; Langlotz–Hirmer, Pl. 20 right; Gàbrici, Pl. LIX. 4 and 9.— This interpretation of the rectangle in question is borne out by the—otherwise problematical, and unique—figure Gàbrici, Pl. LVI. 2. A woman dressed like the more developed figurines of the type under discussion is standing with both arms raised sideways. Thereby the folds of her long and wide chiton are spread out in a sweeping curve; the rectangular strip, hanging from her shoulders, remains unaffected.

[2] e.g. Gàbrici, Pl. LXII. 8; van Ufford, Figs. 33–4; Louvre, B548.

[3] e.g. Louvre B554; B.M. 1109. K. Hadaczek, Oest. Jh. v (1902), 207 ff. collects illustrations of this 'common Greek' use of shoulder-pins; enormously large and rich samples come from Etruria (e.g. G. Becatti, Oreficerie antiche (1955), tav. A and no. 243).

[4] See Langlotz–Hirmer, Pls. 19 and 20 (right) and von Matt[1], Pl. 106; B.M. 1109; Louvre B554, B555, B558.

[5] e.g. Louvre B552, B553, B558; B.M. 1107 (?); Gàbrici, Pl. LXXVI. 6 and 10; Marconi, Agr. arc., Pl. XV. 9 and p. 57, Fig. 33 (twice) have no décor; Louvre B554, Gàbrici, Pls. LXVII. 2 and LXX. 14, Langlotz–Hirmer, Pl. 19 have only the discs, or rosettes, on the shoulders. Cf. below, p. 125, n. 1.

[6] See Blinkenberg, 592 f.

[7] This is easily imaginable for figurines like e.g. Louvre B552, B443, B558; unfortunately, none of these figurines appears to have survived with its paint intact. What scant information about traces of paint I have found, never suggested an elaborate rendering of the décor, and the assumption becomes improbable in the light of an observation which will be offered shortly (below, p. 125 and p. 134, n. 4).

[8] Louvre B550; B.M. 1112; Blinkenberg, L'Image . . ., Fig. 4 (Oxford); Marconi, Agr. arc., p. 57, Fig. 34; Not. Scav. (1956), p. 244, Fig. 2b.

[9] Louvre B546.

clasps (although this has often been asserted). How indeed, if they were, could they run across the chest horizontally and in parallel? Add that they are found even on some figures which have no shoulder-clasps at all.[1] Nor, evidently, are they extended necklaces. They are fixed to that strange upper garment (sewn on to it, presumably), the edges of which they never overlap. This observation is quite obvious with regard to the lower registers;[2] with regard to the uppermost, one may hesitate, but on consideration it is found to apply there—at the top-edge of the garment—likewise.[3]

The pendants attached to these strings as a rule cover the whole chest. On average figurines, especially those taken from 'tired' moulds, they may appear merely as so many elevations, longish or round; on a number of well-worked ones they are clearly defined.[4] They are: discs, globules,[5] acorns, corn- and wine-jars, crescents, bull's and ram's heads as well as heads of sileni. These pectorals then are the third significant feature of the type; in addition to the front-strip with its clasps and the *ad asse* shape. To be made to stand, the type-figure so far described had only to be broadened at its lower end, or even throughout, and perhaps even given feet. A fair number of standing ones do exist;[6] the vast majority, however, have been given a sitting posture; which was not difficult. Here again we meet with the two alternatives previously mentioned.[7] If the figure was only slightly bent in the middle, it was sufficient to thicken its lower part (struts were not used with this type) to keep it upright while intimating a sitting posture;[8] far more often, though, the image was properly seated on a small stool or a bench which is often covered by a cushion and sometimes has a more or less elaborate back.[9]

The basic type just described was gradually developed towards a more naturalistic representation.[10] There are figurines with arms faintly intimated by the sleeves of a wide chiton;[11] others on which arms and hands,

---

[1] Louvre B550 and B553; B.M. 1102; Marconi, *Agr. arc.*, Fig. 34.

[2] See e.g. Louvre B549; B.M. 1109 and 1111; Langlotz–Hirmer, Pl. 20 (right).

[3] See note 1 above; moreover note that the top string and pendants, which coincide with the curved upper edge of the front-piece, by-pass the clasps on Louvre B549, the London 'Goddess' (pictured in Higgins, *Greek Terracotta Figures*, Pl. 9, and now also in his *Greek Terracottas*, Pl. 37. 1; our Plate 15*b*) and Gàbrici, Pl. LIX. 9 and 14.

[4] For good illustrations of good samples see e.g. Langlotz–Hirmer, Pl. 20b; von Matt[1], Pl. 106; B.M. 1109; Orsi, *Gela*, p. 711, Fig. 536; Blinkenberg, *L'Image*..., pp. 28 f., Figs. 5 f.

[5] e.g. Gàbrici, Pls. LVII. 5 and LXII. 8.

[6] Standing figures are: Louvre B546–8 (Agrigento), Langlotz–Hirmer 20a and b (Agrigento), Marconi, *Agr. arc.*, p. 57, Fig. 34 (three statuettes).   [7] Above, p. 114.

[8] Such figures are B.M. 1111 and 1112; Louvre B550 and 551; Gàbrici, Pl. LXXV. 14; Marconi, *Agr. arc.*, Pl. XV. 9; *Not. Scav.* (1956), 366, Fig. 13.

[9] In some instances it is quite clear that, as suggested, the statuette was first fashioned standing and thereafter bent into a sitting position; see e.g. Louvre B552–4. The figure van Ufford, Pl. 34 has survived without the seat to which evidently it was none too firmly attached.   [10] Cf. van Ufford, pp. 81 f.

[11] e.g. van Ufford, Fig. 34; Louvre B549.

more or less concrete, are added to the abstract trunk;[1] and finally some which are very similar to the *seduta*; even though the pectoral, and the rigidity of the body, still witness to their different ancestry.[2] It is possible to elaborate a typological sequence from the all but abstract *ad asse* to the richly elaborated *seduta*; but it would be wrong to assume that figures of the former kind must always be older, and the more developed ones correspondingly more recent. None of them is anything like as old as is the primitive type of the body (which being far less developed than even Nikandre—with no arms and no modelling of the body—would have to be dated earlier than the seventh century); in fact, the whole bulk of these terracottas seems to come from a comparatively short period; say, about 530–460 B.C.[3] Within this period, a figure primitive in the main may exhibit developed details; e.g. the standing, shapeless body of Louvre B546 has fully-fashioned sleeves, arms, and hands; the same is true of B548, which, moreover, has a head of a type which is frequently found with figures of the most richly developed variety;[4] on the other hand, the latter sometimes retain the primitive, block-like shape of the body without arms.[5] There is, then, here no straight progress from abstract to naturalistic representation. The primitive form continued to be retained, wholly or at least in detail, no doubt because of its aura of specific sanctity; and this alone can account for the emergence of this type at a time when the general development of art had long outgrown its venerable primitiveness.

It is tempting to relate this type to the other *ad asse* types found in Sicily. The plank-like shape of the body—whether standing or bent into a sitting posture—compares with that of the Corinthian figures which we discussed first; some of these moreover wear an ornament (in the shape of pellets) which affords the only Sicilian analogy—not a perfect one, it is true—to the pectoral of the so-called 'Lindia'. The 'goddess combined with her chair', on the other hand, provides an analogy for the amalgamation of a contemporary head with a highly archaic rendering of the body. From these data, so one might infer, the type under discussion was developed in the latter half of the sixth century;[6] in confirmation, one

---

[1] e.g. Louvre B558.

[2] e.g. the 'Sicilian goddess, about 500 B.C.' (above p. 120, n. 3; our Plate 15*b*), or Blinkenberg, *L'Image* . . . , p. 29, Fig. 6, or B.M. 1102 and, even more so, 1149 and 1150 (the latter without polos and pectoral but with indication of the upper garment). Some figures could reasonably be connected with either type; e.g. B.M. 1090 and 1118.

[3] Cf. below, p. 138, n. 4.

[4] e.g. the 'Sicilian goddess' quoted above, note 2, or van Ufford, Fig. 35.

[5] e.g. B.M. 1099; Gàbrici, Pl. LVII. 5.

[6] I see too late that I am not the first to consider a connection between the Corinthian and the 'Lindia' types. P. Orlandini, in commenting (*Not. Scav.* (1956), 211, no. 5, Fig. 9b) on one of the former found at Gela declares it 'l'archetipo del tipo muliebre seduto con *polos* e lunghe collane di *bulle* e *kardia*'; which implies the rejection of Blinkenberg's thesis.

would particularly stress the similarity, pointed out above, p. 116f., between a Corinthian body *ad asse* found at Selinus and one from Akragas, now lost, with characteristics of the so-called 'Lindia'.

This connection is not in fact really solid. The drawing of the lost Agrigentine figure indicates a curvature of the outline of the body, narrowest about the waist, such as I do not recall seeing on any specimen of the 'Lindia' type and is actually excluded by the characteristic shape of its upper garment. The Corinthian figure, too, shows this curved outline; moreover, it lacks the upper garment. The same is probably true also of the other specimen.[1] In view of these differences one is bound to acknowledge that this isolated specimen resulted from the combination of two different types. The décor—two chains with pendants—characteristic of the so-called 'Lindia' has been applied to an *ad asse* figure of a different kind. After all, that lost figurine wore a large gorgoneion and was thereby identified as Athena; no figurine true to the 'Lindia' type is thus characterized.[2] Generally, moreover, the 'Lindia' type has somewhat more 'body'; i.e., the 'board' or 'plank' is thicker than it is with the Corinthian figurines *ad asse*. In short, the two classes, though comparable, are unrelated.

The antecedents quoted can serve as analogies for the type under discussion, but they cannot by themselves account for its emergence. The creation, development, and wide appeal of so peculiar a representation bespeaks some specific and powerful motive—on which it would be useless to speculate as long as the character and purport of the figurines of this type have not been investigated. And this is anyhow our main concern.

3. CHARACTER AND VARIETY OF THE FIGURINES OF THIS TYPE

Since there is so little variation in the rendering of the body, the identification of the deity, or deities, represented by this type has to be based on the examination of the heads (and of the attributes, that is, the garment and décor; on which later). Apart from a few untypical yet

---

[1] The strip of material covering the front may be held to be indicated by the double lines along the outer sides of the rather imperfect drawing. This, though, is doubtful, both in view of their shape and shading and of the absence of the corresponding horizontal line near the bottom. It rather looks as though the draughtsman aimed, however unreasonably, to indicate on both sides the thickness of the figurine.

[2] To Blinkenberg obviously this drawing provided a main prop for his theory; hence it has to be stressed that the figure which it shows is not true to type and that not one among the typical ones is characterized as Athena. One of them, Gàbrici, Pl. LIX. 7, wears three small gorgoneia. They are of course a traditional item of ancient jewellery; besides, buildings as well as human beings and deities were placed under their magic protection. *Postscript*: For a recently found figurine of the 'Lindia' type adapted so as to represent Athena see Detached Note V, below, p. 399.

significant instances and some of imperfect characterization, there are
three main types; namely (a) a round and friendly face, not young;
(b) a more elongated but still rather full one, equally womanly but more
solemn, and (c) a narrow-faced and youngish one. The first two we hold
to represent Demeter; the third, Persephone.[1] We need hardly repeat
that, in different places, the goddesses may have been worshipped under
various specific names and that the justification for defining them as we
are doing is in what we know about the sanctuaries at Selinus, Akragas,
and Gela from which so many of these terracottas come.

The first type seems to be known, so far, from Agrigento and Gela
only.[2] The Agrigentine shows, like some of the 'Rodia seduta' type, the
chubby face of a friendly peasant woman. Round like a full moon, and
brightened by a benign smile, it radiates goodness and bounty; reminding
one of the kourotrophos from Caltanisetta.[3] The type is Rhodian;[4] but
in this particular form, with its exuberant and almost plebeian geniality,
it asserts a character of its own. It may be ascribed to the last quarter of
the sixth century and may well have been prompted by some cult-
image, on which the coroplasts felt free to base their variations—the
figure standing or seated; the head with polos or also without it; the
smile more or less broad.[5] A variant—differing from the preceding
in being without arms—which has more recently been found at Gela
(Carubazza),[6] repeats more nearly an Ionian (?Milesian) form of the
round face and has no polos; its expression is less rustic and more dignified
but still benign.

The second type stresses the dignity of the great goddess rather than her
affability. Almost always she is enthroned, and the elaborate rendering
of the chiton and its sleeves (with or without indication of arms and

[1] The contrast is strikingly illustrated by Langlotz–Hirmer, Pl. 20a and b.—Against the
proposed distinction it might be urged that a youthful female who, on a red-figured Attic
cup at Bruxelles (H. Metzger, Recherches sur l'imagerie athénienne (1965), p. 26, no. 61; Pl.
XII/2), is represented depositing ears of corn on an altar, is by its inscription defined as
Demeter. I submit that the genitive ΔΕΜΕΤΡΟΣ indicates, not the person offering but, the
goddess to whom the offering is presented (cf. Metzger, ib., pp. 108 ff.). The person making
the offering might be Kore (as on two lekythoi, Metzger, ib., p. 22, nos. 47 and 48, Pls. X/1
and IX/2) or also a human worshipper: she wears the very diadem which, on the Ninnion
plaque, distinguishes not only the goddesses but also the leader of the mystai.
[2] Excellent photographs in Langlotz–Hirmer (Pl. 20, right) and von Matt[1] (Pl. 106); two
further instances of the type apud Marconi, Agr. arc., Pl. VII, nos. 9 and 10. The ugly little
figure, Gàbrici, Pl. LXXV. 14, may be quoted as an unsuccessful attempt, at Selinus, to
reproduce the same type; its grim expression, as evidence of poor workmanship.
[3] Langlotz–Hirmer, Pl. 21 (left); cf. above, p. 112.
[4] See in particular Blinkenberg, Pl. 96, Figs. 2127 and 2137.
[5] Louvre B555 (from Gela) has a truly infectious smile.
[6] Not. Scav. (1956), 244, Fig. 2a. It has not the slightest similarity with those to which the
editor refers (p. 245, nn. 2 and 3: Orsi, Gela, Figs. 533 (fragments of a different seat) and 534;
Marconi, Agr. arc. pp. 56–8); except that the latter, however different, do at least belong to
the 'Lindia' type.

hands) enhances the nobility and richness of her appearance.[1] The face is sometimes almost fat,[2] but always longish rather than round; its majesty often combined with womanly beauty.[3] The glance of the goddess sometimes goes straight forward;[4] more often, with a slight downward bent of the head, she seems ready to heed the entreaties of her worshippers;[5] occasionally one may discern a hint of a smile.[6] The polos, never lacking, is high and often richly decorated. This very definite type, too, is unlikely to have been invented by some coroplast. Some cult-image must have given rise to it; a Sicilian one, no doubt; for it does not recur elsewhere. This assumption is supported by the find of a life-size terracotta head of the same kind at the Gaggera[7] which most probably belonged to a large votive statue deriving from the same original as the figurines. They are evidence of a more advanced art than the first type— one might date them in the first quarter of the fifth century—and witness to another aspect of, and attitude to, the same goddess. She remains the mistress and dispenser of the gifts on which all life depends; but it is her majesty which is now predominantly felt and expressed.

If, now, the reader will contemplate a representative of the third type, such as Langlotz–Hirmer, Pl. 19, the difference of shape and expression must strike him. This narrow face, with lean cheeks descending from high cheek-bones; this very regular and entirely unmoved face; young but confined within itself and without a breath of sympathy—conveys the very antithesis of the character expressed by the other two. Divine it is no less than they; but here is the divinity of total nothingness. Its impact is reinforced by the plainness of the whole figure—no arms; no bulging folds of the chiton underneath the flat top-cloth; and no décor (apart from the large, disk-shaped shoulder pins holding the top-garment). By contrast, the previous two types are indeed—but very rarely—found armless but practically never without those characteristic pendants covering the chest. My material obviously is far too incomplete for apodictic statements to be based upon it; even so, it may be tolerably representative. As far as it goes, it suggests that the Demeter-heads are normally added to comparatively elaborate bodies with full décor;[8] while plain, board-like bodies without

---

[1] The only standing, and less elaborate, figure of this type that I can quote is Louvre B548; besides, B.M. 1111 is only 'almost seated'; seated but plain are the very small figurines Gàbrici, Pl. LXXVI. 6 and 10.

[2] Blinkenberg, *L'Image* . . . , p. 29, Fig. 6; Louvre B549.

[3] 'Sicilian goddess' (Higgins, *Greek Terracotta Figures*, Pl. 9, above, p. 121, n. 2; our Plate 15b); Gàbrici, Pl. LIX. 9; B.M. 1109; also 1099; *Kokalos*, xii (1966), Pl. XI. 3 (Bitalemi).

[4] As note 2 above.

[5] Van Ufford, Fig. 34; Ashmolean Mus. no. 1891, 694 (our Plate 16a), Blinkenberg, ib., Fig. 5); Louvre B548.　　　[6] B.M. 1111.　　　[7] Gàbrici, Pl. LIV; cf. esp. B.M. 1109.

[8] My evidence has been quoted on the preceding pages. Exceptions are: Louvre B558 (arms; no décor; head type B) and three of Gàbrici's very small and rough figurines, Pls. LXXV. 14, LXXVI. 6 and 10.

arms and with little or no décor normally have a Persephone-head.[1] There appears to be a ratio in this distribution. It militates, for one thing, against the assumption[2] that décor not rendered plastically might have been indicated in paint; but it does not by any means imply that Persephone statuettes are always plain and without décor. The opposite is true. On Langlotz–Hirmer's next plate (20, left) we find the goddess represented in the same style as before; standing this time, with arms and hands faintly indicated. Again: a narrow, youthful face; deeply serious though not as severe as the previous one.[3] Sadness lies on it, as though Persephone were sharing in the sorrow at the ending of life and hope which she must enforce.[4] And she wears the rich pectoral—summarily rendered—which is Demeter's emblem. What does this mean?

The figurine Louvre B546 is almost overloaded with it; the only one known to me with as many as four bands, each with nine, ten, and more pendants hanging from it. The maker of this comparatively late figurine[5] —its date may be early in the fifth century—seems to have expended more care on the elaboration of detail—also on arms, sleeves, wristlets, and hands—than on the animation of the face; which is regular and dignified but without deeper expression. Its eyes, though, look at the spectator: this Persephone is not separated from the realm of the living. More striking is the head on the elementary body, without any indication of hands and feet, and only one row of disc-shaped pendants, of B550. It is a sensitive, even sweet, maiden's head; withdrawn and yet with the hint of a smile.[6] How variously, and how meaningfully, the notion of death could present itself to Greeks! In the untypical figurine Brit. Mus.

---

[1] Entirely without décor: Langlotz–Hirmer, Pl. 19; van Ufford, Fig. 33; Marconi, *Agr. arc.*, Pl. XV. 9; ib., p. 57, Fig. 33; Gàbrici, Pl. LXVII. 2; Louvre B552 and B554; B.M. 1108. Similarly plain shape, with little décor: Louvre B547, B550, B553; B.M. 1112; Blinkenberg, *L'Image* . . . , Fig. 4; also, likewise from Selinus, the figurine at Berlin pictured by V. Müller, *Frühe Plastik* . . . (1929), Pl. XXXII, no. 350.

[2] Above, p. 119, with note 7.

[3] Quite as severe as Langlotz–Hirmer, Pl. 19 are van Ufford 32 and Gàbrici, Pl. LXVII. 2.

[4] One may find a similar blending of sentiments in the fragment, Marconi, *Agr. arc.*, Pl. X, no. 2 and, different in style but similar in expression, in the statuette *Not. Scav.* (1956), 367, Fig. 13, likewise with pectoral. This figure is probably somewhat older; say, of *c.* 520 B.C. Its finder, though, would put it as early as the first half of the sixth century (ib. p. 369), for reasons of style and because it was found, at Gela, outside a child's sarcophagus near to which (apparently in another rock-grave) was a coffin containing 'frammenti . . . di due scyphoi corinzi del tipo "siracusano" '. Comparing the plan on p. 357, I wonder how safe this inference is, and even if the sherds in question are contemporary with the figurine, opinions on the date of the late-Corinthian import at Syracuse are divided (Dunbabin, pp. 259 ff. and literature quoted there). To the best of my knowledge, no absolute date, fixed by stratigraphy or securely dated finds, is available on which the chronology of this type of terracotta could be based; it has therefore to be inferred by considerations of style. For my part, I cannot visualize heads with an expression as differentiated as is seen on even the most primitive among these terracottas to have been produced in the first half of the sixth century.

[5] Cf. above, p. 121.   [6] Cf. now *Kokalos*, xii (1966), Pl. XI. 4.

1102, with the summary indication of three rows of pendants, it assumes the features of a most lovely girl, withdrawn yet alluring, and the same holds good for one from the Gaggera,[1] a seated one, who appears to be weighted down by the large, globular pendants which cover her chest.

In examining the representations of Demeter and Persephone in the type popularly called 'Lindia' a similar range of concepts and sentiment has emerged as previously in reviewing the 'Rodia seduta'. This time, though, it appears to be bound up, somehow, with the peculiar characteristics of garment and décor. If we care more fully to understand these figures, with their strange combination of features ancient and contemporary, we have to try and account for these characteristics. This involves resuming the question raised by C. Blinkenberg.

4. Origins of this type

Blinkenberg's thesis—as urged above, p. 117—cannot be retained in view of the absence of any trace of the alleged 'Athana Lindia' at her supposed place of origin. How many terracottas, by contrast, have been found, on the Akropolis and generally in Athens, reflecting the 'ancient image' of the city-goddess or, at any rate, its general appearance![2]

Even so, Blinkenberg's approach, though probably too narrow, was basically correct. Some outstanding model must lie behind this very peculiar type, and this model did not originate in Sicily. To see any one of these Sicilian statuettes, in the shapelessness of their bodies and the profusion of their décor, especially when this décor is not elaborated into distinct shapes but reduced to mere roundish or longish elevations, is to be reminded of the notorious image of the Ephesian Artemis. They are not descendants of the Ephesian Artemis; but the evident analogy suggests where we have to look.

To take first the characteristic upper garment. It is no more than a plain and straight, rectangular strip of material (slightly tapering towards the bottom in the minority of cases where it had to be adapted to a βρέτας-shape slightly narrowed at or above its base). We inferred that

---

[1] Gàbrici, Pl. LXII. 8 = van Ufford, Fig. 33. The figurine from Gela at Oxford (our Plate 16a; Blinkenberg, *L'Image* . . . , p. 27, Fig. 4) is in this category; likewise Louvre B547 and B551–4.

[2] F. Winter, *Arch. Anz.* (1893), 144; C. J. Herington, *Athena Parthenos* (1955), p. 24; *B.M. Cat.* on no. 655.—To make matters worse, figurines variously dependent on the later image of Athana Lindia,—in the manner of Phidias, have emerged at Lindos (Blinkenberg, *L'Image* . . . , pp. 41 ff.; id., *Lindos*, i, nos. 2332–6 and 2866–70) and Kamiros (*Clara Rhodos*, iv (1931), 210, Fig. 223), and three replicas of one of these types have gradually emerged at Gela (Orsi, *Not. Scav.* (1907), 38; Orlandini, ib. (1956), 246 with note 7 and Fig. 5a, which compares with *Lindos*, no. 2870). If the original of these very rare Sicilian replicas of the later Rhodian image is found at Rhodes, why not likewise the model of the exceedingly frequent alleged replicas of the old image?

a similar piece has to be assumed to have covered the back. The point, as will be seen, is not essential to our argument; but we shall proceed on the assumption that it is valid. If so, our terracottas are wearing that *scapulare* which the Virgin Mary brought down from Heaven in A.D. 1156, to be for Carmelite monks the distinguishing vestment and a surety of deliverance from Purgatory. She had been anticipated, though, by the Byzantine emperors who, ever since the days of Justinian II, wore a garment, glittering with gold, of the same shape (it may have been called *loros* or *lorion*).[1] This is, after all, the most primitive form of clothing that man could have devised, as soon as he had taught himself, or his woman, to weave a straight piece of cloth. He had only to take a strip twice his own length and cut a slit into the middle for his head: there was the *poncho* for the *gaucho* and the *omophorion* for the orthodox clergy; or he might prefer to take two strips, each of less than his own length, and pin or strap them on his shoulders: there was the garment worn by our terracottas and Byzantine emperors and Carmelite monks—and still others. One might proceed to sew it up on the sides to below the armpits: thus the wearer's body would be inside a woven tube, which might be shorter or longer; one might in the end even add sleeves: the result would be a kind of pull-over. This is what happened; the 'pull-over' was worn by Greeks in certain cults—especially Dionysiac, which includes theatrical costume—and even, at times, by Athena, and it became, besides, a popular and even plebeian garment;[2] the long tube encases the body of the Ephesian Artemis, and other deities. This kind of garment was normally *worn on top* of a long chiton (as it is also on the Sicilian terracottas); it was thus an ἐπένδυμα or ἐπενδύτης.

Therewith we are on the field covered by H. Thiersch's classic study *Ependytes und Ephod* (1936), the precious side-issue of the comprehensive disquisition on *Artemis Ephesia* (i, 1935) which he did not live to complete. To his immense learning I owe most of the material and ideas now to be presented, and it is with genuine trepidation that, in some respects, I venture to go beyond the trail blazed by him.[3]

[1] The best known representation of it is on an ivory plaque, now in the Bibliothèque Nationale, with the coronation of Romanos II and Eudoxia, pictured e.g. in Ch. Diehl, *Manuel d'art byzantine* (1910), pp. 616 ff., Fig. 308 and D. Talbot Rice, *Byzantine Art* (1935), Pl. 33b. On the indefinite meaning of the word *loros–lorum*, J. J. Reiske's comment (on Constantinus Porphyrogennetus, *De caerim.* ii. 657 ed. Bon.) still deserves to be noted. Voigt, in his commentary on the *De caerim.* i, p. 71, translates 'écharper'; P. S. Schramm, *Herrschaftszeichen und Staatssymbolik*, i (1954), p. 26 says 'Binde'; R. Delbrück, *Die Antike*, viii (1932), 20 describes the *lorum* as a 'Galakostüm der Damen'. Whatever its name, to us the salient fact is the existence of this garment at Byzantium.   [2] John 21: 7.

[3] The interested reader will find in Thiersch's essay an invaluable collection of illustrations and of references to relevant literature, much of which is inaccessible to me; e.g. for the Byzantine imperial dress on pp. 172 ff. and 211 ff.; cf. Pl. LIV. 2–4; for Attic vases and other illustrations of the Greek ependytes on pp. 29 ff. and 203 f., with Pls. XXI–XXVIII and LIV. 1. Thiersch concentrates on the tube-like shape of the garment, which is indeed the

The feature about the Ephesian Artemis which comes first to mind is of course those *mammae* which, as we saw, are analogous to the décor, or jewellery, on the Sicilian statuettes. M. Meurer showed in 1914[1] that on the Ephesian idols they are, likewise, not monstrous excrescences of the body but a part of the rich décor which is attached to the outer garment. The analogy is weakened by the fact that on the Ephesia the whole front of the round body is covered with a profusion of various décor; it is stronger with the—generally similar—cult-image of the Aphrodite of Aphrodisias,[2] for this shows the décor confined to a rectangular strip which lies on top of the richly folded chiton and reaches from the neck down to below the knees; on the shoulders it is fastened by clasps. Even more relevant is the image of Jupiter Dolichenus at Baalbek, which is well known from excellent replicas.[3] His richly decorated outer garment does indeed cover the whole body; it is, however, perfectly clear that essentially it consists of one panel on the front and a corresponding one on the back: they are joined by narrow side-strips which do not share in the meaningful mythological and astrological décor of the two panels.[4] The armour-like appearance of the outer garment on all these statues is evidence that on the original cult-images it was rendered in metal; no doubt gold.[5] The extant copies date from the recrudescence of oriental religions under the Roman Empire, and even their representations on coins do not antedate the second century B.C. Even so, no one will doubt that this type of cult-image was not invented in the Hellenistic age but, though in a modernized form, continued an age-old tradition; in fact, a set of outstanding Rhodian gold-plaques[6] of the seventh century B.C. represents the 'Mistress of Beasts' in this shape.

So far, then, we have evidence of ancient and rigid Anatolian and Syrian cult-images which exhibit two main characteristics of the Sicilian terracottas: the ependytes and a profusion of décor attached to it; and of adoption of this type of image by Eastern Greeks (Ephesus; Rhodes).

most frequent, especially among Greeks, and is accurately defined as a 'second, shorter chiton' (p. 2: the Old Syriac translation of John 21 : 7 actually renders *ependytes* by 'chiton', and the combination χιτὼν ἐπενδύτης occurred in a late-classical comedy quoted by Pollux vii. 45 [vol. ii, p. 843 Meineke]); only in his *Addenda*, p. 196, does he consider the primitive form of separate strips for front and back in which we are mainly interested. It is surprising that, with his immense learning and industry, Thiersch should have failed to notice the relevance, to much of his argument, of the Sicilian terracottas (he did notice, p. 152, Punic imitations and, for once, completely misinterpreted them); otherwise he would no doubt have accounted for them far more competently than I can hope to do.

[1] *Röm. Mitt.* xix (1914), 200 ff.
[2] Thiersch, *E. u. E.*, pp. 59 ff.; Pls. IX–XII; our Plate 17a.
[3] Thiersch, ib., pp. 73 ff. and 196; Pls. XIII–XIX.
[4] See esp. Thiersch, Pls. XV, XVI. 2 and XVIII. 2; our Plate 17b.
[5] Cf. Thiersch, p. 51.
[6] F. H. Marshall, *B.M. Cat. of Jewellery* (1911), Pl. XI, nos. 1107, 1121, 1126, 1128–30, etc.; R. A. Higgins, *Greek and Roman Jewellery* (1961), pp. 111 f. with Pls. 19d, e, and 20.

This is not sufficient fully to account for the emergence of the Sicilian type, for the following differences remain:

1. The Eastern statues referred to, and many more of the same class,[1] are standing; of the Sicilian terracottas, roughly half represent the goddess seated;
2. the Eastern statues are round, but the Sicilian flat (the former perpetuating the shape of a tree-trunk, the latter that of a plank or board);[2]
3. the former have arms, but not so the latter (except in their later development);
4. the former grow narrow, in a strong curve, towards the base; the latter rarely so and, if at all, to a far less degree and in a straight line;
5. the characteristic décor covers the whole ependytes of the Eastern statues, but the chest only of the Sicilian terracottas or even only the upper part of it; on a proportion of these it is entirely lacking.

The first difference may be disregarded since, as already observed, a standing βρέτας is the original form of the various Sicilian types; the others, however, are such as to preclude any direct dependence of the Sicilian upon these Asianic images. The analogies noted retain their significance, but more specific intermediaries remain to be sought.

The décor worn by the Sicilian terracottas may fittingly be called a pectoral, but it is decisively different from the finery to which this term is currently applied: those necklaces, in particular, with an abundance of chains and pendants hanging from them, which spread from Egypt to Cyprus and Greece.[3] Among Greek jewellery one may indeed easily find almost all the various kinds of pendants which have previously been noticed on the terracottas;[4] but the fact that on the latter they are fixed—

---

[1] Collected and discussed by Thiersch, pp. 3 ff. and 54 ff.

[2] I fail to see—especially in view of H. Brunn's (*Griech. Kunstgeschichte*, ii (1897), pp. 83 f.) sensitive comment—why this traditional derivation is frowned upon by many contemporary archaeologists; e.g. by V. K. Müller, *Röm. Mitt.* xxxiv (1919), 106. His observation in *Frühe Plastik* . . . , p. 178, that at all ages abstract and naturalistic art co-exist or alternate, though true in itself, does not invalidate Brunn's argument.

[3] M. Meurer, *Röm. Mitt.* xix (1914), 207 ff. argued the derivation of the décor on the Sicilian terracottas from these pectorals. One will admit that the over-all effect of e.g. the great Egyptian pectoral found at Enkomi, Cyprus (*Excavations in Cyprus*, 1900, Pl. V; *B.M. Cat. of Jew.* no. 581) is similar; that the type is frequent in Cyprus (e.g. on the limestone statue from Arsos, in *The Swedish Cyprus Expedition*, iii (1937), Pl. 185; cf. the terracottas ib., Pl. 203. 1 and 7 and Pl. 205, and in H. B. Walters, *B.M. Cat. of Terrac.* (1903), Pl. XIV, A88 and A89) and was in vogue in Greece in archaic (e.g. *B.M. Cat. of Jew.* no. 1461; cf. 'pappades' like B.M. 767 and Peloponnesian terracottas as mentioned above, p. 116) and classical times (Higgins, *Jewellery*, Pls. 26 f. and 33; *Collection Stathatos*, iii (1963), 167; cf. P. Amandry, ib., 233). But the fundamental difference of cultic symbols affixed to a cultic garment remains.

[4] Above, p. 120.—The reader may easily check this by perusing the *B.M. Cat. of Jew.*:

presumably by hooks—to strings, or bands, across the ependytes constitutes a fundamental difference; they are therewith no longer trinkets but a cultic ornament,[1] expressive of ideas connected with the relevant cult. The analogy, previously noted, of the necklaces on *ad asse* figures imported from Corinth[2] therewith loses much of its significance for the present problem; even when 'pellets' similar to those on the cruder ones among the figurines under review are attached to them and even when the string holding them is not a necklace but is attached to shoulder-pins.[3] We still have to look for instances of the different, cultic pectoral.

The fact that the primitive Sicilian type does not render arms, hands, or feet may be compared with the same feature on many prehistoric relics (especially from the Balkans, Thessaly, and Troy) in illustration of the persisting, or recurring, tendency to abstract representation, but no one would suggest a genetic relation between objects so far distant in time and character. In the Greek sphere there are indeed a few instances which have actually been compared[4]; they are however so different in general as to make the coincidence in this detail insignificant.[5] The Sicilian type may well be termed 'primitive' or 'abstract': it is at the same time a complete and perfect artistic creation; the absence of the extremities, an 'early' or 'primitive' feature from a historical point of view, is not a deficit but an element of this creation, together with ependytes, décor, and the *ad asse* shape. If its place within the Greek tradition is to be identified, one has to look for creations comparable with it as a whole and not only in details.

here it will suffice to refer, once more, to Higgins, ib., Pl. 26 f. (bull's heads, acorns, pomegranates, eggs); ib., 34b (gorgoneia); also *B.M. Cat. of Jew.* nos. 1416, 1460, 1601 and, for discs on 'pectorals', nos. 76, 761, 763, 1414 ff.

[1] V. K. Müller stressed this difference in *Röm. Mitt.* xxxiv (1919), 92; cf. ib., 101 ff. his criticism of Meurer's (above, p. 129, n. 3) argumentation.

[2] Above, p. 129, n. 3.

[3] e.g. the crude figurine in C. Waldstein, *The Argive Heraion*, ii (1905), Pl. 42. 8, with the pendants in the form of 'pellets', may appear very similar to a Sicilian one like e.g. Blinkenberg, *L'Image* . . . , Fig. 4, and yet it belongs to a different class.

[4] By Müller, *Frühe Plastik* . . . , pp. 175 ff.—Hermae obviously are in another category not here relevant.

[5] Some entirely 'abstract' Spartan ivories (Müller, ib., Figs. 348 and 349 = *BSA*, xiii (1906–7), 94, Fig. 27a and xiv (1907–8), 23, Fig. 8 = F. Poulsen, *Der Orient und die frühgriechische Kunst* (1912), p. 85, Fig. 84 and p. 139, Fig. 153 = Dawkins, *The Sanctuary of Artemis Orthia*, pp. 218 and 247, Pls. CXVII ff. and CXXIII. 2)—most of them round (after Sidonian models; cf. D. Harden, *The Phoenicians* (1962), Pls. 64a and 65), but one square—belong to completely different traditions which do not touch upon the Sicilian; the same holds good for the incredibly crude figurines from Thera (Hiller von Gaertringen, *Thera*, ii (1903), 304 f.; note Poulsen's ingenious explanation, pp. 137 f., of the absence of arms). On several of the Ephesus ivories, arms and hands are only faintly indicated, being clearly an additional feature hardly affecting their basic, round shape; which anyhow makes them irrelevant in the present context. The Sicilian armless figurine, Gàbrici, Pl. XXXVII, 2, a local product, in all its poverty may derive from some better model, but the marked rendering of the breasts and the thick, long curls falling on to them puts it into a class apart from the so-called 'Lindia'.

One may gain a notion of the Eastern archetype of the Sicilian figurines by striving to visualize the ancient image, or images, of Hera in her age-old Samian sanctuary, for which there is comparatively rich evidence from literature, coins, an inscription, and excavations.[1] The oldest, according to Kallimachos,[2] was 'a plank (or board) unwrought by sculptors' knives': γλυφάνων ἄξοος cανίς. Nikandre's Delian statue is by no means the only one known to preserve, only slightly elaborated, the shape of a wooden board; one may further quote, again from the Heraion at Samos, a large marble statue (Hera?), and a small wooden one;[3] furthermore, the Athenian Palladion (as known from the prize amphoras), and, from Sicily, the fragments of large terracotta statues.[4] All these, however, are more advanced than the type we are seeking, in that the elementary shape of the plank begins in them to be moulded into a human form; mainly by a narrowing of the waist (often belted) and by the rendering of arms and feet. A notion of the more elementary form may be conveyed by the immensely expressive relief, on a Boeotian pithos, of a goddess with raised arms:[5] her body is nothing but a shapeless board, almost square, decorated with a lozenge pattern, and there is no indication of feet. Some scholars infer from Kallimachos' words an even more shapeless, oldest agalma; in fact, a piece of unwrought wood; but the word cανίς will not bear this interpretation; a piece of wood (ξύλον, πρέμνον) to become a cανίς has at least to be cut. There is thus a marked difference between pure natural objects felt to be the embodiment of some deity (such as the Eros of Thespiai, an unwrought stone, or the herma in its primitive form) and even the oldest Samian cult-image. One may, even so, take Kallimachos literally and assume that it (and likewise, according to him, the old image of Athana Lindia) had the entirely abstract form of a rectangular board (comparable to an undecorated stele); the fact that the Sicilian terracottas combine an abstract body with various heads of a comparatively advanced style could conceivably be traced to a model consisting of an abstract 'body' and no more. Since, however, it is known that both the Samian and the Rhodian ancient images were annually bathed, clothed, and adorned, one would incline to assume that they had some intimation of the human form; be it as little as on the 'menhir' of

[1] Thiersch, pp. 10 f. and Pl. III, 1–5; Overbeck, *Schriftquellen* (1868), nos. 340–4; E. Buschor, *Ath. Mitt.* lv (1930), 1 ff. The German excavation of the Heraion, while yielding dramatic results, has also shown the problems of the cult-image(s) to be more complicated than the evidence previously known would have led one to think. This topic has been dealt with in a most instructive and stimulating essay by D. Ohly (*Ath. Mitt.* lxviii (1953), 25 ff.; cf. ib., 77 ff.), who also (p. 46) republishes the inscription (C. Michel, *Recueil d'inscr.* (1900), no. 832; also *SGDI*, 5702). It would have been a great help to be able to use also the publication, by the same (ib., lxvi (1941), 1 ff.), of Samian terracottas; but this volume proved unobtainable.

[2] Fr. 100 Pf.   [3] *Ath. Mitt.*, lxviii (1953), 79 and 85; Buschor, i. 72 f.

[4] Orsi, *Gela*, p. 594, Fig. 402; id., 'Daedalica Siciliae', *Mon. Piot*, xxii (1916), 143 ff.; Pace, ii. 7 ff.   [5] Pictured e.g. in L. Alscher, *Griech. Plastik*, i (1954), Pl. 36.

Lewidhi in Arkadia[1] with the outline of a face carved out of the otherwise crude stone; nor need Kallimachos' words imply more than that the oldest image was 'shapeless' by contrast with the elaborate 'Skelmian work'; the latter being, according to the *Diegesis*, a 'statue' (ἀνδριάς); the former, a 'xoanon' (and not a shapeless piece of wood; the ξύλον 'out of which it was made' is mentioned immediately afterwards). The most primitive among the Sicilian terracottas may reproduce an ἄξοος cανίc of this kind . . . but we have to beware of arguing in a circle. Fortunately, there is some further evidence for the Hera of Samos.

The German excavations have uncovered, close to the back-wall of the small, oldest temple, a square foundation which was preserved, with remarkable consistency, to the very end of antiquity; similar foundations were traced in the two successive giant temples which, in the sixth century, superseded the modest earlier structures. It is plausible that these foundations were bases for cult-images. The fourth century inscription refers to two images, 'the Goddess' and 'the Goddess at the back'; the former 'owns' an amazing amount of garments and décor, but the latter only one himation. One will conclude that 'the Goddess' is the ancient wooden image whose place was devoutly kept through the ages, while the latter is the statue of one of the great temples. This conclusion can be harmonized with the representations on Samian coins.[2]

They date from the first century B.C. to the third A.D. and show, with variations in detail, one and the same ancient statue of the Goddess. The general impression is similar to that of the images of Artemis, Aphrodite, etc., on the coins of Ephesus, Aphrodisias, etc., previously referred to; but there are notable differences indicative of the combination of Greek and Asianic traditions. Judging by the majority of the Samian coins—for some of them are adapted to the Ephesian type—the lower part of the Samian image was not, as with the Asianic ones, circular and curving from the waist to the base, but straight and broad and thus—though apparently with rounded edges like Nikandre—reminiscent of the shape of the ancient cανίc; at any rate, there was no indication of the waist.[3] The Goddess is wearing a long and wide chiton which completely covers her feet; the elaborate rendering of its rich folds could not have been a feature of an

[1] Discovered by D. Burr Thompson, see *Am. Journ. Arch.* xxxi (1927), 168, who compared it with the primitive statuettes from Thera mentioned above, p. 130, n. 5.

[2] Thiersch, Pl. III. 1–5; *Ath. Mitt.* lv (1930), Pl. 3, Fig. 2; ib., lxviii (1953), Beilage 4; cf. our Plate 18c.

[3] My description is contradicted by the interesting Roman brick-stamp reproduced and discussed by D. Ohly (*Ath. Mitt.* lxviii (1953), pp. 38 and 46; Beilage 4. 1). I venture to differ with his assertion that this outline sketch conveys a truer notion of the statue than do the coins; for where, in Greek sculpture, is there a comparable statue with its body built up of 'separate, stereometric components'; namely, an ovoid heavy block resting on a narrower cylinder? I prefer to take the enlargement, on the stamp, of the upper part of the body for a crude indication of its particular significance; namely, as bearer of the décor (on which presently).

archaic image but may be ascribed to the imagination of the die-cutter. On top of the chiton, and down to the knees, is a tube-shaped ependytes which, in turn, is overlaid with a rich décor. Unlike the Anatolian images, it covers the chest only; below the waist the ependytes appears to have been decorated with a lozenge-pattern.[1] And this décor consists of three or four rows of ball-shaped pendants. The same arrangement occurs on one of the archaic Rhodian gold-plaques representing the winged 'Mistress of Beasts';[2] for the circles and half-circles, in granulation technique, on the chest of this figure are likely to signify the same kind of décor.

This statue of the Samian Hera thus appears to have shown several of the characteristic features which recur with the Sicilian terracottas; namely, the rectangular outline of the body; the ependytes on top of a long chiton and the peculiar décor covering the chest. Even so, this statue cannot be held to give an adequate idea of their postulated Eastern model; for while much of the detail and refinement which the coins indicate, may be attributed to successive die-cutters, there can be no doubt that, unlike the posited model, the image which they reflect rather than reproduce had arms. Arms, it is true, which look like an inorganic addition to its rigid rectangular shape; and indeed—being stretched forward from the elbows onward—they had to be supported by struts.[3] The literary tradition makes it possible to discern the more primitive state of this image, without the elaborations seen on the coins; for Kallimachos addresses it—one and the same image—as the originally 'unwrought plank' which became a 'well-wrought work' through 'Skelmian' art; concurrently, Aethlios, a Samian chronicler perhaps of the fifth century B.C.,[4] told that the ancient xoanon 'became a statue' ($\dot{\alpha}\nu\delta\rho\iota\alpha\nu\tau\omicron\epsilon\iota\delta\dot{\epsilon}c$ $\dot{\epsilon}\gamma\acute{\epsilon}\nu\epsilon\tau\omicron$) in the time of King Prokles; that is, in hoar antiquity.[5] This can hardly mean anything other than that, 'when the sculptor's art had progressed' (see the *Diegesis*), a sculptor was charged to transform the ancient abstract image into a more realistic one;[6] perhaps his name was Smilis,[7] for which 'Skelmis' (as has long since been recognized) is a synonym. The retention of very primitive features and their combination with more naturalistic ones thus become understandable.

---

[1] Thiersch (p. 10) inferred this detail from one of the coins (his Fig. 3) and commented (pp. 102 ff. and 202) at length upon its frequent occurrence, throughout the ages and together with its variant, the chess-board pattern, on ceremonial dress. Perhaps our earlier discussion of the lozenge pattern is here relevant.

[2] *B.M. Cat. of Jew.* no. 1107; Higgins, *Jewellery*, Pl. 19E.

[3] The struts—so it appears from the coins—were disguised by snakes coiled round them; cf. the Spartan ivory plaque pictured by Dawkins, Pl. XCIII. 2.—Archaic terracottas from Lokri, like Langlotz–Hirmer, Pl. 6 (cf. von Matt², Pls. 114 and 116), show the same posture.

[4] Quoted in the Kallimachean *Diegeseis* ad loc. (p. 105 Pf.) and by Clem. Al. *Protr.* iv. 46. 3. Aethlios may well have been Kallimachos' source.

[5] See Pausanias vii. 4. 2.

[6] Thus R. Pfeiffer, *Die neuen Diegeseis* (1934), p. 19.

[7] Paus. vii. 4. 4.; Clem. Al. *Protr.* iv. 47. 3; Athenagoras 17.

This then was 'the Goddess' of Samos, who retained her original place throughout Antiquity, with her primordial dignity unaffected by the erection of later and no doubt grander images. An 'unwrought' xoanon from origin, subsequently worked into a more elaborate—but still highly archaic—statue, her secondary, and permanent, appearance is reflected on the coins, while the primitive xoanon was of a kind with the archetype of the Sicilian terracottas. They indicate chiton, ependytes, and décor (the older ones schematically, the later ones elaborately—as do the Samian coins). On the Samian image these were not sculptured; for these are the garments and ornaments which, as the inscription tells, the Goddess actually 'had'. The breast-décor in particular may be found in the πρόϲλημμα παραλουργὲϲ ἀμφιθύϲανον (II, § 15, line 20). The word πρόϲλημμα is not known from anywhere else; which is not surprising if it denotes so rare an object. One may infer that the whole *kosmos* was attached to a piece of purple-coloured material which either was itself the ependytes or was fixed on to it.[1] The statue was normally clad and adorned with these paraphernalia (also the polos, μίτρη, is mentioned), and thus it is depicted on the coins; but they were taken off at the annual ceremonies, when it was bathed in the sea;[2] as was done with Athena's ancient image at the Attic Plynteria. The Rhodian gold-plaques previously referred to afford a welcome parallel in that among them there are representations of the same idol with and without its *kosmos*.[3] A similar ceremony in Sicily could account for the fact that among terracottas otherwise identical, some are with, and some without, décor;[4] anyhow, the general impression of one of the richly decorated terracottas and of the ancient Samian image is so similar as to put the close affinity between their archetypes beyond question.[5]

It would be strange indeed if the actual ancient image of the Samian Hera had afforded the model for the Sicilian terracottas. There is no

---

[1] D. Ohly (*Ath. Mitt.* lxviii (1953), 36 and 46) interprets πρόϲλημμα as a small jacket, such as is indicated on some ancient statues at Samos and elsewhere—but not on the Hera image as shown on the coins, where indeed the abundant décor leaves no room for it; besides, this kind of garment would naturally be called ἀμφίβλημα or περίβλημα; of which in fact the Goddess owned at least one (II, § 10, l. 18). By contrast, the word πρόϲλημμα suggests something 'attached to' something else (rather than 'worn around the body'). It is ἀμφιθύϲανον: this word could presumably indicate that the πρόϲλημμα had a border of tassels; but remembering the description, *Il.* 15. 309, of the aigis as ἀμφιδάϲεια because it is covered all over with θύϲανοι, and *Il.* 2. 448, where a hundred golden θύϲανοι are said to hang on it, 'each of them worth a hecatomb', one may consider whether θύϲανοι here designates the pendants by which the ependytes is 'covered all over'.   [2] Athenaeus 672 d.

[3] *B.M. Cat. of Jew.* nos. 1107 and 1126; our Plates 18a and b.

[4] The usual polos is lacking with the terracottas Louvre B552–4; one may infer a ceremony at which it too was removed. If it is acknowledged that on some figurines the very ependytes is not indicated (above, p. 118, n. 5), one may infer that it too was taken off at certain occasions; as was Athena's peplos at the Plynteria.

[5] Compare e.g. the coin Thiersch, Pl. III. 3 (cf. our Plate 18c) with Langlotz–Hirmer, Pl. 20 or Louvre B546 and B548.

specific connection between Samos and Sicily (apart from a lively import of perfumes in the sixth century); and the terracottas no more represent Hera than Athena. What, I hope, has come into view is, rather, the exact kind of image which the terracottas reproduce and develop. It was a xoanon, small as all these early wooden idols are known to have been; essentially a plank with no hands or feet but with the rich and peculiar apparel of ependytes and pectoral.[1] A remarkable fusion, in fact, of Greek and Anatolian traditions, yet one which arose most conveniently on the Eastern shores of the Aegaean.[2]

5. TELINES

Why was an Eastern image, or two, of this type repeated by figurines widely spread in Sicily and (practically) nowhere else? All art in Sicily, obviously, is dependent on Eastern models, and one may infer that the models of this type presented originally the same goddesses as their Sicilian descendants. Even so, it is puzzling that no Eastern terracottas exist which could have served as models for this Sicilian type; while for all others they exist by the hundreds and thousands. That Eastern image apparently was not, in the East, reproduced . . . Why not? And why was it reproduced in Sicily? And a further puzzle. That image was very ancient; it probably antedated the year 700 B.C. If it, or close replicas, reached Sicily at all—as evidently they did—they must have been brought there by some of the first colonists. If replicas of it were broadcast in Sicily at all—as indeed they were—, why did this not happen until about a hundred and fifty years later? Why indeed, on all the replicas of that highly archaic (or, rather, geometric) image, are the heads late-archaic or even early-classical? Bodies of, say, 700 B.C. with heads of 550, or 500 B.C. or even later.[3]

It may reasonably be held that for this early period our knowledge of Sicilian history and civilization is too scanty to admit of any answer to

[1] We may here discount the large veil peculiar to the Samian image; it constituted that *habitus nubentis* which Varro (*apud* Lactantius i. 17. 8) noted.

[2] The non-Greek root of the particular décor of these statues is underlined by its keen reception by the Phoenicians (as well as by the Jews), both in their replicas of Sicilian statuettes and on Tanit figurines like the one from Ibiza pictured by Harden, Pl. 78.

[3] Ancient, and even very ancient, types of representation are often retained in religious art—the Korinthian *ad asse* figurines are a case in point, and so are the Boeotian geometrizing terracottas—and, quite naturally, these representations change gradually, though slowly, in parallel with the developing style of art in general, and that particularly with regard to facial expression. The Christian crucifix is an obvious instance, and so are the Athenian Panathenaic amphorae; from our field we may refer to two Lokrian types which will be discussed later (below, p. 160f.). A specific motive for the retention of a particular ancient type is evident in some of the instances just quoted and is likely to have existed in every case. The type under discussion has distinctive features which invite the search for its origin and are bound to guide it. They are: its sudden emergence and impact, with no antecedents, in either Sicily or the East, to either its primitive body, with ependytes, or its contemporary head, and still less to the combination of both.

these questions. Equally reasonably, though, it may be urged that the facts just summarized bespeak some significant event. The sudden emergence and the wide and lasting appeal of these terracottas is not sufficiently explained by the assumption that one day, about 550 B.C., some potter hit upon the idea of producing this odd type of figurine, combining an Eastern geometric body with contemporary heads, and that the product of his fancy met with outstanding success. This success presupposes an outstanding appeal, and this appeal, in turn, presupposes some particular fact or experience, which caused Greeks all over Sicily to hail these strange, new-and-old images as particularly adequate representations of the 'chthonic deities'. This granted, it may still be held that our ignorance prevents us from identifying that pregnant fact. Actually, however, we possess one piece of information which seems to fit all facets of the puzzle.

The terracottas in question, while found all over Sicily, are so frequent at Akragas and its mother-city, Gela, that their origin has often, and reasonably, been sought there. In addition to these and other *Kleinfunde*, the Santuario Ctonico as well as San Biagio provide evidence of an ancient and outstanding cult, at Akragas, of the goddesses represented by these particular terracottas. For Gela, its mother-city, there exists, in addition to a whole series of such sanctuaries,[1] a notable piece of literary evidence.

Herodotus, in an often quoted passage (vii. 153), tells the following. One of the founders of Gela (his name, Deinomenes, is known from elsewhere)[2] came from the small island of Telos, which lies off the promontory Triopion (the place of the famous Knidian Demeter sanctuary). Gelon, the tyrant of Gela and Syracuse, was his descendant. The priesthood of the 'chthonic deities' was hereditary in the family ever since one of Gelon's ancestors, Telines by name (obviously called after the island), had been rewarded with it because he had put an end to some civic strife 'using not any power of (armed) men but the 'sacred things' (ἱρά) of these deities'. Herodotus professes himself ignorant as to whence Telines obtained these *sacra*, but we may trust the statement in another source[3] that the first Deinomenes had brought them to Sicily from Triopion.

---

[1] Cf. above, p. 90, n. 1.

[2] *Etym. Magn.* s.v. Γέλα.

[3] Schol. Pind. *Pyth.* ii. 27b. The passage as a whole is indeed, as Drachmann ad loc. notes, absurd; but the statement about the *sacra* brought by Deinomenes from Triopion—which is irrelevant to the scholiast's silly argument—must rest on an older tradition. A wealth of information about this famous sanctuary was at the command of Alexandrian scholars (Kallimachos' sixth hymn is one illustration of it). Even if an Alexandrian commentator on Pindar had merely inferred this statement from Herodotus, he would be likely to have been correct, for his description of Telos as lying 'off Triopion'—which is by no means the most natural—may imply that Herodotus knew of the tradition that the *sacra* originated there but was sceptical about it. To us, on the other hand, this tradition has the appeal of intrinsic probability.

'Sacrorum nomine tam Graeci quam Romani signa et imagines deorum omnemque sacram suppellectilem dignari solent.'[1] The ἱρά which Telines wielded were sacred images and symbols; he must then have been a priest of the 'chthonic deities' even before his historic exploit, and if these *sacra* had been handed down among the Deinomenids from the days of their founder-ancestor, this must have been their family-cult. If none the less Telines was rewarded with the position of 'hierophant', this can only mean (as has been concluded long ago)[2] that the family-cult of the Deinomenids was received into the state-cult at Gela and they became its hereditary officers.

Telines' exploit must have left a profound impression; seeing that Herodotus was told of it so much later, and with some picturesque detail; there is in fact no other event in early Sicilian history of which a comparably realistic tradition survives. And indeed: a revolution which threatened to disrupt the Geloan state—part of the population had left the city and occupied a fortress, Maktorion, nearby—overcome not by force of arms but by the 'chthonic deities' and their servant: this must have impressed the people of Sicily as a miracle demonstrating their power.

The cult, now public, required a sanctuary; the sanctuary, images of the saving goddesses. Those ancient images which the first Deinomenes had brought from the Triopion (replicas no doubt of xoana in the 'chthonic' sanctuary there); which had been handed down in the secrecy of the family-cult of his descendants; and which had proved their efficacy at the day of Maktorion: they, and none but they, could provide the type for the new images. They were themselves too small—had not Telines carried them with him to the insurgents?—and too archaic to inhabit the new public sanctuary; hence they returned, so one may assume, to the domestic shrine from which they had been taken on that one, momentous occasion. But the artist who fashioned the new images was charged religiously to reproduce their over-all shape and décor; as in past days Smilis had done when he was set to renew that image of the Samian Hera to which the xoana from the Triopion must have been closely similar. The rigid and geometrical form of their bodies was to be retained, and combined with heads expressive of the character of the goddesses; with a differentiation of which there cannot have been a hint in the Triopian originals. The artist achieved this difficult task in a manner which must excite admiration, for he succeeded in amalgamating the old and the new into a convincing and organic whole. He worked most probably in clay; for, since Sicily has no marble, baked clay, richly

---

[1] C. A. Lobeck, *Aglaophamus*, i (1829), p. 51; cf. *Hermes*, xci (1963), 233.

[2] Holm, i. 153 and H. Stein (1866) *ad* Hdt. vii. 153, l. 16 are unlikely to have been the first to state this conclusion.

painted, was used there predominantly also for large statues;[1] and he devised for Demeter that round, friendly face, developed from Ionian models, which so fully brings out the goodness of the mother and protectress of all that lives and grows. For Persephone he created that narrow and severe face which characterizes the Goddess of Death and for which I for one cannot indicate any antecedent.[2]

It is understandable if these new images made an overwhelming impression. Gleaming with the bright paint which accentuated their strange garments and the patterns on them, as well as their wonder-working jewellery; with faces expressive, powerfully as never before, of their profoundest essence: here they were, the goddesses who had shown their saving might by the miracle of Maktorion; strangely remote in their archaic and ritualistic bodily appearance and finery yet close to their idea as it was alive in the hearts of the contemporary worshippers. Thus these images are likely to have exercised a similar appeal as did, later on, those at Florence, Lourdes, or Nizhnii-Novgorod. Thereafter, what wonder if people all over Sicily craved for replicas of them, and coroplasts, for about a century, repeated, varied, enriched (or corrupted) the Geloan models? It is, moreover, highly likely that, apart from small terracottas, large-size replicas were also dedicated in many sanctuaries;[3] and that these too would develop and vary the basic pattern. These by turns could be imitated, more or less freely, by the producers of small terracottas; and an endless series of variations on the Geloan theme could thus originate.

A guess, all this, admittedly.[4] If it is credited with some probability,

---

[1] A full list (though now no longer complete) of the Sicilian evidence for large terracotta statues is in W. Deonna, *Les statues de terre cuite* (1908), pp. 45 ff.; cf. Dunbabin, p. 275.

[2] Perhaps Demeter was represented seated beside Persephone standing; cf. above, p. 121. Parallels for this combination exist; cf. above, p. 109, n. 4, and also the Geneleos group in Samos; not to mention typical later reliefs and vase paintings representing these very goddesses; see e.g. Metzger, *Recherches* . . . , pp. 21 f. (nos. 41 and 44), 34 ff., and 42 f.

[3] Our 'second Demeter-type' in particular would reasonably be traced to a new, more classical, variety which could well have been a cult-image—I will not guess, where.

If this hypothesis is considered, the dates of Telines' exploit and of the earliest terracottas of this type have to be equated. Both are conjectural. For the latter cf. above, p. 121. As for Telines, his date has been progressively lowered by successive scholars; and indeed Herodotus could hardly have been supplied with the curious and realistic detail which he transmits, if the event which made Telines famous took place (as used to be assumed) in the seventh century (thus still Dunbabin, p. 64). Recently, though, R. van Compernolle (*Études de chronologie et d'historiographie sicéliotes* (1960), pp. 393 ff.) has given reasons which seem cogent to me for regarding Telines as the grandfather of Gelon. A date about 540 B.C. for the events under discussion therewith becomes an acceptable possibility.

Addendum: This suggestion has been borne out in a welcome manner by P. Orlandini's recent results at Bitalemi (above, p. 106, n. 5). The 'Telines figurines' appear, all of them, above the date-line of '550 o poco dopo'; the terracottas immediately below are Rhodian import. What is more, this 'date-line' consists in a thick, artificial layer of compressed clay, which seals off the loose sand below and serves as a base for sacred buildings, where previously there had been an open temenos only. Exactly the same—'una completa trasformazione'—happened, perhaps the class of terracottas which occasioned it might henceforth be termed the 'Telines figurines'. It has been hard enough to write about them without falling back upon the precarious 'Athana Lindia'.[1]

6. THE PECTORAL

A new facet of their religious significance has at any rate come into view; its full appreciation requires, in conclusion, a brief consideration of their characteristic pectorals. They are, as has been seen, much more than mere ornaments. Impressive by their size and sheen—the gold on the original images intimated, no doubt, by bright paint on the terracottas— they were an integral part of the hieratic apparel. One may compare the breast-shields, covered with divine images and symbols, which were worn by priests of Attis, Kybele, and Sabazios,[2] for these προϲτηθίδια καὶ τύποι[3] were imitations of the décor worn by Kybele herself.[4] Among the extant illustrations of this custom a Pergamene statue of Kybele[5] is to us of special interest, for it exhibits, on the middle of the body, a triangular shield covered with ten roughly oval elevations[6] which are much like those on many 'Telines figurines'. A similar shield, but rectangular and with thrice three globules, covers the breast of a fragmentary, post-classical, terracotta statuette (Kybele? 'from Asia Minor?').[7] These, then, are some further pointers at the Eastern element in our terracottas. Their

at the same time, at the chthonic sanctuary in Predio Sola, and also the large, similar sanctuary at Madonna dell'Allemanna was built at this time (for the date see D. Adamasteanu, *Not. Scav.* (1956), 387). Three suburban chthonic sanctuaries, to the South, East, and North of Gela, newly built 'between 550 and 540 B.C.' and 'quasi contemporaneamente' (*Kokalos*, xii (1966), 16 f., 24, and 33 f.)! The Deinomenids evidently took their new public priesthood seriously . . .

[1] One last argument against Blinkenberg's thesis may, in conclusion, stand here. Its main prop was in the fact, twice reported in the Lindian Chronicle, that the local image was provided with ὅρμοί. These he identified with the 'pectoral' on the Sicilian terracottas. But ὅρμοί are 'chains'; the word could suitably denote necklaces, even large ones (so on the 'ancient image' of Athena on the Athenian Akropolis); but hardly this vast décor, of which the holding 'chains'—if such there were—would form the least significant part. The obvious term would be κόϲμος, or κόϲμος προϲτηθίδιοϲ, or even προϲτηθίδια, or θύϲανοι.

[2] Cf. V. Müller, *Röm. Mitt.* xxiv (1919), 93 ff.; Thiersch, p. 134, n. 1 (both referring to Blinkenberg, *Archaeol. Studien* (1904), p. 113). The standard example is the Roman relief of an *archigallus* in the Museo Capitolino, pictured e.g. in the *Bilderanhang* of H. Lietzmann's *Handbuch zum N.T.* vol. i (1912), Pl. VII; another one is pictured *Oest. Jh.* xviii (1915), p. 75, Fig. 47.

[3] Polybius xxi. 37. 5 Hultsch (xxii. 20. 6 Dindorf); cf. Herodotus iv. 76. 4 ἐκδηϲάμενοϲ ἀγάλματα.

[4] Cornutus, *Theol. Graec.* 6 (καρδίαν . . .) καὶ ἄλλουϲ τινὰϲ τύπουϲ περὶ τὸ ϲτῆθοϲ αὐτῆϲ περιτιθέαϲιν.

[5] The subject of V. Müller's article quoted in note 2 above, illustrated ib., p. 83.

[6] Their arrangement (4, 3, 2, 1) suggested a Pythagorean symbolism to O. Weinreich, *Röm. Mitt.*, xxxvi/xxxvii (1921-2), 153—in vain. It is the natural result of the triangular shape of the shield, which recurs on the relief of Zeus Stratios (below, p. 140, n. 2), with a similar arrangement of the 'breasts', yet without any Pythagorean symbolism.

[7] Thiersch, Pl. XXXIX. 2; cf. ib., pp. xviii and 152 (on wrong track); Winter, ii. 57. 1.

apparel belonged originally to the great Asianic goddess in several of her many individualizations; their 'pectoral' in particular was adopted by Greeks for the model statues at the Triopion (if our hypothesis be allowed), as well as for the Samian Hera, in combination with the ependytes and not as a separate plaque like those worn by Kybele;[1] even so, it is in the same category.

The pendants are, on the terracottas, often indicated in a summary fashion and, besides, hard to identify on many pieces which were cast in 'tired' moulds. They must still have conveyed, if not an exact likeness of the décor on a particular cult-image, at any rate an impression concordant with the notions of the goddess which the figurines represented. On the Samian Hera as well as on the Sicilian terracottas the décor covers the space which on the Roman statues of the Ephesia is covered by that repulsive cluster of breasts; these then have to be understood as a naturalistic interpretation of the older, globular pendants. One may hesitate to accept this interpretation as correct, seeing that the globular décor is not worn by female deities only: it recurs also on the image of the 'Zeus of Labraunda', both on local coins and on a relief from Tegea;[2] one need hardly recur, though, to a hypothetical bisexuality of Asianic deities to envisage the possibility that a geometrical symbol indicative of fecundity could have been applied to deities of either sex.[3]

On the Sicilian terracottas it is, in a rigidly globular form, not frequent;[4] but the discs, which are frequent, are sometimes so bulky[5] that they may be taken for the same symbol; moreover, the impression left by the mass of figurines whose chests are covered with rows of similar bulky objects, cylindrical or oblong, pointed or rounded, is the same. These objects often remind one of the manner in which various fruits are represented on Lokrian reliefs,[6] so that one may feel tempted to interpret them as apples, pomegranates, pears, or almonds. We can hardly presume to decide whether, at the time, these non-naturalistic, or half-naturalistic,

[1] The same holds good, according to Thiersch (pp. 120 f.), for the ḥoshen of the Hebrew High-priest; its development into a separate plaque occurred later; as in the Greek instances just mentioned. It must however be admitted that on some late 'Telines figurines', and especially on Punic and Cyrenaic imitations (such as B.M. 1471–3; Louvre C182; Thiersch, Pl. XXXIX. 1), the bulky décor could easily be taken for a separate 'pectoral'; a pectoral adorned with 'breasts').

[2] Both dating from the fourth century B.C.; see A. H. Smith, *JHS*, xxxvi (1916), 65 ff.; our Plate 18*d*; M. Meurer, *Röm. Mitt.* xxix (1914), 204 ff.; the coins also *apud* Thiersch, Pl. IV. 9–11; the relief, in J. T. Wood, *Discoveries at Ephesus* (1877), 270.

[3] One may compare the problematical terracotta fragment from Taranto (pictured in A. Levi, *Le terracotte . . . di Napoli* (1926), p. 27, no. 93, Fig. 29) representing a reclining youth adorned with a necklace and large pendants which look like breasts rather than like 'acorns'.

[4] See, however, Gàbrici, Pl. LVII. 5 and LXII. 8 (= van Ufford, Fig. 33).

[5] e.g. B.M. 1109; Blinkenberg, *L'image* . . . , p. 27, Fig. 4.

[6] See e.g. the basket at the feet of the fruit-gatherer on the tablet pictured in von Matt[2], Pl. 137 and in *Ausonia*, iii (1908), 224 f., Figs. 73 f.; the reproduction, in clay, of a similar basket, found at Medma, is exhibited in the Museo Nazionale, Reggio, vitrine 10.

shapes were felt, consciously or subconsciously, to suggest fruits or the female breast—or non-material symbols; but a general intimation of fecundity is felt spontaneously and unambiguously.

This intimation is substantiated by those figurines whose pendants are given the shape of particular concrete objects, such as corn-vessels and wine-jars or the heads of bulls, rams, or sileni. These can indeed be paralleled from actual Greek and Etruscan jewellery; but this particular selection from current types unequivocally points in the direction which appeared to be intimated by the more abstract pendants.[1] The pectorals, then, of these Sicilian terracottas are not mere trinkets but indicate, symbolically, the essential character, or δύναμις, of the Goddess; as does the profusion of sculptured symbols on the garments of the Roman statues of Asianic goddesses and gods.

With the 'Telines figurines', the essential aspect thus intimated is— Life, and all that produces, maintains, and enriches it.[2] This is perfectly natural with images of Demeter, but most remarkable with Persephone. For here are not Demeter and Kore, the Eleusinian pair, both together the bringers of rich harvests; not Mother and Daughter, so similar to each other that they could be described, at Lindos, as Damateres.[3] So they may have been at the Triopion; but not in Sicily, for there they are differentiated as the Mother of all Life and the Queen of Death. The great artist who, in sixth-century Gela, so profoundly contrasted them: how could he adopt this identical symbolism? And the people of Sicily, who through many decades continued to dedicate to the two goddesses replicas—varied but always retaining the type—of this great model: how could they be satisfied with this paradox—the Queen of Death, Persephone: Giver of Life?[4]

---

[1] I am not sure about the purport of one frequent form; namely, the discs; though perhaps they should generally be regarded as equivalent to the globules just mentioned. Some students indeed have regarded them as representing Kybele's tympana, but the rarity, in Sicily at this period, of indubitable representations of this goddess is against this interpretation. And, after all, discs are about the most frequent item in all jewellery.—A few terracottas have a crescent-shape pendant. At its meaning in Sicily one can only guess. It too is of Eastern origin; Greeks took it over from the VIII–VII century onward (Higgins, *Jewellery*, p. 155). W. M. Ramsay, when discussing its occurrences in Roman times (*Journ. Rom. Stud.* viii (1918), 141 ff.) doubted whether it generally symbolized the moon.

[2] This symbolism may be underlined by the large ornamental pattern which often covers the shoulder-clasps of these figurines. In some cases (von Matt[2], Pl. 106, twice; also Orsi, *Gela*, p. 711, Fig. 537) it is that two-spiral motif whose occurrence, at Castelluccio, occasioned our inquiry. One may at any rate ask whether Greeks of the sixth century B.C. were aware of its primeval symbolical meaning—which, after all, we found surviving in our own days.

[3] See M. P. Nilsson, *Opuscula*, ii. 552 on the Hellenistic dedication to the Damateres with Zeus Damatrios.

[4] The fact (noted above, p. 125) that the décor is often absent from Persephone, but not from Demeter, statuettes may be indicative of a consciousness of this paradox with a proportion of the worshippers.

(g) PROTOMES ('MASCHERE')

Neither designation fits this type precisely, but the former is preferable because it does not invite inappropriate associations. The type is exceedingly frequent in Rhodes; it may have originated and developed there;[1] at any rate, its wide spread over the shores of the Aegean (e.g. Klazomenai, Elaious, Olynthos) and beyond (especially Boeotia and Athens) is indicative of a flourishing export-centre in the East. It came into use, so it seems, in the last quarter of the sixth century[2] and continued, in some places, down to the age of Alexander the Great. In its most elementary form it consists of a head—it is always a female head—applied to a flat plaque; of this, though, I know only one instance, and that in Sicily.[3] In the normal form, as described by Blinkenberg,[4] the plaque—much higher than broad, with parallel sides—is concave more often than flat; its rounded upper edge coincides with the veil which covers the head (or, usually, a diadem on the head) and forms a broad rim, on both sides, down to the straight lower edge.[5] Gradually, the outer sides were curved more and more so as to intimate neck, shoulders, and body;[6] finally, in the second half of the fifth century, the (upper part of the) body and the garment were shaped and arms added; often with the traditional oriental gesture of the fingers touching the breasts.[7] Like all terracottas, these too were richly painted, and some extant samples of the older kind enable us to visualize their original appearance; with their features, and especially eyes and lips, vividly brought out, the hair set off, the veil covered with decorative patterns and, sometimes at any rate, a necklace or two painted on the shapeless surface underneath the head.[8] Very often a hole at the top indicates that they were intended to be hung up on the wall of a temple or on a tree in a temenos.

[1] Blinkenberg, i. 36 and 591, regarded the majority of the Lindian protomes, in view of the quality of their clay, as import from 'Ionia' (whatever that much abused word may mean). If another place than Rhodes is supposed to have been the centre of fabrication and export—a place so far unidentified—it could be assumed to have supplied the models for certain Sicilian types which do not recur in Rhodes; especially for the 'round faced' one presently to be mentioned.

[2] See P. Orlandini, *Mon. Ant.* xlvi (1963), 33, n. 1.

Addendum: On the basis of the Bitalemi stratigraphy this date will have to be moved back, for the Rhodian originals, by *c.* thirty years, since such have been found within, and close to, that layer of clay which establishes the 'date-line' of *c.* 550–540 B.C.

[3] Gàbrici, Pl. XLIX. 2. For an older (and unrelated?) Attic type see now Higgins, *Greek Terracottas*, p. 44.

[4] *Lindos*, i. 588 ff.   [5] e.g. B.M. 135; Louvre B215 ff.

[6] e.g. Blinkenberg, nos. 2513–16.

[7] e.g. B.M. 237 ff. In Sicily (Palermo) I noted only one 'maschera' of this type (Winter, p. 251. 2).

[8] Gàbrici, pp. 218 f. with Fig. 113; Blinkenberg, i. 592 and, better, *Clara Rhodos*, iv (1931), 228, no. 113 with Pl. IV; also B.M. 137.

Mistaking these strange objects for masks, the venerable Ed. Gerhard[1] proclaimed them images of Demeter Kidaria; but how could the implement of an obscure cult in Arkadia[2] have spread, from the East, all over the Aegean and to Sicily? None the less Gerhard was widely followed.[3] Going to the opposite extreme, Blinkenberg[4] declared them to be mere 'abbreviations' of complete statuettes and, like these, representations of human worshippers (if nothing else, the fact that many among the later ones repeat the gesture of the oriental *déesse nue* ought to have made him pause). Of late, P. Orlandini has incisively opposed both these views.[5] While still describing them as 'masks', he asserted that 'generally they represent one of the great chthonic deities, Demeter or Kore–Persephone', at any rate in Sicily, though elsewhere they could have represented other goddesses.

These are not masks. It is implicitly wrong in defining them to disregard the greater, shapeless part below and around the head. The impression made by Egyptian mummies with the portrait of the dead and, still more, by Phoenician anthropoid sarcophagi is undeniably similar. Orsi[6] would derive the 'maschere' from these; but I will not burden the text with the vexed and unsettled question of origins.[7] The objects in the form in which they emerge in Sicily at almost every excavation, must themselves reveal their purpose and meaning.

While there can be no doubt that this kind of terracotta, like all others, originated far away to the East, the hundreds (and probably thousands) of Sicilian samples, so the experts assure us, were all of them made locally[8]; and while those found elsewhere repeat a very few standard forms of face—in the main, a rather triangular, narrow one[9] and,

---

[1] *Ann. Istit.* 1857, 212.

[2] At Pheneos: Paus. viii. 15. 3. *Κίδαρις*, the Persian (!) word for a high head-dress (tiara), suggests a polos. The protomes, as a rule, have no polos (but a diadem); if any, it is not high.

[3] P. Marconi even invented a 'Sanctuary of Demeter Kidaria' on Rhodes in which, according to him, these 'masks' were 'exceedingly frequent' (*Agr. arc.*, p. 56, cf. *Agrigento*, p. 174).

[4] Lindos, i. 37 and 589 f.

[5] *Mon. Ant.* xlvi (1963), 30 f. (with literature).

[6] *Mon. Ant.* i (1892), 936; similarly *Gela*, p. 687.

[7] Blinkenberg, i. 36 and 589, sought their origin in Cyprus; for still another hypothesis see H. R. N. Smith, *Hesperia*, viii (1949), 353.—If one looks for Eastern prototypes, Phoenicia itself does not seem—apart from the anthropoid sarcophagi—to provide usable evidence, and the Punic samples are derived from Sicily; thus e.g. the one pictured by Harden, p. 198, Fig. 61: its Rhodian prototype is in Blinkenberg, no. 2522; while Fig. 60, with an Egyptian head, may be a Punic adaptation of the Greek shape. The same may hold good for Harden, Pl. 77; unless indeed the vague date 'seventh to sixth century B.C.' implies that it antedates the origin of the Greek protomes; in which case it could intimate the existence of Phoenician antecedents.

[8] Van Ufford 72, quoted approvingly by Orlandini, *Mon. Ant.* xlvi (1963), 33; now however see above, p. 142, n. 2, *Addendum*.

[9] Such as B.M. 134, Higgins, *Greek Terracottas*, Pl. 26A.

subsequently, a full and even fattish one[1]—with little variation and to the point of dreariness,[2] the Sicilian exhibit an amazing variety of shape and expression. They were of course produced in the mass, many of them with so little care as to be void of significance;[3] even so, it is evident that the coroplasts made, and their public welcomed, ever fresh attempts at conveying an all but inexpressible divine reality in its diverse and even contradictory aspects. The extant tokens of this endeavour deserve an exhaustive study; it is really not enough to group these protomes according to e.g. the rendering of the hair (covered by the veil, or indicated by 'dog-teeth', or waving lines, etc.). This cannot here be attempted; but the examination of a few outstanding samples may, even so, serve our purpose.[4]

The impression which these 'protomes' convey is largely determined by that specific feature, the empty space below the head, which puts them in a different class from masks.[5] Shape growing out of shapelessness, a head hovering over nothingness: you cannot but sense therein a symbolic significance.[6] It stands out most strikingly in what appears to be the oldest class, dating from the last third of the sixth century. It is characterized by the round, and practically circular shape of the face (a set of near forty of these has been found at the Predio Sola, Gela;[7] many more have come to light at other sites in Gela[8] and elsewhere[9]). To regard this type as the continuation of the round-faced loveliness of the 'Samian korai',[10] or the friendliness of the 'Rodia seduta', is to discount, for the sake of one superficial common feature, the complete difference of character and expression, down to palpable detail in the rendering of lips,

---

[1] Such as B.M. 141, Higgins, ib. Pl. 26B. This, as far as I know, does not occur in Sicily (even Gàbrici, Pl. LVI. 8 and Mon. Ant. i (1891), Pl. IX. 13, from Megara Hyblaia, are different).

[2] There are, it is true, some exceptions; e.g. the old woman, Blinkenberg, no. 2510 (if indeed this head comes from a protome) or the smiling young girl, ib. 2508; but compared with the range of variety in Sicily these mean little.

[3] e.g. Gàbrici, Pl. XLVIII. 1; LVIII. 7.

[4] Here again, the way has been shown by Orsi (Gela, 685 ff.). The profundity of his remarks cannot be rivalled; but significant new types have been discovered since he wrote: they tell of aspects which could not be realized sixty years ago.

[5] The gradual elaboration, on specimens a century and more recent, of this space into the semblance of a realistic bust is a corruption of the original, symbolic concept of these 'protomes' no less than in the case of the 'faceless goddess' of Cyrene.

[6] 'Le type a été très en vogue,—probablement parce qu'il était facile à fabriquer, donc bon marché!': thus van Ufford (p. 72, justly censured by P. Orlandini, Mon. Ant. xlvi (1963), 30, n. 9). As though there had not been elaborate 'masks' which must have been quite as costly as ordinary statuettes! And average and inferior statuettes, cheaper than a good 'mask'!

[7] Orlandini ib., pp. 10 ff.; Pls. I–V (excepting a few items); our Plate 19a.

[8] Orsi, Gela, Pl. XLIX, centre; Pl. L, 4 (our Plate 19c; Not. Scav. (1962), 386, Fig. 63.

[9] Louvre, B563 (Selinus).

[10] As van Ufford (p. 45) does; cf., e.g., B.M. 57–62.

nose, cheek, not to mention the body. Presumably this class of protomes, too, derives from some 'Ionian' model;[1] the closest analogy known to me is in the famous fragment of a marble head from Ephesus now in the British Museum;[2] and how different is even this! These 'maschere' then must speak for themselves; be it only through Orsi's or Orlandini's photographs.

Those heads hovering above nothingness: they are not young not old; they are ageless and outside time. We spoke, inadvertently, of their 'expression' and 'character'—but there is no 'character', nor 'expression'; not joy, nor sadness; not kindness, nor any menace. But an immense seriousness . . . What here emerges above nothingness is—Nothingness itself. The totally different, the absolute otherness: here it is become shape, and even a face.

Hence, its geometric and abstract structure and, therewith, its mask-like appearance; mask-like not as the representation of this or that individuality human or divine, but as the chilling concretization of what is behind it; namely, the naught. Formally, and not formally only, it compares with the mask of Medusa; except that on these protomes there are no terrifying paraphernalia; what they convey is too serious for terror. A symbol they are, final, like the faceless images at Cyrene. Sometimes they smile, but their smile 'non è espressione di sentimento' . . . (Orsi).[3]

It is on the lips also of the grandest and most elaborate piece of this class, the 'regina delle maschere archaiche' (justly so styled by its finder, the excavator of the Predio Sola),[4] again without imparting as much as a hint of 'sentimento' to the soulless, symmetrical face. This figure has a trait peculiar to itself; namely, below the head but nearer to the lower edge than to it, the plastic rendering of two horizontal rows of pendants touching, but not exceeding, the edge of the broad veil on either side. It has already been said[5] that necklaces of an everyday kind were painted on some, and perhaps many, Rhodian protomes; but this is different. The pendants in the upper row are clearly bull-heads; those below are schematized and hence not easily identified ('pendagli piriformi con goccia sferica', says the editor); perhaps they represent amphorae;[6] between them are small, raised discs. This then is a pectoral like those

[1] Cf. above, p. 142, n. 1.

[2] D. G. Hogarth, *Excavations at Ephesus* (1908), Pl. 16. 6; E. Langlotz, *Frühgriech. Bild-hauerschulen* (1927), Pl. 61; G. M. A. Richter, *Greek Archaic Art* (1949), Fig. 265. The type is repeated on the terracotta Louvre B249.

[3] *Gela*, p. 686. Orsi makes it clear also how the original colouring would not soften but deepen their impact. This can now be checked by originals with their paint preserved; see above, p. 142, n. 8.

[4] Orlandini, ib., p. 19, no. 31 with Figs. 11–13; our Plate 19*b*.

[5] Above, p. 142.

[6] The interpretation of these and similar pendants as phalli—which I have once or twice

worn by the 'Telines statuettes'; the arrangement, too, is the same, and the space between the edges of the veil can be taken to suggest the ependytes. We know the import of this décor. The question on which the preceding section ended therewith poses itself with enhanced force: what does it mean that the symbol of unquenchable life is worn by this ultimate impersonation of the antithesis of Life? For, surely, the 'regina delle maschere' does not represent Kore, the friendly corn-maiden.

We may approach the meaning of this *coniunctio oppositorum* in considering other protomes which reveal other facets of the same reality. P. Marconi unearthed, in the potter's workshop by the so-called Temple of the Dioscuri (that is, in the Santuario Ctonico) at Agrigento, the mould of a 'maschera' which is pictured, together with a cast taken from it, by von Matt.[1] It belongs to a type frequent in Rhodes and elsewhere.[2] The first Sicilian replicas may have been simply 'taken off' from an imported specimen; but this Agrigentine mould yields a figure with an expression of its own. The plaque remains plain, the head unadorned (but for ear-rings) with no plastic indication of the hair. It is no longer circular but, from the temples down to the chin, almost triangular. 'Volti monotoni e rigidi, compenetrati di un arcano mistero': Orsi's characterization applies even here; yet with a difference. Here is no longer a mask-like abstraction, but no individualized face either. Even so, this is a face; the face of a deity, youngish, beautiful in its regularity and anything but void of 'sentimento'. There is not indeed any emotion about it; the 'arcano mistero' which Orsi perceived in his different finds: here it is present as a boundless sadness; a sadness unrelieved by any outburst. For, it constitutes the very essence of this image, its absoluteness, beauty, and majesty. Another realization, then, of Persephone.

The aspect here realized recurs, enhanced, in two other works which are not protomes. One is a statuette, 32 cm. high, of a seated goddess which was found at Carubazza (Gela) together with other terracottas which we have previously mentioned.[3] It is, formally, a development, so far unparalleled, of the 'Telines' type, the body being very similar in par-

heard suggested—seems less than probable to me. That wine-jars are meant—here as well as in many similar instances—is likely in view of indubitable representations of vessels on some figurines (e.g. von Matt[1], Pl. 106) and of extant archaic pendants thus shaped (e.g. G. Becatti, *Oreficerie antiche* (1955), Pl. LXXVII, no. 313).

[1] Von Matt[1], pl. 105. If Marconi, *Agr. arc.* p. 174, Fig. 104 represents the same, the difference between the two pictures would amount to a devastating indictment of the unreliability of photographic reproduction. Marconi, though, speaks of 'talune matrici'; perhaps, then, he reproduced a different one from von Matt, though one of the same type. Anyhow, von Matt pictures the face looking downward, and this is correct, for this impression was bound to arise when the plaque was hung on a wall, as it was intended to be.

[2] See B.M., no. 134 with Higgins's comment (cf. ib., 108), and G. M. A. Richter, *Greek Archaic Art*, 1949, Fig. 266, both from Rhodes. Another Sicilian instance comes from Feudo Nobile, Gela (*Not. Scav.* (1960), 233, Fig. 22. 1).

[3] *Not. Scav.* (1956), 245 with Fig. 4 (D. Adamasteanu); cf. above, pp. 123 n. 6., 125, n. 4.

ticular to that of the 'round-faced' Demeter figurine from the same place;[1] the arms, though, are intimated by sleeves[2] and the chiton and the feet are rendered with greater detail than is usual with this type. The goddess wears the polos and, on her chest, a row of pendants like those on the Demeter figurine just mentioned.[3] The wonder about this statuette is its head. It is in the tradition of Polycletus.[4] Regular, great features; a nobility beyond words; remoteness and sublimity; absolute beauty in absolute sorrow. Persephone.

The other—created a generation earlier—is the head from a terracotta statue of near life size from Agrigento (now in Palermo) which is likely to have come from the pediment of a temple in the city of Persephone.[5] Not even Hirmer's mastery has succeeded, on two excellent plates, in capturing its essence, and I have exhausted my vocabulary. Go and see— that transcendent beauty frozen in the breath of the other world; those lips that have answered the embrace of the King of the Dead; and feel the glance of the eyes which have taken in what no one living sees.

The transcendent reality which the oldest protomes conveyed in a sym-bolic form is present in these masterpieces in the person of the goddess and the intimation of her myth. What they hint, or imply, becomes explicit, if on a less profound plane, in the combination of many other works which exhibit partial aspects of the same infinite phenomenon.

The wide range of character and quality which distinguishes the Selinuntine production in general stands out also in the protomes; they sometimes show, besides, a type of head which recurs on other kinds of terracottas. We may consider some significant varieties, drawing occasionally also on other sites.

The mask-like oldest type is lacking at the Gaggera. A roundish type of face does indeed occur;[6] but it is a face and not an abstraction; serious, remote, and marked, so it seems, by an overwhelming experience. The same head recurs with a type of standing figure[7] of which very many

---

[1] Ib., p. 244, Fig. 2a.

[2] Fore-arms, not originally belonging, have been crudely fixed on so as to hold some object now lost. The sleeves on the other hand are of the usual kind, with herringbone folds, as e.g. on Louvre B546 and B.M. 1109.

[3] The seat too appears to have been of the kind usual with 'Telines statuettes' but, judging by the photograph, there was no indication of an ependytes. Most of the middle part of the figurine is lost; but the dress apparently was a long chiton with sleeves, and no more.

[4] Chronologically there is no difficulty about this; the site yielded coins of the age of Timoleon, as well as the terracotta of the ('second') Athena Lindia, dependent on Phidias' Promachos (above, p. 126, n. 2).

[5] Langlotz–Hirmer, Pls. VIII and 44. Langlotz's comment on Hirmer's photographs is here, as always, instructive—and still, in a way, disappointing. For, what help towards the appreciation of this great work comes from references to Smyrnaean coin-types and a terracotta-head, perhaps thirty years older, at Olympia, seeing that a terracotta statue for a temple in Akragas obviously was made there and witnesses to the tendencies of those for whom it was made?   [6] Gàbrici, Pl. L. 1.   [7] Ib., 7; cf. 4.

fragments were collected; this, then, must represent Persephone (or Pasikrateia, as she seems to have been called at Selinus); there is, moreover, a related type of statuette[1] which is marked by the same expression of unapproachable remoteness. All these wear a high polos. Some of the protomes from Bitalemi likewise deviate from the earlier mask-like scheme. Theirs is an elongated type of face, of similar severity;[2] even so, the transition from abstract symbolism to individualization implies a decisive lessening of the distance between deity and man. Some cognate protomes[3] even show the hint of a smile, and it is no longer the smile of Medusa, bringer of death.

Severity gives way to quiet, deep sadness on the life-size face of another protome from the Gaggera,[4] fashioned about the turn of the sixth century; the face of a young woman whose loveliness seems veiled by a knowledge which dims this world of light and life: she gazes into it, through it, beyond it. Another one[5]—'di importazione ionica' according to Gàbrici, but repeatedly copied and varied locally[6]—similar in expression, is even lovelier, with the faint hint of a smile; 'un sorriso che no riesce'; one from Megara Hyblaia,[7] finally, has an expression of almost tragic suffering on its classical features.

How far we are, with these individualizations, from those symbolical representations with which our survey started! And yet they all convey aspects of the same divinity. Nor is their variety a mere concomitant of changing taste and style; for the 'regina delle maschere', culmination of abstract realization, is likely to be about contemporary with those just surveyed, and if an inferior sample[8] could now and then stir apprehension lest Blinkenberg's pedestrian view could after all be correct (the protomes representing human dedicants), some outstanding piece soon emerges to confirm what is inherently evident: in all its varieties, this peculiar and indeed unique form continued to convey what it had conveyed from origin.

Gàbrici's Plate LIII shows one of these indubitable pieces; the head, 19 cm. high, from a very large protome. This time it is the goddess that stands out; the goddess beyond terror and grief, calm in the fullness of her divinity.[9] Some other protomes, far inferior in quality,[10] show her in the

---

[1] Ib., Pl. XLVIII. 4 and 7.

[2] Orsi, *Gela*, Pl. XLIX. 8 and 9; our Plate 20*a*.   [3] Ib. 7 and 10; our Plate 20*b*.

[4] Gàbrici, Pl. LXV. 2; our Plate 21*a*.   [5] Id., Pl. XL. 6; our Plate 21*b*.

[6] Id., p. 217 and Pl. XL. 9.   [7] *Mon. Ant.* i (1890), Pl. IX. 10.

[8] e.g. the little one from Megara Hyblaia pictured by Orsi, *Mon. Ant.* i (1890), 805, with a gay smile on its very ordinary face.

[9] A similar expression may be found in Pl. VII. 4 of Marconi, *Agr. arc.* while ib. 5 and 6 show the old, mask-like round type losing its rigidity and becoming individualized. The more one sees of these 'maschere' the less one understands that they could be called 'stereotyped'.

[10] Gàbrici, Pl. LXVI. 2 and 3, cf. 1 (a bust). The even poorer types Pl. LVI. 4, 6, 8 presumably aim at the same concept.

likeness of a friendly young woman, smiling, a trusty benevolent helper for other women. Again a totally different aspect emerges with Plate LVIII. 4: the face of an amiable girl with, perhaps, a hint of sorrow foreknown rather than experienced. This leads on to the charming youthful head, Gàbrici's Plate LXIV. 3;[1] the head of a bright, lively maiden who seems to be looking into the world with gay and hopeful expectation, totally ignorant of those depths which left their shadow on the images of Persephone previously quoted. And yet this is the same goddess. The head indeed does not come from a protome; it belonged to a statuette or bust; but having been found in the sanctuary of Malophoros, whom else could it represent? For this is no mortal maiden; these features and eyes gleam with the sheen of divine brightness. Add that the head—judging by its shape and the presence of a number of perforations at the top—originally appears to have worn the polos.[2]

Different in style but very similar in character are two, almost identical, terracotta heads from the necropolis del Fusco, Syracuse.[3] A maiden again; maturer than the one from Selinus, but with the same expression of hopeful anticipation. Who could she be—she that accompanied the dead into their graves? Add to these one of the 'maschere' found by Orsi at Bitalemi.[4] The head alone remains, and it is quite different from all the others. It is the head of a young woman, most unusual in its position (it is leaning sideways) and expression. Love for which the maiden just described appeared to be destined, has gripped and overpowered her. Persephone, loving; it seems blasphemous, and certainly incomprehensible.

The range of the concept 'Persephone' revealed by her Sicilian representations—from the abstract mask of ineluctable Death to the youthful features of a loving maiden and, again, from the all but abstract xoanon with the head of the Queen of Death in her inflexible grandeur to the lovely image of the seated bride—is amazing indeed. It presupposes, evidently, the identification of Persephone and Kore; but if this appeared problematical and incomplete in Greece, it baffles the understanding in Sicily. The Eleusinian concept (and others in Mainland Greece and the East, as far as they are discernible) laid all stress on the Mother–Daughter relationship, and centred on Demeter's distress, her search, triumph, and joy so predominantly as to reduce the absence and return of the Daughter to a sorrowful but temporary interlude, its impact all but wiped out in the happiness of reunion. But 'to be carried off by the Lord of the Nether-

[1] Also Langlotz–Hirmer, Pl. 35 (with the designation, 'Demeter or Kore' to which the commentary, p. 65, adds 'Meter–Kybele', as a further alternative. As though all these names were equivalent, and irrelevant!).
[2] Cf. Gàbrici, p. 278 and the head-gear of B.M. 1109.
[3] Von Matt[1], p. 13; one of them in Langlotz–Hirmer, Pl. 38.
[4] *Gela*, Pl. XLIX. 2; our Plate 20c.

world' and 'to enter through the gates of Hades' really is to suffer death,[1] and the archaeological material is evidence of the radical earnest with which the finality of death was accepted in Sicily. The fact that its divine reality, Persephone, could none the less be perceived also as Kore, the tender Maiden, signifies an awareness of some supreme divine force which could make possible the *coniunctio oppositorum*. We have in fact met, incidentally, with some pointers at the presence of this divine force; we may here recall, in particular, that the goddess of the 'maschere' always wears the veil which is the distinction of brides and married women.

That divine agent, unifier of realms separate and opposed to each other, is Aphrodite. She made it possible for men to understand and to master their existence in the tension between an unmitigated realization of Death and the awareness of an unquenchable source of Life. This understanding found its classical expression in the mythology, worship, and art of Epizephyrian Lokri, which was followed all over Sicily. Our concluding chapters will therefore be centred on Lokri; in preparation, though, some Sicilian monuments remain to be considered.

(*h*) 'GRANDI BUSTI' AND OTHER MONUMENTS

The lovely, late-archaic terracotta statue of a seated goddess, piously and painstakingly reconstructed out of (incomplete) pieces which Orsi had discovered near Grammichele,[2] gives some notion of the form in which Greek religion appealed to the native population in the hinterland of Syracuse. Part of the body and most of the face are modern,[3] but enough of the original remains to identify Persephone. The object which she held in her right hand against her young body can only have been an apple or, rather, a pomegranate; the head was gently bent forward, ready to listen to the prayers of worshippers. The 'bruttissima statua' which Orsi found in the same neighbourhood[4] shows how, haltingly at first, the Siculi responded, while the powerful, and wholly un-Greek, mother-goddess from Megara Hyblaia[5] illustrates the earthbound sentiments and traditions which they contributed to the common stock of Sikeliote religious consciousness. I am not sure that this product of a primitive surrealism is rightly placed in the tradition of the Maltese symbolic art, but it is clear at a glance that the equally (if not still more) powerful 'Meteres' at Capua[6] witness to the same primitive mentality as the Megarean goddess; that is, to an Italiote mentality.

---

[1] Consider Sophokles, *Ant.* 807 ff.

[2] *Mon. Ant.* xviii (1908), 24 ff.; Langlotz–Hirmer, Pl. 39; von Matt[1], Pl. 164; Pace, ii. 41 f., Figs. 39–41.   [3] Orsi, ib., p. 28, n. 1.

[4] *Mon. Ant.* vii (1897), Pl. iii; Pace, ii. 153, Fig. 142; cf. above, p. 73.

[5] Langlotz–Hirmer, Pl. 17; von Matt[1], Pl. 52.

[6] Langlotz–Hirmer, Pl. 167. For these see J. Heurgon, *Recherches sur . . . Capoue préromaine* (1942), pp. 330 ff.; especially his characterization (pp. 334 f.) of the 'déesses mères en qui

To point the contrast between native and Greek, see the statuette Gàbrici, Pl. LIX. 8.[1] A lovely young woman, seated, with a babe in her arms. It stretches a hand up to her breast; she is looking in front of herself with a forlorn, dreaming gaze. This Greek Madonna: who is she? Who could she be, at this sanctuary, but Persephone? For this is no mortal woman—as he will agree who compares the frequent representations of human mothers carrying or leading their offspring to a sanctuary.[2] But if so, who, and whose, is the babe?[3] Persephone kourotrophos: the paradox about the goddess grows ever more extreme.

A pointer to its meaning is given by the series of 'grandi busti',[4] a type confined to Sicily[5]—and Lokri. These busts, usually of near life size, were made from the first half of the fifth until well into the fourth and even the third century. They are thus, in their majority, more recent than the evidence with which we are mainly concerned. Deficient in the profounder significance conveyed by many relics of the preceding age, they have, even so, the merit of making explicit, albeit on a more superficial plain, essential aspects implied rather than expressed by them. Their distinctive feature is the combination of an elaborate female head with the upper part of a body entirely shapeless[6] and without arms. We are not here concerned with the question of their origin,[7] nor with the—

se manifestaient, dans la pensée des Méditerranéens, les énergies créatrices de la Nature', etc., and his report about the over 6,000 terracotta figurines found there, including about 600 kourotrophoi of the kind in question, with one (as Langlotz–Hirmer, Pl. 167 f.) to twelve babes in their arms, and thousands of representations of dedicants offering pigs, apples, doves, and baskets; note also that the male god associated with this goddess is Zeus Meilichios (364).

[1] Our Plate 21c. From a grave on Monte Bubbonia comes the comparable terracotta Syracuse no. 24905 (our Plate 21d).   [2] Above, p. 96.

[3] The answer, in my view, is not 'Dionysos–Iakchos, the son of Zeus and Persephone': that myth (if it existed in Sicily in archaic times; cf. Detached Note IV, below, p. 401) involves a very different sentiment.

[4] The statuette Gàbrici, Pl. LXI. 4–4a conveys a similar hint; it is relegated below the text in view of its poor quality. It is a standing female figure with high polos; the arms, which were added separately, are lost. She wears a belted himation which however leaves the body to appear almost naked except for the part covered by the overfall. Neither a priestess nor a worshipper could be thus represented, and the serious squarish face, unsmiling and unbeautiful, forbids any thought of Aphrodite. It is Persephone the bride as visualized by a coroplast of limited ability. The head is closely similar to that of the bust which Gàbrici suitably put beside it (no. 5) and also to that of the protome ib. 2; both of which can only represent this very goddess.

[5] Basic on these is the article by G. E. Rizzo in *Oesterr. Jahreshefte*, xiii (1910), 63 ff.; besides, Marconi, *Agrigento*, pp. 182 ff.; Pace, ii. 81 ff. W. Deonna, *Les statues de terre cuite* (1908), pp. 43 ff. contains a list of the specimens then known, largely based on Orsi, *Mon. Ant.* vii (1897), 245.

[6] Occasionally a narrow necklace is indicated, but—judging by the comparatively few of which the 'bust' is actually preserved (e.g. Langlotz–Hirmer, Pl. 36)—the body remains shapeless and undecorated throughout the classical period (as also in Lokri). For later developments see below, p. 156.

[7] Italian scholars incline to regard them as a Sicilian development of the 'maschere' or 'protomes' just discussed (thus lately P. Orlandini, *Mon. Ant.* xlvi (1963), 31 f.). This is

indubitable—dependence on classical Attic sculpture of the heads on all but the oldest among them; but with their significance.

P. Orsi, at an early stage of his dealings with them,[1] pondered whether they 'referred to' the cult of Aphrodite or the 'Eleusinian goddesses'; subsequently[2] he held that they 'represented' Demeter and Kore, and this view has been generally accepted.[3] I wish to qualify it by the suggestion that they all represent Persephone, and that the evident striving of the coroplasts after improved characterization (which has been eloquently described by Marconi[4] and Pace[5]) was guided by the wish to express, with the means of a progressing art, her characteristics as a universal goddess.

As a rule (to which there are exceptions) she wears a high polos; very often of a shape—open at the top and with rims below and above—which justifies its designation as *modius*, and hence as a symbol of rich harvests. The oldest *busti* known are those found by Orsi at Grammichele,[6] but nobody will suppose the type to have been invented there; others come from Agrigento, Gela, Akrai, and Syracuse, and the oldest among these are only slightly, if at all, more recent.[7] They were found in the two 'chthonic' sanctuaries of the city of Persephone, and the *favissa* at Grammichele proved, by its general contents, to belong to the same category. This is already a powerful hint as to the identity of the goddess represented.

Orsi's early hesitations were perfectly justified, for there are among the 'grandi busti' such as—in a different context—would naturally be taken to represent Aphrodite; in fact many of these heads show (within the limits of what are productions of artisans and not of great masters of sculpture) a beauty which would become Dione's daughter. It is, however, self-evident that all images of this very peculiar kind, all of them emerging at 'chthonic' sanctuaries, must be held to represent one and the same goddess, unless indeed any of them were found to exhibit thorough and exclusive differences.

indeed perfectly possible. A 'protome' of the concave kind had only to be broadened in the region of the shoulders and to be provided with a back however simple to be turned into a *busto*. Just this can in fact be seen happening gradually both at the Gaggera (Gàbrici, Pls. XLVIII. 2; LXI. 5; LXV. 1) and at Lokri (see the instructive series presented by Orsi, *Not. Scav.* (1913), *Supplemento*, 70 ff.); at the former place, though, the typical form, with the body quite shapeless, has not been found. If these *busti* originated in the West, the significance of the only relevant literary passage customarily quoted in this context, Pausan. ix. 16. 5 (on which below, p. 153), is greatly reduced. If, on the other hand, any student should wish to consider the possibility of their having originated in the Orient, he will find suggestive material in Thiersch, p. 86.

[1] *Mon. Ant.* vii (1897), 243 ff.   [2] Ib., xviii (1908), 11.
[3] e.g. by Pace, ii. 83; Orlandini, *Mon. Ant.* xlvi (1963), 11.
[4] *Agrigento*, pp. 183 f.   [5] ii. 83.
[6] *Mon. Ant.* vii (1897), Pls. V and XVIII; pp. 11 f. with Pl. I; one of these is also in Pace ii. 74, Fig. 82.
[7] Marconi, ib., p. 182, Fig. 115 = Pace, ii. 82, Fig. 80.

The two outstanding ones from Grammichele, with polos and modius respectively, represent maidens unlike in their features but equal in their loveliness tempered with austerity; the same description can apply to the oldest one from Agrigento, notwithstanding its thoroughly different style. Who this divine maiden is requires no saying. The austerity which marks these oldest *busti* gives way, in the later ones, to other characteristics; a loveliness which could suggest Aphrodite;[1] a dignity that would fit Hera;[2] which means that majestic dignity and the power of Love were realized in Persephone. Occasionally, indeed, the coroplasts succeeded in combining these features, to an extent, in one figure.[3]

The unshapely part below the heads of these busts is accounted for, genetically, if they are assumed to be a development of the (earlier) 'protomes' with their analogous, vacant lower part; but why was this unsightly piece retained even while the head was constantly refined and elaborated? Dedicants and spectators must have found some significance in it. It cannot, as with the protomes, be taken for a symbolization of the shapeless sphere of Death, for the goddess of these busts is not characterized as the Goddess of Death; nor, if the *busti* originated in the West, can Pausanias' (ix. 16. 5) report about an image ὅcον ἐc cτέρνα of Demeter Thesmophoros at Thebes or pictures of Gaia half emerging from the ground (as on the Attic Erichthonios vase) be cited for anything more than suggestive parallels. Valid parallels though these are. Since the goddess represented is Persephone, one might suspect an allusion to Kore's return from the Netherworld, comparable to the renderings of this scene on some vase-paintings.[4] However, the intimation of a particular mythical happening would not be in keeping with a representation which aims to represent the lasting essence of a goddess rather than one particular scene from her myth; nor could this interpretation account for the absence of arms from all these busts. They are in fact different from all of the various representations of a deity rising out of the earth. More adequately, and in analogy with the symbolic implication of the corresponding part of the protomes, the shapeless part of the busts may be held to convey the notion of the shapeless χθών whose essence is visualized in the person of this goddess; not—in the aspect rendered by this class of monuments—as the abode of Death but as the womb and cradle of Life.[5] Thus Persephone appears to a large extent to have taken the place of Demeter.

[1] Marconi, *Agrigento*, Figs. 116 and 119; Pace, ii, Figs. 85 and 87.

[2] Marconi, ib., Fig. 118; Pace, ii, Fig. 86; B.M. 1180.

[3] See Pace, ii, Figs. 83 and 84: majestic when viewed from the front; maidenly charm in profile.   [4] Above, p. 82.

[5] As an analogy one may quote the statuettes of nymphs, found in quantity at Lokri (von Matt², Pls. 124 f.), modelled down to the knees only. Like Persephone, they are emerging from the element of which they are the divine reality.

It is remarkable indeed that, among all these *busti*, there is not one that would necessarily have to be held to represent Demeter. They all represent maidens or youngish women; some of them more mature than others[1]—as we found it also in other images of Persephone; but none with those features by which we found Demeter characterized in other and, *nota bene*, older representations; the good mother, the genial helper of women is not found among the *busti*. There is, of course, the double-bust from Agrigento in Syracuse.[2] Its two heads were cast in the same mould, but one of them was subsequently, and rather crudely, worked over by hand so as to make it appear older; with bent nose and wrinkled neck but no hint of geniality. The immediate urge to recognize a combined image of Mother and Daughter is countered by the consideration that this would be a strange way of characterizing Demeter. G. E. Rizzo[3] accordingly held two aspects of the one Persephone to be represented. His argument that double images always represent the same person twice is questionable indeed, for the opposite view could well be maintained by reference to many double hermae and to plastic vases combining the heads of e.g. a negro and a Greek, or satyr and nymph, or man and woman.[4] The question calls for consideration within a wider frame.

It may be suggested, first, that the double-bust is of comparatively recent origin. Rizzo[5] indeed would date it early in the fifth century, finding in it 'tratti dell'ultimo arcaismo'. I have not found this view contradicted, but I cannot see anything 'archaic' about this bust; on the contrary, its pathetic expression, and especially the 'illusionistic' treatment of the excessively rich hair, seem to me dependent on the style of Skopas and to point to a date in the latter half of the fourth century. And indeed, if it is not a product of the fifth century, it could not have been made before the resettlement of Akragas by Timoleon. If it was made during the rule of Timoleon, it has a striking contemporary analogon in a series of small Syracusan silver coins (two litrae) which the experts ascribe to his period.[6] They show, on the reverse, a free horse, symbol of liberty regained, and above it either an ear of grain or a star. The obverse has a representation unique in Sicily, namely, a 'Janiform' female double-head. The two heads are not identical, one of them being more youthful than its counterpart. Demeter and Kore? Or 'expression de la nature double de la divinité chthonienne' (J. Marcadé)?

---

[1] Thus especially Marconi, *Agrigento*, Fig. 118.

[2] Our Plate 22a. [3] Ib. (see p. 151, n. 5), p. 76.

[4] Much relevant material has been presented, and thoughtfully discussed, by J. Marcadé, *Bull. Corr. Hell.*, lxxvi (1952), 596 ff. under the heading *Hermès doubles*; cf. below, p. 170, on a Lokrian double-bust.

[5] *Oesterr. Jahreshefte*, xiii (1910), 72 f.

[6] *B.M. Cat. Coins, Sicily*, p. 186, nos. 283–6; Holm, iii. 659, nos. 319 f.; Hill, p. 150 and Pl. XL. 4; J. Marcadé, ib., p. 620; our Plate 22b and c.

When, in 344 B.C., Timoleon prepared to set out for Sicily from Corinth, 'the Goddesses' told the priestesses of Kore in a dream that they would accompany him; hence the city declared one of his ships 'sacred to the Goddesses'. When he was at sea, by night, 'the sky broke open and shed a bright fire upon his ship, and out of it rose a torch like those used at the mysteries and moved ahead on his course to Italy', in proof of the divine presence. No doubt this report of Timaios, preserved by Plutarch,[1] correctly renders what Timoleon believed or, at any rate, what he desired to be believed, and it is hard not to conclude that the several emblems on the coins in question aim to impress just this belief.[2]

Some thirty years later Agathokles burned his fleet in Africa, ostensibly, as a sacrifice to Demeter and Kore, since they were 'the goddesses who own Sicily'.[3] To these two historical reports attesting the authority of the two goddesses may be added the fragment of a Hellenistic relief found at Catania. It is inscribed ΔΑΜΑΤΡΙ ΚΑΙ ΚΟΡΑΙ and shows the two goddesses (receiving worshippers, no doubt, in the standard form of post-classical votive reliefs), with Kore holding the torch.[4] This illustrates the Eleusinian concept, of which otherwise there is so little pre-Roman evidence in Sicily. The meagre evidence here presented may indicate it to have been propagated by Timoleon and on this basis the Akragantine double-bust may be assumed to represent Demeter and Kore. It is not a certain diagnosis, even in view of the Timoleontean coin,[5] and if it is correct, this is, among the *busti*, an isolated exception.

For it is becoming increasingly clear that the production of *busti* of the traditional type went on, at any rate, to the end of the third century. Essential evidence has come from Morgantina, and not from there

---

[1] Plut. *Timol.* 8.

[2] Janiform heads on Greek coins otherwise seem to be all but confined to the region about the Hellespont. There are archaic types from Tenedos, male and female or two females, one older, one younger (*B.M. Cat. Coins, Troas*, Pl. XVII; J. Marcadé, ib., p. 642, Fig. 19) and, from Lampsakos, both archaic and later ones with two female heads (*B.M. Mysia*, Pls. XVIII. 9–11 and XIX. 10 and 13; I can see no difference between the heads; except, perhaps, on the archaic one, Pl. XVIII. 11). At Athens, the Lampsakos type was imitated on a few small coins issued by Hippias (*B.M. Attica*, Pl. II. 10 and p. 5; cf. B. Head, *Hist. Num.* (1911), pp. 529 ff. and P. Gardner, *A History of Greek Coinage* (1918), 160). It is possible to establish a historical connection between Athens and Lampsakos; it is far less easy to see how Timoleon could have been inspired by a Lampsakene coin-type.

[3] Diodor. XX. 7.

[4] Published by G. Libertini in a study of representations of the two goddesses combined, *Ephem. Arch.* (1932), ii. 720 ff.

[5] The basic fact after all is that a double-bust was originally made with two identical, youthful heads. Such a bust, of small size, and certainly Sicilian, is now in Catania (G. Libertini, *Il Museo Biscari*, i (1930), no. 1014, Pl. CX); its two, youthful heads are reasonably taken to indicate 'la nature double de la divinité chthonienne'. The same would apply to the larger bust in its original state, and he that altered one of its heads in the aforesaid, and rather inept, manner may be held to have aimed at making explicit this 'twofold nature' rather than at portraying Demeter.

only.[1] A potter's workshop in the small town at Scornavacche (Prov. Ragusa) had samples ready for baking at the moment of its destruction about 280 B.C.[2] and these samples are indistinguishable from the—supposedly classical—ones from Agrigento. Similar *busti* were smashed on the floor of the Demeter sanctuaries (as the excavators call them) when the Romans destroyed Morgantina in 211 B.C.[3]

To some extent, these *busti* underwent the same development as the protomes and the 'faceless busts' at Cyrene; the shapeless body was elaborated in more and more naturalistic forms. 'Morgantina has produced a considerable number of fully modelled 'busti'.[4] The Syracuse Museum houses three of them; all are greater than life size, and one is of colossal dimensions (not published). Others are approximately life size. Subject faces frontally, with arms placed parallel and cut off above the elbows. She is fully clothed, and her dress falls in a V-shaped fold between her breasts and is girt immediately below'.[5] The faces on this late type of *busto*[6] are individualized and they are without polos; the traditional form then has been humanized so that one may wonder whether a goddess or a priestess is represented.

In this variety, the original symbolic power is largely lost. The shapeless, older form, however, also continued to be used. Three of this kind were found in the smaller 'Demeter' sanctuary at Morgantina (which was in use from *c.* 300 to 211 B.C.),[7] with painted scenes on the front of the bodies, suggesting embroidered clothing; one of these scenes, characteristically, being the rape of Kore. The larger sanctuary yielded more;[8] those from Scornavacche have already been mentioned, and the beautiful head of one found at Centuripe is pictured by von Matt (Pl. 169); its headgear—two intertwined snakes—indicates the goddess of the dead; a large modius, the giver of fruitfulness. This shapeless type must have been *en vogue*, even at this late period, as an outstanding expression of Sicilian religion; it is reproduced even on a small terracotta altar found at Phoenician Solus and dedicated to Tanit, the chief goddess of Carthage.[9]

For the present argument the decisive point is this. The heads on all of these *busti*—whether traditional or naturalistic—always represent a

---

[1] For the following, Profs. E. Sjöquist and D. White have greatly helped me both by their publications and by personal advice.

[2] A. Di Vita, *Kokalos*, iv (1958), 91 ff. (esp. 96); Pls. 38 f.

[3] See e.g. Pl. 2 in *Greek, Roman and Byzantine Studies*, v (1964), 277 (D. White).

[4] 'Only one other Sicilian site has yielded such busts: Centuripae; see G. Libertini, *Centuripe* (1926), 8 ff. (D. White)'

[5] Quoted from a letter of D. White.

[6] For a photograph of one of them see *Am. Journ. Arch.* lxii (1958), Pl. 32, Fig. 20.

[7] R. Stillwell, *Am. Journ. Arch.* lxvii (1963), Pl. 36, Fig. 17 and p. 170.

[8] R. Stillwell, ib., lxiii (1959), 169 with Pl. 41, Figs. 10 and 11.

[9] See Pl. 105, Figs. 18–20 and p. 347 in *Am. Journ. Arch.* lxxi (1967) (D. White).

maiden or young woman; lovely often, or beautiful, friendly or also majestic—but representations expressive of the character of the Mother are sought in vain.

This holds good not only for the *busti*. The Eleusis-type relief at Catania (just mentioned) stands alone; apart from it there is, after the early fifth century,[1] nothing in Sicily analogous to the Demeter of Knidos or to Eleusinian representations on reliefs and Attic vases. The Daughter appears to have usurped all the Mother's domain or—putting it more objectively—traces of the Mother are all but non-existent.[2] There is Kore everywhere but, so it seems, not Δήμητρος Κόρη.

The coins tell the same. Enna alone continues to represent ΔΑΜΑΤΗΡ;[3] for the rest, King Pyrrhos had to come from Epirus to secure her a place together with her daughter.[4] Otherwise, Kore–Persephone rules supreme. The female head characteristic of Syracuse, and so difficult of interpretation in the earlier fifth century, is unequivocally identified ever since, towards the end of the century, the great die-cutters (Phrygillos, Euainetos, etc.) crowned it with ears of grain and barley-leaves.[5] 'From henceforward, the head of Persephone becomes the most important of all Syracusan coin-types';[6] it is elaborated in beauty and ever fuller characterization and adopted all over Sicily.

The ascendancy of Persephone, which was noted in surveying the 'Telines figurines', the 'protomes' and, now, the 'grandi busti' and coins, is in agreement with the indications of the scanty oldest literary evidence and especially Pindar.[7] She appears to have been worshipped as a giver of Fruitfulness and Life no less than as the great deity of Death, and in an enigmatic union with Aphrodite.[8] She has become the universal Goddess of Sicily.[9]

---

[1] The date, approximately, of the last Demeter terracottas.

[2] The relief above the Athenian decree (*IG*, ii. 2, 18) of 394/3 B.C. honouring the tyrant Dionysios I is often said to show Sicily represented by Demeter. It is however anything but evident that the (broken) female figure facing Athena *is* Demeter; she may as well be Sikelia (as e.g. Svoronos held; see his comment on Pl. 205 and in his catalogue of the sculptures in the National Museum at Athens; cp. ΣΙΚΕΛΙΑ on the later 'alliance coins' and, afterwards, on those inscribed ΣΙΚΕΛΙΩΤΑΝ, for which see E. Sjöquist, *Museum Notes* (American Numismatic Soc.), ix (1960), 53 ff.). [3] Holm, iii. 674 f. nos. 399 f.; Hill, p. 178.

[4] Holm, iii. 691, n. 463; Hill, p. 163, Pl. XII. 6. Pyrrhos was using a type from his homeland (*B.M., Thessaly*, Pl. XX. 1). [5] Cf. above, p. 100 n. 7.

[6] Hill, p. 102. It is inscribed ΚΟΡΑΣ on one of Agathokles' issues, Hill, Pl. XI. 4 and p. 157.

[7] A peculiarity of the report about Timoleon's divine protectresses (Plut. *Timol.* 8; cf. above, p. 155) seems indicative of the combination, in Timoleon's propaganda, of traditions Sicilian and Eleusinian. It is 'the priestesses of Kore' (and not 'of Demeter and Kore') to whom the two goddesses reveal their intention, and the seers who afterwards expound their appearance declare that 'the goddesses' were joining in the enterprise 'because Sicily was sacred to Kore' (and not 'to the Two Goddesses').

[8] A type of fully modelled *busto* at Morgantina, the head of which is pictured in *Am. Journ. Arch.*, lxiv (1960), Pl. 28, Fig. 30 (cf. ib., p. 133), shows a beautiful maiden-goddess with polos and veil holding (as I learn from D. White) a dove against her body. Persephone with the bird of Aphrodite: we shall presently find the same union at Lokri.

[9] As such, her images could serve the Carthaginians for dedications to their Tanit, as the

V. LOKRI

(a) A FEW GENERALITIES

No coroplast ever produced a piece more wonderful than the bust of Aphrodite holding the child Eros which may be seen in the Museo Nazionale at Reggio–Calabria. Even Hirmer's photograph[1] cannot fully convey its expression of divine majesty, in purity and beauty, combined with motherly tenderness and pride. There is no other vision comparable to this of the goddess of Love—with one exception (the reader will guess which; and it probably comes from the same orbit).[2] If not an original masterpiece, this is, at any rate, the congenial rendering of some master-piece of early-classical sculpture; the cult-image of a temple in the region where this bust was made.[3] It was made, and found, at Rosarno, north of Reggio, the ancient Medma; a colony of Lokri Epizephyrii. Orsi's excavations of graves and a *favissa* there[4] have produced terracottas so similar to those found at Lokri that the art of the colony can serve to illustrate that of the mother-city.[5] This Aphrodite therefore may stand

Solus arula (above, p. 156) and imitations of 'Telines figurines' show (cf. also D. White, *Am. Journ. Arch.*, lxxi (1967), 346 ff.). The statue dedicated by the suffete Milkyaton (now in Turin; Harden, pp. 90 and 201; Pl. 44; also D. White, ib., Pl. 106, Fig. 27) is not with certainty quoted in this context. It is customarily asserted to be dedicated to Persephone, but this is nothing more than a guess of Lenormant; the inscription (*Corp. Inscr. Sem. I*, i, no. 176) does not identify the goddess, and the dedicant may have intended Tanit. The statue itself is not of a type used for representations of Persephone.

[1] Langlotz–Hirmer, Pl. 96; with Langlotz's comment and indication of literature ib., p. 79 (add S. Ferri in *L'Italia antichissima*, ii (1930), 173).

[2] See B. Ashmole, *Journ. Hell. Stud.* xlii (1922), 248 (though I confess myself one of those heretics who feel unable to believe in the genuineness of the Boston throne).

[3] It is a wise maxim not, as a rule, to take terracotta figurines for faithful replicas of great works of sculpture, since the coroplasts aimed to produce images of this or that deity rather than replicas of specific works of great art; but this rule has its limitations. The coroplasts were bound to start from certain established notions, and these notions could not be un-affected by authoritative images. We have ventured, in the preceding pages, to trace the origin of several types to specific cult-images; types which, once established, were freely varied. Two instances may be quoted in justification of this procedure. At Garaguso (between Potenza and Metapontum) a charming little marble goddess was found, seated inside a small temple or aedicula (von Matt², colour Pl. I; Langlotz–Hirmer, Pl. 52 f.). Either an object of worship itself or the replica of a larger one, it was found together with a number of terracotta replicas which had been placed in front of the 'tempietto'. And the Apollon Philesios by Kanachos is reasonably held to be reliably reproduced by, among other things, a bronze statuette (now in the British Museum; F. Winter, *Kunstgeschichte in Bildern*, 220. 6). The sculpture under discussion, notwithstanding its outstanding quality, is not an independent original (as Langlotz held). In the Antikenmuseum in Basel is a terracotta, apparently from Lokri, which repeats the same motif (K. Schefold, *Führer* . . ., p. 128, no. 177. 10); hence a common original has to be posited.

[4] *Not. Scav.* (1913), *Supplemento*, pp. 55 ff.

[5] This was stated e.g. by Dunbabin, p. 163; it must be self-evident to anyone who has seen finds from both places, and it is essential as long as many of the finds from Lokri remain

here first, as a symbol of the spirit of this fascinating city or, at any rate, of one significant facet of that spirit.[1]

We may take our cue from Pindar (*Ol.* x. 13 ff.) in rapidly recalling its characteristics: the Lokrian *atrekeia* in obeying the strict laws, laid down by Zaleukos, of an aristocratic government and the rigorous mode of life enjoined by them; the devotion to the Muse (Kalliopa) — and indeed a faint echo at least of Lokrian musical arts still survives;[2] and the war-like prowess[3] which became legendary with the victory over Kroton at the river Sagra. Moreover there are the tantalizing hints at certain prerogatives of women: the matrilinear descent acknowledged in Lokrian families; the ritual office of 'cup-bearer' (*phialephoros*) reserved for noble maidens[4] . . . I do not wish to enter into the much-discussed problems given with these fragmentary pieces of information,[5] but we shall have to bear them in mind. They may perhaps be connected with the erotic tendencies in Lokrian poetry; although we have to concede it to Bachofen that gynaecocracy (if the term be applicable to Lokri) is anything but synonymous with licentiousness. It is significant that the school of Pytha-goras flourished in Lokri even though the master himself, according to the legend, was denied entry.[6]

Archaeology has decisively enriched the faint picture arising from the scanty and chancy literary evidence. The persistingly plain equipment of Lokrian graves has confirmed the adherence to Zaleukos' stern laws; the recovery of much excellent bronze work has demonstrated their out-standing craftsmanship in an unsuspected field;[7] but quite particularly it has shed light on Lokrian religion.

Orsi's excavations (it is Orsi always) have substantiated the supreme devotion paid by the Lokrians to Persephone.[8] At the foot of the steep hill

unpublished. The Lokrian style—developed, probably, on bronzes before it was adopted by the coroplasts—is so clearly marked that one is surprised occasionally to find it mistaken by experts: A. Levi, *Le terrecotte . . . di Napoli*, 1926, p. 5, no. 12 (Pl. I) = Langlotz–Hirmer, Pl. 70 is Lokrian; cf. von Matt[2], Pls. 128 (Lokri) and 102 (Medma); Orsi, l.l., Figs. 88 f., 106, 125, 136, 142.

[1] W. Oldfather, *Real-Encycl.* xiii. 2, 1351 observes that there is little evidence for the cult of Aphrodite in Lokri. I suspect that, very competent though he was, he may here have taken too narrow a view.

[2] See the summary by Oldfather, ib., 1359.

[3] Cf. also Pind. *Ol.* xi. 18.

[4] Polyb. xii. 5.

[5] I could not anyhow go beyond Dunbabin, pp. 183 ff.

[6] On this point see now W. Burkert, *Weisheit und Wissenschaft* (1962), p. 95.

[7] Some samples are in von Matt[2], Pls. 130–6 and Langlotz–Hirmer, Pls. 89–92 and 126 f.

[8] This must not, obviously, be taken to mean that the worship of other gods was neglected. A great temple (at Marasà, in the lower city) was decorated with the statues (? akroteria), now in Reggio, of the Dioscuri (von Matt[2], Pls. 119 f.; Langlotz–Hirmer, Pls. 122 f.); it was therefore supposed to have been dedicated to these divine protectors of the city but has now been found to have been sacred to Zeus (*Klearchos*, xxiii–iv (1964), 21 ff.); the Dioscuri though may still claim a second one (Marafioti, von Matt[2], Pl. 121). Some terracottas

called La Mannella,[1] at the far end, inland, of the city and just outside its walls, he discovered the traces of a small building and a *favissa*, both abounding with dedications to her (many though had been stolen previously). The building cannot have been the vaunted 'most outstanding Greek sanctuary in Italy'—that must have lain on the top of this or the neighbouring hill (Abbadessa)—but its treasury; the location is strikingly similar to San Biagio at Agrigento, with the Demeter temple above and its *favissa* below.[2] The examination of 1675 graves in the Lokrian necropoleis yielded further evidence of the same devotion, and at Medma Orsi discovered the *favissa* 'in località Calderazzo' and graves, already mentioned, of the same character.[3] It is proposed to deal summarily with the main features of his (and some other) finds; they are analogous to Sicilian ones previously considered, though different in the thoroughly Lokrian style of representation and pregnant with enlightening indications of a profound and radical theology.[4]

(*b*) ARCHAIZING TERRACOTTAS, 'MASCHERE', AND 'GRANDI BUSTI'

A highly archaistic type of standing female has been found in quantity at La Mannella.[5] It is analogous to the Sicilian 'Telines figurines' in its combination of a very ancient form of the body with a far later kind of head; but here the similarity ends. The bodies of the Lokrian figurines— they are often large, measuring up to *c*. 60 cm.—are cylindrical like the Cheramyes type, not flat like Nikandre; the upper parts were worked separately and hence often survive without the body. The heads on them, covered by a low polos, are far from the varied and expressive characterisation of their Sicilian counterparts; they repeat one rather dull type of face surrounded by the old-fashioned 'Etagen-Perücke' and indicative, in the modelling of the long nose and rounded cheeks and chin, of a date in the latter half of the sixth century. This quiet face, with the hint of a smile, could be held, though rather youngish, to be Demeter's; it is the

representing Athena which Orsi found at a little temple at the lower end of Regione Mannella led him to ascribe this sanctuary to her (*Not. Scav.* (1910), *Suppl.*, 62 ff.; A. de Franciscis, though, adds a 'forse' to this ascription in his survey in *Encicl. d'Arte Antica*, *s.v.* Locri, iv. 673); for evidence, variously cogent, of other cults see Oldfather, ib., 1350 ff.

[1] Von Matt[2], Pl. 138.

[2] On this point an article by Y. Béquignon on 'Déméter acropolitaine', in *Rev. Archéol.* (1958), ii. 149 ff. may be compared.

[3] *Not. Scav.* (1913), *Suppl.*, 55 ff.

[4] For the reader's convenience I shall, wherever possible, refer to the volumes of von Matt–Zanotti-Bianco (von Matt[2]) and Langlotz–Hirmer (of which the latter alone indicates relevant literature), although I shall have to quote some pieces exhibited in the museums at Reggio and Lokri of which no published reproductions are known to me.

[5] Von Matt[2], Pls. 114 and 116; Langlotz–Hirmer, Pl. 6.

indubitable prevalence, in other representations, of Persephone which suggests the same ascription also for these (for, under the circumstances, *tertium non datur*). If so, the Daughter has assumed, in these older Lokrian images, much of the character of the Mother, while there is, in these statuettes, hardly any hint at her dread aspect as the Queen of the Dead.

This, though, is very much present in another archaizing type: namely, the seated goddess combined with her chair, of which von Matt pictures a characteristic sample from the same place.[1] This is indeed 'the Goddess', as she is styled, simply and meaningfully, in several dedications found at La Mannella;[2] Persephone, pitiless, remote, almost mask-like. An enthroned statuette, with a body similarly archaizing and a head of, perhaps, 510 B.C. has the same expression of unapproachable majesty.[3]

The 'maschere'—or 'protomes', as we preferred to call them—found at Medma[4] have counterparts from Lokri itself.[5] None of them could be mistaken for one of Sicilian origin; but taken together they cover, more or less, the same range of symbolical expression.[6] There are those—they are, so it seems, among the older ones—which convey the unmitigated image of death;[7] one at least among those from La Mannella,[8] and perhaps many more, look like death masks, with eyes broken. A 'dead Persephone':[9] and, indeed, did not the bride of the Lord of the Netherworld pass through the Gates of No Return? On other protomes her rigid, lean features (comparable to the 'Telines' Persephone previously considered)[10] seem gradually to return to life; a slightly rounder face and the hint of a smile begin to appear;[11] and as the shapeless plaque begins to assume bodily form, with arms resting on it, also the face becomes fully live and—though it remains serious—even friendly;[12] one hand gracefully holds up a flower—but it is the 'flower of Death', the lotus; the other, maybe, a small wreath; for whom?[13]

---

[1] Von Matt[2], Pl. 117.—For Sicilian samples of this type see above, p. 115. Orsi, *Not. Scav.* (1913), *Suppl.*, p. 84 states that these 'statue a leggio' had been found, at Lokri, 'by the dozen'; or even 'by the hundred'—these as well as the type with 'tubular' bodies—according to *Bull. d'Arte*, iii (1908), 419.

[2] For these inscriptions cf. Orsi in *Saggi* for J. Beloch (1910), pp. 166 f. and *Not. Scav.* (1909), 321; one of them is pictured in von Matt[2], Pl. 143.

[3] Reggio, Mus. Naz.

[4] Orsi, *Not. Scav.* (1913), *Suppl.*, pp. 70 ff.; cf. above, p. 158, n. 5.

[5] Reggio, Mus. Naz.

[6] The round, 'Ionian' type of the 'regina delle maschere' though does not occur in Lokri.

[7] Orsi, ib., p. 70, Fig. 77.

[8] Reggio, Museo Naz.; our Plate 23a.

[9] Orsi (ib., p. 73, Fig. 82) interpreted one of his finds—a crudely worked one—as the image of 'una vecchia arcigna . . . gli occhi chiusi'. Could it be that, here too, a 'dead Persephone' was intended?

[10] Above, pp. 124 and 138.

[11] Orsi, ib., Fig. 78; Reggio, Mus. Naz.; Naples, Mus. Naz., no. 141067.

[12] e.g. Orsi, ib., Fig. 79; Naples, no. 20644.   [13] Orsi, ib., Fig. 81.

Orsi showed (as already noted)[1] how the 'maschere' could, and probably did, develop into the 'grandi busti'. The Lokrian ones[2] are unmistakably different from the Sicilian; but it is the same strange type of an elaborate head and neck on a bulky, shapeless, and armless lower part; and even though the Lokrian *busti* exhibit the faintest indication of breasts, and some of them—even some comparatively early ones— indicate dress and arms (on the breast) by paint or in low relief[3]—this part can only metaphorically be called a 'bust' or 'body'. Since generally it is without representational value, it must have some symbolical import, and it may be suggested again that it intimates the element, or sphere, which is personalized in the goddess whose head rises above it. The Lokrian heads vary greatly in expression and character, from severity to youthful sweetness and charm; always, though, they are youngish rather than matronal. Persephone, then, and not Demeter, is represented as the 'chthonic' deity by these *busti*, and indeed one of them holds a pomegranate and a flower of lotus.[4] The dread might of the Queen of Death is felt less and less in them, but an unsmiling seriousness and an indescribable air of mystic remoteness remain.

So singular a type, representing the same goddess, with the same range of characteristics, could not have arisen in Sicily and Lokri—and only there—independently. It would be vain, with insufficient data, to inquire into its place of origin; it is far more relevant to observe that the communion in the use of these symbols is conclusive evidence of a communion of religious concepts. There is, of course, no practical problem in this communion across the Straits; besides, there is the perennial, close relation between Lokri and Syracuse and its recurrent involvement in Sicilian politics. Not to burden the page with references, from Pindar onward, which everybody knows, it may here only be recalled that Orsi found the treasury at La Mannella to have been built of Syracusan sandstone; probably, then, the blocks were sent from there in token of veneration for the great Lokrian goddess. We shall soon quote further evidence for her hold over Sicily.

(c) OTHER TERRACOTTAS

The identification of the images so far adduced was not difficult, because their particular form was sufficient indication that they represent a deity, and which. Matters become somewhat more problematical with representations which lack the various kinds of traditional hieratic symbolism; for an average Lokrian terracotta head may often leave you

[1] Above, p. 151, n. 7.   [2] Orsi, ib., pp. 80 f., Figs. 88 ff.; von Matt[2], Pl. 102.
[3] Orsi, ib., Fig. 81; B.M. 1208.
[4] B.M. 1208; cf. Orsi, ib., Fig. 81.

uncertain as to whether it represents a divine or a human being, and indeed whether a female one or a male.[1] Orsi, who characterized[2] their 'masculine and vigorous structure, robust squareness and solid flesh' with his usual perceptiveness, stressed that not rarely a female head was turned into a male one merely by the addition of a beard; a fact which may add a feature to one's notion of the people of Lokri. Where a whole figure survives, or has been safely reconstructed, the distinction between representations human and divine is often guaranteed by posture, attributes[3] and, with many products of high quality, by that *je-ne-sais-quoi* which makes you feel certain of the divine character even of an isolated head.[4]

For example, the charming figurine, from Medma, of a woman carrying a dove by its wings, and, in the other hand, a bowl[5] proclaims itself a human dedicant by stance, rough dress, and a general absence of dignity. Contrast with it a *seduta*, likewise from Medma and very similar in features and stature.[6] She, too, holds a bowl; but it is a different one: namely, of the kind which a thousand representations show to have been an outstanding implement of Lokrian cult; the phiale, that is, which it was the prerogative of the noblest maiden to carry. Here is a dove, too; not painfully grabbed by the wings but freely standing on the lady's lap.[7] Her seat is a throne, its feet ending in lions' claws and its high back decorated with palmettes. Obviously she is a goddess; but—as Orsi observed[8]—the dove does not prove her to be Aphrodite.

He did indeed find figures which represent the Goddess of Love almost as unequivocally as the masterpiece which we contemplated first; one[9] with two doves settled on her throne on either side of her shoulders, and with features of a nobility and beauty which pales the, by comparison, somewhat rustic charm of the figure just cited and many of the same type. Even nobler, in spite of its desperate fragmentation, was one with two young Erotes nestling against the shoulders of the goddess.[10]

Aphrodite then, in her own right, shared in Persephone's Lokrian cult; but Persephone herself adopted Aphrodite's symbolic bird; for the more common run of *sedute* represent her. This is clear from their different

[1] Orsi's excellent plates (ib., p. 108, Figs. 124–47) convey an impression of the wide range of variety within the unmistakable Lokrian style of the (first half of the) fifth century.

[2] Ib., p. 109.

[3] The polos, though, is hardly ever worn by Lokrian figurines of the type under discussion.

[4] e.g. von Matt[2], Pl. 96 = Langlotz–Hirmer, Pls. 60 f.

[5] Orsi, ib., p. 86, Fig. 96; Langlotz–Hirmer, Pl. 67.

[6] Ib., p. 93, Fig. 104 *bis* = von Matt[2], Pl. 100.

[7] On a closely related figure, Orsi, ib., p. 94, Fig. 105, the dove spreads its wings, unhampered yet unwilling to use its freedom.

[8] Ib., p. 96.   [9] Ib., p. 95, Fig. 95 our Plate 23*b*.

[10] Ib., p. 129, Fig. 172. This drawing gives no idea of the beauty of the fragment, which meantime has had a small piece added to it; see our Plate 23*c*.

characterization; from their vast numbers;[1] and from the other attributes, apart from phiale and dove, with which they are frequently equipped. The same seated goddess sometimes holds a cock—Persephone's bird;[2] or a small box, or chest;[3] of a kind which, like the phiale, was an outstanding implement in Persephone's Lokrian cult; finally, the head which, on some protomes, is undoubtedly recognized as Persephone's recurs with some of these *sedute*.[4] She is (as on the *busti*) characterized, sometimes more as a lovely maiden[5] and sometimes more dignified.[6] The authority of the goddess is felt in all of these (rather large) images; the shadow of death, not. As though that mystic veil had been lifted, all of them look out, freely, into the world of the living.

Strangest of all: in the place of cock or dove or chest, some of these figurines wear still another symbol. Between the breasts of the goddess stands, free, naked, winged—Eros;[7] in the same shape, that is, in which we first saw him on his mother's arms. Or he is seen hurrying, with a chaplet in his hand, along the ritual chest held by the goddess.[8] Has, then, Persephone adopted not only Aphrodite's bird but also her son? On one fragment,[9] indeed, Eros and dove have both settled on her. The enigma of a union of the goddesses of Death and of Love presented itself in Sicily; it poses itself in an extreme form at Lokri. Its solution is in the Lokrian tablets; a solution which, alas, we are able to grasp only imperfectly—if at all.

(d) THE TABLETS (PINAKES)

They are widely known today; some well-preserved ones, at any rate, which recur in the picture books.[10] A complete survey and a comprehensive interpretation cannot be attempted before Dr. Zancani-Montuoro has published her immensely laborious work; nor are they here required. We shall consider those aspects bearing upon our theme on the basis of the available material; that is, mainly, the comprehensive older publications by Orsi[11] and Quagliati[12] and the summary survey which Dr.

---

[1] Von Matt[2], Pl. 99, gives an impression of the vast quantities of fragments still awaiting reconstruction in the Reggio Museum. And these are only the remains, or part of them, from the comparatively minor site at Medma!

[2] Orsi, ib., p. 92, Fig. 104; now also in Higgins, *Greek Terracottas*, Pl. 38A.

[3] Orsi, ib., p. 91, Fig. 103.

[4] Compare von Matt[2], Pl. 102 (middle) with Orsi, ib., Figs. 103 f.

[5] Ib., Fig. 105 (a desperately inadequate photograph).

[6] Ib., Figs. 103 f. (ditto); Langlotz–Hirmer, Pl. 22.   [7] Ib., p. 96, Fig. 108.

[8] Ib., Fig. 109.   [9] Ib., p. 99, Fig. 112.

[10] Von Matt[2], Farbtafel, p. 10 and Pls. 137, 140–2, 144–8; Langlotz–Hirmer, Pls. 71–5 and IX.

[11] *Bull. d'Arte*, iii (1908), 406 ff.   [12] *Ausonia*, iii, 1908 (app. 1909), 136 ff.

Zancani-Montuoro has given in the *Enciclopedia dell'Arte Antica*,[1] as well as her articles, there quoted, on several points of detail.[2]

The vast majority of the pinakes come from the thesauros at the foot of La Mannella, where Orsi secured what had not been removed by generations of clandestine diggers and spread all over the world. They were, then, votive-offerings destined to be hung on the walls of Persephone's temple or on the trees of her temenos. Some more were found in local houses and graves; still others (as we shall have occasion to stress) in Sicily.

It is clear, and accepted, that the pinakes show, in successive scenes, the myth of Persephone, from her abduction to her enthronement as Queen of the Netherworld; her Lokrian myth, of which many details remain obscure and which is thoroughly different from the Eleusinian. Here is no Demeter—indeed no certain Lokrian representation of Demeter has so far been found.[3] This means that the very essence of the Eleusinian religion is lacking—the Mother's despair, search, and wrath, resolved into final joy and reconciliation on the Daughter's return. The Lokrian Maiden does not return.[4] She finds her final elevation, worshipped by all gods and men, by the side of Hades; the frightened girl becomes the great goddess, the Queen of the Dead. Seated on her infernal throne, on her face an expression of profound seriousness, she holds in her hands rich ears of grain and the cock, emblem of fecundation.

The maiden became goddess, and Persephone, Queen of Death, became the giver of Life—through her marital union with the Lord of the Netherworld.[5] This marriage is in the centre of the cycle (too evidently so

[1] Vol. iv, 674 ff.

[2] The collection of the Museo Nazionale in Reggio is arranged according to her reconstruction of ten main types of representation. No photographs of these are available; they are however summarized in *Enc. dell'Arte Ant.* and also by Zanotti-Bianco (von Matt[2], p. 130).

[3] This cannot imply that Demeter was unknown at Lokri; in fact, Orsi found an Attic vase of 530–520 B.C., decorated with the Eleusinian myth, at La Mannella (G. Procopio, *Archeologia Classica*, iv (1952), 153 f., Pls. XXX f.; Metzger, *Recherches* . . . , pp. 8 f.; Pls. I. 2 and II). What it does mean is that, in Lokrian cult and theology, the Daughter alone embodied the whole vast sphere of divine reality which elsewhere was perceived in the united persons of Mother and Daughter. One may illustrate this, however imperfectly, by a comparison with various forms of Christian devotion; namely, the divine Mother and her Son worshipped equally at some places while at others the cult of one of them is more or less completely eclipsed by that of the other.

Addendum: This, and much more on the same basis, was written before, through the kindness of the authoress, I was able to read the article 'Persefone e Afrodite sul mare' by P. Zancani-Montuoro (from *Essays in memory of Karl Lehmann* (1964), 386 ff.). One of the two pinakes there reconstructed, however difficult its interpretation, almost beyond doubt shows Demeter in search of her daughter. This unique type confirms that the Eleusinian form of the myth was indeed known at Lokri, but it does not show that it was adopted there; on the contrary, it serves, by its isolation, to underline the pre-eminence, throughout the bulk of the local evidence, of Kore–Persephone.

[4] For literary and archaeological parallels see Detached Note VII, below, p. 400.

[5] The motif of two doves, facing each other, which occurs on two different types of pinakes (P. Zancani-Montuoro in *Atti e Mem. della Soc. Magna Grecia* (1954), p. 104, Pl. XIV and Quagliati, *Aus.* iii (1908), 229, Fig. 81), may symbolize this.

to require a rehearsal of the evidence) and this marriage—the union of Life and Death—is the work of Aphrodite.[1] On her light chariot, 'drawn by a pair of Loves, male and female',[2] Hermes guides her—he knows the way—to the Netherworld; the love-genii bring her dove and a jar of fragrant ointment, emblems and means of her power. And Aphrodite meets Persephone,[3] and the Paphian goddess proffers her son, winged Eros, to the bride; he stretches out his little hands to her, and with eager hands she receives him. Thus Eros became Persephone's own; as we saw him, on her breast, on many a statuette.

The meaning of this scene is immediately obvious; it may be illustrated by comparing a Tarentine relief less than a life's span more recent.[4] A bride is sitting on the nuptial couch; Aphrodite has entered the room and, looking fixedly towards the bride, she sends from her right hand Eros to bring her a taenia. The consummation of marriage happens by the agency of Eros and the grace of Aphrodite. Thereafter, the Maiden is *matrona*—the distinction is expressed and maintained on the tablets with amazing finesse—and, henceforth, the unageing queen of the other world, whence she bestows life and fertility for those above. Eros stays with her. When Hermes once more appears,[5] to offer, like the other gods, his felicitations, Eros stands on her outstretched arm, greeting the divine messenger with his right arm (the left hand holds the lyre: music, so we are given to understand, has its origin where all life originates). But Persephone's hand holds up the flowering lotus; she still is the Goddess of Death.

Giver of life and fertility, after her wedding, to the world above, her marriage is sterile; Persephone bears no child. It must be so, for Persephone is herself Death; she can foster, by Aphrodite's grace, all life on earth; but Death itself cannot procreate its antithesis. Persephone thus is

---

[1] With Roman poets, from Ovid (*Met.* v. 363 ff.) to Claudian, the *raptus Proserpinae* is the work of Venus, and it is so represented on many sarcopnagi (see R. Foerster, *Der Raub . . . der Persephone* (1874), pp. 131 ff.). It is hard to say whether or no this feature derives from Lokrian, or some other, Greek poetry; it may, or may not, have been in the hypothetical epic mentioned below, p. 168.

[2] This is B. Ashmole's formulation (*Proceed. Brit. Acad.* xx (1934), 105); it cannot be translated into Greek, and yet he must be right; for 'Eros and Psyche' (thus Langlotz–Hirmer, p. 73) is too profound a concept to be applied to these charming putti. This was noted, in a different and wider context, by E. Petersen in *Röm. Mitt.* xvi (1901), 57 ff.; esp. 77 ff. He observed that this pair is found drawing the chariot of Aphrodite especially when—as here—the goddess is on her way to bless a marriage: very properly, Eros is joined, particularly in this context, by his female counterpart. One may, however, hesitate to follow Petersen in calling this companion of Eros 'Nike', for—notwithstanding Ἔρως ἀνίκατε μάχαν—she seems a stranger to erotic iconography. G. Kleiner, who (*Tanagrafiguren* (1942), pp. 170 ff.) traces the Hellenistic Eros putti to the fourth and late fifth century (but not to the Lokrian tablet; cf. H. Metzger, *Les représentations dans la céramique attique du IVᵉ siècle* (1951), pp. 54 f.), likewise speaks of 'Nike', but 'Peitho' may be more suitable; cf. e.g. Plutarch, *Coniug. praec.* 138 d and *Quaest. Rom.* 264 b; Pausan. v. 11. 8.   [3] Quagliati *Aus.* iii (1908), 191, fig. 42.

[4] Rumpf, *Die Religion der Griechen* (1928), Fig. 135.

[5] Orsi, *Bull. d'Arte*, iii (1909), p. 147, Fig. 12.

the fostermother rather than the mother of all life. This true and deep insight—that through Love, Life grows out of Death while Death itself remains irrevocable—becomes visibly real on those plaques which show her lifting the lid of a large round basket to find in it, with joyful surprise, a babe or, more correctly speaking, a tiny but well-grown child, sitting up in some versions and standing in others. It is not her child, obviously. Who is it, and whose? Adonis has been suggested and also, time and again, Iakchos;[1] but it cannot be either. The story of the child Adonis as reported in pseudo-Apollodorus[2] and illustrated on an Etruscan mirror and a South Italian vase[3] cannot be reconciled with the indications of the pinakes concerning the relations between Persephone and Aphrodite; it would intolerably exceed and break the complete and meaningful cycle of the scenes represented on them, to which no subsequent quarrel of the two goddesses with a final arbitration by Zeus could possibly be added; and it would anyhow be excluded if in fact the child in the basket is, on some plaques, a girl. This fact alone would suffice also to disqualify Iakchos. Since however the urge to discover 'Orphic mysteries' seems powerful enough to overcome this obstacle, we may urge the incompatibility of everything that the tablets show and intimate with the myth which tells of Persephone, a daughter of Zeus and Demeter who, raped by her heavenly father, gives birth to Dionysos–Zagreus (identified with Iakchos not before Hellenistic times—if then) and who afterwards is ceded to Hades–Pluto.[4] Some plaques of outstanding beauty show Dionysos, in the fullness of his might, before Persephone, saluting the newlywed; the giver, he, of the vine as she of grain. Where, in this context, is there room for Dionysos–Zagreus–Iakchos, the babe, to be torn and devoured by the Titans?[5]

[1] e.g. by N. Putorti, in *L'Italia antichissima*, xi (1937), 3 ff. (Iakchos, 'orfismo'—and all that; as, before, by G. Giannelli, *Culti e miti della Magna Grecia* (1924), p. 193).

[2] iii. 183 ff. Wagner, after Panyassis; cf. Preller–Robert, i. 360, n. 2.

[3] See Preller–Robert, ib., n. 3; Gruppe, ii. 865, n. 4.

[4] Dionysos and Iakchos were identified, at any rate, in the cult of the Attic Lenaia; but this Dionysos is very explicitly the son of Theban Semele; the ritual cry Ϲεμελήϊε Ἰάκχε πλουτοδότα (schol. Aristoph. *Ran.* 479) forbids any thought of Persephone and Zagreus. The same identification prevailed, for a while, at Eleusis (Soph. *Ant.* 1115, 1120, 1152). It must have given a special point to the opening chorus of the *Frogs*; but there is, in all this, no hint of the Orphic Zagreus (whose standing with modern mythographers would not be what it is, if Fate had allowed Aischylos' *Lykourgeia* to survive rather than Nonnos' perverse *Dionysiaka*).

[5] And since we are touching on this sore point, let it be said that the interpretation of the c. 30,000 Tarentine 'Funeral banquets' as representations of the 'holy family' Persephone, Dionysos, and their child Iakchos rests on no evidence whatever. No marital association of Dionysos and Persephone is attested anywhere, except in two late Latin sources (*Mythogr. Vat.* ii. 41 and schol. Stat. *Theb.* iv. 482); according to these, their offspring is—Hermes. According to Nonnos (and no one else) Iakchos is indeed a son of Dionysos; but his mother is a pallid nymph named Aura and not Persephone. Finally, according to the Orphic Hymn 53 (illusions about whose evidential value are no longer legitimate), Dionysos sleeps 'by the house of Persephone' for two full years—which presumably means that he lies as dead—before rousing his thiasos again. That helps neither for Taranto nor for Lokri.

We must then, so it seems, resign ourselves to being unable to identify
the specific myth pictured in the tablets of Persephone finding the child
in the basket; even so, this scene stands out as a beautiful and meaningful
detail of the Lokrian vision of the goddess of Death who, herself childless,
through marital love became the giver and fosterer of all life. A myth,
though, must have existed which contained this scene as well as the
others which are illustrated on the tablets, a myth transmitted, most
probably, in the form of an epic poem and, certainly, relived in cult and
rite. I am not suggesting the enactment of scenes of, for example, abduction and 'Sacred Marriage'; but there are those ever repeated representations—as parts of larger scenes and also by themselves—of cultic
implements and sacrificial animals; the cocks; the bowls (phialai); the
baskets (kalathoi); and particularly those boxes or chests (kistai), small
and great, which we have found the statuettes of the goddess holding, as
she does also on certain tablets.[1] On others, these chests contain the
marital garment;[2] baskets and vessels stand on them, for Persephone's
use[3]; a very large one stands beside her while she adorns herself for her
wedding[4]—a kind of *cista mystica*, which must have conveyed some particular significance in both myth and rite, and hence is also represented
separately, both on pinakes[5] and by small models.[6] Hardly less frequent
are representations of a basket (kalathos), normally filled (or being
filled) with fruits; mainly apples and pomegranates. Cista and kalathos:
we cannot guess at their specific role in the Lokrian myth, except in the
barest outline; but we know something of their importance, at many
places, in the cult of Demeter—which, here again, is found transferred to,
or usurped by, the younger goddess. In her cult they must have been used,
and the myth which is illustrated on the pinakes must have provided the
reasons for this use.

(e) OTHER LOKRIAN RELICS

A type of terracotta unknown in Sicily has been found at La Mannella
and elsewhere in Lokri; namely, female figurines entirely naked.[7] They

---

[1] Orsi, *Bull. d'Arte*, iii (1909), p. 413, Fig. 5.

[2] Von Matt[2], Pl. 145; Langlotz–Hirmer, Pl. 75.   [3] Orsi, ib., pp. 423 f., Figs. 20–4.

[4] Ib., Fig. 28; cf. Quagliati, *Aus.* iii (1908), 105, Fig. 46.

[5] Orsi, ib., Figs. 21–3; Quagliati, ib., p. 227, Figs. 77 and 78.

[6] Naples, Mus. Naz., Inv. 20684 (Levi, p. 23, Fig. 24); B.M. 1226; now also in Higgins,
Greek Terracottas, Pl. 38B.

[7] *Addendum*: Of late, figurines of the same type have become known from a restricted area
in Central Sicily; their reference to a specially Lokrian institution (see text) therewith becomes even less acceptable. D. Adamasteanu, in publishing them (*Kokalos*, iv (1958), 55 f.
and Pl. 12, Fig. 21) describes them as 'statuette-bambolle'. The objections against this designation are enhanced by the fact that they are represented sitting on what looks like an altar.
The interpretation attempted, in the text above, of the Lokrian nudes is not, to my mind,
negatively affected by their occurrence in Sicily and elsewhere (below, p. 169, n. 7).

are in a half-sitting position, with the arms pressed along the body.[1] The head—if any—is decorated with a diadem or polos; often, though, it is missing, and it may be doubted whether in all these cases it has simply broken off or whether the body alone was the object of representation; the same question arises with others which are without hands or feet. Orsi repeatedly declared them to be dolls;[2] but they are very different from those naked figures, found (as far as known) in the graves of children and unmarried girls at Lokri[3] as well as in countless other places, which are convincingly so interpreted; in particular, their limbs are not movable and their position is different. They do not strike one as intentionally lascivious, nor are the sexual characteristics particularly stressed; they are in no way comparable to the prehistoric figurines which we have discussed, nor to the oriental *déesse nue* and her Greek successors; even so, their erotic quality is, I think, obvious; particularly when it is remembered how very rarely one meets with female nudes in Greek sculpture prior to the fourth century. Oldfather[4] suggested that they are representations of hierodules. The assumption that the institution of hierodules existed at Lokri rests on an uncertain inference from two short texts: first, the report, in Justin, that the Lokrians, hard pressed in a war with Rhegion (in 477 B.C.), swore in case of their victory to prostitute their daughters 'on the day of Venus';[5] second, the assertion, by Klearchos of Soloi,[6] of Lokrian libertinism—which is too vague (and contrary to all that is known of Lokrian *atrekeia*) to deserve credence; nor has it any obvious connection with the assumed institution. Even if this bold inference were allowed, the significance of the institution would remain to be considered; for nothing suggests, and everything known discourages, the assumption that a Lokrian temple—and indeed Persephone's temple! —could have served as a glorified *lupanar*; as the Aphrodite-temple at Corinth, with its international harbour, is likely to have done. The figurines in question[7] may indeed be seen in some relation with the

---

[1] *Bull. d'Arte*, iii (1909), 14; *Not. Scav.* (1911), *Suppl.*, p. 20, Fig. 18; *Not. Scav.* (1917), 105, Fig. 7; our Plate 24a.

[2] *Not. Scav.* (1911), *Suppl.*, p. 20; ib. (1913), *Suppl.*, pp. 50 and 53.

[3] e.g. *Not. Scav.* (1913), *Suppl.*, p. 40, Fig. 50.   [4] *Real-Enzykl.* xiii. 2, 1350.

[5] Justin. xxi. iii. 2; cf. schol. Pind. *Pyth.* ii. 36. It is not impossible that Pindar's own words contain an allusion to it. 'Since the war was prevented by Hieron's intercession, the barbarous oath could be left unfulfilled': thus A. v. Stauffenberg, *Trinakria* (1963), p. 215; but Justin's phrase 'quo voto intermisso . . .', etc., hardly implies this evasion; *intermittere* is not synonymous with *neglegere*.

[6] Athen. 516 a.

[7] Identical figurines from Taranto and Cyrene are in the Louvre (C200–4 and C249) and in the B.M. (1437–41 and 1500–1); in the Mus. Naz. at Naples are samples from Taranto, Ruvo (our Plate 24a), Cumae, Capua, and Nocera (Levi, nos. 200, 314, 467, 588, 792); for Rhodes (Kamiros) finally see *Clara Rhodos*, iv (1931), 284. The wide spread of the type is one of several facts which discourage the assumption that customs and traditions of the native Siculi gave rise to this 'matriarchal' feature of Lokrian life.

'erotic' aspects of Lokrian religion and institutions which have so far been noted; but hardly in the narrow manner suggested by Oldfather. They may be taken for another symbol of what is emerging as a central article of the Lokrian mythical theology; namely, the triumph of Life over Death through Eros.

This interpretation is thoroughly supported by the fact that these naked figurines have been found not only in the sanctuary of Persephone but also in graves; and that quite frequently.[1] Whether Egyptian *ushabtis*, of similar appearance, were put into graves merely *pour le divertissement de Monsieur*, I am not competent to decide; but no explanation on these lines could account for the Lokrian figurines; be it only because they have been found also in the grave of a young girl.[2] Reference to other gifts placed in Lokrian graves will serve to confirm and clarify the proposed interpretation.

A unique double-bust representing Persephone and Hades was found in one of them.[3] It may be compared, formally, with the two Sicilian ones previously mentioned; in the Lokrian grave, it places the dead under the protection of the deities whose realm he is entering. Statuettes representing Persephone 'in the usual manner'—and hence passed over by Orsi in a brief sentence[4]—were found in many Lokrian graves; a bust of 'Kore', carefully secured by being placed inside a bowl and covered by its lid, was interred between three of them:[5] the goddess is guarding her new wards. Represented by a 'grande busto', she similarly guarded a young child at Medma;[6] in the same grave, and next to her, lay one of those naked *sedute*! In another grave[7] she was found, at one end, seated on a very large chair, with a patera (phiale) in one hand, a fruit (pomegranate or apple) in the other, and the polos on her head; at the other end, again, lay 'una donna nuda seduta'.

It is hard to believe that these figurines, in graves, are not all equally meaningful, and the meaning which we inclined to ascribe to the naked ones derives probability from the presence of Aphrodite in neighbouring graves. The reader may recall our reference to her fragmented representation, from Medma, with an Eros on each shoulder.[8] It belongs to a type recurrent at Lokri and Medma, but not elsewhere, which may derive from a cult-image;[9] two replicas of it come from graves at both places.[10] On the Lokrian one (which is a free and inferior variant), one of the putti holds a lyre; the other is female; they thus recall the pair drawing

---

[1] Orsi, *Not. Scav.* (1911), 18, Fig. 18; ib. (1913), *Suppl.*, pp. 50 and 53; ib. (1917), 44 and 105, Fig. 7.

[2] *Not. Scav.* (1917), 105.   [3] *Not. Scav.* (1911), *Suppl.*, p. 70, Fig. 51.

[4] *Not. Scav.* (1913), *Suppl.*, p. 50.   [5] Ib., p. 9, Fig. 8.

[6] *Not. Scav.* (1917), 48, Fig. 17.   [7] Ib., 44, Fig. 11.

[8] Above, p. 163, with note 9.   [9] Orsi, *Not. Scav.* (1913), *Suppl.*, p. 129.

[10] *Not. Scav.* (1917), 61, Fig. 36, and 152, Fig. 57.

Aphrodite's chariot on one of the pinakes and also, on another one, Eros with his lyre on Persephone's arm. The pair of winged 'genii', one male and one female, recurs on an askos found in the grave of a Lokrian youth;[1] another one yielded an image, more than half a metre high, of Aphrodite, her head crowned with the polos, and her dove settling on her right hand.[2]

The religious meaning in these funeral gifts is evident; it stands out most impressively in some others of particular significance. In two graves (nos. 587 and 612) of the Lokrian necropolis *in contrada Lucifero*, Orsi found bronze statuettes, one male, one female, of exquisite workmanship and emphatic expressiveness.[3] Both had served as handles, or decorations, of some unknown, and presumably wooden object (could it have been a replica of the ritual cista?); and both are—in different ways—in an attitude of fervent prayer. The female statuette lay on the left forearm of the skeleton of (so it seems) a very old woman; its expression is determined by the 'large and solemn gesture of salutation and adoration' with which the erect, standing woman raises the straight right arm and hand in what Orsi convincingly described as a gesture of proskynesis (in the original, Greek sense of the word). The other statuette lay above the head of a skeleton; it is a naked male figure, kneeling, with both arms bent upward in fervent supplication.[4] It seems impossible in these remarkable figurines not to see representatives of the dead invoking the goddess whose realm they are entering in fear and trust.

Three other graves (nos. 1614, 1433, and 739) yielded precious candelabra made of bronze over an iron core. It is not in fact certain that these remarkable objects—they consist of a heavy and long central shaft with branch-like excrescences—are candelabra;[5] but the interest of this

---

[1] *Not. Scav.* (1911), *Suppl.*, p. 83, Fig. 17.

[2] Ib., p. 17; apparently a Rhodian alabastron like B.M. 62.

[3] *Not. Scav.* (1913), *Suppl.*, pp. 10 ff., Figs. 11 and 13.

[4] Orsi (ib., p. 13) posited an original standing not kneeling; and indeed this would be the normal posture for a Greek praying, since kneeling in the oriental manner (A. *Pers.* 152; Eur. *Or.* 1507, *Phoen.* 293) before gods or men was regarded as bigotry and unworthy (A. *Sept.* 95, 185; Theophr. *Char.* 16. 5). There are however two exceptions. The suppliant προσπίτνει the person invoked (often embracing his knees, e.g. Eur. *Suppl.* 10); equally understandably one might kneel when invoking the dead (e.g. Soph. *El.* 453, Eur. *Hel.* 64) or the deities of the Netherworld (often beating the ground with one's hands, like Althaia invoking Hades and Persephone, *Il.* 9. 566 ff., cf. Eur. *Tro.* 1305 ff.). O. Walter illustrated the latter alternative from Attic fourth-century reliefs (*Oesterr. Jahreshefte*, xiii (1910), *Beibl.* 229 ff.; add K. Schauenburg, *Arch. Jahrb.* lxviii (1953), 57): the deities thus invoked are—apart from the Asianic Men—Zeus Philios or Meilichios, Artemis, and the goddesses of Eleusis; the persons praying, almost always women. Representations of this kind are, according to him, generally rare; nor does he quote any early instance. In view of these facts the kneeling posture of the figurine under discussion is reasonably interpreted as one of supplication; and indeed Orsi himself noted various details, also of facial expression, which favour this interpretation. At the same time, the position of the arms is one of prayer; the supplication then is addressed, by the kneeling suppliant, to a deity of the Netherworld. "Νῦν δ' ἱκέτης ἥκω παρ' ἀγαυὴν Φερσεφόνειαν."   [5] Orsi discusses the point in *Not. Scav.* (1913), *Suppl.*, p. 29.

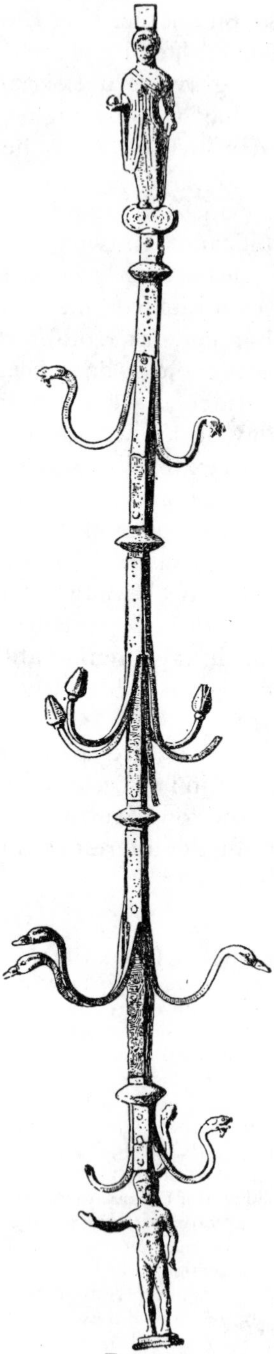

question pales before their religious significance, which is put beyond doubt by the find-circumstances of one of them.

The smallest (1614)[1] is 39·5 cm. high; it had lost its bronze covering and most of the 'branches'. It lay by the forearm of the skeleton. The top of the shaft is surmounted by a large lotus-bud of bronze just beginning to open; around it were four winding 'branches' ending in small, similar but closed buds. The second (from a cremation, grave no. 1433),[2] 48 cm. high, has lost the three orders of curving branches along its stem (but for their rudiments); its shaft, too, is topped with a bronze bud. The third (from grave no. 739)[3] is a masterpiece of the Lokrian toreutic art—and more than that; and it is almost perfectly preserved. It is no less than 1·225 m. high. Four times four 'branches' issue from its stem. The lowest of them end in snakes' heads: harbingers of death; the next—longer than all others—in geese's heads: Aphrodite's birds, which also figure on the pinakes;[4] the third, in lotus buds, some closed, some opening (we know their meaning); the uppermost and shortest branches again end in snakes' heads, markedly smaller than those at the lower end. All this structure rests on the head of the statuette of a sturdy naked youth; and it is crowned, at the upper end of the stem and high above even the nearest snakes, by a standing female figure on a square basis decorated with volutes. The youth has the right arm raised;[5] his posture is precisely like that of the well-known statuette of a praying Arkadian

[1] *Not. Scav.* (1917), 26 f. with Fig. 44.
[2] Ib., 126 with Fig. 31.
[3] *Not. Scav.* (1913), *Suppl.*, pp. 27 f. with Figs. 31 and 33; our Fig. 3.
[4] e.g. von Matt[2], Pl. 144.
[5] Von Matt[2], Pl. 136. Dr. Zancani-Montuoro (see below, p. 173, note 2), p. 200, n. 2 describes the goose as an 'animal sacred to Persephone'; an alternative which I do not wish to exclude, seeing that, on one type of the pinakes, a large goose stands between the legs of her throne.

FIG. 3.

shepherd;[1] he is praying. The female figure, from her dress and posture, might be a human maiden; but she holds, in her outstretched right hand, a large pomegranate, Persephone's fruit. Her serious countenance confirms it: she is Persephone.

This great object was found lying along the side and legs of the skeleton of a grown-up man; his hands held—they 'clutched' it, says Orsi—the female figure at its upper end. Is not the symbolism clear or, rather, the faith thus expressed?[2] The dead man is praying to Persephone; he will have to go the long, lone way; to pass the horrors of death, helped at first by Aphrodite's might, but then travelling ever more deeply into the unknown; but he will penetrate it and, in the end, reach the goddess whose image he is clutching: the Goddess of Death who is the Giver of Life.[3]

VI. THE GODDESS OF SICILY

Reflecting a myth which we discern dimly and partially, Lokrian art shows in an organic context those features which in the Sicilian images of Persephone appeared contradictory and enigmatic—the stern goddess of the Netherworld and the loving bride; the Queen of Death and the giver

[1] Reproduced, e.g., in Rumpf, Fig. 143, after K. A. Neugebauer, *Antike Bronzestatuetten* (1921), Pl. 23.

[2] Herein may lie the analogy between the 'candelabra' and the strange object, made up of palmettes and spiralling branches and crowned by a large flower of lotus, which Persephone is seen holding in one of the scenes represented on the Lokrian pinakes. Dr. Zancani-Montuoro, who reconstructed and discussed this type (in *Paolo Orsi*, published in 1935 by the *Archivio storico per la Calabria . . .* , pp. 202 ff., Fig. 1 and Pl. XIV), compared this object with the three 'candelabra' and concluded that, whatever it be, it could hardly be a candelabrum. Perhaps they all are ritual implements, their shape determined by their symbolism. The one held by Persephone could very well be held to convey the forces of Life growing in the shadow of Death.

[3] In another grave (no. 934) of the same cemetery Orsi (*Not. Scav.* (1913), *Suppl.*, p. 45) found a similarly expressive though completely different token; namely, the wonderful terracotta of a maenad (von Matt[2], Pl. 127; Langlotz–Hirmer, Pl. XI), in the hand of, perhaps, a young woman. It is a unique work of unknown origin but certainly not Lokrian. She who was thus buried expected in another life to join the thiasos of Dionysos. Here, then, we meet with the first symptom—an isolated one—of the impact, at Lokri, of a new religion— a century after the date of the monuments with which we have been dealing (for the late-archaic figurine of a girl dancing or, rather, running which Orsi (ib., p. 14, Fig. 14; cf. the bronze statuette of a running girl from Dodona, B. Ashmole, *Proc. Brit. Acad.* xx (1934), Fig. 6) found in the hand of another girl's skeleton, has nothing dionysiac about it). Dionysos, the giver of the wine, stands before Persephone, the giver of grain, on the beautiful Lokrian pinakes already referred to (above, p. 167); understandably so, for as the giver of wine and rapture, the son of Semele held sway, according to Sophokles (*Ant.* 1119), over Italy. As the giver of a blissful after-life, however, he is otherwise known, in the West, only from the late-archaic funeral inscriptions from Pozzuoli and in a chamber grave at Cumae (Jeffery, p. 240, nos. 7 and 12). The people of Cumae appear to have brought his cult from Euboea (Wilamowitz, ii. 62).

of fruitfulness and life. It is this wide, or even universal, concept of the goddess which made it possible for her to be worshipped as the chief deity of Lokri;[1] for no community as vigorous as this could conceivably find its divine ideal in a concept of Death absolute nor, alternatively, in an Eleusinian Maiden, the friendly adjunct of the great Demeter. There can be no doubt that the particular features of the Lokrian character—of which we have caught some glimpses—enabled this people to grasp this kind of universality about their goddess; in a manner which everyone concerned may ponder for himself, learning *quantum satis* from J. J. Bachofen.[2] This much, though, may be taken for granted: that particular character of the Lokrians and their vision of the goddess are not easily explained as either inherited from their mainland forebears or adopted from local natives; for these alternatives have been sufficiently discussed to establish the fact that the evidence, archaeological and historical, is against either of them.

In terms of mythical realization, the Lokrian universal concept of Persephone is expressed in her relation to Aphrodite. It is not that the two goddesses became one; Aphrodite was, and remained, the second great goddess of Lokri. At the same time, though, Persephone has been seen to exhibit features of Aphrodite. The mythical expression for this widened concept was in the visit by Aphrodite, the handing-over of Eros and the marriage of Hades and Persephone.

The age of Romanticism was better attuned to appreciate a concept of the unity of Death and Love than is ours. One of its sons, Ed. Gerhard, wrote a long essay on *Venus Proserpina*[3] in which he brought together the literary and archaeological evidence for a personal union of the two goddesses. Neither, unfortunately, amounts to much. According to pseudo-Aristotle, *Mirab*. 133,[4] Herakles set up a dedication, in the land of the Aenianes in Thessaly, to Κυθήραι Φερϲεφαάϲϲηι. The style of his alleged inscription suggests anything but its archaic origin; its transmitted wording is 'vehementer corruptum',[5] and the context in which it is quoted makes any reference to Persephone preposterous. This had been argued even before Gerhard adduced the epigram, and under G. Hermann's

---

[1] The universal character of the goddess of Lokri finds, perhaps, the fullest expression, in a terracotta, 20 cm. high, which is reproduced on our frontispiece. Orsi recovered it at Rosarno–Medma. It is the best representative of a type of which the same spot yielded 'alcune diecine' of further samples, and it is elaborated—especially its hands and feet—with a finesse which suggests an original in bronze; it may then very well be the reproduction of a cult image. The right hand holds 'il mistico frutto del papavero', the left, a fillet (Orsi, *Not. Scav.* (1913), *Suppl.*, pp. 89 f. and Fig. 99).

[2] An attempt in this direction has been made by G. Säflund, on the last page of his *Aphrodite Kallipygos* (English edition (1963), p. 56, with notes on pp. 81 ff.).

[3] First published in *Hyperboreisch-Römische Studien*, ii. 121 ff.; reprinted in his *Archäologischer Nachlass* (1852), 119 ff. (which I am using).

[4] Ed. O. Apelt (1888), p. 83.   [5] G. Hermann, *Opuscula*, v (1834), p. 180.

critical scalpel Φερϲεφάαϲϲα vanished from the text for good. Slightly more substantial is the evidence of Plutarch,[1] who compares the Roman funeral goddess Libitina to an (otherwise unknown) Greek Aphrodite ἐπιτύμβια[2] of whom, he says, a little image existed at Delphi; the dead were called up to receive libations at it.[3] Plutarch deserves credence here, seeing that he was a Delphic high-priest; but this isolated fact concerns Aphrodite rather than Persephone.[4] The images, finally, in which Gerhard found his goddess represented belong to the vast class of statues and statuettes which are now generally called 'korai', and which cannot be identified as representations of a specific goddess (and least of all one so feebly attested) unless they exhibit specific characteristics and attributes.[5]

On the preceding pages, hundreds of different representations of Persephone have been presented, many of them exhibiting, in various ways, features also of Aphrodite. It remains for us to demonstrate that the Lokrian theology, which combined these features into a meaningful whole, was accepted in Sicily.

P. Orsi (again and always Orsi) excavated the ruins of Kamarina in 1899 and 1903. The graves in the necropolis Passo Marinaro there were rich in terracottas. One of them—it was the 444th to be opened!—though small, yielded 'two seated figurines with high polos in a rigid hieratic style; one of them with two rows of pendants, the other with a dove on the chest' (we would now call them a 'Telines figurine' and, perhaps, a 'Rodia seduta'); moreover, two dolls (real dolls) and—the main find—'a grand seated image of Aphrodite'.[6] It was, in fact, a typical sample of the Persephone images from Medma and Lokri; but this find was made before the same Orsi excavated there. He recognized that the figure was not Sicilian; he even thought, tentatively, of Medma,[7] from where he had seen some 'dispersed finds'. His erroneous designation was understandable, for a winged Eros, with a chaplet in his left hand and a dove on his right, is pictured on the body of the youthful goddess; in the

---

[1] *Aet. Rom.* 23; cf. *Numa* 12. 1.   [2] Read ἐπιτυμβιδία.

[3] To these two texts, L. R. Farnell (*The Cults*, ii (1896), p. 754, n. 110) added Clement's curious allegation of a cult, at Argos, of 'Aphrodite the Grave-robber' (τυμβώρυχοϲ), as well as other testimonies even more obscure, and less relevant, to bear out the preposterous assertion (p. 652) that 'we find in Greece the frequent worship of Aphrodite as a divinity of death and the lower world'; with the corollary (p. 653): 'it does not appear that the Greeks have added anything new to the tradition which they received' (namely, from the Orient).—Gruppe, ii. 1358, n. 1, quoting this and other evidence for 'Aphrodite als Todesgöttin', is himself duly reserved about its relevance.

[4] G. Koerte (in *Archäol. Studien . . . H. Brunn* (1893), 1 ff.) used the same evidence to account for an exceptional, archaic image of a naked Aphrodite in the necropolis of Orvieto (Volsinii).

[5] This observation was made, against Gerhard, by J. J. Bernoulli in 1873 (*Aphrodite*, pp. 63 ff.); twelve years before the find of the Athenian korai proved him right. Cf. A. Rumpf, *Archäologie*, ii (1956), 30.

[6] *Mon. Ant.*, xiv (1904 [1905]), pp. 868 ff., with Fig. 74; our Plate 24*b*.

[7] Ib., p. 871, n. 1.

manner which we now know so well. The correct identification is dictated, not only by her serious and withdrawn expression but by the phiale held, on her lap, in her right hand and by the sacred cista in her left.[1] Here, then, is a Lokrian representation of the goddess put into a Sicilian grave together with others made locally.[2]

But the fullest proof for the acceptance of Lokrian imagery—and, therefore, also of Lokrian theology—comes from the farthest Greek city in Sicily, Selinus. I shall not go into detail. On Gàbrici's plates LXVIII– LXXIV are copious samples of the many hundreds of Lokrian terracottas from the Gaggera[3]—originals, copies and imitations of Lokrian models; the goddess standing or seated; holding phiale, cista, dove, apple, pome- granate, lotus; often with Eros on her hand and upon her garment; her body sometimes hidden underneath a heavy peplos and sometimes modelled underneath a thin chiton as though it were Aphrodite's;[4] her face now more severe and withdrawn, now friendly, lovely, and some- times actually smiling. Even Lokrian pinakes were dedicated at Selinus; witness the fragment of one representing the abduction of Kore, pictured by Gàbrici, Pl. LXXVII. 5.

These Lokrian products obviously were not accepted and dedicated to the goddess and put into graves in Sicily merely because they were pretty; if that had been the motive, many other pretty things were to hand. They were thus accepted because the people of Sicily found in them the best and fullest expression of that vision of Persephone which so many other votive statuettes, imported ones as well as locally made ones, had intimated profoundly but incompletely; the vision of the Queen of Death who, through Love, had become the giver of Life.

It is the Greek vision of the Goddess of Sicily. We had to go to Malta to find her fullest realization from pre-historic times; to Lokri, for her classi- cal Greek image. The prerogative of women there, however obscure, may be not unconnected with the emergence of this most universal concept of the Goddess; it affords, moreover, at the very least, an analogy to the predominance of women among her Sicilian worshippers. Its emergence —as we saw[5]—is not open to a simple historical explanation; this god- head was not 'taken over from the Siculs of Calabria', nor brought from

---

[1] The statuette is pictured also by Pace, ii. 44, Fig. 42, with the unaccountable description 'Demeter of Enna, with Nike'.

[2] I cannot tell whether the latter represented Demeter or Persephone.

[3] One of the seated figurines is pictured in van Ufford, Fig. 46; a head, Fig. 65. I saw one in the Museo Pepoli at Trapani (no. 5291), presumably likewise from the Gaggera.

[4] Gàbrici, Pl. LXXI. 9 is here instructive. It is a local make, imitating the typical Medma *sedute*; of imperfect proportions. The fully modelled body, and especially the breasts, would suit Aphrodite, and so would the dove on her hand; but the face could never be that of the goddess of Love; its serious and somewhat withdrawn and even suffering expression charac- terizes Persephone.

[5] Above, p. 174.

mainland Lokris by immigrating Greeks. It is the sublime expression of a vision which was perceived and worshipped throughout Greek Sicily; a vision of the perennial godhead of those lands; the ancient Goddess now seen by Greek eyes, received by Greek minds and fashioned by Greek hands.

In the course of the fifth century a new, Corinthian type of terracotta was widely adopted in Sicily for her representation;[1] a slim and tall standing figure, in a flowing, sleeved chiton, with the polos on her head and various objects in one or both hands. It is not a type of particular artistic merit, but it brings out the basic features just summarized plainly and fully. For example, one found in the necropolis of Megara Hyblaia, now in the Museo Nazionale at Syracuse,[2] supports a dove with her right hand and holds an apple in her left. Aphrodite? The symbols would suggest her, but the serious, unsmiling face contradicts the suggestion. Other specimens hold a pomegranate and a flower of lotus,[3] confirming the alternative designation; and indeed one connoisseur asserts, even with regard to samples from Corinth, that a 'connection with Demeter and Persephone is in every case probable'.[4] It means that the one goddess was felt to combine, with her own, the features of Aphrodite and Demeter; we recall her representations even as a madonna-like kourotrophos. Thus Sicily was (if we interpret the evidence rightly) in the fifth and fourth centuries predominantly the patrimony of Persephone,[5] as Pindar said; thereafter, under the impact of Athens, Eleusis and, later, Rome, the other goddesses reasserted their individualities.

But the ancient Goddess remained.[6] At Easter, in Syracuse, churches and houses are decorated with the sign of the 'palumba' (the Sicilian word for 'columba', 'dove') and all confectioners bake cakes and sweets in this

---

[1] Cf. van Ufford, p. 50 and Pl. 29.   [2] See Plate 24c (inventory no. 11520.)

[3] Cf. Higgins, *Greek Terracottas*, Pl. 35E.

[4] R. A. Higgins, in *Cat. Brit. Mus.*, on no. 905; not unaware, of course, that the same type was made into a representation of Artemis by the addition of different attributes (bow and fawn), as in B.M., no. 907; see now *Greek Terracottas*, p. 82 with Pl. 35D.

[5] I lack the boldness in evidence to quote the much debated female head on early Syracusan coins, which some call Arethusa, some Artemis, some Kore. It definitely *is* Kore on coins from c. 400 B.C. onward—crowned with ears of corn!—and it is named 'Arethusa' occasionally in the fifth century; but does this prove, or disprove, that the older ones always represent Arethusa?

[6] The so-called 'after-life' of ancient cults in Sicily has been the subject of many specialists' studies; for a summary see Pace, *passim*, especially iii. 466 ff. The most grandiose demonstration of this continuity is in the cathedral of Syracuse built on the foundations, and resting on the columns, of the Deinomenid temple of Athena; but it is felt no less live in local custom, rite, and shrine. Orsi (*Gela*, 576) sketched the continuing cult at 'S. Maria di Bitalemi' in a few moving lines; lately W. Fuchs (*Arch. Anz.* (1964), 704) commented about the same place, where 'to this day the women come, carrying their children on their left shoulder, as the terracottas show it'. U. Zanotti-Bianco and P. Zancani-Montuoro tell of similar surviving customs in and about Paestum, and indeed the Hera of Paestum and Foce del Sele is thoroughly comparable to the Sicilian Persephone; but I have forbidden myself to enter their province.

shape, for the delight of young and old. If you ask them what it means, the answer comes spontaneously and predictably: the dove means the Holy Spirit. You may feel puzzled at this: is Easter the Feast of the Holy Spirit? Does not Scripture and Rite assign it a different day? And you recall the goddess of spring and life who carries the dove. . . .

Go to the Palazzo Bellomo; admire its memorials of Sicilian art since the Middle Ages. See that fifteenth-century Madonna with the Son on her arm; he stretches out to her an apple with his right hand and a dove with his left. Ask that gentle priest what these symbols mean. 'The apple recalls Eve's sin in paradise; the dove is the Holy Spirit.' And you recall the Lokrian goddess with her child; and Eros with wreath and dove; and Persephone with the babe in her arms or, again, with Eros and holding apple and dove. And you think your own thoughts.

BOOK TWO

EMPEDOKLES' *KATHARMOI*

οὐκ ἂν ἀνὴρ τοιαῦτα cοφὸc φρεcὶ μαντεύcαιτο
ὡc ὄφρα μέν τε βιῶcι τὸ δὴ βίοτον καλέουcιν
τόφρα μὲν οὖν εἰcὶν καί cφιν πάρα δειλὰ καὶ ἐcθλά·
πρὶν δὲ πάγεν τε βροτοὶ καὶ ἐπεὶ λύθεν οὐδὲν ἄρ' εἰcιν.

I. EMPEDOKLES OF AKRAGAS

HE was a genius—the town-planner from Gela who, in the second decade of the sixth century, selected, from among the countless hills lining the southern coast of Sicily, the site for the city of Akragas. Standing where, two thousand years later, the Duomo was to overlook the shrunken town, he conceived, by an inspiration equal to any artist's or poet's, the design of a grandiose city on the vast terrain at his feet. The place in fact fulfilled to perfection the requirements which, ever since Mycenaean times, Greeks sought to meet in building their towns.[1] The high rock-plateau (now Colle di Girgenti) on which he was standing was the predestined akropolis; its enormous and unscalable northern fall, together with the mile-long sweep of the neighbouring Rupe Atenea, would on the north and east shield the town below the southward slope of the akropolis. These gigantic ramparts had been carved out by the river Akragas, flowing at the bottom of the guarding precipices; the high banks of its tributary, the Hypsas, though less enormous, and less regularly shaped, afforded corresponding protection from the west, and even where, to the beholder on his height, the calcareous slope appeared to merge into the coastal plain, the sea had left, in ages past, the sandstone edge of a former coast, providing boundary and defence even there. Between them, these residues of the eternal strife of water and rock enclosed an irregular quadrangle ready to accommodate a city much larger than classical Athens. As such, and with parallel streets meeting at right angles, the un-named planner (long before Hippodamos) designed it; thus it was laid out, and where, in our days, the oldest foundations of streets and houses have been uncovered, their size, solidity, and precision make the later, Roman rebuilding appear shoddy and flimsy.

The river-god Akragas, whose waters—much more abundant then than, owing to deforestation and erosion, they are now[2]—had carved out this natural fortress, together with his tributary all but surrounded it; he went on to irrigate the fertile plain below, and he created, on joining the sea, the roadstead where merchants from Gela had long ago established a small emporium; henceforth, wares were to flow, through it, to and from Africa and the Aegaean; he was therefore naturally felt to be the ancestor and protector of the new city. It took its name from him (Gela, Selinus, Himera, Heloros, Medma and many other Western Greek cities

---

[1] The evidence has been collected, and discussed, in an instructive manner, by E. Blumenthal, *Die altgriechische Siedlungskolonisation . . .*, in *Tübinger Geographische Studien*, Heft 10 (1963)

[2] On this general Sicilian feature cf. P. Orsi, *Mon. Ant.* xvii (1906) 7 with note 2.

honoured their life-giving rivers in the same manner[1]); its inhabitants felt what Pindar and Empedokles echoed: theirs was 'the city of (the river) Akragas'.

His gift they strove to utilize and embellish; even before its classical age this was, in the words of the young Pindar, 'the fairest among the cities of men'. The line of fortifications followed and, where necessary, completed the ramparts carved out by him, and where natural protection was weakest, that is, along the southern boundary, there arose, in the course of the fifth century, that row of temples whose ruins are, to this day, the glory of Sicily. In their time, shining with the brightness of the whitish gypsum covering their sandstone structures, and with the rich colouring of their sculptures and ornaments, they witnessed to the devotion and pride of the citizens and their trust in their divine protectors; for the temples stand immediately behind the walls; so closely, indeed, as in some places to leave hardly room for a single person to pass. Thus they proclaimed, to friend and foe, that the gods were the defenders of Akragas; as the golden Gorgoneion on the south wall of the Athenian akropolis placed Athena's city under the protection of her goddess.[2]

The splendour of the life in the city is described in Diodoros (xiii. 81–4). It corresponded with the splendour of these monuments; besides, and primarily, they bespeak that religious devotion which has been illuminated, at least in some aspects, in our previous chapters. This devotion found its expression in cult and rite, centring on abundant sacrifices, and these sacrifices we must strive vividly to put before our minds, for they had an evident and decisive impact upon Empedokles.

We may visualize him—the nobleman, the thinker, the physician—in his city. His mind and thought stand out in his surviving verses, and some details in the biographical tradition deserve credence and can be integrated with the image of his time and milieu; as E. A. Freeman and J. Bidez have shown. An impressionable youth at the time of Theron's rule and Pindar's visit; a man at the fall of the tyranny, conspicuously active in the ensuing struggles for the establishment of a democratic order: we need not dwell on details which are as significant for his character as they are familiar; and any lingering questions about the compatibility, within one person, of the characteristics of a democratic leader and a conscious aristocrat; of a 'scientist' and a 'miracle-worker' and, finally, of the authorship of books allegedly diametrically different in purpose and content: these cannot usefully be taken up until the evidence has been considered afresh; which will be done in the following chapters. Here, though, we may ponder the impact upon Empedokles of the religious traditions observed by the people of Akragas and by all Greeks.

---

[1] See Stephanos Byz., s.v. Ἀκράγαντος.
[2] Paus. i. 21. 3; cf. Preller–Robert, i. 193 and n. 3.

Imagine what went on in their sanctuaries; for example, in that
'Chthonic Sanctuary' to which we have previously referred, trying to
recover the sentiments and ideas centring on it; now let us consider the
reality of the cult. The temenos is studded with low altars, square ones
and round ones, with holes, deep into the ground, in their centre. There
enter devout women (we know them from the terracottas), each of them
carrying in her arms, like a pet, a small piglet. They bring it to one of the
altars; its head is pressed across the hole and its throat cut; its life-blood
flows into the deep, to please the deity below. Then faggots are heaped
on the altar, the little body is burned on it; blood and sizzling grease drip
into the ground. This goes on all over the sanctuary, at all times. And
there are many sanctuaries throughout the town, all with their altars;
and altars in front of every house, and sacrifices everywhere; the grandest
at those shining great temples—the altar in front of the giant temple of
Zeus is more than 160 feet long and 50 feet wide, to accommodate easily
a whole hecatomb at one time and any time. Akragas is a rich town and
a devout town; and the richer and the more devout, the richer are its
offerings; not small piglets only and hens and lambs, but goats, cows,
bulls . . . their useless parts burning for the gods, while the worshippers
feast on the good parts. To this day one seems to see on the weathered
altar-stones the marks of the axes which, at one expert stroke, severed the
heads of victims; and the profusion of blood flowing over them, and the
fires burning on them, have left them discoloured. The glorious city, in its
continuous worship, must have resounded with the shrieks of dying
animals; its air reeking with the stench of blood and burning carcasses.

Sympathy with animals is rare among Southern people today, and so it
was in Antiquity. This notwithstanding, there is evidence of feelings of
remorse at the enormity of this kind of worship, and attempts to appease
these feelings are reflected in the stories of victims forcing their way to the
altar or at least willingly bowing to the deadly stroke; the same motive
stands out in the fictitious lawsuits against the axe which dealt the stroke
and therewith put an end to the innocent cult of an earlier and gentler
age, traces of which remained in the bloodless sacrifices prescribed for
certain deities at many places.[1] Empedokles could not acquiesce in these
evasions. He felt overwhelmingly the horror in honouring by murder the
presumed givers of life, and he perceived: this worship is crime, the gods
who exact it are false; the world under their sway is on the path of
corruption.

This was his 'Ur-Erlebnis'; no mere 'sympathy with animals', but an
inborn consciousness of the sacredness of all life. Aroused by his finding

[1] Pausan. i. 24. 4 and 28. 10; Theophrast. *ap.* Porph. *De abstin.* ii. 28 f. and 9 f. (ib. 10
αἰτίαι . . . πλήρεις οὐκ εὐαγῶν ἀπολογιῶν); cf. L. Deubner, *Attische Feste* (1932), pp. 158 ff.;
A. B. Cook, *Zeus*, iii (1940), pp. 570 ff.

it denied and defiled in honour of the gods, this consciousness determined the direction of his thought and governed his adoption, or rejection, of traditions historic and poetic, religious and philosophical, and it
became the vital centre around which all his insights and experiences
crystallized into a consistent whole. The world is all Life, and its fullness
is in the gods; Empedokles, then, must comprehend it in all its forms and
show the true essence of the gods and the true manner of worshipping
them. In the five books of his poem he committed to words the comprehensive vision in which he grasped the eternity of divine being together
with the eternity, in periodic change, of this world of matter; conveying
it as a revelation to his friends and to all those willing to listen, for by
revelation he had conceived it.

If, in the preceding passage, we have in some points gone beyond what
is commonly accepted, the following pages will supply the reasons for the
views here adumbrated. In accordance with the theme of this book, we
shall concern ourselves with the last two scrolls of Empedokles' poem,
whose theme was the interconnection of the two worlds, of Being and
Change; or, to use the modern term, the Empedoklean theology. These
two books are usually cited by the separate heading '*Katharmoi*' and they
are actually set off from the rest by a special, and different, dedication; it
is therefore perfectly possible that, notwithstanding the over-all unity
of the dominating conception, they were written on a different occasion,
and no doubt later, than the part commonly known as the '*Physika*'.

It is not proposed, in the following pages, to influence or enhance the
reader's appreciation by paraphrase and emphatic elaboration of the original
words. He who is insensitive to poetry has as little chance of understanding
Empedokles as he who with equal fluency translates a corrupt text and
a sound one, and the genuine student will resent being told what he can see
for himself. It is proposed, therefore, *pro viribus* to be useful to the latter in
passages whose understanding is not obvious, or not commonly agreed—and
there are surprisingly many of these. This endeavour will necessarily include
irksome considerations of detail. On this point I make no apologies. 'Le dieu
est dans le détail': this axiom is particularly relevant where the gist of a comprehensive and concentrated creation is to be recovered from a small proportion of fragments.

Everything that is here going to be proposed rests on foundations laid by
earlier students, from Sturz and Karsten (whose commentary remains indispensable) to Diels (especially his full presentation of the evidence in the
Poetae Philosophi) and, particularly, Wilamowitz; for his reconstruction and
discussion of the *Katharmoi*, concentrated and lucid, a ripe masterpiece of his
old age, is widely quoted indeed, but it has by no means, so far, been fully
appreciated; hence I shall often resume, and always start from, his contribution—which I have no wish, nor ability, to supersede. However, since the
Vorsokratiker are in the hands of every student, the following notes are given,

as far as possible, in the order and on the basis of the text contained in this standard work. A reconsideration of the proper arrangement, and indeed of the relevance to the *Katharmoi* of individual fragments, will, in some instances, inescapably impose itself; but a fresh attempt at the reconstruction of the poem as a whole can only be attempted when the detailed interpretation of all the fragments has been completed.

The most recent edition, with translation and comment, by J. E. Raven, presents a problem. In accordance with the design of the volume of which it forms part (Kirk–Raven, *The Presocratic Philosophers*), it contains less than one half of the fragments which figure in Diels; yet none of these is really dispensable. Its perplexing feature however—leaving aside details of text and interpretation—is in the arrangement of those fragments which have been included. Concerning the original place, within the context of the *Katharmoi*, of the surviving fragments, a fair amount is known for certain, and much more is open to reasonable inference. Diels's presentation is not indeed beyond criticism, but it represents what has, in the main, been established by three half-centuries of fruitful studies, and important modifications have, since then, been made by Wilamowitz. By this standard, the order of the fragments in the latest edition seems chaotic, and it is telling that the verses which are certain to have formed the opening of the poem stand at the very end of this selection. It appears to have seemed irrelevant to the editor (and he is by no means alone in this failing) that Empedokles was a poet—a great poet—in the tradition of Homer and Hesiod; that, beyond metre, vocabulary, and style, the very concept and presentation of his theme was determined by this fact; and that, in particular, for the description of scenes outside the sphere of everyday life, there existed a tradition of epic poetry which provided the very possibility of grasping, and expressing, the transcendental in the concreteness of myth. Hence it is hazardous, and in fact impossible, to determine the bearing of any fragment from the *Katharmoi* without attention to its place within the poem and without asking in which situation it was spoken, and by whom—for it is perfectly clear that not all of the surviving verses were uttered by Empedokles in his own person. He who disregards this caveat places himself in the same quandary as those trying, on the basis of selected quotations, to systematize the thought of, for example, Euripides or Shakespeare, without asking whether the verses in question were spoken by Hecuba, or Theseus, or Polonius, and in which situation.

The 'Kirk–Raven' volume has rapidly gained the authority of a widely-used textbook. This fact, together with the indubitable distinction of its editors, obliges us, in considering the individual fragments of the *Katharmoi*, to take account of this latest edition—obviously without harking back to the apparent precariousness of its general layout. The patient reader is now invited, with his copy of the *Vorsokratiker* before him (and, preferably, also the *Poetae Philosophi*, and Karsten's commentary, and Wilamowitz's essay), to reconsider, one by one, the fragments of the *Katharmoi* and to see whether in clarifying his own understanding, the following notes can be of any use to him.

II. COMMENT ON THE FRAGMENTS

The main editions referred to in the following are:

Sturz: *Empedocles Agrigentinus*, ed. M. F. G. Sturz, 1805.

Karsten: *Empedoclis Agrigentini carminum reliquiae*, ed. S. Karsten, 1838.

Stein: *Empedoclis Fragmenta*, ed. H. Stein, 1852.

Diels[1901]: *Poetarum philosophorum fragmenta*, ed. H. Diels, 1901, pp. 149 ff.

Bignone: E. Bignone, *Empedocle*, 1916.

DK: *Die Fragmente der Vorsokratiker*, ed. Diels–Kranz, 9. Aufl., vol. i, 1960, pp. 354 ff.

Wilamowitz: U. von Wilamowitz-Moellendorff, *Die Καθαρμοί des Empedokles*, in *Sitz.-Ber. der Preuss. Akad. der Wiss., Phil.-Hist. Klasse*, 1929, pp. 626–61; here cited from the reprint in his *Kleine Schriften*, i, 1935, pp. 473 ff.

Kranz[1949]: W. Kranz, *Empedokles*, 1949.

R: J. E. Raven, in G. S. Kirk and J. E. Raven, *The Presocratic Philosophers*, 1957, 348 ff.

Fr. 112 DK (478 R). vv. 1–2. It is sad to find the very beginning of the poem—which was correctly interpreted by Karsten in 1838—mistranslated as never before in 1957 (R p. 354). 'Friends who dwell throughout the great town of golden Akragas, up by the citadel': this rendering, once attempted, ought to have stirred second thoughts and a reconsideration of the original. If Empedokles' addressees lived 'up by(?) the citadel', could he possibly say, in the same breath, that they dwelled 'throughout the great town of Akragas'? Moreover, it would be hard, in this translation, to understand 'golden Akragas' as anything but the name of the town. But Empedokles means the river. Ξανθός is an epithet, not of towns but of rivers, from Homer onward to Horace's *flavus Tiberis*. The translation in DK is open to objections no less grave. There it is assumed, after Wilamowitz, that κατὰ ξ. Ἀκράγαντος means 'sprawling downward along the (river) Akragas'. Wilamowitz himself admitted that he could not support this meaning by any parallels—and indeed I should call it linguistically impossible; moreover, knowledge of the site or a glance at a detailed map shows that materially too it would be wrong: the city did not and could not thus 'sprawl' (DK, perhaps with a view to escaping this objection, render ἄστυ by 'Stätte' ['site', 'spot']—a wholly inadmissible device). And the inconsistency in situating Empedokles' friends both 'down by the river' and 'up on the height' is as glaring here as in R.

Akragas is concretely the city, or even the abode, of the river-god Akragas—the ἱερὸν οἴκημα ποταμοῦ (Pind. *Ol.* ii. 10).[1] In that city, and

---

[1] Cf. what was said on this point above, p. 181 f.

on its citadel: that is where Empedokles' friends live.¹ For this specification in indicating an abode cf. *Il.* 16. 719 ὃς Φρυγίηι ναίεσκε ῥοῆις ἔπι
Cαγγαρίοιο and H. *H. Ven.* 227 ναῖε παρ' Ὠκεανοῖο ῥοῆις ἐπὶ πείραcι
γαίης. For the verb ναίω with κατά cf. *Il.* 2. 130 Τρώων οἳ ναίουcι κατὰ
πτόλιν, *Od.* 8. 551 οἳ κατὰ ἄcτυ καὶ οἳ περὶ ναιετάουcιν and H. *H.* xv. 7
κατὰ καλὸν ἕδος . . . Ὀλύμπου ναίει; for the 'inversion' ἄcτυ κάτα cf. *Od.*
17. 246 (and, perhaps, 16. 466).²

v. 3. The verse ξείνων αἰδοῖοι λιμένες, κακότητος ἄπειροι was inserted
here, from Diod. xiii. 83. 1, by Sturz; it is not in the one extant source
of the present passage, Diog. Laert. viii. 62 (nor in *A.P.* ix. 569, where
vv. 1–6 are supposed to derive from D.L.). If it belonged here, it is hard
to believe that Diogenes (or his source, Herakleides Pontikos) could have
omitted this verse, or that it could have dropped out in his extant manuscripts. Acknowledging this, Wilamowitz posited the currency, in Antiquity, of widely different texts of the poem; Diogenes (Herakleides)
using one from which the verse was absent, while Diodoros (i.e. Timaios)
found it in his copy—a large assumption to account for a problem to
which there may well be a simpler solution. The question whether or not
the verse belongs here would anyhow remain open; for there is nothing
to enforce the assumption that Timaios found it at this place. The
opening address is satisfactory and complete without it, and the insertion
—against the only extant witness (or, possibly, witnesses)—rather over-
loads it, the actual greeting thus being postponed until the fourth verse.
Karsten indeed asserted that 'no other place could be more suited for this
verse', and all later critics followed suit; even Wilamowitz agrees: 'The
insertion is convincing, since the verse is quoted in evidence of the
φιλανθρωπία of the Akragantines.' This is not an impressive argument,
seeing that there was no need, after v. 2, to mention their generosity, and
Empedokles could have turned to his addressees again, for instance, at
the end of the poem, as he did in the *Physika* (fr. 110).

Anyhow, what does the verse mean? 'Unversed in wickedness, havens
of respect for strangers' (R): the smoothness of this as well as of other
current renderings tends to gloss over some dimly felt problems of interpretation, and the inversion of the original order of the two clauses shows
that the words rendered 'unversed in wickedness' are supposed to amplify
the preceding 'mindful of good deeds'. There may be a temptation to support this understanding of κακότητος ἄπειροι by reference to Pind. *Ol.* xi.
17, where the citizens of Italian Lokroi are commended to the Muses:
they will find there no φυγόξεινον cτρατὸν μήτ' ἀπείρατον καλῶν. In this
passage, however, καλά has a specific connotation: the Lokrians are

¹ For the combination of πόλιc and ἄcτυ cf. *Il.* 17. 144, etc.
² There are many other instances of κάτα following its noun; e.g. *Il.* 20. 221, *Od.* 19.
345.

devoted to 'music'.[1] Could Empedokles, by contrast, have used κακότης as the general opposite of 'virtue'? This assumption is necessary for this interpretation but, in Empedoklean thought and style, it is impossible. We shall return to this point in discussing frs. 144 f.; here it may suffice to state that, in archaic and classical poetry, κακότης never conveys the notion which later on, in prose and especially in philosophy, was expressed by κακία. Rather, κακότης is the 'ill' which affects me or is within me, or which I do to someone else; its specific connotation was, in every instance, bound up with the current standard and system of values—which did not entail a concept of general moral 'badness'. Hence the normal connotation of κακότης, from Homer onward, is 'harm', 'hardship', 'ill'.[2] It may mean 'cowardice' in some few places in Homer;[3] it certainly does so with Solon and Aischylos;[4] but this particular form of κακότης could not suit the present context. It has to be interpreted in the light of valid parallels. On the model of, e.g. *Il.* 17. 41 ἀπείρητος φόβοιο, H. *H. Ven.* 133 ἀπειρήτην φιλότητος, Aisch. *Ch.* 371 πόνων ἄπειρον, id. fr. 350 νόcων ἀπ., and Theogn. 1013 ἀπ. ἄθλων, etc., κακότητος ἄπειροι can only denote men who 'have not experienced [i.e. are untouched by] hardship': Empedokles' addressees are possessed of long-standing wealth; contrast the ἀτιμίη and κακότης—'dishonour and misery'—which, according to Tyrtaios (fr. 6. 10 Diehl), are the lot of cowards, or the κακότης, 'poverty' and 'misery' which, instead of ἀρετή, 'wealth', is reaped by those making the wrong choice among Hesiod's Two Ways (*Op.* 287).

The first half of this verse, ξείνων αἰδοῖοι λιμένες, is characteristic of Empedokles' style. The stranger—like the suppliant; like woman—is traditionally αἰδοῖος: he is weak and therefore is met—by people who acknowledge the demands of αἰδώς—with respect and willingness to help (H. *Od.* 19. 191; Aisch. *Suppl.* 489). If Empedokles had written ξείνων αἰδοίων (as Bergk conjectured), this would have been in accordance with tradition and with the normal, 'passive', connotation of the adjective. On this assumption, however, it is impossible to account for the transmitted *lectio magis ardua* αἰδοῖοι; the poet, so it appears, varied the traditional phrase. The notion of αἰδώς, like that of χάρις, is bipolar; the sentiment stimulated by the appeal of the weak, or the beautiful, emanates from one responding to this stimulus—in the present case, from the host, who is αἰδοῖος in that he acts in accordance with the call for αἰδώς. Of this, 'active', connotation of αἰδοῖος there is, in epic poetry, only one instance, *Od.* 17. 578, which is quite different from the one under discussion. Even so, Empedokles was not alone in using this particular alternative;

---

[1] χαίροντα μουcικῆι schol. A.

[2] One illustration for a hundred: the 'misery' (κακότης) from illness or incarceration as described in Hes. *Scut.* 42.

[3] Thus probably also in *Od.* 24. 455: the fathers 'had not the courage' to curb their sons.

[4] See Plut. *Sol.* 30; Aisch. *Prom.* 1066.

Aischylos had unambiguously thus described a host,[1] and Sophokles was later to do the same.[2] Empedokles, moreover, stressed the fact that, out of αἰδώς, strangers were, at Akragas, well received—'harboured'—by the daring catachrestic use of the noun λιμήν.

The Akragantines were hospitable and rich; the verse thus fully summarizes the subject of Timaios' digression. Its former half could have suitably completed Empedokles' opening address, but the stressing of their affluence would have been out of place in it. This is a further argument against the current intrusion of this verse into fr. 112.[3]

From this exordium it is clear that Empedokles is not writing (or reciting) this poem at Akragas. The circumstantial description of their abode alone suffices to show that he is sending it to his friends from abroad, as Pindar sent *P*. iii to Hieron. The scenes described next, then, did not take place in his home-town (cf. especially v. 7); and indeed, if they had, why should he describe what the addressees had witnessed? And yet that is what, according to the latest translation, he is supposed to have done.

vv. 4–6: 'I go about among you all, an immortal god' (R): this makes an odd piece of information. Empedokles—as we just noted—was not in Akragas when he wrote this; but whether he was or was not, he could not have written and told his friends there that he was 'going about among them all'. And quite apart from the material incongruity, what Greek could possibly have expressed this alleged meaning by ἐγὼ δ' ὑμῖν θεὸς ἄμβροτος . . . πωλεῦμαι μετὰ πᾶςι? The Greek words, in this order, are a categorical protest against a rendering which tears apart what belongs together and connects what, in the Greek, is separate. Does it need arguing that μετὰ πᾶςι τετιμένος is a unit not to be broken? Cf. *Il*. 23. 649 τετιμῆςθαι μετ' Ἀχαιοῖς; also *Il*. 13. 461; *Od*. 11. 495 ἔχει τιμήν . . . μετὰ Μυρμιδόνεςςιν; 13. 128 μετ' ἀθανάτοιςι θεοῖςιτ τιμήεις; H. H. Dem. 366 τιμὰς δὲ ςχήςειςθα μετ' ἀθανάτοιςι. Empedokles is 'going about, honoured by all as is fitting'. The correct rendering of the much discussed ὥςπερ ἔοικα has been re-established by K. Reinhardt.[4] It is more than doubtful if this phrase could mean 'as, with regard to me, it seems'; if it could, the result would be nonsense. *Il*. 23. 649 τιμῆς ἧς τε μ' ἔοικε τετιμῆςθαι παρ' Ἀχαιοῖς illustrates the real meaning. The problematical use of the first

---

[1] *Suppl.* 491 αἰδοῖον πρόξενον; cf. vv. 29 and 641 and Pind. *I*. ii. 37.

[2] *O.C.* 273 ὦ ξένοι αἰδόφρονες.—For the whole concept of *Aidōs* see the essay thus entitled by C. E. von Erffa in *Philologus*, Suppl. Bd. xxx. 2 (1937).

[3] From a note in DK, I learned with satisfaction that H. Fränkel too objects to the insertion of the verse at this place. But it rather takes one's breath away to find in the latest, long-awaited edition of Diogenes (ed. H. S. Long, vol. ii (1964), p. 422), the note *'del.* H. Fränkel' referring to the following verse—the most frequently quoted of all, whose genuineness nobody could dream of questioning.

[4] *Class. Philol.* xlv (1950), 171; reprinted in *Vermächtnis der Antike* (1960), p. 102. Diels and others had previously thus understood it.

person may be paralleled by *Od.* 22. 348 ἔοικα δέ τοι παραείδειν, which I incline to render 'it is fitting that I should sing'. Even so, the difficulty of this particular feature may still encourage one to consider whether, after all, the plain third person in *A.P.* xi. 569 is original and the *lectio difficilior* in the Laertius manuscripts a mere corruption;[1] but the meaning (as reproduced in R) is beyond doubt.[2]

There remains the dative ὑμῖν at the beginning of the phrase. It is, in the context, a mere 'ethical dative'[3] marking—after the greeting—the beginning of Empedokles' message and practically incapable of being rendered in modern English. The meaning can be paraphrased, if crudely, by 'listen!' or 'I tell you'.[4] This was stated by Wilamowitz—in vain. Taken out of their context, the words ἐγὼ δ' ὑμῖν θεός could be taken to mean 'I am a god to you', or even 'I am your god'—by readers imbued with the thought and wording of the Old Testament. It is unlikely that any Greek could have thus mistaken the phrase,[5] even if he quoted it in evidence of Empedokles' ἀλαζονεία;[6] in its original context this interpretation is inadmissible.[7] If his addressees regarded Empedokles as a god, it was futile to inform them of their view; if they did not, it was absurd as a statement and useless as a claim since, with Greeks at least, the acknowledgement of a deity is a matter, not of the god's claim but, of man's perception. Wilamowitz, then, is right: the pronoun ὑμῖν is merely 'inserted briefly' to underline that Empedokles is addressing his friends. If, then, this dative does not have any limiting effect[8] (in asserting that Empedokles is a god 'in the eyes of' his friends), his absolute claim of divinity is all the more startling. If he had wanted to say that he was 'honoured by all *like* a god', many Homeric passages could have served as models;[9] in fact, no more was needed but for that unemphatic ὑμῖν to

---

[1] In v. 6, the *Anthology* has a corrupt reading in agreement with one of the three main Diogenes manuscripts.

[2] In DK the abstruse rendering 'so wie ich *ihnen* dünke' is immediately followed by the correct one (in brackets); as though both meant the same.—Cf. also v. 37 of the *Hymn* of Kleanthes.

[3] Perhaps this is meant by the—rather ambiguous—translation in DK. Van Groningen (*Class. et Mediaev.* xvii (1956), 52) likewise takes ὑμῖν to be an 'ethical dative'; I could not, however, accept his interpretation (Empedokles 'badine . . .; un spirituel clignement de l'œil . . .').

[4] Cf. the stock example, Hdt. v. 30 Ἀρταφρένης ὑμῖν Ὑστάσπεω . . . ἐστι παῖς.

[5] e.g. Plotinus (iv. 7. 10) quotes it in illustration of the divinity of the soul recognized by Empedokles; he did not then mistake him as stating that he was a god 'for' or 'to' or 'in the eyes of' his friends.   [6] Sextus Empiricus i. 302, Diog. Laert. viii. 66.

[7] One notes with regret that a scholar as distinguished as C. H. Kahn (*Archiv f. Gesch. der Phil.* xlii (1960), 5, n. 6) does not notice this but merely quotes, without examination, two of the older translations.

[8] The dative is not on a level with κείνοιϲιν in fr. 128. 1 (on which below, p. 207).

[9] θεὸς ὡϲ τίετο δήμωι *Il.* 5. 78, 10. 33, 11. 58, 13. 218, 16. 605, *Od.* 14. 205; θεὸν ὡϲ τιμήϲουϲιν *Il.* 9. 297 (cf. 155, 303 and *Od.* 5. 36, 19. 280, 23. 339); τιμὴν δὲ λελόγχαϲιν ἶϲα θεοῖϲι *Od.* 11. 304.

give way to ὥσπερ. The uniqueness of Empedokles' claim stands out in the very avoidance of the well-known Homeric phrase. The hearers are, instead, reminded of two other authoritative texts. Demeter, in the Eleusinian hymn (v. 120), begins the speech in which she—the goddess in disguise—half reveals herself χαίρετ'· ἐγὼ δ' ὑμῖν μυθήσομαι (and a little before this line occurs the verse (111) οὐδ' ἔγνων· χαλεποὶ δὲ θεοὶ θνητοῖcιν ὁρᾶcθαι). The allusion, in Empedokles' χαίρετ'· ἐγὼ δ' ὑμῖν θεὸc ἄμβροτοc serves to stress the fact that his poem conveys the revelation of a deity;[1] and this is confirmed by the further allusion to Il. 24. 460 (Hermes speaking) . . . ἐγὼ θεὸc ἄμβροτοc εἰλήλουθα.

The 'due honour' given him 'by all' finds its expression, first, in the fillets and crowns with which they decorate him. Such décor was not in fact applied to divine images only; the people who thus honoured Empedokles need not, in this way, have acknowledged him as a god. They honoured the 'divine man' in the same way as they honoured victors in battle or at the great games, and Empedokles regards this homage as a confirmation of his own conviction.

v. 7. Here again Wilamowitz has spoken in vain; and yet he was right— even more than he himself realized. The verse is corrupt even in the better manuscripts of Diogenes Laertius—and R (following Diels) reproduces the inferior ones. The interpolation ⟨εὖτ'⟩ in them mends the metre, spoils the style, and disrupts the context. What is the reference of the pronoun τοῖcιν in R's text supposed to be? It could only be πᾶcι v. 5— which is evidently impossible (R translates after Diels 'these my followers'; but no 'followers' have so far been mentioned and the pronoun 'these' has no reference). Even so, in the Greek, this orphan of a pronoun, τοῖcιν, must be supposed to be resumed, in the next verse, by ἀνδράcιν ἠδὲ γυναιξί; how could it be?[2] TOICINAMAN is corrupt; ἄν has been mistaken as equivalent of ἐάν and doubled (ἀμ') either by dittography or in an effort to fill up the metre. We need a connection with the preceding verse and, moreover, a word that can be resumed, and specified, by ἀνδράcιν ἠδὲ γυναιξί. Wilamowitz's reconstruction πᾶcι δὲ τοῖc ἄν ἵκωμαι is even better than he realized, because not only does it satisfy these requirements, but, moreover, provides an analepsis of πᾶcι in v. 5. There ought then to be a colon (not full stop) after v. 6. What is given with the situation thus becomes explicit: those that 'give Empedokles due honour' and crown him are the inhabitants of the cities which he visits,

---

[1] Incidentally, this parallel confirms the interpretation (just urged) of the pronoun ὑμῖν in Empedokles: it is analogous to ὑμῖν μυθήcομαι in the hymn.

[2] DK now print the text of the better manuscripts of Diogenes Laertius, marking ἀμ' as corrupt and subjoining a translation which is deservedly furnished with a question mark. The reference of τοῖcιν to a (non-existing) precedent is rightly abandoned; even so, the pronoun is too feeble to serve as a general reference for the specification 'men and women' afterwards.

and this is how they 'revere him'.[1] Text and translation in R imply that crowds following Empedokles were seized by a sudden urge to 'revere' him when he entered a city. In fact, the text does not suggest the notion of Empedokles being followed by large crowds on his wanderings from city to city: οἱ δ' ἄμ' ἔπονται in v. 8 is said of the inhabitants of the cities which he enters. Vast crowds of them follow him in each town and ask for what they regard as 'gain'; for practical advice, that is, such as one sought from oracles, and for relief from prolonged illness.[2] 'They are not coming to him as a physician of souls' (Wilamowitz); but in approaching him as they do they are proclaiming him a healer and seer.

The preceding observations may be summarized in a tentative and unpoetical translation:

1. Friends who dwell in the great city of the yellow (river) Akragas
2. on the citadel, you who care for right deeds,
4. I greet you. An immortal god, mortal no more,
5. I am going about honoured by all, as is fitting (for me),
6. (by being) garlanded with fillets and verdant wreaths,
7. and by all (inhabitants) of whatever flourishing cities I come to,
8. by men and women, I am revered . . .

Fr. 113 DK. Here I find it impossible to follow Wilamowitz. He held that ἐπίκειμαι, for which the meaning 'to insist' is not otherwise attested, must be taken to mean 'I attack'; hence he inferred that a passage preceded in which Empedokles attacked some critics of his divinity and that τοῖσδε refers to these. The latter assertion is hard to accept and this fact weakens the whole thesis. The deprecatory reference to his own superiority in the following line implies that, up to this point, Empedokles had enlarged on this superiority. This would have naturally emerged in the continuation of the first fragment; he is approached by countless supplicants—and he is able to help them all. Τοῖσδε, a neuter pronoun, is naturally taken to refer back to details, mentioned by Empedokles, of his ministry which made

---

[1] The *attractio relativi* in τοῖc (for τῶν) is harsh—if less so than in fr. 115. 5; cf. *Il.* 5. 265 and 23. 649 (quoted above). Concerning the grammatical structure of these verses, I venture to differ from Chantraine, *Gramm. Hom.* ii (1953), paras 74 and 346.

[2] In the phrase πεπαρμένοι ἀμφ' ὀδύνῃσιν (brilliantly and beyond cavil recovered, from the corrupt wording in Clement of Alexandria, by T. Bergk), Wilamowitz described ἀμφ' as an adverb ('all over'). This view, I suspect, will prove untenable on comparing the numerous parallels; they show that the Greeks (those at least who first coined and adopted the metaphor) took the notion of 'piercing pains' far more concretely than we do; the sufferer is 'pierced' by them, or 'spitted' on, or around, them as is the nightingale clawed by the hawk, πεπαρμένη ἀμφ' ὀνύχεϲϲιν, in Hesiod's fable (*Op.* 205) or the leopard περὶ δουρὶ πεπαρμένη in Homer (*Il.* 21. 577); cf. the standing Homeric phrase ὀβελοῖϲιν ἔπειραν with, or without, ἀμφί: the piercing spit is in the centre, with the pierced meat around it. In the metaphor, pains take the place of the spit. In Apollonios of Rhodes (iv. 1067), Medea's heart is πεπαρμένον ἀμφ' ὀδύνῃσιν; in his Empedoklean model, the sufferers themselves are said to be thus 'spitted upon (lit. "around") their pains'.

his superiority stand out palpably. The traditional understanding of the words under discussion thus appears to be correct,[1] and if the required acceptance of the verb ἐπίκειμαι is otherwise unattested,[2] it is sufficiently supported by the analogous use of (πολὺς) ἔγκειμαί τινι in e.g. Herodotus and Thucydides. With μέγα . . . πράσσων cf. *Od.* 19. 324, Hes. *Op.* 402, Eur. *I.A.* 346, Ar. *Ran.* 302. One may, then, translate:

> But why do I insist on this, as though it meant any great achievement
> That[3] I am superior to mortal men who are liable to manifold destruction?

Kranz and others rightly compare Hes. *Theog.* 35.

Fr. 114 DK. Here Wilamowitz has freed us from an unfortunate conjecture of Diels. To understand the last verse (and fr. 133) one has to try and grasp the implication of the words πίστις and πειθώ. The upshot of an examination of their use by Parmenides and Empedokles may be summarized as follows.[4] The verb πείθω means 'to make one accept something as true'. The things (objects) around man call to be grasped according to their real being (ἀληθείη). When this πίστις, or πειθώ, of the objects (Parm. 2 [4]. 4, Empedokles 114) is received by man's perception (to use this term for want of any proper equivalent for φρήν), man is possessed of a (subjective) πίστις. But man is liable to error: his (personal) πίστεις may be ἀληθεῖς or ψευδεῖς; and so, therefore, may be the words by which he endeavours to convey his πίστις to others (i.e. πείθειν); they may convey δόξαν ψευδῆ or πίστιν ἀληθῆ; the criterion being in the ἀληθείη (reality) of the object behind the words.

The second half of this fragment then means that the 'onrush' (impact, ὁρμή) of the 'persuasiveness' (πίστις) with which the 'truth' in Empedokles' words strives to enter the 'mind' (φρένα) is wearying and of a kind which men are not eager to admit (δύσζηλος; L–S–J are very wrong on this word).[5]

Fr. 115 DK (471 R). v. 1. Wilamowitz stressed that in Hippolytos and Plutarch—two independent witnesses—the verse begins ἔστι τι, while

---

[1] The manner in which Sextus quotes this fragment does not indeed prove it to have followed soon after the first, but lends probability to this assumption; which rests, in the main, upon the plausibility of their interconnection.

[2] *Addendum:* I ought to have checked this assertion by Wilamowitz. As Professor E. R. Dodds reminds me, it is refuted by Hdt. v. 104.

[3] Here again, DK put the correct translation 'daß', for εἰ, in brackets beside 'wenn'—which is meaningless unless it be taken as a loose synonym of 'daß'. Empedokles knows that he *is* superior.

[4] Cf. Verdenius (*Mnem.* Ser. iv, vol. i (1948), 10), who refutes the assumption that, with the Presocratics, πίστις could denote a 'religious faith'.

[5] In abandoning Diels's conjecture and, largely, also in their translation, DK follow Wilamowitz. They retain however Diels's splitting up of the sentence translated above (after Wilamowitz), taking ὁρμή to be the subject of its latter part only and ἀληθείη to govern the first. Here too, I submit, Wilamowitz was right, for ἀργαλέη καὶ δύσζηλος cannot be separated from each other.

only Simplicius gives the inoffensive ἔcτιν. Since Empedokles has synaloephe of τι in fr. 17. 30, where it cannot be expelled,[1] he accepted it here too. Differing from him, I cannot help feeling that the pronoun is stylistically unwelcome or even wrong; for Empedokles is not going to mention 'some' oracle of Ananke, not one among many, but the one and only which determines his own lot and that of all men; he adds a whole verse to stress its import.[2] The pronoun τι added seems to weaken the power of the whole preamble;[3] why then should Empedokles have sought the metrical difficulty which results from its addition? Hence, however strange the recurrence of the dittography, one may feel justified in not following Wilamowitz here.

v. 4. This verse is an insult to Greek style; on consideration, no way will be found left but to agree with Wilamowitz who rejected it. What Greek poet would have followed up the flowing grandeur of vv. 1–3 with this jumble? And Empedokles was a great poet. Diels's invention, νείκεϊ, stands where he put it, a lump without any connection forward or backward. The conjunction τε after it is wrong (if Empedokles had added other types of wrongdoers, he would have continued ἤ καί . . .), and the alleged dependence of the dative νείκεϊ upon the participle ἁμαρτήcαc (taken as ὁμ-) is not within the possibilities of Greek style. The order of words in Greek verse is free; irrelevant it is not. Diels's device is further discredited by the fact that Νείκεϊ stands, genuine and powerful, at the end of the fragment; this is enough by itself to refute its anticipation at this earlier place.

The great editor of the *Doxographi* and *Vorsokratiker* was not invariably at his best when dealing with textual matters. The present verse may, with little exaggeration, be described as Diels's invention. Of the two witnesses which preserve this part of the fragment, Plutarch (*De exilio, in fine*) has no trace of it, v. 3 being followed immediately by 5.[4] Hippolytos —who alone (though in an odd rearrangement) preserves the whole fragment—omits v. 3. Instead he—or rather, the one poor, surviving manuscript—has

ὃc καὶ ἐπίορκον ἁμαρτήcαc ἐπομώcει.

---

[1] Wilamowitz (*Verskunst*, p. 608) compared ἆcτῠ ἐρῐκῠδέc in an oracle, Hdt. vii. 220.

[2] It is stressed also by the unique catachresis in the word χρῆμα, which may be compared with χρῆcιc as used by Pindar *Ol.* xiii. 76.

[3] It is instructive to contrast this dubious τι with Alcman's ἔcτι τιc cιῶν τίcιc, where the pronoun has concrete force; the poet is sure of the existence of divine vindication but refrains from elaborating the manner of its action (cf. Aisch. *Ag.* 182 που). No comparable justification for the added pronoun offers itself in the context of Empedokles.

[4] It is true that Plutarch gives an extract only: viz. vv. 1, 3, 5, 6, 13 (of the current numbering). Vv. 2 and 7–12 were outside the purpose of his citation. It is practically certain, though impossible to prove, that his text of Empedokles contained nothing between vv. 3 and 5; and *De esu carn.* i, 996 b excludes that Plutarch could have found any other guilt of the daimons mentioned in it than the φόνοc of v. 3.

It would then be correct to say that the text from which Hippolytos quoted had an alternative for Plutarch's v. 3—and we all know that to combine alternatives is, as a rule, the worst thing a textual critic can do. Besides, if the two verses are combined, the question remains open what fault caused the fall of Empedokles' daimon; if only v. 3 is retained, it is answered in accordance with the trend of the whole poem.

Materially this fragment of a verse (the spelling mistakes in the manuscript are easily put right) has something to commend it. The whole passage is evidently inspired by, and partly worded on, the model of Hesiod (*Theog.* 793 ff.), describing the punishment of gods who swear a false oath by Styx.[1] It could seem natural for Empedokles to retain that particular Hesiodic feature; moreover, in Pind. *Ol.* ii—the doctrine of which has striking similarities with Empedokles—those οἵτινες ἔχαιρον εὐορκίαις are particularly marked out (vv. 66–72). Generally the sanctity of the oath was one of the earliest and greatest moral rules;[2] how then could its occurrence in Empedokles be denied?

These arguments are annihilated by the simple fact that the *s*-aorist of ἁμαρτάνω is attested, for the first time, in the Septuagint; no one would dream of defending it in the text of Empedokles. And yet, in the verse quoted by Hippolytos this is clearly what ἁμαρτήσας is meant to be. It has been put in the place of Hesiod's ἀπολείψας so as to fit *Theog.* 793 into the Empedoklean context—and this cannot have been done in pre-Hellenistic times. Diels's attempt to interpret it as ὁμαρτήσας is, first, against all probability because he posits an out-of-the-way meaning and form in the place of what is, in the context, the natural one. The false oath is a 'sin': this makes sense; but what is one to make, here, of the notion of 'accompanying'?[3] Diels endeavoured to bestow a meaning upon it by filling-up the verse with that νείκεϊ which we have already dismissed;[4] moreover, one has only to see how the verb ὁμαρτέω is actually used elsewhere to realize that νείκεϊ ὁμαρτεῖν, 'to accompany strife', simply is not Greek. Diels's device, then, is unworkable, and it would be hard to think of any other. The upshot is that Hippolytos was quoting from a corrupt text; what he gives in the place of the genuine v. 3 cannot be Empedoklean (this conclusion had been drawn, before Wilamowitz, by Knatz).[5] The

---

[1] With Empedokles v. 12 cf. Hes. *Theog.* 800.   [2] *Il.* 3. 279; 19. 260, etc.

[3] From a purely linguistic point of view (and only from it), Diels's alternative is admissible. The Bacchylides papyrus has (18. 46) ἁμαρτεῖν with the meaning of ὁμ-, and there are inscriptional instances of this vocalization which, besides, may have occurred in Euripides' *Skiron* (Hesych., s.v.). If these instances were considered insufficient to support the same spelling in Empedokles, the conjecture ὁμαρτήσας would, in itself, be easy enough—the rare aorist ὡμάρτησεν occurs in Hes. *Theog.* 201—but Hippolytos wrote ἁμαρτήσας, and it is only too obvious what meaning, in its context, this word was intended to convey.

[4] The obvious supplement would be δαίμων ὅς κ'. This, if correct, would show that the verse was not part of the Empedoklean text, but added as a parallel.

[5] See Wilamowitz, p. 484. The defence of this verse attempted by W. Rathmann

Hesiodic parallel may have been cited by some ancient commentator and hence, altered and corrupted, finally penetrated into the text used by Hippolytos.

vv. 3 and 5:[1] The 'attractio inversa' in εὖτέ τιc . . . δαίμονεc οἴτε κτλ. is hard indeed. If the order of the two verses were inverted, parallels would be available;[2] as it is, only *Il.* 18. 429 ἦ ἄρα δή τιc, ὅcαι θεαί εἰc' . . . ἀνέcχετο can, to some extent, be compared; but even this makes an imperfect parallel.[3] The best defence for this form of the verse would be (to my mind) in the observation that, with the—syntactically isolated— nominative δαίμονεc, it intimates, strikingly, that vast realm which is the gods' and separate from the world into which the transgressor is banished by the law of Ananke; any alteration, so it might be argued, must weaken its expressive power, however strange, or even unique, its structure may be from a grammatical point of view. It may be held that, even so, the structure εὖτέ τιc . . . μιήνηι δαίμονεc οἴτε is beyond the possibilities of Greek poetical idiom. What, then, constrains us to adopt it—seeing that the old conjecture δαίμων (Heeren, Sturz) effects a legitimate one?[4] The reading δαιμόνιοι in the fantastically corrupt manuscript of Hippolytos' *Refutationes* may as well be traced to δαίμων οἵ as to the plural (and δαίμοναc in his paraphrase proves nothing either way). Plutarch, it is true, attests δαίμονεc οἵ, but the extant evidence for his *De exilio* is likewise extremely faulty; there are four obvious faults in the five verses quoted from the present fragment, and this may easily be the fifth; for an original δαίμων οἵ was almost bound to be changed into the plural.[5] The more I consider this passage, the more I become convinced that we ought to return to this reading, which was adopted also by Stein, while Diels did not deem it deserving of a place even in his apparatus criticus.

vv. 6 ff. With regard to ὥραc in v. 6, Wilamowitz commented: 'in der Bedeutung von ὥροc, singulär'. He was not explicit enough to prevent the traditional rendering 'seasons' from being retained; but a moment's consideration should suffice to prove him right. To state that the 'daimon' was banished for so-and-so-many 'seasons' would have been unsuitable, for this vague term is unsuited to indicate a span of time;

(*Quaestiones Pythagoreae* . . . (1933), pp. 98 ff.) fails to meet, or even to see, the salient points of the indictment.

[1] Using the traditional numbering, notwithstanding the ejection of the current v. '4'.

[2] *Il.* 10. 416; 14. 371; H. *H. Dem.* 66.

[3] To say that the genitive δαιμόνων—which would make the grammar normal—'would not easily fit the verse' (Wilamowitz) is not a sufficient excuse. After all, Empedokles, like Hesiod, admits a trochee in the first foot of the hexameter (fr. 112. 6 ταινίαιc); besides, one ought not to seek excuses for Empedokles such as could be valid with a versifying schoolboy.

[4] Cf. e.g. *Il.* 24. 650; *Od.* 19. 40.

[5] Corruptions similar to the one here posited are, in the same essay, μακάρων for Μάκαροc 603 d and γυναῖκεc for γύναι 604 e. For the general, poor quality of the evidence for this section of the *Moralia* see the Preface of the Teubner edition (vol. iii (1930), p. xxiii).

moreover, it has often been noted that the period indicated compares with the 'three myriads' of years—or, synonymously, the χρόνος μυριέτης—of suffering endured by the Aischylean Prometheus.[1] Ὧρος was used by Hellenistic poets with the connotation 'year', and Lykophron's (1153) χιλίωρος χρόνος stands for χιλιέτης χρ.[2] It is not given, though, that Empedokles is indicating a fixed cycle of 30,000 years. Μύριοι is likely here, as in all older Greek, to connote an unconscionably large number rather than a definite figure; the difference between 'countless' and 'thrice countless' is one of emphasis. Thus Hesiod[3] told of a 'countless' host of daimonic watchers—rather than of precisely 30,000—and Aischylos, as just noted, used 'a myriad' and 'three myriads' synonymously. If this understanding is correct, Empedokles would not exclude variations in the duration of the long penance undergone by the fallen 'daimons', and his catachrestic use of the word ὥρα may emphasize this latitude.

Besides, there arises in these verses the question whether, in describing the lot of the fallen gods, Empedokles spoke of one (representative) 'daimon', or whether he used the plural. Μίν (v. 6)[4] is singular in epic poetry (though in the Odyssey it is twice used with reference to δώματα) but can be plural in Pindar and Bakchylides. Cφέ (v. 9), normally plural, is used for the singular in tragedy from Aischylos onward. Hippolytos, the only *ad verbum* witness for vv. 7–8, has the unambiguous plural φυομένους in 7 and the equally unambiguous singular μεταλλάccοντα in 8. Adaptation is easy at the former place but impossible at the latter. Since the number has to be equalized, we write φυόμενον in v. 7 (with Stein).[5] If, then, Empedokles here had the singular, he was continuing in the form initiated by εὖτέ τις in v. 3 (and this is a further argument for reading δαίμων in v. 5); he was also remaining within the epic tradition of his use of the pronoun μίν. If this holds good also for cφέ in v. 9, he changed over here to the plural; which—in view of the general application of what precedes—is possible but hardly probable.

v. 11. ἀκάμαντος Plut.; φαέθοντος Hippol. 'The commonplace word would have to give way, even if Plutarch (who gives the choice alternative)

---

[1] Schol. Aisch. *Prom.* 94, etc.

[2] Cf. L–S–J, s.v. ὥρα, 3.

[3] Hes. *Op.* 252, cf. 122.—The distinction between the two connotations ('numberless' and '10,000') by means of different accentuation is hardly more than a grammarian's fad; anyhow we cannot know how Hesiod and Pindar accented the word.

[4] Corrupted to μέν in Hippolytos and Origen.

[5] This conjecture receives some slight support from Celsus *apud* Origen viii. 53, who puts γινομένην because he embodies vv. 6–7 in a discussion of the purification of the ψυχή.—He who uses, in parallel, the indeclinable English participles 'being born' and 'changing' may be untroubled by the sequence of plural and singular in his Greek text.—Φυόμενον . . . εἴδεα, by the way, is 'growing into [i.e. 'turning into', 'becoming'] all manner of shapes'; cf. fr. 35. 14 θνῆτ' ἐφύοντο. And it is, of course, the 'daimon', and not the εἴδεα θνητῶν, that 'exchanges various paths of life' (*contra* DK). The individual 'mortal forms'—say bush, fish, man—do not change one into another, but the 'daimon' exchanges one such form for another.

were not anyhow the better witness.' Thus Wilamowitz. One cannot put it more concisely and cogently. And still the trite wording of the inferior witness stands in our editions.

v. 13. The beginning of this verse is transmitted in three varying forms; Wilamowitz set them out and settled the problem. Thereafter a pastiche of the inferior variants ought no longer to appear in our texts.

These are the variants:

(*a*) ὡc καὶ ἐγὼ δεῦρ' εἶμι   Philoponos and Asklepiades;
(*b*) τῶν καὶ ἐγώ εἰμι   Hippolytos;
(*c*) τὴν καὶ ἐγὼ νῦν εἶμι   Plutarch.

Form (*a*) is impossible because ὡc is hopelessly prosaic and cannot be replaced by any conjecture (τώc would be quite as bad). Form (*b*) is unmetrical. The currently accepted insertion of νῦν from (*c*) spoils the sense; for Empedokles could conceivably have said 'I am one of these'; but to make him say: 'I am *now* one of these' is to charge him with vague talk.[1] Besides, as Wilamowitz ad loc. observes, 'the critic ought not to mess up variants but choose among them'. In fact, what Hippolytos offers is not a genuine variant at all. He who reads his quotation in its context, will see that Hippolytos had good reason, for his purpose, to put τῶν at its beginning and to omit νῦν; in consequence, his τῶν has as little authority as has ὡc in (*a*); it has, besides, lost any possible reference since the singular has been restored in the preceding verses. The absence, here, of νῦν does not discredit it where it is found in a different and suitable context. The form preserved by Plutarch (anyhow the best witness) gives exactly what is wanted and can account for the emergence of the others: 'This way I myself am now going.'[2] The original τήν was replaced by δεῦρο in the text used by the commentators of Aristotle; in the one used by Hippolytos, εἶμι was mistaken for εἰμί. And thus we are, to this day, offered a text where the meaningful designation, by Empedokles, of his lot as a 'journey' (through the elements) is expelled in favour of the mere auxiliary verb (as though the poet were, with a bow, introducing himself to the audience), and an obnoxious metrical stop-gap.

---

[1] It would be no help either if, in this composite wording, the particle νῦν were described as introducing (as it often does) a particular situation which illustrates a general rule. The present passage does not really fall under this definition; and one has only to give its proper weight to the particle thus understood (translating e.g. 'As you see [or 'well, then . . .'], of these daimons I, too, am one') to appreciate the intolerably prosaic quality, clashing with the pathos of the preceding verses, of the wording adopted by DK and R. Besides, the particle νῦν preserves its temporal connotation even where it is used in this manner (see e.g. *Od.* 5. 448 and 8. 330), and Empedokles is one of the 'daimons', not 'now' but always; but he is 'now' on the way, just described, of atonement.

[2] The sceptical question in DK 'can εἶμι in epical language mean "I am on a way"?' is not really shattering. Cf. e.g. *Od.* 6. 102, 131; 10. 191; Hes. *Theog.* 972 (Plutos) εἶc' ἐπὶ γῆν τε καὶ εὐρέα νῶτα θαλάccηc; *Op.* 208.

Fr. 117 DK (476 R). v. 2. The balance of the vast evidence[1] shows that the verse ended

> . . . καὶ ἔξαλος ἔμπορος ἰχθύς.

In particular, the witness of Clement alone has not sufficient weight to sustain the variant εἰν ἁλὶ ἔλλοπος ἰχθύς against all others. Add that 'it is not permissible to take one word from one variant and one from another' (Wilamowitz)—and yet DK and R persist in doing just this. The variants εἰν ἁλὶ φαίδιμος ἰχθύς in Cyril and, similarly, ἐ. ἁ. νήχυτος ἰ. in Olympiodoros, with some other, equally late and irrelevant ones, merely serve to confirm that the peculiarity of the authoritative reading provoked alterations. The gloss ἔλλοψ being a favourite with Hellenistic Greek poets, any later interpolator could devise what we find in Clement on the model of ἔλλοπας ἰχθῦς (Hes.) *Sc.* 212 (or some similar passage); as others devised other alleviations.

'The fish that jumps out of the water as it makes its way' is the dolphin, the sacred animal of Apollo. The noun ἔμπορος retains its verbal implication as in the passages quoted by L–S–J, s.v. ii; cf. cυνέμπορος[2] and also παραίβατις ('she that goes beside') in Theocr. iii. 32. The adjective ἔξαλος could have been suggested by *Od.* 11. 134.

Fr. 118 with 121 (472 f. R). Here I shall try to advance slightly on the foundations firmly laid by Wilamowitz[3] (and blandly disregarded by editors). The argument to be convincing will have to be lengthy; hence the resulting text may stand in front of it:

> Κλαῦσά τε καὶ κώκυσα ἰδὼν ἀσυνήθεα χῶρον.
> ἔνθα Φόνος τε Κότος τε καὶ ἄλλων ἔθνεα Κηρῶν·
> ⟨. . . . .⟩
> Ἄτης ἂν λειμῶνα κατὰ σκότος ἠλάσκουσιν.

The most important source for the whole text is in the comment of Hierokles on vv. 54 ff. of the *Carmen Aureum*:[4]

Man has fallen from bliss, as Empedokles the Pythagorean says (quoting φυγὰς θεόθεν . . . πίσυνος, fr. 115, 13 f.)· ἄνεισι δὲ καὶ τὴν ἀρχαίαν ἕξιν ἀπολαμβάνει, εἰ φύγοι τὰ περὶ γῆν καὶ τὸν "ἀτερπέα χῶρον" (ὡς ὁ αὐτὸς λέγει)

> ἔνθα Φόνος τε Κότος τε καὶ ἄλλων ἔθνεα Κηρῶν·

εἰς ὃν οἱ ἐμπεσόντες

> Ἄτης ἀνὰ λειμῶνα[5] κατὰ σκότος ἠλάσκουσιν.

---

[1] Fully indicated in *Poet. Philos.* ad loc. (not so in DK); note especially Calcidius *in Tim.* (p. 218, 11 Wasz.) *ex undis* and the identical use of the rare adjective ἔξαλος by Oppianus, *Hal.* ii. 593 describing the battle between dolphin and bonito.

[2] Especially in Plat. *Phaed.* 108 b 8 (see Burnet ad loc).

[3] Bergk (*Kl. Schriften*, ii. 42), Karsten and Stein had long ago blazed the trail.

[4] Reprinted in Mullach, i. 470.

[5] Hence ἂν λειμῶνα rightly Bentley; ἐν(ι) λειμῶνι in the other citations.

We may note first that, according to Hierokles, it is not the Κῆρες that 'roam on the field of Ate',[1] but fallen souls. Moreover, he embodies the first verse into a phrase of his own; that is, he does not give us the specific context in which Empedokles spoke of the 'joyless place'. The missing subject and verb which preceded the accusative χῶρον emerge in Clement, *Strom.*, p. 516 P. He gives a series of quotations denouncing this world of change. After one from Herakleitos there are three from Empedokles. The first is

$$\text{Κλαῦcά τε καὶ κώκυcα ἰδὼν ἀcυνήθεα χῶρον (fr. 118 DK).}$$

Empedokles, then, told of his own experience. The 'daimon' who is his true self wept and lamented when he saw 'the strange (unwonted) place' —a place, evidently, to which he was transferred immediately after his banishment.[2] The conclusion that the verse-endings ἀτερπέα χῶρον in Hierokles and ἀcυνήθεα χῶρον in Clement are variant forms of one and the same passage is inescapable (it was drawn by Stein and supported by Wilamowitz). They must both be referring to the same scene, since Hierokles is likewise speaking of the place 'on to which (the souls) fall'. Two so nearly identical verse-endings are unthinkable within one and the same context. Final proof of this inference is provided by Proklos *In Remp.* 614 e and 616 b (on the λειμών in Plato's myth!), ii. 157. 24 Kroll:

$$\text{τοῦτον Ἐμπεδοκλῆς ἰδὼν τὸν λειμῶνα παντοίων αὐτὸν εἶναι κακῶν πλήρη καὶ εἶπεν}$$
$$\text{καὶ εἰπὼν ἀνώιμωξεν·}$$

$$\text{ἔνθα Κότος τε Φόνος τε[3] καὶ ἄλλων ἔθνεα Κηρῶν}$$
$$\text{Ἄτης ἐν λειμῶνι κατὰ cκότος ἠλάcκονται.[4]}$$

Ἀνώιμωξεν in Proklos echoes κώκυcα in Empedokles and proves the interconnection of frs. 118 and 121. The variant ἀτερπέα in Hierokles proclaims its spurious origin, while Clement preserves the expressive original adjective (used here for the first time in Greek literature). Empedokles modelled this passage on one from the beginning of the Homeric Nekyia (*Od.* 11. 93 f.)

$$\text{τίπτ' αὖτ', ὦ δύcτηνε, λιπὼν φάος Ἠελίοιο}$$
$$\text{ἤλυθες, ὄφρα ἴδηι νέκυας καὶ ἀτερπέα χῶρον;}$$

---

[1] The translation 'Field of Doom' may suggest 'Judgement'—which would be very far from the connotation of Κῆρες. I know of no English equivalent; for 'Vale of Tears' is equally remote from the original.

[2] This, then, was the prelude to Empedokles' incarnations. The verse was thus suited for use, by Epicurus, in illustration of the newly-born babes' reaction to the unpleasant impact of cold air (Sextus Emp. *Adv. Math.* xi. 96), but to claim this as its original setting (H. S. Long, *Am. Journ. of Philol.* lxx (1949), 58) is fantastic. In Lucretius' reproduction of the Epicurean tenet (v. 226) there is no trace of the Empedoklean phrase.

[3] It is impossible to establish the original order of Φόνος and Κότος (cf. Hierokles above).

[4] The active only is Homeric and original.

—for he, like Odysseus, had left the 'Realm of Light' to see that of Death—but Empedokles varied the model. In the text which Hierokles used the Homeric phrase had reasserted itself (perhaps owing to a marginal quotation; cf. above on fr. 115, v. 4).

The passage just quoted from Proklos seems to show that, contrary to our initial inference, vv. 2 and 4 of the current texts of fr. 121 succeeded each other. This impression appears to be borne out by a reference in Synesios, and it was endorsed by Wilamowitz. I wish to show that a verse (or possibly more) stood in between—but not what is currently printed as v. 3. The condensation of the original sequence by the two authors just mentioned was due, I submit, to their special purpose (on which later).

I would appeal, first, to the reader's sensibility. Empedokles 'saw the unwonted place where fiends[1] roam about on the Field of Ate'. That 'place', presumably, *is* the 'Field of Ate'; but, if so, is not this manner of stating the fact suspicious, with the pronoun 'where' duplicating the explicit indication 'on the Field'? Is not, moreover, the change from aorist to present, from κλαῦϲα and κώκυϲα to ἠλάϲκουϲιν, indicative of some missing link? And is it suitable that these fiends should be said to be 'roaming in the darkness' of the Stygian scene—which after all is their habitat? Is not this aimless and hopeless motion appropriate, rather, for souls banished into it? What appears to be demanded by the style and structure of these two verses can be supported by parallels in the description of the Netherworld in the sixth book of the *Aeneid* (which has such marked affinities with Empedokles). There the Roman equivalents of Empedokles' *Κῆρεϲ habitant* (v. 275) at the entrance of the *orcus*; but the *innumerae gentes* of souls awaiting incorporation 'fly around', like swarms of bees, on the *campus* (v. 709;—the λειμών!) by the river Lethe. Empedokles then—so we infer—sees 'the place where Κῆρεϲ ⟨dwell⟩ [the Greek sentence is—or at least, can be—complete without a verb]; ⟨there [or, e.g., 'next to them'], banished souls⟩ roam about on the Field of Ate'; this supplement to the preserved words, is, I submit, called for by grammar, style, and the Vergilian parallels. And it is what Hierokles— see the text quoted above, p. 199—expressly and unambiguously indicates.[2] Nor is he the only witness to confirm the assumption. Julian (*Or.* vii. 226 b) extols the perfect Cynic who looks down, as though from the height of Olympus, upon τοὺϲ ἄλλουϲ "Ἄτηϲ ἐν λειμῶνι κ. ϲκ. ἠλάϲκοντας"; the quotation would have been inapplicable, if his text had described the Κῆρεϲ as 'roaming on the Field of Ate'. And Synesios (*Ep.* 147) expressly mentions τοὺϲ ἀνθρώπουϲ ἡμᾶϲ "Ἄτηϲ . . . ἠλάϲκοντας": men and not

---

[1] This is not a sufficient equivalent of Κῆρεϲ; but 'Fates' is worse.

[2] 'E quibus colligere probabiliter licet v. ἠλάϲκουϲιν non referendam esse ad Φόνοϲ et Κότοϲ, sed ad homines sive daemones e coelo in terram delapsos (οἱ ἐμπεϲόντεϲ), adeoque hos versus non ita jungendos esse, ut facit Synesius . . . sed a se invicem dirimendos' (Karsten, p. 165).

Κῆρες.[1] Moreover, Theon of Smyrna and Philo[2] quote the verse ἔνθα . . . Κηρῶν as a phrase complete in itself—such as we hold it to be—to denote the sublunar world. This would hardly have been possible if, in Empedokles, this verse had been the incomplete first half of a sentence.

The preceding arguments are not invalidated by the fact that Proklos and Synesios, once each, quote vv. 2 and 4 combined. The former (as quoted above) wanted to illustrate the fact that the 'Field' is 'full of evils'; he had, in his context, to cite the last verse (because it contains the cue-word λειμών) with the first; any intermediate reference to the exiled souls was foreign to his purpose. And Synesios, at the beginning of *De Provid.*, simply could not include any such reference; as anyone will see who troubles to read his quotation in its context.[3]

Considerations of style and of mythography thus combine with the positive indications of some sources to show that, in the original text, one verse (or possibly more) stood between ἔθνεα Κηρῶν and Ἄτης ἀν λειμῶνα. Proklos once[4]—alone among so many witnesses for this passage —quotes the verse ἔνθα Φόνος κτλ. with a second, otherwise unattested one. But this new verse, far from filling the gap, proclaims its own spuriousness. Whatever ἔργα ῥευστά may mean—the expression is obscure beyond hope of elucidation[5]—this unmythical notion cannot be grouped with the mythical Κῆρες, Φόνος, and Κότος; for these are persons. Νόσοι could very well gain mythical reality; with Σήψιες, the same would be hard to believe; with ἔργα ῥευστά it is impossible (who indeed could suppress a smile when visualizing that Stygian scene where, according to DK's translation, 'Unglücksgeister . . . und das Wirken des Rheuma hin und her schweifen'—'spirits of distress and the effect of rheumatism'!). In fact, Proklos does not say that this pair of verses comes from Empedokles. He quotes it, without any indication of its provenance, in evidence of the healing power of Apollo in the sublunar world;[6] that is, in a context quite

---

[1] His quotation in *De Provid.* teaches the same; see below, note 3.

[2] Quoted in Diels, *Poet. phil.* ad loc. Philo's reference is preserved, in a corrupt form, in Eus. *Praep. Ev.* viii. 14. 23 (p. 390 c = i. 468. 14 Mras).

[3] Ed. Terzaghi (1944), ii, p. 65 (cf. *Poet. Philos.*, p. 105 and DK in front of. fr. 121): Θέμιδος νόμος (cf. Ἀνάγκης χρῆμα, fr. 115. 1) . . . καὶ τὰς ἐκ τῆς ἑτέρας μερίδος . . . φύσεως ἀνάγκῃ ἐς τοὺς ξυγγενεῖς αὐλισθῆναι κευθμῶνας, ἔνθα Φθόνος . . . ἠλάσκουσιν; Synesios' prefatory words anticipate what we infer to have stood between vv. 2 and 4.—There can be no doubt that the imitation by N. Muzalon (see P. Maas, *Byz. Zeitschr.* xxxv (1935), 6) is based on Synesios l.l., seeing that he, like S., has Φθόνος instead of Φόνος. Muzalon therefore is not a witness *sui iuris*.

[4] In *Cratyl.*, p. 97 Pasq.

[5] As is shown sufficiently by the long series of unconvincing attempts at explanation.

[6] Therewith, renderings of ἔργα ῥευστά like 'Inundations' (Diels) and 'Deluges' (R) are excluded, and likewise Karsten's '*res fluxae*' (or '*opera fluxa*'), which he presented as synonyms for the term ῥευστὴ οὐσία (or φύσις) in Plutarch (*Aet. Rom.* 268 d; *Adv. Col.* 1116 c) and other late writers. The adjective is at home in the Aristotelian School, contrasting 'changeable' matter with permanent essence (Arist. fr. 207 R.; Diels, *Doxogr.*, p. 307. 24 ff.). Sextus Empir. *Hypotyp.* 217 and 219 (80 [74] A 14 DK) cannot prove it to have been used by Pro-

incommensurable with the Empedoklean. We know however that Empedoklean verses were not rarely embodied in later poems—e.g. the *Carmen Aureum* (fr. 112. 4), *Orphica* (frs. 127 and 141), Lucretius (frs. 114, 124, 133). It stands to reason that Proklos derived this quotation from some such late poem.[1]

One may still consider whether, in addition to the necessary subject of ἡλάϲκουϲιν, the lacuna could have contained further 'personifications'—specifications, as it were, of the *Κῆρεϲ* in the preceding verse. The comparable passage in the *Aeneid* (vi. 273 ff.) could be quoted in support of this guess, and since Vergil instances, among others, also *pallentes morbi*, he could even seem to suggest that *Νόϲοι* might have figured in this lost passage[2] (serving as a model for the unfortunate verse in Proklos). This assumption, however, is countered by strong or even prohibitive arguments. The 'condensed' quotations of vv. 2 with 4 in Synesios and Proklos (*In Remp.*) suggest that very little stood between these two verses; what is more, the verse ἔνθα . . . Κηρῶν is so concentrated and exhaustive as to make any elaboration of its content incredible. *Κότοϲ*, the world-power of Strife, and *Φόνοϲ*, the deadly guilt which it engenders; to these two joined 'hosts of other fiends'; what else could be added to this horror, without weakening its impact? Add finally that, unlike Vergil, Empedokles introduces the negative forces active in this world, together with their opposites, at a later point and in a similar mythical form (frs. 122 f.); he could not here have anticipated himself.

After all this (and after Wilamowitz), it would be futile to argue the obvious fact that the mythical scene from which these verses come, was located in Hades—whatever interpretations the Neoplatonists, and their successors, may have put upon it.

Fr. 119 DK. ἐξ οἵηϲ τιμῆϲ τε καὶ ὅϲϲου μήκεοϲ ὄλβου

This dolorous evocation of the daimons' lost home appears to have been

tagoras, and how this technical term could have been joined to Empedokles' demons remains unimaginable.

[1] Karsten (p. 166) comments: 'Versus . . . Empedocle indignus mihi videtur; profectum credo a seriore quodam χρηϲμολόγῳ qui interdum Empedoclis versus tamquam splendidos pannos suis neniis adsuere soliti erant. Namque istud ϲήψιεϲ ἐργατερευϲτά olet seriorem aetatem.' W. Kranz[1949] made a valiant attempt to save the verse for Empedokles by means of an ingenious interpretation which aims to avoid the objections to which the previous ones are exposed. According to him (p. 22), Empedokles here presented 'the first attempt at systematising illnesses, dividing them into three groups; namely such as are due to an excess of dryness, or of moistness, or finally to 'rotting' (ϲήψιεϲ)'. Leaving aside the wider problems which this interesting suggestion raises, we may wonder if the present context was suitable for this pithy sketch of a new medical theory; the decisive fact, however, remains that no one could have recognized the meaning 'illnesses caused by excess of moistness' ('rheumatism', for short, according to DK i. 501) in ἔργα ῥευϲτά and that this obscure concept could under no circumstances be joined to the mythical personages of the preceding verse.

[2] 'Quae in Empedoclea hac descriptione desiderantur, suppleri paene possint e Vergiliana descriptione Orci', etc., Karsten, p. 166.

uttered by Empedokles on seeing them 'roaming the Field of Ate' (so also fr. 124). Stählin's restoration of the words following upon the quotation in Clement (ὧδ' ἐλθών for ὧδε λιπών) permits of the guess that the next verse may have begun ὧδ' ἐλθόντες or ὧδε λιασθέντες (cl. fr. 2, v. 8). Plutarch and Hippolytos quote the fragment in the context, respectively, of 'forgetting' and 'remembering' the soul's heavenly origin. The latter is likely to correspond with its original setting, for in the typology of eschatological myths like the present, the 'forgetting' of former existences normally and reasonably happens at, or after, a new incarnation and not earlier (Pl. *Rep.* 621 a; Verg. *Aen.* vi. 715). Empedokles, then, may with these words have deplored the anguish of the banished, sharpened by the recollection of their past state. They were to lose that recollection; while Empedokles, different from the common lot, was privileged to retain it. On the model of later eschatologies one may imagine that, when the time came, he was prevented by his divine guide from drinking, with the others, from the waters of Lethe.

Empedokles goes through the Netherworld accompanied by a divine guide. This follows from

Fr. 120 DK—or, rather, from the words with which Porphyry introduces the quotation. He is following the Neoplatonic manner when he makes ψυχοπομποὶ δυνάμεις, rather than concrete ψυχοπομποί, speak this phrase. Empedokles, of course, would not have introduced any δυνάμεις but concrete mythical persons—or, rather, a person. One could not imagine more than one person speaking these words, and more than one guide would anyhow, here again, be contrary to the typology of *katabaseis*, down to Vergil and Dante.[1] The word ψυχοπομπός suggests that Empedokles' guide was Hermes, and this inference is supported by Hippolytos, for in the passage, just referred to, from the Naassene homily[2] fr. 119 is quoted in the course of an interpretation of the figure of Hermes Psychopompos.

The consideration of the trend of the poem as a whole being reserved for the next chapter, the very obvious fact may however here be noted that a 'Cave' is not a 'Field' . . . Likewise it may be observed, with regard to

Frs. 122 and 123,[3] that the pairs of opposites personified in these lists of divinities are essentially different from the Κῆρες whose habitat is on the 'Field of Ate'. By ἔνθ' ἦσαν (122. 1) they are located in the 'Cave'. On the other hand, in

---

[1] The individual *daimones* who, according to Pl. *Phaed.* 107 d 6, quoted by DK i. 501, accompany the souls to the place of judgement are irrelevant to the present context.

[2] *C. Haer.* v. 7, p. 103 Miller.

[3] For a detail of the text of fr. 122. 4 see below, p. 217, n. 1; as to fr. 123. 3, the persuasiveness of Bergk's conjecture ζωπή, for ςο(μ)φή(ν), has been enhanced by the occurrence of this form in Kallimachos' *Iamboi* (frs. 191. 31 and 194. 59 Pf.).

Fr. 124 DK, ἔριδες and cτοναχαί (which might as well be given capital initials) recall rather the scenery of the 'Field'. The sympathy pervading these verses, and in particular the opening ὦ πόποι, indicate that they are spoken by Empedokles himself surveying that scene.[1] The sentiment is as in fr. 119, which was assigned, above, to the same context.

Frs. 125 and 126 DK. These are suitably considered together.[2] The fact that, according to 126, a female 'daimon' carries out the ἐνcωμάτωcιc, was bound to cause difficulty as long as fr. 125 was supposed to describe the same scene, since there a male 'daimon' seemed to be found in the same role (ἀμείβων). The difficulty resolves itself when the relevant observations of Kranz and Wilamowitz are pursued.

Ἐκ ζῳῶν ἐτίθει νεκρά cannot mean 'e vivis mortua facit' (Karsten; leg. fecit?), nor 'aus Lebendigem machte er Totes' (Kranz). Τίθημι is here used as in θέντα κυρίωc ἔχειν (Aisch. *Ag.* 178); it means 'laying down as a law, ordaining'.[3] It follows that an infinitive has to be added to what Kranz rightly divined to have followed; e.g.

⟨ἐκ δὲ νεκρῶν ζώοντα ∪ – ◡◡ – ∪ φύεcθαι⟩.

Νεκρὰ εἴδεα, like the εἴδεα θνητῶν in fr. 115. 7, are the 'forms' of transitory, earthly life; cf. fr. 35. 14 (of the *Φυcικά*)

αἶψα δὲ θνήτ' ἐφύοντο τὰ πρὶν μάθον ἀθάνατ' εἶναι.

Ἀμείβων, then, here means 'causing them to change'; cf. fr. 21. 14 τόcον διὰ κρῆcιc ἀμείβει and *Il.* 14. 381.

Who 'laid down' this law of change? The νόμοc can hardly have been given by Νόμοc personified. The subject could have been θεόc; but this generalizing designation is too vague to fit the concrete mythical situation. E. Bignone[4] met all requirements by suggesting Κότοc—the negative world-power (also called Νεῖκοc) that caused the fall of Empedokles and of all creatures.

A general law being here pronounced, these verses could not be uttered by Empedokles who, in this part of the poem, is speaking as a witness of mythical scenes. He could report what he heard said—when and by whom? This question will be considered later. Enough for the time being, if it is realized that fr. 125—belonging to a different context—does not in any way clash with 126. The female 'daimon' who is said to have 'clothed'

---

[1] For the reasons indicated, I hesitate here to follow Wilamowitz who would attribute these verses to Empedokles' divine guides.

[2] The fact that fr. 125 is quoted, by Clement, in the midst of a series of fragments from the *Katharmoi* is proof that this one too comes from there.

[3] Cf. Pind. *Ol.* iii. 22, vii. 61; L–S–J s.v. τίθημι, vii.

[4] p. 277 (the above will show that, beyond this, I cannot agree with Bignone's interpretation of this passage).

the daimon(s) with flesh[1] may have been called Φύcιc or Φυcώ (cf. fr. 123. 1). If she was—the inference from Plutarch's and Porphyry's comments is tempting but far from necessary—the connotation would not have been that of 'Nature' but, in accordance with Empedokles' use of the word (esp. fr. 8), that of 'Becoming' and 'Birth'.

Fr. 128 DK (466 R).[2] Not without regret does one meet, both in R and DK, two faults, one of which had been corrected centuries ago, while the other was forced, by Diels, upon a sound tradition. In v. 8 ἀκρήτοιcι must indeed be regarded as transmitted since it is implied by ἀκρίτοιcι in Porphyry and Cyril and ἀκράτοιcι in Eusebius; but how could Empedokles have described the blood with which altars were drenched, as 'unmixed'? This adjective could only have been used if sacrificial blood could alter-natively, like wine, have been 'mixed'—which is inconceivable. In v. 8 it comes from v. 6; Empedokles could not have repeated the word so soon, and at the same place in the verse. Fabricius's conjecture ἀρρήτοιcι is described, in the app. crit. of DK, as 'wohl richtig'. Indeed it is; and ought to be put into the text.[3] In v. 10, ἐέδμεναι is transmitted unani-mously by Porphyry (ΕΕΛΜ- being the most obvious of slips for ΕΕΔΜ-), Cyril and Eusebius (in whose copy of Porphyry the verb was correctly spelled). It is true that this form cannot pass the tests of modern philo-logy; it is formed by 'false analogy' of ἐέλδωρ, ἔεδνα, ἐέρcη, etc. This is not a sufficient reason for replacing it by a monstrosity like ἐνέδμεναι.[4]

The above is, once again, a mere paraphrase of Wilamowitz's observa-tions. However, I venture to differ with him on one pregnant detail of interpretation. He observes: 'Theophrastos explains Κύπριc as Φιλία; but he cannot mean the cosmic potency (Aphrodite) of the Φυcικά, since under her absolute rule there are neither gods nor men but only Cφαῖροc μονίηι περιηγέϊ γαίων' (fr. 27. 4). This is one of the (apparent) differences between the two poems which led Wilamowitz, like many others, to regard their ideologies as irreconcilable. But what Empedokles here says does not by any means enforce the conclusion drawn by Wilamowitz. At the early stage in the history of mankind whose cult Empedokles describes Aphrodite alone was worshipped. This statement does not neces-sarily exclude the existence of other gods;[5] it certainly does not imply that there existed, at the time, no other power in the universe than Aphrodite. This 'Golden Age' fits into the doctrine of the other poem if we assume

---

[1] On this concept see Detached Note IX, below, p. 405.

[2] On fr. 127 below, p. 232 ff.

[3] The recurrent incompleteness of v. 3 (due to the intercalation of Theophrastos' comment ἤ ἐcτιν ἡ Φιλία) shows that Athenaeus (or his source), like Porphyry, drew this quotation from Theophrastos' *De pietate*.

[4] It is not excused by DK's reference to fr. 137. 6: κατέδομαι is legitimate; ἐνέδομαι is not.

[5] On vv. 1–3 see below, p. 207.

that Empedokles is describing an early stage in the transition from the absolute rule of Love towards that of Strife, whose growing power becomes evident in the gradual adoption of bloody sacrifice and the worship of evil gods who previously had been powerless or even non-existent. Wilamowitz is perfectly right in saying that under the absolute rule of Love no individualization could take place within the kosmos; the fact that, in the state here described, it has taken place implies that Strife has begun to be active in it. By a lucky chance, enough survives of the text to bear out this conclusion. The statement that 'the altar was not drenched by the unspeakable murder (blood) of bulls' is followed by the assertion that 'this was the greatest pollution among men: to crush away life and eat noble limbs'. This evil, then, though abhorred, was conceivable at this stage; it could even occasionally have happened. This could not be so 'under the cosmic rule of Love, when Strife is wholly excluded'.[1] Love indeed is dominant at the dawn of humanity; but the first stirring of Strife is already felt. Had it been otherwise there would have been no humanity.

In this context, the precise meaning of v. 1 is of some relevance. 'To (with) them, no Ares was god nor Kydoimos nor ... , but Queen Kypris.'[2] This means, at any rate, that the other gods were not recognized, i.e. not worshipped. Greek gods are the realities of the world, perceived in personal forms. This was an age without violence and strife—which these gods represent; in the sense, then, that at this age they would have stood for nothing, they 'did not exist'. Are we to understand that also in a concrete, mythological sense, Empedokles taught that they 'did not exist' at all—that, in consequence, he taught successive 'theogonies' in time? It is conceivable that he represented them, rather, as eternally existing like their prototype, 'Strife'; powerless at certain periods, like him, and increasing, like him, at others. There are, however, arguments which compel the view that Empedokles presented a succession of 'theogonies'. Theophrastos (*ap.* Porphyr. ii. 21) describes the later stage with the words ἐπεὶ δὲ Ἄρης καὶ Κυδοιμὸς καὶ πᾶσα μάχη καὶ πολέμων ἀρχὴ κατέσχεν. This by itself is, for the present question, ambiguous; but when, introducing the quotation, he says of Empedokles περὶ τῆς θεογονίας διεξιών, a mythology in the manner of Hesiod is clearly indicated. Empedokles, then, described the history of civilization as a history of the gods and their cult. The Hesiodic prototype is evident, as elsewhere in the *Katharmoi*, so in the first verses of the present fragment; we may then draw the conclusion that the increasing preponderance of 'Strife' was

---

[1] R, p. 349.

[2] Βασίλεια is attribute, not predicate, to Κύπρις, as is, in the preceding verse, βασιλεύς to Ζεύς; otherwise the concinnity of the whole passage is needlessly destroyed. The text then does not say that Kypris was 'queen', but that Queen Kypris was the sole deity to the men of yore.

realized, in the relevant part of the poem, in the emergence, that is, the birth, of those gods whom the 'Golden Age' did not know.[1]

Fr. 129 DK (263 R). Stylistically this passage gains greatly when, as Stein suggested, the order of vv. 2 and 3 is inverted. Ἐπιήρανος in v. 3 joins on naturally to εἰδώς in v. 1 : 'he knew things numberless and was highly competent in wise works of all kinds';[2] with v. 2 in between, this sequence is interrupted and v. 3 hangs in the air both syntactically and with regard to its subject-matter. Again, vv. 4–6 illustrate the 'outstanding mental power' owned by Pythagoras and hence follow naturally upon v. 2, but not so upon v. 3. The latter order results in a hiatus of both syntax and substance, for these verses do not really illustrate his 'manifold wise works'.

As far as intrinsic considerations go, Stein's transposition has thus everything to commend it.[3] A powerful argument against it is however given with the fact that Diog. Laert. viii. 54, i.e. Timaios, quotes vv. 1 and 2 (and these only) in the same order in which Porphyry and Iamblichus found them in their common source. Even so, the gain from Stein's conjecture appears so great that it deserves to be presented for renewed consideration.[4]

The meaning of the last three verses was correctly indicated ('mentis infinitam vim') by Diels in *Poet. Philos.*; not so in DK (while R remains prudently ambiguous).[5] Wilamowitz observed truly: 'The dative καί τε

---

[1] Cf. fr. 21. 12.—The problem might be simple if v. 3 were transmitted complete. It is possible, as DK, p. 501 suggest, that the rest of the verse contained nothing but *epitheta*; but it could as well have run 'but Queen Kypris ⟨alone held sway⟩' or even '⟨was the only deity⟩'.

[2] Here Wilamowitz effected idiomatic Greek by adding τ' after σοφῶν.

[3] It is significant that R (p. 219) prints the traditional arrangement of these verses but translates Stein's rearrangement.

[4] It is not absolutely necessary to assume that Timaios read the verses in the same order as the Neoplatonists. Supposing that Stein's arrangement represents the original, it is conceivable that the second verse was dropped by Timaios, or by Diogenes, or even merely in the archetype of our Diogenes-manuscripts.

[5] One will not, I expect, deny that the word πραπίδες, as here (and fr. 110. 1) used by Empedokles retains, to some extent, its basic and concrete meaning 'diaphragm'; but the wording seems to forbid the interpretation 'tense the diaphragm', which M. Detienne (*La notion de Daïmon* . . . (1963), pp. 79 ff.) would attribute to it; thus detecting, in the footsteps of A. Delatte and others, in Empedokles the evidence for a Pythagorean 'discipline de type chamanique' culminating in 'une maîtrise du souffle'. The preceding verse, according to which Pythagoras was possessed of 'a vast treasure of *prapides*', would make no sense, if the connotation of the last word were centred upon its physiological aspect rather than upon the notion of mental capacities. 'With' these capacities Pythagoras 'reaches out' to penetrate the universe of time and space; as Achilleus (*Il.* 23. 99; cf. 16. 834) reaches out (ὠρέξατο) 'with' his arms to embrace the shade of Patroklos. These verses then were legitimately interpreted, in the common source of Porphyry (*Vita Pyth.* 31) and Iamblichos (*Vita Pyth.* 66 f.), as evidencing the superhuman powers of perception, arising from his superior 'organization' (διοργάνωσις), with which Pythagoras was endowed; but they do not indicate the techniques employed by Yogis and shamans.

δέκ᾽ . . . αἰώνεccιν is hard to construe'; presumably, though, it became plain in the context of what followed (there may have been e.g. a participle like γιγνόμενον or -να). At any rate, this verse does not by itself refer to Pythagoras' ('ten or twenty'!) reincarnations—how could this reference possibly have been combined with the preceding clause 'whenever he strained with all his mind' (cf. fr. 2. 8)—but it defines the range of his mental power: Pythagoras 'saw what happened in ten or twenty lives of men'; he was thus comparable to the seer who ᾔδει τά τ᾽ ἐόντα τά τ᾽ ἐccόμενα πρό τ᾽ ἐόντα (*Il.* 1. 70). The particular turn which Empedokles gave to the traditional formula may even so imply a hint at Pythagoras' teaching: the range of his 'seeing' was so wide because he was able to remember his previous incarnations. The spontaneous impression that an indefinite number of generations is meant is borne out by the Homeric models of the Empedoklean phrase, *Il.* 9. 379 and 22. 349.

᾽Εν κείνοιcιν at the beginning compares with οὐδέ τιc ἦν κείνοιcιν Ἄρηc in fr. 128, but Pythagoras did not live at the dawn of history. Empedokles, then, gave a story, in the Hesiodic vein, of successive γενεαί of men; and this (as we saw from Porph. *De abst.* ii. 21) was subsumed under the concept of the progressive debasement of gods and worship, from the pure offerings of the age governed by Love (fr. 128) to the bloody sacrifices of his own day (frs. 136–9). The κείνοι at the beginning of fr. 129, one may infer, were the men of the generation preceding Empedokles' own; a better generation, like that of the heroes preceding Hesiod's Iron Age.

It is very obvious that, in following Diels's arrangement, we are being carried into a context totally different from the fragments previously commented upon. This holds good also for the following. Fr. 130 is, like 128, from a description of life under the rule of Love; and from the same context comes

Fr. 78 DK—as had been suspected by Karsten (p. 268), accepted by Stein, rejected by Diels, and reasserted by Wilamowitz. The latter no more than hinted at the solution of the problem given with the traditional combination of fr. 78 with fr. 77, and DK still print the unfortunate combination of the two as devised by Sturz. Hence we have to take up the problem afresh.

In the course of the first conversation reported in the third book of Plutarch's *Quaest. Conviv.* a speaker (Trypho) maintains that ivy is suited, by its 'coldness', to counteract the effects of wine (647 a). Against him, Ammonios argues (648 b ff.) that it is, rather, 'fiery and warm' and hence perennial (ἀειθαλήc 648 e). This view is finally countered by Plutarch himself (649 a ff.): ivy is essentially 'moist'; and he proceeds (649 c–d) to account for its evergreenness with arguments drawn, largely, from Empedokles. The passage shows that Empedokles used the word ἐμπεδόφυλλον to denote 'perennial', and that he accounted for the fact that some plants are perennial by positing a special conformation of their 'pores' conserving their 'moistness'. This problem, and its treatment, evidently belongs to the *Physika*, and happily a doxographic report survives to confirm this.[1]

W. Capelle has convincingly shown[2] that for the whole 'problema' Plutarch used a source which, in turn, drew largely on Theophrastos; it is therefore very likely that, in the last resort, we owe to him this summary of a passage in the *Physika*. The likelihood becomes a certainty in view of the parallel in Aetius; but in Theophrastos' extant writings this summary has not survived. In *De caus. plant.* i. 13. 2 Theophrastos quotes a different passage from Empedokles in a different context. The question there is not: why are some plants perennial?—but: what is the relation between the change of seasons and the germination of plants? It appears, so Theophrastos says (13. 1), that trees keep budding in mild and soft weather. This fact leads him to a 'theoretical consideration', the main point of which, to us, is this.[3] Supposing that the most favourable climatic conditions were to prevail all the time: would not the cycle of the seasons come to an end? Would not the trees, instead, have buds, flowers, and fruits simultaneously at all times? Thus the words of the poets (cf. *Od.* 7. 117) would not appear fantastic, nor what Empedokles says—who posits a climate similar to spring persisting—ἀείφυλλα καὶ ἐμπεδόκαρπα . . . θάλλειν καρπῶν ἀφθονίῃσιν κατ' ἦρα[4] πάντ' ἐνιαυτόν.

By analogy with fr. 77 it is clear that ἐμπεδόκαρπα, with Empedokles, means 'in fruit throughout the year'. But how could scholars yield to the temptation to foist ἐμπεδόφυλλα, from 77, upon this different quotation? It is odd indeed that Empedokles appears to have followed ἐμπεδόκαρπα with καρπῶν ἀφθ. κτλ.—so much so that a verse or more may be supposed to have stood in between; it could e.g. have contained an enumeration of various trees, as in *Od.* 7. 115 f. But what justification is there for ousting the variation, within fr. 78, between ἀείφυλλα and ἐμπεδόκαρπα, and interpolating the ugly parallelism which even Wilamowitz printed? The one word called 'fr. 77', ἐμπεδόφυλλον, comes from the *Physika*. Fr. 78 comes from the description of an ideal scene like the garden of Alkinoos; that is, of the 'Golden Age' in the *Katharmoi*. The fact that Theophrastos quotes it in a discussion of the effect of the ἀήρ upon plants is no excuse for changing the corrupt κατ' ἦρα, in the citation, into κατ' ἠέρα; Empedokles'

---

[1] Aetius v. 26. 4; DK A 70 (p. 296. 23).

[2] *Philologus* lxix (1910), 274 ff.

[3] The text from paragraph 1 (end) onward is corrupt, but I trust that the above summary meets the salient points made by Theophrastos. In the absence of reliable information about the manuscript-evidence I refrain from any attempt at emendation.

[4] Thus the manuscripts—as far as can be seen from the edition by A. E. Dengler (1927).

trees did not grow 'in the air'.[1] But the dative ἀφθονίηισι needs a support-ing adjective. Scaliger four hundred years ago restored κατήρεα.[2]

Fr. 78, from the *Katharmoi*, then should read:

⟨δένδρεα δ'⟩ ἀείφυλλα καὶ ἐμπεδόκαρπα τεθήλει

⟨. . . . .⟩

καρπῶν ἀφθονίηισι κατήρεα πάντ' ἐνιαυτόν.

Empedokles did not write these verses merely in order to add an idyllic feature to the description of the world under the rule of Aphrodite. If fruits grew throughout the year, her devotees were never short of pure fare and pure offerings; they were, to use Theophrastos' words,[3] πρὸς cυνεχῆ εὐcέβειαν ἕτοιμα.

Fr. 131 DK. These verses are preserved only by Hippolytos; in a state of corruption which, I suspect, has not been entirely cured yet. I wish to suggest (after Th. Bergk)[4] that a verse has dropped out after v. 2.

The infinitive ἐλθεῖν in v. 2 calls for a governing verb, and since ◡◡ – is lacking either before or after μελέτας, it was natural to try and supply one in this lacuna. It was tempting, moreover, to assume the effect of haplography and to insert a past tense of μέλειν. Here Schneidewin, who inserted ἔμελε, was outdone by Diels. His μελέτας ⟨μέλε τοι⟩ is as beautiful a sample of haplography as it is an abominable cacophony—such as Empedokles could not possibly have devised; and, besides, 'an aorist is required' (Wilamowitz). It was no doubt an improvement when P. Maas and Wilamowitz put ἅδε in the place of Diels's μέλε; even so, the resulting phrase seems impossible to me. 'It has pleased you that my endeavour should go through the (a) mind': this makes as little sense in English as in Greek. It is easy enough to translate '. . . to let my endeavour go through your mind'; but the Greek will not yield this meaning, for it has no equivalent for either 'let' or 'your' (τοι being absorbed by ἅδε); besides, the whole phrase διὰ φροντίδος ἐλθεῖν, with the connotation here required ('favour' rather than 'consider'), sounds un-Greek. On the model of διὰ μάχης ἐλθεῖν ∼ μάχεcθαι, it is permissible to assume that διὰ φροντίδος ἐλθεῖν could stand for φροντίζεcθαι (though hardly in epic style?). In that case, however, the subject of the phrase would have to be 'the

[1] The fact that Theophrastos adds, in his own words, the information that Empedokles accounted for the miraculous flora by a persisting spring-like climate (ἀήρ) cannot justify the conjecture κατ' ἠέρα. Nor can I see any satisfactory way of extracting the notion 'spring' from the transmitted letters, notwithstanding the epic and lyric evidence for ἦρος, εἴαρος, and ἦαρος; for κατ' ἦαρα could conceivably stand for 'in the spring', but not for 'as in (permanent) spring'.

[2] Cf. Eur. *El.* 498.—Beck's conjecture κατήορα is less good; as anyone must agree on examining the evidence for the use of either adjective.

[3] *Apud* Porph. *De abstin.* ii. 13.

[4] In his review of H. Stein's edition (*N. Jahrb.* lxviii (1853), 21 ff.); reprinted in *Kl. Schriften*, ii (1886), p. 65. Bergk compares the fragment with *Il.* 10. 278 ff.

Muse' and not, as is actually the case, Empedokles' 'endeavour'.[1] And, finally, while the Muse certainly had favoured that endeavour, the φροντίς 'through' which it 'went' surely was his and not hers?

It appears to be impossible to fill the lacuna in v. 2 in such a manner as to obtain a complete and satisfactory phrase. If in consequence the loss of a whole verse after it is assumed, it may be observed that (a) the normal form of the protasis in invocations like the present one is εἴ ποτε . . . ἔδωκας; that (b) the noun φροντίδος calls for an epithet,[2] and that (c) the verb ἐλθεῖν calls for some specification as to 'where' or 'how' Empedokles' endeavour 'went'; for it is very likely that here, as in fr. 35. 1, the traditional image of the 'way', or 'journey', of the poetical work was used.

The following reconstruction (largely after Bergk) is offered merely to illustrate what seems to be required by sense and style, and with no pretence at recovering what Empedokles wrote:[3]

> εἰ γὰρ ἐφημερίων ἕνεκέν τινος, ἄμβροτε Μοῦσα,
> ἡμετέρας μελέτας ⟨καθαρῆς⟩ διὰ φροντίδος ἐλθεῖν
> ⟨οἶμον ἀν᾽ εὐσεβίης πάρος εὐμενέως μοι ἔδωκας⟩
> εὐχομένωι, νῦν αὖτε, κτλ.

The fragment is certain to come, as Diels held, from the *Katharmoi*,[4] although his demonstration was less cogent than it could have been. For one thing, he robbed himself of the strongest argument by asserting that ἐφημερίων τινός in v. 1 is neuter. A strictly logical contrast with ἀμφὶ θεῶν in the last verse appears indeed thus to be gained; an earlier poem would be stated to have centred on a theme of an 'ephemeral' kind, while now Empedokles is about to speak about the gods. This interpretation, however, is impossible, first, because the 'postposition' ἕνεκεν is ill suited to introduce the theme of a poem; secondly, because the only other instance of the neuter used without a noun, namely the Homeric phrase (*Od.* 21. 85) ἐφημέρια φρονεῖν, is not sufficient to support the presumed use of the neuter as a full noun; thirdly, and mainly, because Empedokles could not possibly have described any one of his poems—and least of all the *Physika*—as 'a thing subject to the changing day'.[5]

The masculine ἐφήμερος is frequently used as a noun denoting 'man', the unstable creature of the day. The alternative form ending on -ιος, which conveys the same meaning,[6] is very rarely so used (Aisch. *Prom.*

---

[1] Μελέτας cannot be taken as a genitive, since a preposition (περί) would thus be required; not to mention the dialect.

[2] Bergk supplied 'ἀδινῆς (vel καθαρῆς)'. [3] Cf. frs. 3 (4). 2–5 and 110. 2.

[4] It is no objection that Hippolytos quotes it in a summary of Empedokles' doctrine which is based upon *Phys.*: he quotes fr. 115, from the *Katharmoi*, in the same context (and similarly fr. 117 in i. 3, with 'Love', 'Strife', etc.; likewise, in vii. 30, fr. 110 follows the cue-word καθαρμοί.

[5] Cf. H. Fränkel's suggestive discussion of the uses of ἐφήμερος in *TAPA*, lxxvii (1946), 131 ff. = *Frühgriechisches Denken* (1955), pp. 23 ff.

[6] Cf. R. Strömberg, *Greek Prefix Studies* (1946), p. 135.

546; Aristoph. *Av.* 687), but Empedokles so used it at the beginning of the
Physika, fr. 3 (4). 4 *DK*. By the repeated use of the choice word—and that,
once in a proemium, and again in the context of an invocation of the
Muse, with ἐυχομένωι in fr. 131 resuming ἄντομαι from fr. 4¹—Empedokles
made it clear that he was referring to that earlier passage; what he had
done 'for the sake of' Pausanias, he now proposes to do 'about' the gods.
The parallel is not exact, and the inconcinnity is mirrored by the use of
ἕνεκεν and ἀμφί respectively. It is therefore conceivable that fr. 131 continued with a dative ('to my friends') after ἀμφαίνοντι.² This assumption,
though tempting, is not, however, necessary, for the word ἐφήμεροc so
normally calls forth the contrast between man's transient nature and the
abiding existence of the gods³ that this must have been felt predominantly
also in the present passage, its logical unevenness notwithstanding.

Therewith it has already been implied that fr. 131 must come from the
Katharmoi. And indeed, it could not have occurred in the *Physika*. This
poem is, from beginning to end, addressed to Pausanias, and Empedokles
could not anywhere in it disparage his addressee by the derogatory term
ἐφημερίων τιc. Fr. 131, then, is a reference from the later to the earlier
work like Hesiod's from *Op.* 11 to *Theog.* 225 or, generally, the reworking
of the Pandora story.⁴ And it has the form of a proemium. The beginning
of the *Katharmoi* is extant; fr. 131 cannot find its place there. It must,
then, mark the beginning of a later main section. We shall shortly offer
some evidence suggesting the old, and probably original, division of the
poem into two books;⁵ fr. 131, I infer, comes from the proemium of
Book ii.

Fr. 133 DK (480 R). 'It is not possible to reach to god and set him before
your eyes': what could have made R put this translation in the place of

---

¹ In view of this reference, I have inserted a further motif from fr. 4 (ἐυcεβίη) in the tentative supplement of 131. 3.

² In this case the verse ξείνων αἰδοῖοι λιμένεc, κτλ., which is currently but wrongly inserted
in fr. 112, could have found its place shortly after the fragment under discussion.—Schneidewin was probably right in changing its last word to ἀμφαίνοντι. The phrase is, in any case,
derived from Homer: φαῖνε δ' ἀοιδήν (*Od.* 8. 499), νοήματα φαῖνε (*Il.* 18. 295), etc. (as is fr. 17.
15 πιφαύcκων πείρατα μύθων, cf. *Od.* 22. 131 etc.). Homer uses ἀναφαίνω similarly; see especially
Il. 1. 87 θεοπροπίαc ἀναφαίνειc. The compound ἐμφαίνω, on the other hand, is essentially
a prose-word of the fourth century and later, with a somewhat different nuance of meaning,
viz. of 'showing forth', 'exhibiting', some constituent quality. The only other early instance
of ἐμφαίνω happens to be in Empedokles (fr. 17. 15; both missing in L–S–J). But even if
Simplicius is correct there, the connotation is the one just sketched and therefore different
from the place under discussion. Hence this parallel is hardly sufficient to support the manuscript reading ἐμφαίν. in fr. 131. Schneidewin's easy alteration yields exactly the meaning that
Wilamowitz stipulated, viz. 'presenting'; it is in the Homeric tradition, and the parallel *Il.*
1. 87 implies, once again, that Empedokles is 'presenting' something more than an ordinary
ἀοιδή (cf. above, on fr. 112. 4).

³ e.g. Aisch. *Prom.* 82 and 945; Pind. *Nem.* vi. 1 ff.; Semonides, fr. 1.

⁴ Note that in 115. 2 Empedokles resumes a motif (ὅρκοc) from *Phys.* 30 and in 146. 3 one
from *Phys.* 21. 10–12.   ⁵ Below, p. 236.

that given in DK and L–S–J (s.v. πελάζω B 3)? How is one to imagine the action indicated? Supposing that this were feasible, how could the Greek words, thus understood, yield the (supplied) verb 'to set'? And could πελάζομαι θεόν mean 'I reach *to* God?' Would not πρός be required, or the dative?[1]

The middle πελάζομαι is rare. In three instances in tragedy[2] it is intransitive (and followed, if anything, by the dative). In epic poetry there is, as far as I know, only one instance (*Il.* 17. 341); it is all the more relevant since there only do we find the same aorist as in Empedokles. In this passage, the middle voice has the same, transitive connotation as the active predominantly has in Homer: Aeneas wishes to prevent the Greeks from 'bringing the body of Patroklos to their ships (μηδ' . . . Πάτροκλον νηυσὶν πελασαίατο). The difficulties just mentioned in the rendering of the Empedokles fragment vanish when this one, valid parallel is applied to it. 'It is impossible to bring near to us the Divine [so that it becomes] reachable in our eyes.' This understanding of the verse was established by Diels in 1880.[3]

In the following verse, one regrets to find Karsten's conjecture ᾗπερ still in the texts, instead of Clement's ἥπερ. The alteration is minute, but it impairs the meaning. Empedokles should not be supposed to have said '. . . the way by which the way of persuasion leads . . .' The relative does not refer back to an individual noun ('eyes' or 'hands'), but to the whole of the preceding statement that sense-perception exercises the most immediate appeal—or, in Empedokles' words 'this (which) is the . . . way of persuasion'.

Fr. 134 DK (467 R). Consideration of the evidence for this fragment can serve to establish its wording and its original context. The evidence is late but comparatively rich—in fact, fourfold. The fragment is quoted in full by Ammonios and Tzetzes (three quotations by the latter; in one of them, though, *Chil.* vii. 522 ff., the first three verses are merely summarized; otherwise they agree *ad verbum*); moreover, Olympiodoros quotes the first verse in his commentary on Plato's *Gorgias* (p. 29 Norvin), and the full text of the quotation—but without v. 2—is added in the margin of the archetypal manuscript, Ven. Marc. 196. The similarities and differences between these citations are such as to suggest that they were not derived one from another but go back, separately, to a rather late common source; presumably a book containing selected Empedoklean pas-

---

[1] It is little help that Euripides once (*Andr.* 1167) construes the active πελάζω, on the model of ἱκάνω, with the accusative; πελάζειν δῶμα is a simple, local concept, very different from the notion of 'reaching to God'.

[2] Aisch. *Sept.* 144; Eur. *Or.* 1274; *Rhes.* 776.

[3] *Hermes*, xv (1880), 172 (comparing Homeric ἐν ὀφθαλμοῖσιν ὁρᾶσθαι, *Il.* 1. 587, 3. 306, etc., with ἐν ὀφθ. ἐφικτόν in Empedokles).

sages of specific interest to Neoplatonists and, perhaps, interspersed with comment.[1]

On the one hand, all these witnesses agree in certain faults. These are, for once, recognized and put right beyond cavil because Empedokles, in this passage, iterated—though with some variation—two verses from the *Physika* (fr. 29). In v. 2, ἀπαὶ νώτων γε stands condemned in view of the otiose particle, evidently inserted to mend the metre. Fr. 29 (i.e. Hippolytos) preserves the genuine ἀπὸ νώτοιο, proving that, moreover, the preposition has been altered for (invalid) metrical reasons; as so often in Homer and Hesiod, where ἀπό and ὑπό are legitimately lengthened before a liquid consonant. Empedokles followed the Homeric usage here as in fr. 115. 6 ἀπὸ μακάρων. At the end of the same verse the active ἀΐccουcιν is in bad style; fr. 29 is here again right in giving the middle form, for the phrase is modelled on Hes. *Theog.* 150 χεῖρες ἀπ' ὤμων ἀΐccοντο; cf. also *Il.* 6. 510 ἀμφὶ δὲ χαῖται ὤμοιc ἀΐccονται; the faulty active in fr. 134 may have been anticipated from v. 5 καταΐccουcα. These agreements in error show that the witnesses to fr. 134 derive from one common source.

On the other hand there is, among these witnesses, an amount of variation which cannot convincingly be traced to slips or whims of the copyists.[2] By this fact the derivation of the witnesses one from another is excluded.

According to three witnesses (Ammonios, Olympiod. text and marg.) the fragment begins οὐδέ (or οὔτε) γὰρ ἀνδρομέῃ; Tzetzes instead has, twice, οὐ μὲν γὰρ βροτέῃ—offering a trite adjective (cf. frs. 20. 1 and 100. 17) in the place of the choice Homerism of the others. For reasons of metre, the particle μέν is now necessary, and therewith the whole variant is proved spurious, for thus the following verse does not join on satisfactorily. It is, however, unlikely, and indeed incredible, that Tzetzes, quoting twice the same wrong incipit, relied on nothing but his own invention; and this all the more so since he expressly cites the fragment as coming from 'the third book of the *Physika*' (we shall presently turn to this point). He did not find this in Ammonios or Olympiodoros; he must, then, have drawn upon a book in which the beginning of the fragment was written thus faultily, and since the other witnesses quote the correct form from, ultimately, the same source, both forms must have been in it; that is, it—or some copy of it—contained glosses. Tzetzes used a copy in which the gloss had penetrated into the text. The same inference suggests itself at the very beginning of this verse and, again, in v. 3.

The first word is οὐδέ in the text of Olympiodoros only. The full quotation in the margin of the outstanding manuscript (of *c.* A.D. 900) of his commentary has οὔτε; the same is in Ammonios. The former is right, for

---

[1] A similar suggestion was made by K. Horna (*Wiener Stud.* xlviii (1930), 10) and, with reference to fr. 115, by Wilamowitz (p. 482).

[2] Of the latter kind though is Tzetzes' καί (for οὐ) in v. 3 (and, equally, Hippolytos' γούνατ', for γοῦνα, in fr. 29).

οὔτε in v. 1 could not be continued by οὐ μέν in v. 2. The variant οὐδέ: οὔτε is trite; even so, it is unlikely that the latter two witnesses should have committed the same fault in the same place independently. If, then, they copied it from different copies of one and the same (*ex hypothesi*) florilegium, this is likely from the first to have had the faulty particle in the text and its correction in the margin; whence it penetrated into the text of some copies, while others retained οὔτε.

In v. 3 χέρες, instead of πόδες, is probably too weakly attested—by Olympiod. marg. only—to represent more than a, possibly suggestive, variant;[1] but the alternative cτήθεα for μήδεα at the end of the verse is, at any rate, an authoritative variant and, beyond this, stands a good chance of being correct. Cτήθεα is written, as a variant, above μήδεα in one of the four manuscripts selected by Busse for his edition of Ammonios (p. 249. 9). If information about the many other manuscripts[2] were available, some could be expected to give cτήθεα in place of μήδεα, for *pectora* in the Latin translation is proof that it stood in the Greek manuscript used by William of Moerbeke. This reading might be no more than a secondary adaptation to *Il.* 18. 415 cτήθεα λαχνήεντα, but probably is something much better. In fr. 134, the adjective λαχνήεντα is genuine beyond doubt, and so is μήδεα γεννήεντα in fr. 29. This makes sense, if Empedokles varied the whole phrase, and not the adjective only: μήδεα γεννήεντα in fr. 29, and cτήθεα λαχνήεντα in fr. 134; thus the two passages stand in meaningful contrast. In the florilegium from which the extant evidence for fr. 134 appears to be drawn, the parallel passage from fr. 29 may have been quoted in the margin, or in a subjoined exposition; whence μήδεα could penetrate into the text of derived copies.

It appears that, in that source, the provenance of every passage quoted was indicated, as is customary in good florilegia; thus it can be explained that Tzetzes was able—he alone—to state that fr. 134 comes from 'the third book of the *Physika*', as also we learn from him alone that fr. 6 comes from the first.[3] These indications are not in Ammonios nor (for

---

[1] K. Horna (l.c., 5) argued that χέρες is genuine, taking the place of v. 2 which, so he held, was wrongly inserted, in the other witnesses, from fr. 29. Seeing that thus the two peculiar features are traced to one and the same cause, this suggestion is well worth pondering; it would be in line with the other difference between frs. 29 and 134 to be mentioned in the text above; even so, its basis is precariously, or even forbiddingly, slight, and the resulting wording stylistically precarious.

[2] Such are listed in Busse's *Supplementum Praefationis*, pp. ix ff.—I am leaving out of consideration Busse's puzzling note ad loc., according to which the passage containing the fragment under discussion is omitted in 'A¹FG¹'; the manuscripts which he uses being called A, F, G, M, all of which are explicitly cited ad loc., excepting only F.

[3] Apart from Tzetzes, only Simplicius gives information of this kind (frs. 17, 62, 96) and, once, Aetius (fr. 8).—Diels's rejection of Tzetzes' testimony has been briefly criticized by Wilamowitz, p. 498, and was rejected by Bignone (pp. 631 ff.). With regard to fr. 6, Diels strove to dismiss Tzetzes' statement by suggesting that he had drawn it from the similar ascription of fr. 8 by Aetius. This device will not stand scrutiny. It implies that Tzetzes

fr. 6) in Aetius; but there is no reason to assume that Tzetzes invented them. Therewith it is confirmed that he did not draw his citations of fr. 134 from Ammonios. In view, however, of their close textual interrelation they must have drawn upon different copies of one and the same source. Ammonios did not copy out the indication 'from *Physika*, Book iii' from it; Tzetzes did—in one of his three citations. This source was not a complete text of Empedokles; otherwise Tzetzes would have given larger samples of it to posterity. Consequently, it was a selection. Tzetzes drew from it, perhaps, also his citation of fr. 6 and, at least, one further, unique piece of evidence; namely, the otherwise unattested but genuine variant μελάγκουρος in fr. 122.[1] Quotations by Neoplatonic writers from frs. 115, 117, and 121 are likely to come from the same 'florilegium'. The comparative scarcity of quotations from it makes one suspect that it was not very full; it may have centred on particular aspects of Empedokles' philosophy and, on the other hand, have contained extracts from other Presocratics; such as 'Pythagoras' and 'Orpheus', as well as Parmenides and Xenophanes. I refrain from pursuing this hypothesis. At any rate, the survival of some semi-independent evidence for Empedokles down to the 12th century has to be acknowledged; the evidence from Tzetzes being confirmed by the quotation in the margin of Cod. Marc. 196[2] and, besides, by a letter of Michael Italicus.[3]

troubled to fish out, from the end of Book i of pseudo-Plutarch's *Placita*, the heading of a fragment which he did not quote and prefixed this to another one which he quoted from the very beginning of the same book. This is too abstruse even for Tzetzes. The natural inference is that he found the heading of each fragment where he found the fragments themselves.

[1] Tzetzes applies twice, in closely similar passages, the Empedoklean adjective to the noun ἀσάφεια (used by him in a rhetorical context); namely (a) *Chiliad*. xii. 574 (ed. Kiessling, p. 462) and (b) *Proleg. in Aristoph.* 136 c (ed. Kaibel, *Com.* i. 1. 28 = Aristophanes, *Com.*, ed. Cantarella, i (1949), p. 56. 83). At the former place the manuscripts, as far as known, have μελάγκορον (see Tzetzae *Epistolae*, ed. Pressel (1851), p. 139, for the Paris manuscripts; the same is in Cod. Graec. Monac. 338, fol. 256ᵛ, according to information kindly supplied by the Direktor der Handschriften Abteilung der Bayerischen Staatsbibliothek); at the latter, μελάγκουρον. Tzetzes' middle-Greek synonym, which Cantarella, l.c., convincingly corrected to κουτ⟨ρ⟩ούλαν, i.e. 'bald', 'shorn', is not far from the mark; for Empedokles appears to have visualized Obscurity personified with 'shorn black hair'.—Regarding fr. 50 DK—likewise transmitted by Tzetzes alone—the reserve expressed in the app. crit. is highly justified; for Tzetzes makes it quite clear that he is merely guessing at the authorship of Empedokles 'or someone else', and the verse itself has no specific Empedoklean characteristics. On the other hand, it is here worth recalling that the same Tzetzes was able to transmit several Hesiod fragments (81, 161, 237 Rz.), drawing on sources lost to us.

[2] The thorough differences of wording are proof that this quotation, too, was not drawn from Ammonios. Marc. 196 stems from some particularly scholarly centre, to which T. W. Allen (*Journ. of Philol.* xxi (1893), 48 ff.) traced eight other outstanding manuscripts, among these the Paris. 1807 of Plato. They are furnished with explanatory notes drawn from authoritative sources—as a perusal of the Platonic scholia and of Norvin's apparatus in his editions of Olympiodoros easily shows. Similarly as in the passage under discussion, a short verse-quotation by Olympiodoros is given in full in the margin on p. 235. 18 Norvin; cf. also p. 19. 23, and Busse's *Praefatio* to his edition of Simplicius, *Phys.*, vol. ii, based pre-eminently upon a manuscript of the same group, Ven. Marc. 226.

[3] See K. Horna, l.c., 9; cf. fr. 160 DK.

Since Tzetzes has been found drawing on authentic evidence, his ascription of fr. 134 to the third book of the *Physika* has to be taken seriously. So did all editors prior to Diels, who transferred the fragment, because of its 'theological' content, to the *Katharmoi*. This was a *petitio principii* indicative of the preconceptions of the age; in the heyday of nineteenth century science, a 'scientific' work like the *Physika* could not be visualized as culminating in 'metaphysical' speculation; the witness to the contrary had to be silenced—by abuse rather than by argument.[1] Meantime it has been realized that even on the showing of Diels's own collection of the fragments, the *Physika* was not confined to 'scientific' demonstration; it begins and ends on a religious note (frs. 3 f. and 110 f.); the divine names of the elements are anything but irrelevant decoration, and the whole presents itself as a religious revelation.[2] The agreements and differences in the descriptions of the Sphairos (fr. 29) and of the world-god (fr. 134) suggest that the same *essentia* is being shewn under a new aspect, and the most important one; and indeed it would be uniquely fitting if the detailed interpretation of the kosmos culminated in the revelation that the god Sphairos (fr. 31)—composed of the elements ever swayed by Love and Strife—was, in essence, One Mind permeating all its parts.[3] On the other hand, the ascription of fr. 134 to the *Katharmoi* seems inadmissible quite apart from Tzetzes' testimony. Its second part, according to Theophrastos,[4] was περὶ τῆc θεογονίαc καὶ τῶν θυμάτων[5]— fr. 128 shows in what manner; and I for one find it impossible to visualize the godhead described in fr. 134 in this mythological framework; still less in the preceding κατάβαcιc εἰc Ἅιδου. Fr. 134, then, has to resume the place which Tzetzes and, following him, the earlier editors assigned to it;[6] with it, likewise, fr. 133, for these two make one, practically inseparable whole. Whether or not further fragments (namely, 131 and 132) have to be similarly re-transferred will be considered together with the reconstruction of the *Katharmoi* as a whole.

Fr. 135. DK in their translation follow Wilamowitz in suggesting that the extant μέν-clause was followed by the contrasting statement: 'but (δέ) on

---

[1] K. Horna, l.c., 6 f., presents an impressive collection of the epithets heaped by Diels upon Tzetzes.

[2] This has been shown most excellently by C. H. Kahn, *Archiv f. Gesch. d. Philos.* xlii (1960), 6 ff.

[3] Wilamowitz considered changing the transmitted ἀΐccονται in fr. 29 to ἀΐccοντο, no doubt in view of ἔην in v. 3. The contrast with the present adopted in fr. 134 would be fitting; the former passage describing a passing stage in the unending process of the material world; the latter, its permanent divine essence. Anyhow, the basic identity underlying periodic change is mirrored by the two passages being identical in part and again, and decisively, different.

[4] *Apud* Porphyrius, *De abstin.* ii. 21 (ed. Nauck, 1886, p. 150. 17).

[5] For this quotation cf. below, p. 240, n. 4.

[6] This conclusion was drawn, as by Bignone and Horna, so by C. H. Kahn, l.c., p. 6, n. 8.

earth people do not obey'.[1] I venture to doubt it. This grandiose statement of a universal law could not really be weakened and reduced almost
to a mere preamble by a following δέ-clause asserting its neglect by mankind or the variety of laws current among them.[2] Empedokles, rather,
seems to have added emphasis to its proclamation by using 'μέν soli-
tarium' (equivalent, almost, to μήν). So Homer does very frequently,[3] and
often this μέν, with him as here, is preceded by ἀλλά.[4] This need not
indicate a contrast with what precedes the clause thus opening, but it
does so not rarely.[5] In the present passage such a contrast is exceedingly
likely to have existed, for the words τὸ πάντων νόμιμον suggest that νόμιμα
observed only sporadically had been mentioned before. The words with
which Aristotle introduces the quotation, τοῦτο γὰρ οὐ τιcὶ μὲν δίκαιον τιcὶ
δ' οὐ δίκαιον, can be quoted in support of this conclusion; however hopeless it be to try and recover the original wording from them.[6] Moreover,
the extant verses must have been followed by an indication of the substance of the universal law: namely, the absolute sanctity of life. There
is, of course, no doubt that Empedokles did state that this world-law was
being neglected in his day; but he cannot have done so by a mere δέ-
clause following upon fr. 135.

Fr. 136 DK (468 R). This fragment and the following are preserved by
Sextus Empiricus (*Adv. Math.* ix. 129). They are the passionate appeal of
a preacher striving to controvert what is, to his fellow men, the normal
expression of devotion. 'Murder' he calls their sacrifices; 'ill-sounding'
with the cries of the slaughtered victims, δυcηχέα—as was, with Homer,
the noise of battle.[7] He invokes them to 'visualize' that, in eating sacri-

---

[1] DK, though, strive to keep nearer Aristotle by supplying '(but the human laws . . .)'.

[2] One realizes the impossibility when recalling Soph. *O.T.* 865 ff.

[3] Cf. Denniston, *Greek Particles*, pp. 360 ff.

[4] e.g. *Il.* 1. 125, 8. 374; *Od.* 3. 317, 4. 349, 5. 290, 12. 156.

[5] e.g. *Od.* 4. 694, 15. 405; cf. Denniston, l.c., p. 378.

[6] Sturz and Karsten, who made the hopeless attempt, deduced from Aristotle that
Empedokles had said of his world-law that 'it was not just with some and not-just with others,
but . . .'. It is clear that this mechanical transcription of Aristotle's words results in a muddle
of contradictory negations; besides, clauses opening with ἀλλά . . . μέν seem always to be
preceded by a more definite incision than this reconstruction would allow. Diels concluded
from Aristotle, feebly supported by Hippol. vii. 31 (a passage which in *Poet. Phil. Fragm. ad*
B 131 he characterized as '*explicatio inepta*'), that 'Empedokles himself used the word δίκαιον or
δικαιοcύνη' in this context. This is highly improbable; seeing that in the preserved verses,
where it would be suitable, if anywhere, Empedokles uses νόμιμον, and that δίκη and all its
derivates do not occur even once in the extant fragments (fr. 2. 4 is not an instance). Which
is highly significant. And still Diels's note is carried on from one edition of the *Vorsokratiker*
to the next (though now augmented by the rider 'Differently Wilamowitz')—together with
a reference to Rohde's *Psyche* which cannot cause anything but bewilderment and fruitless
search.

[7] Fr. 100. 19 Empedokles uses the same word with its alternative Homeric nuance, 'emitting an impeded, gurgling sound'—as of men dying.

ficial meat (and all meat eaten was sacrificial) they 'devour', like wild
beasts, each other; what they consider to be acts of piety arises, in fact,
from ἀκήδειαι, that is, the absence of that consideration which man owes
to man and in particular to his kin. The conviction dictating this inversion of values—the conviction of the unity of all life—culminates in the
vision of frantic murder among relatives:

Fr. 137 DK (469 R).[1] vv. 1–4 present, with unique pathos, the traditional
pious action of the *pater familias* offering sacrifice on behalf of his household as the ritual murder of a son by his father; vv. 5–6 urge, in the same
terms, the horror of all consumption of flesh: it is murder among kinsfolk.[2]

The understanding of vv. 1–4 is hampered, first, by Diels's conjecture
ὁ δ' αὖ νήκουϲτοϲ in v. 3.[3] The manuscripts of Sextus attest ὅδ' ἀνήκουϲτοϲ.
Bergk recognized that the rare, original adjective νήκουϲτοϲ (cf. νηλεήϲ,
νήπιοϲ, νῆϲτιϲ, νήνεμοϲ)[4] had been replaced by the current form ἀνήκουϲτοϲ; hence he restored ὁ δὲ νήκουϲτοϲ—'sine dubio recte', as Diels judged
in 1880.[5] It is hard to guess what, twenty years later, made him change his
mind and print, in the *Poetae Philos.*, that δ' αὖ which remains in DK and
R to this day. Diels could not have been unaware that δέ is metrically
unobjectionable;[6] besides, the seemingly simple addition of the single
letter υ had lost its basis by Bergk's explanation of the transmitted
α-privativum; finally, the intrusive particle is here out of place, for none
of the nuances which are elsewhere conveyed by the frequent combination
δ' αὖ fits the present context. The sacrificing father, deaf to the imploring
cry of the victim, carries out his murderous intention and proceeds to
prepare the nefarious meal for his family; he does not do so 'again' or
'in turn' or 'for his part'.

The grave and difficult problem in these verses is given with the uncertain wording after v. 2 νήπιοϲ; its imperfect solution has obscured the
action described and blunted its impact.

The manuscripts of Sextus Empiricus, who is alone in preserving the

---

[1] The discussion of this fragment was published previously in the *Festschrift* for A. Lesky
(*Wien. Stud.* lxxix (1966), 38 ff.). Thereby I gained the benefit of some valuable comment by
the addressee as well as by Professor A. Dihle and Dr. H. Cancik, which in the following
I have striven to utilize.

[2] Diels's note (*P. Phil.*, ad loc.) 'ante v. 1 alios commemoratos fuisse docet v. 5' betrays bad
taste; how could vv. 5 f. be imagined, with a description of further murders, to continue the
preceding scene—which in fact they generalize!

[3] Discarded by Wilamowitz only.

[4] In the extant Greek literature, the adjective νήκουϲτοϲ seems to survive only in Arat. 173
(with passive connotation); but the derived verb, in *Il.* 20. 14 νηκούϲτηϲε θεᾶϲ, confirms
Bergk's diagnosis.

[5] Hermes, xv (1880), 172.

[6] Cf. e.g. *Il.* 4. 274 δὲ νέφοϲ; similarly 6. 469, 11. 378; Chantraine, *Gramm. Hom.*, i³
(1958), § 70.

whole fragment, and in particular the passage under review, fall into two classes deriving separately from one, often corrupt archetype.[1] One class is represented by the single manuscript N, of the 13th or 14th century; the other, by E and L which are still more recent; besides, there are Renaissance copies of no evidential value. Consequently, the reading of the archetype, whether corrupt or not, may survive either in N or in EL (if not in both); errors being frequent in each class.[2] In the passage under discussion, N reads οἶδα πορεῦνται, the other two οἱ δὲ πορεῦνται. These are two attempts at making sense of one and the same series of letters, with a difference only at the fourth letter; namely ΟΙΔΑΠΟΡΕΥΝΤΑΙ (ΟΙΔΕΠ- in EL). Since οἶδα is obviously wrong, there is some probability that the reading of EL is not an authoritative variant but arose from an attempt at correction, presumably in the margin of the (presumably late-13th century?) archetype of our manuscripts; hence ΟΙΔΑ is likely to be nearer the original than ΟΙΔΕ. All modern attempts, however, at tackling the same problem moved from the obvious uselessness of οἶδα to the assumption that the first letters represented οἱ δέ or οἱ δ'. Thereupon one was left with the third person plural of some doubtful verb— πορεῦνται or ἐπορεῦνται or ἀπορεῦνται. The first is vox nihili. The second was alleged by Th. Bergk, on the isolated model of Il. 23. 212 τοὶ δ' ὀρέοντο, to mean 'they rush up'.[3] Realizing the unsuitability of this connotation, Diels in 1880, after quoting other useless suggestions,[4] proposed φορεῦνται (which actually comes to about the same); but he returned to Bergk's reading in 1901; in the third edition of the Vorsokratiker finally he accepted the reading of N, interpreting its letters as ἀπορεῦνται, and this has so far remained in the texts. It must put any attentive reader in a state of ἀπορία, for vague and illegitimate translations, like 'sie sind verstört' (i.e. 'benumbed' or 'troubled'?) or 'distracted' can serve to allay—or certainly to betray—the editors' uneasiness but cannot clarify the described situation. How could those who are in the act of sacrificing (θύοντες) be said to be 'rushing up' or 'perplexed' or 'distracted'? And indeed, who are they? 'The people', according to R; but there is no hint in the text to justify this assumption and how could they, these unknown ones, all of a sudden take over the sacrifice? DK, alternatively, propose 'attendants', and so did Wilamowitz, adding 'every Greek knew the procedure followed at sacrifices'. This is undoubtedly true but cannot make up for the lack of a reference for the lonesome pronoun οἱ. And even supposing that famuli were meant, what part are they

---

[1] This sketch is based upon Mutschmann's Praefatio of the Teubner edition.

[2] For example, N has two faults in the first verse of fragment 136 (παύcacθε πόνοιο).

[3] For the (equally unavailing) derivation from ἐπόρημι see Wien. Stud. lxxix (1966), 40, n. 6.

[4] Hermes, xv (1880), 172, quoting ὃc δὲ πορεῦται, οἱ δὲ πονεῦνται and even ὑc δὲ βόηcεν.

supposed to be playing? The father speaks the ritual prayer (ἐπευχό-μενος); the father raises the victim up to the altar (ἀείρας); the father slaughters it (cφάζει v. 2; cφάξας v. 4) and, finally, carves it up. What, then, is left to be done by the *famuli*? And yet they are supposed to be engaged, not upon any subsidiary task—which would anyhow be outside Empedokles' theme—such as the preliminary washing of hands or the sprinkling of barley, but in carrying out the very sacrifice (θύοντες, v. 3); and, worse still, in carrying out their professional task they 'do not know what to do'—for that is what ἀπορεῖcθαι means. 'Every Greek knew about sacrificing'—except, so it seems, these professionals (who could not even be expected to 'feel hesitations'—supposing that this meaning of the verb were admissible).

It is legitimate to consider whether, before the preserved verses, some other persons could have been mentioned to which the pronoun οἵ could refer; but this proves to be highly improbable, first, for stylistic reasons. The scene centres on the two persons, father and son; they are both introduced before the pronoun, and, after the words under discussion, the sacrificing father is again in view—but no trace of the supposed by-standers;[1] it passes belief that, in between, the pronoun could have referred, right across the pathetic presentation of father and son, to other persons mentioned previously. Moreover, whether they were *famuli* or 'people' or 'family-relations', or whosoever, the inescapable fact arises again that there is no conceivable employment for these dummies.

This, of course, is the salient point. Here is no room for any others to 'rush up' or 'sacrifice' or 'be perplexed' or 'look on' or 'implore'.[2] The horrific scene imagined by Empedokles is between father and son, and between them alone; it may have been prefaced in some general manner, but the intrusion of any additional persons can only weaken its impact and is, in fact, refuted by the resulting inconsistencies.[3] It follows that the letters ΟΙΔΑ in v. 2 no more imply a plural pronoun than the perfect οἶδα, and that the transmitted end of the verse cannot originally have been the third plural of a verb. What the faulty letters do, or did, originally represent may be inferred, first, from a consideration of the sound wording before and after them; at the same time, the plural θύοντες calls for correction, for it is as destitute of any reference as is the preceding finite verb.

---

[1] It has already been observed above, p. 220, n. 2, that the last two verses anything but indicate their previous appearance.

[2] The λιccόμενος in v. 3 obviously is the victim; the plural ending in some manuscripts without authority is a Renaissance conjecture (if not a plain slip) which leaves the sentence in ruins.

[3] This applies also to the recent attempts, by van Groningen (*Mnemos.* IV. ix (1956), 223) and Cataudella (*Riv. di Filol.* N.S. xxxviii (1960), 32) to extract an acceptable meaning from Diels's reluctant text.

Before the corrupt passage, the father is the acting person, and thus again after it. At the latter place he is introduced by ὁ δέ; consequently, the intervening words must have centred upon the son. This inference is at once confirmed by the participle λιccόμενον, which can only refer to him; thereafter, G. Hermann's easy correction θύοντοc (for -τεc) has to be accepted,[1] yielding at once a most convenient reference for the following ὁ δέ. The alteration is so easy as to all but impose itself, but the syntax of the resulting wording is problematical,[2] for the person implored is, after λίccομαι, always indicated by an accusative. I submit that Empedokles may have here used the genitive on the analogy of δέομαι, so as to avoid an accumulation of accusatives (whose number will anyhow increase with the progress of the present discussion). Thus Euripides, once (*I.A.* 1242), follows ἱκετεύω with a genitive. If this explanation should seem unsatisfactory, an alternative—to be proposed in due course—may be taken into consideration.

Now for ΟΙΔΑΠΟΡΕΥΝΤΑΙ. In these problematical letters lurks some detail concerning the son. Before them, the father was seen praying and about to slaughter (cφάζει) his victim; after them, he has, notwithstanding its entreaty, carried out the slaughter (cφάξαc)—'not listening to the cries'. These cries must have been mentioned before; and indeed, what else could have been said about the victim but that it shrieked? Λιccό-μενον does not express this but was, so it appears, added epexegetically—the victim 'shrieks imploringly'.

The results of the preceding analysis are confirmed by a testimony which has been strangely neglected, although it was briefly mentioned by Karsten and printed by Diels in the *Poetae Philosophi*. In ch. 197 of his commentary on the *Timaeus*, Calcidius,[3] following Porphyry, reproduces the present fragment freely but completely. Its first four verses correspond with the following three hexameters:

> Mutatos subolis mactat pater impius artus
> Dis epulum libans. Saeva prece territa mugit
> Hostia, luctifica funestatur dape mensa.

v. 2 *mugit*, G.Z.: *mente* MSS.

[1] A corruption of the same, trivial kind recurs, in the same Sextus, in Empedokles fr. 2, v. 3, namely ἀθρήcaντοc for -τεc (corr. Scaliger).—Karsten ad loc. maintained that the participle must derive from θύω 'to rage', the homophonous verb 'to sacrifice' having ῠ. This is wrong, for the vowel of its present stem is normally long. The form under discussion infringes, it is true, a rule laid down in L–S–J, s.v. θύω A, according to which 'trisyllable cases of the participle have ῠ'. This rule, however, is based, so it appears, on a mere two instances, and there are other forms (most of them duly quoted ib.; add Pindar, fr. 78. 2) likewise with ῠ. All these are in fact illustrations of a metrical licence which is by no means confined to this verb (see Chantraine, *Gramm. Hom.* i. 372). In short, there is no reason to doubt its accepted connotation in the present fragment.

[2] This was rightly stressed to me by Professors Dihle and Lesky. I regret having been unable to find out where and how G. Hermann accounted for his conjecture.

[3] Ed. Waszink (1962), p. 218; cf. ib., *Praefatio*, pp. xc sqq., also lxxii sq. and app. crit., p. 219.

All the main elements of the Greek text are there, though rearranged—but there is no trace of any persons, other than father and son, 'rushing on' or 'undecided'; where they seemed to appear in the Greek, Calcidius enlarges upon the terror of the victim. I have allowed myself to replace the transmitted, meaningless *mente* by a verb which seems required by both syntax and style, to balance *funestatur* in the next line;[1] but my argument does not hinge on, or require, this conjecture. Even without it, Calcidius confirms what emerges from a sympathetic reading of the Greek: the scene described by Empedokles was confined to those two persons, father and son, alone; and the corrupt passage, in which undefinable interlopers were supposed to make their appearance, actually described the reaction of the victim. In the original Greek this could have been conveyed, in the available two dactylic feet, only if λιccόμενον was added epexegetically to another participle, the meaning of which was 'screaming'. Such a combination of participles is in the style of Empedokles (fr. 2, vv. 3 ff.) and Homer; cf. e.g. *Il.* 21. 324 f. θύων ‖ μορμύρων or 18. 259 f. ἰαύων ‖ ἐλπόμενοc.[2] The ending of a participle of the required kind emerges on deleting the last of the transmitted letters—an easy operation such as has been carried out successfully in other places.[3] Casting around for a suitable participle ending on -εῦντα, none nearer to the transmitted letters is likely to offer itself than τορεῦντα, and anyone accepting this (or a similar synonym) will recognize οἰκτρά in the preceding letters. I presented this diagnosis confidently in the *Festschrift Lesky*;[4] since then, Dr. H. Cancik has shown me, by his incisive critique,[5] that it stands in need of careful evaluation.

The crucial parallel for the assumption that in Empedokles the notion of 'crying' could have been expressed by τορέω is Aristophanes, *Pax* 381 εἰ μὴ τετορήcω ταῦτα καὶ λακήcομαι. It is evident that the verb here denotes some kind of vocal utterance; moreover, the scholion ad loc. confirms that the verse is a skit on tragic phraseology. This use of the verb is thus proved to have been legitimate in high poetry, although we have evidence only for its use with the concrete connotation of 'piercing'.[6] The adjective

---

[1] The scribe who originated the fault appears, on reaching the last word in v. 2, to have been misled by looking at the end of the following line.

[2] Cf. Chantraine, *Gramm. Hom.* ii (1953), p. 322, § 468; Schwyzer, *Syntax* (1950), p. 406; Kühner–Gerth, *Syntax* (1898), ii. 103 f.

[3] e.g. at the end of v. 30 of the *Hymn* of Kleanthes: φέροντεc F: -νται Meineke (the original ending had been misspelled -ντε and this was 'corrected' by the addition of -c); exactly the same corruption has emerged in v. 448 of Menander's *Dyskolos*. Cf. also the last verse of the present fragment, where the fact that in Homer the dual is occasionally used for the plural was admirably used by Karsten to correct the faulty ending of ἀπορραίcαντα. Comparable is Euripides *El.* 871 ἐξενέγκωμαι for original -μεν; cf. also the variants in *Hipp.* 1285. The ends of verses are particularly exposed to corruption; see Wilamowitz, *Einleitung in die griech. Tragödie* (1887–1910), p. 218 with notes 193 and 194.

[4] *Wiener Stud.* lxxix (1966), 44.   [5] Above, p. 220, n. 1.

[6] *Il.* 11. 236; *Hymn. Merc.* 119 etc. (cf. τετραίνω, τείρω, and lat. *tero*). The relevant

τορός, and its adverb, are in classical literature frequently combined with μῦθος, ἔπος, λέγειν, ἀγγέλλειν, etc., to convey the notion of a 'clear', 'distinct' utterance;[1] hence one might well conclude that the verb τορέω, when used metaphorically, means 'speaking clearly' (not 'loudly'). This is in fact the explanation given by the scholion to Ar. *Pax* 381 (κατείπω . . . cαφῶc); it could seem to take away the basis of the proposed emendation in Empedokles—until the constant substratum of the strangely differing connotations of the Greek root is realized.

We speak of a 'penetrating' voice—scarcely aware of using a metaphor—but more frequently of a 'bright' or 'clear' one, with a metaphor from the field of vision. This is not usual with Greeks; they use the concrete notion of 'piercing'. This basic and concrete notion of adjective and adverb remained alive (though more frequently, in extant classical texts, with the compound διάτορος) with poets speaking of nails 'piercing through and through';[2] of Prometheus' shackles;[3] of Oedipus' pierced feet.[4] The same notion stands out when terror,[5] or the sound of a trumpet,[6] or a human voice, are described as 'piercing'. Of the latter usage, oddly enough, no classical instance appears to survive (this situation, though, will presently be remedied); anyhow, its frequent occurrence with later, classicist authors is evidence for lost classical models. Porphyry[7] tells of the τορόν—the piercing, bright quality—of Plotinus' voice; Lucian[8] combines φωνὴ λαμπρὰ καὶ φθέγμα τορόν; Thetis, according to Philostratos,[9] ἐβόα τορόν when lamenting Achilles and, finally, the oratory of Polemon was, according to the same,[10] τορὸν ἤχουcα ὥcπερ ἡ Τυρcηνικὴ cάλπιγξ.

The 'piercing', 'penetrant' voice is, implicitly, 'distinct' and 'clear'. This fact—decisive in the present context—is in itself perfectly understandable, and particularly so when the quality of Southern speech and the musical character of the Greek language are recalled; high pitch is equivalent with 'clarity' and 'distinctness'[11] The last passage just quoted from Philostratos can serve for illustration. It is an echo of classical models like Aisch. *Eum.* 567 and Soph. *Aj.* 15 ff., where Odysseus similarly

entries in L–S–J are, as always, most helpful but, owing to various misstatements, have to be used with circumspection.

[1] Thus e.g. in Eur. *Ion* 696.—The evidence from tragedy is collected and helpfully discussed in E. Mielert, *Ausdrücke für Wahrheit und Lüge in der attischen Tragödie*, Diss. München (1958), pp. 89 ff.

[2] Aisch. *Suppl.* 944; Soph. *Indag.* 309. [3] Aisch. *Prom.* 76. [4] Soph. *O.T.* 1034.
[5] Aisch. *Prom.* 181. [6] Aisch. *Eum.* 567. [7] *Vit. Plot.* 2.
[8] *Bacch.* 7. [9] *Her.* 12. [10] *Vit. Soph.* i. 25. 10.

[11] I am opposing the suggestion that the meaning 'distinct' of τορός rests on the basic notion of 'penetrans animum' or also of 'geistiger Durchdringung' (thus E. Mielert, l.l., p. 92, quoting Groeneboom on Aisch. *Eum.* 567). This all-too abstract derivation breaks the evident connection between, and indeed identity of, expressions like τὸ τορὸν τῆc φωνῆc and λέγειν τορῶc. Their common basis is in an identical impact on the senses and not in an abstraction which cannot apply to those instances nearest to the basic concrete connotation of τορός.

likens Athena's voice to an 'Etruscan trumpet'; not because of its power but because of its clarity: it is 'well-intelligible' to him; he readily 'grasps it with his mind'. The high-pitched, 'piercing' sound is 'distinct' and 'intelligible', and vice versa; this is why, in Attic drama, τορός and τορῶc so frequently convey the notion of 'clarity' of speech.[1] Thereafter we may with fair confidence quote Aristophanes, *Pax* 381 (and its tragic model) in support of our interpretation of the Empedoklean *crux*; τορεῦντα would mean 'emitting a high-pitched ('piercing') sound'. The rarity of this use of the verb is an argument for, rather than against, its attribution to Empedokles.[2]

In conclusion, the syntactical function of the genitive θύοντοc may briefly be reconsidered. If the possibility of its dependence upon λιccό-μενον is denied, it may be taken for a *gen. abs.*: 'the son cries imploringly, while the father proceeds with the sacrifice'. Λίccομαι often stands absolute,[3] and the absence of a genitive noun is not without parallels where, as here, the reference of the participle is self-evident.[4]

Frs. 138 and 143 DK. These two fragments are quoted together by Aristotle (*Poet.* 1457[b]13); they were both attributed to Empedokles by Vahlen, because Theon of Smyrna who, more fully, quotes the second, ascribes it to him. This is reasonable, since Aristotle subsumes both of them under one (anonymous) εἴρηκεν.[5] Aristotle also shows that the participle ταμών

---

[1] I doubt that, when applied to 'interpreters' (Aisch. *Ag.* 616 and 1062) the adjective means 'clear', 'distinct' in the same way, for in this case there is no question of a 'piercing' sound perceived by listeners; if anything, the interpreters, if they are to be 'clear', must have 'pierced' the obscurity of the utterance which they clarify. I should, however, connect this use of the adjective rather with its more general connotation of 'able', 'competent' (for which see L–S–J, s.v. II); its basis being in the notion of an action (whichever it be) carried out as efficiently as by a drill 'piercing' a piece of wood (compare the use in American slang of the adjective 'cute'). In the case of an interpreter, the result would indeed be in making 'clear' what had been obscure, but this would be because he is 'efficient' and 'competent' at his task. Differently again, the ὀνειρόμαντιc in Aisch. *Cho.* 32 is τορός indeed, but not because the omen is 'clear'—it is expounded afterwards by interpreters. But it 'makes the hair stand on end' and materializes in a cry; it is, then, 'piercing' as is φόβοc in *Prom.* 181.

[2] An unconvinced reader may care to consider the alternative οἰκτρὰ γοεῦντα. The transition of an -άω verb to -έω would not lack ample parallels (Chantraine, *Gramm. Hom.* i. 361; K. Meister, *Die homerische Kunstsprache* (1921), pp. 77 f.); even in Akragas, an inscription attests τιμεῖν, and if Wilamowitz's bold reconstruction of fr. 154a is accepted, the participle κυκέων (for -άων) would provide a parallel in Empedokles; cf. moreover γοήμεναι, γοεδνόc, and γοερόc. Combination of οἰκτρόc and γόοc is usual, e.g. Aisch. *Pers.* 688; Soph. *Ai.* 629; (cf. *Od.* 4. 719 and 8. 540); Plato (*Phaedr.* 267 c) uses the adjective οἰκτρόγοοc, and Hesychius even attests the participle οἰκτρογοοῦντοc (which could suggest οἰκτρογοεῦντα for Empedokles). The objection to this alternative is in its greater distance from the transmitted letters and in its inferior expressiveness.

[3] e.g. *Il.* 1. 502; Bacch. v. 100; Soph. *El.* 1380, *O.T.* 650; Eur. fr. 773. 53.

[4] *Od.* 17. 489, cf. *Il.* 13. 291, and often in plural; see Chantraine, *Gramm. Hom.* ii. 322, § 469; Kühner–Gerth, *Syntax*, ii. 84, Anm. 2.

[5] I find no justification for the note in DK (p. 369 app. crit.) according to which Wilamowitz regarded fr. 138 as 'unempedokleisch'; the passage referred to suggests the opposite.

in 143 stood in the nominative; the accusative in Theon was occasioned by his context. Wilamowitz stressed—so far in vain—that the trochee caused by ἀτειρέϊ following cannot be removed by inserting ἐν (with Karsten). He inclined to accept the metrical irregularity; but it is extremely improbable that Empedokles could have adapted the Homeric verse-ending (*Il.* 5. 292) χαλκὸς ἀτειρής only to produce a glaring metrical fault, while disregarding the suitable alternative offered by the standard formula ταναήκεϊ χαλκῶι, which in *Il.* 23. 118 is followed by τάμνον. P. Maas has shown[1] that this wording has to be restored in Empedokles and offered a suggestive explanation for the troublesome fact that the wrong adjective appears in the single manuscript of Theon and in one of the two of the *Poetics*, where the other preserves the satisfactory reading almost unimpaired (τανᾳκεϊ B).

Fr. 138 could, but need not, refer to the slaughter of a victim;[2] fr. 143 prescribes a particular rite to be observed in securing water for purifying ablutions.

Fr. 139 DK (470 R).[3] The involuntary humour in the translation in DK: "... ehe denn meine Lippen der Gedanke an den gräßlichen Frevel des Fraßes umspielte"[4] forcibly points to the difficulty of the transmitted wording. How could anyone be said to 'think around his lips'? The verb cannot be replaced by any other (μαστεύσασθαι Karsten), for it is guaranteed by Homeric prototypes (esp. *Od.* 12. 373); nor can the prepositional phrase be connected with βορᾶς preceding (on the model of θεὸς διὰ κόλπου); for 'feeding' does not take place '*around* the lips'. The troublesome preposition can be eliminated by assuming, with H. Fränkel, that περί arose from πρίν misread—as could easily happen in minuscule writing—and that its correction in the left margin was wrongly prefixed to the beginning of the verse. If, then, with Fränkel, we carry out the emendation presumably intended by the ancient corrector, the verse reads

σχέτλια ἔργα[5] βορᾶς πρὶν χείλεϲι μητίϲαϲθαι.

The dative χείλεϲι now makes a fitting indirect object, as in νόϲτον

---

[1] *Byz. Zeitschr.* xxxvi (1936), 456; cf. *Hermes* xv (1880), 174, n. 2, where the wording of the passage in Theon is established.

[2] ψυχή is 'life', not 'soul' (it is important indeed that the latter term is non-existent in Empedokles); accordingly, the sword, cutting the veins, can be said to 'scoop off' the life; with a similar metaphor as in frs. 128. 10 and 137. 6.

[3] Nauck's alteration of the transmitted οἴμοι ὅτ' οὐ at the beginning of the fragment to ... ὅτι οὐ is not necessary; it is enough, with R, to adjust the accentuation (... ὅ τ' οὐ); cf. *Il.* 16 433 οἴμοι ἐγών, ὅ τε μοι, κτλ. (Chantraine, *Gramm. Hom.* ii. pp. 286 and 289).

[4] Kranz[1949] (p. 134) instead makes Empedokles deplore that he had "solche Greuel ... gedichtet im Liede": a stark mistranslation which, besides, makes nonsense of the whole fragment.

[5] Empedokles respects the digamma in ἔργον in fr. 17. 23 (not so in 112. 2 and 129. 3).

'Οδυccῆϊ . . . μητιόωca[1] and the whole phrase: 'before I devised awful fare for my lips' suits the context. The verses are spoken by one who has been made to realize the true nature of sacrifices as described in fr.137.

Frs. 140 and 141 DK. Together with fr. 143 (see above), these are the only extant prescriptions concerning details of 'purity' in everyday life. There may have been many more since, as Wilamowitz observed, the title 'Katharmoi' seems to imply, primarily, a set of rules of this very kind; if few such survive, this could be because later readers were interested, rather, in the philosophical and religious content of the poem. The denunciation, anyhow, of bloody sacrifices—no doubt with the commendation of such offerings as were used in the Golden Age (fr. 128. 4–7) —naturally falls under the same heading; which, besides, may have had wider implications.—The style of an impassioned homily stands out, as in frs. 136 f. and 139, so here, especially in the twofold vocative δειλοί, πάνδειλοι; the poem was meant for a much wider public than Empedokles' noble friends at Akragas.

Fr. 142 DK (479 R). Looking at the wording of this fragment in DK, 'von Diels sehr unsicher ergänzt', one inclines, with Wilamowitz (506, n. 1), to dismiss it as too obscure for any profitable consideration; for not only is Diels's completion of the latter half of the second verse materially without base and abstruse in its result; but what can be safely recovered raises grave doubts.[2] The purpose of the Epicurean author who quoted this fragment is not indeed, as Wilamowitz asserted, obscure; he writes as a grammarian. After citing the end of Kallimachos' *Epigr.* 7 as an instance of one predicate referring ἀπὸ κοινοῦ to two subjects, one in the singular and the other in the plural, he proceeds to illustrate the same figure of speech from a passage in Empedokles, thus providing a hint for the completion of the mutilated second verse. The wording of the first is clear:

τὸν δ' οὔτ' ἄρ τε Διὸς τέγεοι δόμοι αἰγ[ιόχοιο];

in the second, one seems to read

οὔ]τε π[ο]θ' Ἄ⟨ι⟩δου δέ[χεται . . .]κ[. . .] cτέγος . . .

This scans, if the epic Ἀΐδεω is put in the place of the Attic form; it fits into the required grammatical category and, in itself, yields an acceptable meaning. The notion of an evildoer for whom there is no room either on Olympos or in Hades recalls, to some extent, fr. 115. 9–12; it certainly

---

[1] *Od.* 6. 14; cf. *Il.* 15. 349, H. H. *Apoll.* 325a.
[2] One will consult also Bignone's transcript (p. 506), whose widely different reconstruction is hardly in complete agreement with his own indications.

does not fit the frame of the *Physika*. The adoption of traditional mythological notions by Empedokles is, however, surprising. It definitely forbids tracing these verses to the description of the lot of the fallen daimons or to the novel 'Theogony' in the *Katharmoi*; but they may conceivably come from a warning for those who transgress the 'universal law' of fr. 135.

Frs. 144 and 145 DK. Plutarch and Clement gave the cue for the misinterpretation of these verses which has been taken up and pursued by all modern students; to culminate in Kranz's assertion:[11] "Der christliche Ausdruck 'Sünde' ist hier nicht unpassend, weil wir in der Tat christlicher Sphäre nahe sind." The protest of the original words calling for an entirely different understanding was overborne by translations in which stark error was cloaked in soothing ambiguity. Or is νηcτεῦcαι really rendered adequately by 'sich ernüchtern' (the un-German coinage suggesting 'ridding oneself of drunkenness'); κακότηc by 'colpa' (Bignone) or 'Sünde', and ἀλύειν by 'irre sein' (that is, 'to be mad', but seems to suggest 'erring')? The upshot of these distortions is a fanatic's pronunciamento: 'since you are erring in sins, you shall never be relieved from grievous suffering'—which fits Clement's protreptic argument, but hardly agrees with the spirit and trend of Empedokles' revelation.

With Homer, and down to the end of classical times, ἀλύειν does not mean 'to err', i.e. 'roam about aimlessly' (as it does with Polybios and later); it denotes a state of violent emotion, usually grief. If the following κακότηcιν is taken to mean 'sins', the combination of verb and noun makes nonsense of the whole phrase ('since you are grieving about your sins, you will not be relieved from suffering'). But κακότηc does not mean 'sin'; it comprises what is conceived of as 'bad', τὰ κακά. To the realistic thought of the Archaic Age, 'bad is as bad does'. 'Bad' is what is felt as adverse and weakening, as are e.g. old age, illness, and, in particular, poverty; *e contrario*, ἀρετή, the sum of ἀγαθά, is, with Hesiod (*Op.* 287–9), in 'affluence'. Empedokles' noble friends in Akragas were κακότητοc ἄπειροι; they 'did not know hardship', as we saw above, in discussing fr. 112. 3. The conclusion drawn from the material presented there applies here; it is borne out, furthermore, by the plural κακότηcιν. Who could, on consideration, find here a plurality of 'anti-virtues', as in a Stoic catalogue of ἀρεταί and κακίαι? And it is borne out by the combination of κακότηcιν with the adjective χαλεπῆιcιν. To translate this by 'schwere Sünden' is to eschew the original, and the substitute 'schlimme' or 'widrige' is nothing but a sop to the scholastic conscience.

Χαλεπόν is what is felt as a burden or a sore, is reacted upon with sentiments of anger and grief, and demands strain and effort if its impact is to be overcome. Accordingly this adjective could not, in the present context,

11 *Empedokles* (1949), p. 361.

be combined with the concept of 'sins'—which those allegedly 'erring' are supposed to indulge in. Pain, sorrow, suffering are χαλεπά; as above fr. 112. 12, so e.g., ἄλγος *Od.* 2. 193, πένθος 6. 169, πόνος 23. 250, Hes. *Scut.* 44, δύα Aisch. *Sept.* 228. These samples show what kind of κακά must be expected here to be covered by the noun κακότητες; the kind, namely, from which men were free, νόσφιν ἄτερ τε κακῶν καὶ ἄτερ χαλεποῖο πόνοιο, until Pandora opened her box (Hes. *Op.* 91 ff.); those men of the Golden Age who lived like the gods, careless, κακῶν ἔκτοσθεν ἁπάντων (see ib. 110 ff.). This, then, is here meant by κακότης. Men who, according to Homer (*Od.* 19. 366), ἐν κακότητι καταγηράσκουσιν are not therewith said to age 'in sin'; nor was Ixion, whom wrongdoings ἐς κακότατ' . . . ἔβαλον (Pi. *P.* ii. 35), thrown 'into sin'; nor did the 'Orphics' (fr. 229 Kern) aspire to 'breathe afresh from sin'—but 'from hardship', ἀναπνεῦσαι κακότητος.[1] The most striking verbal parallel to the present passage is, in Alkaios (59 B.), the girl lamenting ἔμε δείλαν, ἔμε παίσαν κακοτάτων πεδέχοισαν—she, too, is by no means accusing herself of 'all sins'.[2] And it is characteristic that the adjective δειλός occurs there, as δείλαιος here and as δειλός in frs. 132 and 141; cf. 124.[3]

Thus every one of the significant words in fr. 145 calls for an understanding and points to associations which are irreconcilable with the current interpretation. If, instead, we translate: 'Ye that are writhing in troublous hardships will never relieve yourselves from wretched pains', this rendering is at any rate coherent and in agreement with the indications of the Greek—as far, that is, as Clement chose to quote it. But the question previously raised remains even after the words are properly understood: can Empedokles be supposed in these terms to have inveighed against his listeners and readers? Is it not, rather, fairly obvious that Clement cut the sentence short to suit his polemical argument? Empedokles, I submit, went on with εἰ μή or πλήν or πρίν: "ye will find no

---

[1] Thus also fr. 230 K. ἀναψῦξαι κακότητος, the meaning of which is established by the parallel (or even citation) in Plato, *Leg.* iv. 713 e 6 οὐκ ἔστι κακῶν αὐτοῖς οὐδὲ πόνων ἀνάψυξις (-φύξις MSS.).

[2] Cf. (Pl.) *Axiochus* 366 a 5, where αἱ ἐντὸς κακότητες are 'internal diseases'.

[3] The assertion that, in Empedokles, 'δειλός is regularly used for the misery of those who violate the precepts of purification' deserves the briefest refutation only because it was presented by so distinguished a student as C. H. Kahn (*Archiv f. Gesch. der Philosophie*, xlii (1960), 8, n. 12). He is perfectly right in discerning, in the *Physika*, the linguistic symptoms of a mystical revelation. The terms ὅσιος, καθαρός, ἐποπτεύειν, in frs. 2, 3, 110, are significant in this respect; but δειλός, in frs. 2. 2 and 110. 7, is not. It is true that in fr. 141 Empedokles deplores as δειλοὶ πάνδειλοι those who disregard the taboo on beans; but he uses the same word in fr. 124 in commiserating with mankind in general—not because of their impurity but because of their congenital entanglement in Strife and consequent woe. According to fr. 132. 2, he is δειλός, 'unfortunate', that holds inadequate views about the gods. This fragment is indeed a variant of the traditional benediction of those initiated, with its correlative, the commiseration over those profane; but the adjective here again carries no hint of any notion of 'impurity'. Nor does δειλός in fr. 145. 2, nor τὰ δειλά in 2. 2 and 110. 7 (cf. 15. 3). It should really be sufficient to consult L–S–J, s.v.

relief ⟨unless [or 'until'] ye follow my teaching⟩". It is a form of utterance natural to all prophetic exhortation; as a close parallel we may quote the Platonic variation on the Empedoklean theme, *Tim.* 42 c, according to which he who, μὴ παυόμενος κακίας, has sunk into an animal-body, ἀλλάττων οὐ πρότερον πόνων λήξοι πρὶν . . . εἰς τὸ τῆς . . . ἀρίστης ἀφίκοιτο εἶδος ἕξεως; similarly *Epist.* vii. 326 c 7 κακῶν οὖν οὐ λήξειν τὰ ἀνθρώπινα γένη πρὶν ἄν, κτλ., after *Rep.* v. 473 c 10, cf. *Phaedo* 107 d 1; also e.g. *Il.* 1. 98, 22. 265; Aisch. *Prom.* 165, 175, 755.

Thereafter it will be clear that, likewise, fr. 144 DK νηστεῦσαι κακότητος cannot mean 'to abstain from sin'; there exists no passage—certainly not in pre-Hellenistic Greek—where κακότης conveys this meaning. The 'badness' which it denotes is normally a feature of the situation;[1] in the (rare) instances where it is attributed to a person, it amounts to 'cowardice', and not until late in the fifth century is this notion widened so as to stand for the opposite of 'virtue' (ἀρετή)—but only with a few prose authors[2] (Attic philosophers use κακία instead). It is therefore unthinkable that in fr. 144 κακότης could denote 'sin'; not even Plutarch took it thus. The context of his quotation (*De ira* 464 b) does not fully show how he understood it[3] and we do not know where he found it; it may be that by his time it had become a 'winged word', exposed to all kind of misinterpretation.

To interpret a phrase consisting of a mere two, problematical words from an unknown context is a precarious proposition indeed. Since, however, the concepts involved are important, we may seek help from a consideration of the meaning of νηστεύειν. It does not primarily denote 'fasting', still less a ritual fast (although it was suited early to cover also this specific aspect). He νηστεύει who is taking, or has taken, no food—be it by chance, from poverty, for dietetic or whatever reason; νήστης or νῆστις is a person (or even a fish) with an empty stomach. And it is a feature of Greek speech, so frequent that a metaphor is hardly felt in it, to describe the 'partaking' in anything as 'tasting' of it—as one glance at L–S–J s.v. γεύομαι will show. This verb is connected with e.g. δουρὸς ἀκωκῆς, ὀϊστοῦ, χειρῶν, ἀλλήλων, ὕμνων, στεφάνων, etc., and also with πόνων, μόχθων, πένθους, etc.; that is, it is practically synonymous with 'to experience', or 'to share'. The adjective to denote its negative is ἄγευστος.

[1] e.g. *Il.* 3. 366 Menelaus desires to revenge on Paris the ill which he has caused (κακότητος).

[2] Such as Gorgias and Demokritos; in poetry I find it first in Aratos, v. 121. The juridical term κακότης, 'bad-intent' is again another matter.

[3] Plutarch proceeds to commend a considered abstinence from anger. This he prefaces by the analogy of vows of abstinence from sex, wine, and lying, and the Empedoklean words serve to introduce this set of ideas. Clearly then the operative association, with Plutarch, lay in the word νηστεύειν, with the connotation of 'abstaining', and if he considered the meaning of κακότης at all, he would seem to have taken it to imply 'badness' in all fields of human behaviour.

Here one thinks at once of Soph. *Ant.* 583 εὐδαίμονες οἷσι κακῶν ἄγευστος αἰών—and I submit that this is indeed the vital parallel to the passage under discussion—but there are many other relevant instances; such as, e.g., ἄγευστος τερπνῶν, χαρᾶς, φιλίας, ἐλευθερίας.[1] Ἄγευστος, then, like ἄπειρος, ἀπείρητος, ἀπόκληρος, stands for *expers*—but there is no corresponding verb, derived from any one of these stems. The place of γενέσθαι negatived is filled by νηστεύειν. Νηστεῦσαι κακότητος, then, corresponds with κακῶν ἄγευστος and κακότητος ἄπειροι, and each and all of these phrases mean *malorum expertem esse*.

Where in Empedokles fr. 144 stood nobody can tell for certain. The *Katharmoi*, though, would seem more likely to have afforded a setting for it than the earlier poem; and if so, the two words could have occurred in the description of life in the 'Golden Age', when men ἐνήστευσαν κακότητος—as, according to Hesiod (*Op.* 115), they τέρποντ' ἐν θαλίῃσι κακῶν ἔκτοσθε ἁπάντων; but they could equally well have stood in any other passage referring to the recovery of that state of bliss.

Frs. 146, 147, and 127 DK (476 and 475 R). The first two—both quoted by Clement (in *Strom.* iv and v)—fit together so perfectly that they were justly supposed, by Stein and Wilamowitz, to form one context. The opening words εἰς δὲ τέλος show that earlier, inferior stages were indicated before this verse, and the specification of the highest and last has so close an analogy in Pindar, fr. 133 Sn. (and not only there), that the reproduction of some older doctrine, presumably Pythagorean, has to be acknowledged.[2] Fr. 147 is the noble conclusion of an extensive description of the stages by which the fallen daimon achieves his return to his original abode; the reader or hearer realizes that Empedokles has reached the final stage of this long journey; he is thus given the solution of the riddle entailed in the apparent hybris of Empedokles' claim to divinity combined with his description of himself as an 'errant fugitive' at the beginning of the poem. This solution, though, is not given by Empedokles speaking in his own person, as at the beginning of the poem; fr. 117, then, belongs to another context. But Wilamowitz was right in suggesting that fr. 127 had its place 'not very far before 146'. The proof comes from an out-of-the-way text.

The first among the fragments, preserved by Stobaeus, from the Hermetic writing called *Kore Kosmou* (fr. xxiii Nock–Festugière) contains, within the framework of a muddled apocalypse about the creation of the world and man's lot in it, a section (38–42) about the return of souls to heaven. While the first three chapters of this section describe their rise to higher,

---

[1] See, apart from L–S–J, s.v., Wyttenbach's note on Plut. *De lib. educ.* 13 B, much of which has gone into the *Thes. Ling. Gr.* s.v.

[2] The similarity with *Od.* 17. 384 (cited by Diels) is, I suppose, purely accidental.

or fall to lower forms of existence after their first embodiment in human beings, the last (42)[1] implies their gradual ascent, beginning with plants and animals. 'The most just among you,' so this chapter begins, 'capable of changing into the divine, will be, among men, just kings, genuine philosophers, ⟨good⟩ founders and lawgivers ⟨of cities⟩,[2] truthful seers . . . and expert musicians [this list is swelled by types which bear the stamp of the superstition of the Roman period]; among birds, eagles . . . , among quadrupeds, lions . . . , among reptiles, "dragons" [snakes, that is, of a special, harmless type] . . . , among fishes, dolphins . . . .' In each case, a lengthy description aims to show why the relevant animal is suited to house the just soul: the eagle does not kill its kin; the lion shows a divine quality in that it needs no sleep; the 'dragon' casts off its coil and, moreover, hurts no man; etc. Festugière, whose penetrating analysis[3] we have been following, shows in a very learned and instructive manner the affinity of these odd bits of natural history with popular lore such as survives in Aelian and the *Physiologus*—and thereupon classes the whole section as 'épisode zoologique'.[4]

This is to miss the essential quality and purpose of this curious passage. Undoubtedly it is the tendency of this kind of lore to assimilate the nature of animals to human character-types; but by no means primarily to just and noble ones. The dolphin, indeed, is always described as 'philanthropic'; the snake, not so; nor do the lion and eagle normally exhibit such features as would bring them near to divine righteousness. And why, among so many animals figuring in popular lore, were just these four chosen? It is very obvious that each of them is meant to represent the highest of its class—and Empedokles is found to have chosen the same, at any rate, in the two classes concerning which his teaching survives: namely the lion among mammals (fr. 127) and the dolphin among fishes (fr. 117). He mentioned also birds as hosts of fallen daimons (fr. 117)— though here we have no direct evidence as to which he regarded as the highest—and even plants (frs. 117 and 127), among which the laurel houses the just daimon ready to progress to a higher incarnation (and therefore the laurel must not be harmed: fr. 140).

The *Kore Kosmou* passage, then, exhibits a coherent piece of that

---

[1] Ed. Nock–Festugière, vol. iv, p. 13. 14–p. 14. 12.

[2] Reading ⟨πόλεων⟩ κτίσται καὶ νομοθέται ⟨χρηστοί⟩, after Theiler.

[3] l.c. vol. iii, pp. cc ff.

[4] Ib., pp. cxcviii and ccii.—Festugière would derive the philosophical warp of the folkloristic canvas from the Platonic myths in the *Republic* and *Phaidon*. This is not correct (but for the fact that all later eschatologies are to some extent affected by the Platonic), for in this case the exclusive consideration of 'the most just' representatives of each class of living beings has to be discounted. In the Platonic variety of these doctrines, the incarnation in any animal is a retaliation for human shortcomings, while the system in *Kore Kosmou* 42 implies the attainment of the highest form within each class as the final step on the way to the next higher grade. Festugière himself notes (p. cciv, n. 1) one of the crucial objections to his interpretation.

doctrine (Pythagorean, as we guessed before), the Empedoklean version
of which survives fragmentarily in the texts here discussed. Either can be
supplemented from the other. The Hermetic piece indeed bears the
marks of its late composition in the expansions previously mentioned;
besides, one notices in it the adoption of further details from that perennial fund of popular lore on which some of the early Pythagoreans had
already drawn in elaborating their doctrine of transmigration. These are
excrescences easily removed; the identical common stock remains. We
may note that Oppian (*Hal.* ii. 539–42) likewise presents eagle, lion,
dolphin, and 'dragon' as the acknowledged 'lords' of the four parts of the
animal life; thereafter we can cite the late text in confirmation of the
conclusion that Empedokles' poem contained a systematic description of
the stages of the ascent, from vegetable life through animals and man, of
the fallen daimon, and that he assigned the highest rank among birds to
the eagle, and, most probably, among reptiles to the innocuous snake
called *pareias*.[1] The conclusion is, in its general tendency, confirmed by
Sharastani;[2] the combined evidence can outweigh the opposing testimony
of Aelian,[3] who introduced the notion of the 'lot' determining reincarnation in plants or animals under the influence of the myth in Plato's
Republic. Down to animals, and even fishes, lot or choice could indeed be
imagined to determine the further lowering, in the scale of beings, of souls
which after their fall had been reborn in human bodies; but the inclusion
even of plants[4] is an indication that Empedokles' fallen daimons had to
begin their penance at the lowest rung of the ladder. And it may be noted
that Empedokles presented the same gradation of the natural world in the
Physika (see frs. 20, 21, 23)—setting the stage, so to speak, for the passage
of the daimon. The summit—which Empedokles feels he has attained—is
in the realization of perfected humanity. As he defined and lived it, as
Pindar[5] and even the late Hermetist delineate it, and even in Plato's
ironical perversion,[6] it bears essentially Apollonian features: healers and
seers, leaders of men and founders of cities, poets and musicians—all of
them upholders of purity—the perfection of their striving is embodied in
the Delphic god; add that dolphin and laurel (though not snake and
eagle) are sacred to him. We seem here to obtain a hint to bear out that
particular attachment to Apollo which Ammonios[7] ascribes to Empedokles
and which, in a Pythagorean context, one would expect.

Fr. 148–154 DK. Even though some of these may confidently be traced to
the *Katharmoi*, they teach little. 148 ἀμφιβρότην χθόνα at any rate cor-

---

[1] This must be what, in *K.K.* p. 14. 5, is meant by 'dragons'; cf. Festugière ad loc., p. 39.
[2] Quoted by DK, p. 358, *ad* fr. 117.   [3] Quoted by DK, p. 362. 10 (fr. 127).
[4] Proclus (*In Remp.* ii. 333. 8 Kr.) rightly stresses this difference between Plato and
Empedokles.   [5] Fr. 133.   [6] *Phaedr.* 248 d ff.
[7] Quoted in DK, p. 365. 15 *ad* fr. 134.

responds with fr. 126, and 151 ζείδωρος Ἀφροδίτη covers the central concept of the reign of Kypris (fr. 128. 3), when men were not tempted to kill animals since all their needs were satisfied (cf. frs. 130 and 78).[1] Fr. 154a, in Wilamowitz's bold reconstruction[2] from the corrupt text of a Plutarchean draft, results in a verse of Empedoklean ring. It conveys, like fr. 125, the notion of some male daimon determining the constituents of human existence.

Fr. 158 DK. I believe that Stein was right in extracting this fragment from Hierokles. The commentary on the *Carmen Aureum*, vv. 54–60 continues, after the passage set out above (p. 199) for frs. 118 and 121, with the words quoted by DK before fr. 158. Hierokles illustrates man's situation between the higher and the lower world from Herakleitos, Empedokles and finally, Plato's *Phaidros*. The recollection of the chariot-myth, dear to the Neoplatonist, has coloured also his second section (πτεροῤῥυήςεως), which otherwise is couched in his own prose interspersed with Empedoklean fragments from the beginning of the *Katharmoi*. The words concluding it, ὀλβίου αἰῶνος ἀμερθείς, are poetical. They are not, as Diels alleged, a citation from Homer; but they are modelled on *Il.* 22. 58 μὴ ... φίλης αἰῶνος ἀμερθῆις. There was no reason for Hierokles to effect, on his own, this variation on the Homeric theme; these words are as naturally identified as Empedoklean as are the other three quotations with which he studded this passage. For his didactic prose, Hierokles adapted the poetical word-order. Originally, αἰῶνος ἀμερθείς must have formed, as in Homer, the end of a hexameter; the adjective probably followed at the beginning of the next verse, its long termination shortened by a following vowel, as e.g. in fr. 114. 2.

The substance of this fragment, the analogy, in phrasing and sentiment, with fr. 119, and the Hieroklean context show that it refers to the loss of the daimon's true home. It could have stood in the transition from the proemium, frs. 112 and 113, to the narrative beginning with fr. 115, or soon after the latter; Empedokles relating how, 'bereft of blissful existence', he was led down to the 'Field of Ate'. The words of Hierokles make the latter alternative more probable.

---

[1] Frs. 149, 150, 153 fit the *Physika*, and so does 153a, notwithstanding Theon's different assertion; 152 is uncertain. Fr. 154, as Kranz rightly observed (DK, i. 501; cf. his *Empedokles* (1949), p. 145), is proved to be Empedoklean by A 70 but belongs probably to *Phys.*; for the combination of a primeval state of the earth and of mankind (which would fit even Democritean and Platonic speculations) could hardly have had a place within the mythology of the *Katharmoi*. Fr. 154c could come from the description of the age of Kypris; the ascription to Empedokles, though, is uncertain and the present tense would, if anything, rather suggest the *Physika*; 154d (read '154e') = *Orph. Fragm.* 354 Kern cannot be reconciled with the Empedoklean mythology.

[2] *Hermes*, xl (1905), 165 = *Kleine Schriften*, iv (1962), p. 212; cf. above, p. 226, n. 2.

III. RECONSTRUCTION

(a) THE ORIGINAL

THE attempt at recovering the outline of the *Katharmoi* reasonably begins by visualizing the edition of Empedokles' works from which the extant fragments ultimately derive. Apart from general ascriptions to the *Physika* (fr. 1. 85. 103 f.) and the beginning of the *Katharmoi* (fr. 112) there are precise references to the *Physika* Book i (pseudo-Plutarch, fr. 8; Simplicius, frs. 17 and 96; Tzetzes, fr. 6), Book ii (Simplicius, fr. 62), and Book iii (Tzetzes, fr. 134). These data may be combined with the indications contained in the list of Empedokles' works which survives, though in a reduced form, in Diog. Laert. viii. 77 and in the *Suda* (Suidas), s.v. Ἐμπεδοκλῆς:

> D.L.: τὰ μὲν οὖν Περὶ φύcεωc αὐτῶι καὶ οἱ Καθαρμοὶ εἰc ἔπη τείνουcι πεντακιcχίλια, ὁ δὲ Ἰατρικὸc λόγοc εἰc ἔπη ἑξακόcια.

> Suda: ἔγραψε δι' ἐπῶν Περὶ φύcεωc τῶν ὄντων βιβλία β'· καὶ ἔcτιν ἔπη ὡc διcχίλια· Ἰατρικὰ καταλογάδην· καὶ ἄλλα πολλά.

These two versions supplement each other, and the hitch which emerges in their combination is easily removed. The two main works together are stated to have comprised 5,000 verses, and the 'two books of *Physika*' 2,000; the *Katharmoi* (one book?) must then have comprised 3,000 verses. This implication is evidently absurd, and Diels's attempt at eliminating it[1]—he would reduce the sum total to 3,000 verses by changing πεντακιcχίλια to πάντα τριcχίλια—misses the mark stylistically, palaeographically, and materially. The known data have only to be put together to yield the true solution. The evidence is that (a) two Empedoklean books comprised two thousand verses; that is, one thousand verses each, and (b) The *Physika* and *Katharmoi* together comprised five thousand verses; in, so one will conclude, five books. These indications have to be combined with the fact that (c) three books of *Physika* are independently attested. This would leave two for the *Katharmoi*, and this conclusion tallies with fr. 131—which must come from the *Katharmoi*—exhibiting the characteristics of a proemium. Where there is a proemium, there a book is more than likely to have followed. Fr. 131 did not stand at the beginning of the *Katharmoi*; hence it intimates, by its very existence, the existence of a second book of the same.

[1] *Sitz. Ber. d. Berlin. Akad.* (1898), 398.

These considerations lead one to conclude that the passage in the *Suda* has lost one line through homoioteleuton. It should read:

ἔγραψε . . . Περὶ φύσεως τῶν ὄντων, βιβλία ⟨γ΄· καὶ ἔστιν ἔπη
ὡς τρισχίλια· καὶ τοὺς Καθαρμούς, βιβλία⟩ β΄· καὶ ἔστιν ἔπη
ὡς δισχίλια, κτλ.[1]

Simplicity and material suitability combine to bear out this restoration. Three books of the *Physika* and two of the *Katharmoi*, each of them comprising one thousand verses, that is, 5,000 in all: thus the evidence is consistent. All too consistent, indeed; for who would easily believe the works of Empedokles to have been so evenly proportioned? In fact, these uniform figures are one of the convergent indications which prove these statements to come from the Περὶ ποιητῶν by Lobon of Argos[2]—who, according to Crönert, 'ludum non genuinam de poetis commentationem proposuit'; a παίγνιον, according to O. Crusius;[3] a *Schwindelbuch*, parodying the scholarly labours of Kallimachos. It would appear to afford a highly dubious basis for the textual history of Empedokles.

But its statements are in agreement with the independent evidence about the three books of *Physika* and the two of *Katharmoi*.[4] Lobon's figures can, and have to, be regarded as approximate (and, indeed, he appears to have presented them as such; note the wording ἔπη ὡς δισχίλια in the *Suda*, and its parallels). For the rest, some confidence in Lobon's statements concerning Empedokles can be vindicated by a rapid survey of the other remnants of his book. It is perfectly true that they contain much that is fanciful, but the notion of his German critics that this—apparently laborious and quite extensive—work was written 'convivalium in usum' or as a parody seems unrealistic. Perhaps Lobon aimed to supplement rather than to parody the *Pinakes* of Kallimachos by providing information about literary creations which were not mentioned in that standard work for the excellent reason that they did not survive. Consequently, what Lobon disclosed concerning mythical and half-mythical poets and writers like Thamyris and the Seven Sages was bound to be *Scheingelehrsamkeit*. He endeavoured to win credit for his fancies by bringing the account down to extant authors and combining genuine information about them with inventions of the kind which he had perforce to present for their ghostly predecessors. Consequently he

---

[1] This conjecture was published in *Mnemos.* xviii (1965), 365.

[2] Cf. esp. the entries Thales, Parmenides, and Panyassis in Crönert's collection of Lobon's fragments (see next note). The early origin of this information is, at any rate, confirmed by the fact that the length also of the alleged prose-work is given in ἔπη and not in στίχοι.

[3] W. Crönert in *Χάριτες für Leo* (1911), 123 ff. (basic); preceded by E. Hiller, *Rhein. Mus.* xxxiii (1878), 518 ff. and followed by O. Crusius, *Philologus*, lxxx (1925), 176 ff.

[4] This assertion does not rest on a vicious circle; the reconstruction of the *Suda*-article is, I trust, valid even in reference to the parallel passage in Diog. Laert. only; just as the ascertainment of three plus two books is independent of Lobon.

credited many also of the historical poets, such as Xenophanes and Parmenides, with writings in prose, Sophokles with a book on the chorus, Pindar with tragedies, and most of them, sweepingly and vaguely, with 'many other works'. These are fancies indeed; but they are presented together with statements which are supported by independent evidence and hence, e.g. in the case of Epimenides (Diog. Laert. i. 111), Solon (ib. 61), and Panyassis (*Suda*), widely accepted, notwithstanding the conclusiveness of Crönert's basic criticism. Lobon's statements about the works of Empedokles may be accepted with similar, qualified confidence; though much scepticism would be justified with regard to his alleged book about medicine, for this detail is suspiciously reminiscent of similar ones regarding Pittakos, Solon, and Epimenides.

However, even if Lobon is distrusted, there is sufficient evidence for an edition in five rolls—three for the *Physika* and two for the *Katharmoi*—which remained in use throughout Antiquity.[1] Of an authoritative Alexandrian edition there is no trace, and an argument against positing it is in the fact that Lobon's rough estimate of ἔπη was cited in the handbook on which Diogenes Laertius and the source of the *Suda*-article ('Hesychius') drew; otherwise its place would probably have been taken by a precise indication of ϲτίχοι. This is not to say that the text handed down was fluctuating and basically uncertain like that of e.g. Theognis, or of *Volksbücher* like the stories of the Seven Sages or the Alexander Romance. Wilamowitz[2] indeed stressed the 'baffling amount of variant readings' and the recurrence of misplaced verses which, according to him, showed 'that the text never had the benefit of a scholarly recension and edition'. He may have overstressed the bearing of his observations. The one instance of a 'fluctuating verse' adduced by him from the *Katharmoi* is illusory,[3] and if those from the *Physika* are accepted, it may be remembered that the same phenomenon occurs also in texts which descend from Alexandrian scholarly editions—not only in medieval manuscripts but also in papyri of e.g. Homer and Euripides.[4] Neither this fact nor the occurrence of verbal corruptions could justify any fundamental distrust in the text of Empedokles circulating in Antiquity. The works of Empedokles were propagated and read from the fifth century onward[5] and

---

[1] The transmission by separate rolls made it possible for Plutarch (*De exil.* 607 c) to quote verses from the beginning of the *Katharmoi* (fr. 115) as standing ἐν ἀρχῆι τῆϲ φιλοϲοφίαϲ. He apparently regarded Empedokles' 'theology' as basic to his 'physics' and kept the scrolls arranged accordingly.

[2] l.c. 514 and *Hermes*, lxv (1930), 245 = *Kleine Schr.* iv (1962), p. 513.

[3] See above, p. 187.

[4] One instance of many is the wrong order, in the papyrus of Euripides' *Hypsipyle*, of vv. 5–10 in fr. 20/21 (noted by Wecklein, *Sitz. Ber. Bayr. Akad., Phil.-hist. Kl.* (1909), 26 and again, independently, by the present writer; see D. L. Page, *Greek Liter. Papyri* (1941), p. 76).

[5] See D. Tarrant, *Class. Rev.* xxxvii (1923), on an Empedoklean echo in Aristophanes' *Aves* 700.

there is no reason why the texts on which Plato and Aristotle, Theophrastos and Aratos,[1] Hermarchos, Lucretius and Vergil relied should have been of imperfect authenticity. They were not, of course, copied as frequently as Homer or Hesiod; this very fact could help to preserve them intact. We today have to grapple with the vast amount of corruption which affected the transmission of those later writers from whom we cull the debris of his works, and these writers may themselves occasionally have drawn upon imperfect copies or selections; but beyond all this, if only we can reach it, there lies firm ground.

The division in particular of the two main works into three and two books is 'pre-Alexandrian'. It is attested by Lobon and hence may be traced, at any rate, to the fourth century. It is unlikely to have been devised by some scholarly editor of that period—seeing that the very existence of 'editors' of the Alexandrian type in pre-Alexandrian times is not recorded; it could conceivably have been generally adopted because it was used in copies propagated from an early centre of book-production, that is, from Athens. But I do not see why, even so, this division should not go back to Empedokles' autographs. The *Physika* as well as the *Katharmoi* were too long for single rolls. If, then, they had to be divided, the author is likely to have divided them in the manner which corresponded best with their size and structure, and the persistence of this division is most readily understood if it was authentic.[2]

(b) IDENTIFICATION OF FRAGMENTS

Only one of the Empedoklean fragments is explicitly ascribed to the *Katharmoi*. It may therefore appear vain to base an interpretation upon Diels's ascriptions—as we have done. We found reason to exclude two only of the fragments included by him, and added one or two others. On this point, the current German standard work on Greek literature proclaims an extreme scepticism; its author would allow only eleven out of Diels's *c*. forty ascriptions.[3] A more recent American student goes even farther:[4] 'Very few of the fragments', he says, 'can be assigned with any certainty to the work from which they came. . . . Since an editor must arrange them in some order, the most logical procedure is to gather the fragments concerned with the physical universe in one group and those

---

[1] Wilamowitz, *Hellenistische Dichtung*, ii (1924), p. 265.

[2] The standard division of the Homeric epics was no doubt fixed by the Alexandrian editors, but many of their divisions result in artistic units too organic to be attributed to editorial cutting. 'Rhapsodies' like the first and fifth books of both *Iliad* and *Odyssey*—to mention only these—are likely to have been transmitted in separate rolls for many centuries prior to the Alexandrian editions. And Empedokles could have followed this usage.

[3] Schmid–Stählin, *Geschichte der Griechischen Literatur*, i (1929), 318 would allow only frs. 112–14, 136–41, and 144 f. to come from the *Katharmoi*.

[4] H. S. Long, *Amer. Journ. of Philol.* lxx (1949), 144.

concerned with religious matters in another group', but this 'admirable method of arrangement' is, according to this writer, far from likely to coincide with Empedokles' own. The sceptical argument thus presented has a persuasiveness which obliges us to review the reasons for accepting, by and large, Diels's ascriptions.

The indubitable and invaluable fr. 112, preserving the very first eleven verses of the *Katharmoi*, yields a string of further safe identifications. It shows, first, that the poem was addressed to Empedokles' Akragantine friends; fr. 114 beginning, like 112, ὦ φίλοι, must therefore come from the same.[1] More pregnant hints are given with the subject-matter of these verses. In them, Empedokles proclaims himself a god and describes, in evidence, the impact of his person; fr. 113, quoted by Sextus immediately after 112, clearly belongs to the same context. That startling and provocative claim could not remain without a sequel. It had to be substantiated: how could the man Empedokles be a god? And how became the god a man? Fr. 115 preserves the beginning of the required elucidation,[2] which is seen to have been the mythical story of the fall of a divine being and his return (warranted by 112) to his pristine state. Two sets of fragments are therewith drawn into the frame of the *Katharmoi*: namely, those continuing the mythological opening of 115 by a description of the scenery and act of incarnation (119–26; also, less certain, 116), and, secondly, those concerning the passage of the incarnated daimon through various phases of existence (117, 127, 146 f., and, in a wider sense, 145).

A separate and different theme is indicated by the very title the *Katharmoi*; whether it be original or not, it shows, first, that the rules of taboo, frs. 140 f. and 143, had their place in this poem. The concern with defilement and purification stands out likewise in the emphatic passages about sacrifice (135–9), whose provenance from the *Katharmoi* anyhow has never been doubted.

Finally we learn from Theophrastos[3] that Empedokles enlarged upon 'the theogony and the sacrifices'.[4] The latter topic covers the points just instanced, and the long fr. 128 by which, happily, Theophrastos illustrated his statement, shows how the 'theogony' was bound up with the

---

[1] The 2nd person plural in frs. 124, 136, and 145 is irrelevant in the present context, for the persons addressed in them are not the addressees of the poem. On the other hand, the use of the 2nd person singular marks nine fragments as coming from the *Physika*.

[2] Its place early in the poem is, moreover, attested by Plutarch (above, p. 238, n. 1).

[3] *Apud* Porphyry, *De abstin.* ii. 21.

[4] I am quoting these words in the order advocated by Bernays and adopted by Nauck and DK (p. 362. 22). It commends itself as implicitly reasonable, but the MSS. (followed by Diels in *Poet. Philos.*, p. 158) put the 'sacrifices' before the 'theogony', and Theophrastos, or Porphyry, may well have thus written, because sacrifices were their subject in this passage. Whatever order of the words they may have preferred, Empedokles could not have spoken about sacrifices first and subsequently about the origin of the gods to whom the sacrifices were offered.

subject of 'sacrifices'. At least frs. 128, 130, and 78, describing the situation and the sacrifices under the rule of Kypris, are therewith secured for
the *Katharmoi*, and fr. 129 appeared on consideration likewise to fit the
theme of successive ages of gods and men. Here, however, we have
reached the problematical ground of 'theology'.

In discussing[1] fr. 134, the older view, according to which
this fragment—and with it, at least, 133—belongs to the *Physika*, was
upheld against Diels, who traced the whole set of 'theological' fragments,
131–4, to the *Katharmoi*. In fact, though, the strongest argument which
could be quoted in support of Diels's view has not previously been mentioned; and, on the other hand, those who, following Tzetzes' citation,
placed fr. 134 in the *Physika*, joined to it the whole 'theological' set. These
two points call for examination.

Regarding the first, the relevance of fr. 114 is decisive. This fragment is
unlikely to belong to the context in which DK present it. The statement
of personal certainty of a truth which could not be expected to meet with
ready assent is unlikely to have prefaced the recital of the crucial but
personal experiences of Empedokles' daimon. It appears, rather, to
introduce the exposition of some disconcerting general theme.

Fr. 133 is as certain to belong together with 134 as anything in this
hypothetical context could be. Bentley observed that fr. 133 is strikingly
paralleled by Lucret. v. 101–3. If the reader will look up this passage,
he will at once see that the preceding verses 97–100 easily match fr. 114.
One is thus tempted to assume that Lucretius' model consisted of frs. 114
and 133 combined, and that, therefore, 114, 133, and 134 formed one
context; and since 114 is sure to come from the *Katharmoi* (ὦ φίλοι), this
would appear to hold good for the whole composite passage.

Pondering the arguments previously marshalled,[1] one will, I expect,
feel that, none the less, fr. 134, with 133, could only come from the
Physika. One would then account for the Lucretian parallel by the
assumption that, in the *Physika*, fr. 133 was preceded by verses very similar
to fr. 114—but not by fr. 114 itself. This is not after all unbelievable.
Empedokles could very well have prefaced his revolutionary teaching
about deity with similar words when presenting its—*sit venia verbo*—
metaphysical aspect (in the *Physika*) and again before the new 'Theogony'
in the *Katharmoi*.

The question whether frs. 131 and 132 ought to be re-transferred,
together with 133 f., to the *Physika* is decided in the negative, if the view
previously argued (above, p. 212) is accepted that fr. 131 could not
appear in the *Physika* because in the work addressed to him Pausanias
could not be referred to as ἐφημερίων τις. This view is confirmed by
a further observation. Fr. 134 delineates the one, all-comprehensive

[1] Above, pp. 218 f.

world-god. Empedokles may have styled him 'Apollo' or θεός or even τὸ θεῖον; at any rate, here is only one deity. Equally, the subject of fr. 133 is in the singular—τὸ θεῖον, according to Clement. Frs. 131 and 132, by contrast, announce the true account of 'the gods': ἀμφὶ θεῶν and θεῶν πέρι; and these gods could not have been the personalized forces of nature of the *Physika*. The plural outstandingly fits the successive 'births of gods' narrated in the *Katharmoi*. Hence frs. 131 and 132 should be left where Diels put them. A few minor fragments remain, the uncertain relevance of which has been discussed previously;[1] in the main, the adopted selection of fragments from the *Katharmoi* appears to be vindicated.

(c) THE ARRANGEMENT OF THE FRAGMENTS

The fragments identified as coming from the *Katharmoi* will naturally be arranged, by and large, according to the topics which emerged in the preceding examination. It is evident that the mythical narrative of the incarnation of fallen daimons followed immediately upon the account of their fall in fr. 115. On the other hand, the pathetic description and denunciation of bloody sacrifices, and following from it, the series of ritual injunctions, are so different in their setting and ethos that they must have stood widely separated from that first main topic. They indicate, for contemporaries, the way of redemption; being the upshot of the teaching presented in the epic, they must have formed its conclusion. The 'Theogony' showed the gradual decline from pure worship to the bloody sacrifices of Empedokles' own day; that is, it preceded the denunciation of these sacrifices. Fr. 131 comes from the proemium of a section in which the 'true'—that is, a new—view of the gods was set forth; it can only have preceded the 'Theogony'. And since we have convinced ourselves that the *Katharmoi* consisted of two books, that proemium must have stood at the beginning of Book ii, the outline of which thus becomes discernible: it comprised teaching, censure, admonition, and legislation given by Empedokles speaking in his own person but not, as before, narrating the experience of his daimon.

The first book comprised the mythical account of the fall and incarnation of Empedokles' daimon; Empedokles related what he had seen and heard and was enabled, differently from ordinary men, to remember. Accordingly he reported, in this book, words and actions of other mythical beings. This is attested at least in one instance (fr. 120); it must be true of others. In particular, only a divinity could reveal (as in Plato's *Republic*) the details about the long way to final restoration lying before the lapsed. The often cited words (fr. 117) in which Empedokles himself recalls previous stages of his migration are out of place in this mythical

---

[1] Above, p. 234 f.

context; he must have referred to his experience, as a warning example, in the latter part of Book ii.

Within this wider frame, the finer details of the arrangement will settle themselves as the details of narrative and argument emerge into clarity. The place of some fragments (112 f.; 122 f.; 158) is fixed by the manner and context in which they are cited. Occasionally the choice between alternative possibilities may depend upon considerations of style. For example, the 'universal law' (fr. 135) could conceivably have been proclaimed early in the course of the revelation, in Book i, of the stages of transmigration. We know, however, from Aristotle, that these verses were embedded in a longer passage of a rather argumentative character. This hardly agrees with the style of a revelation uttered by a divinity; hence these verses are far more likely to have served as the foundation, in Book ii, of the Empedoklean *regula vitae*.

In the following I offer a text of the *Katharmoi* based upon the preceding discussion, with a twofold apparatus indicating (*a*) the sources for each fragment and (*b*) variant readings and conjectures (omitting, for the sake of clarity, what seemed irrelevant). The reader is invited to consider whether, with the adopted arrangement, the outlines of an organic structure appear to emerge. The proper place of a few fragments remaining doubtful, these are marked by an asterisk added to their current number.

VI. CONCORDANCE OF FRAGMENTS

KATH. A′

G.Z.	DK	Page
1	112	(186 ff.)[1]
2	113	(192)
3	115	(193 ff.)
4	158	(235)
5	118+121	(199 ff.)
6	124	(205)
7	119	(203 f.)
8	120	(204)
9	122+123	(204)
10	116	(256)
11	126	(205)
12	148	(234)
13	125	(205)
14	154a	(235)
15	145	(229 ff.)
16	127	(232 ff.)
17	146+147	(232 ff.)

KATH. B′

G.Z.	DK	Page
18	131	(211 ff.)
19	112 v. 3	(187 ff.)
20	114	(193)
21	132	(241)
22	135	(218)
23	128	(206 ff.)
24	144	(231)
25	151	(235)
26	130	(241)
27	78	(209 ff.)
28	129	(208)
29	136	(219)
30	138	(226)
31	137	(220 ff.)
32	142	(228)
33	139	(227)
34	117	(199)
35	143	(226)
36	140	(228)
37	141	(228)

DK	G.Z.
78	27
112	1 & 19
113	2
114	20
115	3
116	10
117	34
118	5
119	7
120	8
121	5
122	9
123	9
124	6
125	13
126	11
127	16
128	23
129	28
130	26
131	18

DK	G.Z.
132	21
133	*Phys.* iii. 213 f.
134	*Phys.* iii. 214 ff.
135	22
136	29
137	31
138	30
139	33
140	36
141	37
142	32
143	35
144	24
145	15
146	17
147	17
148	12
151	25
154a	14
158	4

[1] The page numbers in brackets refer to the discussion of each fragment in this book

ΕΜΠΕΔΟΚΛΕΟΥΣ ΚΑΘΑΡΜΟΙ

⟨ΚΑΘΑΡΜΩΝ Α´⟩

1 (112 DK)   Ὦ φίλοι οἳ μέγα ἄστυ κάτα ξανθοῦ Ἀκράγαντος
        ναίετ᾽ ἀν᾽ ἄκρα πόλεος ἀγαθῶν μελεδήμονες ἔργων,
[3] 4 χαίρετ᾽· ἐγὼ δ᾽ ὑμῖν θεὸς ἄμβροτος οὐκέτι θνητός
        πωλεῦμαι μετὰ πᾶσι τετιμένος ὥσπερ ἔοικα
        ταινίαις τε περίστεπτος στέφεσίν τε θαλείοις·
        ⟨πᾶσι δὲ⟩ τοῖς ἂν ἵκωμαι ἐς ἄστεα τηλεθάοντα
    8 ἀνδράσιν ἠδὲ γυναιξὶ σεβίζομαι· οἱ δ᾽ ἅμ᾽ ἕπονται
        μυρίοι ἐξερέοντες ὅπηι πρὸς κέρδος ἀταρπός·
        οἱ μὲν μαντοσυνέων κεχρημένοι, οἱ δ᾽ ἐπὶ νούσων
        παντοίων ἐπύθοντο κλυεῖν εὐηκέα βάξιν,
  12 δηρὸν δὴ χαλεπῆισι πεπαρμένοι ⟨ἀμφ᾽ ὀδύνηισιν⟩.

2 (113 DK)   ἀλλὰ τί τοῖσδ᾽ ἐπίκειμ᾽ ὡσεὶ μέγα χρῆμά τι πράσσων
        εἰ θνητῶν περίειμι πολυφθερέων ἀνθρώπων;

3 (115 DK)   Ἔστιν Ἀνάγκης χρῆμα, θεῶν ψήφισμα παλαιόν,
        ἀίδιον, πλατέεσσι κατεσφρηγισμένον ὅρκοις·
  3 [4] εὖτέ τις ἀμπλακίηισι φόναι φίλα γυῖα μιήνηι
    5 δαίμων οἵτε μακραίωνος λελάχασι βίοιο,
        τρίς μιν μυρίας ὥρας ἀπὸ μακάρων ἀλάλησθαι
        φυόμενον παντοῖα διὰ χρόνου εἴδεα θνητῶν
    8 ἀργαλέας βιότοιο μεταλλάσσοντα κελεύθους.
        αἰθέριον μὲν γάρ σφε μένος πόντονδε διώκει,
        πόντος δ᾽ ἐς χθονὸς οὖδας ἀπέπτυσε, γαῖα δ᾽ ἐς αὐγάς
        Ἠελίου ἀκάμαντος, ὁ δ᾽ αἰθέρος ἔμβαλε δίναις·
  12 ἄλλος δ᾽ ἐξ ἄλλου δέχεται, στυγέουσι δὲ πάντες.
        Τὴν καὶ ἐγὼ νῦν εἶμι, φυγὰς θεόθεν καὶ ἀλήτης,
        Νείκεϊ μαινομένωι πίσυνος . . . . .

1 1–11 Diog. Laert. viii. 62   1–6 Anthol. Pal. ix. 569   1–2 Diog. Laert. viii. 54 (. . . ἐναρχό-
μενος τῶν Καθαρμῶν φησιν)   4 (et part. 5) Diog. Laert. viii. 66, Sext. Empir. Adv. math. i. 302,
et Lucian., Philostr., Plotin., Tzetzes   10 et 12 (om. 11) Clem. Al. Strom. vi. 30   **2** Sext.
Empir. (post fr. 1. v. 5 τετιμένος) : καὶ πάλιν· ἀλλὰ κτλ.   **3** 1–2, [4]–14 (ordine tur-
bato) Hippol. Refut. vii. 29   1. 3. 5–6. 13 Plut. De exil. 17   1–2 Simplic. Phys. 1184 d)
9–12 Plut. De Is. 26; singulos vel binos vv. cit. multi (vid. Poetae Philos. ad loc., Wilamowitz
l.c. 481 sq.)

1 [3] ex Diod. xiii. 83 falso inser. Sturz (vid. fr. 19)   5 ἔοικα Diog. Laert. : ἔοικεν Anth.
Pal.   7 ⟨πᾶσι δὲ⟩ τοῖς Wil. : τοῖσιν ἅμ᾽ Diog. Laert. (+εὖτ᾽ recc.)   11 κλύειν mss. : κλυεῖν
Wil. χαλεπῆισι et ⟨ ⟩ Bergk (Opusc. ii. 14, Kl. Schr. ii. 7, coll. Archil. 104 (84), Apoll. Rh. iv.
1067, Orph. Lith. 490) : χαλεποῖσι πεπ. Clem.   **3** 1 ἔστιν Simplic. : ἔστι τι Plut. Hippol.
5 praef. ὃς καὶ ἐπίορκον ἁμαρτήσας ἐπομώσει (‘v. 4’) Hippol. ‖ δαίμων οἵτε Heeren : δαίμονες οἵ
τε Plut., δαιμόνιοί τε Hipp.   7 φυόμενον Stein : φυομένους Hippol., γινομένην (paraphras.)
Celsus   11 ἀκάμαντος Plut. : φαέθοντος Hipp.   13 τὴν . . . εἶμι Plut. : τῶν καὶ ἐγώ εἰμι
Hipp., ὥς κ. ε. δεῦρ᾽ εἶμι Philoponus

4　(158 DK)　．．．．．．．．　αἰῶνος ἀμερθείς
　　　　　ὀλβίου　．．．．．．．．．．

5　(118 et　Κλαῦcά τε καὶ κώκυσα ἰδὼν ἀcυνήθεα χῶρον.
　121 DK)　ἔνθα Φόνος τε Κότος τε καὶ ἄλλων ἔθνεα Κηρῶν·
　　　　　⟨ἔνθα δ' ἄρ' αἰνὰ πεcόντες ἀπ' αὐγῆς δαίμονες οἰκτροί⟩
　4　Ἄτης ἂν λειμῶνα κατὰ cκότος ἠλάcκουcιν.

6　(124 DK)　῍Ω πόποι, ὦ δειλὸν θνητῶν γένος, ὦ δυcάνολβον·
　　　　　τοίων ἔκ τ' 'Ερίδων ἔκ τε Cτοναχῶν ἐγένεcθε.

7　(119 DK)　ἐξ οἵης τιμῆς τε καὶ ὅccου μήκεος ὄλβου

8　(120 DK)　'Ηλύθομεν τόδ' ὑπ' ἄντρον ὑπόcτεγον　．．．

9　(122 et　῍Ενθ' ἧcαν Χθονίη τε καὶ 'Ηλιόπη ταναῶπις
　123 DK)　Δῆρίς θ' αἱματόεccα καὶ 'Αρμονίη θεμερῶπις
　　　　　Καλλιcτώ τ' Αἰcχρή τε Θόωcά τε Δηναίη τε
　4　Νημερτής τ' ἐρόεccα μελάγκουρός τ' 'Αcάφεια
　　　　　Φυcώ τε Φθιμένη τε καὶ Εὐναίη καὶ ῍Εγερcις
　　　　　Κινώ τ' 'Αcτεμφής τε πολυcτέφανός τε Μεγιcτώ
　　　　　καὶ Φορύη Cωπή τε καὶ 'Ομφαίη　．．．．

10*　(116 DK)　⟨καὶ⟩ Χάρις ⟨ἢ ∪∪–⟩ cτυγέει δύcτλητον 'Ανάγκην

11　(126 DK)　(δαίμων . . .)
　　　　　cαρκῶν ἀλλογνῶτι περιcτέλλουcα χιτῶνι

---

4 Hierocles *In Carm. Aur.* 24 (ὀλβίου αἰ. ἀμ.)　　5 1 Clem. Al. *Strom.* iii. 14; cf. Epicur. ap.
Sext. Emp. xi. 96　　2 et 4 Hierocles *In Carm. Aur.* vv. 54 sqq. (praef. ἀτερπέα χῶρον), Synes.
De provid. i. 1, Proclus *In Remp.* ii. 157 Kr.　　2 Philo *De provid.* (ap. Eus. *Pr. Ev.* viii. 14. 19:
libere), Theo Smyrn. p. 149. 4 H., Procl. *In Crat.* p. 97 Pasq. (add. αὐχμηραί τε νόcοι καὶ cήψιες
ἔργα τε ῥευcτά ['v. 3'] versum ab Emped. alienum)　　4 Julian. *Orat.* vii 226 b, Themist.
Orat. xiii. 178, Synes. *Epist.* 147, p. 283 c　　6 1–2 Clem. Al. *Strom.* iii. 14 (post fr. 118 et
125)　　2 Timon fr. 10 Diels et Porph. *De abst.* iii. 27　　7 Plut. *De exil.* 17, Clem.
Al. *Strom.* iv. 12, Hippol. *Refut.* v. 7 (brevians)　　8 Porph. *De antro nymph.* 8 (praef. αἱ
ψυχοπομποὶ δυνάμεις λέγουcιν)　　9 1–4 Plut. *De tranq. an.* 15, 474 B　　2 Plut. *De Is.* 48,
370 D　　4 respic. Tzetzes *Chil.* xii. 574 et *Proleg. Aristoph.* p. 56. 83 Cantar.　　5–7 Cornutus
17　1–4 ('fr. 122') et 5–7 ('fr. 123') coniunx. Bergk　　10 Plut. *Quaest. conv.* ix. 5, 745 C
11 Plut. *De esu carn.* ii. 3, 998 C; Porph. ap. Stob. *Ecl.* i. 49. 60

---

5 2 φόνος τε κότος τε Hier. Synes. (φθόνος Synes.): κότος τε φόνος τε Theo, Procl. (bis)
3 exempli gratia suppl. Zuntz　　4 ἂν λειμ. Bentley: ἀνὰ λειμ. Hier., ἐν λειμῶνι cett.
6 1 ὦ (post γένος) Scaliger: ἢ Clem.　　2 ἔκ τ' Timon, Porph.: ἐξ Clem. ‖ ἐγένεcθε Clem.:
γενόμεcθα Porph., πέπλαcθε Timon　　7 ὅcου Plut.: οἴου Clem.; om. Hipp.　　9 4 μελάγκ-
κο(υ)ρος Tzetzes: μελάγκαρπος Plut.　　7 Φορύη Karsten: Φορίη Corn. ‖ Cωπή Bergk:
cόφ(ι)ή (accent. var.) Corn. mss.; Cόμφη Th. Gale　　10 supplem. tent. Zuntz coll.
Hes. *Theog.* 361

12* (148 DK) . . . . . . ἀμφιβρότην χθόνα . . .

13 (125 DK) Ἐκ μὲν γὰρ ζωῶν ἐτίθει νεκρὰ εἴδε' ἀμείβων
⟨ἐκ δὲ νεκρῶν ζώοντα ∪ – ‿‿ – ∪ φύεϲθαι⟩.

14 (154a DK) ὠδῖνάϲ ⟨τ'⟩ ὀδύναϲ ⟨τε⟩ κυκέων ἀπάταϲ τε γόουϲ τε

15* (145 DK) Τοιγάρτοι χαλεπῆιϲιν ἀλύοντεϲ κακότηϲιν
οὔποτε δειλαίων ἀχέων λωφήϲετε θυμόν
⟨πρὶν κὲν . . .⟩

16 (127 DK) Ἐν θήρεϲϲι λέοντεϲ ὀρειλεχέεϲ χαμαιεῦναι
γίγνονται, δάφναι δ' ἐνὶ δένδρεϲιν ἠϋκόμοιϲιν

17 (146 et 147 DK) εἰϲ δὲ τέλοϲ μάντειϲ τε καὶ ὑμνοπόλοι καὶ ἰητροί
καὶ πρόμοι ἀνθρώποιϲιν ἐπιχθονίοιϲι πέλονται.
Ἔνθεν ἀναβλαϲτοῦϲι θεοὶ τιμῆιϲι φέριϲτοι
4 ἀθανάτοιϲ ἄλλοιϲιν ὁμέϲτιοι αὐτοτράπεζοι
†ἐόντεϲ†, ἀνδρείων ἀχέων ἀπόκληροι, ἀτειρεῖϲ.

⟨ΚΑΘΑΡΜѠΝ Β'⟩

18 (131 DK) . . . .
εἰ γὰρ ἐφημερίων ἕνεκέν τινοϲ, ἄμβροτε Μοῦϲα,
ἡμετέραϲ μελέταϲ ⟨καθαρῆϲ⟩ διὰ φροντίδοϲ ἐλθεῖν
⟨οἶμον ἄν' εὐϲεβίηϲ πάροϲ εὐμενέωϲ μοι ἔδωκαϲ⟩
4 εὐχομένωι, νῦν αὖτε παρίϲταϲο, Καλλιόπεια,
ἀμφὶ θεῶν μακάρων ἀγαθὸν λόγον ἀμφαίνοντι
⟨? scil. τοῖϲ φίλοιϲ⟩

19* (112. 3 DK) ξείνων αἰδοῖοι λιμένεϲ, κακότητοϲ ἄπειροι

12 Plut. *Quaest. conviv.* v. 8. 2, 683 E   **13** Clem. Al. *Strom.* iii. 14 (post fr. 118)
14 Plut. *De esu carn.* ii. 1, 996 E (cf. Hes. *Op.* 67)   **15** Clem. Al. *Protr.* 2. 27. Hoc fr.
post 31 (137 DK) locum habuisse potest   **16** Aelian. *Nat. anim.* xii. 7 et Schol. in
Aphthonium inedita (ap. *Orphica* ed. Hermann p. 511)   **17** Clem. Al. *Strom.* iv.
150 ('fr. 146') et v. 122 ('fr. 147'; quod citat Eus. *Praep. Ev.* xiii. 13. 49); in unum
coniunxit Stein   **18** Hippolyt. *Refut.* vii. 31   **19** Diodor. xiii. 83 (de Agrigenti-
norum divitiis et liberalitate disserens, Timaeum secutus). Hoc fragm. loc. habuisse potest
sub finem libri

---

13 2 exempli gratia suppl. Kranz, Zuntz   **14** Verba parum certa. ‖ ⟨τ'⟩ et ⟨τε⟩ add.
Wil. ‖ κυκέων Wil.: κυκεών Plut. mss.   **15** 3 πρὶν κὲν vel πλὴν vel sim. suppl. Zuntz
16 1 ἐν θήρεϲϲι Schol. Aphth.: ἐν θηρϲὶ δὲ Ael.   2 δ' ἐν Schol. Aphth.   **17** αὐτοτράπεζοι Eus.: ἐν τε τραπέζαιϲ Clem. Al. ms.   2 de ἐόντεϲ (εὖντεϲ) dubitare licet; an leg.
εὔφρονεϲ?   **18** 2 et 3 e.g. suppl. Bergk, Zuntz   5 ἀμφαίν. Schneidewin: ἐμφαίν. Hippol.
6 tent. Zuntz

20 (114 DK) Ὦ φίλοι, οἶδα μὲν οὕνεκ' ἀληθείη πάρα μύθοις
οὓς ἐγὼ ἐξερέω· μάλα δ' ἀργαλέη γε τέτυκται
ἀνδράσι καὶ δύςζηλος ἐπὶ φρένα πίςτιος ὁρμή

21 (132 DK) Ὄλβιος ὃς θείων πραπίδων ἐκτήσατο πλοῦτον,
δειλὸς δ' ὧι σκοτόεσσα θεῶν πέρι δόξα μέμηλεν

22 (135 DK) ἀλλὰ τὸ μὲν πάντων νόμιμον διά τ' εὐρυμέδοντος
αἰθέρος ἠνεκέως τέταται διά τ' ἀπλέτου αὐγῆς.

23 (128 DK) Οὐδέ τις ἦν κείνοισιν Ἄρης θεὸς οὐδὲ Κυδοιμός
οὐδὲ Ζεὺς βασιλεὺς οὐδὲ Κρόνος οὐδὲ Ποσειδῶν,
ἀλλὰ Κύπρις βασίλεια . . . .
4 τὴν οἵγ' εὐσεβέεσσιν ἀγάλμασιν ἱλάσκοντο
γραπτοῖς τε ζώιοισι μύροισί τε δαιδαλεόδμοις
σμύρνης τ' ἀκρήτου θυσίαις λιβάνου τε θυώδους
ξανθῶν τε σπονδὰς μελίτων ῥίπτοντες ἐς οὖδας.
8 ταύρων δ' ἀρρήτοισι φόνοις οὐ δεύετο βωμός,
ἀλλὰ μύσος τοῦτ' ἔσκεν ἐν ἀνθρώποισι μέγιστον
θυμὸν ἀπορραίσαντας ἐέδμεναι ἠέα γυῖα.

24 (144 DK) . . . . νηστεῦσαι κακότητος

25 (151 DK) . . . . . ζείδωρος . . . . . Ἀφροδίτη

26 (130 DK) ἦσαν δὲ κτίλα πάντα καὶ ἀνθρώποισι προσηνῆ,
θῆρές τ' οἰωνοί τε, φιλοφροσύνη τε δεδήει

27] (78 DK) ⟨δένδρεα δ'⟩ ἀείφυλλα καὶ ἐμπεδόκαρπα τεθήλει
. . . .
καρπῶν ἀφθονίηισι κατήρεα πάντ' ἐνιαυτόν

20 Clem. Al. *Strom.* v. 9   21 Clem. Al. *Strom.* v. 140. Post 18 (131 DK) locum habuisse potest   22 Aristot. *Rhet.* i. 13, 1373ᵇ6 ("ὡς Ἐ. λέγει περὶ τοῦ μὴ κτείνειν τὸ ἔμψυχον . . .")
23 1-8 Theophrast. ap. Porph. *De abstin.* ii. 21   1-7 Athen. xii. 510 c (ex Theophr.)
8-10 Porph. ib. 27 (unde Eus. et Cyril.)   24 Plut. *De cohib. ira* 16, 464 ʙ
25 Plut. *Amat.* 13, 756 ᴇ   26 Schol. Nicander *Ther.* 452   27 Theophrast. *De caus. plant.* i. 13. 2

---

23 2 οὐδὲ Κρόνος οὐδὲ Athen.: οὐδ' ὁ Κρ. οὐδ' ὁ Porph.   3 vers. decurt. Porph., Athen.
6 ἀκρήτου Athen.: ἀκράτου Porph.   7 ξανθῶν . . . μελίτων Athen.: ξουθῶν . . . μελιττῶν Porph.   8 ἀρρήτοισι Fabricius: ἀκρίτοισι Porph. bis (ita Cyr.: ἀκράτοισι Eus.: ἀκρήτοισι Scaliger)   10 ἠέα Vigerius: ἠΐα Porph. (Eus. Cyr.)   26 2 οἰωνοί Sturz (cf. fr. 21. 11 DK. 23. 7 DK): ἄνθρωποι (ᾆνοι) mss. (cf. v. 1)   27 1 ex Theophrasti paraphrasi versum restit. Karsten et G. Hermann ‖ post v. 1 lac. indic. Zuntz   2 κατήρεα Scaliger: κατ' ἦρα Theophr. mss.

28 (129 DK) Ἦν δέ τις ἐν κείνοισιν ἀνὴρ περιώςια εἰδώς
3 παντοίων τε μάλιστα cοφῶν ⟨τ'⟩ ἐπιήρανος ἔργων
2 ὃς δὴ μήκιστον πραπίδων ἐκτήςατο πλοῦτον·
4 ὅππότε γὰρ πάςῃςιν ὀρέξαιτο πραπίδεςςιν
ῥεῖ' ὅ γε τῶν ὄντων πάντων λεύccεκεν ἕκαστον
6 καί τε δέκ' ἀνθρώπων καί τ' εἴκοςιν αἰώνεςςιν
⟨γιγνόμενα ..⟩ . . . .

29 (136 DK) Οὐ παύcεcθε φόνοιο δυςηχέος; οὐκ ἐcορᾶτε
ἀλλήλους δάπτοντες ἀκηδείῃςι νόοιο;

30 (138 DK) χαλκῶι ἀπὸ ψυχὴν ἀρύcας . . . . . .

31 (137 DK) Μορφὴν δ' ἀλλάξαντα πατὴρ φίλον υἱὸν ἀείρας
cφάζει ἐπευχόμενος μέγα νήπιος οἰκτρὰ τορεῦντα
λιccόμενον θύοντος· ὁ δὲ νήκουστος ὁμοκλέων
4 cφάξας ἐν μεγάροιςι κακὴν ἀλεγύνατο δαῖτα.
ὡς δ' αὔτως πατέρ' υἱὸς ἑλὼν καὶ μητέρα παῖδες
θυμὸν ἀπορραίcαντε φίλας κατὰ cάρκας ἔδουςιν.

32 (142 DK) τὸν δ' οὔτ' ἄρ τε Διὸς τέγεοι δόμοι αἰγ[ιόχοιο
οὔ]τε ποτ' Ἀΐδεω δέ[χεται ...]κ[...] cτέγος ...

33 (139 DK) Οἴμοι ὅ τ' οὐ πρόcθεν με διώλεcε νηλεὲς ἦμαρ
cχέτλια ἔργα βορᾶς πρὶν χείλεςι μητίcαcθαι

34 (117 DK) ἤδη γάρ ποτ' ἐγὼ γενόμην κοῦρός τε κόρη τε
θάμνος τ' οἰωνός τε καὶ ἔξαλος ἔμπορος ἰχθύς

---

28 1–6 ex uno fonte Porph. *Vita Pyth.* 30 et Iambl. *Vita Pyth.* 67   1–2 Diog. Laert. viii. 54
(ex Timaeo)   29 1–2 Sextus Emp. *Adv. Math.* ix. 129; cf. Calcidius *In Tim.* 197
30 Aristot. *Poet.* 21 (1457ᵇ13)   31 1–6 Sextus Emp. *Adv. Math.* ix. 129; cf. Calcidius *In
Tim.* 197   1–2 Plut. *De superst.* 13 (μορφὴν ... νήπιος), Orig. *C. Cels.* v. 49 (φίλον ... νήπιος)
32 Pap. Herculan. 1012 col. 18   33 Porph. *De abstin.* ii. 31   34 *Athen.* viii. 365 e,
Clem. Al. *Strom.* vi. 24, Diog. Laert. viii. 77, Hippol. *Refut.* i. 3. 2 (partim citant multi; vid.
Poet. Philos. ad loc.)

---

28 v. 3 ante v. 2 trp. Stein   3 ⟨τ'⟩ Wil.   5 ῥεῖ' ὅ γε Cobet: ῥεῖα γε Porph. Iambl.
7 exempli gratia add. Zuntz   31 2 οἰκτρὰ τορεῦντα Zuntz: οἶδα (vel οἱ δὲ) πορεῦνται S.E.
mss., territa mente (mugit ci. G. Z.) hostia Calc.: οἱ δ' ἐπορεῦνται Bergk, alii alia   3 θύοντος
G. Hermann: -τας S.E. ‖ ὁ δὲ νήκ. Bergk: ὅδ' ἀνήκουστος S.E.   5 ἀπορραίcαντε Karsten:
-ντα S.E.   32 2 lectura et supplem. incerta ‖ ΟΑΙΔΟΥ (? i.e. -θ' Ἀΐδου) pap.
33 2 cχέτλια ἔ. β. πρὶν H. Fränkel: πρὶν cχέτλι' ἔ. β. περὶ Porph.   34 1 κούρη τε
κόρος τε Athen. [et Philostr., Cy., Themist.]   2 ἔξαλος (vel ἐξ ἁλὸς) ἔμπορος Athen., Diog.
Laert. (ἔμπυρος mss.), Hippol. [et Procl., Philopon.]: εἰν ἁλὶ ἔλλοπος Clem. solus [pro ἔξαλος
(sic etiam Calcid.): εἰν ἁλὶ etiam Cyr., Olympiod. v.l.; pro ἔμπορος (ἄμφορος Olympiod.
v.l.): φαίδιμος Cyr., νήχυτος Olympiod. v.l., etc.]

35 (143 DK) κρηνάων ἄπο πέντε ταμὼν ταναηκέϊ χαλκῶι

36 (140 DK) . . . . δάφνης φύλλων ἄπο πάμπαν ἔχεςθαι

37 (141 DK) δειλοί, πάνδειλοι, κυάμων ἄπο χεῖρας ἔχεςθαι

35 Theo Smyrn. *De arithm. Plat.* p. 15. 7 Hiller   ταμὼν . . .χαλκῶι *Arist. Poet.* 21, 1457[b]14
36 Plut. *Quaest. conv.* iii. 1. 2, 646 D   37 Gellius, *N.A.* iv. 11. 9; Didymus in *Geopon.*
ii. 35. 8 (" 'Ορφέως")

____

35 ταμών Arist.: ταμόντα Theo (in orat. sol. contextu) ‖ ταναηκέϊ Margoliouth (? sic Theo
ms. ante ras.): τανάκει Arist. ms. R; ἀτειρέϊ Arist. ms. A et Theo ms. post ras.   37 πάνδειλοι
om. Did.

APPENDIX

ΕΚ ΤΟΥ Γ´ ΤΩΝ ΦΥΣΙΚΩΝ

133 DK   οὐκ ἔςτιν πελάςαςθαι ἐν ὀφθαλμοῖςιν ἐφικτόν
     ἡμετέροις ἢ χερςὶ λαβεῖν, ἧπέρ τε μεγίςτη
     πειθοῦς ἀνθρώποιςιν ἁμαξιτὸς εἰς φρένα πίπτει.

134 DK   οὐδὲ γὰρ ἀνδρομέηι κεφαλῆι κατὰ γυῖα κέκαςται·
     οὐ μὲν ἀπὸ νώτοιο δύο κλάδοι ἀΐςςονται,
     οὐ πόδες, οὐ θοὰ γοῦν᾽, οὐ ϲτήθεα λαχνήεντα·
4   ἀλλὰ φρὴν ἱερὴ καὶ ἀθέϲφατος ἔπλετο μοῦνον
     φροντίϲι κόϲμον ἅπαντα καταΐϲϲουϲα θοῆιϲιν.

133 Clem. Al. *Strom.* v. 82 ("τὸ . . . θεῖον, ὁ Ἀκραγαντῖνός φηϲι ποιητής, οὐκ" κτλ.). Cum fr.
134 coniunxit Bergk   134 1–5 Ammonius *De interpret.* 13 (p. 249 Busse; versio
lat. Moerbekiana, ed. Verbeke p. 442), Tzetzes[a], *Chil.* xiii. 79 sq.; Tzetzes[b], *Epist.* 98 (p. 88
ed. Pressel)   1. 3–5 Olympiod. *In Gorg.* (p. 29 Norvin) ms. marg.   1 Olympiod. l.c. text.
2–3 cf. fr. 29 (Hippolyt. *Refut.* vii. 29)   4–5 Tzetzes[c], *Chil.* vii. 522 ff. ("Ε. τῶι τρίτωι τῶν
Φυϲικῶν").

____

134 1 οὐδὲ Olymp. (text.): οὔτε Ammon., Olymp. (marg.): οὐ μὲν Tzetzes[ab] ‖ ἀνδρομέηι
Ammon., Olymp. (text. et marg.): βροτέηι Tzetzes[ab]   2 ἀπὸ νώτοιο fr. 29: ἀπαὶ νώτων γε
Ammon. (ab humeris Moerb.), Tzetzes[ab] ‖ ἀΐϲϲ(ϲ)ονται fr. 29 (cf. *Il.* 6. 510): ἀΐϲϲουϲιν Ammon.
Tzetzes[ab] (cf. v. 5)   3 πόδες Ammon., Tzetzes[ab] (ut fr. 29): χέρες Olymp. (marg.) ‖ καὶ
(ante μήδεα) Tzetzes[ab] ‖ ϲτήθεα v.l. Ammon. ms. A, pectora Moerb.: μήδεα (ut fr. 29) cett.

V. PARAPHRASE

THE purpose of the following is to adumbrate the outlines of the poem as in the study of the fragments they seemed to emerge to the present writer. The reader will for himself have pondered the fragments and the possible relations between them; if a different picture should have commended itself to him, a comparison with the present attempt may serve towards the attainment of an improved result.

No one can 'reconstruct' a work of genius. Every word in the extant fragments of the *Katharmoi* bespeaks the individuality of a poet and thinker of unique verve and original inspiration. If ninety out of every hundred of his verses were preserved, the recovery of the remainder no doubt would overtax our power of divination. As it is, only one, roughly, out of every twenty verses of the poem survives (namely, about 56 and 52 out of the, roughly, thousand verses of each book).[1] Hence the present task is in no way comparable to that achieved in refashioning, out of hundreds of fragments, the figure and base of the 'Nike of Samothrake'; it may be likened, rather, to the endeavour of assigning to a small number of surviving pieces their places within a large relief or mosaic and, with luck, identifying the subject of the whole composition. Even though, in view of lacunae as large as they are in the *Katharmoi*, the quite unexpected and unattested could conceivably have had a place somewhere in the poem, this limited purpose seems capable of realization, for none of the extant fragments fails to convey some significant and pregnant detail. The hypothetical words by which we shall interconnect them do not pretend to be more than faint and minute shadows of what the poet may have said. Or, rather, they take the place of the colourless cement into which the surviving pieces of a mosaic are inserted by the restorer; who may even connect, by an outline-drawing, the preserved head and feet of, say, a human figure without claiming to have recovered the original.

Following the order which emerged as the most probable we shall not, as a rule, stress uncertainties of arrangement which have been discussed previously, but some remaining, more general problems will be taken up at the appropriate places.

BOOK I

From afar, Empedokles greets his friends, noblemen in his city of fr. 1 Akragas –and immediately asserts as a fact the startling claim: 'a god, no longer a mortal', he is wandering among mankind, 'honoured as is his

---

[1] Even if Lobon is disbelieved, these figures cannot be very far wrong, and the argument remains the same even if we allow six hundred or twelve hundred hexameters for each book.

due'. He finds this claim confirmed by the manner in which he is received and revered in town after town; the people turn to him as a seer and healer and (so, no doubt, he must have continued his report) he is able to satisfy all their requests and hopes.

It may be that some of the expressions used by Empedokles in this proemium appealed for a specific understanding by the knowing ones among his addressees. The words 'a god, no longer a mortal' recall the formula θεὸς ἀντὶ (or ἐκ) βροτοῖο which we know from the so-called 'Orphic' Gold Leaves; in presenting himself as a seer and healer he may be evoking the doctrine of redemption which becomes explicit at the end of the book (fr. 17 = 147 DK) and of which echoes come from Pindar (fr. 133) and, later, Plato (*Phaedr.* 248 d); and it may be for the same reason that he describes his friends as 'concerned with good doings' (as well as, later on, as 'havens for strangers'), for Pindar similarly praised Theron of Akragas at the end of the similarly esoteric *Ol.* ii. All these may be allusions to a persuasion to which his addressees, or some of them, adhered.

The assertion of his divinity remains none the less startling; for nothing could be more erroneous than the view that Greeks of his age, who saw 'everything full of gods', could have forgotten the exclusive distinction between man and god. Until, in the end, it proves to flow from a deepened concept of the very essence of Greek religion, Empedokles' claim is fr. 2 hybris; the more accentuated, so it seems, when, a little later, he checks himself, averring that his achievements—the achievements of a healer and seer—mean little in one so endowed. What, then, is it that distinguishes him from 'men mortal and subject to all kind of destruction'? The question may or may not have been explicitly formulated (he may have hinted that 'deprived of blessed existence' (fr. 4) he is now nearing the end of a long journey); it is, at any rate, unavoidably posed by this challenging opening.

fr. 3 The answer to it transfers the listener into a new dimension. How the mortal man Empedokles could be, at once, 'a god, mortal no more' and a 'vagrant, banished from the gods': this is expounded by no reasoned argument, but through myth; the myth experienced by all, recalled by him alone.

The 'Revelation to Pausanias' (which we call *Physika*) had shown that universe in which men live—live 'what they call life'—in its never-ceasing change and its eternity; had reproduced it as it stood out to the penetrating and all-embracing gaze of the inspired beholder, who discerned the interaction of divine essences in the life-process of the whole, down to the structure and operation of its smallest constituents—with gods, men, and beings of all grades of complexity emerging from imperishable components and again dissolving into them. The myth of the

Katharmoi comprises a different reality. It begins and ends with gods not waxing and waning, but 'immortal and indestructible' (fr. 17); there, with them, is the home and eternity of that principle and substratum of all beings incarnate which exists separate from their bodies and all the actions, sensations, and thoughts which are conditioned by the body; from there it is exiled into the foreign and inimical world of the elements —the universe described in the *Physika*—and to that realm it strives to return.

In modern terminology this concept would probably be defined as a transcendental reality—and thereby be robbed of its Hellenic concreteness and meaning. Empedokles sees that *essentia* which undergoes incarnation in bush or fish, lion or man, as a god from among gods eternal; called 'long-lived daimon' not because his existence is finite but because his divine status is intermittent and because, foregoing divine impassibility, he must accept involvement in earthly toil and strife; he is again 'god' (θεóc, fr. 17, v. 3) when he has finally overcome this involvement. One trespass, and one only, causes his downfall; the negation of divine perfection is—murder.

Stories like that of Apollo banished for slaying the Python may have provided the germ, or distant background, for this 'Law of Ananke'[1]; but the gods visualized by Empedokles—as later-on by Epicurus—living 'far from human sorrows' in timeless bliss cannot be imagined in the entanglement of passion. Their fall is caused by the alien power which acts as *principium individuationis* throughout the material universe; 'Strife', Νεῖκοc, reaches into their other-worldly realm and causes the pollution and penance of daimons like Empedokles', enforcing their long, toilsome journey through the hating elements back to eternity. How a force determining this world of change could be conceived of as impinging upon the eternal: this crucial question will be considered when the Empedoklean vision has been followed up in its entirety.

⟨When the daimon Empedokles became guilty of the pernicious crime, fr. 4 the Decree of Ananke was executed upon him.⟩ 'Bereft of the state of bliss', ⟨he was led—probably by Hermes—to⟩ a place of darkness and fr. 5 horror, the 'Field of Ate', abode of the Furies who are the bane of life on Earth. The same, awful place receives the exiles condemned to go through that life.

The various notions of a 'field' (λειμών) in the Netherworld all derive, in the last resort, from the *Odyssey*. That famous phrase κατ' ἀcφοδελὸν λειμῶνα, recurring twice in the 'Nekyia' (11. 539 and 573), combined with the description of the 'Elysian field' (πεδίον, 4. 563), suggested the bright λειμών, blissful sojourn, according to Pindar, Aristophanes, and

---

[1] It is formulated (as noted above, p. 195) with reference to Hes. *Theog.* 793 ff.

'Orpheus',[1] of the deceased initiated. Two verses from the beginning of the 'Smaller Nekyia' (24. 13 f.) define the ἀςφοδελὸς λειμών to which Hermes leads the shades of the slain suitors as the habitat of the 'phantoms of the dead', the εἴδωλα καμόντων. Empedokles adopts and develops this trait, and so does Plato; according to the concluding myth of the *Republic* (614 c 2; 616 b 2) the souls assemble on 'the' λειμών before reincarnation—and after judgement and penance; while according to the *Gorgias* (524 a 2; cf. 523 e 4) they go there immediately after death and undergo judgement there.

Popular imagination, as reflected e.g. in the opening scenes of Aristophanes' *Frogs*, and in stories about the descent of Herakles and Orpheus, visualized the way into Hades as haunted by monsters. The Empedoklean myth combines this tradition with the Homeric descriptions of the 'field', resort of the deceased, at its entrance. The combination is natural and may antedate Empedokles; with him, however, the place of fantastic monsters is taken by personifications, akin to the children of Night in Hesiod, of the evils which haunt life on earth. The myth thus modified had, through Vergil (*Aen.* vi. 274 ff.), a long after-life; it is bound up with the un-Homeric concept of the dead returning to Earth for another life: those embarking upon it are fated to breathe under the sway of evil.

To these 'Gates of Hell', then, Empedokles was conducted by his guide who, one guesses, interpreted the place to him; he came to grasp that the
frs. 6, 7 shades roaming among its inhabitants were awaiting incarnation, and his
fr. 8 realization of their fated woes, in poignant contrast with their lost state of bliss, broke forth in words of dolorous compassion.

'We have arrived in this roofed cave': so Empedokles is told by his guide.

On consideration, this short phrase reveals much. He who said these words must have said more. Otherwise the mere fact of a change of locality could have been reported by Empedokles himself; anyhow, the change was not worth mentioning unless thereby the scene was set for some significant happening. ⟨'Here you are to be given a body'⟩: thus the speech must have continued. Together with other 'daimons', Empedokles has been brought to the place of incarnation.

It is clear from the fragments that two different places, 'field' and 'cave', were mentioned; it is equally clear that the act of incarnation was described (fr. 11), and that this could not have been located in the 'field' —that region of eternal gloom to which the shades of the deceased repair. The new—or renewed—belief in their revival entailed additions to the Homeric image of the Netherworld; as in Plato's and later myths, so with Empedokles. That the place of incarnation, with him, was the 'cave' is not an absolutely certain inference. So much is missing from his poem that

---

[1] *Apud* Diodor. i. 96. 5; cf. Dodds, *Plato's Gorgias* (1959), p. 375, and below, p. 332.

the 'cave' conceivably could have been the scene of other happenings beyond our divination,[1] while the incarnation could have been located at still another, unknown place. If this faint possibility, unsupported by any evidence, is disregarded, the 'cave' was the scene of all the happenings related in the remaining part of the First Book of the *Katharmoi*.

Caves have no outstanding significance in Greek—as distinct from oriental and pre-Hellenic—religion and mythology.[2] Pan and the Nymphs live and are worshipped in caves; Dionysos and his cortège may feast in them;[3] but no profound symbolism is connected with them, and of particular caves in the Underworld there is no other evidence. The Platonic simile of the Cave in *Rep*. vii has of course been compared, especially by Neoplatonists; in fact, though, it is totally unrelated, for it was suggested by the stage of a puppet-theatre or shadow-play. The Netherworld as a whole could quite naturally be visualized as a large cave; this is normal in oriental mythology and common with Latin poets, but very rare in Greek (cf. Apoll. Rhod. ii. 735—an imperfect parallel). It would appear hardly less natural to conceive of various recesses in it as of so many *speluncae*; this again is usual in Roman poetry (an elaborate example is the cave of Cacus in Vergil's *Aen*. viii),[4] but I know of no Greek instance. Even so, the Empedoklean innovation becomes less surprising in the light of these parallels; besides, the analogy of cave and womb may have contributed towards it. The—possibly significant—similarity with the Orphic 'Cave of Night' will be considered below.[5]

The world in which the fallen daimon must live is dominated by Philia fr. 9 and Neikos in their perpetual interaction; all life in it is accordingly marked by contrariety. The absolute contrast between the daimon's true,

[1] The analogy of Platonic and later myths could tempt one to locate scenes of judgement or punishment in the 'cave': it will be argued later that such were not a feature of the *Katharmoi*.

[2] Assertions to the contrary are indicative of the persisting spell of Neoplatonic speculation and in particular of Porphyry's *De antro nympharum*. Chasms and rifts—frequent in the limestone of Greece and Asia Minor—were naturally held, at many places, to be entrances to the Netherworld and hence described as 'Plutonia'; as the way by which Pluto abducted Kore, or by which Herakles or Orpheus descended to Hades and returned. Like Pan and Nymphs in their caves, and like Nereids, Naiads, and Dryads, such tales evidence nothing more, nor less, than the pious awe stirred by all nature and particularly by striking natural phenomena. The Phrygian Kybele was worshipped in artificial caves suggestive of her original abode; not so the Greek Demeter; still less Persephone. The 'black Demeter' of Phigalia (Pausan. viii. 42) is an exception; she has usurped the place of the local nymph (see now R. Stiglitz, *Die Großen Göttinnen Arkadiens*, 1967, Sonderschr. hg. v. Oesterr. Arch. Inst. xv; esp. p. 127), and Pherekydes (7. A8 and B6 DK) is an outsider to Greek tradition.

[3] For reproductions of Διονυσιακὰ ἄντρα, which became popular in the Hellenistic period, see Athenaeus iv. 148 b, v. 200 c, and Plutarch, *De sera* . . . , 565 E; for nymphaia see the Attic dedicatory reliefs (listed in Roscher, *Lexikon* . . . iii. 555 f.), Menander's *Dyskolos*, and the models of grottoes found at Lokri (P. Arias, *Not. Scav.* (1946), 138 ff. with Figs. 23 ff.; also *Arch. Anz.* (1941), 650 f.). The Cretan 'Zeus' and his caves are pre-Hellenic survivals.

[4] Cf. J. Kroll, *Gott und Hölle* (1932), pp. 220 and 390 ff.; also p. 521 (on Claudian).

[5] Detached Note VIII, below, p. 403.

'heavenly' existence and his exile on Earth became manifest when, after his fall, he was transferred to the sombre abode of the Kēres. The place from which subsequently he enters life on Earth is haunted, so Plutarch tells, by other genii. If you ponder the implications of the pairs of their names cited by Plutarch and Cornutus, you will find in them a comprehensive and poetical summary of the contrasting facts and tendencies which constitute this life; they will condition the daimon's impending incarnate existence. And you may consider the possibility that this list of names was concluded, like similar ones in Hesiod,[1] by a less stereotyped verse contrasting the dominating forces of 'Necessity' and 'Grace'; although admittedly the structure of this verse—with one of the names in the accusative—makes this assumption problematical.

fr. 10

fr. 11   The act of incarnation was described. Empedokles was clothed by a female daimon (possibly called 'Physis') with 'the foreign garment of flesh',[2] the 'soil wrapping the mortal'; and not he alone but, like him,

fr. 12   a host of others. This one would infer from general grounds of poetical economy; from the analogous scenes in Plato's *Republic* and *Phaidros*, and from the number of shades, previously mentioned, 'roaming the field of Ate'; it will presently be confirmed in considering the following fragments, especially fr. 15. This essential and grandiose scene cannot be imagined without some superior deity presiding over it, and this inference will likewise presently be confirmed.

frs. 13–17   Five fragments show that the lot awaiting the incarnated and the law governing their long journey through many forms of earthly existence were set out at length. This revelation could only come from a deity, and the given setting for it was an address to the crowd of the newly-incarnated; they are directly addressed in fr. 15. The scanty remains of this great speech can hypothetically be connected as follows:

⟨'You, daimons, have fallen because you yielded to the power of 'Strife';

fr. 13   hence you are now subject to his ordinance.⟩ He laid down that live forms shall grow out of dead ones and, by turns, dead ones out of live. ⟨You are doomed to be involved in this alternation. In the place of the bliss of your

fr. 14   former state, your lives will be full of sorrow; for he, Κότος,⟩ has blended pains and torments and deceit and weeping ⟨which shall be with you at all times⟩.

fr. 15   Verily, then, writhing in hardships you will not be relieved from your sufferings ⟨unless you abide by the counsel which I shall give you'⟩.

fr. 10   It would be possible at this point to insert fr. 10. It could here have been stated that the exiled, by their trespass, had put themselves under the yoke of Ananke, and it could have been added that a force opposed to it did, for their good, exist; for 'Grace hates unbearable Ananke'; through

fr. 16   her a way, however long, out of their plight was open for them. At any

---

[1] Hes. *Theog.* 231, 263, 361.
[2] For comment on this concept see Detached Note IX, below, p. 405.

rate, the speech went on to show how, ascending through ever higher stages of earthly life, and fulfilling the best possibilities of each, the daimon could finally regain his original state and become, once more, 'a god with the other immortals, released from human woes, eternal'. fr. 17

With these sublime verses the book, I suppose, ended. There was no reason for weakening their impact by a trivial continuation ('and thereupon each of us started upon his allotted journey') or *fabula docet*. Reader and hearer comprehend the truth of what had seemed hybris and paradox: Empedokles, the man, the healer and prophet, is 'an exile and a vagrant' —and a god.

Which deity could have pronounced this paramount speech? There is much to encourage the assumption that it was spoken by Persephone herself. The scene was set in her realm; it is there that those destined for rebirth were gathered and 'clothed with flesh'. The doctrine—if the all-too prosaic term be allowed—which becomes reality in the Empedoklean myth has its closest parallels in Pindar and in the verses inscribed on the Gold Leaves; not only in its general outline but in characteristic detail. One recalls at once Pindar's οἷσι δὲ Φερσεφόνα, κτλ.: the final decision about the lot of the defunct is hers; moreover, *Ol.* ii. 59, too, may hint that she is the supreme judge;[1] while on the Gold Leaves the opening address is to the 'Queen of those below', whose supreme authority stands out in them from beginning to end. Even so, the assumption may appear paradoxical that in the *Katharmoi* the way to the final conquest of Death was shown by the very Queen of Death; but this is, after all, her role also with Pindar and on the Gold Leaves. The concept of Persephone as a giver of Life no less than of Death was, as we have seen, alive among Western Greeks, and particularly so in the city of Empedokles, of which she was the chief goddess. The profundity and wide significance expressed in her cult—with which he had grown up—could have inspired Empedokles in attributing to her the culmination of his revelation.

This is a hypothesis; alternatives to it are discussed in a Detached Note.[2] If the hypothesis is correct, the imagination dimly visualizes a scene of unique grandeur—which the pen refuses to elaborate.

BOOK II

Before the extant part of the proemium no more need be lost than one verse ('Once more I invoke thee, O Goddess'). fr. 18

The explicit reference to the *Physika* is a hint that the poet proposes to resume, from a new angle, the subject of the earlier poem. The *Physika* had revealed the forces and processes determining all life on Earth,

---

[1] Above, p. 86.   [2] Below, p. 405.

culminating in the delineation of the world-deity comprising and permeating the whole of it. The first book of the *Katharmoi* had shown man—the god-man—essentially at home in another reality yet fated to go through *this*. His fall was due to murder; from murder he must keep free if he is to regain his divine state—and murder is being committed by men day in, day out. Not indeed in public life, where it is restrained by public law; but in the relation which matters above all others: the relation between men and gods—where it is called sacrifice and is accepted by all as the very essence of 'worship', εὐcεβίη.

Empedokles therefore is compelled to undertake an excessively revolutionary task: to controvert the accepted traditions of public and private worship. No revaluation more fundamental could be contemplated; he purports to denounce the current rites and the gods demanding them; the sacred foundations of common life—it rested on the traditional worship—are to be overturned and the tables of a new code to be erected upon their ruins. Only a god could sanction an endeavour so bold. The opening invocation of the Muse is thus anything but a formality; Empedokles is to speak his 'good word' about the gods under divine inspiration.

fr. 19   He addressed this book—fr. 20 (ὦ φίλοι) confirms it—like the preceding one, primarily to his Akragantine friends. Our fr. 19 (112. 3 DK) may therefore have followed here. Since however it is possible that a greeting to the same friends concluded the poem, this verse could as well have had
fr. 20   its place in that context. At any rate, the poet is aware that his teaching about the gods is bound to be contrary to the notions of his public. Hence
fr. 21   he solicits their goodwill; he knows that it is the truth and that bliss and doom for any man depend upon his approach, right or wrong, to the gods —as the expounders of the mysteries were wont to assert, a basic formula of whose preaching (ὄλβιος ὅς . . .) he makes his own.

The reversal of all traditional religion—for that is what his teaching
fr. 22   amounts to—flows from one ultimate persuasion: the sacredness of all life; which he proclaims as a law different in kind from the many and various customs accepted and rejected by mankind. Later propagators of vegetarianism, like Porphyry, were to find themselves hard put to it when striving to demonstrate a *consensus gentium* on this point; but Empedokles proclaims it—if once more, and with every reserve, we may apply a terminology based on our different and less concrete mode of thought— as a transcendental truth. He sees it 'stretched out throughout the universe'; it is of a kind with the 'heavenly laws unborn and unageing' to which the Sophoclean chorus (*O.T.* 865 ff.) appeals. Aristotle informs us that this law forbade the killing of what is alive, and the fragments 29, 31, 33 make it quite clear that the 'murder' envisaged was committed in offering bloody sacrifice. This basic tenet cannot have remained

unstated at the point which our paraphrase has reached, and this inference is confirmed by the words with which Theophrastos[1] prefaces a quotation from the beginning of the following, myth-historical section (our fr. 23); they sound like a free rendering of the context from which Aristotle drew his citation.

Before this absolute law, present worship and the gods demanding it frs. 23 ff. stand condemned. This startling indictment is not stated baldly. Empedokles opens up the way for persuasion (fr. 20) into reluctant minds by showing the present state to be the outcome of an age-long process; indictment, rejection, and a fresh resolve flow from a mythical history of gods and men. This history claims assent in that it is based upon an authoritative Hesiodic myth and in line with that interpretation of the universe which Empedokles had given in the *Physika*. The myth is recast in the light of that interpretation. Hesiod's narrative of the Golden and the following Ages provided the basic concept of progressive deterioration and is called to mind by characteristic details both material and verbal;[2] but a different relation, at each stage, between gods and men is stressed from the first—no Kronos existed at this Golden Age—and stands forth throughout: the fault of the subsequent generations of men is anything but their failure to sacrifice.[3] The Empedoklean recasting showed a succession not of men only but, determining them, of gods. The series of 'theogonies', with the rule of Kypris followed by the emergence of gods more and more brutal, was bound up with the interaction of the world-forces of Philia and Neikos, and corresponded with the gradual change of men's attitude to the divine.[4]

Empedokles' vision of an earliest mankind peaceful and blest, serving in purity a pure godhead, and its gradual progress in ever-increasing brutality, is (though inspired by Hesiod) a concept of high originality and perennial suggestiveness. Here was the model to be variously, and even contradictorily, developed by those who endeavoured to reconstruct the history of human civilization; from Demokritos and Plato to Dikaiarchos, Epicurus, Poseidonios, and Seneca. The purpose of Empedokles, though, was not primarily historical. The essential aspect, to him, was that of pure worship depraved, and the purpose, a reform of the cult of his day. In this respect his follower was Theophrastos. His Περὶ εὐcεβείαc, which J. Bernays recovered from Porphyry, bears the marks, as is natural, of a different age and mind; the reconstruction of past ages has gained from the researches and discussions of a century and more, and the presentation witnesses to the refinement of a subtle and keen mind trained

---

[1] *Apud* Porph. *De abstin.* ii. 27, p. 157. 14 Nauck.
[2] e.g. fr. 24, cf. Hes. *Op.* 113 and 115; frs. 25 and 27, cf. *Op.* 117 f.
[3] Contrast Hes. *Op.* 136 ff.; also 187.
[4] Cf. Theophr. *apud* Porph. loc. cit. 22, p. 151. 8 ff. Nauck.

in the traditions of philosophy and rhetoric. Basically, though, the method and purpose of Theophrastos are the same as Empedokles'—with the one fundamental reservation that the pupil of Aristotle ascribes the changes in human behaviour to material causes. According to him, bloody sacrifices began when, under the stress of famine and war (due, perhaps, to overpopulation) men turned to cannibalism and, next, began to eat the flesh of animals; while to the Akragantine prophet the history of the cult is, at the same time, the history of the gods—indeed, a function of it. While according to Theophrastos[1] 'the deity was angered' by the adoption of bloody sacrifices, the gods accepting them are, with Empedokles, themselves evil.

His subject in this section was defined, by Theophrastos,[2] as περὶ τῆς θεογονίας καὶ τῶν θυμάτων; the very articles which the latter adds to the two nouns betray that, at the time, Empedokles' refashioning of the Hesiodic prototype was remembered as striking. We can still, from the remaining fragments, recover a shadow of his full and poetical description of the earliest stage, and Porphyry's words[3] 'as long as Philia . . . ruled, nobody committed murder, but when Ares and Kydoimos and all kind of warring originated,[4] nobody spared anyone' indicate the trend of what followed: the emergence and advance of gods akin to Neikos and the corresponding corruption of mankind. The description of these successive ages of men and gods is lost (but for the verses in praise of Pythagoras).[5] It culminated in the passionate denunciation of the corruption of Empedokles' own day; this stands out in verses that call for no paraphrase.

The part dealing with 'theogony and sacrifices' thus concluded, it has become abundantly clear that man's true vocation could not be fulfilled in surrendering self to the cosmic cycle which is governed by Neikos and leads more and more deeply into corruption. From here on Empedokles spoke directly to his contemporaries. 'For him that commits this trespass there is no room among the gods on high or below': thus he may have continued;[6] and proceeded to instance his own experience in evidence of the suffering caused to the immortal essence of man by the disregard of the most absolute of laws (fr. 22).

The rest is lost. No doubt positive injunctions concerning the right way of worship followed, but the slight remaining fragments merely show that

frs. 23-7 remaining fragments...

frs. 28-31 cessive ages...

fr. 32 and leads...

frs. 33 f. trespass...

frs. 35-7 of worship...

---

[1] *Apud* Porph. loc. cit. ii. 8, p. 138. 11 Nauck.

[2] loc. cit. ii. 21, p. 150. 17 Nauck; for the wording see above p. 240, n. 4.

[3] After the passage cited in the preceding note; i.e. ii. 22, p. 151. 8 Nauck.

[4] Cf. Hesiod, *Op.* 145 ff.

[5] For the placing of the Pythagoras-fragment 28 (129 DK) see above, p. 209. It is conceivable that the age which, though late, produced the 'divine man' was analogous to Hesiod's 'fourth age' (*Op.* 157 ff.), marked by a temporary, last improvement preceding final corruption.

[6] Our fr. 15 (145 DK) could have had its place in this context.

the need to avoid pollution was stressed and the observation of traditional taboos enjoined as a means towards the recovery and preservation
of original purity.[1]

[1] Among the extant fragments there are no specific moral injunctions. The implications
of this fact will be considered later (below, p. 265). Two points of detail, though, may be
taken up here. We may feel that the conviction of the sacredness of life must imply the advocacy
of pacifism. His loathing of war is evident from fr. 23, but no fragment survives to tell whether
Empedokles elaborated this implication or whether, despairing of its realization during the
present world-cycle, his exclusive aim was to free suffering mankind from staying on in
a world inescapably dominated by Strife. Actually, one highly problematical, non-ritual
injunction is reported by Hippolytos: he asserts that Empedokles denounced marriage and all
sex relations. When it is read in DK (*ad* fr. 115, p. 356. 30 ff.; cf. *ad* fr. 110, p. 352. 11 ff.), this
assertion may seem, and has seemed to some, worth considering; it evaporates when it is read
in its original setting. Hippolytos' crazy design to discredit 'heretics' by showing up their
doctrines as identical with those of one or the other pagan philosopher has borne for us
a wonderful harvest of precious fragments; but one must not forget his design when using his
evidence. His whole representation of Empedokles is bent so as to fit Marcion, and the
Greek's alleged asceticism has its origin in nothing but Marcion's. Hippolytos equates
Marcion's 'evil Creator' with the Empedoklean Neikos, 'who makes many out of One'
(vii. 29; p. 250. 99 Miller), and Marcion's 'good God' with unifying Philia. Marcion pro-
hibited procreation so as not to further the works of the 'evil Creator'; Empedokles' Philia
strives to extract souls from the cruel regime of Neikos; hence Empedokles—always according
to Hippolytos—enjoined abstinence from all ἔμψυχα—and sexual abstinence! 'For marriage,
according to Empedokles, divides the One and makes many, as I have shown': thus, trium-
phantly, Hippolytos (p. 252. 48) sums up his fabrication. Need one still elaborate its incompatibility with the whole of Empedokles', and indeed all Greek thought? Hippolytos is not
saved by Aristoxenos' (fr. 25 Wehrli, from Gellius iv. 11. 10) perverse interpretation of
Empedokles' fr. 141 DK; see Wehrli ad loc.

VI. SOME GENERALIA

'. . . et glimt af guds ansigt;
af det realiserede menneske.'

THE preceding may, it is hoped, be of use to some students who seek to realize their own picture of Empedokles. This at any rate has been the purpose of the writer; who has no ambition to see his personal impressions become part of 'the common stock of knowledge', and hence feels strongly tempted at this point to regard his task as concluded. The following hints are reluctantly added for those who may care to test their own conclusions by a comparison with his. By way of a *caveat*, we may begin with the following reflection.

Being, infinite, is one thing, and inexhaustible; a man's perception of it —less or more comprehensive according to his vision—is another; yet a third thing is the extent and manner in which he may give expression to that perception. If he does so by means of words, these will stir reactions more or less adequate according to the listener's aptitude. If, across a gulf of two thousand years, the echo of a few words, torn out of a comprehensive and profound utterance, is to become at all audible, and even meaningful, much creative sympathy will be required from the listener. And if, finally, the listener makes bold to try and convey his impressions by means of words, these will in turn be subject to similar qualifications. Thus the whole process of communion between past and present appears beset with forbidding obstacles. It is in the unceasing effort at overcoming them that the vision once enshrined in a man's inspired words can revive our own vision.

Concerning Empedokles, it will have become clear that certain well-worn questions have been posed prematurely and discussed, if not without gain, yet with no chance of a final solution. As long as the content, form and specific character of the *Katharmoi* remained obscure—they were in fact hardly considered—the meaning of passages on which a particular argument turned was liable to be qualified, in a manner unknown, by the context—the ignored context—of which originally they formed part. A case in point are the statements about gods, which have been systematized irrespective of whether they came from the 'revelation' in the first book of the *Katharmoi* or from the 'theogony' in the second or from the first or third book of the *Physika*; and yet their bearing was in each case different from all others.

With similar inconclusiveness, and with unflinching assurance, it has been asserted and, in turn, denied that the 'field' and 'cave' to which the 'daimon' was brought on his banishment were meant to be on Earth—or indeed to be mere metaphors denoting 'Earth'—or, alternatively, in Hades. The question is settled when the verses in question are found to have formed part of a 'Nekyia' or 'Katabasis', in the tradition of Homer and later poets. When outstanding scholars like E. Rohde and C. H. Kahn object that there is no room for a Netherworld in Empedokles' cosmology (is this so sure?), and that, with him, the place of penance is on Earth (which is true),[1] their protest may be met by a consideration of the significance of this myth. It was open for Neoplatonic allegorizers to find its scenery on Earth,[2] and modern expounders, once they have grasped it in its own right, are at liberty to analyze and assess it in accordance with their notions; but Empedokles recalls and retells it with the same—and certainly no less—conviction, 'realism', and emphasis as would have applied to any 'real' happenings; his Hades is as real as the murder committed by human sacrificers, or the process of respiration (fr. 100 DK), or the exile of banished daimons and their return. This is not allegory; it is myth. A region of being experienced with, at least, the same intensity as any happening in the elementary universe has revealed itself to him in this form, and thus he reproduces it. No alternative way for conveying it was open. The truth of myth is separate from, and beyond, the truth which is grasped and conveyed διὰ λόγου. It was waning at the time; here, miraculously, it stands forth, once more, with traditional and new vitality. The same miracle happened, at the same time, on the Athenian stage; there, as here, the unleashed energies of thought which were soon to make the gods withdraw from the world of man were answered by the most powerful resurgence of myth. This was its final manifestation, or nearly so; for Plato's eschatological vision, so genuinely expressive of the transcendental (and so largely inspired by Empedokles[3]), is yet (or so it seems to me) impaired by rationalistic amendments designed to exonerate God—who is the Good—from responsibility for the imperfections of man and his world. What came later was artistic fancy, moralizing allegory, and the personalized terrors and speculations of fearful small minds—until the new god brought his new myth. Who would dare, by allegorical exposition, to relieve Dante of his hell and his heaven? Empedokles' Hades is no less definitive.

His myth is not an imitation of Orphic models. The fantastic series of Orphic theogonies could not be combined—as we saw—with either the timeless existence of 'eternal gods' (frs. 3 and 17) or the succession, beginning with Aphrodite, of gods emerging in the world of the elements

---

[1] E. Rohde, *Psyche*, ii² (1921), p. 178, n. 1; H. C. Kahn, *Archiv f. Gesch. d. Philosophie*, xlii (1960), 20, n. 50.

[2] Or even, for Epicureans, in the nursery; cf. above, p. 200, n. 2.

[3] Note, e.g., specific echoes of our fr. 17 (DK 147) in Pl. *Phaed.* 69 c 7, 81 a 9, 84 b 4.

(fr. 23, and frs. 21. 2 and 23. 8 DK); and of Dionysos, so outstanding in Orphic theology, there is no trace in Empedokles. Likewise, the way to 'eternal drunkenness in Hades', which Orphic missionaries opened up by their purifications,[1] is incommensurable with the progress of the Empedoklean 'daimon'; nor does the myth in the *Katharmoi* leave room for what seems to have been a cherished trait of their preaching; namely, the pedantic elaboration of the terrors and punishments of hell for those uncleansed by their rites.[2]

The concept of punishment—and therefore also of judgement—awaiting the dead is alien to the concept of transmigration. It arises naturally where the popular belief is held that the dead live on in the Netherworld; for the elementary desire to see the manifest injustices of life evened out finds scope in the prospect of a just retribution after death. Combined with a primitive fear of death, this prospect was bound to stir the desire to secure the best, and avoid the worst, lot in Hades. The Eleusinian mysteries seem to have satisfied this desire, and so did 'purifiers' who claimed the authority of Orpheus for their rites.

The different persuasion—which may have been held by some early Pythagoreans—that the *psyche* wanders endlessly from one body to another[3] could be combined with the belief in periods of reward and punishment in between one incarnation and the next; but—as far as speculations of this kind were indulged in at all—the obvious form of a retribution for merit and demerit would on this basis be through incarnation of a type higher, or lower, than the preceding one. This latter doctrine was inherently given when incarnation was conceived, as by Empedokles, as a penance exacted from a divine being; whose supreme punishment and suffering is in being kept from its eternal home and whose supreme reward and goal is the return to it and the recovery of its divine self. It undergoes incarnations higher or lower according to desert; for other judgements and punishments there is no room or reason.[4]

It is credible that the common persuasion took this particular form with, at any rate, a notable part of the early Pythagoreans.[5] I cannot indeed find any explicit literary evidence to bear out the assumption, but their concern with righteousness and ritual purity would therewith appear

---

[1] Plato, *Rep.* 363 c; cf. Antisthenes *apud* Diog. Laert. vi. 4; and so on down to AERACURA.

[2] Plato, *Rep.* 363 d; 364 e; Diodor. i. 96. 5.

[3] Arist. *De an.* 407b22 (58 B 39 DK); Porph. *Vita Pyth.* 19; schol. *Il.* 16. 857.

[4] The two forms of eschatology—the Eleusinian, for short, and the Empedoklean—were conflated by Plato (in *Rep.* and *Phaedr.*) in an effort to express, in one myth, his belief in the divine origin and immortality of the individual soul and the vindication of righteousness.

[5] As W. Burkert, *Weisheit und Wissenschaft* (1962), pp. 110 ff. pertinently stresses, the extant evidence excludes the existence of a unified Pythagorean dogma. The agreement, in essentials, of certain early witnesses (on which presently) is, in view of this fact, all the more significant; the absence of a dogma is evident in the disagreement between Pindar and Empedokles concerning a purgatory in between incarnations (which also the Gold Leaves imply).

to have its motive in the striving after a definite and supreme goal. Admittedly the desire to secure a higher, and avoid an inferior, form of incarnation could conceivably account for their canons of behaviour; but why should Empedokles have included the praise of Pythagoras in his description of a former age, unless he worshipped him as his precursor?

It is not, then, by chance that among the Empedoklean fragments there is not one telling of sinners punished and just men rewarded in the other world—apart from the primal fall and final restitution. Indeed, if such statements had occurred in the *Katharmoi*, there is no doubt that they would have been cited by later theologians, from Plato onward to Plutarch and Plotinus, Clement and Origen. The Empedoklean daimon regains his pristine divinity when he achieves perfect 'purity'. The title of the poem is therefore likely to have had wider implications than the observance of taboos which was enjoined at its end; 'purification' meant ridding the soul of all the accretions and distractions given with its incarnation.[1] To achieve it was a matter of right life and right worship, and the prime purpose of the poem was in inculcating the true notion of, and relation to, the divine; once this is achieved, 'das Moralische versteht sich von selbst'. The absence—as far as the extant fragments go—of moral injunctions does not indicate that in Empedokles' teaching relations to fellow men were irrelevant. What Pindar (*Ol.* ii. 94 ff.) hints in praising Theron as εὐεργέτας (and develops ib. 69) is implied in Empedokles addressing his friends as ἀγαθῶν μελεδήμονες ἔργων, and as Theron gave 'delights numberless' to his people, so Empedokles achieved his consummation in serving the needs of people wherever he went.

On consideration, the whole of the persuasion here surveyed—from primitive taboos to a reformed theology, and all this aiming to restore the soul, from its incarceration in alien bodies, to its original divinity—this persuasion, which is common, in essentials, to Pindar, Empedokles and, later, Plato, can only go back to the teaching of Pythagoras; and indeed Empedokles is described as a Pythagorean in many sources.[2] We know all too little about early Pythagoreanism to define this fact in detail; as it is, Empedokles can convey a general notion of this Pythagoreanism rather than vice versa. He paid tribute to Pythagoras as to no other man,[3] but he was too great a genius to be suspected of merely versifying another's teaching. His own thought was stimulated—as Theophrastos stated[4]—by

---

[1] Cf. Aristoxenos, fr. 26 Wehrli, on the Pythagorean notion of purity and, for its significance, P. Boyancé, *Le culte des Muses* (1937), *passim*.

[2] e.g. Diog. Laert. viii. 54 (Timaios); ib. 55 (Neanthes); Gellius iv. 11. 9; Hierokles *ad Carm. Aur.* v. 24, etc.   [3] Fr. 28 (129 DK).

[4] Simplicius, *Phys.* 25. 19; 31 A 7 DK; *Doxogr.*, p. 477. 18. Diog. Laert. viii. 55 (28 A 9 DK) does not prove the reference to Pythagoras to have been added by Simplicius. Similar though the two passages are, and both Theophrastean, they differ in purpose and context;

Parmenides no less than by Pythagoras. Parmenidean inspiration stands out throughout the work of Empedokles; from the 'ontological' foundations of his cosmology down to details of embryology; from the reduction of the world-process to the interaction of opposites to the concept of an eternal essence of man;[1] and, as generally in the poetical form of his utterance, so particularly in his mythology; from the supreme, creating 'daimon' Aphrodite down to the impersonations of opposites;[2] all this melted down into his own vision; a vision perceived and conveyed as myth.

The word through which this myth could be perceived and conveyed was Hesiod's.[3] With all its newness and revolutionary fervour, the Empedoklean message presented itself as an interpretation, or re-interpretation, of, mainly, the *Theogony*; even where it controverted its teaching. The younger prophet owed to the elder his grasp of the universe of gods and men, of heaven and earth, and the means for putting it into words; this debt he avowed and proclaimed, joining his own teaching to that tradition which, through the ages, gave Greeks their first clue for their understanding of reality. To appreciate this conscious and fundamental dependence one has to try and read Hesiod as Empedokles read him.

The *Theogony* is so very much more than a pedantic catalogue of deities and personifications! When the genealogies, their interrelations, and the stories attached to some of them, are appreciated with the serious and sympathetic attention which the gravity of the theme and the concentrated power of its presentation demand, they stand out as a complete and profound image and interpretation of existence. Modern expounders may, and indeed are bound to, try and reproduce this image by prosaic paraphrase, but in doing so we can never match the concise and pregnant meaning of the original. Such is the superiority of myth over logos and of poetry over prose.

We have previously noted the Hesiodic prototypes of various Empedoklean passages—the catalogue of female divinities in the 'Cave',[4] compared with Hesiod's enumeration of Nymphs and Okeanids,[5] affords

Simplicius surveying the number of principles posited by Presocratic philosophers, while Diogenes seeks to account for the poetical form used by Empedokles. The latter quotation may go back to Theophrastos' separate book about him.

[1] Simplicius, *Phys.* 39. 18, quoted in DK *ad* 28 B 13.

[2] Cf. K. Reinhardt, *Parmenides* (reprint 1959), pp. 17 ff.; H. Schwabl, *Wiener Stud.*, lxx (1957), 278 ff.; K. Deichgräber, 'Parmenides' Auffahrt . . .', in *Abhandl. Akad. Mainz* (1958), 711 ff.

[3] Some readers may care to compare the following with the essay *Homère, Hésiode et Pythagore* by M. Detienne (1962), who discusses the significance, for the Pythagoreans, of the epic poetry from a different angle and on the basis, largely, of different evidence.

[4] Fr. 9 (122 f DK).   [5] *Theog.* 240 ff. and 349 ff.

an instructive instance—; we now proceed to sketch the fundamental significance of Hesiod for the essential elements of the Empedoklean conception—the fall of the daimon; the state of the world into which he is banished, and his final restitution.

Hesiod saw the present state of the world established and maintained by the order of divine powers under the rule of victorious Zeus. This order may be jeopardized; for 'Strife and Hatred', Ἔρις καὶ Νεῖκος, may invade the divine sodality (vv. 782 f.) and tempt its members to repudiate that order. It is maintained; for Zeus wields an ineluctable 'bond' (ὅρκος), the Stygian oath; the god who would contravene it is annihilated. Hesiod describes his doom in verses of magical intensity (vv. 794–806): until a 'year' (period) is completed, the transgressor lies 'breathless, speechless, not partaking of any fare, shrouded in an evil sleep ("coma")'; he is as though not-being. Thereafter, cut off for a 'great year'[1] from the company of the gods, he must face toils ever more grievous; in the end, though, he returns to 'the ranks of the Immortals whose abode is on Olympos'.

The impact of destructive Neikos upon the supramundane realm of the gods; expulsion of the transgressor, who forfeits his divine status and, cut off from his heavenly origin, must undergo toil upon toil, but finally, on completing his penance, is readmitted to his primordial demesne: it is evident that here is the inspiration for Empedokles' myth of the destiny of man. The banished god described by Hesiod is—Man; all men are banished gods. In developing this 'creative interpretation', Empedokles could feel that he remained within the authoritative Hesiodic frame; that he was describing in concrete detail that long period of penance which the master had merely adumbrated (*Theog.* 799 f.). Accordingly he stressed his discipleship by echoing that very passage and by resuming the central terms νεῖκος and ὅρκος.[2]

The daimon is thrown into this world which, by its constituent law, is dominated by ever increasing corruption; it is not, then, ruled by that perfect deity from whose dominion the essential man stems—but by others. The series of 'theogonies', in which Empedokles set out the emergence of gods ever more brutal, and described the worship, ever more brutal, given to them, is generally, and obviously, in the tradition of Hesiod's *Theogony*, but is conceived and elaborated, in its main trend and in detailed traits, on the model of the passage in the *Works and Days* (vv. 109 ff.) which recounts, with vehement conviction and shattering realism, the decline of mankind from its Golden Age onward. Here,

---

[1] With Göttling and Merkelbach (*Stud. Ital.*, xxvii–xxviii (1956), 292) I would punctuate, in v. 799, before μέγαν; reading ἄλλος ἐξ ἄλλου (accepting a trochee) in v. 800 and regarding the 'great year' of v. 799 as synonymous with the 'ennaeteris' in v. 803.

[2] Νεῖκος Emp., fr. 3 (115 DK), v. 14 ~ *Theog.* 782; ὅρκος Emp., ib., v. 2 ~ *Theog.* 784 and 805; Emp., ib., v. 12 ~ *Theog.* 800.

again, a startling new concept is seized and presented as a fresh interpretation of a well-known and authoritative Hesiodic text, and the dependence stressed by the resumption of specific motifs and allusions to well-known formulations.[1] Empedokles the revolutionary remains the disciple of the ancient *vates*.

Man's final recovery of his original divine state was (as mentioned) prefigured, succinctly, in the Hesiodic model for the myth of his fall and penance (*Theog.* vv. 803 f.), but the lustre of other Hesiodic passages contributed to that note of triumph and bliss on which the Empedoklean myth ends.[2] The 'daimon' had been man before recovering his divinity; the sublime verses depicting his rehabilitation,

> ἔνθεν ἀναβλαστοῦσι θεοὶ τιμῆισι φέριστοι
> ἀθανάτοις ἄλλοισιν ὁμέστιοι, αὐτοτράπεζοι,
> εὔφρονες, ἀνδρείων ἀχέων ἀπόκληροι, ἀτειρεῖς,

recall descriptions of Herakles' apotheosis—Herakles, the son of the highest god, who likewise, through toils, gained divinity—which Empedokles found in his Hesiod; such as

> . . . ἐν Οὐλύμπωι νιφόεντι·
> ὄλβιος, ὃς μέγα ἔργον ἐν ἀνθρώποισιν ἀνύσσας
> ναίει ἀπήμαντος καὶ ἀγήραος ἤματα πάντα[3]

and

> νῦν δ' ἤδη θεός ἐστι κακῶν δ' ἐξήλυθε πάντων
> ζώει δ' ἔνθα περ ἄλλοι 'Ολύμπια δώματ' ἔχοντες
> ἀθάνατος καὶ ἄγηρος . . .[4]

The formula ἀθάνατος καὶ ἀγήρως summarizes, in Hesiod's reports, the divinity attained by other humans;[5] Empedokles' concluding adjective, ἀτειρεῖς, varies it; as his description of the divine fellowship of hearth and table, to which the purified exile is readmitted, resumes Hesiod's beautiful verses about the fellowship of the gods and early mankind:

> ξυναὶ γὰρ τότε δαῖτες ἔσαν ξυνοὶ δὲ θόωκοι
> ἀθανάτοις τε θεοῖσι καταθνητοῖς τ' ἀνθρώποις.[6]

Once more it becomes clear that the whole of the Empedoklean myth, with its deep roots in Hesiod's poetry, and, at the same time, in Pythagorean and Parmenidean thought, is worlds apart from whatever can be

---

[1] Cf. above, p. 207.   [2] Fr. 17, vv. 3 ff. (146 f. DK).

[3] Theog. 954 f. (Paley's conjecture ἀνθρώποισιν, for ἀθανάτοισιν, removes the need for laboured explanations and yields the concise formula for Herakles' achievement).

[4] *Pap. Ox.* 2075; see now *Fragmenta Hesiodea*, ed. Merkelbach *et* West (1967), fr. 25, vv. 26 ff. and fr. 229.

[5] *Theog.* 949; *Pap. Ox.* 2075 with 2481; fr. 23(a), v. 24 (cf. v. 12) Merkelbach *et* West. Pindar's fr. 143 is of the same inspiration.

[6] Fr. 82 Rzach; fr. 1, vv. 6 f. Merkelbach *et* West.

made out with any confidence concerning the trend and substance of early Orphic speculation and mythology.[1] The hypothetical possibility[2] that one crucial scene in the pilgrimage of the Empedoklean daimon could have been modelled upon an Orphic antecedent is therewith markedly reduced in plausibility (and the alternative that Persephone presided over the incarnation becomes correspondingly probable). One point of coincidence, though, remains: namely, the rejection of ἔμψυχος βορά; a coincidence, this, with others also, and especially the Pythagoreans.

The myth, then, in the *Katharmoi* is, first, truly myth and not an allegory; it is, moreover, in the tradition of Homer and Hesiod, and developed mainly on a Pythagorean basis; it is not Orphic, and it is primarily—Empedoklean. Myth, in fact, the *Katharmoi* is as a whole; for the myth of the fall and incarnation of the daimon filled its first book, and the 'theogonies', the first part of the second; the remainder flowed from this reproduction of 'Heaven' and of history in the mirror of myth.

Its relation to the *Physika* makes another point which has been keenly discussed on a basis insufficient for a final solution. When considering various details we have time and again been led on to lines previously pursued by e.g. Bignone, Schwabl,[3] and Kahn in opposition to those who would detect irreconcilable differences between the two poems. They cannot, it is true, be fitted one into the other so as to make the fate of the individual daimon part and parcel of the world-process—for the simple but profound reason that the essence of man reaches into another dimension and is anchored in it; the dimension which finds its expression in myth. Even so, the experiences of the daimon in passing through the world of the elements are bound up with the laws by which it is governed, in a manner which makes the *Physika* the indispensable complement of the *Katharmoi*, and vice versa. The relation between the two poems may therefore be compared with that between λόγος and myth in Platonic dialogues; with the important reservation that in Empedokles there is no definite distinction between these: are Philia and Neikos myth, or not? And are the other four 'elements'? The *Physika* and *Katharmoi*, thus interconnected, make one whole covering the Empedoklean concept of the world, his 'philosophy' (to use the later term), in its totality; as the Parmenidean is covered by the two parts of his poem.[4]

---

[1] I regard the verses quoted by Proclus, *In Remp.*, ii. 388 ff. Diehl (frs. 223 and 224 Kern) as post-Empedoklean (they anyhow do not intimate the final deification of reincarnated souls) and Servius, *In Aen.* vi. 565 (fr. 295 Kern) as erroneous (for 'Orpheus' read 'Hesiod').

[2] Considered in the Detached Note VIII, below, p. 403.

[3] *Wiener Studien*, lxx (1957), 278 ff.

[4] The interrelation between Hesiod's *Erga* and *Theogony* (for which cf. e.g. W. Jaeger, *Paideia*, i (1934), pp. 98 ff.) may also here be relevant.

This in fact is the most illuminating analogy; and that, obviously, not by chance.[1] The analogy is far from complete; but the times surely have passed when, like the *Physika* and the *Katharmoi*, the two parts of Parmenides' book were supposed to be incompatible; when his account of 'Doxa'—by far the more extensive of the two—was contrasted with the 'ontology' of the first part as though it were an irrelevant *lusus ingenii*. He who has experienced the ineffable truth of Being can never forget that, seen against this background, man's life is from beginning to end in the realm of mere appearance, where nothing is stable and in the full sense existing; where therefore every word is deceptive. And yet his very knowledge of absolute Being enables Parmenides to account for this world of seeming in terms adequate to it; deceptive, that is, as this being–non-being is deceptive—and thus relatively true, and more true than those used by men uninitiated into the mystery of Being.

Thus the two parts also of Parmenides' work were complementary; but Parmenides was less favoured by the Muse than his successor Empedokles.[2] She dictated to him the myth of his journey to the gates of light, the myth which conveys the fact of his illumination; but of its content she allowed him to 'breathe short-winded accents' only: that Being is and Non-being is not . . .; she did not empower him to hold up to men an image of the ineffable in the mirror of myth.

Empedokles' prayer was answered by Kalliope. She gave him to grasp and voice, in the sweep of one all-embracing vision, the universe from smallest particles to the whole of the kosmos living and moving in unending cycles, and in it, the goal and consummation of universal life, that creature which, to him, was the prime motive of search, inspiration, and despair: in a divine world, man divine; his divinity the issue of another sphere[3].

According to an authority in these matters,[4] 'nothing is changed in the whole ideology (scil. of transmigration) by the fact that Empedokles speaks of δαίμων and not of ψυχή'. Really? In an age when the transmigration of the *psyche* was known to be Pythagorean dogma; when *psyche* was widely recognized as the live unity of consciousness, thought, and sensation essentially constituting the human person[5] and, as such

---

[1] Cf. above, p. 268.

[2] If to some reader the notion of the Muse should happen to be confined to its allegorical depravation by a later, godless age, he may correct it by turning to W. F. Otto, *Die Musen* (1956).

[3] This concept is hinted at also in the *Physika*; see Detached Note X, below, p. 406.

[4] K. Ziegler, in Pauly–Wissowa–Kroll, *RE*, xviii. 2, 1373, s.v. *Orphische Dichtung*; similarly M. P. Nilsson, *GGR* i². 745, n. 3.

[5] In Ionia: Anakreon 4; Hipponax 42; Simonides 29. 13; Bacchylides xi (xii). 48; cf. Wilamowitz, *Der Glaube der Hellenen*, i². 370 ff.; in Athens: e.g. Aisch. *Pers.* 841, *Prom.* 693; Soph. *O.T.* 64, 727, 894; *Ant.* 317, 559, etc.; Pindar, *Pyth.* iii. 61, *Nem.* ix. 32, *Isthm.* iii/iv. 53 (71b).

was held to be immortal also outside Pythagorean circles;[1] could the avoidance of this term by Empedokles have been due to a mere whim? Was it not, rather, because his concept was different from others', and particularly from the contemporary Pythagorean? What in man thinks and feels is still body and dependent on bodies; this traditional, realistic view Empedokles, as before him Parmenides, made his own[2] (incidentally anticipating and overcoming modern materialism); hence he could not term '*psyche*' what intuitively and definitely he knew to be eternal in man and all creatures and independent of any body; at the same time, its Pythagorean associations made the term unusable, with him, even to denote the centre of 'psychic' functions.[3]

Nor was his designation of that eternal substratum chosen at random.[4] 'Daimon' is that divine force, indistinct but indubitable, whose presence and impact is felt continually both within man and without. He that is alive to the trends pervading his existence and aware how small a part of it obeys his reasoning and his designs, perceives it in natural phenomena, in tragic disaster and unhoped-for salvation. And he knows when this power breathes kindly upon his life; he prays that he may be εὐδαίμων at all times; for there is a particular δαίμων determining his course, for each and for all. 'The daimonic' thus is without number; not sufficiently personalized to receive a cult, it still may be perceived individually wherever its agency is felt; as in nature and human experience, so in the after-life of the dead;[5] they too—the heroes—are 'daimones' in view of their persisting potency; and so are the gods; they, likewise, in the manifestation of their power rather than in the absoluteness of their individualities.

A divine potency stripped, for an aeon, of his divine identity: this is the Empedoklean daimon.[6]

---

[1] Heraclit. B 36, 45, 107, 117; Pind. *Ol.* ii. 70; fr. 133; Herod. ii. 123; Eur. *Suppl.* 532, and the epigram on the fallen of Potidaea.

[2] Cf. H. Fränkel, *Wege und Formen* . . .[2] (1960), pp. 31 and 173 ff.; H. Kahn, l.c., 13 ff.

[3] Pythagoras and his early followers termed 'psyche' the transmigrating and immortal element in man (Xenophanes B 7. 5 DK; cf. 'Philolaos' B 14); the same was, unavoidably, also the potency of sensation and thought. The two are neatly distinguished, as 'daimon' and 'psyche', by the Pythagorean speaker in Plutarch's *De genio Socratis* 591 e. This systematization, no doubt, is much older, but no evidence permits tracing it back to the time of Empedokles. It may rather have been derived from him.

[4] Here again I am touching upon a field to which J. Detienne has recently made a substantial contribution (*La notion de Daïmon dans le Pythagorisme ancien* (1963)); which again (cf. above, p. 266, n. 3) will be found to contain a valuable collection of material, and suggestive observations, resulting from a thoroughly different approach and purpose.

[5] Eur. *Alc.* 1003; Plato, *Crat.* 398 b.

[6] Hippolytos (i. 3. 1) alleges that Empedokles 'said much about the nature of daimons that they are very many and move about administering what happens on earth'. This isolated piece of evidence is irreconcilable with what is known about Empedokles' 'daimonology' and I incline to disbelieve it. It is actually a succinct statement of popular lore (not unrelated to Hes. *Op.* 122 ff.); it may derive from a summary of general Pythagorean

There is not really just one, 'the' ideology of 'the' transmigration of souls.[1] The distinctive features of the Empedoklean stand out when it is contrasted with, say, the Indian, which aims, by renunciation ever more complete, to set man free from the 'wheel of births' and thus to fit him for the supreme goal of annihilation; Being is felt to be Suffering; release is sought in Non-being. Compassion for human suffering is a basic motive also with Empedokles; its effect, the opposite: not abnegation is enjoined but active fulfilment of the highest potentialities at each stage, to make the next higher attainable; the highest realized in man is deity realized.

Another instructive analogy may be recalled. An Isaiah and Jeremiah condemn the contemporary cult and demand its reform with a vehemence similar to Empedokles'; but the Jew is actuated by devotion to a sovereign god whom men must strive to please, while the Greek has his eye on man and judges the gods by his ideal.

A reform of the cult; a purified notion of the gods; an interpretation of the ways of the universe; a teaching of immortality: all these are interrelated themes of Empedokles' proclamation. In his day, he preached and lived it; to posterity it remained, as his 'philosophy', in the five volumes of his poem—a mirror perpetuating, through the magic of words, his vision of the infinite Being. Its heart is in his vision of Man. Try to understand why the Greeks saw the divine in human shape; how it is that so often we are unable to tell whether an early statue represents man or god; then re-read the verses voicing Empedokles' compassion for mankind beset by strife and despair and, by contrast, his description of the peaceful happiness of a past age; feel his revulsion at the defilement of man in the portrayal of the sacrificer murdering his kin: thus you may seize a glimpse of that light in which Empedokles perceived the divinity of man and, through it, the divinity of all Being. In Homer it had stood out in unselfconscious glory; the questionings by the awakening mind dimmed it; before it was finally obscured, it shone with ultimate radiance in the manifestations of fifth-century inspiration. Empedokles, Sophokles, and Pheidias are brothers; on the watershed of the ages they caught, for the last time and for all time, the essence of Man in the mirror of myth and image.

Over against the divine completeness of the Homeric world, the profound change stands out, as in the defiant attitude of Aeschylean heroes, and indeed in the whole tension of the tragic universe, also in the clash between the Empedoklean essential man and the hating elements through which he must seek his way back to his origin. This contrast cannot be

conceptions; but it is hard to see how this doctrine could have had a place anywhere in Empedokles' poem.

[1] Cf. above, p. 264.

over-emphasized; nor ought it to be confounded with a Pauline hatred of the flesh[1] or with Indian transcendentalism. The mind which with untiring intensity scrutinized τὰ φυcικά and discerned, throughout them, the workings of divine *essentiae* was not estranged from the world of the senses; but he felt all the more deeply, within a material universe perfectly organized, the imperfection of man—whose perfect shape had been revealed to him. In the light of this revelation, all life stood out to him as sacrosanct, for he saw all creatures groping, painfully and by stages, after that perfect shape. Its consummation and eternity he saw where Homer had seen it, on that otherworldly Olympus 'where there is neither wind nor rain nor snow, but eternal radiance';[2] where the ideals for which there is no place on Earth have their refuge and permanence.[3]

The Homeric vision of the unassailable abode of the gods lent colours to the Empedoklean; it is the realm of that perfection which he remembers (as Euripides and Plato were to do) as his true home. The irreconcilable contrast between that reality which man experiences in his highest moments and the environment in which he spends his time on earth stands out—in the mythical form in which Empedokles apprehended it— in the impact of the alien force of Strife upon the denizens of that realm of perfection. The notion of this impact tallied with the authoritative teaching of Hesiod; but as conceived by Empedokles, this realm categorically could not be subject to the periodic interaction of the opposing forces which dominate the world of the elements. The fall of the daimon Νείκεϊ οὐλομένωι πίcυνοc is the mythical expression, true by its very inconcinnity, of that irreducible polarity.[4] If one cares to guess how exactly, in the myth, the Empedoklean god could have become guilty of murder, one may imagine that he accepted bloody sacrifice offered to him. The world of change could impinge upon the eternal and divine, if at all, by false worship.

The vision of man divine is foreign to our age. It gripped Empedokles; it illumined the world for him—and it gave him the certainty of his own consummation. Such inspiration is not for us to fathom. In his own age—

---

[1] Cf. above, p. 261, n. 1.

[2] *Od.* 6. 42 ff.; cf. ib. 4. 561 ff., depicting Elysium in similar hues.

[3] Hesiod, *Op.* 256; cf. Soph. *O.T.* 867.

[4] C. H. Kahn, loc. cit. 19 ff., argues, like Cornford and others, that Empedokles presented Philia-Aphrodite as the governing deity of the 'realm of the gods'. To me it seems evident that she is indeed the deity in the world of the elements which man must follow if he is to regain his divine state; but the very notion of a perfect reality (a 'realm of the gods') is controverted if it too were subjected to antithetic forces; that is, to Philia and Neikos. The essential purpose of man: is it not in transcending that reality which is determined by them? To acknowledge this central motive seems more important to me than to free Empedokles' 'system' from an inconsistency which in fact is given with that basic motive. It seems supremely symptomatic that φόνοc is the guilt of the daimon as well as of the sacrificer (fr. 3 = 115 DK, v. 3 and fr. 29 = 136 DK).

an age supremely sensitive to the distinction between man and god—no voice was raised accusing him of hybris or atheism; at Olympia, the *Katharmoi* was recited before the assembled Greeks. What we have grown blind to; what the Romans called *vates*; the θέϲπιϲ ἀοιδόϲ whom the Muse ordained, as her prophet, to sing the wonders of the world—was present in him. Those who followed Empedokles, the healer and seer, the noble-man, thinker, and poet, perceived that he was what he taught and 'revered him as was his due'. There was no 'deification' such as god-less ages, later-on, were to bestow by way of title and flattery; on him was, at the kairos of his fulfilment, that radiance which is the gods'.

The legend of the leap into Etna is true—symbolically. Man perfected sheds the alien garb and is with his own.

BOOK THREE

THE GOLD LEAVES

KG

Erde du meine Mutter und du mein Ernährer der Lufthauch
Heiliges Feuer mir Freund und du o Bruder der Bergstrom
Und mein Vater der Äther: ich sage euch allen mit Ehrfurcht
Freundlichen Dank· mit euch hab ich hienieden gelebt·
Und ich gehe zur anderen Welt euch gerne verlassend·
Lebt wohl Bruder und Freund· Vater und Mutter lebt wohl.

I. INTRODUCTION

F E W are the treatments of Greek religion which do not touch upon the 'Orphic Gold Leaves' (traditionally so-called) and many are the discussions devoted to the whole or to particular aspects of them.[1] A fresh presentation and discussion of these impressive documents may even so be worth attempting. Nine out of every ten students presumably rely upon the wording repeated, from one reprint to the next, in the *Vorsokratiker* (1 [66] B 17–21 DK[9])—which is incomplete and in several important points misleading, and even Olivieri's far superior edition[2] is now, fifty years after its appearance, capable of certain improvements.

I have examined, letter by letter, the lamellae kept in the museums at Naples and London.[3] As a result, I have been filled with admiration for the competence and thoroughness of the scholars, Italian and English, who issued the authoritative transcripts fifty or eighty years ago. Almost throughout I was able to confirm their readings; in some few places I had to take over from them what I could not confidently make out myself; the comparatively few points in which I was led to differ from them do not materially affect the resulting text. The one exception to this general statement is in the tablet containing the (wrongly so-called) 'Orphic Demeter hymn', which is unrelated to all the others. If, then, I cannot offer any startling new readings, I may at any rate feel confident about the textual basis for a new effort at interpretation.[4]

The interpretation of these texts has never, so far, overcome the effects of the accident that the first of them was published in 1835 when, in the aura of Creuzer and E. Gerhard, it was natural to hail it as a testimony to 'Orphic' mysteries. In consequence, the lamellae found at Thurii in 1879/80 and in Crete since 1893 were at once furnished, by D. Comparetti,

---

[1] For ample indications of older literature see Olivieri and Kern (cf. next note); for more recent literature see M. P. Nilsson, *Geschichte der griechischen Religion* (henceforth *GGR*) ii (1950), pp. 223 ff. Much, of course, will have to be cited in the following.

[2] *Lamellae Aureae Orphicae*, in Lietzmann's *Kleine Texte*, no. 133 (1915). O. Kern, in his *Orphicorum Fragmenta* (1922), pp. 104 ff., draws upon Olivieri; hence his text is far better than DK (except for his no. 47, p. 117); but Kern bewilders the reader by his attempt to combine the reconstruction and transcript, even of the more poorly written specimens, into one.

[3] I have not been able to do the same for those kept in Athens. Nor was this at all called for, seeing that they are available in modern editions which are completely reliable.

[4] I might have been able, aided by my excellent lens, to settle the remaining uncertainties, if the authorities in Naples and London had not felt unable to permit me to take the lamellae out of their frames and to clean them. They have apparently been kept in these frames ever since they reached the museums. During this long time, dust and fluff have settled on them, and the covering thick glass plates have turned dim and spotty. By these annoying facts the decipherment is made generally difficult and, in several problematical passages, impossible.

with the same label; which was applied unhesitatingly also to some late-comers of the same class published as recently as 1958 and 1963. The widespread and various efforts at interpretation, though by no means fruitless, were prejudiced by the general acceptance of this designation with its vast and vague implications. The protest of Wilamowitz[1] indeed found some echo in M. P. Nilsson's authoritative account,[2] but it has not so far called forth any fresh and detailed interpretation; today as eighty years ago it is being asserted and, in turn, denied, on the basis of the same traditional appraisement, that these texts are extracts from some Orphic poem, or book of poems, which one may, or may not, aim to reconstruct.[3] We had better start afresh, divesting ourselves of preconceived notions as completely as possible.

Before applying the methods of literary analysis, one ought to realize the very special, and indeed unique, character of the object. These lamellae are essentially not manuscript copies reproducing, with incidental corruption, some poetic original (even though their inscriptions may prove apt for consideration also under this aspect); what essentially they are can only emerge in the course of the investigation. But they are at any rate small gold foils, inscribed with minute letters, which have been found in graves. This fact, and the specific features of the burials to which they were added, are bound thoroughly to affect, or even to determine, the interpretation and will therefore have to be taken into consideration for each site (as far as known) separately. In accounting for the very existence of these inscribed gold leaves, the testimony of archaeology proves likewise indispensable.

Metals were, for obvious reasons, used as writing materials less frequently than stone, papyrus, wooden boards, or animal hides; but they were so used, and that by no means rarely.[4] The disc, kept at Olympia, on which Iphitos had inscribed the law of the games[5] has its extant counterpart in an inscribed fifth-century bronze disc found at Lusoi in Arkadia;[6] bronze plaques (larger than our gold leaves) inscribed with legal texts or dedications are frequent;[7] of the use of the same durable material for

---

[1] *Der Glaube der Hellenen*, ii[2] (1955), pp. 184, n. 1, and 200 f.

[2] *GGR*, ii. 225: 'In Wirklichkeit sind die Spuren spezifisch orphischer Lehren recht schwach'; none the less the texts are (ib. 224) comprised under the term 'orphische Dichtung'.

[3] e.g. Nilsson, l.l.; W. K. C. Guthrie, *Orpheus and Greek Religion*[2] (1952), p. 171; J. H. Wieten, *De tribus laminis aureis* (1915), p. 148.

[4] See L. H. Jeffery, *The Local Scripts of Archaic Greece* (1961), pp. 55 f. and the literature quoted there, p. 50, n. 6.

[5] Plut. *Lyc.* 1; Paus. v. 20. i.

[6] *I.G.* v. 2, 387 (cf. ib. 390 and 566); O. Kern, *Inscriptiones Graecae* (1913), Pl. 21: a list of πρόξενοι.

[7] Instances are pictured by Kern, l.l., Pl. 8. 10. 21; many more may be found in Arangio-Ruiz and Olivieri, *Inscriptiones Siciliae et M. Graeciae* (1925).

large public documents the tables of Heraklea form the grandest but not by any means the only instance.[1] The oldest Greek letter extant, of about 400 B.C., is written on a leaden lamella; so are many questions addressed to oracles (e.g. at Dodona); and the exciting recent find of gold plaques, inscribed in Punic and Etruscan, at Pyrgi[2] has demonstrated that even in archaic times the most precious metal would occasionally be used to commemorate dedications; for the Hellenistic age this had been known already from the Ptolemaic foundation plaques of the Osiris temple at Canopus[3] and of the Alexandrian Serapeion[4].

All these are comparable to the Gold Leaves as far as the writing material is concerned, but not as to their purport. In the latter respect, the *Defixionum Tabellae* afford an analogy—those curses inscribed on leaden tablets and deposited in graves and chthonic sanctuaries, whence they could be expected most readily to come to the notice of the infernal deities whom they invoke to harm the writers' enemies. They are found in all parts of the Greek world, from Sicily (Selinus) and Magna Graecia, Epirus and Athens, to Asia Minor and Syria; ranging in time from the 5th century B.C. to the Roman age. Lead indeed—so Sir Mortimer Wheeler reminded me—is shiny like silver when fresh; but it turns black, and is likely to have been chosen for pernicious purposes because of its resulting dark colour and dead heaviness. The analogy, then, to the Gold Leaves afforded by these tablets, though suggestive, is very much *e contrario*—the material being lead not gold; the wording, a curse not a blessing, aimed not at the dead in his grave but at some living persons above.

E contrario, essentially, is the analogy also of another set of objects which materially are so similar that they have here to be presented in some detail; for this similarity has, not unnaturally and very markedly, affected the appraisal of the 'Orphic' Gold Leaves. I shall quote some samples.

The British Museum keeps, among its ancient jewellery and next to the famous Petelia Gold Leaf (no. 3155) and that of Caecilia Secundina (3154), another one (3153) which was found at Amphipolis.[5] It is quite as small as its two fellows and has, within its height of 2·1 cm., an inscription of ten crowded lines, which begins Βαρουχ Αδωναι Ουριηλ Γαβριηλ Μιχαηλ, κτλ.; it contains the typical magic names Αβρασαξ and

---

[1] See e.g. Kern, l.l., Pl. 22 and cf. below, p. 294.

[2] Pallottino, *Archaeologia Classica*, xvi (1964), 49 ff.; G. Colonna, *Boll. d'Arte* series iv, anno l (1965), 86 ff.

[3] *Catalogue of the Jewellery Greek, Etruscan and Roman in the Departments of Antiquities, British Museum*, by F. H. Marshall (1911), no. 2111; Dittenberger, *Or. Graec. Inscr. Selectae*, no. 60.

[4] A. Rowe, in *Ann. du Service des Antiquités. . . .* (1946), Cah. 2; id., *Rylands Bull.* xxxix (1957), 509.—For a dedicatory inscription on a silver plaque see below, p. 333, n. 2.

[5] *B.M. Cat.*, p. 378.

Ἀβλαναθαναλβα, but also the Greek words παντὸς δαιμονίου ἀρϲενικοῦ καὶ θη[λυγενοῦϲ] and ends Μελχιαϲ ἅγιε θεέ, ἁγίων μόνος αἰώνων φύλαξ εἶ διὰ ἀρε[[α]]τάν.[1] A similar gold leaf was found inside the vase-shaped pendant no. 3150 (depicted on Plate LXXI, for comparison with 3155); of its inscription, only ἀγαθῆι τύχ[ηι . . .] Ιαω Αδω[ναι . . .] Σαβαωθ can still be made out, and ἐρωτῶ Ιαω at the end.

Another similar plaque was unearthed in a Roman camp in the village of Gellep on the Lower Rhine (between Düsseldorf and Duisburg); it was published by F. Siebourg with a detailed commentary and an instructive survey of similar objects.[2] This gold leaf (of 8·4 × 5·7 cm.) was extracted, tightly rolled up, from a small and oblong golden case (6·0 × 0·8 cm.) with three loops; evidently, then, it was designed to be worn, by a chain, around the neck. The Petelia leaf has been handed down with a similar case[3] (this fact occasioned obvious but none the less mistaken conclusions), and it is but one of many parallel instances. The inscription on the Gellep plaque, in crude Greek letters, is arranged, underneath the series of the seven vowels, in eight vertical columns, suggesting the shape of a naiskos and yielding puzzling sequences like ΣΕΣΕΝΓΕΝΒΑΡϕΑΡ, ϕΘΩΣΟΥΘ and ΘΛΙΑΑΒΑΥ but also, as parts of various columns, the plain names ΙΑΩ, ΣΩΘ, and ΒΗΛ. Siebourg's painstaking investigation led to the result that in fact all of these rows of letters convey the names of gods and demons Egyptian, Jewish, Phoenician, and Babylonian, which recur in the Magic Papyri and on other amulets.

For, of course, these Roman gold leaves are amulets.[4] The magic power of the letters inscribed on them—the seven vowels representative of the divine planets,[5] the names of demons and gods, the stranger the stronger —is to defend the bearer[6] against the ever-threatening attacks of evil demons, or (though here we might rather speak of 'talismans') to guaran-

---

[1] For details see the excellent commentary in the *B.M. Cat.*, p. 379. Part of a similar text is on the damaged gold strip, ib. 3152.

[2] *Bonner Jahrbücher*, ciii (1898), 123 ff. (improving on A. Gerstinger, *Wiener Studien*, viii (1886), 175–86). Much of the information given by Siebourg is repeated in *Studies in honor of E. K. Rand* (1938), pp. 245 ff. (D. M. Robinson).

[3] The close similarity will be seen on comparing Siebourg's photograph (Pl. VII. 9) with Pl. LXXI in the *B.M. Cat.*, or, better, Pl. 9 in Guthrie's book (above, p. 278, n. 3). The chain of the Petelia case is preserved.

[4] C. Bonner, *Studies in Magical Amulets* (1950) is now the outstanding work in this field (for the magical names just quoted see p. 201), but has comparatively little on the type here under discussion (and nothing on the 'Orphic' leaves). O. Jahn's classic article on the *mal'occhio* (*Ber. der Sächs. Ges., phil.-hist. Kl.* vii (1855), 28 ff.) remains the unsurpassed introduction to, and characterization of, this unattractive but important field.

[5] Cf. Bonner, p. 187.—A small gold leaf found at Vars (Angoulême) in the sixteenth century proved, when unrolled, to be inscribed with the seven vowels arranged, in ever-changing order, in seven columns; see Siebourg, l.l. 136; Cabrol, *Dict. d'Arch. Chrét.* i (1907), 1794.

[6] The θεῖοι χαρακτῆρες are invoked, together with angels and gods, to avert evil on the Damascus Gold Leaf presently to be mentioned; cf. Bonner, p. 195.

tee the favour of helpful ones, for purposes general or specific. For example:

Ad coli dolorem scribere debes *in lamina aurea* de grafio aureo infra scriptos characteres.

ΛΨΜΘΚΙΑ

ΛΨΜΘΚΙΑ

ΛΨΜΘΚΙΑ

luna prima vigensima *et laminam ipsam mittere intra tubulum aureum.*

This prescription against colic is in the *Liber de Medicamentis* compiled, probably in Gaul about A.D. 400, by one Marcellus ('Empiricus'), a good Christian and *magister officiorum* under the emperors Arcadius and Theodosius II.[1] More than a century later, in the age of Justinian, Alexander of Tralles[2] gives similar advice for averting gout: προφυλακτήριον ποδάγρας· λαβὼν πέταλον χρυσοῦν, σελήνης ληγούσης, γράφε ἐν αὐτῶι τὰ ὑποκείμενα· (the text, entirely in the style of many spells in the Magic Papyri, is too long for citation) . . . εἶτα ὅμοιον τῶι πετάλωι cωληνάριον (i.e. *tubulum aureum*) ποιήcαc κατάκλειcον καὶ φόρει περὶ τοὺς ἀcτραγάλουc.[3] In accordance with these specific prescriptions, a gold leaf extracted from a case like those from Gellep and Petelia—it was found in a grave in Picenum—is inscribed with a spell, for once in Latin, *ad oculorum dolorem*[4]; another one, from Salonika, contains a love-charm;[5] while two others, one in Madrid (from Rome) and the other from Regensburg (in a silver container), are again designed for general protection. The former[6] reads πᾶν ΙΕΡΟΝ (i.e. μιαρόν) πνεῦμα καὶ κακοποιὸν καὶ φθοροποιὸν ἀπάλ⟨λ⟩ας⟨c⟩ον ἀπὸ τῆς (the rest meaningless); the latter, as far as legible, is covered with divine names of the familiar, so-called 'Gnostic' kind, such as Φαρθιαω, Ιαβοχ, Ιαω, Cαβαωθ, etc.[7] This type of amulet—together with many others—remained in use among Christians. An often quoted sample,[8] in its golden container, came from Beirut; its inscription begins ἐξορκίζω cε ὦ Cαταναc . . . ἐπὶ τὸ [sic] ὀνόματι τοῦ κυρίου θεοῦ ζῶντος and ends Χ(ριcτο)Σ ΝΙΚΑ. Another one, from Damascus,[9] may or may not be Christian (the editor ascribes it to the fourth–sixth century); it

---

[1] Ed. G. Helmreich (1889), p. 319. 26. I owe the reference to F. Siebourg (l.l. 196); before him it was indicated by O. Jahn, l.l. 43, n. 50; who cites earlier treatments inaccessible to me.—Amulets against colic are discussed by C. Bonner, l.l. 62 ff.

[2] Ed. Puschmann (1879), ii. 583 (Siebourg, l.l.). Cf. Bonner, l.l. 75.

[3] Two pages before, Alexander suggests, for the same purpose, a gold leaf inscribed with a verse from the *Iliad* (2. 95).

[4] *Not. Scav.* (1887), 157 (Siebourg, p. 135).

[5] Siebourg, p. 134, n. 1 (in Vienna; after Wessely, *Wiener Studien*, viii (1886), 180).

[6] *I.G.* xiv. 2413, 13.   [7] Siebourg, pp. 126 and 135.

[8] Dom F. Cabrol (l.l. 259 and 1795) gives pictures and text of the gold leaf (shaped like a double page in an opened codex) and its golden container.

[9] P. Perdrizet, *Rev. Ét. Gr.* xli (1928), 73.

reads ἐπικαλοῦμαι Ιαω Μιχαηλ . . . and, after some magical signs, κύριοι ἀρχάγγελοι θεοι (? leg. θεῖοι) καὶ θιοι (leg. θεῖοι) χαρακτῆρες ἀπελάσατε πᾶν κακὸν καὶ πᾶσαν . . . ἀπὸ τῆc . . . (rest illegible).

Apart from these (and our survey has not been exhaustive), a number of silver leaves of exactly the same kind has been found (some of them in their containers), and also a few of bronze; all with inscriptions of the same type, or types, as on the golden ones.[1] The Magic Papyri and ancient authors likewise contain prescriptions for inscribing λεπίδες, or πέταλα, or λάμναι of gold, silver, bronze, lead, tin, or even papyrus, with spells for protection and furtherance in general, or for the aversion of specific illnesses and other dangers; or with love charms.[2] And all this forms only a tiny and untypical proportion of the immense mass of charms and amulets, serving the same purposes and providing the closest parallels for the—more or less abstruse—wording on the various Roman gold leaves just instanced. He who, for a while, has immersed himself in the quagmire of late-Roman superstition will therefore, on studying these, find himself on familiar ground. On turning to the texts on the so-called 'Orphic' Gold Leaves he must feel transferred into a different world.[3]

This difference will be accentuated by the following investigation. However, it stands out only on comparing the relevant inscriptions; these apart (which, of course, is to leave aside the essential *differentia specifica*) the two types are indistinguishable. There is therefore a strong and legitimate urge to seek for some connection between them.[4] But such is hard indeed to establish.

Disregarding, for the moment, the immense difference of purpose and quality (both types indeed sometimes accompanied the dead into their graves; even so, the one is designed for the living, the other for the dead),

---

[1] e.g. the silver foil found at Badenweiler (A. Wiedemann, *Bonner Jahrb.* lxxix (1885), 215 ff.; Siebourg, ib. ciii (1898), 135) with the familiar Caβαώθ, Cηcενγεμβαρφαραγγης, Aβλαναθαναλβα, etc., and, still in Greek letters, the request cερουατε αβ ομνι περεκουλω; another one, from Beroea, with its silver 'tubular container', was published by D. M. Robinson (*Studies in honor of E. K. Rand* (1938), pp. 245 ff., with plate), who indicates further samples, both silver and bronze (ib. 246, n. 1). It is inscribed with the usual kind of magic names—Aβλαναθαναλβα recurring again—whose bearers are to protect one Euphiletos.

[2] F. Siebourg, l.l., pp. 136 ff. quotes eight such prescriptions; see esp. his no. 8 = *Pap. Gr. Mag.* iv. 258, vol. i, p. 80 Pr.; cf. ib. p. 158, line 2706 (λεπίδα ἀργυρᾶν as phylakterion); no. 12 = *P.G.M.* x. 26, vol. ii, p. 53 Pr. (λάμνα χρυcᾶ ἢ ἀργυρᾶ); no. 13 = *P.G.M.* vii. 580, vol. ii, p. 26 Pr. (phylakterion πρὸς δαίμονας, πρὸς φαντάςματα, πρὸς πᾶςαν νόcον καὶ πάθος, ἐπιγραφόμενον ἐπὶ χρυcέου πετάλου ἢ ἀργυρέου ἢ καςcιτερινοῦ ἢ εἰς ἱερατικὸν χάρτην). Marcellus (Siebourg, p. 138, no. 17) prescribes a *lamella aurea*, inscribed ΟΡΥΩ ΟΥΡΩΔΗ, against eye-soreness, but (ib., no. 18) a *lamina argentea* for gout; *P.G.M.* i 190 offers a choice between a lead *petalon* and 'hieratic paper'.

[3] K. Wessely alone, to the best of my knowledge, has felt able to lump them together (*Wiener Studien*, viii (1886), 178, on the Petelia tablet) 'vielleicht der schönste Text auf einem Goldblättchen, und ganz verständlich in 12 Hexametern abgefaßt'. This valiant understatement is illustrated by the subsequent (faulty) rendering of the Beirut amulet.

[4] This was rightly stressed by F. H. Marshall in the Introduction to the *B.M. Catalogue* (p. xlvii). It will be hard to get beyond his concise and thoughtful discussion.

there is, first, the vast span of time separating the 'Orphic' from the 'magical' gold leaves; the former coming from the fourth (and some from the third) century B.C., the latter from the third and the following centuries A.D.[1]—with one startling exception; which is, in fact, invalid.

A 'very small' gold leaf,[2] which even in the latest discussion (1958) is said to come from the fourth century B.C., was found after the First World War in the course of building operations at Brindisi.[3] Its inscription—damaged on the lower right hand side—is as follows:

ΧΕΝΤΕΜΜΑ

ΤΕΦΡΕΙΧΕΝ

ΤΕΦΡΑΙϹ[.

ΒΑΥ[.....

The first editor, D. Comparetti, was able to interpret this as Greek; others as Ausonian, Sicel, pre-Greek, pre-Indo-European, or 'unknown'. This guess-work came to an end when A. Scherer[4] confirmed what Olivieri had suggested: this is a magic formula and, in fact, Egyptian, in part if not throughout.[5] Egyptian magic at Brindisi, in the fourth century B.C.! One may wonder that this implication did not stir any doubts about the alleged date of the amulet; and indeed, one glance at the shape of its letters ought long ago to have convinced some thoughtful beholder that it must come, rather, from the fourth century A.D. The report of its discovery shows that the early dating rested on no archaeological evidence—no stratigraphy, and no conjoined, early find—but on the astonishing assertion of the first editor that the writing must antedate the introduction, in South Italy, of the Ionic alphabet.[6] Such is the authority of an *editio princeps*.

The long gap of time separating the 'Orphic' from the 'magic' gold leaves thus remains unbridged; and while the former have at least one

[1] One or two of the latter have been ascribed to 'cent. ii–iii A.D.'.

[2] No exact measurements have been given.

[3] Comparetti, *Not. Scav.* (1923), 207 (with facsimile); Olivieri, *Riv. Ind.-Gr.-It.* vii (1923), 215 (which I know only through the brief reports of P. Kretschmer and P. Vetter, *Glotta*, xiv (1925), 203 and xv (1926), 9); J. Whatmough, *Pre-Ital. Dial.* ii (1933), p. 362; id., *The Foundations of Roman Italy* (1937), p. 353, n. 2; U. Schmoll, *Die vorgriechischen Sprachen Siziliens*, (1958), pp. 44 and 127, fig. 4.

[4] In a contribution (p. 44, n. 2) to the thesis of U. Schmoll.

[5] Scherer compared a magic formula against podagra contained in *Hippiatr.*, p. 69, c. 440 (no. 213 in R. Heim, *Incantamenta magica* (= Suppl. xix, (1893, of *Jahrb. f. klass. Philol.*) p. 536 χεντιμα τεφηκεν τεφρα γλυκαινε, and suggested that the first word is Egyptian ḫntj 'the first'; to which Schmoll added an explanation, likewise on an Egyptian basis, of the following two syllables; (ḫntj ỉmntjw 'Totengott'). My colleague E. A. E. Reymond agreed with the former suggestion ('perhaps ḫntj m mꜥ "the first in the place" ') and would trace τεφ to dj'·f 'may he give'.

[6] What could possibly have occasioned Comparetti's assertion? Was it the fact that the inscription does not happen to contain the letters η and ω?

late successor in the tablet of Caecilia Secundina (which is contemporary
with the first large crop of 'magic' gold amulets and adapted to them),
there are no pre-Roman 'magic' gold leaves, let alone any that are contemporary with, or earlier than, the 'Orphic' ones. They would, in
theory, form the proper counterpart of the leaden *defixiones*, and seeing
how vast is the number of these also in the earlier period, the total lack of
evidence for the existence of this counterpart would be inexplicable, if
gold amulets of the type in question had existed in the classical age of
Greece.[1]

They are product and symptom of the oriental superstition which
engulfed the collapsing Roman Empire; but among the endless variety
of older oriental magical implements—from Babylonia, Syria, Palestine,
Egypt—I have failed to find any of this particular type; while the
'Orphic' ones are—as stated—materially identical. Are we, then, to
reverse the argument and assume that they afforded the model for the
later amulets?[2] F. H. Marshall inclined to this view;[2] but this, too, has its
difficulties. The practitioners of late-Roman witchcraft were so different
a caste, and rooted in traditions so different, from those Greeks to whose
mentality the 'Orphic' leaves witness . . . And even the material identity
of the earlier and later leaves may be deceptive. All of the former are
golden; but we have already noted that the same spells as on the late
gold leaves may be written on silver, bronze, lead, or tin; on amulets of
different kinds; and indeed on papyrus or clay or leather.[3] The cheaper
materials, naturally, were used predominantly, and, though they are
more perishable, a great number of them remain.[4] Writing the spells on
metals would ensure their durability and increase their presumed efficacy;
no 'Orphic' models were needed to suggest this variety of the standard
material.[5] The wearers of these various types of amulets were perfectly
conscious of their basic identity.[6]

[1] P. Perdrizet rightly urges (*Rev. Ét. Gr.*, xli (1928), 75) that Theophrastus would not have
presented his Deisidaimon without a gold amulet, if such had been in use at the time.

[2] Cf. above, p. 282, n. 4.

[3] Above, p. 282, n. 2. Cf. also *P.G.M.* ii. 126. 15 (gold); ib. 172. 279 (silver); ib. 168. 179
(lead; also ib. 170. 233); ib. 169. 189 (clay); ib. 175. 361 (leather); etc. Papyrus (χάρτης) is
quoted too often for citation.

[4] For some samples see *P.G.M.* ii, pp. 177 ff.

[5] Add that the late amulets were by no means standardized as to form and size, as the
older Gold Leaves appear to have been. e.g. an amulet from Beirut, now in the Louvre,
consists of a thin silver ribbon, 37·5 cm. long and only 3 cm. high, with 120 lines of writing
(Bonner, l.l. 101). Still larger is one from Thessaly (*I.G.* ix. 2, 232) designed to protect a house.
And there are those many gold trinkets and pendants of various shapes (e.g. pyramids,
bullae, lunulae) which serve the same purpose and have similar inscriptions to those found on
cut stones, on papyri, and on the (comparatively rare) metal foils. The latter are therefore
reasonably regarded as a plain alternative for the customary papyrus and leather leaves.

[6] Artemidorus (*Onirocrit.* v. 26, p. 307. 11 Pack) tells of a man who, in a dream, ἔδοξε τοῦ
Cαράπιδος τὸ ὄνομα ἐγγεγραμμένον λεπίδι χαλκῆι περὶ τὸν τράχηλον δεδέσθαι ὥσπερ σκυτίδα
(a leather amulet). He dreamt, of course, what he and his fellows were in the habit of doing.

The old Gold Leaves thus appear to be *sui generis*. If one feels that some antecedent has to be posited, he is reduced to guessing. Mahometans to this day wear extracts from the Koran, written on parchment, as amulets; sometimes elaborately decorated and kept in richly adorned containers.[1] From Roman times onward, Jews and Christians used their Holy Books in the same way, and the phylacteries (*thephillin*) worn by the former attest a similar usage even earlier. The British Museum has some small Phoenician gold cylinders which, as W. H. Marshall suggested,[2] may well, like their Roman counterparts, have contained amulets. These are not themselves preserved, but others are. They are not gold leaves inscribed with sacred texts, like the Greek, but long metal strips, or plaques, with images and symbols of Egyptian gods or, alternatively, with representations like those on Babylonian seal cylinders.[3] It would be hazardous on this material to base a theory of the dependence upon oriental prototypes of the Greek Gold Leaves.

Perhaps the adoption of this type of grave-goods ought rather to be viewed against the background of national Greek traditions. We noted above that, in ancient Greece, writing on metal lamellae, even gold ones, was by no means unusual. The adoption of gold in particular for objects deposited in graves is unlikely to have been a mere ostentation of riches.[4] The bright and imperishable metal no doubt was chosen to symbolize the perpetuity of life, just as its opposite, the dark and heavy lead, was used

---

Cf. also the instances where alternatives are prescribed, as e.g. *P.G.M.* ii, p. 129. 24 and above, p. 282, n. 2.

[1] E. A. Wallis Budge, *Amulets and Superstitions* (1930), p. 34, Pl. II, depicts a seventeenth-century container, made of silver and inscribed with Koran verses which, with its chain, may well be compared with the Petelia plaque.

[2] *B.M Cat.* xlviii, with reference to the Phoenician gold pendants nos. 1556 ff. (of the seventh–sixth century B.C., from graves at Tharros, Sardinia). They are not in fact identical in shape with the Roman amulet cases, but are none the less likely to have served the same purpose.

[3] E. A. Wallis Budge, l.l. 250 ff.; D. Harden, *The Phoenicians* (1962), p. 212 with Pls. 90 and 95.

[4] This is likely to apply also to the ornamented thin gold bands and plaques which adorned the bodies of some Greeks of the geometric period and the caskets containing their ashes; see D. Ohly, *Griechische Goldbleche des 8. Jahrhunderts v. Chr.* (1953), esp. pp. 68 ff. It was not customary with Greeks—as it was in the ancient Orient—to add gold in profusion to burials; it is therefore legitimate to seek for some specific reason, and preferably a religious one, where any is found. It is probably due to mere chance that, at the very time when the 'Orphic' Gold Leaves accompanied the dead buried at Thurii, gold foils carrying the image of the local 'Great Goddess' (Hellenized as Aphrodite, or Demeter, or Artemis) were put into the rich graves of the ruling class in the Hellenized cities of the Russian Black Sea coast (for this symbol, and the addition of enormous gold treasures, were traditional there); and yet it is remarkable that these graves are, like the Thurian, grand tumuli, such as were not erected in contemporary Greece but had been customary in the Mycenaean age. It is tempting to assume that, where this custom is found in Greece, it was brought from the North (Trebenishte stands out, chronologically, as intermediate). Even so, it is hard to envisage a direct, material connection between Pantikapaion and Thurii; more likely the mediator, for the latter, was Homer.

to promote destruction and death. It does not, in fact, seem unreasonable to assume that the 'Orphic' lamellae were consciously devised as a positive counterpart to the traditional *defixiones*. This new departure implies a new attitude to death and after-life.

Tens of thousands of Greek graves have been investigated, but gold leaves of this type have been found in four places only; their use, then, was anything but common. These four places, however—Thurii and (perhaps) Petelia, Pharsalos, and Eleutherna—are widely distant, and yet the lamellae found at them are most closely interrelated and witness to a very specific persuasion; they must then have emanated from some specific circle, or group, of people who, at those distant places, adhered to beliefs and customs of their own. And, finally, this closely defined group did not flourish only during that comparatively early and short time to which all (or almost all) of their relics have to be ascribed; its persistence right down to the later age of the Roman Empire is attested by one isolated lamella.

Who were these people? Their relics, so slender and yet so characteristic, may tell. In attempting the interpretation of these relics, the material just surveyed may serve as a useful foil, even though it has proved insufficient to settle the question of their origin.

LIST OF GOLD LEAVES

GROUP A

1. Ἔρχομαι ἐκ καθαρῶν ... (Thurii): p. 4 Olivieri; no. 18 DK; no. 32c Kern: below, p. 300 ff.

2. ,, ,, ...(,,): p. 9 Ol.; no. 19 DK; no. 32d Kern: below, p. 302 ff.

3. ,, ,, ...(,,): p. 10 Ol.;÷DK; no. 32e Kern: below, p. 304 ff.

4. Ἀλλα' ὁποταμ ψυγή ...(,,): p. 16 Ol.; no. 20 DK; no. 32f Kern: below, p. 328 ff.

5. Ἔρχεται ἐκ καθαρῶν ... (Rome): p. 18 Ol.; no. 19a DK; no. 32g Kern: below, p. 333 ff.

GROUP B

1. Εὑρήceιc δ' Ἀιδαο ... (Petelia): p. 12 Ol.; no. 17 DK; no. 32a Kern: below, p. 358 ff.

2. ,, [÷] ,, ... (Pharsalos): *Ephem. Arch.* (1950), 99: below, p. 360 ff.

3–8. Δίψαι αὗος ἐγώ ... (Eleutherna): cf. p. 14 Ol.; no. 17a DK; no. 32b Kern: below, p. 362 ff.

GROUP C

Πρωτόγονος τᾶι ματρί ... (Thurii): p. 22 Ol.; no. 21 DK; no. 47 Kern: below, p. 344 ff.

II. PREFATORY TO GROUPS A AND C

OF the lamellae contained in the first group, A1–3 are closely interrelated, A4 differs thoroughly but centres on the same theme, and A5 is a degenerate descendant about six hundred years more recent than the rest. Again, A1–3 were found in one and the same tumulus, A4 in a neighbouring one together with C, which is inscribed with a completely different and enigmatic text; A5, finally, was found, towards the end of the last century, in Rome, near S. Paolo fuori le Mura.

The river Crati, the ancient Krathis, flows into the Gulf of Taranto at the northern end of what is now called Calabria. About 7 km. from its mouth it is joined by a tributary from the north, the Coscile; ancient maps, however, show that in the sixteenth century the two rivers reached the sea separately. Their beds are, or were, constantly changing, and the coastline being pushed forward owing to enormous masses of sediment carried down, creating marshes which, annually inundated, were a breeding ground of malaria. All this is being decisively changed by the admirable work of amelioration which has been carried out, for more than thirty years, by the 'Bonifica'; and all this is of immediate relevance to my subject, for if the Crati is the ancient Krathis, then the old name of the Coscile was Sybaris, and the city of that name—the grandest of Magna Graecia until its destruction in 510 B.C.—lies buried under these swamps, and also its successor, Thurii, founded by Perikles in 444/3. This conclusion had been drawn and generally adopted for a very long time; it had been disputed occasionally, but was finally proved correct when U. Zanotti-Bianco discovered, in the Parco del Cavallo about 4 km. from the mouth of the Crati, some remains of a heroon dedicated to Kleandridas—a decisive discovery, made in 1932, but, owing to the iniquities of public life, not published until 1962;[1] decisive because Kleandridas, the father of the famous Spartan Gylippos,[2] was one of the founders of Thurii and a commander of its army.[3] Zanotti-Bianco found, at the same place, also some fragments of archaic art antedating the foundation of Thurii by a century; they can only be evidence for Sybaris.

---

[1] U. Zanotti-Bianco and P. Zancani Montuoro, 'La campagna archeologica del 1932 nella piana del Crati', in *Atti e Memorie della Società Magna Grecia*, N.S. iii–iv (1960–1), Roma, 1962. I treasure a copy given me by the venerated author shortly before his lamented death. It contains also an invaluable map of the site.

[2] Thuc. vi. 63.

[3] For the evidence see e.g. E. Ciaceri, *Storia della Magna Grecia*, ii (1928), pp. 346 f. and 377.

We are happily concerned no further with the location of Sybaris. It was, however, the first serious attempt at ascertaining it which led to the discovery of the five lamellae. This enterprise was, in its decisive earlier stage, placed in the capable hands of Francesco Saverio Cavallari (1809–96).[1] He had been, in his early years, together with his father, among the assistants of that great begetter of Sicilian archaeological studies, the Duke of Serradifalco (1783–1863), with whom he explored the sites most famous to this day (recovering, among other things, seven metopes of the temples E and F at Selinus). In his later years he became director of the museum in Siracusa; his assistant and, finally, successor was P. Orsi . . . Cavallari, then, early in 1879, surveyed the whole region from various vantage points and soon concentrated upon a somewhat elevated plateau south of the Crati and c. 4 km. above its junction with the Coscile. It formed part of the property of a Baron Compagno; a large medieval mansion called Favella della Corte lies roughly in its centre. This terrain, the 'Caccia di Favella', Cavallari found studded with graves, and since on it he collected many sherds and pieces of terracotta but nothing of archaic style, he drew the correct conclusion that he had found the necropolis of Thurii (though it was wrong to assume that the city itself lay on this plateau—a conclusion of which Cavallari was innocent).[2] Among the graves he noticed four large, round elevations which the local population called *timponi*—preserving the Greek word τύμβος. These he decided to explore, and it is in two of them that the Gold Leaves were found.

He attacked first the northernmost tumulus, called Timpone Paladino. It yielded three pieces of 'vasi finissimi con pitture del V secolo'[3] and blocks which he held originally to have covered the bottom of a grave. He concluded that the site had been disturbed by earlier diggings and transferred his efforts to the Timpone Grande at the opposite end of the necropolis, less than 2 km. to the south-west.

I wish I could convey to the reader my admiration for the carefulness, competence, and accomplished technique with which this excavation was carried out. One has to read the day-by-day report of the foreman[4] to feel

---

[1] His reports, and those of his successors, were currently published, in *Not. Scav.* (1879), 49 ff., 77 ff., 156 ff., and ib. (1880), 68 ff., 152 ff.; they are embodied, with different pagination, in the *Atti . . . dei Lincei*, Ser. iii, *Memorie* iii (1879), 215, 243, 294, 328, and v (1880), 11, 316, 400. Cavallari produced a most instructive map (*Memorie* v. 20, Pl. V) and careful drawings of the Timpone Grande (ib. Pl. VI; our Plate 25).

[2] Accepting the tradition (Strabo 263) that the Crotoniates directed the waters of the Crati over the ruins of Sybaris, Cavallari (*Memorie* v (1880), 18) concluded that Thurii could not have been built on exactly the same ground. He assumed its place to have been built slightly to the west and below the necropolis, around a fountain ('del fico') which he identified with the spring Thuria (Strabo ib.).

[3] *Memorie* iii (1879), 217. On the next page the same are ascribed to '4th–5th century'.

[4] Ibid., 218 and 243 ff.

that Cavallari was fully master of what we regard as the modern strati-
graphical method,[1] and to share in the excitement of those working under
him, laboriously and systematically, towards an outstanding discovery.
Cavallari was not always himself present, for he went out to explore other
parts of the terrain, but his firm direction is felt at every point.

With the number of workmen growing from fourteen to twice that
figure, and occasionally more, the work took forty days, for the Timpone
Grande measured, at the time, 28 m. in diameter and was still almost
$9\frac{1}{2}$ m. high.[2] It was cut into from the top and one side and was found to
contain eight main strata, each of them consisting of a layer of ashes and
carbon topped by earth (more than $\frac{1}{2}$ m. thick), with clay (or, near the
top, pebbles) above it.[3] Cavallari drew the conclusion that the person
buried had been honoured with repeated sacrifices above his grave, and
that on these occasions the height of the tumulus was increased by adding
layers of the same kind as the original one; the clay and pebbles in particular being designed to prevent rain water from penetrating into the
structure. Sherds of vases with marks of burning testified to libations, and
the find, in one of the interior layers, of plant roots could suggest that the
growing tumulus was each time decorated with flowers. The dead man
inside it must have been worshipped as a hero.[4]

His tomb was finally found at the bottom and in the centre of the *timpone*. It was a plain, but massive, oblong structure of large tufa blocks.
Its side walls were only 30 cm. high but nearly $\frac{1}{2}$ m. thick, enclosing
a space 1 m. wide and 2·30 m. long, and covered by three ponderous
slabs higher at the centre (26·5 cm.) than at the edges (18 cm.), effecting
an outline similar to that of a temple. A few small black vases were found
outside it.

On 23 March 1879, a Sunday, in the presence of the 'egregio ispettore
avv. Tocci', the 'sindaco' of near-by Corigliano, and 'grande quantità di
spettatori', the tomb was opened. No water had penetrated into it and
it had remained unaffected by the enormous weight of the earth heaped
upon it.[5] The ground inside its low walls was found to have been somewhat

---

[1] General Pitt-Rivers worked with similar precision, about the same time, at Cranford
Lodge; nor was Schliemann at Troy (from 1875 onward) unmindful of stratigraphy.

[2] The measurements are from the drawing (*Memorie* v, Pl. VI, after p. 20). Zanotti-Bianco
gives a photograph of its appearance in 1932 (l.l., Parte i, Pl. IIa).

[3] The drawing (*Memorie* v, Pl. VI) specifies the presence of carbon and ashes in only four
of the eight 'calotte'; but according to *Memorie* iii. 218 'agli strati di argilla quasi costanta-
mente si sopraonevano gli strati di carbone, ove si rinvenivano i frammenti di vasi
bruciati'.

[4] The absence of funerary gifts agrees with the observance, at Lokri, of the laws of Zaleukos
(above, p. 159); the periodic worship, with one of the laws of Charondas as cited by Stobaeus
(*Flor.* 44. 40; iv. 2, 24, p. 153. 10 Hense ". . . τῆι τῶν κατ᾽ ἔτος ὡραίων ἐπιφοραῖ").

[5] Cavallari suggested that originally the tumulus would have been still much bigger and
its sides steeper; he considered a diameter of 40 m. and a height of 14 m. possible (thus
I noted from *Not. Scav.* (1879), 259; I cannot identify the passage in the *Memorie*).

deepened. The coffin (whose heavy bronze locks were found) had been placed in this depression; the dead man whose skeleton lay stretched out in it was facing east. By his chest were two silver medallions decorated with female heads 'con capelli radianti ed ornamenti al collo';[1] as well as a few tiny pieces of gold which probably had decorated his garment. Apart from two small wooden boxes ornamented with inlaid palmettes the grave contained no offerings; but close by the head of the skeleton lay an inscribed gold lamella, folded nine times over, with another one, folded 'like an envelope', wrapped into it:[2] our text C with A4 inside it. When unrolled, A4 measured 54 × 29 mm., and C 812 × 3 mm.[3] A pyre had been built over the coffin, libations were poured over it; when it had burned down, the remains of the hero were left untouched, but a snow-white sheet was spread over them (the 'bianchissimo lenzuolo' was found intact in 1879, but disintegrated when touched by the excavators). Thereafter the three large tufa slabs which had stood upright beside the pyre were lowered to cover the tomb and earth was heaped over it in a wide circle and topped with clay, to form the basis of the ever-growing Timpone Grande and the place for the cult of the hero who, from its centre, had started on the way to Persephone.

After ascertaining that the earth around the grave contained no further relics, Cavallari proceeded to explore the Timpone Piccolo, 265 m. west of the Timpone Grande. This was still 5 m. high, with a circumference of 52 m. Digging into it at four points, through 'terra vegetale', a rotted skeleton was soon found at each of them. There followed, at greater depth, the same alternation of clay, earth, and carbon as at the Timpone Grande, but not with the same regularity. Attempts from other points produced further remains of bodies deposited haphazard rather than buried, but no real tomb such as the colour of the earth, mixed with carbon and ashes, led the diggers to expect. Cavallari concluded that prolonged investigations were required for which there was no time, and hence broke off the campaign on 9 April. Apparently the malaria season was approaching. It was a great pity, for the Timpone Piccolo was still to yield three gold leaves—but not to Cavallari. The campaign was resumed in December 1879[4] and rather summarily reported;[5] the direction was in the hands of an 'ingegnere L. Fulvio' who himself, at a crucial moment, was 'partito per Napoli'. The result is sadly plain. The task was evidently far more complex than at the Timpone Grande, and neither the progress of the work nor the stratigraphy of the tumulus become clear

[1] Could they have represented the city-goddess of Thurii (in a similar style to the 'Arethusa' on Syracusan coins), or perhaps Aphrodite or even Persephone?

[2] *Memorie* iii. 328.

[3] The indications concerning these measurements have been inverted by Olivieri, pp. 15 and 22.   [4] *Memorie* v. 316 (*Not. Scav.* (1880), 68).

[5] *Memorie* v. 400 ff. (*Not. Scav.* (1880), 152 ff.).

from the report. I shall try to summarize what can be elicited from this inferior evidence; it involves skating over certain contradictions in it.

The Timpone Piccolo consisted of plain earth in its upper part (for about 4 m.), and along its outer sides (at least 0·75 m.). In this layer a considerable number of persons (more than ten) had been carelessly interred. This fact is apparently unrelated to the original purpose of the tumulus, which seems subsequently to have been used for the easy disposal of bodies in some emergency, such as war or epidemic.[1] Below the layer of earth were 'two strata, clearly distinct; the upper one of clay, the lower one of gravel mixed with sand and lime; each measured about 60 cm.'[2] Within this lower, twofold part three tombs similar to that in the Timpone Grande were found. It is exasperating that their relative places within the tumulus are not made clear; of the third grave there is no description at all. The other two, however, are said to have been identical in structure. The tufa framework was like that in the Timpone Grande, and so were, roughly speaking, the measurements, except that the side walls, and hence the interior of the chambers, were much higher: namely 1 m. and 1·22 m. respectively. The interior walls were painted white, with (in the second grave) a yellow socle below. The bottom of the tomb found first was level with the natural ground; the second, so we are assured, lay considerably deeper and must therefore have been earlier;[3] about the position of the third we are told nothing. The implications are important for the relative dates of the burials. The one found first contained the lamella A1, which both from its content and appearance—it is by far the most carefully written of all the Thurii plaques and, in fact, of all yet known—one would incline to regard as the earliest, while the writing on the one from the second tomb (our A3) is, to say it in one word, a scandal. If Cavallari had directed this excavation, we would know which of the three tombs lay in the centre of the timpone and, in consequence, was the original one.[4] As it is, the assumption that it was the one found first may be supported by the fact that its bottom was level with the natural ground, and one may suggest that the grave which was found deep in the natural soil need not have been the oldest, for it could

[1] However imperfectly known, the woeful history of Thurii can suggest many such occasions. One may think of the wars of Pyrrhos, or even of Hannibal; Comparetti (*Laminette Orfiche* (1910), p. 3, note) provides some support for the latter suggestion. In the near-by 'Timpone 3' (on which below) was found a small silver cylinder containing two rolled-up silver lamellae without inscriptions (cf. *Memorie* v. 401, note). Analogies for this exist, according to Comparetti, only in Carthaginian dominions (Malta, Sardinia—and Rome (booty?)).

[2] *Memorie* v. 402.—This statement makes it difficult, or even impossible, to accept the suggestion (ib. 401) that the whole Timpone Piccolo was the product of several small tumuli growing into one; a suggestion which otherwise could derive some support from *Il.* 23. 245 ff.

[3] The report adds some puzzling details about the stratification; what is said about the second tomb (p. 403, second para.) is not easily reconciled with the statement about the first (p. 402, first para.).

[4] With the reservation mentioned in the last note but one.

conceivably have been built by tunnelling from the edge of the existing timpone. The question of the succession of the three graves, then, remains ambiguous.

Anyhow, each of the three tombs contained the remains of one person in the same position as in the Timpone Grande, with a gold lamella by his right hand—and nothing else; except that in the four corners of the first tomb were small hollows filled with ashes of bones and plants, tokens of funeral sacrifices. Only the lamella found last (our A2) was folded over once, the other two being quite uncreased, in marked contrast with those from the Timpone Grande. Another difference—and it is an important one—is inferred, safely enough, from the silence of the report. It has not a word about any traces of a coffin,[1] nor any mention of carbon or ashes inside the graves. The dead in the Timpone Piccolo, then, in contrast to the one in the Timpone Grande, were inhumed not cremated.[2] This indeed would be the normal and natural procedure with this kind of sepulchre, for after cremation the remaining bones were usually collected and buried in a vessel or box; for a burial like that in the Timpone Grande, with the corpse cremated in its coffin and left, thus, in the tomb I know of no parallel.

This brings us to the wider question of the purpose and significance of these timponi. Tumuli are anything but the rule among Greeks; so that those seeking to illustrate Homeric usage[3] have to point to some few, untypical instances—Drachmani in Phokis, Aphidna, and the southern slope of the Athenian Akropolis—none of which is really like those at Thurii. For one thing, none has a solid, built, grave inside. One will think, rather, of the Etruscan circular graves and their later, Roman successors, such as the mausolea of Augustus and Hadrian. Their outward appearance is certainly similar; but there is the fundamental difference that these grandiose tumuli contained vast and luxurious habitations for the dead, and not, like those at Thurii, low and plain tombs. The same difference prevails with regard to the Mycenaean tholoi (which besides, like the Etruscan, were sunk into the earth), the enormous tumuli in Lydia and Phrygia (Gordion; Alyattes), and the luxurious kurgans in South Russia. The closest similarity, after all, will be felt to prevail with regard to Homeric burials; what happened at the burials of Patroklos and Hektor must have been very similar to the funeral ceremony at the Timpone Grande.

Even there, essential differences remain. There was no cremation at

---

[1] The word *cassa sepolcrale* is indeed used twice (*Memorie* v. 408, n. 1, and 403, below middle), but it is clear from the context that each time the grave-chamber is meant.

[2] The traces of ashes found outside the tombs are naturally taken as evidence for sacrifices burned at the funeral ceremonies, or later.

[3] H. L. Lorimer, *Homer and the Monuments* (1950), p. 106, n. 5; similarly E. Mylonas in his contribution to Wace and Stubbings, *A Companion to Homer*.

the Timpone Piccolo; and no solid tomb in the Homeric tumuli. Most characteristic, finally, is the absence, from the Thurii graves, of any kind of votive gifts and equipment for an after-life of the hero in his grave. Commemorative feasts and sacrifices continued to be carried out above it; none the less, it seemed destined to be only the starting-point for the journey to the other world, the journey being indicated by the one precious gift accompanying the dead—the Gold Leaves. Their study may elucidate the origin and purpose of these sepulchres which have so many similarities with traditions Greek and non-Greek, and yet are, as a whole, unique.

I have left to the last the question of the chronology of the lamellae, which is as important as it is difficult. With the means at present available it can be solved only within a fairly wide margin.

The problem is not indeed very difficult with regard to the late descendant of this tradition, the Caecilia Secundina tablet[1] (A5). Its engraver wrote 'by means of a blunt point',[2] as though with a stilus on a wax tablet. The cursive but clear writing may be traced to the middle of the third century A.D. in view of its slant to the right, the special form of the combination of AI and EI, and the long downward prolongation of I and P. The whole style reminds one of certain hands in the Heroninos Correspondence of about A.D. 260;[3] a specific similarity is in the writing of Εὔκλεες Εὐβουλεῦ on the tablet and the final greeting in one letter (no. 259) of this correspondence, pictured also by W. Schubart.[4] In dating the bulk of the older tablets one has to rely on (a) archaeological evidence and (b) the style of the lettering; both are less telling than could be wished, but the general adoption, on all of the plaques, of Ionian H and Ω point to a date in the fourth century, or, at any rate, not early in the 5th; they are, then, indeed products of Thurii and not of Sybaris.

The lettering on the various lamellae from Thurii shows very wide differences, from the careful and regular, firm shapes on A1 to the thin and spidery on A4, and the careless scribble on A3 and C. These, however, are varieties in the quality of the workmanship; the underlying style is the same in all. They are all angular letters with no attempt at ornamentation (such as the 'apices' on Ptolemaic letters from c. 250 B.C. onward); the sigma in particular is always 'broken' and never round; the cross-bar of A straight; and all letters are, in principle, of equal height. The difference of quality may, but need not, be indicative of different times of origin. The assumption, in particular, that A1 is older than the

---

[1] See Plate 28, or W. K. C. Guthrie, *Orpheus and Greek Religion*[2] (1952), Pl. 10.

[2] *B.M. Cat.*, p. 380, no. 3154; ascribing the tablet to the '2nd–3rd cent. A.D.'

[3] See *Papiri Fiorentini*, vol. ii; esp. no. 259 (p. 226); also no. 153 (p. 110); 218 (p. 186); 238 (p. 207).

[4] W. Schubart, *Palaeographie* (1925), p. 150, Fig. 115.

others is, as we saw, not necessarily excluded by the stratigraphy of the Timpone Piccolo; but even if this uncertain assumption is made, there is so far nothing to tell how great a difference of time would correspond with the differences of quality.

To fix, or approximate, the date of the writing one will look around for comparable material. One would wish, first of all, to compare the lettering on these lamellae with that on similar plaques; but such are scarce, and the few that can be pointed out are themselves no more securely dated than those from Thurii; besides, the exceedingly small size of the letters on the Gold Leaves may be expected to affect their shapes. In this respect, only the lettering on coins affords a parallel, and an expert in this field might indeed be able to draw useful conclusions from it; to my limited knowledge, though, the letters on coins seem too standardized to afford any specific chronological indication. An Archaic bronze plaque from Policastro[1] and two more, of the sixth and fifth centuries, from Mycenae and Thetonium (Thessaly),[2] at any rate convey, by the thoroughly different style of their lettering, a warning against ascribing similarly early dates to our lamellae. A fifth-century bronze disc found at Lusoi in Arcadia[3] reinforces this warning, but a bronze plaque found at the same place,[4] though much larger, is definitely comparable. Unfortunately, however, the experts are divided about its date, ascribing it to the fourth or third century; and it is anyhow obvious that the date which we are seeking to fix must lie within these limits.[5] More helpful is a comparison with the 'oldest Greek letter', that small leaden plaque (7×4 cm.) found near Athens, which A. Wilhelm dated to the first half of the fourth or even to the end of the fifth century.[6] Its regular, upright, and angular letters compare in particular with those on our plaque A1, while their more rigid shapes and wider spacing—even nearer to stone inscriptions than in A1—suggest a slightly later date for the latter. Of the *Defixionum tabellae*, likewise on lead, those inscribed in the fourth century[7] are generally comparable, but from the poor photographs available I am unable to extract a date more specific; besides, an uncertain factor is implied by the possibility of local variations. The accounts, inscribed on smallish bronze plaques, of the temple of Zeus at Epizephyrian Lokri date themselves to the time of Pyrrhos' campaigns in Italy.[8] Their regular, upright letters, at a first sight, convey a similar impression as our A1, but

---

[1] Arangio-Ruiz and Olivieri, *Inscriptiones Siciliae et M. Graeciae* (1925), p. 47; cf. below, p. 355, n 4.

[2] O. Kern, *Inscriptiones Graecae* (1913), Pls. 8 and 10.

[3] Ib., Pl. 21a; cf. A. Wilhelm, *Oesterr. Jh.* iv (1901), 74.

[4] Kern, ib., Pl. 21b (a better photograph is in *I.G.* v. 2, 390).

[5] I leave out of consideration Kern, ib., Pl. 22a, c, d.

[6] Kern, ib., Pl. 26c; for a full discussion see A. Wilhelm in *Oester. Jh.* vii (1904), 94 ff.

[7] A. Wilhelm, ib. 105 ff.

[8] A. de Franciscis, *Klearchos*, iii (1961), 17 ff.; ib. iv (1962), 66 ff.

a closer inspection reveals characteristics indicative of a later date. The various Lokrian letters differ in size; omikron in particular shrinking into a small circle; sigma sometimes shows a curved back, alpha a broken middle bar; the second downward hasta of pi vies in size with the first; the left bars of delta and lambda join the right descenders below the top. These plaques, then, are more recent than those from Thurii. At the other extreme, the earliest possible date for the latter would be about the end of the fifth century, both in view of the general character of the site (connected with Thurii and not with Sybaris), and of the use, on the plaques, of the Ionian alphabet[1] (which, however, to judge from the coins, was used at Thurii from the first).

Inscriptions on stone suggest the same. They will often be found comparable when hailing from the fourth century; not so when from the fifth (the earlier half, at any rate), but the style continues, on them, into the third century. Of letters written with pen and ink, finally, only the oldest extant are comparable; that is, the Timotheus papyrus, the 'Curse of Artemisia', and the Elephantine marriage-contract of 311 B.C.[2] These parallels lead us back to the second half of the fourth century, and probably early rather than late in it—if indeed the comparison is considered valid. It gains support from the dramatic recent discovery, near Salonika, of a commentary on the Orphic Theogony,[3] the very elegant, angular writing of which most experts (not all) would put even earlier than the Timotheus; it may be compared with the plaque A1.

This survey has shown that letters small and great, on metal, stone, and papyrus, do agree in their general style and its development, but also that this style of writing (no doubt maintained by school-teaching) remained constant throughout a long time. The lamellae show no trace of cursive writing; their generally angular writing and in particular the absence of 'sigma lunatum', rounded ϵ and ω, are a definite indication, at any rate, of a fourth-century date; nor would one choose to move too near the end of that century, seeing that the place of the 'broken sigma' is not taken, on any one of the Thurii plaques, by that alternative form which consists of one simple angle, for this form occurs on the Artemisia papyrus and on the lamella from Pharsalus which, as we shall see, is safely dated to c. 350–320 B.C. Our comparisons of necessity applied predominantly to the regular writing on A1 and suggested a date for this plaque before rather than after 350 B.C. If the analogy of Attic inscriptions is valid, a date not later than the middle of the fourth century is suggested for A1

[1] A. Olivieri indeed suspected the presence, on plaque C, of some Chalkidian letters; but this almost certainly was a mistake; see below, p. 345.

[2] W. Schubart, *Papyri Graecae Berolinenses* (1911), Pls. 1 and 2; id., *Palaeographie* (1925), pp. 98 ff. and Figs. 64 f.; C. H. Roberts, *Greek Literary Hands* (1955), Pl. 1.

[3] See S. G. Kapsomenos in *Gnomon* xxxv (1963), 222 f.; *Bull. Amer. Soc. Papyrol.* ii (1964), 3 ff., and *Archaeol. Deltion*, xix (1964), 17 f.

also by the fact that, on it alone, the ending -ου is expressed by a mere omikron.

It is not a certain conclusion. Even on coins of Agathokles we still find ΑΓΑΘΟΚΛΕΟΣ and, generally, we do not know how long before 350 B.C. this style of writing prevailed and how long after 350 engravers may have retained it; nor can we tell what distance in time—if any—is indicated by the various coarser forms of writing on the other tablets. The palaeographical argument thus seems to place them all somewhere between *c.* 400 and 320 B.C., with some preference for the middle of the century, and, for A1, perhaps earlier. A more precise and reliable date would be welcome, for it does matter whether we connect the Gold Leaves with the great days of Thurii about the beginning of the century, or with its political decline after the débâcle at Laos;[1] with its brief respite under the shield of Alexander the Molossian, or with its subsequent sufferings at the hands of the Lucanians and the Spartan Kleonymos. It remains to consider the archaeological evidence.

As previously noted, Cavallari reports that in the Timpone Paladino he found pieces of Attic red-figured 'vasi finissimi' of the fifth or fourth century.[2] On the other hand, a small, third timpone near the Timpone Piccolo, which 'had lost its shape owing to agricultural work', and which was cursorily attacked by workmen who could be spared from the excavation of the latter, yielded remains of inferior, non-Attic pottery—'Lucanian and Apulian'—and also fragments of a cup with palmettes not painted but stamped:[3] this suggests a date about 300 B.C. or even later; especially since here also the (? Punic) silver cylinder and lamellae were found. These indications, then, point to the very beginning and to the end of the fourth century—which, at different places of the necropolis, would be perfectly possible. Zanotti-Bianco in 1932 tested the upper layers of both Timpone Grande and Timpone Piccolo and recovered a few pieces of pottery and terracotta; they were apparently too poor for a definition more specific than his 'il tutto databile al IV sec. a. C.'.[4]

Inside the Timpone Grande, Cavallari found, again, pieces of red-figured pottery which he ascribed, at first, to the fourth or fifth century, but later, with detailed argumentation, to the 5th.[5] Outside the tomb lay black-varnished ware (which cannot be ascribed a specific date; it may have been held suitable for libations at funeral sacrifices, for it recurred frequently in both timponi). A decisive indication of the date could probably be gained from the silver medallions found inside the tomb; but

---

[1] The finest Thurian coins date from this period, suggesting that defeat and subservience to barbarians were not synonymous with economic and cultural decline.

[2] *Memorie* iii. 217 f. At the same place pottery 'with black figures on white ground' was found. This description need not indicate Attic lekythoi; it would fit a much later Italic ware equally well.

[3] *Memorie* v. 401.   [4] L.l. (see p. 287, n. 1) 10.   [5] *Memorie* iii. 218; ib. v. 18.

no reproduction of them exists.[1] If Cavallari was right about the Attic vases at its top, the timpone must have stood high about 400 B.C., but it is hard to feel sure, and no other pointer is known.

The Timpone Piccolo yielded many sherds, and also two small heads of terracotta, of which one gains no clear idea.[2] The surprise is the report of the find, outside the third and last tomb, of a plate 'of Lucanian make', decorated in the centre with the figure, red on black, of 'a winged, hermaphroditic genius with a wreath in his hand'—which suggests, rather, a typical Apulian Eros; it is asserted that, from its style, it could not antedate the third century.[3] If this is correct, the Timpone Piccolo— or, at the very least, this grave in it (with lamella A2—which is not the worst of the three) has to be dated later than 300 B.C.

The uncertainty of these indications could be overcome if the finds could be examined by some expert. They were all transferred, carefully numbered, to the municipio di Corregliano Calabro, where F. Lenormant saw them in 1880;[4] but this, unfortunately, is the last that has been heard of them. On the basis of the reports one would have to conclude that the Timpone Grande is earlier than the Timpone Piccolo; although both the quality of the writing on the plaques found in it and their content would have led one to expect the opposite. One need hardly, though, with Cavallari, place it as early as 400 B.C., seeing that his judgement about the age of the vase-sherds found in it may have been over-optimistic and that he himself at first considered a fourth-century date for them. As to the Timpone Piccolo, one would love to see the 'Lucanian' plate found in it before assigning it a third-century date; which seems inadmissible, at any rate, for the writing on the lamella A1. Until further information, the most acceptable conclusion may be that it was erected not later than the middle of the 4th century over the tomb which contained the lamella A1 and that the other two tombs were added considerably later and perhaps as late as the turn of the century.[5]

On this uncertain argument the latest Thurian Gold Leaves would be roughly contemporary with those large Apulian amphorae which exhibit a fairly standardized picture of the Netherworld, with Pluton and Kore in a central aedicula and, around it, various mythical figures; for these vases were produced, according to an authoritative view,[6] about 340–310 B.C. They can thus illustrate notions of Hades current at the time in the neighbouring Tarentine province (even though their repertoire is Attic),

---

[1] Cf. above, p. 290, n. 1.   [2] *Memorie* iii. 294; ib. v. 401.   [3] *Memorie* v. 403.

[4] F. Lenormant, *La Grande Grèce*, i (1881), p. 323. Lenormant (ib. 322) assumes that the Timpone Grande was erected 'around 400 B.C.'; but this part of his admirable work appears to be wholly based on the *Notizie degli Scavi* of 1879 rather than on his personal judgement.

[5] M. P. Nilsson thus would, to an extent, be justified in discussing the lamellae in the Hellenistic section of his *GGR* (ii. 223 ff.).

[6] R. Pagenstecher, as quoted by Nilsson, *GGR* i². 824, n. 5.

but beyond this they contribute little or nothing towards the interpretation and dating of the Gold Leaves[1].

The gold plaques were, immediately after they had been discovered, examined by Professor Barnabei, whose excellent transcripts and facsimiles were used for the original publication (with comments added by D. Comparetti)[2] and by all successors, except Kern, even after the publication, in 1915, of Olivieri's excellent edition, in which some troublesome errors of Barnabei's were corrected, and important and difficult passages (especially in C) for the first time deciphered. In the preceding section I have confessed how little these predecessors left for me to revise. The main task still open is that of an interpretation no longer prejudiced by the comment in the *editio princeps*, and its aftermath. This task is difficult and, in places, all but impossible because the texts inscribed on the Thurii lamellae are unique; some essential points of detail cannot be satisfactorily settled in the absence of instructive parallels, such as Pharsalos and Crete have recently provided for the long-known plaque B1 (Petelia). There is a glimmer of a possibility of unearthing helpful further evidence also for the A-series. Cavallari alleged the existence of a great number of further timponi to the east and north-east of the Caccia di Favella and thereby fired the imagination, of e.g., V. Macchioro and E. Ciaceri[3] with the spectre of a 'gigantic Orphic necropolis' awaiting exploration. This spectre vanished when U. Zanotti-Bianco[4] showed, by his tests in 1932, that these timponi are in fact sand dunes. Even so, the fact remains that the real timponi stand in an extensive necropolis. Its numerous graves no doubt have been ransacked by the local people in search of antiquities ever since (at least) 1880;[5] even so, they deserve that thorough exploration which was eloquently advocated by F. Lenormant in 1881[6] and by D. Comparetti in 1910.[7] This could be expected to settle the questions of chronology with which we have had to grapple. With luck it might even lead to the discovery of further gold leaves; for these were produced *en masse* (as will soon be shown), and where could they have gone if not into these graves? I have told, in the epilogue of this book, how my hope of conducting this exploration was finally dashed; may others be luckier.

[1] See Detached Note XII below, p. 411.
[2] *Memorie* v. 403 ff.; for lamella C (published later) see below, p. 344.—It was an injustice that Barnabei's excellent work was currently ascribed to Comparetti (e.g. by G. Murray and F. Lenormant); his small facsimiles (*Memorie* . . . v. Pl. 3, p. 412) give a more adequate general impression of the leaves than do photographs.
[3] See next note.
[4] L.l. 7 ff.; with a florilegium of the hopeful utterances of the scholars referred to in the text above (he could have added F. Lenormant, l.l. 319 f.).
[5] F. Lenormant, l.l. 319: 'Les paysans y font souvent des recherches et en retirent des vases à figures rouges, pour la plupart de l'époque de la décadence.' This statement is worth remembering also with reference to the dating of the timponi.
[6] l.l. 327.   [7] *Laminette orfiche,* at the end of the Preface.

III. TABLETS A1–A5

(a) A1–3, TEXT

T H E three texts from the Timpone Piccolo, A1, A2, A3, are represented below in transcript and reconstruction. The latter does not aim to restore a perfect wording—the grave problems inherent in this attempt will emerge in the commentary—but to present in our mode of writing the wording at which the engravers appear to have aimed, even where its style or metre appear to be at fault. It will at once be seen that none of them succeeded in producing a fully satisfactory text. Even A1—by far the most careful—omits and interchanges letters and wrongly repeats whole phrases; A2 is lazy and careless, and A3 has produced nonsense which, without the other two, would in many places baffle any attempt at interpretation. The details will become clear on studying the transcript, with the notes added to it, and comparing the reconstruction, the photographs,[1] and Olivieri's excellent facsimiles. Except in a few flagrant instances, the differences between reconstruction and original will not be found stressed in the latter; they can be seen by looking at the left page.

[1] Plates 26 and 27. When consulting the photograph of A3, it must be remembered that this plaque (paper-thin, like all of them) has been inscribed on both sides. Hence the letters pressed through from the back form, together with the actual writing, a bewildering crisscross of lines on either side.

A1. *Transcript*

Napoli, Museo Nazionale 111625.   Plate 26*a*
Timpone Piccolo.   51 mm. × 36 mm.
Not. Scav. (1880), 155 = *Memorie* v. 403; *I.G.* xiv. 641.1. *G.D.I.* ii. 1654; G. Murray
ap. J. Harrison, *Proleg.*² (1908), p. 667 (cf. 585); D. Comparetti, *Laminette orfiche*
(1910), no. 1; A. Olivieri, *Lamellae aureae orphicae* (1915), p. 4, facsim. p. 26, A;
O. Kern, *Orphic. fragm.* (1922), p. 106, no. 32c; Diels–Kranz, *Vorsokr.* 9, i (1960),
p. 16, no. 18a.

l. 1	ΕΡΧΟΜΑΙΕΚΚΟΘΑΡΟΚΟΘΑΡΑΧΘΟΝΙΒΑ	v. 1
2	ΣΙΛΕΙΑΕΥΚΛΗΣΕΥΒΟΛΕΥΣΤΕΚΑΙΑ	2
3	ΘΑΝΑΤΟΙΘΕΟΙΑΛΛΟΙΚΑΙΓΑΡΕΓΩΝ	3
4	ΥΜΩΝΓΕΝΟΣΟΛΒΙΟΝΕΥΧΟΜΑΙ	
5	ΕΙΜΕΝΑΛΑΜΕΜΟΡΑΕΔΑΜΑΣΕ	4
6	ΚΑΙΑΘΑΝΑΤΟΙΘΕΟΙΑΛΛΟΙΚΑΙΑΣ	(2)
7	ΣΤΕΡΟΒΛΗΤΑΚΕΡΑΥΝΟΝΚΥΚΛΟ	5
8	ΔΕΞΕΠΤΑΝΒΑΡΥΠΕΝΘΕΟΣΑΡΓΑ	
9	ΛΕΟΙΟΙΜΕΡΤΟΔΕΠΕΒΑΝΣΤΕΦΑ	6
10	ΝΟΠΟΣΙΚΑΡΠΑΛΙΜΟΙΣΙΔΕΣΣΠΟΙ	7
11	ΝΑΣΔΕΥΠΟΚΟΛΠΟΝΕΔΥΝΧΘΟΝΙ	
12	ΑΣΒΑΣΙΛΕΙΑΣΙΜΕΡΤΟΔΕΠΕΒΑΝ	(6)
13	ΣΤΕΜΑΝΟΠΟΣΙΚΑΡΠΑΣΙΜΟΙ	
14	ΣΙΟΛΒΙΕΚΑΙΜΑΚΑΡΙΣΤΕΘΕΟΣΔΕ	8
15	ΣΗΙΑΝΤΙΒΡΟΤΟΙΟΕΡΙΦΟΣΕΣΓΑΛΕΠΕΤΟ	9
16	Ν	

l. 7 ΚΥΚΛΟ, ll. 9 et 12 ΙΜΕΡΤΟ, ll. 9–10 ΣΤΕΦΑΝΟ, cf. l. 13: *o* pro *ου* (fort item l. 2
ΕΥΒΟΛΕΥΣ)   N.B. ll. 6–7 ΑΣΣΤΕΡ- et l. 10 ΔΕΣΣΠΟΙΝ-   Scriptio
plena ll. 5 et 11, sed apostrophus ll. 8, 9, 14, 15

AI. *Reconstruction*

1   Ἔρχομαι ἐκ κοθαρῶν κοθαρά, χθονίων βασίλεια,

2   Εὐκλῆς Εὐβουλεύς τε καὶ ἀθάνατοι θεοὶ ἄλλοι·

3   καὶ γὰρ ἐγὼν ὑμῶν γένος ὄλβιον εὔχομαι εἶμεν.

4   ἀλλά με μοῖρ᾽ ἐδάμασσε [καὶ ἀθάνατοι θεοὶ ἄλλοι]
              καὶ ἀστεροβλῆτα κεραυνῶι.

5   κύκλου δ᾽ ἐξέπταν βαρυπενθέος ἀργαλέοιο,

6   ἱμερτοῦ δ᾽ ἐπέβαν στεφάνου ποσὶ καρπαλίμοισι,

7   δεσποίνας δ᾽ ὑπὸ κόλπον ἔδυν χθονίας βασιλείας.
    [ἱμερτοῦ δ᾽ ἀπέβαν στεμάνου ποσὶ καρπασίμοισι]

8   "ὄλβιε καὶ μακαριστέ, θεὸς δ᾽ ἔσηι ἀντὶ βροτοῖο."

9   ἔριφος ἐς γάλ᾽ ἔπετον.

Dittographias v. 4 (ex 2) et post v. 7 (ex 6) del. Kaibel   v. 4 κεραυνῶι G.Z. (κεραυνῶ
Dieterich): ΚΕΡΑΥΝΟΝ (cf. l. 1 ΚΟΘΑΡΟ pro -ων)

A2. *Transcript*

Napoli, Museo Nazionale 111623.   Plate 26*b*
Timpone Piccolo.   47 mm. × 28 mm.
I.G. xiv. 641. 2; Comparetti, no. 2; Olivieri B; 32d Kern; 19 DK.

l. 1	ΕΡΧΟΜΑΕΚΑΡΩΙΣΧΟΝ	v. 1
2	ΚΑΘΑΡΑΧΟΝΙΩΝΒΑΣΙΛΗΕΙ	
3	ΕΥΚΛΕΚΑΙΕΥΒΟΥΛΕΥΚΑΙΘΕΟΙΔΑΙΜΟΝ̣	2
4	ΕΑΛΛΟΙΚΑΙΓΡΑΕΓΩΝΥΜΩΓΕΝΟΕΥΧΟΜΑ	3
5	ΙΟΛΒΙΟΙΕΙΝΑΙΠΟΝΑΙΔΑΝΤΑΠΕΙΓΕΣΕΙ	4
6	ΕΡΓΩΙΕΝΕΚΑΟΥΤΙΔΙΚΑΩΝ (vac.)	
7	ΕΙΤΕΜΕΜΟΡΑΕΔΑΜΑΣΑΤΟ	5
8	ΕΙΤΕΑΣΤΕΡΟΠΗΤΙΚΡΑΥΝΩᴺ	
9	ΝΥΝΔΙΚΕΤΙΙΚΩΠΑΙΑΓΝΗΦΕΣΕ	6
10	ΦΟΝΕΑΝΩΣΜΕΙΠΡΟΦΩΠΕΙΨΗ	7
11	ΕΔΡΑΙΣΕΣΕΥΑ Γ ΕΙ Ω Ι	

Literae parum aequales, lineis tenuibus et passim duplicibus exaratae. Scriba piger unam saepe hastam plurium loco incisit, ut e.g. Ι pro Ν (ll. 1, 5, 6, 11) vel Ρ (l. 9) evaderet; praeterea literas invertit (ll. 2 et 4) et passim omisit vel corrupit
l. 1: ultimas in hac linea literas ΣΧΟΝ fuisse putabam, quarum ultima valde dilatata est; post quam quae ΩΝ legerunt priores, ea lineae non literae esse mihi videbantur l. 2: nihil ante ΚΑΘ (falsa DK in app.) l. 3: literae partim cum l. 2 literis mergunt; lamella in fine huius lineae mutila l. 7: post ΜΟ, lit. Ι ruga hausta esse potest l. 8: lit. Ν in fine supra lineam, spatio in linea minime deficiente

A2. *Reconstruction*

1   Ἔρχομαι ἐκ καθαρῶν καθαρά, χθονίων βαςίλεια,

2   Εὖκλε καὶ Εὐβουλεῦ καὶ θεοὶ δαίμονες ἄλλοι·

3   καὶ γὰρ ἐγὼν ὑμῶν γένος εὔχομαι ὄλβιον εἶναι·

4   ποινὰν δ᾽ ἀνταπέτεις᾽ ἔργων ἔνεκ᾽ οὔτι δικαίων·

5   εἴτε με μοῖρ᾽ ἐδάμασς᾽ εἴτ᾽ ἀστεροπῆτι κεραυνῶ(ν).

6   νῦν δ᾽ ἱκέτης ἥκω παρ᾽ ἁγνὴν Φερσεφόνειαν

7   ὥς με πρόφρων πέμψηι ἕδρας ἐς εὐαγέων.

v. 1: in ΚΑ⟨θα⟩ΡΩΙΣ (lam.) ΙΣ pro Ν incisum; dein ΧΟΝ(?ΩΝ) falso q.s. Χ⟨θ⟩
ΟΝΙΩΝ praeripit   v. 6: παρ᾽ ἀγανὴν cj. Diels   v. 7: pentametrum (leg. ἕδρᾰς) **agn.**
Kaibel

A3. *Transcript*

Napoli, Museo Nazionale 111624. Plate 27
Timpone Piccolo. 46 mm. × 25 mm.
I.G. xiv. 641. 3; Comparetti, no. 3; Olivieri C; 32e Kern (not in DK).

Recto 1 ΕΡΧΟΜΑΙΕΚΑΘΑΡΩΚΑΘΑ 1

2 ΟΒΑΣΙΛΥΡΡΥΚΛΕΥΑΚΑΕΥ 2

3 ΒΟΛΕΥΚΑΙΘΕΟΙΟΣΟΙΔΜΟ

4 ΝΕΣΑΜΟΚΑΙΓΑΡΕΩΥ 3

5 ΙΓΕΝΟΣΕΥΧΟΜΑΕΝΑ

6 ΟΛΒΙΟΠΟΙΝΑΝΝΑΤΑΠ 4

7 ΕΤΕΕΡΓΩΟΤΙΔΙΚ

Verso 1 ΑΩΝ ΕΤΜΕΜΟΙΡΑ 5

2 ΕΤΕΡΟΠΗΤΙΚΗΚΕΡΑ

3 ΥΝΟ ΝΥΝΔΕΚΗΚΩ 6

4 ΙΙΚΩΠΑΡΑΦΣΕΦ

5 ΩΣΛΛΛΕΡΟΦΠΕ ΨΕᴹ 7

6 ΕΔΡΑΣΕΣΕΥΠΩ

Opisthographon est, literis in utraque parte incisis in utraque eminentibus; 'la qual cosa ne rende oltramente difficile la lettura' (Barnabei, *Memorie* v. 404). In lamina aversa siquae literae in fronte incisae maiores extabant, scalptor spatia vacua reliquit.

Literas punctis notatas in lin. 2, 6, 7 (recto) et 3 et 4 (verso) distinguere non potui; itaque Olivierii in his lectiones expressi.

Recto: l. 1: ΕΡ (non ΕΙΡ: quod Ι legebant, versae lamellae lineola est) l. 3: ΔΜΟ vel ΔΛΛΟ, et similiter l. 4: ΑΜΟ vel ΑΛΛΟ l. 5: prima lineola non est ligatura (pro ΜΩΝ) sed scalptoris pigritiae monumentum; pro Γ legi potest Π (cf. verso 6) vel ΓΙ

Verso: l. 4: ΙΙ pro Η (i.e. ΗΚΩ bis; ΙΚΕΤΗΣ om. l. 5: ΛΛΛ pro Μ l. 6: Π Ω: voluit ΓΩ (pro ΓΕΩΝ)

A3. *Reconstruction*

1   Ἔρχομαι ἐκ καθαρῶν καθα⟨ρά, χθ⟩ο⟨νίων⟩ βασίλεια

2   Εὖκλε [υα] καὶ Εὐβουλεῦ καὶ θεοὶ ὅσοι δαίμονες ἄλλοι·

3   καὶ γὰρ ἐγὼν ὑμῶν γένος εὔχομαι ⟨ὄλβιον⟩ εἶναι· [ὄλβιον]

4   ποινὰν δ' ἀνταπέτεισ' ἔργων ⟨ἔνεκ'⟩ οὔτι δικαίων·

5   εἴτε με μοῖρ' ⟨ἐδάμασσ'⟩ εἴτ' ΕΡΟΠΗΤΙ [ΚΗ] ΚΕΡΑΥΝΟ.

6   νῦν δ' ⟨ἱ⟩κ⟨έτης⟩ ἥκω παρ' ἁ⟨γνὴν⟩ Φερσεφ⟨όνειαν⟩

7   ὥς με πρόφρων πέμψηι ἕδρας ἐς εὐαγέων.

v. 2 : ὅcοι e scalptoris errato ; vid. comment.   v. 3 : ὄλβιον transposui ; cf. A2   v. 4 ⟨ἔνεκ'⟩ ut A2 ; ⟨ὑπὲρ⟩ melius fuit   v. 6 ἁ⟨γνὴν⟩ cf. A2 ; item de v. 7

(b) COMMENTARY ON A1, A2, A3

A3 represents the same wording as A2, with minor differences and many faults. Corruptions apart, A1 agrees with them in the first three verses, and its fourth verse corresponds with the fifth in A2–3. The preceding (fourth) verse in A2–3 does not recur in A1, and after their coincidence in the next verse (A1, v. 4 ~ A2–3, v. 5), the two versions diverge, the last four verses, and concluding formula, of A1 being totally different, in wording and substance, from the two verses (vv. 6–7) on which A2–3 ends. There is a rationale to these differences; as will be seen.

Style and language are predominantly Homeric; not so the vocalization ποινάν in A2–3, v. 4, and, perhaps, the acc. plur. ἕδρας with (Doric) ᾰ ib., v. 7. A1 alone writes κοθαρός (as *Tab. Heracl.* i. 103) and has the widespread but non-Homeric infinitive εἶμεν. These features, together with the spelling o for the ending -ō of the gen. sing.[1] and the doubling of c before consonant in ἀccτερόεντος and δεccποίνας—a frequent feature in all dialects[2]—suggest that A1 is older than the other two tablets, and the superior quality of the writing may point to the same conclusion. We noted in the introductory chapter[3] that the archaeological evidence, imperfectly known as it is, does not indeed bear out this conclusion but may be reconciled with it. The verses are spoken to Persephone by the soul, ψυχή; hence the feminine gender in v. 1; only the last verse in A1 (not in A2–3) is addressed to the soul.

V. 1. 'Out of the pure I come, pure Queen of them below':

I could wish that this often-quoted rendering appeared here for the last time, never to be heard again. It reduces the noble and profound original to a platitudinous ditty and can serve, if anything, only to show how much harm can be done by a misplaced comma.[4] The speaker does not set out to tell the goddess from where he has journeyed,[5] addressing her with a most unsuitable adjective (for Persephone is ἀγνή indeed but not καθαρά); but he states with all possible emphasis that he himself is 'pure'. 'Here I stand before you', so the soul says, 'καθαρὰ ἐκ καθαρῶν'; the comma then has to be put after, and not before, καθαρά.[6] According to Plato,[7] the soul fit to see the ideas has similarly to be ἀγαθὴ καὶ ἐξ ἀγαθῶν and ἀρίστη τε καὶ ἐξ ἀρίστων. The same mode of expression is

---

[1] Perhaps also in ΕΥΒΟΛΕΥ, v. 2.

[2] Schwyzer, *Griech. Gram.* i. 216.

[3] Above, p. 297.

[4] E. Rohde, *Psyche*, ii. 218, n. 1 stressed this in vain.

[5] Contrast *Il.* 24. 287 οἴκαδ' ἱκέσθαι ἄψ ἐκ δυσμενέων ἀνδρῶν.

[6] This was done already by Kaibel, followed by Rohde and others, opposed by Comparetti (originally) and others; see the summary by Olivieri ad loc. (only part of the literature quoted by him is accessible to me).

[7] Pl. *Phaedr.* 246 a ff., 249 e, 274 a.

frequent elsewhere, particularly in tragedy;[1] e.g. Soph. *Phil.* 324 κακίϲτου κἀκ κακῶν, 874 εὐγενὴϲ κἀξ εὐγενῶν; Aristoph. *Ran.* 731 πονηροῖϲ κἀξ πονηρῶν. The connecting particle is not *de rigueur*: Soph. *Ant.* 471 ὠμὸν ἐξ ὠμοῦ πατρόϲ; [Eur.] *Rhes.* 185 ἐξ ἀφθίτων ἄφθιτοι, 388 ἐϲθλὸϲ ἐϲθλοῦ παῖϲ; Theognis 185 κακὴν κακοῦ; Andokides, *De Myst.* 109 ἀγαθοὶ ἐξ ἀγαθῶν.[2] Basically this type of expression enhances the qualities indicated by describing them as inherited; even so, it is not, perhaps, necessary to assume—though it is possible—that those buried with these lamellae belonged to family-cult communities.[3] At any rate, they called themselves καθαροί, and their expectation of Persephone's favour centred on their consciousness of being 'pure'. This rendering in fact blurs the special nuance of the adjective. The state of ritual and mental 'purity' required of the worshipper who appears before the gods is normally indicated by the adjectives ὅϲιοϲ, ἁγνόϲ, or εὐαγήϲ; Orphics in particular, according to Plato,[4] described themselves as ὅϲιοι (and this is an argument against rather than for describing the present texts as 'Orphic'). The special nuance of the adjective καθαρόϲ is in denoting purity in some particular respect and from some particular pollution; one may be καθαρὸϲ τὰϲ χεῖραϲ, or τὸ ϲῶμα, or ἀπὸ φόνου, or ϲυνουϲίαϲ, or παρανόμων;[5] but for its use, as here, to denote a perfect and general state of, say, 'holiness' I cannot find any true parallel.[6] The believers, then, for whom these tablets were made, conceived of man as liable to some specific and pernicious pollution which they, the καθαροὶ ἐκ καθαρῶν, had overcome. What they held this pollution to be, it is too early to consider, but the very use of the word καθαρόϲ suggests that they sought purification by ritual means; though not necessarily only by these. One is reminded of the teaching of 'those who instituted the τελεταί', which, according to Plato,[7] condemned the uninitiated to lie, after death, 'in mire', while the initiated and 'cleansed' (κεκαθαρμένοι) will be with the gods; likewise, the

---

[1] E. Bruhn, *Anhang zu . . . Sophokles* (1899), p. 159, no. 263; also Lobeck, *Aias* (1866), p. 389, *ad* v. 1304.

[2] ΚΟΘΑΡΟ in A1, taken by itself, would have to be transliterated κοθαροῦ; but the normal gen. plur. in this type of phrase (sing. only in specific references), together with -ΩΙ in A2, -Ω in A3, and -ΩΝ in A5 (Caecilia Secundina), is indicative of a scribal slip in A1. In view of this evidence, P. Friedländer's defence of the gen. sing. as analogous to ἐν καθαρῶι (*Arch. Anz.* (1935), 30) cannot carry conviction; the less so when the connotation of the latter phrase is remembered.

[3] This, according to Olivieri, l.l., was the view of H. Alline. A suggestive analogy is in Plato, *Leg.* vi. 759 c (. . . ἐκ καθαρευουϲῶν οἰκήϲεων, κτλ.).					[4] *Rep.* 363 c–d.

[5] Ἁγνόϲ and ὅϲιοϲ are used in the same way, but also, quite currently, absolutely to denote a general state rather than the effect of a specific 'purification'; as καθαρόϲ hardly ever is. The difference is clear from the derived nouns: ἁγνεία and ὁϲία (or ὁϲιότηϲ) denote a general state of 'purity' or 'piety'; κάθαρϲιϲ and καθαρότηϲ do not.

[6] Pausanias viii. 44. 5 mentions gods popularly called οἱ Καθαροί at Pallantion in Arkadia; who they were, and why thus called, he professes himself unable to tell. Much later, and down to the Middle Ages, Christian sects did thus describe themselves. The analogy is suggestive indeed but not immediately applicable.					[7] *Phaed.* 69 c.

terminology of 'purifiers' (καθαρταί) like Epimenides and of mysteries like the Eleusinian[1] comes to the mind. Nor can we fail to remember that (and the reason why) Empedokles' poem was given the title Καθαρμοί,[2] and we may note that Alexander Polyhistor, in summarizing a Pythagorean doctrine,[3] reports it to have contrasted the lot of souls καθαραί and ἀκάθαρτοι. This specific terminology thus seems to point to a specific region—with which we have become familiar—within the wide fields of concern with 'pollution' and 'purity';[4] and indeed the source just cited explicitly states the identity of the taboos observed by 'those who carry out purifying rites in temples' and by the Pythagoreans.[5]

Unlike most of the rest, this first verse succeeds in expressing a dominant and profound sentiment with originality and in a perfect form; here is no Homeric tag, such as abound in what follows. This is true also of the address to the goddess as χθονίων βασίλεια. No goddess is thus styled in Homer and Hesiod; a possible model may be found in Hesiodic references to Ζεὺς βασιλεύς (rather than in the different application of the word βασίλεια to Hera in the insignificant 'Homeric' Hymn xv);[6] however this may be, this verse is one beautiful and organic whole.[7]

V. 2, at once, is below this level. In A1 it runs smoothly enough, but there is no justification, in the context of the lamella, for the two nominatives which are prefixed, in lieu of vocatives,[8] to the Homeric formula[9] which is its latter half. It would have been so easy to write Εὔκλεες Εὐβουλεῦ τε; as indeed was done, six centuries later, for Caecilia Secundina (A5); why

---

[1] Adopted e.g. by Plato, *Phaed.*, l.l.; also ib. 80 d 6 and e 2, 81 b 1 and d 2, 82 c 1, 83 e 2, etc.

[2] '(Empedocles οἴεται . . .) θείους δὲ καὶ τοὺς μετέχοντας αὐτῶν (*scil.* the gods?) καθαροὺς καθαρῶς': this formulation in Stobaeus' (i. 35. 20 W.—the presumed Aetius; Diels, *Doxogr.* 303. 28 = DK 31 A 32) diluted summary points in the same direction.

[3] Diog. Laert. viii. 31 (DK i. 451. 6); on the date (? 4th cent.) of his source see the summary by C. H. Kahn, *Anaximander* (1960), p. 190, n. 1 and now K. von Fritz, *PW.* xxiv. 234 and W. Burkert, *Weisheit und Wissenschaft* (1962), 47 ('3rd cent').

[4] On this cf. E. Rohde, *Psyche*, i. 288, n. 1; ii. 71 ff.   [5] Diog. Laert. viii. 33 (end).

[6] Cf. Aisch. *Pers.* 632 βασιλεῦ τ' ἐνέρων. In the Orphic hymns, Persephone is indeed styled ὑποχθονίων βασίλεια (29. 6), but this fact is not indicative of any ancient tradition. The verbal repertory of this late poetaster is extremely limited, and hardly any one of the many goddesses addressed by him escapes the designation 'queen'. This is true not only of 'Melinoe' (71. 10 καταχθονίων βασίλεια), 'Ipta' (49. 4), and Hekale (1. 5), but of Athena, Artemis, Leto, Selene—and the rest. A parallel of greater interest would be the inscription, *I.G.* xiv. 450, underneath a clay statue, Περσεφόνη βασίλισ[σα] Καταναί[ων]—if only the wording and indeed the genuineness were credible.

[7] This notwithstanding the fact that its recurrent incision, resulting in a succession of anapaestic words, would have offended the refined ear of a Kallimachos.

[8] The specific conditions under which vocative forms are found replaced by nominatives (Ζεῦ πάτερ 'Ηέλιός τε is, comparatively, the closest analogy) do not here apply; as a glance at the grammars will show; e.g. Kühner–Gerth, i. 48; Schwyzer, ii. 63; Chantraine, *Gram. Hom.* ii. 36. Nor does the recent, comprehensive work by J. Svennung, on *Anredeformen* (1958) contain anything that could justify the irregularity in A1.

[9] *Il.* 3. 298, 308, 18. 116; *Od.* 14. 53, 119, etc.

was it not done here? Could the verse possibly have been current in this form? Is it a quotation from some descriptive context, not adapted to the present context? Or has a slip, however odd, of the engraver to be acknowledged? A2, at any rate, shows that syntactically the nominatives in A1 stand for vocatives.

The divergent forms of the same verse in A2 and A3, while free from the faulty nominatives of A1, are highly problematical in their latter half. At the beginning, the heteroclitic form Εὔκλε of A2 has some attraction, seeing that the alternative Εὔκλε⟨ες⟩, though easy in itself in view of the omission in A2 of many other letters, would involve the crasis καὶ Εὐ-, which in Homer, at any rate, would not be admitted;[1] but the original form, behind these variations, must have been as in A5.

In lieu of καὶ ἀθάνατοι θεοὶ ἄλλοι in A1, there is καὶ θεοὶ δαίμονε⟨ς⟩ ἄλλοι in A2, and ΚΑΙΘΕΟΙΟΣΟΙΔΜΟΝΕΣΑΜΟ, i.e. καὶ θεοὶ ὅσοι δ⟨αί⟩μονες ἄλλο⟨ι⟩ in A3; neither of which will scan. DK and Kern, following Radermacher,[2] transfer ὅσοι (A3) before θεοί; one could wish that they had told the reader what they supposed ὅσοι θεοὶ δαίμονες to mean. 'As many gods as are daimons'? Or 'all god-daimons'? It may be suggested, rather, that A2 and A3 both set out to render the same, written *Vorlage* and that A2 did so perfectly (but for omitting one letter). In A3, ΟΣΟΙ is indeed read as reliably as possible, but it needed only the slightest aberration, on the part of the careless engraver, to produce this word instead of ΘΕΟΙ;[3] which is to say that it may be discounted as being a dittography (like ΚΗΚΕΡΑΥΝΟ in v. 5 and ΗΚΩ *bis* in v. 6). The intended wording then would have been, as G. Murray saw,[4] καὶ θεοὶ ⟨καὶ⟩ δαίμονες ἄλλοι; the connecting particle (? written *per compendium*) must either have been accidentally omitted by both engravers—or it had been skipped already in their *Vorlage*.

Anyhow, this form differs from A1 by introducing 'daimons' in addition to 'gods', and one easily assumes that the χθόνιοι δαίμονες ἁγνοί[5] are

[1] The corrupt sequence of letters at the corresponding place in A3, ΕΥΑΚΑΕΥ, most likely implies ΕΥ⟨Κ⟩Λ⟨Ε⟩ ΚΑ⟨Ι⟩ ΕΥ-.—The vocative Εὔκλε, of nom. Εὐκλῆς, was defended by Bücheler, *Rhein. Mus.* xxxvi (1881), 334 (reprinted in his *Kleine Schriften*, ii. 412), by reference to alternatives like Πατροκλῆς: Πάτροκλος, Ἰφικλῆς: Ἴφικλος, etc. and to *Euklói* on an Oscan tablet; the objection that, even so, the alternative Εὐκλῆς: Εὔκλος in one and the same text, and even in the same place, could seem improbable he countered by pointing to Διόκλου and Διοκλεῖ in the Homeric *Hymn on Demeter* vv. 153, 474, 477 (and there is, of course, the constant alternation, in Homer, of the various forms of the name Patroklos, -es, etc.). One may add that, beside the frequent personal name Εὐκλῆς, the name Εὔκλος (? also Εὐκλοῦς) of an allegedly pre-Homeric soothsayer is attested by Pausanias (x. 12. 6, 14. 3, 24. 3) and by Hesych., s.v. ἐμπυριβήτης.

[2] *Rhein. Mus.* lxvii (1912), 472.

[3] 'ΘΕΟΙ misread as ΟΣΟΙ: cf. the reverse confusion at Plato, *Gorg.* 492 b 2' (E. R. Dodds).

[4] *Apud* J. Harrison, *Proleg.*, p. 668 (middle); but 'ὅσοι seems miswriting for καί' (p. 669) is not a convincing diagnosis.

[5] Aisch. *Pers.* 631.

meant. This fact raises questions to be taken up in the interpretation of the whole context of vv. 1–3; but the priority of the wording in A1 is surely self-evident. The unaltered Homeric formula must have preceded its alteration; besides, the latter form, with its tedious repetition of καί, cannot have given rise to the superior wording in A1.

V. 3 in itself raises no problems. It is, again, modelled on a Homeric formula,[1] which always ends on εὔχομαι εἶναι; hence the place of ὄλβιον in A1, before these two words, is likely, again, to represent an earlier form of this verse than its position between them in A2.[2] The connection, however, by καὶ γάρ, of this verse with what precedes it is problematical indeed. 'I am of your race': what is the causal relation between this statement and what has been said before? We have here to consider the material content of these verses.

With Persephone, the soul addresses, by name, Eukles and Eubouleus. For the former there is no direct evidence except Hesych., s.v. Εὐκλῆς· ὁ Ἅιδης.[3] This name has duly been compared with the more frequent Κλύμενος = Hades; which is well compatible with the indications about Euklos on the Oscan tablet from Agnone.[4] Thereafter, the temptation was irresistible, to some, of finding in the third deity the (presumed) offspring of the infernal couple, Dionysos,[5] and therewith confirmation of Orphic theology dominating the tablets. But Dionysos is not said in any source to have been the child of Hades and Persephone nor, if evidence is respected —and there is considerable evidence— can Eubouleus be claimed, in our texts, to be Dionysos. He is Dionysos, certainly, in the Orphic Hymns (29. 8, 30. 6, 52. 4); he is Adonis, too, in them (56. 3), and also father of Dionysos (42. 2), and of Artemis = Tyche (72. 3); he is also Pluto (18. 2). In some even later verses, quoted from 'Orpheus' by Macrobius,[6]

---

[1] Od. 14. 204, 21. 335; Il. 21. 187, 14. 113, 6. 211 = 20. 241.

[2] In A3 it is anyhow misplaced; in the reconstruction it has been placed as in A2 because these two appear to reproduce the same Vorlage.

[3] E. Schwyzer, Rhein. Mus. lxxxiv (1935), 111 (note) suggested that in Hesych. Εὔκολος· ... Ἑρμῆς παρὰ Μεταποντίοις the name might originally have been Εὔκλος. If this suggestion is considered, one would have to think of Ἑρμῆς χθόνιος and thus not be far from what the same Hesychius reports about Εὐκλῆς. G. Radke, Die Götter Altitaliens (1965), pp. 114 f., quotes further literature and, to my mind, doubtful hypotheses.

[4] Cf. above, p. 309, n. 1.—J. H. Wieten, De tribus lamellis ... (1915), p. 33 objected that Euklúí paterí was unlikely to be identical with Εὔκλος–Εὐκλῆς because his name follows upon those of a number of fertility deities. O. Skutsch however assures me that the combination of Euklos pater and Dis pater with these deities is as natural with Oscans as that of Greek Pluto with Demeter. Bücheler's thesis is accepted also by Schwyzer (see preceding note).

[5] 'Dionysum Zagreum (Iacchos) intellego, Plutonis et Persephones filium': thus Olivieri ad loc., while J. Harrison (ib. 587) found no difficulty in equating the two with Dionysos, Zagreus, Phanes—the lot; the 'one god of Orphism'. When we are presented with the evidence—pre-Neoplatonic evidence—we shall believe it and be grateful to be shown an easy way out of the intricacies of these texts—by means of the equation of everything with everything. Meantime, cf. above, pp. 81, n. 5 and 167, n. 4.

[6] Sat. i. 18. 12 (Orph. fr. 237 Kern; cf. fr. 239).

Eubouleus is, besides Phanes, Dionysos, and others, a name for the universal deity, personified in the sun-god, of dying paganism. But this blending of all divinities, resulting in the annihilation of that definiteness of form which is the hall-mark of genuine Greek religion (whatever theories philosophers, sophists, and allegorists might apply to them) cannot without compelling evidence be thrown back by more than half a millennium to be applied to the interpretation of the present texts. In the religion of the Classical Age Eubouleus is not Dionysos,[1] and Dionysos is not Hades (those who quote Herakleitos in support of the latter identification betray a naivety which is out of place in interpreting him).[2] The valid evidence for Eubouleus has been fully presented by E. Rohde;[3] it shows him to have been worshipped, in various places, as a, or the, god of the Netherworld (identical with, or associated with, Hades–Pluton) together with Demeter, Kore, and other deities; not rarely he is called Zeus Eubouleus. His name is an euphemism like that of (Zeus) Meilichios; his special role at Eleusis has been often discussed, and the 'Eleusinian trinity' of θεός, θεά and Eubouleus may well be compared with that of Eukles, Persephone, and Eubouleus in the present verse; it does not follow, though, that the tablets testify to a specific Eleusinian mythology. The Lord of the Netherworld ('Zeus Chthonios') was invoked, originally, by various, euphemistic names at various places. With the increase of contact and exchange between tribes and places, these various realizations of one deity were largely absorbed into one dominating concept, Eubouleus becoming Zeus Eubouleus as Malophoros became Demeter Malophoros. At some centres, though, they joined themselves, retaining their individualities, to the dominating local deities. A multitude of chthonic deities, similar to each other and none the less distinct, could thus come to be worshipped at one and the same place.[4] This is what happened at Eleusis and also at Thurii.

The following words, καὶ ἀθάνατοι θεοὶ ἄλλοι, suggest an assembly of

---

[1] 'We do not find it [the name Eubouleus] attached to this deity [Dionysos] in a single recorded public cult': Farnell, *Cults* . . . v. 128. Eubouleus is mentioned in the Gurôb papyrus; he cannot be Dionysos there either, for εἶς Διόνυσος follows. Plutarch (*Quaest. Conv.* vii. 9, 714 c) alleges that 'in very ancient times' Dionysos was called Eubouleus because '*in vino veritas*'; he appears unaware of any 'chthonic' associations; and indeed the epithet was thus used (if not frequently) of gods and men; e.g. of Themis and Nereus (Pind. *P.* iii. 27 and *I.* vii. 32; Bacchyl. i. 7); of men e.g. Bacchyl. xiv. 37, [Eur.] *Rhes.* 105; Plato, *Rep.* 428 b (εὔβουλος and -εύς are synonyms). The oldest evidence for a cult of Dionysos Eubouleus is (*pace* L. Farnell) a dedication to him, now lost, by the wife of a 'hierophantes' Antiochos (*C.I.G.* ii, no. 1948). It is unlikely to antedate the third century of our era, for the dedication is τῷ ἐπιφανεστάτῳ θεῷ Διονύσῳ (*sic*). This phrase is a shibboleth indicative of a late origin, as will be seen on comparing the (likewise lost) inscription *C.I.G.* ii. no. 1392 (*I.G.* v. 1, 1179).

[2] Cf. Detached Note XI, below, p. 407.

[3] *Psyche*, i. 207 and 210; see also Nilsson, *Opuscula*, ii. 551.

[4] The kommos in Aischylos' *Choephoroi* conveys powerfully the notion of a vast multitude of chthonic deities; see especially vv. 359, 399, 405.

gods which it is hard, even so, to visualize. In the Homeric epics this phrase is always joined to the name of Zeus and intimates all of the Olympians without specifying any other one from among them. How could the soul before Persephone be addressing them together with her? Nor could a host of chthonic deities suitably be denoted by the Homeric formula. Perhaps the insertion, in A2–3, of the word δαίμονες was intended to alleviate this difficulty; the soul could indeed be supposed to be facing, in addition to the named triad, a number of δαίμονες χθόνιοι.[1] Even this assumption, though, would not solve the problem given with the mention of θεοί in all three tablets. Why indeed had it to arise at all?[2]

The answer emerges on considering v. 3. 'I am of your race': so the soul proclaims. But nowhere is mankind said to be the offspring of Hades and Persephone; and indeed this would be unthinkable. Those seeking to interpret these texts on the lines of Orphic theological speculation indeed have an answer. They assume the following implications: Dionysos, the son of Persephone (and of Zeus, be it noted; not of Hades) is killed and devoured by the Titans; man's body contains particles from their ashes (after Zeus had burned them with his thunderbolt) and hence an admixture of the body of Dionysos. The assumption, however, that the soul could claim, before Persephone, to be ὑμῶν γένος ὄλβιον on this basis seems more than the text could possibly bear out; in particular, the pronoun would be wrong (it would have to be coῦ) and the adjective ὄλβιον highly inappropriate; nor could the soul really expect to curry favour with Persephone by claiming descent from the murderers of her child. If we forget these mythological antics, the words seem to speak simply and plainly for themselves. 'I am of the race of the blessed gods', so the soul says; and these gods are not those of the Netherworld—but the Olympian ἀθάνατοι θεοὶ ἄλλοι.

This, then, is why the 'immortal gods' are introduced in this context. It remains true that their mention does not fit the situation; nor are matters improved by the addition of δαίμονες. But the possibility of

---

[1] This suggestion gets no support from the only epic passage where, in the same phrase, δαίμονες takes the place of θεοί (the two words are never combined): in *Il.* 1. 222 the connotation is that of the standard phrase. The same is true of H. *H. Merc.* 381, and in the Demeter-hymn, 338, the return of Kore μετὰ δαίμονας means her regaining the upper world and does not designate the δαίμονες χθόνιοι.

[2] The formula, typical among the curses on lead tablets found at Knidos by Newton, Δάματρι καὶ Κούραι καὶ θεοῖς τοῖς παρὰ Δ. καὶ Κ. illustrates the problem: these of course are all of them 'chthonic' deities. On the other hand, no help comes from the formula θεοὶ δαίμονες, so frequent in Italy on sepulchral inscriptions of the Roman age, for this is the Greek rendering of *Dis Manibus* (*I.G.* xiv. 1612 is even headed *DM*, in Latin letters, instead of the usual ΘΔ). Nor, finally, can 'daimons' be here suitably understood in the Empedoklean sense, that is, as the divine essences of deceased humans; for these have indeed to face the judgement of Persephone but they cannot be visualized among her entourage. Whatever he meant by 'daimons', some rewriter of these traditional verses must have been so concerned to insert them as to disregard the resulting obscurity.

imagining a gathering of Olympian and chthonic gods, however unsuitable to the specific situation, is realized on recalling the characteristic concept of Persephone in Magna Graecia as outlined in an earlier chapter: the severe goddess of death now visualized as being also a loving giver of life and thus at one with the Olympians. The Lokri tablets, and in particular those showing Persephone with her divine visitors, illustrate the ideology underlying this problematical verse.

There remains the problem of the connection of v. 3 with the preceding. After what has been said about the intervening verse, the connection between vv. 1 and 3 is clear enough. It is effected, again, by means of a Homeric tag; καὶ γὰρ ἐγών occurs in *Il.* 2. 377, 6. 365 and *Od.* 7. 24 (also H. *H. Merc.* 450); the meaning is: 'I may venture thus to address you . . . because I (like you) am of divine race.'[1]

The inconcinnities mentioned obtrude themselves to the critical reader; they seem to preclude the derivation of these verses from the context of some older poem, but they were evidently irrelevant to the believers. They were content to be given, in a traditional poetical form, the assertion of certain tenets which were essential to them; namely: (1) the soul is of divine origin; (2) after death it will face the decision of Persephone; (3) it may face it with trust, for during life on earth it has kept 'pure'.

A2–3, v. 4: This verse is not by chance lacking in A1—as will be seen later. It is a painful instance of a brief prosaic statement—ποινὴν ἔργων ἀδίκων (or, rather, ἀδικίας) (ἀπ)έτεισα—drawn out so as to fill a hexameter. Compounds with ἀνταπο- are foreign to classical and earlier poetry;[2] ἀνταποτίνω in particular is not otherwise recorded prior to the Christian era;[3] ἕνεκα is a bad stop-gap, and οὔτι δικαίων is worse. That verse certainly does not come from any poetical model; and yet the idea so poorly expressed by it must have been felt to be essential. It calls to mind Pindar's αὐτίκ' (after death) ἀπάλαμνοι φρένες ποινὰς ἔτεισαν (*Ol.* ii. 57) and οἷσι δὲ Φερσεφόνα ποινὰν παλαιοῦ πένθεος δέξεται (fr. 133). The former of these passages indicates a punishment for faults committed on earth which is inflicted by a judgement immediately after death; that this is the same ποινά which Persephone 'accepts', is by no means certain. The soul speaking on our tablet, anyhow, is expected immediately after death to be appearing before Persephone; its 'penalty' therefore was 'paid' before death. What this penalty was, and for what 'injustice' it had to be paid, can be considered only in the context of the poem as a whole.

---

[1] I owe this interpretation to Professor Dodds, who disposed of an erroneous attempt of my own and, for ample parallels, referred to J. D. Denniston, *The Greek Particles*[2] (1954), pp. 60 f.; cf. also *Rhein. Mus.* xciv (1951), 339 ff.

[2] This statement can be countered—not very efficiently—by reference to ἀνταποδίδωμι in (Hom.) *Batr.* 186.

[3] J. H. Wieten (see above, p. 310, n. 4), p. 78, would emend this to π. δ' αὖτ' ἀπέτεισα; but in a verse in which almost everything is bad it seems useless to refurbish one detail.

A1, *v. 4* = *A2–3*, *v. 5*. The variants and corruptions in the texts of this verse have caused trouble which is reflected even in L–S–J. The transmitted wording is

A1 Ἀλ⟨λ⟩ά με μο⟨ῖ⟩ρα ἐδάμας⟨c⟩ε καὶ [. . . .]¹ ἀccτεροβλῆτα κεραυνόν.

A2 Εἴτε με μο⟨ῖ⟩ρα ἐδαμάc⟨c⟩ατο εἴτε ἀcτεροπῆτι κ⟨ε⟩ραυνῶν.²

A3 ΕΤ ΜΕ ΜΟΙΡΑ   ΕΤ   ΕΡΟΠΗΤΙ [ΚΗ] ΚΕΡΑΥΝΟ.

The Homeric model-verses are

Il. 18. 119 Ἀλλά ἑ μοῖρα ἐδάμαccε καὶ ἀργαλέοc χόλοc ʺΗρηc
(Achilleus speaking of Herakles);

Il. 16. 849 Ἀλλά με μοῖρα ὀλοὴ καὶ Λητοῦc ἔκτανεν υἱόc (Patroklos).

For the end of the verse cf.

Od. 5. 128 Ζεὺc, ὅc μιν κατέπεφνε βαλὼν ἀργῆτι κεραυνῶι, many other verses ending on κεραυνῶι³ (it is, of course, always the thunderbolt 'of Zeus'), and particularly

Il. 15. 117 Εἴ πέρ μοι καὶ μοῖρα Διὸc πληγέντι κεραυνῶι κεῖcθαι
(Ares speaking).

It is clear at a glance that: (*a*) εἴτε . . . εἴτε in A2–3 is an inferior alteration of ἀλλά . . . καὶ in A1; (*b*) the accusative κεραυνόν in A1 is impossible, since the thunderbolt is the means, not the object of the divine action (its object being με); (*c*) the middle form ἐδαμάccατο in A2, though (in other contexts) Homeric, is in our verse secondary, seeing that the metre is spoiled by it. Moreover, (*d*) the verse-ending in A2–3 is corrupt, for ἀcτεροπητήc, 'he with the lightning', is Zeus; the word cannot be applied to the thunderbolt itself; add that it could never form a dative in -τι.⁴ Since, however, the dative κεραυνῶι forms a standard verse-ending in Homer, it is possible that this was here intended and that the preceding word has been wrongly adapted to it.

The Homeric models show that in the second half of the verse a subject noun is required in parallel with μοῖρα in the first half.⁵ It can only have been ἀcτεροπῆτα; a nominative of the type κυανοχαῖτα, νεφεληγερέτα, etc.,⁶ and closely similar to cτεροπηγερέτα Ζεύc *Il.* 16. 298. This conclusion is

¹ It ought not to be necessary to argue that the repetition in A1 of καὶ ἀθάνατοι θεοὶ ἄλλοι from v. 2 is a scribal error (even though it still figures in DK), seeing that it is absent from A2 and A3; and how could the 'other gods' be joined to Moira, which is not a god (cf. Wilamowitz, *Der Glaube* . . .² i. 359)?

² The Ν is added above the line although there was room on it; indicating, perhaps, that it was not in the *Vorlage* (cf. A3); for there is no other instance of a letter thus placed on A2.

³ e.g. *Od.* 5. 131; 7. 249; 12.387.

⁴ It was excessive to devise, merely for this corrupt passage, an entry ἀcτεροπήc in L–S–J.

⁵ Cf. also *Od.* 22. 412 τούcδε δὲ μοῖρα ἐδάμαccε θεῶν καὶ cχέτλια ἔργα and the formula-verse (three times in *Il.*) . . . ἔλλαβε πορφύρεοc θάνατοc καὶ μοῖρα κραταιή, which recurred also in the *Ilias parva* (fr. 18 Kinkel, Tzetz. *ad Lycophr.* 1263).

⁶ This conclusion was first drawn—for A2—by G. Kaibel in *I.G.* xiv. 641, followed by E. Rohde, *Psyche*, ii. 218 and many others. The form in -τᾰ, in lieu of the Homeric -τηc, may have occurred in some epic poem known to the author of the verse under discussion but lost to us.

supported by A1, where ἀστεροβλῆτα provides, at any rate, a nominative
of the postulated kind—and, besides, has given rise to certain
mythological novelties: namely, the phantoms of a 'Sternschleuderer',
of 'Sternzeugung', or a 'star-flung thunderbolt', which necessitate a
brief discussion.

Modern etymologists may be right in connecting the word-group
cτεροπή–ἀcτραπή 'lightning' with ἀcτ(ε)ρ- 'star'; even though I for one
cannot quite believe it. To Greeks at any rate, from Homer onward,
stars and lightning were separate things; Zeus ἀcτεροπητήc throws the
thunderbolt and not stars. Ἀcτεροβλῆτα in A1, if it is more than a slip, or
whim, must be synonymous with ἀcτεροπῆτ(ι) in A2—which is derived
from (ἀ)cτεροπή and not from ἀcτήρ; it would then have to be regarded as
a syncopated form of ἀcτερο(πο)βλῆτα.¹ The derivation from ἀcτήρ, 'star',
leads to absurdity. Adjectives derived from βάλλω end on -βλήc² or -βλητόc,
and their connotation is normally passive.³ Among them we find, in the
prose of Aristotle and his followers, κεραυνοβλήc and even ἀcτροβλήc—
which means 'scorched by midsummer-heat' (i.e. the dog-star). On these
compelling analogies, ἀcτεροβλῆτα κεραυνόν in the unemended text A1
would describe the thunderbolt, just possibly, as 'throwing a star',
though rather as 'hit by a star'; both these alternatives are clearly
absurd. Nor is the thunderbolt 'flung by a star'; but by Ζεὺc ἀcτεροπητήc.

If, then, ἀcτεροπῆτα (with, perhaps, the synonym -βλῆτα) is the subject
of the phrase under discussion, namely, the 'thrower of the thunderbolt',
it remains to consider which word was intended after it, and variously
missed, by the three engravers. Dieterich,⁴ who accepted Kaibel's reading
ἀcτεροπῆτα in A2, followed it with κεραυνῶν (partic. praes.). This evidently has good transcriptional authority and makes good sense, but is
open to the objection that active forms of the verb κεραυνόω are not
attested from epic and other poetry, and even its passive only once in
Hesiod, and rarely in lyric poetry.⁵ Hence my preference is for the dative
κεραυνῶι, which is fairly easily extracted from the three or, rather, four
existing variants⁶ and supported by many Homeric parallels—such as are
wanting for the participle.

The connection, in A1, of this verse with the preceding, by ἀλλά, is

¹ This was suggested by E. Rohde, l.l.
² A full list and discussion of them may be found in E. Fraenkel, *Geschichte der griech.
Nomina agentis*, i (1910), pp. 78 ff.
³ The only exception seems to be Aristophanes' comic coinage ἀcπιδαπόβληc.
⁴ A. Dieterich, *De hymnis Orphicis* (1891), p. 31 (reprinted in his *Kleine Schriften* (1911),
p. 92).   ⁵ Hesiod, *Theog.* 859, Pindar, *Nem.* x. 8.
⁶ The psychological reason for the engraver putting KEPAYNON in A1 may be that he
took ΑΣΤΕΡΟΒΛΗΤΑ for an accusative; A2 may originally have intended the dative and
added the N afterwards (perhaps from another *Vorlage*); KEPAYNO finally in A3 may, in
view of his fantastic carelessness, stand for the dative as well as for anything else.

taken over from the Homeric models. Its bearing must not be tested too severely—there is no particular, contrasting relation between the two—but it may be felt to afford a passable start for a fresh statement. Very differently A2–3. It appears that, after the statement 'I have paid the penalty', the continuation by means of ἀλλά was felt to be inappropriate. If the person who devised the alteration merely wanted to avoid the appearance of a contrast between the two statements, he could have introduced the second by εἶτα (retaining καί after the verb); if he wanted to indicate that death by lightning was the punishment undergone by the speaker, εἴγε (likewise continued by καί) would have been acceptable. The twofold εἴτε however effects a quite inadmissible distinction ('*either* by lot *or* by Zeus' thunder'); besides, the speaker must know whether he died from lightning, or not! I hesitate to draw any firm conclusion as to the process which resulted in this corruption of the wording.[1]

Anyhow, the speaker states that he died from lightning. Those who interpret these texts on the basis of what they hold to be Orphic theology[2] assert that thereby he identifies himself with the Titans destroyed by Zeus' thunder. Which is to say that, on this interpretation, the speaker actually was not killed by lightning—although he states that he was—and that he presents himself as a Titan; which he is not. Could he truly expect thus to deceive the dread goddess of the dead? And if he succeeded, what reason had he to hope for her favour?

We had better take him at his word; those buried with these particular tablets had been killed by lightning. E. Rohde, in his admirable discussion of these texts,[3] suggested that 'in its original form' the text contained in these three tablets was destined for someone thus killed. This restriction is not in fact necessary, for these tablets all come from one and the same tumulus, and this particular feature does not recur in any one of the other tablets. It is perfectly natural to assume that this tumulus, the Timpone Piccolo, was erected over the grave of a person killed by lightning and thereby sanctified[4]—and that two others who, later, found their death in the same way were buried in this most appropriate place.[5]

In the following verses—they are different in A1 and A2–3—the con-

---

[1] I incline to the following diagnosis. After the intrusion of the (bad) verse 4 in the model of A2–3 the original continuation by means of ἀλλά was understandably felt to be unsuitable; hence it was replaced by εἶτα. The engraver of A2—perhaps working from memory—wrongly put ΕΙΤΕ for ΕΙΤΑ and in consequence put a second ΕΙΤΕ in the place of ΚΑΙ. The poor two letters ΕΤ in A3 require little comment. If they are held to imply the same reading as in A2, the error just inferred must have been in the *Vorlage*.

[2] J. Harrison, *Proleg.*, p. 587, al.   [3] *Psyche*, ii. 218, n. 4.

[4] E. Rohde, *Psyche*, i. 320 ff.; ii. 101; A. B. Cook, *Zeus*, ii. 18 ff. and 806.

[5] E. Rohde's alternative suggestion (l.c. ii. 218, n. 4) that εἴτε . . . εἴτε in A2–3, for ἀλλά . . . καί, was due to deliberate alteration—so as to make the text usable for persons not killed by lightning—seems inadmissible to me. The result, as R. notes himself, would be extremely 'ungeschickt', for this use of εἴτε . . . εἴτε would be both ungrammatical and materially absurd. There could be no doubt as to whether the dead had been killed by lightning or not:

ception that the speaker is addressing Persephone is somewhat changed:
the goddess is now spoken of in the third person. This may be taken for an
expression of awe, but a different explanation will commend itself in the
course of our interpretation.

A2–3, vv. 6–7. The meaning of these verses is clear, but their form imperfect. In v. 6, παρ' ἀγνήν must be considered to be the intended wording.
It is easy to correct the metre, with Diels, by writing παρ' ἀγαυήν, and the
verse is indeed likely to have existed, earlier, in this correct form, which is
closer to the model *Od.* 11. 213 and 226 (also *H. H. Cer.* 348). It is,
however, unlikely to have been thus in the written *Vorlage* of A2–3.
Ἁγνὴ Περσεφόνεια stands at the beginning of the verse *Od.* 11. 386
(= *H. Cer.* 337); the same epithet is given to the goddess in inscriptions.[1]
Both ἀγνή and ἀγαυή are sure to have been used in the cult; hence their
interchange in the present passage.

In v. 7, on the other hand, Diels's conjecture εἰc εὐαγεόντων, while
managing to effect a complete hexameter, produces a wording too bad to
have ever existed. Those who, in life, observe ritual purity (καθαρεύουcιν,
εὐαγέουcιν) are καθαροί, ὅcιοι, and εὐαγεῖc; not καθαρεύοντεc nor ὁcιοῦντεc
nor εὐαγέοντεc. The transmitted adjective, then, is genuine. The poem
thus ends on a pentameter, with ἕδρᾱc spoken as a trochee. Doric forms
of this type occur in Hesiod, in *H. H. Merc.* 106 and e.g. in the Rhodian
'swallow-song'; a single pentameter, after a series of hexameters, is found
in some epigrams on stone.[2] A certain amount of metrical variation has
anyhow to be acknowledged in this group of lamellae; there are passages
in prose in A1 and A4, and trochees in A4, v. 5.

The poem thus ends on the same note on which it began; namely,
ritual purity.[3] A 'pure from the pure' enters before the presence of

---

if he was not, formularies were available for people who had died a natural death; for example,
the Homeric phrase τανηλεγέοc θανάτοιο could have replaced the second half of the parallel
verse in A1. Actually, though, this whole verse pretty clearly appears to have been invented,
and intruded into a standard formulary, in order to present a person killed by lightning; it
looses its *raison d'être* if it is applied to others. That the dead had died, this fact needed no
stating.

[1] e.g. on the *defixio*, found in the Gaggera (and mentioned above, p. 74, n. 2), παρ τὰν ἀγνὰν
θεάν ('evidentemente Persefone': S. Ferri, *Not. Scav.* (1944–5), 171); also the dedication, at
Akrai, Ἁγναῖc θεαῖc, I.G. xiv. 204, 'i.e. Cereri et Proserpinae', inscribed on a 'basis parvula';
ib. 431 θεαῖc ἀγναῖc χαριcτήριον Α. Μάλιοc Ἑρμῆc ῥέκταc (Roman); cf. Pausan. iv. 33. 4 (on
which below, p. 373, n. 2).

[2] This is a summary of Radermacher's argument, *Philologus*, lxvii (1912), 473. Kaibel had
thus understood this verse thirty years earlier (*I.G.* xiv. 629).—In the first part of this verse,
the use of πρόφρων has many Homeric antecedents (esp. also with 'giving', 'allowing', and
'accepting'; e.g. *Il.* 8. 175; 13. 359; 23. 647; *Od.* 8. 498; also Hes. *Th.* 419; Parmen. 1. 22),
and so has ἀγαυὴν (*sic*) Φερcεφόνειαν at the end of the preceding verse; but as a whole, these
two verses are not, like verses 2, 3, and 5, made up of Homeric formulae. The use of ἕδραι at
the end likewise is not Homeric but has many parallels in lyrics.

[3] Εὐαγής is he who is free from ἄγοc and thus ἀγνόc and therefore fit to participate in a cult;
the notion of the word thus is closely similar to that of ὅcιοc. In the Homeric Demeter-hymn

Persephone; to the sojourn of the 'pure' he hopes to be sent by her. If we make bold to ask which place this was thought to be, one naturally thinks first of the 'meadows of Persephone' of A4, v. 6. There are, as will soon be seen, certain objections to this assumption—if indeed one is to reckon with any definite and consistent notions of the various parts of the Netherworld. If so, one may alternatively equate the εὐαγέων ἕδραι with the place of the ἥρωες of the Petelia tablet; the station described by Pindar, *Ol.* ii. 61–7 and, one may think, in fr. 129.

This long analysis may have helped, it is hoped, to clarify a few points in this text and to discern some of its antecedents; but it would be a pity if the myopic observation of the details of wording and context were to hamper the appreciation of its simple and profound devotion. These persons faced death in trusting piety: 'Pure I stand before you, deities of death, myself an offspring of the gods: I have paid the amends of injustice; send me, gracefully, to the sojourn of the pure.'

There is no hint in these simple words of any involved and abstruse theological speculation; certainly nothing 'Orphic'; nor even, as far as this poem goes, is there an explicit statement of a belief in reincarnation. The remaining texts will show that in fact this belief was very definitely held; they may also yield some information about two essential facets of this, as of every religion; namely, its rites and its myth.

A1, vv. 5 ff. The concluding part of A1 begins with three verses parallel in structure. Each of them forms a whole in itself, is connected with the preceding by δέ and begins with a noun in the genitive; the endings of the first two are Homeric[1] while that of the last echoes, meaningfully, that of the very first verse of the poem. This lucid structure is emphasized by the brisk and even rhythm which corresponds with the progress of which these verses tell; in words which are, each and all of them, well-defined in themselves and without ambiguity as to their interrelation. This whole, evidently, is of one, definite, and sustained inspiration. The three verses have often been compared with the Eleusinian 'symbolon' ἐνήςτευςα, ἔπιον τὸν κυκεῶνα, ἔλαβον ἐκ κίςτης, κτλ.; but to make this comparison, and to draw inferences from it concerning the purpose of the verses, is to disregard the fundamental difference between a series of prosaic state-

---

(274 and 369) the adverb εὐαγέως indicates the proper observance of rites, and Theokritos (if it is really Theokritos) 26. 30, in a wildly ritualistic poem, paraphrases a ritual formula εὐαγέοιμι cὺν εὐαγέεςςιν, to which Kallimachos (*H. Del.* 96) similarly refers. The verb (also in Eur. *Ba.* 1008) is also used transitively to denote the 'cleansing' of a holy place (ὅπως τὸ τέμενος εὐαγῆται, inscr. Rhodes *I.G.* xii. 1. 677 = Dittenberger, *Sylloge*[3.4] 338). As with all words bearing on the religious sphere—which includes the politic and legal—the implications also of these were affected by the change of religious concepts; see Soph. *Ant.* 521.

[1] Ἀργαλέοιο at end of verse *Il.* 11. 812; 16. 528; *Od.* 24. 531 (ref. to 'wound' and 'war'); ποcὶ καρπαλίμοιcιν *Il.* 16. 342; cf. 809; 22. 166; *H. H. Merc.* 225.

ments of ritual acts performed and the poetic description of a mythical experience.

In v. 6 the speaker declares: 'Coronam exoptatam assecutus sum';[1] that is, he relates his story by the metaphor of a foot-race (ποcὶ καρπαλί-μοιcιν); and he has reached the goal.[2] The preceding verse indicates his starting-point; the following makes clear what the goal is: like an infant which finds safety and rest ὑπὸ κόλπωι of its mother or nurse, thus he has found his haven with Persephone.[3] Since more fantastic interpretations still find credence, the Homeric model and parallels may be presented.

Teucer seeks protection, in battle, from his big brother: *Il.* 8. 271 παῖc ὡc ὑπὸ μητέρα, δύcκεν εἰc Αἴανθ'; Hektor's son, *Il.* 6. 467, . . . πρὸc κόλπον . . . τιθήνηc ἐκλίνθη (cf. ib. 400 and 483); the queen of Eleusis carrying 'infantem in sinu vestis involutum', meets Demeter, *H. Cer.* 187, παῖδ' ὑπὸ κόλπωι ἔχουcα;[4] Eidothea dives into the sea, *Od.* 4. 435, ὑποδῦcα θαλάccηc εὐρέα κόλπον;[5] the goddess of the sea receives Dionysos and Hephaistos *Il.* 6. 136 and 18. 398 Θέτιc δ' ὑπεδέξατο κόλπωι.

Who would think, in these analogous instances, of 'rites of adoption' and 'sacred marriage'? Or acquiesce in Jane Harrison's vague and lachrymose pseudo-poetry, 'I have sunk beneath the bosom of Despoine'?[6] Ships may 'sink beneath' the surface of the sea, but Persephone's ward 'rushes', or 'dives', trustfully for safety to his goddess, as Teucer to his big brother or a child to its mother or nurse.

[1] Thus translated by Comparetti (1910), p. 27.

[2] In epic (and dependent) literature, the verb ἐπιβαίνω, with gen., often conveys the notion of ('ascending', 'setting foot on' and, hence,) 'reaching', 'achieving'; one may thus 'set foot on', not only γαίηc or πόληοc but, εὐφροcύνηc (*Od.* 23. 52), ἀναιδείηc (22. 424), τέχνηc, ὁcίηc (*H. Merc.* 166; 172), εὐκλείηc (*Il.* 8. 285), χορῶν (Ar. *Ran.* 675); the writer of our verse may have had in mind particularly *Od.* 23. 328 ἀcπαcίωc δ' ἐπέβαν γαίηc, κακότητα φυγόντεc. Since the wreath is the normal prize of victors, the word cτέφανοc is obviously suitable; it may however be added that it is used, elsewhere too, metaphorically with the connotation of 'purpose' and 'distinction'. Cτέφανον ὕψιcτον δέδεκται says Pindar (*P.* i. 100) of the man who both fares well and is well spoken of, and Orestes (Eur. *El.* 614; cf. *I.T.* 12) says ἐπὶ τόνδε πάρειμι cτέφανον, 'that (matricide!) is the prize (glory) for which I have come'. With this basis for the interpretation given in the text it will not, I trust, be necessary to enlarge upon the difficulties involved in the various, more fantastic interpretations which have been suggested for this verse and can be found summarized by Olivieri, p. 7 and Wieten, pp. 100 f. It may be added, though, that, on this basis, the spuriousness of v. 6 repeated, on the tablet, after v. 7 is established beyond cavil.

[3] Thus Rohde and again Comparetti, who refers to Dante, *Inf.* xii. 119 *in grembo a Dio*. The image can be illustrated by terracottas of the type Louvre C30 (S. Mollard-Besques, *Catalogue* . . ., i. 87 and Pl. LXI).

[4] Cf. ib. 231, 286.

[5] Comparison with *Il.* 18. 140 δῦτε θαλάccηc . . . κόλπον can serve to prevent overstressing the significance of the preposition ὑπό in the verse under discussion.

[6] 'I passed beneath the breast of the Queen-Mistress of the lower world' (L. R. Farnell, *Greek Hero Cults* . . . (1921), p. 378) may strike some as even worse.

V. 5. The place which the runner after the divine goal has left behind is the κύκλος βαρυπενθὴς ἀργαλέος. It is no secret that these words are widely, though not universally,[1] held to denote a ('Pythagorean' or 'Orphic') 'cycle of births', and there may well be truth in this interpretation; but since so standardized a terminology is liable to obscure the characteristic features of this verse, we may briefly consider it in its own right. It is spoken by the dead, that is, by his soul; its verb could therefore be taken literally, seeing that souls are represented with wings and that Homer often speaks of the soul πταμένη ἐκ ῥεθέων.[2] Πέτομαι, though, can denote any rapid movement—e.g. of man, horses, arrows—and this connotation (which could be felt together with the more specific one) agrees well with the foot-race imagery. The latter, at any rate, demands that some concreteness must have been felt in the notion of κύκλος. Primarily denoting a wheel, the word had long come to be applied to anything circular (or also spheroid); such as, for example, a 'circle' of men assembled in the agora or for hunting—or, on the other hand, the stone-vault of heaven. None of these connotations is here applicable. What the speaker has left behind obviously is life on earth; how could it be described as κύκλος?

There was a proverb current among Greeks and twice quoted as such in the *corpus* of Aristotelian writings:[3] κύκλος τὰ ἀνθρώπινα πράγματα. From Herodotus[4] we learn what it meant: κύκλος ἐστὶν τῶν ἀνθρωπηΐων πρηγμάτων· περιφερόμενος δὲ οὐκ ἐᾶι αἰεὶ τοὺς αὐτοὺς εὐτυχέειν. Less alienated from the life of nature than we are, the Greeks were deeply conscious of its all-pervading rhythm, in day and night, season and year;[5] but Herodotus shows that this was not the point of this proverb (whatever speculations philosophers might attach to it).[6] No part of the turning wheel remains unaffected by its movement; what had been elevated is bound to move downward, and whether you will live to share in the following upward movement is doubtful; the instability of human affairs is the point of this proverb as, in the Middle Ages, of the *Rota Fortunae*.[7]

If, on this basis, it is assumed that, in our verse, κύκλος βαρυπενθής is simply a metaphor for life with its uncertainties and disasters, there

---

[1] J. H. Wieten, pp. 98 f., inspired by J. Harrison, ib. 591, found in it a ritual of the *mystes* surrounded by flames or torches; J. Eitrem, *Opferritus und Voropfer* (1915), pp. 53 f., similarly supposed circular ritual dances to be indicated by this verse and its repetition after v. 7.

[2] The parallel to our verse in Empedokles fr. 2. 4 DK ὠκύμοροι . . . ἀρθέντες ἀπέπταν may be significant, for the aorist ἔπτην is not Homeric (also διέπτη Emped. 17. 5).

[3] Arist. *Phys.* iv. 14, 223ᵇ24; *Probl.* xvii. 3, 916ᵃ28.   [4] Hdt. i. 107. 2.

[5] See the evidence, and incisive discussion, in C. H. Kahn, *Anaximander* (1960), pp. 175 ff. (add 'Musaios' fr. 5 DK from Clem. Al. *Strom.* vi. 738 Pott).

[6] On these see lately S. G. F. Brandon, *History, Time and Deity* (1965), pp. 85 ff., which may be placed into the context described by I. Düring, *Aristoteles* (1966), pp. 321 ff.

[7] This is confirmed by the variant of the proverb cited by the Paroemiographers: τροχὸς τὰ ἀνθρώπινα.

would not remain, in any of the lamellae, any direct attestation of a belief in the transmigration of souls. This 'simple' interpretation, however, is excluded by considerations of style and thought and, besides, by the collation (to be carried out later) of the doctrines in the various texts now under discussion. The word 'wheel' is, in any case, a metaphor. One easily understands that it was applied, as a descriptive *predicate*, to human life with its changes and suffering, but its use as a *synonym* for life presupposes more than the consciousness of life's instability; it has, in addition, a terminological ring which implies some particular doctrine.

One is thus thrown back upon the evidence for the term 'wheel' used in the context of the Pythagorean doctrine of rebirth which A. Lobeck presented on pp. 798 ff. of his *Aglaophamus*, and which served A. Dieterich, E. Rohde, and others to elucidate the verse under discussion. The essential passages are two:

1. Diog. Laert. viii. 14 πρῶτόν τέ φασί τοῦτον (scil. Pythagoras) ἀποφῆναι τὴν ψυχὴν κύκλον ἀνάγκης ἀμείβουσαν ἄλλοτ' ἄλλοις ἐνδεῖσθαι ζώιοις. A. Delatte[1] traced this report to Aristoxenos; this, then, would be evidence almost contemporary with our lamella. One is forcibly reminded of the Empedoklean Ἀνάγκης χρῆμα and related texts.[2]

2. Κύκλου τε λῆξαι καὶ ἀναπνεῦσαι κακότητος.

This, as E. Rohde stated,[3] is the most authentic form of this verse,[4] which was quoted with some variation and corruption, by two Neoplatonists,[5] 900 years later, both of whom ascribe it to 'Orpheus'; i.e. it occurred in some epic fathered on him and expressed the prayer of Orphic initiates to be released from 'the κύκλος'.

---

[1] *Études sur la littérature pythagoricienne* (1915), p. 20. The ascription to Aristoxenos is in fact uncertain, for it is not evident that the reference to him after the next statement covers also this one (F. Wehrli does not include it in his fr. 24). Some support for Delatte's thesis may be drawn from fr. 12 W. (below, p. 336, n. 2); but what matters in the present context is the ascription, in an evidently early source, of the term κύκλος to Pythagoras.

[2] Detached Note VIII, below, p. 403.—In Late Antiquity this concept, like all religion, was dragged down into the sphere of magic. For the κύκλος Ἀνάγκης used by magicians see A. Audollent, *Defixionum Tabellae* (1904), Praefatio, p. lxxiii and W. Gundel, *Beiträge zur Ananke* (1914), 96.

[3] *Psyche*, ii. 124, n. 1 and 130, n. 3.

[4] No compound ἀναλήγω exists; the preposition, or particle, variously prefixed to the verb in the very late quotations of this verse was added by schoolmasters who had forgotten that in Homer the initial of λήγω can lengthen the preceding syllable (*Il.* 9. 191; *Od.* 8. 87).

[5] Simplicius (*In Arist. De caelo* ii. 1, p. 377. 12 Heiberg; Orph. fr. 230 Kern), expounding a reference to Ixion's wheel (τροχός), alleges that the verse describes the task of those gods whom man has to propitiate if he is to be rid of the wheel (τροχός) τῆς εἱμαρμένης καὶ γενέσεως (hence the verb at the end is ἀναψῦξαι). Proclus (*In Plat. Tim.* 42 c–d, iii. 297. 3 Diehl; Orph. fr. 229), speaking of the salvation of the soul from the κύκλος τῆς γενέσεως, quotes the verse as containing, according to Orpheus, the substance of the prayer of those 'initiated to Dionysos and Kore'.

Pythagoreans, then, spoke of the 'wheel of Ananke'. For the specific expression κύκλος γενέςεως I find no earlier evidence than in the Neoplatonic comment accompanying the second quotation[1] (and none for κύκλος γενέςων); but the two texts taken together show sufficiently that κύκλος was a Pythagorean term for life on earth conceived as a doleful series of incarnations.[2] How early, or how late, this term was adopted by Orphic devotees may be decided by those able to date the verse just quoted and to produce evidence, prior to Proclus', of an Orphic doctrine of metempsychosis; but the conclusion that on the Gold Leaf the word κύκλος is used with the Pythagorean connotation of the term is inescapable. Therewith it also becomes clear that the wording of the verses under discussion entails no suggestion of any particular rites—such as a dancing in and out of circles, or a turning of wheels—nor of a celestial journey of the soul. It has come to Persephone, who is χθονίων βαςίλεια; here is no trace of the 'heavenly geography' of Hades as elaborated by later Pythagoreans.

Formally perfect and coherent in themselves, the three verses 5–7 are unconnected with the following and imperfectly connected with the preceding. The latter is not surprising if, as we maintained, v. 4 was devised specially for victims of lightning; anyhow, the sudden introduction of the κύκλος implies a doctrine—why did this soul, but not the others, leave the 'wheel'?—which is not made explicit. One is tempted to conclude that these verses may have been taken out of a poem in which the lot of the privileged soul (and, if so, presumably that of others too) was described. This hypothesis must await discussion until all the texts have been examined in detail; but it may here be noted that the three verbs which the speaker of these verses uses in relating his experiences can all, without the slightest difficulty, be turned into the third person, merely by deleting the final -ν of each of them. These three verses, then, could indeed have been taken out of a descriptive context.

V. 8. He that has been speaking so far is now being spoken to. Since his first words had been addressed to Persephone, one would expect this verse to be her answer, but its tenor is such as to discourage this assumption. Ὄλβιε καὶ μακαριςτέ: thus an outstanding man, or hero, may be hailed by his fellows—rather than a human suppliant by the Queen of the Netherworld.[3] And indeed the fiction of her being addressed is becoming

---

[1] Lobeck, l.l., quotes the same term from Proclus' *Theologia Platonica* (this I cannot check).

[2] Lobeck, l.l., moreover, cites a passage from Cyprian to the same effect ('per diversos circulos'). 'Cf. perhaps also κύκλον ἀνιηρῶν ἐξέφυγες καμάτων in an epitaph from Kertsch, *Journ. Warburg Inst.* (1939), 368–74' (E. R. Dodds).

[3] For the address ὄλβιε see *Od.* 24. 36 and 192, Pausan. x. 24. 2 and, more significant, the typical and well-known praise, as ὄλβιοι, of those initiated into certain mysteries; for μακαριςτός (which is rare), an Attic inscription (quoted in L–S–J) of 446 B.C. praising a brave man

less explicit in the course of the poem until, in the preceding verse, she is
spoken of in the third person; the following words of praise sound rather
like an utterance by some *coetus sanctorum*, such as are seen on catacomb
paintings hailing one newly arrived at the sojourn of the blessed.[1]
Although no such *coetus* is indicated—the δαίμονες intruded in A2–3, v. 2
could fill this place; but they are not in A1—this impression will soon be
supported by a comparison with the lamella A4. First, though, it may be
observed that, very differently from all that precedes it, this verse bears
the mark of a prose-utterance laboriously and imperfectly turned into
a hexameter (as was previously observed with regard to A2–3, v. 4). The
shibboleth establishing this fact is the particle δ' after θεός, indispensable
for the metre but ruinous to the syntax.[2] An equally bad δ' has to do the
same service in A4, v. 3. At this point, in fact, the poetical form of A1
breaks down finally; the poem ends with a statement in prose: ἔριφος ἐς
γάλ' ἔπετον. The conclusion drawn from the style of the last two statements is, again, borne out by comparing A4; they both occur there,
undisguised, in prose. And yet it is these, formally so poor, phrases which
convey that culminating fact: the dead has become god. If we are to
approach this tremendous assertion, we have to attack that much be-
laboured and never solved crux, the formula ἔριφος ἐς γάλ' ἔπετον.

It would be hopeless to try and reproduce, and discuss, all that has
been said about this little phrase;[3] it may serve the present purpose if,
instead, two extreme views are considered: that the dead is stated, by this
'mystic formula', to have been assimilated to Dionysos[4]—or that, as
M. P. Nilsson holds, any discussion is a waste of time because, 'es sich
einfach um einen Ausdruck der volkstümlichen Hirtensprache handelt,
der die Befriedigung eines heißen Wunsches bezeichnen soll'.[5]

'There is no direct evidence', says Nilsson, 'that Dionysos appeared as
fawn or kid.'[6] This statement is slightly exaggerated; there is a brief gloss
in Hesychius Ἔριφος· ὁ Διόνυσος.[7] This, though, has long since been

---

who οὐδένα πημήνας ἐπιχθονίων ἀνθρώπων ‖ εἰς Ἀίδα κατέβα, πᾶσιν μακαριστὸς ἰδέσθαι (I.G. i².
1085; no. 41 Tod). Another instance will soon prove relevant. Plutarch (*De genio Socratis*, 16,
585 e) introduces a Pythagorean speaking of the burial rites without which the members of his
school would despair of ἀπέχειν τὸ μακαριστὸν καὶ οἰκεῖον τέλος.

[1] e.g. on the painting of the *inductio Vibiae* in the Praetextatus catacomb; Christian examples
are cited by L. von Sybel, *Christliche Antike*, i (1906), 266 f.

[2] The particle δέ after an imperative is normal—under certain conditions which do not
here apply; as anyone interested may see for himself by consulting Kühner–Gerth, *Syntax*, i.
50; Schwyzer, *Gram.* ii. 60; Denniston, *The Greek Particles*, pp. 172 and 178 f.

[3] References and fair summaries may be found in Olivieri, ad loc., J. H. Wieten, pp. 119 ff.,
J. Vollgraff, *Med. Akad. Amsterdam*, lvii (1924), 2; V. Macchioro, *Zagreus* (1929), p. 74, n. 1.

[4] 'New born as . . . a kid, one of the god's many incarnations': J. Harrison, *Proleg.*, p. 595;
'l'iniziato è divenuto dio, è rinato Dionysos eriphos': V. Macchioro, *Zagreus* (1929), p. 74.

[5] *G.G.R.*, ii. 225.   [6] *G.G.R.*, i. 539.

[7] Be it remembered that the whole evidence for Hesychius consists in the one, corrupt
manuscript of the fifteenth century from which Musurus printed his edition! Preller–Robert

amended to Ἐρίφ⟨ι⟩oc, because it was reasonably assumed to go back to a statement by the Athenian Apollodoros which survives, fuller but still sadly incomplete, in the geographical lexicon of Stephanos of Byzantium s.v. Ἀκρώρεια. According to Apollodoros, the Dionysos who was called Ἀκρωρείτης in Sikyon was called Ἐρίφιος in Metapontum. To this rather obscure information can be added pseudo-Apollodoros, Bibl. iii. 29 Wagner: Zeus changed the babe Dionysos εἰς ἔριφον to save him from Hera's wrath. That is all; for the epithet εἰραφιώτης, which is sometimes applied to Dionysos, is supposed by most authorities to describe him as bull rather than as kid.[1]

Assuming, on this slender basis, that Dionysos was sometimes imagined in the shape of a kid,[2] and that the person who utters the concluding words on this lamella, in describing himself as 'kid', declares himself to have become Dionysos: in what sense did he 'fall into milk'? Did the community to which the dead belonged practise baptism in milk? The technical obstacles to this practice have long since been recognized to be forbidding; nor was this the moment to mention it. Does he proclaim himself to have been translated to the galactic sphere, and perhaps to the constellation of Capricorn? But the speaker is standing before the chthonian Goddess. Is he, the renatus, rushing to suck the milk of immortality from her lactea ubera? This idea, though quite proper with Egyptian devotees of Isis, makes him shudder who has the slightest notion of Persephone, the goddess of the dead.[3]

The merest summary of these attempts as interpretatio mystica may easily be felt to be sufficient to discourage further efforts in the same direction; and yet the fundamental objection against it still remains to be stated. Even if it is accepted, for the sake of argument, that Dionysos could be called 'kid'—as, in Elis at least, he was invoked as 'bull'—how

i. 714, n. 5 indeed quote Hes. for Διόνυcος· ἔριφος παρὰ Λάκωcιν; this however is a slip: the lemma is Εἰραφιώτης not Διόνυcος (the slip recurs in Farnell, Cults . . . , v. 126 and 303. 85c).

[1] On a Campana relief representing a Dionysiac initiation (J. Harrison, ib. 519, Fig. 147) the tambourine carried by a maenad is decorated with the figure of a buck. It was left for V. Macchioro to claim this emblem as a representation of Dionysos (Zagreus (1929), p. 72, n. 3).

[2] The arguments in favour of this assumption are greatly strengthened, if we permit ourselves reference, in addition, to τράγος and αἴξ; in which case cf. L. R. Farnell, The Cults . . . , v. 107 f.

[3] The originators, and opponents, of the views here summarized can be found in the literature indicated above, pp. 277, n. 2; 278, n. 3. The view quoted last was proposed independently, so it seems, by V. Macchioro, Zagreus (1929), p. 74 (reprint of an earlier publication) and J. Vollgraff, l.l., and pursued by J. Carcopino (La Basilique Pythagoricienne . . . (1929), p. 311, cf. 156). They all refer to the 'mystic interpretation' (originated by Rizzo?) of a panel on the Dionysiac fresco in the Villa dei Misteri which shows a panisca suckling a kid. The kid is not Dionysos, nor a human identified with Dionysos, for the god appears himself on the central wall; the 'bucolic scene' illustrates a feature of dionysiac rapture known from Euripides (Ba. 700).

does it follow that the word ἔριφος here stands for Dionysos? And what has Dionysos to do with milk, and indeed in milk? The suppliant, it is true, has 'become god', and he says: 'I, the kid'. This does not by any means imply that he, the new god, is a kid—and hence Dionysos. The word ἔριφος is part—the subject—of a phrase evidently metaphorical, the meaning of which is sought, and this unified meaning need not by any means involve the equation 'kid = Dionysos'. In fact, this equation is, in the present context, inadmissible.[1] It is permissible to say that Greek mystery-cults aimed to establish some particularly close relation between the initiated and their gods; but quite apart from the fact that so far we have not found any indication that the lamellae witness to any mystery-cult, it is axiomatic that no Greek cult of any kind ever aimed to achieve identity of god and worshipper, alive or dead. That kind of aspiration existed in Egypt, where in the end every man expected after death to 'become Osiris'; there are traces of the same aspiration in Early Christianity; but it is beyond the horizon of Greek religion. The priestesses of the Ephesian Artemis were called 'bees' and those of the Brauronian, 'bears'—perhaps because in ages long forgotten their goddess had appeared in animal form; the ecstatic followers of Dionysos were bakchoi, or bakchai, as was the divine begetter of their raptures; but no man or woman was ever thought to have been transformed into Dionysos[2] or Artemis or any of the great deities. When Greek states recognized super-human qualities in men, they decreed divine honours for them—in their own names;[3] the great queen Arsinoe received a cult, after her death, as Aphrodite Arsinoe, still retaining her human name; and when, finally, powerless Seleucid and Ptolemaic puppet kings were proclaimed Dionysos, Epiphanes or Neos, religion had ebbed out into empty court-ceremonial.[4] These political 'deifications' are anyhow outside the stream of live religion. Where the belief in a higher life after death was held, the dead was thought of as 'being with the gods', even as 'god'—but never as identified with one of the known gods. So it remained to the end of Antiquity, and so we find it in our text: 'You have become (a) god.' It is not by chance but fundamentally characteristic that neither here nor

---

[1] Could it be that those who maintained this interpretation were influenced, consciously or unconsciously, by that type of early Christian representation, the Lamb of God accompanied by twelve other lambs (the apostles) which can be seen e.g. in S. Clemente and SS. Cosma e Damiano in Rome and in S. Apollinare in Classe in Ravenna?

[2] L. R. Farnell, *Greek Hero Cults . . .*, pp. 374 f.: 'union of the mortal with the divinity'; 'the *mystes* . . . partaking of the sacred body of the dismembered deity and assisting in his resurrection'; 'the mystic sacrament of the Orphic societies, by which man and god became one flesh'; '. . . at least we may be sure that it [the "kid in the milk"-formula] alludes to the mystic union of the votary and the god, who was often theriomorphic'; these quotations, all of them referring to the gold plaques, sufficiently summarize the interpretation which—with every respect for the distinguished author—I oppose.

[3] C. Habicht, *Gottmenschentum und griechische Städte* (1956), *passim*.

[4] W. Taeger, *Charisma*, i (1957), *passim*.

in any other Greek text does there occur any formulation comparable with the current Egyptian 'Osiris Pepi' (or whatever the personal name of the deceased might have been).[1]

The dead, then, has not 'become Dionysos'. A string of conclusions hangs on this observation. First, the word ἔριφος does not here denote Dionysos; consequently, there is no hint pointing to Dionysos on this tablet—nor on any other; and therewith, finally, no reason remains for describing the religion to which they witness as 'orphic'. But the question of the 'kid in the milk' remains. That little formula follows upon the announcement 'you have become god', as on A1, so on A4; on the latter tablet it is, moreover, preceded and followed by the acclamation χαῖρε. These contexts suggest that this formula must somehow denote the attainment of a supreme good. This was M. P. Nilsson's conclusion, and he was by no means the first to draw it. His further suggestion, that it stemmed from the language of shepherds, is, however, open to doubt; they were not shepherds who erected these grandiose tumuli. I would tentatively suggest an alternative.

This little phrase has a ring reminding one of proverbs. Here are some comparable ones, mostly drawn from Schneidewin–Leutsch, *Corpus Paroemiographorum* (1839): ὄνος εἰς ἄχυρα.—βοῦς εἰς ἄμητον (or ἐπὶ φάτνην, or ἐπὶ cωρῶι).—βατράχωι ὕδωρ.—γαλῆι cτέαρ and, with the opposite implication: εἰς ἠκονημένας μαχαίρας ἡ αἴξ.—εἰς πάγας ὁ λύκος.—μῦς ἐν πίττηι. With verb: ἐν ὅλμωι ἐκοιμήθην.—εἰς μελίττας ἐκώμασας.—κριὸς τροφεῖ· ἀπέτιcεν.—μῦς πίccης γεύεται. If it be objected that the 'fall into milk' would seem to involve an excessive and indeed a pernicious supply of the 'desired good', it may be urged that such exaggeration, again, is characteristic of proverbs; e.g. γλυκὺ μέλι καὶ πνιξάτω or ἐν μέλιτι cαυτὸν κατακρύπτεις or ἀγαθῶν μυρμηκιά; besides, one may recall the reaction, in Aesop's fable,[2] of the fly that fell into the saucepan.

It may still seem strange that a plain proverb should acquire the dignity of a religious formula, but there is, I suspect, at least one analogy for this. Ἔφυγον κακόν· εὗρον ἄμεινον is a normal *versus paroemiacus*. From Demosthenes we know that it was used in *Winkelmysterien*; from his commentators, that it was recited in Athenian marriage rites; and the paroemiographers[3] offer still other comment on it, from which one may conclude that an ordinary proverb had been received into various liturgical formularies.[4]

A proverb invested with the dignity and the esoteric significance of

---

[1] Cf. S. G. F. Brandon, *Man and his Destiny* (1962), pp. 35 ff.; id. *History, Time and Deity* (1965), p. 22.

[2] No. 177 Hausrath.

[3] Zenobius iii. 98, Diogenianus iv. 74, and parallels, in ed. Schneidewin–Leutsch.

[4] 'The land flowing with milk and honey', the phrase used to denote outstanding bliss, affords a Biblical parallel which has been noted by many students.

a religious formula, the phrase about the 'kid in the milk' sets the seal upon the high eschatological hope which this poem expresses with a beautiful and coherent flow of ideas and imagery, hardly impaired by those minor hitches on which the critical analysis had to insist. The specific ideology of A1, to be appreciated, requires a comparison not only with A2–3 but also with A4, to which therefore we now turn.

(c) TABLET A4

A4. *Transcript*

Napoli, Museo Nazionale 11463. Plate 27*b*
Timpone Grande 54 mm. × 29 mm.
Not. Scav. (1879), 156; *I.G.* xiv. 642; Olivieri A²; 32f Kern; 20 DK.

l. 1 ΑΛΛΟΠΟΤΑΜΨΥΧΗΠΡΟΛΙΠΗΙΦΑΟΣΑΕΛΙΟΙΟ v. 1

2 ΔΕΞΙΟΝΕΣΟΙΑΣΔΕΕ[·]ΝΑΙΠΕΦΥΛΑΓΜΕΝΟΝ 2

3 ΕΙΥΜΑΛΑΠΑΝ[·]ΑΧΑΙΡΕΠΑΘΩΝΤΟΠΑΘΗ 3

4 ΜΑΤΟΔΟΥΠΩΠΡΟΣΘΕΕΠΕΠΟΝΘΕΙΣΘΕΟΣΕΓ 4

5 ΕΝΟΥΕΞ[·]ΑΝΘΡΩΠΟΥΕΡΙΦΟΣΕΣΓΑΛΑ

6 ΕΠΕΤΕΣΧΑΙΡΧΑΙΡΕΔΕΞΙΑΝΟΔΟΙΠΟΡ 5

7 ΛΕΙΜΩΝΑΣΤΕΙΕΡΟΥΣ ΚΑΙΑΛΣΕΑ 6

8 ΦΕΡΣΕΦΟΝΕΙΑΣ

Lamella, quae novies (!) plicata erat, rugis cooperta est, quae lectorem fallere possunt.—
Literae pertenues sed satis diligenter incisae l. 1 : inter ΠΟ et ΤΑΜ spatium ceteris paululo
maius, quo literam (per compendium scriptam) contineri non puto (item olim Barnabei)
l. 2 : in media linea, ante ΝΑΙ, una litera (?Τ) ruga hausta est l. 3 : in initio, litera Ι a lit.
Ε tam procul abest ut scalpelli lapsu effecta esse videatur.—Post ΠΑΝ una litera ruga hausta
est. l. 5 : post Ε Ξ ruga foramen effecit quo una litera hausta esse potest l. 6 : in fine, post
ΠΟΡ, nihil scriptum est neque unquam fuit l. 7 : in fine scalptor spatium vacuum reliquit,
ut deae nomen in ultima linea totum extaret l. 8 : in fine quod ΝΕΦΑΣ, pro ΝΕΙΑΣ,
legerunt priores, id rugae tribuendum est

A4. *Reconstruction*

1 Ἀλλ' ὁπόταμ ψυχὴ προλίπηι φάος Ἀελίοιο,

2 δεξιὸν †ΕΣΟΙΑΣΔΕΕΤ† ⟨ἰέ⟩ναι πεφυλαγμένον εὖ μάλα πάντα.

3 χαῖρε παθὼν τὸ πάθημα τὸ δ' οὔπω πρόςθε ἐπεπόνθεις·

4 θεὸς ἐγένου ἐξ ἀνθρώπου· ἔριφος ἐς γάλα ἔπετες.

5 χαῖρ⟨ε⟩ χαῖρε· δεξιὰν ὁδοιπόρ⟨ει⟩

6 λειμῶνάς τε ἱεροὺς καὶ ἄλςεα Φερςεφονείας.

v. 1. 2 ⟨ἰέ⟩ναι nescio an primus coniecerim; εἰςιέναι iam E. Rohde   v. 1. 5 ὁδοιπόρ⟨ει⟩
G.Z.: -⟨ῶν⟩ priores.

Comment

V. 1. 'ἀλλ': hoc initium nobis manifestum facit e maiore carmine excerpta esse quae sequuntur': thus Olivieri. In fact, a brief consideration of the whole text will easily lead to the opposite of his conclusion. The opening ἀλλ' ὁπόταν indeed sounds as though the verse were the continuation of others preceding; but this impression is countered by many oracles which begin in the same manner;[1] as no reader of Aristophanes can fail to remember: Ἀλλ' ὁπόταν μάρψηι . . . (*Eq.* 197); ἀλλ' ὁπόταν . . . (*Lys.* 770); ἀλλ' ὅταν . . . (*Av.* 967; cf. 'Bakis', parodied ib. 983 by αὐτὰρ ἐπήν . . .). Herodotus provides four instances of the same kind;[2] one more 'Bakis' ἀλλ' ὁπόταν . . . is quoted by Pausanias ix. 17. 5; a Delphic one of the same type by Plutarch.[3] The recurrence of this sonorous yet empty opening on the gold leaf does not prove the text on it to be an oracle; it does show that versifiers could thus fill the first foot of the first hexameter of their productions and give it an air of hieratic dignity. The rest of the verse is modelled on *Il.* 18. 11 ∼ Hes. *Op.* 155 λείψειν (ἔλιπον) φάος Ἡελίοιο; for the one syllable still wanting after the indispensable subject ψυχή the compound προλείπω was happily available. The substance of the whole verse amounts to the two words 'at death'. The verse quoted from 'Orpheus' by Proclus[4] ὁππότε δ' ἄνθρωπος προλίπηι φάος Ἡελίοιο represents a similar adaptation of the handy epic model.

V. 2. The letters marked as corrupt are, but for the last, securely read. It is, I am afraid, as hopeless to try and extract an original wording from them as it is with regard to many passages of the so-called 'Demeter-hymn' (below, p. 344 ff.) found in the same grave. The question is, even so, legitimate whether these letters are a part, however corrupt, of a complete verse, so that this line would have to be regarded as representing two verses, however incomplete. This, I believe, can be answered confidently, and in the negative, on considering the last words in this line. They do not mean 'being right wary of all things'. In epic poetry φυλάσσω, and its middle, with an object-accusative never means 'to beware of', or 'guard against' something, but, always, 'to keep', 'observe', 'bear in mind'. The middle is thus used four times in Hesiod's *Works and Days*, the closest parallel to our verse being v. 491 εὖ πάντα φυλάσσεο.[5] 'Observing carefully everything' the dead is 'to go to the right'. It is lucky indeed

---

[1] A similar observation was made by A. Dieterich, *De hymnis Orphicis* (1891), p. 41, n. 2.
[2] i. 55. 1; iii. 57; vi. 77. 2; viii. 77. 1: 'Bakis'.
[3] *De Pyth. or.* 399 c. These are early instances. On perusing any collection of late oracles one will at once light on further parallels; e.g. *Or. Sib.* i. 190, 230, 336 (Ἀλλ' ὁπόταν φωνή . . .); ii. 154 (ditto); iii. 97 (ditto); iv. 130 (ditto). Nor would Lucian miss the opportunity of a persiflage: *Peregr.* 29 f. Ἀλλ' ὁπόταν Πρωτεύς, κτλ.
[4] *In Remp.* ii. 339. 17 Kroll; Orph. fragm. 223 Kern.
[5] See also Hes. *Op.* 263, 561, 694 and the end of the Homeric *Hymn on Apollo*.

that, before the meaningless letters, ΔΕΞΙΟΝ is perfectly clear, and after them ἰέναι can be claimed to be almost completely extant. This line, then, summarizes the advice which is given fully on the plaques from Petelia and Pharsalos, in which the need to 'keep right' is stressed; it therewith provides welcome evidence that these texts emanate from the same milieu as those from Thurii. The dead is reminded at the entrance of Hades to go to the right and to observe all the prescriptions which he knew from the traditions of his community. This summary advice is drawn-out, so as to effect a proper hexameter-ending, by the addition of μάλα and the use of the perfect participle instead of the present; the verse can be completed by extracting the prefix, or preposition, εἰς from the beginning of the corrupt letters and disregarding the rest; the infinitive (εἰς-)ἰέναι is easily taken *in loco imperativi*.[1] Now δεξιὸν (εἰς-)ἰέναι is certainly not exemplary Greek for 'go to the right', and if this fact is regarded as an objection valid even with a text like this, one may assume that the corrupt letters conceal some expression which effected better Greek—but also a hexameter with seven or eight feet![2] It is a Hobson's choice. What matters, however, is the conclusion that no extensive and substantial element of the text—e.g. something on the lines of the Petelia tablet— can be assumed to be implied by those corrupt letters; for the valid reason that any such substance is actually summarized by the words πεφυλαγμένον . . . πάντα.

Vv. 3ff. The centre of the following obviously is the pronouncement 'you have become a god', with its corollary, the 'kid in the milk' formula, as in A1; the whole here addressed to the dead by, let us say, some 'chorus mysticus';[3] for there is no mention in this text of the presence of the goddess. The pronouncement is both preceded and followed by the acclamation χαῖρε, corresponding to ὄλβιε καὶ μακαριστέ in A1; and it is in prose; a prose which rings more genuine than its laboured counterpart in A1. In fact, the verse preceding it loudly proclaims its origin in a prose formula, awkwardly and ineffectually disguised. Its actual meaning is: 'you now experience what you have never experienced before'.[4] As the verse stands, the noun τὸ πάθημα is, after παθών, a supernumerary, with its article worse than redundant; after it, τό is pressed into service in place of a relative pronoun; the following δ' serves to bridge the hiatus but spoils the syntax; the second syllable of οὔπω duplicates πρόσθε after it; and the concluding pluperfect would have been an aorist but for the requirement of the metre. These stylistic observations are, I feel, sufficient to discourage any attempt to find more in these words than the indicated, comparatively plain meaning. It remains indeed to be considered why

---

[1] This was, more or less, the view taken by E. Rohde, *Psyche*, ii. 220, n. 4.

[2] e.g. δεξιὸν οἶμον δεῖ ς' ἰέναι: sed hoc ludentis est.

[3] Cf. above, p. 323.   [4] παθών is here used as in Menander, *Dyskolos* 954.

the novelty of the experience is stressed at all, seeing that nobody would
expect to 'become a god' more than once; for the moment, though, it may
be noted that these lines are quite unconnected with the preceding, in
which rules for the entering of Hades are hinted at rather than given.
What is described in A1, 2, 3—the arrival before Persephone and the
words to be spoken to her—is here left out; the outcome, confidently
expected, is alone stated.

The text ends with a perfect hexameter, the latter half of which is
borrowed from Homer (*Od.* 10. 509), while the 'holy meadows' are one
of many echoes of the ἀcφόδελοc λειμών in the Nekyia.[1] The connection
of this beautiful verse with the preceding raises a problem. The natural
first urge on the part of the reader is to refer the word δεξιάν in v. 5 to the
same situation as δεξιόν in v. 2; that is, to the choice facing the soul on
entering Hades. This, however, is impossible, for (*a*) this would require
the supplement ὁδοιπορ⟨ήcαc⟩ (or fem.), which is excluded by the metre,
the trochaic dimeter, though surprising, being inescapable;[2] (*b*) the soul
is not here being praised 'because she walked to the right' before but,
obviously, because she 'has become god'; (*c*) she obviously did not 'go to
the groves of Persephone' straight on entering Hades but is to go there
now, after her deification. The matter is clinched by an analogy of detail
in the Platonic myth of Er (*Rep.* 614 c), where the judges in the Netherworld are said to τοὺc μὲν δικαίουc κελεύειν πορεύεcθαι τὴν εἰc δεξιάν.

Those, then, who had declared the dead deified, hail him again and
tell him to go to the right, like the 'just' in Plato's myth. Considering this,
ΟΔΟΙΠΟΡ, which the engraver left incomplete—apparently he wished
to start the last verse at the beginning of a line, as also he allotted a separate line to the name of the goddess at the very end—is better completed
so as to form an imperative.

The concluding verse must be supposed to specify the direction given
to the perfected soul; it is to go to the meadows and groves of Persephone.
As a point of grammar, the admissibility of this interpretation may be
granted; the accusative, without any preposition, indicating the goal

---

[1] See E. R. Dodds, *Plato, Gorgias*, p. 375 and above, p. 253.

[2] On the metre of this passage more will be said below.—The riddling inscription (enu-
cleated by Wilamowitz) on a square silver leaf from Paestum (*I.G.* xiv. 665) τὰc θεοῦ τ⟨ᾶ⟩c
παιδόc εἰμι does not, to my mind, afford more than an incidental parallel to the use of trochees
in A4 (such as is provided also by the chance combination of dactyls and trochees in the Attic
epigram 1387 Peek = 79 Kaibel). P. Friedländer indeed (Fr.–Hoffleit, *Epigrammata* (1948),
p. 166, no. 178) would compare it with the gold lamellae and even connect it with the line
under discussion into a dialogue between Soul and Persephone; on this assumption he presented it as 'the oldest "safe-conduct for the dead"'. This is hardly convincing. Silver is not
gold (and the material appears to be essential) and the mode of writing quite different.
Numerous analogies, like τᾶc Ἥραc εἰμί (cf. L. H. Jeffery, *B.S.A.* (1955), 78) quoted by Fr.
himself, suggest that the silver leaf was attached to some object dedicated to Kore; cf. the
contemporary inscription, from the opposite end of the Hellenized world, Ἀπόλλωνοc ἡγεμόνοc
εἰμὶ τὸμ Φάcι on a bowl discussed by Rostovzeff, *Iranians and Greeks . . .* (1922), p. 128.

being a Homeric characteristic. One would not, though, find in Homer an indication of this kind filling a whole verse as it does here, where, moreover, the direction has already been indicated by δεξιάν. Perhaps, then, this verse (as previously suspected with regard to others) is a citation from some poem. It is too good a verse to have been devised by the compiler of the text on the lamella; nor, obviously, can it from origin have been preceded by the trochees to which we here find it—rather loosely—attached.

The centre and essence, then, of this tablet is the announcement of deification, in prose and in a wording which proves, especially on comparison with A1, v. 8, to be a traditional formula. It is surrounded by acclamations and followed by the order 'go to the right'; the whole adumbrating a scene of Judgement through which the deceased is expected to pass to eternal bliss. The metrical form of these surrounding verses hardly disguises their origin, likewise, in a prose formulary. The prefatory verses summarize rules to be observed on entering Hades; they were probably made up for use on the present tablet. The text is concluded by a verse of totally different quality evoking the sojourn of the deified and introducing, at the very end, the name of the goddess.

Widely different, in form and content, from the other three tablets, this one still breathes the same confidence in a higher life beyond and suggests the same theology. Quite otherwise the last remaining sample of the group under discussion. The late tablet of Caecilia Secundina (A5) none the less deserves a brief discussion; and that not only for completeness' sake. As previously noted,[1] it alone preserves correctly the vocatives Εὔκλεες Εὐβουλεῦ τε which are variously corrupted in A1–3; beyond this, it conveys some important lessons, if mainly by way of contrast.

(d) TABLET A5

The reading is nowhere in doubt, hence it will suffice if the resulting wording is here subjoined.[2]

Tablet A5

Brit. Mus., Dept. of Antiquities, no. 3154.   Plate 28a
From Rome   6·5 × 2·4 cm.
B.M. Cat. of Jewellery, p. 380; G. Murray apud Harrison, Proleg., p. 673; Comparetti (1910), p. 42; Olivieri B² (p. 18); 32g Kern; 19a DK.

> Ἔρχεται ἐκ καθαρῶν καθαρά, χθονίων βασίλεια,
> Εὔκλεες Εὐβουλεῦ τε, Διὸς τέκος ἀγλαά· ἔχω δὲ
> Μνημοσύνης τόδε δῶρον ἀοίδιμον ἀνθρώποισιν.
> "Καικιλία Σεκουνδεῖνα, νόμωι ἴθι δῖα γεγῶσα."

[1] Above, p. 308.
[2] The facsimile in the B.M. Catalogue of Jewellery, p. 380 and the photograph in Guthrie, Orpheus . . . , Pl. 10 may be compared.

Comment

The tablet of Caecilia Secundina,[1] which was incised about six hundred years after the other four,[2] is evidence of the same religion sadly debased. It is the only one among all the remaining Gold Leaves to which Diels's description 'passport for the dead' applies ('Orphic' though it is no more than the rest). It is valuable for this very reason. For one thing, it confirms that the older leaves, far from being chance finds emanating from some conventicles of slight significance, are witnesses to a tradition strong enough to last into the age of the Soldier Emperors; moreover, the interpretation of these texts is greatly helped by this profound contrast: what had, once, expressed a deep and metaphysical devotion has been turned into an amulet.[3]

At the very beginning of the text one may be puzzled to find the verb in the third person replacing the traditional Ἔρχομαι, all the more so since immediately afterwards the person referred to speaks of herself in the first person (ἔχω). This syntactical *contredanse* was necessitated by the alteration which the versifier applied to the traditional form of v. 2. He desired to give brief expression to the necessary claim of divine descent which in the model filled a whole verse (καὶ γὰρ ἐγών, κτλ.). Διὸς τέκος filled the bill for him, and looking at the end of his production one may suspect that he regarded Διός and δῖος as fairly equivalent; I suspect that he was not a Greek and had Latin *divus* in mind. Ἔχω δέ at the end of his verse left a metrical gap to be filled; he knew the Homeric tag ἀγλαὰ τέκνα and boldly borrowed the adjective from it.[4] Presumably he meant it to be taken, contrary to epic usage, for a feminine; after all, he was writing for a lady! The difficulty of syntax and scanning he left to the reader (if any); he may have expected his wording to be as legitimate as Homeric ΑΓΛΑΑΕΡΓΑ and ΑΓΛΑΑΑΠΟΙΝΑ or ΑΓΛΑΑΑΕΘΛΑ. But it was unsuitable, he felt, for Secundina to introduce herself as 'the glamorous child of Zeus': hence he put the verb in the third person, thereby render-

---

[1] Caecilia Secundina has been denied entry in the *Prosopographia Imp. Rom.*[2] by Groag and Stein, where she ought to appear in vol. ii, p. 14. There are many plain Secundini, esp. potters in Gaul and Germany (*PW* iiA 3. 986); besides, this is a cognomen in many respectable families (e.g. Aelii, Aurelii, Claudii), but I have found no Caecilius among these. If, however, it is assumed that Secundina was named after some Secundus, she would have various chances of a distinguished ancestry, right up (as G. Murray and J. Harrison noticed, pp. 585, n. 4, and 674) to the elder or younger Pliny (cf. also Martial vii. 84). Thus, by the way, she could well qualify for the epithet ἀγλαά (i.e. *clarissima*?).

[2] For the date (about A.D. 260) see above, p. 293.

[3] 'It has every appearance of having been rolled up in a cylinder similar to that which contained the Petelia tablet' (F. H. Marshall, *B.M. Catalogue of Jewellery*, p. xlvii); cf. above, p. 280 and below, p. 355.

[4] Its first letter entails the one problem of reading in this tablet; in fact, it is not a letter at all. The engraver's tool seems to have slipped, producing after ΟϹ a deep hook which could have been completed to form an Α. This was not done, but since ΓΛΑΑ after it is indubitable, no other word can have been intended.

ing the intended reference less awkward. The first sentence could now be taken as spoken, by way of presentation, by some infernal *ianitor*, however unsuitable it be that Secundina's speech thereafter begins with ἔχω δέ.

The following sentence, ἔχω δέ . . . ἀνθρώποιϲιν conveys the meaning 'I hold this tablet with its famous verse-inscription'. Here Mnemosyne appears; an intentional echo of the Petelia-text, welcome because, once more, it proves the two sets of plaques to come from one and the same orbit; but how changed and enfeebled an echo. Poetry is the gift of the Muses; Mnemosyne is the mother of the Muses. The original, profound meaning of this mythological concept has here degenerated into a mere metaphor, for 'this gift of Mnemosyne' means 'the poem on this Gold Leaf'. It is intended to serve a specific and important purpose and its value has accordingly to be stressed. This is done by the phrase ἀοίδιμον ἀνθρώποιϲιν; the pale and vague reflection of a tragic Homeric concept.[1] Secundina presents the 'famous poem' and can rely upon its magic efficiency; some infernal voice will address her: 'Go! You have become goddess in accordance with the law.' Here ἴθι corresponds with ὁδοιπόρει in A4 and δῖα, as already noted, stands for *diva* and θεά, corresponding with θεὸϲ ἐγένου in A1 and A4. Symptomatic of the fundamental change in the religious attitude is the fact that here, and here only, the personal name of the dead forms part of the text, while the anonymity of all of the older tablets witnesses to the deeper conception of death as the entrance into a new dimension. Secundina expects to become *diva* in her own right because she is equipped with the magic token; with her, we are in the region of the Magic Papyri and Gnostic amulets. She did indeed belong— as especially the first verse shows—to the very sect (if the word be for once allowed) to which the older tablets witness; but its persuasion had changed, in conformity with the general tendencies of the age.

(e) A COMPARATIVE ANALYSIS OF A1–4

The spirituality of the older documents stands out by contrast. The dead holds the gold leaf in his hand, or it lies near his ear. On the dread journey to the other land the letters on them speak to him. They whisper advice; they prompt him for his meeting with the gods of the Nether-world, and some—two of the four—go on to anticipate the favourable judgement which awaits him. Direction, comfort, and a strengthening for the departing soul: this is the essence of these documents.[2] It was

---

[1] *Il.* 6. 358.

[2] M. Guarducci (*Inscriptiones Creticae*, ii. 315) suggested that the gold leaves, rolled up, were put into the mouths of the persons buried, in analogy with the 'Charon's obolos' in Athenian rite; but if so, why were they inscribed at all? For most of the plaques, anyhow, this suggestion cannot be made to square with the find-reports (as to the Cretan leaves, their precise location in the graves is not known). The question still remains open, why some of the

wrong, and worse than wrong, to misinterpret them by forcing the debased ideology of the one, late specimen upon documents older by more than half a millennium. The ideology underlying them emerges in considering the differences between A1 (with A4) on the one hand, and A2–3 on the other.[1]

A1, 2, 3 have in common the first three verses (but for the intrusion, in v. 2, of δαίμονες and the transposition of ὄλβιον in A2–3), in which the dead presents himself and asserts his divine descent. Also the statement 'I was killed by lightning' occurs in A1 as well as in A2–3, but we saw reason to regard this, with its curious variations of wording, as an insertion made with regard to the special condition of those buried in the Timpone Piccolo. Thereafter the two texts continue on different lines. The essential difference is in the judgement 'You have become god' occurring in A1 and A4 but not in A2–3, and in the statement 'I have paid the amends for injustice' in A2–3 but not in A1 and A4. This reciprocity is not due to chance. He who becomes god has no injustice to amend; he that has to make amends does not become god. Add to this the difference of tone; the triumphant confidence in A1 : 'I rushed out of the wheel; I gained the crown; I find refuge with the goddess' contrasting with A2–3: 'A suppliant I come to Persephone'; and, corresponding with these different dispositions, the certainty of deification on the one hand; the wish to be sent to 'the place of the εὐαγεῖς' on the other. Behind these differences there lies more than a variety of temperament, sanguine or modest; so systematic a set of alternatives reflects a systematic conception of the after-life. There are those who have lived pure and have paid amends for 'injustice': they hope to be with the εὐαγεῖς. And there are those, also 'from the pure', who had no amends to pay and know that they have 'escaped the wheel' and will experience (πάσχειν) what their soul had not experienced on its previous ἀνακυκλώσεις;[2] they will now become gods. It is impossible not to think of Pindar; of οἷσι δὲ Φερσεφόνα κτλ. on the one hand,[3] and of ὅσοι δ' ἐτόλμασαν ἔστρις κτλ. on the other; and indeed of Empedokles. In that one timpone, then, there was buried one who felt that he had completed the series of incarnations (and so, too,

lamellae—namely, those from the Timpone Grande and the Cretan—were found folded over-and-over. If, for the latter, M. Guarducci's suggestion should prove correct (it can hardly be reconciled with the very precise report about the Timpone Grande), the purpose must have been to 'put the right words on the tongue' of the dead person. Or is this treatment of some of the plaques an indication that, already then, one began to regard them as a kind of amulet? The fact that none of the lamellae was designed for an amulet-case (not even the Petelia plaque; as will be seen later) militates against this assumption; on the other hand, certain features still to be considered (below, p. 353) may support it.

[1] To roll them all into one *mixtum compositum* is to debar oneself from understanding them.

[2] The use of this unusual term in Aristoxenos' (?) report about Pythagoras' incarnations (fr. 12 Wehrli; p. 99. 30 DK) agrees with the Pythagorean use of the term κύκλος. The conventional term would be περίοδος.

[3] Taking this as parallel with *Ol.* ii. 61–6.

felt he who was laid to rest, with our tablet A4, in the neighbouring Timpone Grande); the other two, though equally sure of their pure life, hoped for an interval of bliss but expected (after a 'long year' if we may here interpolate the notions known from Hesiod and Pindar, Empedokles and Plato) to return to a life on earth.[1]

This is, in the main, how E. Rohde[2] interpreted these tablets; for some he spoke in vain. I fail to see, though, what made him call this creed 'Orphic',[3] for he did not indulge in those fancies about Dionysos[4] and Zagreus and Titans which others, before and after him, read into rather than out of these texts.[5] An elaborate doctrine of the after-life centring on the belief in a judgement after death and in reincarnation of souls; a doctrine shared, down to striking detail, by Theron and Empedokles; drawn upon by Plato and surviving, however debased, in the Roman Empire: what can it be if not Pythagorean?[6] For one or the other of the

---

[1] The fact that some of those buried with these Gold Leaves had been killed by lightning thus proves not to have been regarded as a determining factor for their after-life. The hero buried, with the plaque A4, in the Timpone Grande was to become a god, and he was not διόβλητος; while two of the three buried in the T. Piccolo (A2 and A3) are not deified, although their lamellae contain (with scribal faults) the same statement ('I was struck by Zeus' thunderbolt') as A1, who is deified. Cf. above, p. 316.

[2] *Psyche* ii. 219 f.

[3] Cf. Wilamowitz, *Der Glaube* . . . , ii². 202.—G. Charles-Picard (*Compt. Rend. de l'Acad. des Inscr.* (1930), 329) denied the 'Orphic' character of the Gold Leaves and described them as 'Eleusinian'. The rejection of the former term obviously does not imply acceptance of the latter. Eleusinian echoes—echoes, that is, of the generally accepted myth of the abduction and return of Kore, with some details specifically Eleusinian and Attic—stand out on the Tarentine amphorae (Detached Note XII, below, p. 411); the abduction of Kore, but not her return, on the Lokrian reliefs (above, p. 165). The Gold Leaves have neither; nor Demeter, nor Kore; but Persephone. I need say no more, I trust, about this thesis of a respected scholar.

[4] For the 'kid in the milk' in particular see his sceptical note, p. 220. 3.

[5] A more or less identical eschatological doctrine is found in Pindar, Empedokles, the Gold Leaves and (developed) in Plato (also, in Stoic guise, in Vergil, *Aen.* vi. 724 ff.); therefore it is Orphic. The reason? It occurs in Pindar, Empedokles, etc.; none of whom hints at Orpheus (except that Plato, in different contexts, violently abuses his votaries). It seems a remarkable instance of arguing in a circle. Where is the evidence, prior to Proclus, for an 'Orphic' doctrine of transmigration? Kallimachos' reference to Zagreus (fr. 43. 117 ff.) by no means implies it; Herodotus (ii. 123) hints at Pythagoreans (and not at 'Orphics'). How late, or how early, the pertinent verses are which Proclus—and nobody before him!—quotes from 'Orpheus' (frs. 223 f. Kern), I do not pretend to know, but Empedokles' *Katharmoi* is clearly among their ancestors, and ψυχὰς ἀθανάτας (fr. 223. 7) sounds terminological and post-Platonic. Cf. the authoritative discussion by K. von Fritz in *PW* xiv. 187 ff.

[6] The one counter-argument I can see is the fact that the hero buried in the Timpone Grande was cremated; contrary to Pythagoras' direction, if Iamblichus' testimony (*Vita Pyth.* 154) is accepted (its credibility is not enhanced by the assertion that Pythagoras was following the Persian magi). This exception (it applies also to the Pharsalos tablet) cannot outweigh the agreements with the essentials of Pythagorean doctrine; it is moreover reduced by the fact that at Thurii the dead was not burned on a pyre and the ashes and bones collected in a vessel (as was done at Pharsalos and was the rule where cremation was adopted), but placed in a large coffin, put in an elaborate grave-chamber, and there burned. The ceremony at Thurii was thus a combination of the two forms of burial, and it conformed with the other prescription mentioned by Iamblichus: Cavallari found the corpse covered with

representatives just quoted this has been asserted by others before;[1] with regard to the Gold Leaves in particular by J. H. Wieten[2] (to whose argument, however, I cannot subscribe). If this view is accepted, some further details fall into their place. The early Pythagoreans were aristocrats; so were those buried in the grandiose tumuli near Thurii and, of course, Pindar and the ruler of Akragas and Empedokles (who could imagine them undergoing the cleansing rites of Orpheotelestae? And subscribing to the laboured mythology of salvation centring on the Orphic Dionysos?).—Another point. There is the Pythagorean tripartition of 'men and gods and such as Pythagoras'[3]—he that was held to be the Hyperborean Apollo;[4] again, there are, at Thurii, among the 'pure', those that become gods and those that, for an aeon, live in an elysium (as heroes, as the Petelia fragment will confirm; cf. Pindar fr. 133), but face renewed incorporation; and, of course, there are the impure; finally, there are, in Pindar frs. 129–31 (as recovered by Wilamowitz[5] and perfected by Snell) the 'three ways'; the one by which Herakles 'went to the gods', the second to the blissful place of the $\epsilon\dot{v}c\epsilon\beta\epsilon\hat{i}c$, and the third leading the $\dot{a}c\epsilon\beta\epsilon\hat{i}c$ to purification through suffering. Are not these altogether facets of one great concept? Men on the threshold of divinity, like Pythagoras and Empedokles; men worthy to become heroes, like Theron; and, finally, mere—men. He that finds no more in this than abstruse speculation, or varying degrees of vanity, has never felt the impact of a great man—to assure him of that original divinity, hidden and mocked by day-to-day experience, which mankind strives, painfully, gradually, to recover. The impact of 'Strife' and 'injustice' upon the realm of divine perfection, Persephone's 'ancient woe' and the gods' fall into corporality: these are so many hints (insufficient for our ignorance) at the myth which symbolized this understanding of essential humanity and its debasement; as 'purity' summarizes the way to its recovery.[6]

a white sheet (which at once disintegrated) and not the customary purple; Pythagoras prescribed white dress at burials. Unfortunately Cavallari does not tell if the sheet was of linen, as Herodotus ii. 81 would lead one to expect (Artemidorus, *Onirocrit.* p. 245. 17 Pack, refers to the $\ddot{\epsilon}\theta oc\ \kappa\alpha\theta$' $\ddot{o}$ $o\dot{i}$ $\nu\epsilon\kappa\rho o\dot{i}$ $\dot{\epsilon}\nu$ $\lambda\epsilon\upsilon\kappa o\hat{i}c$ $\dot{\epsilon}\kappa\phi\acute{\epsilon}\rho o\nu\tau\alpha\iota$. Had the custom changed since classical times?).

[1] 'I miss any reference to Festugière's article in *Rev. Biblique,* xliv (1935), esp. pp. 370 ff. and 385 ff., as well as to his review of Guthrie, *R.E.G.,* xlix (1936), 307, which anticipate some of your results' (E. R. Dodds).

[2] L.l. 9 ff., 25, etc., after A. Delatte, *Études* . . . , pp. 71 and 78 f.

[3] Aristotle, fr. 192 R, i.e. Iambl. *V.P.* 31; D.K. Pyth. 7.

[4] Arist. fr. 191, i.e. Aelian, *V.H.* ii. 26; DK. ib.   [5] *Pindaros,* p. 499.

[6] If the Pythagorean character of the tablets is accepted, people of this persuasion must have continued to live at Thurii, and to celebrate their rites, well after the final collapse of Pythagorean power in South Italy and the 'exodus' of which Aristoxenos tells and which K. von Fritz (*Pythagorean Politics in South Italy,* 1940) dates about 390 B.C. Our historical knowledge is hardly complete enough to entitle us to deny this possibility. On the contrary, the survival of Pythagorean observance has to be assumed to account for the later emergence of the neo-Pythagorean movement. The scholarly concern with it, in the school of Aristotle and

It remains to attempt a guess at the origin of these particular texts. Their recurrence in forms basically identical though varying in detail, especially on the late Secundina tablet, is unequivocal evidence that they were not specially devised for the tablets which happen to survive. A standard formulary must have existed, transmitted from forebears and handed down; two formularies in fact, adapted for the future 'heroes' and 'gods' respectively. They cannot, therefore, be taken in their entirety for a citation from some larger poem (a hymn, as Dieterich suggested, or a 'Katabasis of Orpheus'); an assumption which anyhow is excluded by the fact that some parts of these texts are in prose or, at any rate, in a prose thinly disguised as verse. The distribution of verse and prose is instructive. In the texts A1 and A4, the proclamation of deification and the surrounding acclamations are prose (or betray their original, prosaic form); in A2 and A3 (where there is no corresponding acclamation), the declaration 'I have paid amends for injustice' is prose thinly disguised. Besides, the verse about 'death from lightning' appeared to have been made up for the special purpose of the burials in the Timpone Piccolo, and in A4, from the Timpone Grande, the 'summarizing' second verse seemed likewise to have been composed for the specific occasion.

If you deduct these accessories, and the prose parts, from texts A1–3, there remains a poem, expressive and well—though not perfectly—coherent and containing no more, nor less, than the speech of the dead before Persephone; a poem consisting of A1 (2, 3), vv. 1–3 followed by two alternative conclusions: namely, either A1, vv. 5–7 or A2–3, v. 6 (assuming that ἀγαυήν was the original reading); it is hard to say if one should posit, for the hypothetical model, a further verse similar to, but better than, the last verse in A2–3; for at A2–3, v. 6 the same situation is reached as in A1, v. 7: 'the suppliant before Persephone' (followed, in A1, by prose). A4, finally, begins with a verse which is possibly, and ends with one which is definitely, too good to be ascribed to the person who strove to give a semblance of poetry to some of the prose which makes the main content of this tablet; these one or two verses then may have existed, somehow, independently of this tablet but they cannot be joined to the two coherent poetical texts which have just been isolated.

If the preceding analysis carries conviction, one may copy out and consider the resulting texts, for in this form they can confidently be assumed to have actually existed and to have been handed down for use, adaptation (and gradual corruption).[1] Were they originally composed for this use, or were they extracted from some poetry already existing?

at Alexandria, cannot by itself account for this revival; it presupposes a live continuity. In evidence of it one may refer to the proemium of Ennius' *Annals*.—See now W. Burkert, *Weisheit und Wissenschaft* (1962), pp. 192 ff.

[1] It is possible that the dialectal forms in A1 are older than the common ones on the other tablets, but this inference—if correct (cf. above, p. 306)—would not imply that these texts

The basic poem

a–b

1   Ἔρχομαι ἐκ καθαρῶν καθαρά, χθονίων βασίλεια,
2   Εὔκλεες Εὐβουλεῦ τε καὶ ἀθάνατοι θεοὶ ἄλλοι·
3   Καὶ γὰρ ἐγὼν ὑμῶν γένος ὄλβιον εὔχομαι εἶναι·

a

a4   Κύκλου δ᾽ ἐξέπταν βαρυπενθέος ἀργαλέοιο,
a5   Ἱμερτοῦ δ᾽ ἐπέβαν στεφάνου ποcὶ καρπαλίμοιcι,
a6   Δεcποίναc δ᾽ ὑπὸ κόλπον ἔδυν χθονίαc βαcιλείαc.

b

b4   Νῦν δ᾽ ἱκέτηc ἥκω παρ᾽ ἀγαυὴν Φερcεφόνειαν
(b5   Ὡc με πρόφρων πέμψηι ⟨e.g. εἰc εὐαγέων λειμῶνα⟩.)

(f) VERSE AND PROSE: ORIGINS

In either form this makes a coherent poem, and it is far more important to appreciate its simplicity, intensity, and piety than to speculate about its possible antecedents. If this further step is taken, one may consider whether these small poems could have been produced by extracting verses from some larger, didactic poem which taught the faithful what awaited them after death and how they were to face it. If one cares to pursue this possibility, one may think of that Ἱερὸc Λόγοc[1] in hexameters, which Sotion[2] ascribed to Pythagoras and from which some verses, including the first, are identifiable;[3] further fragments have boldly been traced by A. Delatte[4] and E. Rostagni.[5] Combining these indications with the statement by Ion of Chios[6] that Pythagoras fathered some poems written by himself upon Orpheus, there is reason for admitting the existence of this *Logos* in the early fourth and perhaps even in the fifth

were originally Doric. The Cretan tablets B 3–8 (below, p. 362), which are inscribed in the local dialect and spelling, contain extracts from originals in the traditional epic *Kunstsprache* which luckily are preserved; the transposition into the local dialect, then, is a secondary feature. And what happened at Eleutherna could have happened also at Thurii.

[1] This rather than the *Katabasis* ascribed to the Pythagorean Kerkops (15 DK), because a poem of this type would be unlikely to contain verses like those on the Gold Leaves (similarly Comparetti, *Lam. orf.* 37).

[2] *Apud* Diog. Laert. viii. 7; 14, no. 19 DK.

[3] Diog. Laert. ib. et 22; Porphyr. *Vita Pyth.* 40.

[4] *Études sur la lit. pyth.* (1915), pp. 1 ff.   [5] *Il verbo di Pitagora* (1924), pp. 166 ff.

[6] 36 B 2 DK.

century[1] (though few would make so bold as to ascribe it to Pythagoras himself). The verses traced to it contain, it is true, rules for the conduct of life on earth, but the assumption that it dealt also with the after-life seems permissible,[2] especially also in view of its title.

From this *Hieros Logos*, then, the basic verses (p. 340) on the Gold Leaves might have been extracted. It is a very uncertain guess—their sensitive and poetical imagery (cf. Petelia!) has no counterpart among the dry admonitions surviving from the *Logos*—and anyhow of slight importance; what matters is the appreciation of the texts as we actually have them. It is in this form that they remained authoritative for centuries; nor can the guess just outlined help to answer the remaining question: why is part of the text, and indeed the most important part, in prose?

It is certainly not by chance nor from carelessness. This prose is as much a matter of tradition, with the character of hieratic formulae, as are the verses preceding it (and this notwithstanding the fact that A1 and A4 gave way to the urge to assimilate part of it to the verses). I offer, tentatively, two suggestions which may well be combined.

It may be observed, first, that the words which contain the culmination of the imagined eschatological scene are by no means without form, even though this form is different from that of the preceding verses. Θεὸς ἐγένου ἐξ ἀνθρώπου· ἔριφος ἐc γάλα ἔπετεc: these are two parallel clauses, each of nine syllables and each with three accents. This, strangely enough, is a rhythmic principle which became fundamental in late-antique and medieval Greek poetry; to find it in these early documents is surprising indeed. I forbear speculating about historical implications; the form, anyhow, is there. And it combines itself naturally with the trochaic fall of χαῖρε, χαῖρε before and after (variously altered in both A1 and A4 at the earlier place; omitted at the latter in A1, but developed into a trochaic trimeter in A4).

This form—let us call it a 'rhythmical prose' in contradistinction to the flowing verses preceding it—evidently was felt to be appropriate to the unique and supreme message which these words convey; for they announce deification. There are two analogies to this; both much later but none the less remarkable. Philostratos[3] reports various legends about the manner in which the earthly journey of Apollonios of Tyana, the Pythagorean saint, ended. According to one of them he vanished in a temple of Diktynna in Crete; when his followers approached it, they heard a voice, as though from a choir of maidens, saying cτεῖχε γᾶc· cτεῖχ' ἐc οὐρανόν· cτεῖχε. A call, then, announcing deification; this, too, in 'rhythmical

---

[1] See now W. Burkert, *Weisheit und Wissenschaft* (1962), p. 204.
[2] This was urged, and developed, by Rostagni (l.l. 169, 175, etc.).
[3] *Apoll. Tyan.* viii. 30 (end of chapter).

prose'; three parallel cola with 2, 2, 1 accents respectively. A very similar legend was told when Peregrinus Proteus had voluntarily ended his life at the Olympic games in A.D. 166; from his pyre rose a vulture (was it not, rather, an eagle, as at the funerals of Roman emperors?) saying ἔλιπον γᾶν· βαίνω δ' ἐc "Ολυμπον. Thus according to Lucian,[1] who has the effrontery to pretend that he himself invented the edifying tale. Anyhow, here again is an announcement of deification, this time in two parallel rhythmical cola, each with two accents.

The cardinal prose-passage on the tablets thus appears to conform with a specific tradition. And indeed the transition from verse to prose is a uniquely effective means of conveying the significance of a uniquely important statement. Thus in the canon of the Mass in the Roman Catholic Church, where everything else may be set to music but not the words of Jesus instituting the Eucharist; these central divine words thus stand out in their own unique dignity.[2] It is unlikely to a degree that, in the texts on the lamellae, the transition from verse to prose was devised merely as a means for literary effect; they are not literature anyhow. The analogy just quoted suggests that it is, rather, a ritual feature. The Gurôb papyrus,[3] fragmentary and plebeian though it is, still shows that at the celebration of the *Winkelmysterien* of which it contained the ἱερὸc λόγοc (i.e. the 'order of the service') exclamations in prose alternated with verse. Analogies more relevant can be gleaned from the extensive field of 'acclamations'.[4]

Expressing the sentiment or volition of a crowd or community, in approval or disapproval, admiration or condemnation, emotion and devotion, they are known from the ancient East and from the Roman world far better than from Greece, and can be seen to have crystallized very early from free spontaneity into set forms and wording; a rhythmical prose which came to be chanted, or shouted, in set melodies. From Greece we know of τηνέλλα καλλίνικε used at games, 'Υμὴν ὢ 'Υμέναι' ὢ at weddings, and ὢ τὸν Ἄδωνιν; but nothing otherwise of their cultic use. Of this, though, Egypt affords ample evidence, such as εἷc Cάραπιc, 'no god as great as Sarapis'—the formula applicable to any god or man— while the wide use of *acclamatio* in Roman political life is not here as directly relevant as its large contribution to the Christian liturgy, from

---

[1] *De morte Peregrini* 39. The Doric dialect in both these legends is remarkable. It seems to have conveyed, in this late period, an aura of archaic sanctity.

[2] One may quote, as further analogies, the intentionally monotonous setting of words spoken by Jesus in J. S. Bach's passion music; of the oracle in Gluck's *Alcestis*; of the speaking statue in *Don Giovanni*.

[3] Its rendering in DK (no. 23, p. 19) is faulty to the point of uselessness; one has to turn to the *ed. princ.* A new, revised edition is badly needed.

[4] The studies in this important field have been summarized in a most instructive manner by T. Klauser in his *Reallexikon für Antike und Christentum*, i. 216 ff.; of the earlier literature, E. Peterson, Εἷc θεόc, 1926, remains important.

Κύριε ἐλέησον to Δόξα and 'Amen', and particularly in the service *pro defunctis*; the acclamations uttered at their biers often reappear on their sarcophagi or in the catacombs: e.g. *Vale in pace*; *letaris in pace* (cf. χαῖρε); *anima tua cum iustis*; *agnus sine macula*.[1] Deification indeed was not attributed, *per acclamationem*, to the Christian dead, nor to living Roman emperors; it was done, on the Persian precedent, for late Hellenistic kings. Mithridates was hailed as θεὸς βασιλεύς by the crowds in Asia Minor,[2] and Herod with θεοῦ φωνὴ καὶ οὐκ ἀνθρώπου in Caesarea.[3]

Re-reading the tablets with these facts in mind, a *raison d'être* for their form and content seems to offer itself. The 'hail to the new god' in which they culminate is worded as a ritual formula: whatever the 'kid in the milk' meant, it is not narrative prose but a *symbolon*. Who spoke it? According to the tablets, Persephone or some undefined voices in the Netherworld. But if it was devised, from origin, for the wording of the tablets, why this strict, ritual form?

Perhaps all the verses and formulas on the tablets are part, or echo, of a ritual. J. H. Wieten indeed argued that they are the formulary of a mystery celebration, in which the living were left, with much terror and circumstance, to a mystic death and resurrection, and J. Harrison had preceded him with similar fantasies. I cannot see that the simple and poetical mythology of the tablets can bear the burden of these vast implications. But I can imagine that they contain main items—verses and ritual prose—of a Pythagorean *Missa pro defunctis* celebrated at the burial of those who took the tablets with them to the other world. The Pythagoreans—we know it from Plutarch[4]—buried their dead with particular rites, which were among the arcana of the School and were considered indispensable if a soul was to attain to its 'proper and blissful consummation'. The preservation, through the centuries, of these texts, and the custom of inscribing them on gold leaves to accompany the dead, become understandable—or so it seems to me—as elements, and evidence, of these Pythagorean rites in which the journey of the deceased to Persephone was symbolically enacted.

On this assumption there remains no room for the hypothesis that the verses were extracted from a didactic poem; a hypothesis which anyhow rested on all too slender a basis.

---

[1] I extract these samples from Cabrol–Leclerq, *Diction. Archéol. Chrét.* . . . , i. 245; their analogies with words on the tablets will, I trust, be clear without detailed elaboration.

[2] According to Posidonius, quoted by Athenaeus v. 213 b.

[3] Acts 12: 22; cf. Joseph. *Antiq.* xix. 18. 2 θεὸν προσαγορεύοντες; also the ἰσοθέους προσφωνήσεις by the people of Alexandria, which Germanicus forbade by his well-known edict.

[4] Plutarch, *De genio Socratis*, 16, 585 e (cf. above, p. 322, n. 3). J. Harrison (*Proleg.*, p. 599) was right in drawing attention to this passage.

IV. TABLET C

T HE text inscribed on tablet C is completely unrelated to any of the others, but it was found with those of group A; hence its discussion follows here. This is a task which one would gladly have shunned, for no certain and satisfactory result is attainable. Since, however, excessively faulty renderings of the wording and illusory assertions about its import remain current,[1] I offer the transcript which I made, with Olivieri's at my elbow. I have a fair confidence in its reliability (and any sceptic is free to go to Naples and try for himself); if this is accepted, a detailed rehearsal and assessment of the various traditional interpretations will prove unnecessary.

It will be remembered that the Gold Leaf C was found in 1897 in the Timpone Grande, next to the head of the hero buried there. It was folded nine times over, from its right, shorter side towards the left, and contained inside it the leaf A4, likewise folded. Like the other four leaves it was handed to Professor Barnabei who, in view of the difficulty of reading it, did not immediately produce a transcript, but sent a facsimile to D. Comparetti, who, on this basis, published some observations which at once set the interpretation on the wrong track;[2] for he found evidence of 'la teogonia orfica', especially in the presumed divine names Protogonos, Tyche, and Phanes. In 1902 H. Diels, using a transcript made by H. Siebourg (with others), refashioned the first six lines into his 'Orphic Demeter Hymn';[3] G. Murray followed in the next year with a transcript based mainly on Barnabei's facsimile (which he reproduced on a reduced scale, ascribing it to Comparetti) but also on Diels's text and some readings of his own.[4] Comparetti published Barnabei's facsimile and transcript in 1910;[5] he criticized Diels as well as G. Murray pertinently, but refrained, wisely, from attempting a full reconstruction. In 1915 A. Olivieri published a new transcript—the first notable advance over Barnabei[6]—adding a facsimile drawn by M. Puccetti which was repro-

---

[1] I am referring mainly to DK⁹ i (66) B 21 and Orph. fr. 47 Kern. M. P. Nilsson, *G.G.R*, ii. 231 with note 5, gives expression to a highly justified scepticism; he would no doubt have gone farther if he had relied upon a less imperfect rendering of the text. 'Warum denn "orphisch"?', said Wilamowitz (*Der Glaube* . . .², ii. 200); '. . . und gar ein sogenannter Demeter Hymnus hat doch nicht das mindeste Anrecht darauf [scil. the designation 'orphic'], ist übrigens zum großen Teil unverständlich.' The great old man was right again.

[2] *Memorie* . . . iii. 329.

[3] H. Diels, in *Festschrift f. Th. Gomperz* (1902), pp. 1 ff.

[4] G. Murray *apud* J. Harrison, *Proleg.* 665 f.   [5] *Laminette orfiche*, pp. 12 ff.

[6] *Lamellae aureae Orphicae*, p. 22. In a very few details Barnabei seems to me to have been right against his successor, but the progress achieved by Olivieri was none the less momentous.

duced in 1922 by O. Kern in illustration (or, rather, refutation) of 'Dielesii ingeniosa restitutio, quam omnibus numeris absolutam esse vir summus ipse cautissime negavit'.[1]

The tablet contains, within its height of less than $2\frac{1}{2}$ cm., ten lines of writing. After the fifth line the engraver began to worry about the available space and made the letters less high; towards the end, his confidence restored, he used again larger lettering, drawing out the words, especially at the end of lines. His letters are angular, with thin lines, and irregular in size and position; reading them is often difficult because the scribe (to give him this title) seems to have neither understood nor cared what he was putting down; in some places he incised lines which are unlikely to have meant any letters even to himself (see below on ll. 5, 6, 8 f.). The resulting difficulties are enhanced by the smallness of the lettering and the creases and cracks caused by the folding of the thin plaque. In particular it must be remembered that the slightest prolongation of the top bar must transform a Γ into a T, and vice versa; that ΓΙ and ΤΙ may be almost indistinguishable from Π; two T's may simulate the same letter; two Λ's, a M; and H and N are almost identical. O, varying in size, is written by two downward lines more or less bent which may or may not join, or even cross; it may therefore suggest P or even X and, at the other extreme, a mere Ι. Λ, Δ, and A, of course, are not easily distinguished, and even where one of the three is recognized with fair certainty, the 'scribe' may have put it in the place of one of the other two. These facts account for the, in places, widely differing decipherments presented by different scholars. Comparison of Barnabei's facsimile with Olivieri's will show how differently the same traces may be interpreted by different students. In the transcript below, these uncertain shapes are marked by dots, as are those doubtful for other reasons, such as scratches and other damages to the surface.

Comment

A text more corrupt than this will not easily be found (and it is strange indeed that it should have been placed in the hero's grave, in the noble Timpone Grande, together with the, likewise imperfect, plaque A4 which presages his deification). It has been suspected that the wording was intentionally made incomprehensible, in order to enhance its magic power; but the sequences of meaningless letters bear no similarity to the well-known methods of magical abracadabras, 'Ephesia Grammata', or secret codes. Nor can they, where failing to yield Greek words, be held to

---

[1] *Orphicorum Fragmenta* (1915), p. 117, no. 47.

C. Transcript and Reconstruction

Napoli, Museo Nazionale 111464.   Plate 28b

From Timpone Grande.   81 mm. × 23 mm.

G. Murray *apud* J. Harrison, p. 665; H. Diels, *Festschrift Gomperz* (1902), p. 1; Olivieri, p. 22; 47 Kern ('Carmen Siculum'); Comparetti, p. 12; 21 DK.

Under the transcript stand

  (*a*) the—more or less—certain Greek words;

  (*b*) alternatives and suggestions;

here, a point underneath a letter indicates that an error of the engraver has to be assumed (or that the reading is uncertain); see the transcript and notes. Repeated sequences of letters are marked with a line above the text.

1 ΠΡΩΤΟΓΟΝΟΤΗΜΑΙΤΙΕΤΗΓΑΜΜΑΤΡΙΕΠΑΚΥΒΕΛΕΙΑΚΟΡΡΑΟΣΕΝΤΑΙΗΔΗΜΗΤΡΟΣΗΤ

(*a*) $\Pi\rho\omega\tau o\gamma ovo(\varsigma)$ $\tau\eta\langle\iota\rangle$ $\Gamma\alpha\langle\iota\rangle \ \mu\alpha\tau\rho\iota$ $Kv\beta\epsilon\lambda\epsilon\iota\alpha$ $\kappa o\rho\rho\alpha$ $\varDelta\eta\mu\eta\tau\rho o\varsigma$ $\eta\tau$-

(*b*) $\Gamma\eta\langle\iota\rangle$ $\tau\alpha\langle\iota\rangle$ $\epsilon\varphi\alpha$ $(-\lambda\eta\ddot{\iota}\alpha)$

2 ΤΑΤΑΙΤΤΑΤΑΠΤΑΖΕΥΙΑΤΗΤΥΑΕΡΣΑΠΤΑΗΛΙΕΠΥΡΔΗΠΑΝΤΑΣΤΗΙΝΤΑΣΤΗΝΙΣΑΤΟΠΕΝΙΚΑΙ·

(*a*) $-\tau\alpha\tau\alpha\iota$ $Z\epsilon v$ $\tau v \ \alpha\epsilon\rho$ $H\lambda\iota\epsilon \ \pi v\rho \ \delta\eta \ \pi\alpha v\tau' \ \alpha\varsigma\tau\eta$ $\epsilon)v\iota\kappa\alpha\iota(\cdot$

    $\iota\alpha\tau\eta\langle\rho\rangle$

(*b*) $\pi\alpha\tau\eta\langle\rho\rangle$ $\pi\alpha v\tau\alpha\varsigma \ \tau\eta v$

3 ΣΗΔΕΤΥΧΑΙΤΕΦΑΝΗΣΠΑΜΜΗΣΓΟΙΜΟΙΡΑΙΣΣΤΗΤΟΙΓΑΝΝΥΑΠΙΑΝΤΗΣΥΚΛΗΤΕΔΑΡΜΟΝΔΕΥΧΙ

(*a*) (c)$\eta\delta\epsilon \ \tau v\chi\alpha\iota$ $\tau'\epsilon\varphi\alpha v\eta\varsigma$ $\pi\alpha\mu\mu\eta\varsigma\tau o\langle\rho\rangle\iota \ Mov\rho\alpha\iota(\varsigma)$ $cv \ \kappa\lambda v\tau\epsilon$ $\delta\alpha\mu ov$ $\epsilon v\chi\eta[\varsigma$

(*b*) $\tau\epsilon \ \Phi\alpha v\eta\varsigma$ $(\dot{\alpha})\pi\alpha v\langle\tau\eta\rangle \ \tau\eta\langle\iota\rangle \ c\tau\eta\langle\iota\rangle$ $\delta' \ \epsilon v\chi\eta\langle\iota\rangle$

Line 1. O: one of the uncertain shapes mentioned before the transcript.

Line 2. After ΑΕΡΣΑ ΠΤΑ as read by Ol.: ΠΤΑ (Siebourg) or ΠΙΑ (G. Murray) are not impossible. ‖ After ΔΗ one vertical hasta (like Ι), thereafter a vertical crack which is likely to have absorbed the right half of Π. ‖ At end (after ΚΑΙ) an uncertain letter: Δ? Μ?

Line 3. ΠΑΜΜΗΣΓΟΙ: *sic*; but see above for the near-identity of Γ and Τ. ‖ The *vox nihili* ΓΑΝΝΥΑ could have originated from the engraver's misreading ΠΑΛΙΝ•• in his *Vorlage*. The last letter is right on the edge: the other half of Η may have been cut off. Above ΔΕΥΧΙ appear tiny letters: Δ!M.? (i.e. $\delta\langle\alpha\rangle\mu\langle\omega v\rangle$?).

4 ΣΠΑΤΕΡΑΤΙκΠΑΝΤΑΔΑΜΑΣΤΑΠΑΝΤΗΡΗΝΥΝΤΑΙΣΕΛΑΒΔΟΝΤΑΔΕΠΑΝΤΕΜΟΙΒΗΣΤΛΗΤΕΑΠΛ

(a) πατερ(α)   παντ' αδαμαστα   παντ(η)   -ντα   -οντα δε παντ' εμοι   τλητεα

(b)   παντα δαμα⟨ι⟩ς τα παντ'   (ε)λαβον(τα)   δε παντ' ε⟨π' α⟩μοιβης   π̣α̣[ι-
      ελα⟨ιι⟩ς βροντα   τ̣α̣[ι-

5 ΤΗΜΗΑΕΡΙΠΤΥΡΜΕΜΜΑΤΕΡΛΥΕΣΤΙΣΟΙ··ΕΝΤΑΤΟΝΗΞΣΙΝΝΥΞΙΝΗΜΕΘΗΜΕΡΑΝΕΓΛ·ΥΕΤ

(a) τη μη αερι πυρ   ματερ   εστι σοι   επτα   νηστιν   νυξιν   η   μεθ' ημεραν

(b)   λυες τι σοι   επτατο
      επτατονησιν

6 ΕΠΠΗΜΑΡΤΙΝΗΣΤΙΑΣΤΑΝΖΕΥΕΝΟΡΥΤΤΙΕΚΑΙΠΑΝΟΠΤΑΑΙΕΝΑΙΜΙΛΟΜΑΤΕΡΕΜΑΣΕΠ

(a)   νηστιας   Ζευ   και πανοπτα Α⟨λ⟩ιε   ματερ εμας επ-

(b) εννημαρ   Ολιν⟨μ⟩πιε   αϊε
     επτημαρ   διε

Line 4. Before ΠΑΝΤΑ a slanting K, half below the line, as in Ol.'s facsimile. || After the middle: Barnabei and G. Murray (whose transcripts I did not consult until long after my own attempt) similarly read ΕΛΑΒΔΟΝΤΑ and ΕΛΑΒΡΟΝΤΑ respectively (unavoidably recalling Pindar's ἐλασίβροντα), but the decisive letter after ΛΑΒ is not P (although everyone is free to claim that it ought to be). Siebourg printed P with a question mark, and Ol. put in its place a Π upside down. || At end: ΣΠΛ; perhaps ΤΙΛ; hardly ΣΙΛ (Ol.) or ΤΕΑ (Sieb.); nor ΠΑ (Barnabei and G. Murray); but a tiny cross-bar, easily omitted, would effect this latter reading,

Line 5. Middle: ΣΟΙ··: after a very curious Ο (see on l. 1), and Ι, the scribe filled the space of two letters with meaningless marks (thereafter, clearly, ·ΝΤΑ, probably ΕΝΤΑ, not ΕΠΤΑ—unless one assumes a scribal error). || Near the end, the letter before ΥΕΤ is similarly puzzling.

Line 6. The second letter is again puzzling, but Π is a probable interpretation. || Middle: ΟΡΥΤΤΙΕ: the top-bars of the two Τ's are cut in one line, but the two verticals are too far apart for the whole shape to be called Π. Even so, it is permissible to assume that the *Vorlage* had Π. || After ΠΑΝΟΠΤΑ, G. M. and Ol. read ΔΙΕ (Barn. ΛΙΕ); but the sides of the first letter are drawn down below the cross-bar: ἄιε then may be intended as likely as δίε or Ἅλιε. || ΟΛ: only the right side of Λ is visible (hence Χ̣ Siebourg); Ο, small, is shaped as in l. 1.

C. Transcript and Reconstruction (cont.)

7   ••ΟΥΣΟΝΕΟΕΥΧΑΣΤΑΚΤΑΠΥΡΑΣΗΟΛΚΔΠΕΔΙΩΧΑΜΑΤΕΜΑΝΚΑΛΗΑΔΙΕΡΑΔΑΜΝΕΥΔΑΜΝΟΙ

(a) ακ]ουσον   ευχας   πυρας   πεδιω   εμαν   δ' ιερα   ευδα⟨ι⟩μ⟨ο⟩νοι-

(b)   ⟨ας⟩τακτα   χ' αμα τ'   καλη   διερα   δαμναι

8   ΣΤΑΚΤΗΡΙΕΡΑΜΑΡΔΗΜΗΤΕΡΠΥΡΖΕΥΚΑΙΗΧΘΟΝΙΑΤΡΑΒΔΑΗΤΡΟΣΗΜΣΤΗΟΚΙΝ [vac.]

(a) στακτηρ   ιερα   Δημητερ   πυρ Ζευ και η χθονια   ⟨μ⟩ητρος

(b) στακτηρι   εραμαι

9   •••ΣΝΗΓΑΥΝΗΓΛΑΟΣΕΣφΡΕΝΑΜΑΤΡΙΜΗΓΝΝΤΑΣΝΥΣΧΑΜΕΣΤΩΡΕΛΕΙΣΣΙΡΗΝ

(a)   εc φρενα   ματρι

(b)

10   ΔΙΑφΗΡΤΟΝΟΣΣΜΜΕΣΤΟΝΑΕΡΤΑΙΠΛΜΜΗΣφΡΕΝΑΜΑΡ Τ Ι

(a)   εc τον αερ-   εc φρενα   ματρι

(b)   ες φρενα   ματρι

Line 7. Before the first letter, two more (guess: ΑΚ) have become invisible—if they were ever written. ‖ ΗΟΛΚΔ: this seems the most likely interpretation of the irregular signs (Λ is certain; Κ—if it is Κ—is disfigured by scratches); ΚΔ may have been incised instead of ΚΑ. ‖ ΤΕΜΑΝ: the first (uncertain) letter small, above the line. ‖ At the end, judging by the photograph, ΝΑΙ seems quite as likely as ΝΟΙ.

Line 8. The first letter faint and uncertain: probably Σ, perhaps Ε. ‖ ΧΘΟΝ: perhaps ΚΘΟΝ. ‖ The dotted letters near the end: a scribble, hard to interpret.

Line 9. The same holds good for the first three letters on this line (Ol.'s reading ΗΡΩΣ, though, seemed improbable to me). ‖ After ΜΑΤΡΙΜΗ possibly ΤΙΝΝ. ‖ ΤΑΣ: possibly ΤΗΣ. ‖ ΧΑΜ: possibly ΧΜΜ (scribble). ‖ ΩΡ: poss. ΟΡ. ‖ Ε·Λ uncertain, in crack. ‖ ΙΣΣ: round sigma here?? (otherwise angular). The first of them could be taken together with the preceding Ι to make Κ (leg. εκ).

Line 10. The first letter is unlikely to be Α. ‖ ΜΜ uncertain (on bent surface): ΜΛΙ and other interpretations are possible. ‖ ΠΛΜΜ: Π or ΓΙ (? ΤΙ); the rest uncertain. The last letters are written with ever wider spacing (I regard as scratches what Ol. took for letters).

convey any Italic language,[1] although it is conceivable that the engraver was an Italic native with imperfect command of Greek. Among his innumerable mistakes there are apparent misreadings and inversion of letters (one can thus understand e.g. MAITI for MATPI, l. 1; cf. the very last word on the tablet), and—rightly stressed by H. Diels[2]— the repetition of sequences, either out of sheer slovenliness or because he noticed that he had made a mistake;[3] moreover, his exemplar may have incorporated dialectal variants (seeing that the text strangely mixes Doric with the traditional epic language).[4] This assumption led Diels to an ingenious reconstruction of the first line: TH MAITI ETH and ΓAM (for ΓAI) MATPI EΠA could represent Γῆι μητρὶ ἔφη and the same in Doric; put Πρωτόγονος[5] in front and Κυβελήϊα after it, and an acceptable hexameter emerges. It is not by any means a certain reconstruction—the verb ἔφη has to be assumed to have been mis-spelled both times and even so is hardly suitable in view of what follows; Κυβελήϊα with short alpha is precariously excused by reference to Pindar's[6] Κύκνεια μάχα; nor is it certain that Γᾶι ματρί was intended; the alternatives TH and ΓA(M) could quite as well stand for the article τῆι (τᾶι), and this interpretation commends itself, in view of Κυβελήϊα and Δήμητρος following, as stylistically superior. Even so, this reconstruction of the first line is gold in comparison with all the rest of Diels's presentation, which continues to be broadcast in the *Vorsokratiker*,[7] although it has been put out of court by the publication of Olivieri's transcript fifty years ago.[8] It would be idle to enlarge upon the obvious intrinsic faultiness of this reconstructed text

---

[1] I am indebted to O. Skutsch and O. Szemerenyi for reassuring me on this point, after L. H. Jeffery had presented, in *BSA* (1955), 78 f., four other instances—exciting if not indubitable—of Greek and native (?) words combined on inscriptions from South Italy.

[2] *Festschrift f. Th. Gomperz* (1902), pp. 1 ff.

[3] A small but evident instance is in l. 7: EO before EYXAΣ.

[4] e.g. KOPPA and MATHP but ΔHMHTHP and the article H (l. 8).

[5] Thus rather than (with Diels) the dative: the daughter is 'first-born'—not the mother; cf. Pausanias i. 31. 4 on Πρωτογόνη at Phlya and hence, according to the Methapos epigram, ib. iv. i. 7, at Andania the cult Δάματρος καὶ Πρωτογόνου Κούρας; also the inscription, from Trikka, *I.G.* ix. 2, 305, of the second century B.C., Δήμητρι καὶ Μουνογένη, and Orph. fr. 190 K. Κόρη μουνογένεια. Barnabei, Comparetti, and Olivieri likewise read Πρωτόγονος but took the adjective for the name of the Orphic god.

[6] *Ol.* x. 15.   [7] Also in Kern's *Orphicorum Fragmenta*, p. 118.

[8] The arrogant and disingenuous references to Olivieri's superior work ought to disappear from future editions of the *Vorsokratiker*: vol. i, p. 17 *ad* l. 11 'nach Diels nicht gefördert durch Olivieri'; *ad* l. 15 'nach der letzten Lesung (vgl. Kern z. St.)': the *Lesung* adopted is Olivieri's! The pompous following words about Siebourg's 'fast vollständig korrekte Abschrift', to which Diels himself applied the finishing touch, are given ironical illustration by the very first reading quoted—"πρατοτοτοvo"—being wrong (πρατο- was Diels's conjecture; the tablet has πρωτο-), and by the following notes, which fail to give anything like adequate information about the basis of the text; the final note ('z. 7–10 ist unleserlich oder zusammenhanglos') covering the only two coherent phrases that can safely be made out on the whole tablet. These facts are liable to make the reader overlook the very pertinent sentence: 'Die Herstellung ist überall durchaus hypothetisch.'

(Triballian rather than Greek, to appropriate a classic coinage); but Diels[1] presented the 'Barbarei der Form' as a symptom of 'wie tief diese Bettelpriesterdichtung gesunken ist'; it was destined, according to him, for 'die ungebildete Pöbelmasse'—and yet it was found, written on gold, in a grandiose tumulus, and the absence of a foundation for Diels's diagnosis emerges on comparing his transcript. It is, however, regrettably true that Olivieri's reconstruction does not make sense either, and the same must be said of G. Murray's earlier attempt.

The fact is that no coherent reconstruction is possible on a basis as corrupt as this. The suggestions underneath my transcript do indeed show that more Greek words can be elicited from this jumble than might be expected at first sight; but let it not be thought that these words generally represent what our Triballian was set to copy. For example, ἄστακτα can be read in l. 7 and may in itself seem credible, but not so cτακτηρ(ι) in the next line; and the similarity of the two sequences makes the interpretation also of the former doubtful—which anyhow cannot be made to square with what can be read immediately before. In line 5 the simple words νυξὶν ἢ μεθ᾽ ἡμέραν are read without doubt yet cannot be construed; whether they be taken together or separated, and whether a figure ('seven') be acknowledged before them or not.

This indeed is the most unsettling fact: more often than not Greek words actually extant and, each by itself, unobjectionable do not, in their combination, yield any coherent meaning. The end of the first line reads together with the beginning of the second, quite clearly Δήμητρος ἥττᾱται; none the less, one will think twice before accepting the Attic verb which spoils the rhythm, for even if one made bold after it to read πάντα (for TTATA), the statement 'everything is inferior to Demeter' is not easily fitted into the context (as far as it can be discerned). Again, at the end of the second line and at the beginning of the third, Νίκαιc[2] ἠδὲ Τύχαι τ᾽ ἐφάνης παμμήcτο⟨ρ⟩ι Μοίραι scans as a hexameter, and the slight adjustment of the last word but one gains support from Lykophron 490;[3] but even if Τύχαιc is put for TYXAIT, the meaning of the whole is obscure. Only one victory-goddess exists; what is one to make of the plural? The same holds good for Τύχη;[4] and who could be expected to 'appear' to these incredible mythical figures? One might think of the Sun-god, who seems to be mentioned before, but the resulting scene baffles the imagination; nor is it apparent how 'all-devising Fate' could

---

[1] l.l. (1902), pp. 14 f.   [2] This reading is not really certain; see the transcript.
[3] L–S–J quote παμμήcτωρ, moreover, from *fragm. trag. adesp.* 129 Nauck², where it refers to Ares.
[4] 'Keineswegs landläufig', according to Diels (l.l. 13), who described these unique mythological figures as 'ungewöhnlich, vielleicht volkstümlich' but also as 'Abstraktionen theologischer Weisheit' and 'offenbar Paredroi des . . . Sonnengottes'. He felt 'befremdet' at their appearance but was not thereby actuated to doubt the text which he had constituted.

fit this curious company. Is the Sun-god, accompanied by 'Victories and Fortunes', to be thought of as appearing, rather, to Fate? The most depraved 'Bettelpriesterdichtung' could not contain a verse so completely absurd (it would grow still absurder, if the Orphic Phanes were put in the place of the verb, which is indispensable to the context[1] however obscure). In between these two passages, the combination Ἥλιε πῦρ, however precarious syntactically, may suggest an echo of philosophical allegorism,[2] and a corresponding equation of Zeus and air might be suspected immediately before. Confirmation of a mythology of the elements seems to emerge in l. 5 ἀέρι πῦρ (μεμ⟨ειγμένον⟩?), but this impression is shattered on reaching l. 8, where Demeter appears equated with fire; she whom the wildest syncretism could never identify with the Sun-god. Even so, the impression that fire and air played some significant part in this text, and with them, probably, earth (l. 1; but I find no indication of the fourth element), is not easily rejected (further traces may or may not be in l. 7 ΠΥΡΑΣ and l. 10 ΑΕΡ), but the wording is too corrupt to admit of any specification.

From these frustrating intimations one turns with relief to the two phrases which alone are both clearly legible and materially unobjectionable. The first, and longer, was made out by Olivieri: ll. 6–7 μᾶτερ ἐμᾶς ἐπ(άκ)ουσον ‖ εὐχᾶς; the end of one hexameter and the first word of the next. This imploring prayer is preceded by vocatives which are unlikely not to form part of the same invocation, even though they do not join on immediately and are beset with corruption. The following hypothetical restoration is intended merely to indicate what kind of connection might be conjectured: Ζεῦ ⟨γ⟩εν⟨έτ⟩ορ ⟨μοι 'Ολ⟩ύ⟨μ⟩πιε καὶ ⟨σὺ⟩ πανόπτα ‖ Ἅλιε – ◡◡ – ◡◡ μᾶτερ κτλ. (these supplements involve a general notion of the theme, on which presently). The other safe instance is the short phrase, twice recurring, ἐς φρένα ματρί (ll. 9 and 10). Its repetition at the very end of the text serves to stress the paramount importance in it of 'the Mother'; and indeed this word is the one most frequently recurring; it is also in ll. 1, 5 (vocative) and, perhaps, 8.

Which 'Mother' is invoked, and by whom? This is not a difficult problem, because both the persons in question are named in the first line: Demeter and Kore; the name Demeter recurs besides, in the vocative, in l. 8. The tablet, then, seems to contain an invocation of the Mother by the Daughter; it could only be on or after her abduction by the Lord of the Netherworld.[3] The occurrence, three times, of the vocative 'Zeus' (ll. 2, 6, and 8 (with Demeter)), of the word 'father' (ll. 2(?) and 4), and of 'Helios' (2 and 6(?)) fits this frame;[4] so do some further

---

[1] Similarly Diels, l.l. 14.   [2] Cf. Emped. B 71. 2 DK.

[3] This interpretation must collapse if in line 8 the supplement καὶ ἡ χθονία ⟨βασίλεια⟩ is unavoidable. This, though, is hardly the case; a phrase like βία Πλούτωνος is not unthinkable.

[4] Cf. Hom. H. Dem. 21 and 26.

details but not all. One can imagine, within this context, a place for 'all-inventing Fate' (l. 3) and, after it (if Diels's suggestion is accepted) the invocation cὺ κλυτὲ δαῖμον (Zeus? Pluton?), who 'tamest all and . . . all' (l. 4).[1] This apostrophe could conceivably be followed by the confession πάντ' ἐμοί (or ἐ⟨π' ἀ⟩μοιβῆϲ) τλητέα, and if a reference to 'fasting' is indeed contained in l. 6 (and, perhaps, in l. 5), Demeter's nine-days-fast[2] in search of her daughter could have been mentioned.

The invocations (ll. 6–7) from which the present hypothetical summary started follow. Thereafter the wording is corrupt beyond guessing, but for the repeated invocation in l. 8, another reference to the 'Mother' (ib.) and the iterated phrase ἐc φρένα ματρί; perhaps Kore expressed the wish that her prayer should touch her mother's heart and the poet stated, finally, that this was achieved.

All this is hypothetical, but, I suppose, not inconceivable, and it is clear that what can be made out with some confidence fits into hexametric rhythm. On the other hand I confess myself unable to fit the 'allegorization of elements' into this frame—if indeed this motif has to be acknowledged; nor can I find any place for the 'appearance' of Victories and Fortune(s) (ll. 2–3)—if indeed this is what the corrupt series of letters implies. Corruption there is in any case to an extent which leaves long stretches, particularly in the last lines, quite inexplicable; it forbids any detailed reconstruction of even those motifs which have been discerned with fair confidence and, generally, imposes diffidence in every positive assertion.

It remains baffling that Diels could have presented this text as an 'Orphischer Demeterhymnus'. Even his own questionable reconstruction does not in the least fit his own definition of the 'im antiken Hymnus weitverbreitete Form, die auf den Vocativ der angeredeten Gottheit eine . . . Schilderung der göttlichen Macht folgen läßt'.[3] His 'hymn' does not begin with an invocation but with a descriptive statement and continues with words which indeed contain, inter alia, praise of Helios (evolved from largely untenable readings) but also an assertion of prolonged fasting; all this, according to Diels's text, spoken by Kore addressing Demeter . . . What a 'hymn'! Nor is there anything 'Orphic' about it. No Orpheus need be roused for the equation of Δημήτηρ and Γῆ μήτηρ (which

---

[1] Πάντα δαμᾶ⟨ι⟩c τά ⟨τε⟩ πάντα . . . -νᾶιc. Not, at any rate, πάντα δαμαcτά, ⟨τὰ⟩ πάντα κρατυντά (Diels); the first adjective is non-existent (it ought to be δμᾱτά); the second, likewise, unattested and unbelievable. The negative ἀδάμαcτοc would be legitimate and not unsuitable in relation to Hades, but I cannot fit it into the context. As to Diels's next invention, ἐμβρόντητα, an obvious pun is none too easily suppressed.

[2] 'Εννῆμαρ is elicited from the first letters in l. 6 with no more difficulty than ἐπτῆμαρ and is far more suitable (Hom. H. Dem. 47). Alternatively, the possibility of a reference to Kore rejecting food in Hades (H. H. Dem. 393 ff.) may be considered; her prayer being uttered during her stay in the Netherworld (cf. ib. 343).

[3] Diels, 1902, 15.

is anyhow far from certain to have been in the text), and the further identification of either or both of these with Kybele is known from Euripides; from the Epidaurian hymn; from the cult-image in the Athenian Metroon, and from Kybele statuettes among those of the Sicilian 'Demeter'.[1] Nor, finally, does the fact that the story of Kore's abduction was known in Sicily prove the text to be—as Kern asserted—a 'Carmen Siculum' and 'Orphic'.

If it contains, as suggested, the prayer uttered by Kore when abducted by Pluto (developing vv. 20 ff. of the Homeric hymn), one understands why it accompanied the person buried in the Timpone Grande. He was torn away from among the living as was Demeter's daughter, and like her he expected to return to life; her prayer was his, and he trusted that it was not uttered in vain. The trust in an after-life is the same as in the other tablets, but its mythical equivalent is different. The dead is not here facing and propitiating the guardians of the Water of Life or the Queen of the Dead; he finds the divine type of his fate in the horror of Kore's descent to the realm of Darkness and in her triumphant return to the Light. This is, among all the texts here surveyed, the only instance of the Eleusinian myth; which, as we know, was not confined to Eleusis.[2]

How could a text so amazingly carelessly written have accompanied a prominent person into his grave; a person for whom a grandiose tumulus was built; who, as a hero, received sacrifice and had his monument still further enlarged in subsequent years, and who, according to the second lamella buried with him (A4), was felt to be on the very threshold of divinity? That second text, however, is likewise imperfect, and so indeed are they all, though in varying degrees; from occasional faults (A1) to almost complete meaninglessness (A3 and C). One cannot but conclude that these lamellae were articles of a local mass-production; objects of a beadles' trade like the pictures of the Madonna and of saints sold at Roman Catholic churches. This fact is significant enough, for it implies that they came to be appreciated as material objects rather than as carriers of the words engraved on them. We have previously protested against the designation of the lamellae as 'amulets', and shall continue to urge their essentially different character; but have here to admit that the facts just noted are evidence of the Gold Leaves gradually being accepted for just this. The process comes to its end with the tablet of Caecilia Secundina; but the unconcern about the wording on the Thurii plaques is a first pointer in the same direction. In the next chapter we shall find the dead presenting himself, on the Pharsalos plaque, as

---

[1] Diels (p. 5) quotes Diod. i. 12. 4 (fr. 302 Kern); but see also Eur. *Phoen.* 685 and *Hel.* 1301 ff.; for the Epidauros Hymn cf. P. Maas, *Schriften der Königsberger Gel. Ges.* (1933), 138 [12], and D. L. Page (discussing W. J. W. Koster) in *Class. Rev.* N.s. xiii (1963), 220; for Sicily cf. above, p. 111, n. 7.

[2] Cf. above, pp. 70 and 97.

'Asterios . One may thereby feel reminded of those frequent instances, in the Magic Papyri, of sorcerers presenting themselves as one or the other god or daemon in order to impress unwilling or inimical spirits; in fact, however, as the interpretation will show, the bearing of that statement is so different that it too can be reckoned, if anything, only as a first step towards a magical, instead of a religious, purpose. To appreciate the difference, one has to compare properly magical incantations and amulets, such as the gold plaque from Brindisi with its egyptianizing mumbo-jumbo[1] or any other from among those instanced in the Introduction to the present subject.[2]

Viewed against this background the Gold Leaves retain their primary religious character, even though the clarity and profundity of the original conception appears now to be dimmed by a penumbra of superstition. Perhaps this eclipse began when the words conveying a new vision of man and his destiny were first engraved on gold leaves—carriers, before and after, of magical potencies to combat demonic antagonists.

[1] Cf. above, p. 283.   [2] Above, pp. 279 ff.

V. TABLETS B1–B8

The second main group consists of eight lamellae: the two larger ones from Petelia (B1) and Pharsalos (B2) containing one and the same text with very considerable differences of detail, and six small ones (B3–8), all from the neighbourhood of Eleutherna in central Crete and all of them inscribed with the same three verses, corresponding with the most essential sections of B1 and B2.[1]

(a) PREFATORY ON B1 AND B2

B1. Of all the surviving 'Orphic' Gold Leaves, this one has been longest known. It was apparently found in the eighteenth century, for it was in the possession of the English collector J. Millingen in Rome; whence its inscription was first published (not without considerable mistakes) in 1836.[2] After Millingen's death it finally reached the British Museum; its description in the *Catalogue of Jewellery* (1911, p. 380, no. 3155) is as indispensable as it is generally neglected.

There is no reason to doubt the tradition that it was found at Strongoli, the ancient Petelia,[3] 22 klm. north of Cotrone and *c.* 70 klm. (as the crow flies) south-east of Thurii;[4] this, however, need not have been its place of origin. For it was found rolled up in a golden cylindrical container with a chain attached to it;[5] that is, it was worn as an amulet. We recall that amulets of this form were widely used in the later Roman Empire.[6] I do not know of any earlier one of this type; at any rate, we are bound to accept the judgement of the experts, according to which the Petelia case 'can hardly be earlier than the second or third century A.D.' (when Petelia was a moderately flourishing Roman *municipium*),[7] while 'the inscription on the plaque may pretty certainly be dated to the

---

[1] For an untypical small plaque ('B9') found with B3–8 see below, p. 384.

[2] By G. Franz in *Bullet. dell'Ist. di corrispond. archeol.* (1836), 149 ('proviene da' contorni di Petiglia').

[3] Strabo, vi. 254; Verg. *Aen.* iii, 402; cf. J. Bérard, *La Colonisation grecque* . . . (Bibl. École. Franç. d'Athènes . . . 150), 2nd ed. (1957), pp. 360 ff.

[4] In the 18th century Policastro, the ancient Pyxus (Buxentum), was claimed by a local enthusiast to be the site of Petelia, the foundation of Philoktetes (cf. the preceding note). This claim occasioned some confusion; e.g. an archaic bronze lamella found, in 1783, at Policastro is stated to come from Petelia in *I.G.* xiv. 636 and even in Arangio–Ruiz and Olivieri, *Inscript. Siciliae et M. Graeciae* (1925), p. 147. The gold lamella however appears really to have been found in a grave near Strongoli. Cf. F. Lenormant, *La Grande Grèce*, i (1881), pp. 385 f.

[5] See the photographs in *B.M. Cat.* Pl. LXXI or in W. K. C. Guthrie, *Orpheus* . . . (1952), Pl. 9 (ib., Pl. 8 is an enlarged photograph of the lamella; as also in *Bull. John Rylands Libr.* xvii (1933), Pls. 1 and 2, pp. 73 and 86).

[6] Cf. above, pp. 280 and 334.   [7] Cf. F. Lenormant, l.l. i. 393.

fourth century B.C.'[1] The neglect of these archaeological observations by some students[2] has had a misleading effect upon the interpretation of the lamellae similar to that caused by the false analogy of the Secundina tablet.[3] The Petelia leaf must somehow have been recovered, in the Roman period, from the burial to which it had been added some five hundred or more years earlier (and this obviously need not have been at Petelia). It commended itself for use as an amulet, for objects extracted from graves are commonly credited with outstanding magical virtue. In order to be worn in the usual manner it was folded breadthwise four times over and when, even so, it did not fit into the container destined for it, one corner was simply clipped off. This ruthless procedure resulted in the large lacunae in the last four lines of the inscription; an incurable damage, for no parallel to this section of the text has yet emerged. The angular writing is none too regular—recalling our previous discussion of the palaeography of the Thurii tablets[4] one will date it, like A1, before rather than after the middle of the fourth century—but the engraver has worked conscientiously. There are only one or two slips, and the first five hexameters have a line each to themselves (with a slight hitch at the end of the first); thereafter he realized that the remaining space required a narrower spacing of the letters; even so, he had to squeeze his last line, in minute letters, along the right-hand margin.

B2. The second witness to the same text, by contrast, is among the most recent to become known, for it was discovered after the Second World War and published in 1951.[5] It was found in a grave at Pharsalos, in a beautiful large bronze vase of Attic workmanship which contained ashes and bones and, in addition to the plaque, other funeral gifts. The vase is decorated, in relief, with a representation of the rape of Oreithyia. It belongs to a group which had been studied by G. M. A. Richter,[6] who dated it about 350–320 B.C.; the most frequent representation on them is of Eros and Psyche. It can hardly be doubted that both these mythical subjects were intended as allegories on the lot of the soul after death,[7] for

---

[1] *B.M. Cat.* . . . , p. 381.

[2] e.g. J. Harrison, *Proleg.* p. 574, n. 1, 'doubtless worn by the dead person as an amulet'.

[3] e.g. P. Boyancé who (*Le culte des Muses* (1937), p. 79) describes the tablets as 'ces amulettes si efficaces' and says: 'Ce sont des poèmes destinés à agir par leur vertu magique sur la déesse des enfers, à obtenir d'elle qu'elle exempte des maux et des supplices les âmes des élus.' Poems 'destined to act, by their magic power, upon deities' are of a fundamentally different character (as a comparison with the Magic Papyri can show). The dead person following the advice, and uttering the words, inscribed on his gold leaf is indeed meant to commend himself to the chthonic deities, but not as by a magic incantation.　　　　　　[4] Above, pp. 293 ff.

[5] N. M. Verdelis, *Arch. Ephem.* lxxxix–xc (1950–1), 80 ff. (photo and transcript, p. 99).

[6] *Am. Journ. Arch.* l (1946), 361 ff.; cf. T. B. L. Webster, *Art and Literature in Fourth Century Athens* (1956), p. 104.

[7] This interpretation had been proposed by G. Charles-Picard in an earlier study of these vases (*Monum. Piot.* xxvii (1940), quoted by Richter, l.l. 363, who opposed it); it was reasserted by Webster, l.l. 105.

all these vases appear to have been destined to contain the remains of persons cremated. This kind of allegorism is familiar in the Roman period,[1] beginning with the (Pythagorean?) 'Basilica at the Porta Maggiore'; to find it anticipated at this comparatively early date is quite as surprising as is the find, at this unexpected place, of the tablet itself.[2]

It is even smaller than the others; it passes understanding how the engraver could have managed to write nine lines within 16 millimetres, in letters about one millimetre high. Small wonder that he disregarded the division of verses, found no room for those verses which on B1 have been mangled by Roman scissors and that, even so, he had to condense into prose the content of the essential verses 7–9 of B1. His writing is almost faultless, but for the skipping of four letters in v. 5. At the end of the next line, an I in the place of N may be due to lack of space, and two superfluous *hastae* after the next following word may be accidental scratches. After OYPANOY, finally, at the end of v. 8, he incised only AΣT and followed this by a sign which looks somewhat like his omega; this probably is not a fault but—at the end of the line—a sign indicative of abbreviation, occasioned by the apprehension lest the remaining 1·5 mm. might not suffice even for the condensed ending of the text if the long word were written out in full.

The letters are of the angular type; the sigmas are flat angular hooks. This feature points to a date in the latter half of the fourth century,[3] and this is confirmed by the fact that the vessel in which the tablet was found is securely dated to the third quarter of the fourth century. The Pharsalos lamella thus seems to be a little less ancient than those from Petelia and Thurii (or at least A1). It may be considered contemporary with Aristotle, while the others—or at least most of them—are likely to go back to the age of Plato.

---

[1] It will hardly be necessary—except in token of respect—here to mention the names of F. Cumont and J. Carcopino.

[2] We await with keen anticipation the complete publication of the allegorical commentary on an Orphic poem found at Derveni near Salonika: it seems to be of roughly the same date as the Pharsalos urn and at the very least affords a literary parallel to the allegorical representation on it. Cf. above, p. 295, n. 3 for the literature on it.

[3] Cf. above, p. 295.

(b) TEXT OF B1 AND B2

B1. *Transcript*

Brit. Mus. 3155. Plate 29
From Petelia. 45 mm. × 27 mm.

B.M. *Cat. of Jewellery*, p. 380; *I.G.* xiv. 638; Olivieri, p. 12; 32a Kern; 17 DK.

l.		v.
1	ΕΥΡΗΣΣΕΙΣΔΑΙΔΑΟΔΟΜΩΝΕΠΑΡΙΣΤΕΡΑΚΡΗΝ	1
2	ΗΝΠΑΡΔΑΥΤΗΙΛΕΥΚΗΝΕΣΤΗΚΥΙΑΝΚΥΠΑΡΙΣΣΟΝ	2
3	ΤΑΥΤΗΣΤΗΣΚΡΗΝΗΣΜΗΔΕΣΧΕΔΟΝΕΜΠΕΛΑΣΕΙΑΣ	3
4	ΕΥΡΗΣΕΙΣΔΕΤΕΡΑΝΤΗΣΜΝΜΗΟΣΥΝΗΣΑΠΟΛΙΜΝΗΣ	4
5	ΨΥΧΡΟΝΥΔΩΡΠΡΟΡΕΟΝφΥΛΑΚΕΣΔΕΠΙΠΡΟΣΘΕΝΕΑΣΙΝ	5
6	ΕΙΠΕΙΝΓΗΣΠΑΙΣΕΙΜΙΚΑΙΟΥΡΑΝΟΥΑΣΤΕΡΟΕΝΤΟΣΑΥΤΑΡΕΜ	6,7
7	ΟΙΓΕΝΟΣΟΥΡΑΝΙΟΝΤΟΔΕΔΙΣΤΕΚΑΙΑΥΤΟΙΔΙΨΗΙΔΕΙΜΙΑΥ	8
8	ΗΚΑΙΑΠΟΛΛΥΜΑΙΑΛΛΑΔΟΤΑΙΨΑΨΥΧΡΟΝΥΔΩΡΠΡΟΡΕ	9
9	ΟΝΤΗΣΜΝΗΜΟΣΥΝΗΣΑΠΟΛΙΜΝΗΣΚΑΥΤ[·]ΙΔΩΣΟΥΣΙ	10
10	ΠΙΕΙΝΘΕΙΗΣΑΠ[....]ΝΗΣΚΑΙΤΟΤΕΠΕΙΤΑ[.......]ΗΡΩΕ	11
11	ΣΣΙΝΑΝΑΞΕΙ[.........]ΝΗΕΤΟΔΕΝ[................	12
12	ΘΑΝΕΙΣΘ[.................]·ΟΔΕΓΡΑ·[..............	
marg.	ΤΟΓΛΩΣΕΙΠΑΣΚΟΤΟΣΑΜφΙΚΑΛΥΨΑΣ	

l. 9: Τ[·]Ι vestigia dubia; sed lectionibus Τ[ΟΙΣΟ]Ι vel Τ[ΙΚΑΣΟ]Ι spatium non sufficit; ΣΟΙ (post ΤΟΙ) a scalptore omissum vid.   l. 11:]ΝΗ vel]ΙΗ   In *marg.* ego nil vidi

B1. *Reconstruction*

v. 1   Εὑρήcειc δ' Ἀίδαο δόμων ἐπ' ἀριcτερὰ κρήνην,

2   πὰρ δ' αὐτῆι λευκὴν ἑcτηκυῖαν κυπάριccον·

3   ταύτηc τῆc κρήνηc μηδὲ cχεδὸν ἐμπελάcειαc.

4   εὑρήcειc δ' ἑτέραν, τῆc Μνημοcύνηc ἀπὸ λίμνηc

5   ψυχρὸν ὕδωρ προρέον· φύλακεc δ' ἐπίπροcθεν ἔαcιν.

6   εἰπεῖν· "Γῆc παῖc εἰμι καὶ Οὐρανοῦ ἀcτερόεντοc·

7   αὐτὰρ ἐμοὶ γένοc οὐράνιον· τόδε δ' ἴcτε καὶ αὐτοί.

8   δίψηι δ' εἰμὶ αὔη καὶ ἀπόλλυμαι· ἀλλὰ δότ' αἶψα

9   ψυχρὸν ὕδωρ προρέον τῆc Μνημοcύνηc ἀπὸ λίμνηc."

10   καὐτ[ο]ί ⟨cοι⟩ δώcουcι πιεῖν θείηc ἀπ[ὸ κρή]νηc,

11   καὶ τότ' ἔπειτ' ἄ[λλοιcι μεθ'] ἡρώεccιν ἀνάξει[c

12   .....]νηc τόδε ν[........]θανεῖcθ[

13(?)   ....].οδεγρα.[...........

14(?)   ......]τογλωcειπα cκότοc ἀμφικαλύψαc.

v. 10: fin. vel λίμ]νηc; cf. p. 369, n. 1.   v. 12: Μνημοcύ]νηc speciose *B.M. Cat.* (et ν[ᾶμα, sed lectio utrobique parum certa)

B2. *Transcript*

Athens
From Pharsalos.   42 mm. × 16 mm.
Arch. Ephem. (1950–1), 99.

l. 1   ΕΥΡΗΣΕΙΣΑΙΔΑΟΔΟΜΟΙΣΕΝΔΕΞΙΑΚΡΗΝΗΝΠΑΡΔΑΥΤΗΙ   vv. 1–2

2   ΛΕΥΚΗΝΕΣΤΗΚΥΙΑΝΚΥΠΑΡΙΣΣΟΝΤΑΥΤΗΣΤΗΣΚΡΗΝΗΣ   2–3

3   ΜΗΔΕΣΧΕΔΟΘΕΝΠΕΛΑΣΗΙΣΘΑΠΡΟΣΣΩΔΕΥΡΗΣΕΙΣΤΟΜΝΗ   3–4

4   ΜΟΣΥΝΗΣΑΠΟΛΙΜΝΗΣΨΥΧΡΟΝΥΔΩΡΠΡΟΦΥΛΑΚΕΣΙ   4–5

5   ΔΕΠΥΠΕΡΘΕΝΕΑΣΙΝΟΙΔΕΣΕΙΡΗΣΟΝΤΑΙΟΤΙΧΡΕΟΣ   5–5a

6   ΕΙΣΑΦΙΚΑΝΕΙΣΤΟΙΣΔΕΣΥΕΥΜΑΛΑΠΑΣΑΝΑΛΗΘΕΙΗΙ   5a–5b

7   ΚΑΤΑΛΕΞΑΙΙΙΕΙΠΕΙΓΓΗΣΠΑΙΣΕΙΜΙΚΑΙΟΥΡΑΝΟΥΑΣΤ·   5b–6

8   ΑΣΤΕΡΙΟΣΟΝΟΜΑΔΙΨΗΙΔΕΙΜΑΥΟΣΑΛΛΑΔΟΤΕΜΟΙ   [7–9]

9   ΠΙΕΝΑΠΟΤΗΣ ΚΡΗΝΗΣ

l. 7: post ΞΑΙ lineolae duae directae quae—sicut illa in fine l. 4—scalptoris vitio tribuen-
dae videntur. ‖ ΠΕΙΓ : lit. ν finalis literae insequenti assimilata. ‖ in fine, post ΑΣΤ, figura
quaedam incerta unius lit. spatium implet

B2. *Reconstruction*

v. 1   Εὑρήσεις Ἀίδαο δόμοις ἐνδέξια κρήνην,

2   πὰρ δ᾽ αὐτῆι λευκὴν ἑστηκυῖαν κυπάρισσον·

3   ταύτης τῆς κρήνης μηδὲ σχεδόθεν πελάσηισθα·

4   πρόσσω δ᾽ εὑρήσεις τὸ Μνημοσύνης ἀπὸ λίμνης

5   ψυχρὸν ὕδωρ προ⟨ρέον⟩· φύλακες δ᾽ ἐπύπερθεν ἔασιν·

5a   οἱ δὲ c᾽ εἰρήσονται ὅ τι χρέος εἰσαφικάνεις·

5b   τοῖς δὲ cὺ εὖ μάλα πᾶσαν ἀληθείην καταλέξαι·

6   εἰπεῖν· "Γῆς παῖc εἰμι καὶ Οὐρανοῦ ἀcτ⟨ερόεντος⟩·

(7–   Ἀcτέριος ὄνομα· δίψηι δ᾽ εἰμ᾽ αὖος· ἀλλὰ δότε μοι

9)   πιεῖν ἀπὸ τῆς κρήνης."

(c) TEXT OF B3–B8

Six gold leaves, almost identical and very small (on an average, they are *c.* 60 mm. long and 10 mm. high) come from the region of Eleutherna in Central Crete; at least two of them were found in the same grave and seem to have been incised by the same hand (nos. 3 and 4). Older editions[1] have been antiquated by that of four lamellae in M. Guarducci's *Inscriptiones Creticae* ii. 168 and 314; subsequently two more were published, from the Stathatos Collection, by N. M. Verdelis.[2]

It seems superfluous to duplicate these competent and amply commented editions and their careful facsimiles. These leaves all contain the same wording; scribal errors—of which none is entirely free—are cancelled out by comparison and may here be neglected. These apart, there is only one significant variant; two others, being confined to one and the same leaf (p. 314 Guard.), have, for this very reason, scant authority; seeing that, moreover, this is the most carelessly written of all and differs in shape from the rest (it is a half-disc, all others being rectangular).

Hence it seems permissible to offer a standard text and to relegate the variants to a short apparatus criticus. The wording is in the local (Doric) dialect and spelling (which includes the use of a sign like Z in the place of doubled sigma[3]); it evidently consists, in the main, of three hexameters which are, however, oddly expanded.

In the present numbering, B3, B4, B5 = *a*, *b*, *c* Guarducci, B6 = Guard., p. 314, B7 and B8 = Verdelis 1 and 2. I shall however, for easier reference, retain *a*, *b*, *c*, adding *d* for Guard., p. 314 and call S^1 and S^2 the two from the Stathatos Collection.

The division of verses is entirely neglected in *d* and S^2, which exhibit the most faulty texts; the other four have the first two hexameters on separate lines and allot the fourth and last line to the closing word ἀστερόεντος.

B3–8 (i.e. a–d et S¹, S²)

1   Δίψαι αὖος ἐγὼ καὶ ἀπόλλυμαι· ἀλλὰ πιέμ μοι

2   Κράνας αἰειρόω ἐπὶ δεξιά, τῇ κυφάριccoc.

3   "Τίc δ' ἔccι; πῶ δ' ἔccι;"

4   Γᾶc υἱόc ἦμι καὶ ὠρανῶ ἀcτερόεντος.

v. 1 : Δ. δ' ἤμ' αὖοc καί *d*; ΔΙΨΑΙΑΥΟCΛΛ[·]CCEΓω *c*, ΔΙΨΑΑΑΥΟC . . *S²*, ut δ' ante αὖοc voluisse videantur ‖ ΠΙΕΝ *d*   v. 2: ΑΙΕΙΡΟω *a b*, idem voluerunt *d S¹* : ΑΙΕΝΑω *c* *S²* ‖ ΤΕ *d* (ΤΗ cett.) ‖ ΚΥΠ- *d* (ΚΥΦ- cett.) v. 3: ΓΑΣΗΜΙΤΥΜΤΗΡ (i.e. θυγάτηρ ?) *d* ‖ ΚΑΡΑΝω *S¹*

[1] e.g. Comparetti, *Lamin. orf.*, p. 37; Olivieri, p. 14; Kern, p. 105, no. 32b; 17a DK; cf. Guarducci, p. 168, note.

[2] *Arch. Ephem.* (1953–4, app. 1958), 56 ff.; *Collection Stathatos*, iii (1963), p. 256.

[3] This point was clarified by N. M. Verdelis, *Arch. Eph.* l.l. 59; cf. Schwyzer, *Gr. Gram.* i, pp. 320 and 329. The sign in question had previously been mistaken for a 'broken' sigma

The few textual problems involved may at once be dealt with. Now that the wording at the end of the first line has been established, it need no longer be argued that lines 1–2 and 4 are spoken by the soul and 3 by some unnamed questioner (while B1 and B2 introduce the 'guardians' of the spring). In l. 1 the uncertain attestation of the particle δ' is note-worthy. Its insertion could remove a particularly bad hiatus[1] and cor-respond with B1 and B2; but it appears that Δίψαι αὖος was the standard form adopted in the workshop in which these lamellae were cut and that sometimes attempts were made to remove the hiatus, perhaps not without a knowledge of the fuller text of which B1 and B2 afford (imperfect) evidence; cf. there v. 8.

The variant αἰειρόω:αἰενάω in l. 2 entails a similar conclusion. The latter adjective suits the metre and the context—as many parallel instances show[2]—but it is attested only by two of the six lamellae, while the other four yield a rare word not unsuitable in itself but ruinous to the metre— unless indeed one supposes Ionic (or Lesbian) αἰί to have been expelled by local αἰεί. This again presupposes a faulty local original (or adapta-tion of an original) sporadically emended.

The words printed above as l. 3 are impressive indeed through their parallelism but make no verse at all. They are equivalent to the set form, in Homer, of asking a new-comer to tell his name and parentage by τίς πόθεν εἰς;[3] With this form retained, the combination of these words with l. 4 would yield a perfect hexameter, if the (materially expendable) word υἱός were omitted.[4] One is driven to suspect that an original text in traditional epic language may have been transposed, with imperfect artistry,[5] into the local dialect.[6] The existence, long before the Cretan leaves were incised, of (fuller) versions in the epic language is of course proved by B1 and B2, but, evidently, B3–8 cannot, with their differences

---

(Σ; hence wrong transcriptions and also mis-statements as in Schwyzer, l.l. i. 82 and 321 on ἔϲι, allegedly for Homeric ἔϲϲι); subsequently this broken sigma was supposed to stand, oddly, for ϲϲ, while otherwise a round sigma is used throughout. The sign Z denoting -ss- is by no means confined, in Crete, to these gold leaves. Miss Guarducci (p. 170) noted the point; but the conclusions for the transcription of the texts here considered do not so far appear to have been drawn.

[1] Chantraine, Gramm. Hom. i. 89: there are very few hiatuses of this type in Homer and they are relieved by 'sense-incision'—as this one is not.

[2] e.g. Hes. Op. 595; cf. Kern ad loc.   [3] K. Robert, Hermes, li (1916), 560, n. 1.

[4] Similarly Wilamowitz, Der Glaube . . . , ii. 184, n. 1.—ΓΑϹ ΗΜΙ ΤΥΜΤΗΡ in d may stand for γ. ἠ. θυγάτηρ; a variant of scant authority confined to this inferior specimen, which is alone also in intruding ἠμι in v. 1 (but cf. B1 and B2, v. 8). The alteration, which spoils the metre, does not necessarily imply that the person buried with this lamella was a female (d retains the masc. αὖος in 1); the notion of ψυχή may have occasioned the change, as it occasioned the fem. καθαρά in the A-texts.

[5] The disregard for the metrical form stands out also in v. 4 υἱός, where παῖς (cf. B1 and B2) would at least have preserved the dactylic rhythm.

[6] ΚΑΡΑΝω in S¹ is hardly indicative of a krasis in pronouncing καὶ ὡρ-, which would spoil the dactylic rhythm; more likely the engraver skipped two letters.

of order and wording, be described simply as excerpts from the latter. It is particularly striking that the question addressed to the soul is absent from B1 and worded quite differently in B2 (where, moreover, it will prove, on examination, to be an interpolation). This is a reminder that the few surviving samples of this text convey an incomplete picture of its tradition and variability. The Cretan leaves are particularly valuable because they show the supposedly South-Italian eschatology unexpectedly flourishing, in the third century B.C.,[1] in this island, and because, in their very briefness, they intimate what were felt to be the cardinal points in the longer texts.

(d) THE CARDINAL WORDS

Fountain and cypress; the dead parched by thirst and propitiating the questioner by defining himself: the small Cretan plaques indeed convey the essence of the two larger ones. The latter describe the imagined scene with fuller detail; they identify the spring as that of Mnemosyne and add to it another one which the bearer is to avoid; but their essence is the same. It all culminates in the formula of self-presentation: Γῆς παῖς εἰμι καὶ Οὐρανοῦ ἀστερόεντος. What is it that makes these few words fit to open up the access to the desired spring; to the Netherworld; even to the abode of blessed heroes?

The answer to this question has been sought[2] in comparing a typical Hesiodic verse which speaks of the race of Immortals (or, rather, one of the races)

οἳ Γῆς τ᾽ ἐξεγένοντο καὶ Οὐρανοῦ ἀστερόεντος.[3]

This verse obviously is the model of the one under discussion—formally; but the whole tenor and ideology of the tablets excludes the possibility that, at the entrance to Hades, the soul could have presented itself as a god. Again, a famous fragment from Euripides' *Melanippe the Wise*,[4] and also the song which Apollonius Rhodius puts into the mouth of Orpheus,[5] have been called in evidence.[6] Both these speak of ancestral Heaven and Earth; but they are philosophical, or even scientific, cosmogonies in poetical guise and thus cannot illuminate the specific bearing of our verse, which is about man and not about the kosmos (and man is not even mentioned in the latter of the two texts). The epigram on the fallen at Poteidaia[7] has also been compared; but our speaker, entering Hades,

---

[1] In view of the rounded forms of Є, С, and ⲱ a date about a century later than of our A1, B1, and B2 was suggested for the Cretan leaves by Verdelis (*Eph. Arch.* l.l., 60). Earlier students had ascribed them to the second century B.C. (their ascription, by Dieterich, to the second century A.D. can only be called a curiosity).

[2] J. Harrison, *Proleg.* 575.

[3] *Theog.* 106; cf. 45, 154, 421 and consider *which* gods are thus styled.

[4] Fr. 484 N.²; cf. frs. 839 and 1023.   [5] *Argon.* i. 494 ff.

[6] A. Dieterich, *Nekyia* (1913), pp. 101 ff.   [7] *I.G.* i². 945.

could not fittingly hint that 'the spirit goes up to the aither, the body to earth'; his is a different, mythical situation. Finally, the Titans were, here again, suspected;[1] and indeed they, rather than 'the gods' in general, were 'offspring of Heaven and Earth', in Hesiod as well as according to Orphic theogonies. They, however, were relegated to Tartarus or released to the Isles of the Blessed according to the former, and burned to ashes according to the latter; how could a speaker, in the fourth century or later, present himself as one of them? Besides, it must, reluctantly, once more be stressed that he would have spoiled his prospects of a favourable reception, if the ideology of the Gold Leaves were Orphic; if not, it is impossible to discern any useful purpose in so preposterous a claim. The claimant at the gates of Hades is neither a Titan nor a god but—a man.

In Greek mythology the races of men may have been 'made' by Zeus, or by 'the gods',[2] or by Prometheus;[3] fashioned out of 'water and earth' or clay; they may have grown from trees[4] or from the stones thrown by Deukalion and Pyrrha;[5] they may claim, as autochthones, to have sprung from the soil or the rivers of their district. The Greeks were, on the whole, not greatly concerned about the origin of man;[6] hence this variety of myths,[7] none of which attained wide currency. But many and various as they are, none presents mankind as the offspring of Uranos and Gaia; this primordial couple is, reasonably, the origin of the principal cosmic realities and of the oldest deities but not of man.

This summary survey suggests that the interpretation of the verse under discussion gains nothing from searching the mythographical literature; on the contrary, this search appears rather to have blunted the perceptiveness of students for its clear and deep message. When Oedipus proclaims himself παῖδα τῆς Τύχης,[8] he is very far from appealing to one or other mythological tradition; but the language of myth gives him the means for defining his own essence as, at this stage of his self-realization, he perceives it. Thus here, where, as in Sophocles, any attempt at exposition risks obscuring rather than clarifying what has been given final expression through poetry. Entering the gates of the realm of Death, man declares what is his essence: he is a son of Heaven and Earth. His essence, then, is of both; be it noted, then, that this is not a proclamation of sheer other-worldliness.

'Ein Sohn der Erde bin ich: zu lieben gemacht, zu leiden':

---

[1] See e.g. Olivieri ad loc.   [2] Hes. *Op.* 110 ff.

[3] Kallimachos, frs. 192 and 493 ff.; also in comedies; pseudo-Apollodorus, *Bibl.* i. 45 Wagner.   [4] Cf. Wilamowitz, *Der Glaube* . . . , i². 186 on Hes. *Op.* 145.

[5] Pseudo-Apollodor. i. 48 W.; cf., perhaps, Hesiod, fr. 115 Rz.

[6] S. G. F. Brandon, *Creation Legends* . . . (1963), p. 189.

[7] For further varieties see Preller–Robert, *Griech. Mythol.* i (1894), 78 ff.

[8] Soph. *O.T.* 1080.

it is not flesh and bones only that make him a son of the Earth. And he is aware of another, the heavenly element in his person; it is the unity of the two which constitutes the essence of man. This he proclaims before the infernal guardians, and the way to a higher after-life is opened up for him who has fulfilled this, man's dual potentiality. Such was—as we saw —the persuasion also of Theron; of Pindar; even of Empedokles. In this perspective one understands the combination, in Pindar's poetry, of what seems contradictory—the celebration of victors in games and of the blessed in Elysium; the warning: do not seek to become a god, and the inspired expression of a religion which culminates in man's final deification. Similarly Empedokles; who is so filled with the conviction of man's essential god-head as to describe the body—the body which Pindar celebrated; in whose likeness Phidias recreated the gods, and which he, Empedokles, himself studied, described, and healed with devoted care— as the 'foreign garment' of man's true self; that self which has been condemned to be the plaything of the hating elements . . . even he fulfils all the potentialities of a 'son of the Earth'; fulfils them in that highest degree which will enable him to be, finally, 'god not man'.

Thus, unqualified, the verse stands on the Cretan leaves; this is the confession which 'opens the gates of hell', and if it is accepted that the Gold Leaves are Pythagorean,[1] here is a piece of old-Pythagorean religion. Old-Pythagorean—for although the Cretan leaves are the most recent of all (but for Caecilia Secundina), the other two of the same class, B1 (Petelia) and B2 (Pharsalos), convey, at this point, a less ancient wording.[2]

B1 has, after the verse just discussed, the following:

αὐτὰρ ἐμοὶ γένος οὐράνιον· τόδε δ' ἴστε καὶ αὐτοί.

It seems frankly surprising that the combination of the two verses has (as far as I know) generally been accepted without a murmur;[3] that it has been reproduced in translations and commented upon as though there were nothing wrong with it. 'I am a son of Heaven and Earth, but I am a scion of Heaven': it ought to be sufficient merely to put this sequence before the reader to make him agree, on consideration (if needed), that the second verse is a later addition, quite incompatible with the first; an addition made when it was felt that descent from Heaven was the essential qualification for bliss in the other world.[4] The verse stands condemned also in view of its lame second half: empty verbiage serving to fill the verse. Why indeed should the guardians, before whom the speaker

[1] Above, pp. 337 f. and, for the interrelation between all of them, below, pp. 383 f.

[2] This conclusion is argued below, pp. 376 ff.

[3] 'Not quite; cf. Guthrie, *Orpheus*[2], p. 174' (E. R. Dodds); and indeed G. observes: 'The two halves of this confession do not fit very well together', and draws from his observation a conclusion different from the one suggested above.

[4] Compare the third verse in A1–3.

makes his declaration, 'likewise' know that he stems from Heaven? The preceding verse, though, appears to have been so firmly established in the tradition that it could be neither altered nor eliminated, and hence the two verses had to be accepted together; by faith if not by reason. There is a distinctly theological odour about this; evidence of a swing towards other-worldliness in abandoning the realistic equilibrium of the original conception. One remembers that, at the time when these tablets were inscribed, Attic comedy revelled in pillorying Pythagorean ascetics[1] and Plato directed men's minds towards the other, the true world.

B2 does not have this additional verse; it has, in its place, the brief statement Ἀcτέριοc ὄνομα[2]—which in fact amounts to the same. It is worded like a deposition before the police—the space did not allow any poetical embroidery—but Asterios was not, at the time, a human name.[3] Even so, the mythographers ought not to be ransacked—here as little as with regard to the preceding verse—in search for *points d'appui*. Several mythical Asterioi and Asterions can indeed be found, quite easily, in handbooks and lexica,[4] but none will fit the context. The speaker on this plaque has his name from Οὐρανὸc ἀcτερόειc; his statement then is equivalent to ἐμοὶ γένοc οὐράνιον.

The urge, at the same time, at places so distant, to qualify the traditional wording in the same way though by different formulations is indicative of a change of authoritative doctrine.

(e) OTHER POINTS

The remaining points may suitably be approached in reviewing the two longer texts B1 and B2 and drawing upon the shorter Cretan wording (B3 ff.) where it is relevant. A synoptic rendering of B1 and B2 follows here (p. 368); for B3 see above, p. 362.

At the very beginning all three versions appear to be at variance in a puzzling manner. According to B1, the spring which is to be avoided is on the left; B2 locates the same spring on the right. Both these place the cypress-tree by this spring; but B3 has it by the other—the only one in this text—and on the right. Such wavering is surprising on any count, and particularly so in an eschatological context, where right and left are quite normally synonymous with salvation and perdition.[5] In fact, though, these differences are not as strict as on a first reading they appear.

---

[1] *Athen.* iv, 161 a ff.; 58e in DK i, p. 478.   [2] Cf. above, pp. 353 f.

[3] Perhaps one ought to set down a warning against connecting it with the place Ἀcτέριον near Mount Titanos (!) and not far from Pharsalos . . . Its inhabitants are Ἀcτεριεῖc or Ἀcτεριῶται (*Il.* 2. 735; Strabo 439).

[4] An Asterios, son of Neleus, has recently emerged in the fragments of the *Ehoiai* (*Fragmenta Hesiodea*, ed. Merkelbach and West (1967), no. 33(a), 10).

[5] E. Rohde, *Psyche*, ii. 221 n.; E. R. Dodds, *Plato, Gorgias*, p. 375; commentators on Matt. 25: 33.

Βι (*Petelia*) and Β2 (*Pharsalos*)

1 { Βι   Εὑρήσεις δ᾽ Ἀίδαο δόμων ἐπ᾽ ἀριστερὰ κρήνην,
    Β2   „   ÷   „   δόμοις ἐνδέξια   „

2 { Βι   πὰρ᾽ δ᾽ αὐτῆι λευκὴν ἑστηκυῖαν κυπάρισσον·
    Β2   „   „   „   „   „   „

3 { Βι   ταύτης τῆς κρήνης μηδὲ σχεδὸν ἐμπελάσειας.
    Β2   „   „   „   „   σχεδόθεν πελάσηισθα.

4 { Βι   εὑρήσεις δ᾽ ἑτέραν, τῆς Μνημοσύνης ἀπὸ λίμνης
    Β2   πρόσσω   „   εὑρήσεις τὸ   „   „   „

5 { Βι   ψυχρὸν ὕδωρ προρέον· φύλακες δ᾽ ἐπίπροσθεν ἔασιν.
    Β2   „   „   „   „   „   ἐπύπερθεν   „

5a Β2   οἱ δὲ σ᾽ εἰρήσονται ὅ τι χρέος εἰσαφικάνεις·

5b Β2   τοῖς δὲ σὺ εὖ μάλα πᾶσαν ἀληθείην καταλέξαι·

6 { Βι   εἰπεῖν· Γῆς παῖς εἰμι καὶ Οὐρανοῦ ἀστερόεντος·
    Β2   „   „   „   „   „   „   „   ·

7 { Βι   αὐτὰρ ἐμοὶ γένος οὐράνιον· τόδε δ᾽ ἴστε καὶ αὐτοί.
    Β2   Ἀστέριος ὄνομα·   ÷   ÷   ÷   ÷   ÷   ÷

8 { Βι   δίψηι δ᾽ εἰμὶ αὔη καὶ ἀπόλλυμαι· ἀλλὰ δότ᾽ αἶψα
    Β2   „   „   εἰμ᾽ αὖος· ÷   ÷   „   δότε μοι

9 { Βι   ψυχρὸν ὕδωρ προρέον τῆς Μνημοσύνης ἀπὸ λίμνης.
    Β2   πιεῖν   ÷   ÷   ÷   ÷   „   τῆς κρήνης.

10 Βι   καὐτοί ⟨σοι⟩ δώσουσι πιεῖν θείης ἀπ[ὸ κρή]νης·

11 Βι   καὶ τότ᾽ ἔπειτ᾽ ἄ[λλοισι μεθ᾽] ἡρώεσσιν ἀνάξει[ς . . .

(÷ = om.)

For textual detail see above, pp. 358 ff.

Β2 ends with κρήνης (9); Βι apparently had, after 11, three more verses; they are past recovery.

The Petelia plaque indeed puts the 'wrong' spring 'on the left hand side in the House of Hades'.[1] From v. 4 it is generally, and reasonably, inferred that the 'other' spring is on the right. It seems, therefore, that there is a parting of the roads at the entrance to Hades;[2] odd though it may be that the operative word 'right' is not in this text. It is in Β2. Here the first spring is 'in Hades, on the right'. This, however, does not mean that the indications of Βι are inverted, for this variant is connected with that at the beginning of v. 4: the second spring lies further on in the same direction; that is, likewise on the right, as in all other texts. Β2 thus

[1] 'In', and not 'of', the 'House of Hades', which is the Netherworld. For this use of the genitive cf. Hom. *Il*. 11. 498; 13. 226.
[2] The τρίοδοι in Pl. *Phaed*. 108 a, and similar details of the infernal geography, have of course been compared, and we recall the advice to 'go to the right' in plaque A4.

indicates one straight path and not that 'parting of the ways' which B1 at least implies.

Certain details suggest that the variants in B2 are alterations of a wording like that of B1. As v. 4 stands in B2, the 'water from the lake of Memory' is not called a κρήνη any longer, and yet this designation seems indispensable, and this all the more so, since the last words on this tablet are τῆς κρήνης. In B1 this designation is sufficiently implied by ἑτέραν in v. 4 and hence reasonably resumed in v. 10.[1] Secondly, in v. 1, δόμων ἐπ' ἀριστερά B1 is good Homeric, but ἐνδέξια in B2 is not. This adverb always indicates, in Homer, a movement, or succession, from left to right,[2] but in support of the bare meaning 'on the right' I find no earlier instance than, in Euripides, *Cycl.* 6, the adjective ἐνδέξιος. It is quite unlikely that the correct epic form (B1) could be secondary to the non-epic one (B2). Once the adverb had been introduced into B2, the genitive δόμων had to be changed into the locative dative δόμοις; the opposite sequence would be hard to account for. It is, on the other hand, true that the subjunctive at the end of v. 3 in B2 is vastly better, syntactically, than the optative in B1; the latter being a Homeric form indeed, but here unsuitable because the warning 'do not approach' could not legitimately be expressed by a negatived optative. B2 (that is, here and throughout, the script which the engraver copied) seems here to have aimed to improve upon the objectionable wording of the type B1.[3] If so, he was justified in objecting also to the compound ἐμπελάζειν (of which, in epic literature, H. *H. Herm.* 523 is the only comparable instance); but σχεδόθεν in the place of σχεδόν, designed to fill the gap left by the preposition, goes badly with πελάζειν.[4] Apart from these shortcomings of B2, both texts stand equally condemned in putting μηδέ, for reasons of metre, in the place of μή.

A motive for the thorough alteration (if this diagnosis is accepted) of vv. 1 and 4 by B2 may be found in the urge to introduce into the wording of B1 the notion of 'right', the importance of which, in the ideology of the Gold Leaves, is sufficiently evident from B3 and A4 and 5.[5]

---

[1] It is true that the space in B1 could as well be filled by the supplement λίμ]νης, but it is incredible that this and the preceding verse could have ended on the same word. On the contrary, λίμνης stands at the end of v. 9 (where it is suitable) to avoid such duplication.— Κρήνη, of course, does not only, as πηγή does, denote a natural spring (it does so e.g. in *Hippokrene*) but also any structure supplying running water; even the public water-supply in cities (Kallimachos, *Epigr.* 28).

[2] e.g. *Il.* 1. 597, 5. 189; *Od.* 17. 365, etc.; similarly ἐπιδέξια *Od.* 21. 141. Sometimes only the connotation 'one after another' seems to remain.

[3] Aorist subjunctives on -θα are fairly frequent in Homer (Chantraine, *Gramm. Hom.* i. 462), but almost always with strong aorists. The only s-aorist with this ending is *Il.* 23. 344 παρεξελάσῃσθα. This fact reduces one's trust (if any) in the authenticity of the B2 reading.

[4] Contrast Hom. *Od.* 19. 447 with 4. 439.

[5] For the absence in B2 of δ' in v. 1 see above, p. 363. There is little to choose, in v. 5, between ἐπίπροσθεν B1 and ἐπύπερθεν B2, but this variant once more illustrates the instability of this tradition (so different from the comparative uniformity of the Cretan leaves).

The second, and more extensive, difference of wording between B1 and B2 is in the additional verses 5a and 5b in B2. They may appear, at first sight, to supply a suitable and picturesque detail but prove, on closer examination, to be an interpolation; the shorter text of B1 is older. The reasons for indicting these verses are the following. Οἱ δέ at the beginning of v. 5a is unmetrical;[1] its resumption, in the next verse, in referring by τοῖϲ δέ to the same persons, is lame; τί χρέοϲ, meaning 'why' ('for what need'), occurs in Attic drama but not in epic poetry; besides, this question, though suitable in the situation as, so far, it has developed, does not properly fit the answer. V. 5b is modelled on Il. 24. 407, but the expression 'the whole truth' is meaningless in view of what follows and εὖ μάλα a mere stop-gap (adopted also in A4, v. 2); and, finally, the imperatival infinitive καταλέξαι clashes εἰπεῖν v. 6. It is improbable that all these shortcomings could have been part of the original wording, while it seems plausible that the two verses were added to it from a wish explicitly to motivate the following utterance, by the soul, of the saving formula.[2]

(f) EGYPTIAN ANALOGIES

The individuality and significance of these texts stands out on comparing Egyptian analogies, which are striking enough to have suggested Egyptian antecedents of the B-plaques to some scholars, including even Wilamowitz.[3] Ever since the Petelia tablet became known it has been compared with the formula, inscribed on funeral monuments, Δοίη coι ὁ "Οϲιριϲ τὸ ψυχρὸν ὕδωρ,[4] which in turn has been of interest to students of the Christian term refrigerium denoting the 'refreshment' of the dead in Paradise. Among the studies in this field, the book Le 'Refrigerium' dans l'au-delà by André Parrot (1937)[5] is here of particular interest, because the author presents, with fullness and authority, the oriental antecedents of the Christian concept. Among these, the formula just quoted is, in fact, the least relevant to the present subject, for it does not occur earlier than well in the period of the Roman Empire,[6] and is so different from the ample and characteristic Egyptian tradition—in which Osiris is not the

---

[1] The fact that a few initial trochees, in the place of dactyls, have to be accepted in Hesiod (Wilamowitz, Hesiod Erga (1928), p. 166) hardly suffices to justify this irregularity.

[2] An objection against this diagnosis may be based upon the fact that a comparable question, though differently worded, occurs in B3; it will be taken up later in comparing the three versions in their entirety.

[3] Der Glaube . . . , ii². 200; cf. A. Boettiger as quoted by E. Rohde, Psyche, ii. 391, n. 1.

[4] I.G. xiv. 1488, 1075, 1782.

[5] Originally a series of articles in Rev. Hist. Rel. ciii (1936), 149 and ff.—Further literature is quoted by Guthrie, Orpheus², p. 277.

[6] This must apply—as the barbarized language shows—to the instances from Alexandria (A. Parrot, l.l. 126 f.) no less than to those from Rome. There are no others.

giver of water to the thirsting soul[1]—that it may quite possibly be indicative, rather, of an impact of Greek religious ideas and language on the
Hellenistic Osiris religion.[2] However, the analogies between the tablets
and the Osiris formula would be insufficient to demonstrate their interrelation, even if the latter were assumed to have been in use, in Egypt,
early enough to afford a model for the Greek. Their similarity is confined
to the wish for a cool drink for the dead; and this, as will presently be
seen, is not enough.

Far more suggestive are the similarities between the Greek tablets and
certain details in those illustrated texts which were placed in Egyptian
graves, with increasing frequency, from the second millennium onward.
Deriving, in part, from texts which are found inscribed on the inner
walls of some pyramids, and incorporating collections of spells such as
'*The Book of the Two Ways*' and other 'Guides through the Netherworld'
(which are preserved in the 'Coffin Texts'), these variable compilations
grew into the fairly standardized form of the *Book of the Dead*, which continued to be copied and used in Ptolemaic and even in Roman times.[3]
Certain pictures in it could almost serve as illustrations, and certain
passages as paraphrases, of the section, here under discussion, of the
B-tablets.[4] Concerned lest their dead, at their resting-places on the edge of
the desert, should lack the vital moisture, the Egyptians sought to provide
it for them by including suitable spells and pictures in the *Book of the
Dead*. Hence we find in it representations of the dead, on their way
through the Netherworld, scooping water from a basin between trees,[5]
or catching in a bowl water poured out either by an arm which grows
from a tree beside a large basin,[6] or by a goddess inside that tree.[7]

[1] I cannot find that the stele from Carpentras (A. Parrot, l.l. 123) provides evidence
sufficient to demonstrate the Egyptian origin of the Roman formula.

[2] Cf. E. Rohde, *Psyche*, ii. 391, n. 1.—This possibility would gain in probability if the
inscription (*I.G.* xiv. 1842) in which Aidoneus takes the place of Osiris could safely be held to
represent an earlier form. But who can tell?

[3] A. Parrot, on whom in this section I am mainly relying, drew on the edition by E.
Naville (*Das ägyptische Totenbuch* (1886)). I have supplemented his indications from the following: (a) *The Book of the Dead: The Chapters of Going Forth by Day*, by E. A. Wallis Budge
(1898); (b) *Ägyptisches Totenbuch*, by G. Kolpaktchy (1955); (c) *The Egyptian Book of the Dead*,
ed. T. G. Allen (The University of Chicago Oriental Institute Publications, vol. lxxxii, 1960).
For one who is not an Egyptologist it is difficult indeed to make a reasonable choice between
conflicting renderings of originals far from uniform; even so, I venture to hope that the
following few citations can be trusted to give the gist of the relevant texts with a sufficient
approximation. If, in a few places, I have diverged from Allen's authoritative translation, this
is because I assumed him to be rendering a different form of the text.

[4] A. Parrot, l.l. 106 ff., Figs. 36 ff.

[5] A. Parrot, ib., fig. 37; cf. the analogous illustration in the Papyrus of Ani, of the xv[th] cent.
B.C., reproduced in E. A. Wallis Budge, *The Papyrus of Ani* . . . (2nd edition, 1894), Pl. 16b.

[6] A. Parrot, ib., Fig. 39.

[7] Illustrated e.g. in T. G. Allen's edition, Pl. XXII, and in H. Haas, *Bilderatlas zur
Religionsgeschichte*, Lieferung 2–4, *Aegyptische Religion*, by H. Bonnet (1924), Fig. 136. Both these
illustrations date from the Ptolemaic period.

Chapter-headings like 'To drink water in the divine region below' and prayers like 'O sycamore of Nut, give me your water!' or 'Let me attain the water! Let me drink the water!'[1] accentuate the similarity with the Greek.

When the frequent contacts of Greeks and Egyptians are remembered —the Greek settlements in Naukratis and Memphis; the flourishing trade between the two countries; Greek involvement in Egyptian politics, from the times of Psammetichos onward; the impact of Egyptian sculpture upon the Greek; the statuettes of the grotesque Egyptian god Bès in Greek graves, from archaic times onward, and from Rhodes in the East to Italy in the West—the possibility certainly exists that Greeks could have been affected by Egyptian religious ideas, in archaic times as well as later; one recalls the excessive use which Herodotus makes of this assumption. Settlers at Memphis could have been impressed by the cult of the dead there and even have taken part in it, becoming proselytes like the Jews in Elephantine. And they could tell visitors from the homeland of it; even some Pythagoras . . .

And yet: the similarities of the Greek imagery and the Egyptian are far from proving this possibility to have materialized, for they are countered by fundamental differences. In the Greek, the essential point lies in the presence of guardians, possibly hostile, and their propitiation by that avowal of descent from Heaven and Earth which is the very heart of these texts. The Egyptian has nothing like it; on the contrary: the dead man, on reaching the spring, is at once and most readily refreshed; not only with water but also with fruit and frankincense.[2] The difference stands out most definitely in those representations which are nearest in time to, and even contemporary with, the Greek. They are reliefs, on tablets and *situlae*, showing a goddess—Nut or Nephtys or Hathor— inside a large tree pouring out water for the dead and his soul (his $k\bar{a}$ and $b\bar{a}$)[3] on her right and left.[4] No Persephone could be thought of in her place.

Even so, this notion of a tree at the desired spring appears to constitute a far from obvious coincidence. It is, however, greatly impaired by the fact that the Egyptian texts and pictures always and exclusively exhibit a sycamore and the Greek, with equal consistency, a cypress—and there could not easily be trees more different than these two! Moreover, the Egyptian sycamore is increasingly represented—itself or the goddess in it —as the very giver of the refreshing water, while the Greek cypress seems to have no other function than to serve as a landmark (Wilamowitz[5]

---

[1] Chapters 59 and 62, quoted by A. Parrot, ib. 109 f.
[2] e.g. in the Papyrus of Ani (Pl. 16c Budge); cf. T. G. Allen, l.l., Pl. LXIX (Ptolemaic).
[3] On these cf. lately S. G. F. Brandon, *Man and his Destiny* (1962), pp. 39 ff.
[4] A. Parrot, l.l. 113 f., Figs. 43 f.   [5] *Der Glaube* . . . , ii[2]. 200.

compared it to the pointers which on Hellenistic epigrams guide the wanderer to a spring). This 'white cypress' indeed has never ceased puzzling students; for the cypress is not white[1] and it is about as hard to equate the cypress with the silver-poplar (λεύκη) as with the sycamore. Even if the Greek adjective is taken in its wider and basic sense ('shining'), its application to this dark tree remains unexplained. Nor is it clear why just this tree should here be mentioned. It is nowadays often planted on cemeteries in Greece as well as in the Near East; but Greek evidence for its relation with the Netherworld is as scanty as it is rich for poplar and elm.[2] Greeks reading these words of the Gold Leaves are therefore likely to have recalled, rather, the cypresses in Kalypso's garden[3] and at the cave of the enamoured Cyclops;[4] add that the cypress grows, according to two passages in Theocritus, at springs.[5] At any rate, the analogy between the Greek and the Egyptian tree by the spring grows less striking on closer inspection; add that in the Greek text it appears to stand at or near the entrance of the Netherworld, while the Egyptian sycamore is a station reached after passing through many others.

What, then, remains? The dead, parched by thirst, asks to be refreshed at a spring with a tree near-by and his prayer is fulfilled: this much is common to Greek and Egyptian, and it is not a little. On the other hand, there is that fundamental difference of significance and, corresponding with it, exclusive differences of detail: the readily giving goddess, or tree, over against the dialogue with the guardians culminating in the saving confession; nor has the Egyptian anything corresponding with the choice between two springs in B1 and B2.[6] And the tree is a sycamore as persistently with the Egyptians as, with the Greeks, it is a cypress.

One may incline to conclude that the Greeks (a Greek) borrowed from Egypt the basic motif of the thirsting dead seeking and finding cold water

---

[1] O. Gruppe, *Berl. Phil. Woch.* (1912), 105, asserted that its stem is white; but is this true?

[2] In Rome, the cypress, and its branches, are tokens of mourning and death (e.g. Ovid, *Met.* x. 106 ff.; Pliny, *N.H.* xvi. 60 'Diti sacra'); but the only evidence for similar associations among Greeks which C. Boetticher was able to quote (*Der Baumkultus der Hellenen* (1856), pp. 486 ff.) are a few cursory words in Servius (*Aen.* iii. 681). The great inscription from Andania has shown that the grove of cypresses called Karneiasion (Paus. iv. 33. 5) was from origin dedicated to Hagna and the 'Great Gods', and not to 'Kore', still less to Demeter (Wilamowitz, *Der Glaube . . .*, ii². 528 ff.). One may compare also R. Gruppe, *Griech. Mythologie* (1906), p. 788, nn. 6 ff.; A. B. Cook, *Zeus*, iii. 1 (1940), p. 420; E. Rohde, *Psyche*, i. 220, n. 1; P.–W. iv. 2 (1933) (the fundamental study on which all these draw, by F. Layard (1854), is inaccessible to me); it will be seen that those associations which we owe to Roman poetry and to present-day usage were not valid with the ancient Greeks.

[3] *Od.* 5. 64.   [4] Theocr. xi. 45.

[5] Theocr. xxii. 41 (with λεῦκαι and πλάτανοι, by ἀέναος κρήνη) and *Epigr.* iv. 7. A. S. F. Gow (*Theocritus*, ii. 531) confirms the poet's description by a quotation from the *Geoponica* but subsequently calls Theophrastus to witness that it is 'not very appropriate', since 'the tree dislikes moisture'. Even so, the Gold Leaves and Theocritus confirm each other.

[6] The wading through stagnant hot water, mentioned in some of the Egyptian texts, does not afford a valid parallel.

in the Netherworld and developed it in their (his) own way. This motif, so it could be, and has been, said,[1] suits the climate of Egypt far better than that of Greece, and is therefore likely to have originated there. Here, however, one should remember, first, the concern about, and pride in, good water which is so characteristic of Greeks of all ages. Good, fresh water is 'cold water'—it would be an insult to treat the reader to a collection of instances of the phrase ψυχρὸν ὕδωρ. Secondly, an excellent article with which W. Deonna supplemented A. Parrot's treatise[2] demonstrated, *inter alia*, that the motif of 'the thirst of the dead' is found all over the earth, and at all ages, from prehistory to the present day; in the Alps and in Sweden no less than in India and China. It is, then, by no means confined to people living in a hot climate; even with the Eskimos in Greenland the dead are held to say to a hero who visits them in the Netherworld: 'Bring us ice, for we are suffering from thirst for cold water.'[3] The learned author traces this universal motif to the universal observation that people dying suffer from thirst and demand to drink.

Hence, the similarities remaining cannot be considered sufficiently close to enforce the conclusion that the request for water on the B-tablets was originally suggested by Egyptian prototypes. There is, however, in another group of spells in the *Book of the Dead*, a striking set of parallels to other main items in the Greek Gold Leaves. The words of ch. 122 (anticipated, incomplete and with some differences, in 58) are designed, according to some rubrics, to enable the dead person to 'penetrate into Amenti' (the Netherworld). This chapter has the form of a dialogue. It begins: 'Open the gate(s) to me! . . .'—'Who art thou? Whither goest thou? What is thy name?'— 'Alike to you (O gods) I am . . .', and ends with the wish: 'May I enter . . . to adore Osiris, the Lord of Life.'

The notion of gates, or pylons, guarded by dangerous demons, which the dead man (or his 'soul') has to pass, recurs frequently in the—ever more elaborate—Egyptian concepts of the Netherworld.[4] Ch. 145 of the *Book of the Dead* contains words which are to be addressed to the guardians of each of the twenty-one (!) gates leading to Sekht-Janru (comparable to the Greek Fields of the Blessed) and to the gates themselves.[5] Minor variations apart, the words are the same each time. The speaker begins with a greeting, reveals the names of the gate and its guardian and tells

---

[1] e.g. by Wilamowitz, *Der Glaube* . . . , ii[2]. 200: 'Der Durst nach frischem Wasser weist . . . nach Ägypten'.

[2] *Rev. Hist. Rel.* cix (1939), 53 ff.: 'La soif des morts'.

[3] Quoted from Deonna, l.l. 72; cf. the story of the rich man and poor Lazarus. 'In modern Greek, οἱ διψασμένοι means "the dead" ' (E. R. Dodds).

[4] A kind of 'map' of the Netherworld can be found in many copies of the 'Book of the Two Ways'; see e.g. *Bilderatlas zur Religionsgeschichte* by H. Haas, Lieferung 2–4: *Aegyptische Religion* (1924), Fig. 143.

[5] The scene is illustrated e.g. in the Papyrus of Ani (ed. Budge, Pls. 11 and 12; cf. the editor's comment, l.c. ii[2], pp. 268 ff.).

of his own doings; the guardian, in conclusion, replies: 'Enter; for thou art pure.'

The similarity of the small dialogue quoted first with τίς δ' ἔςςι; πῶ κτλ., and of the second with the welcome addressed to the καθαρὸς ἐκ καθαρῶν in A1, A4, and A5 is certainly striking; even so, there are, here again, essential differences. First, in the setting: the guardians are at the fountain in the Greek, but at various gates in the Egyptian texts; the former knows of no gates; in the latter the refreshing water is not guarded, but readily offered; in the A-texts, finally, the welcome is extended to the suppliant facing the chief deity of the Netherworld and not at any entrance-gates.[1]

Even more relevant is the difference of attitude and purpose; the analogies to the Greek, which appear striking on comparing selected extracts, become questionable when they are seen in their context. When, in ch. 122, the soul describes itself as 'like the gods', the purpose is—here as in hundreds of instances in the *Book of the Dead*, and in countless magical texts—to frighten the demonic questioners. This interpretation is borne out by the words which follow, for the speaker proceeds to quote the names of the boat (i.e. the hearse) which carries him, and of its parts. They all are designed, likewise, to emphasize his irresistible powers. For example, the oar is named 'terror hair-raising'; the steering-oar, 'sail straight on', etc. Truly, then, 'this boat was built for the journey into the Netherworld'—and woe to him that would dare to stop it! The similarity with the Greek dialogue thus proves incidental rather than fundamental; a matter of words rather than of essence.

To know the name is to wield power over its bearer: this is the essential point also in the second text just quoted (ch. 145); for it is by pronouncing their names that the speaker overcomes the gates and their guardians. There follows his assertion that he has bathed at the places where the sun-god, or Ptah, or Osiris, purified themselves; that he wears a magic dress and carries a club of magic wood. What, then, is left for the guardians but to acknowledge his purity and let him pass?

It would be irksome to elaborate the different character of the Greek. The analogy of motifs remains; but in view of these differences one may wonder how much significance one ought to attribute to it, materially and genetically. Striking though they are when taken in isolation, their different context and purport leaves much room for the assumption that they emerged independently in Greece and Egypt. One general aspect, common to both, may, however, be quoted in evidence of their interdependence. In both countries these texts are equally designed to

---

[1] The final aim of the dead Egyptian, certainly, is to 'stand before Osiris' and in ch. 119 (see the relevant illustrations) he anticipates the decision 'this man cannot be kept away from thee, Osiris', but otherwise these Egyptian texts are not comparable with the Greek.

accompany the dead into their graves in order to tell them what awaits them in the other world and how they are to meet it.[1] In Egypt this had been the custom for hundreds and even thousands of years, while in Greece there is no trace of it, apart from the few Gold Leaves, whose texts witness to a set of very specific persuasions. Hence it can reasonably be argued that the narrowly confined and recent Greek usage derives from that older civilization to which Greeks owed so much and which they often proclaimed as their teacher of 'wisdom'. Even this analogy, though, is greatly impaired by the fact that inscribed gold leaves were not used in Egypt in pre-Roman times; neither as amulets for the living, nor as 'guide books' for the dead; and that the Greek Gold Leaves are not comprehensive 'guide books', like the Egyptian, but centre on one single and final situation (and this, their main character, practically forbids the assumption that they were mere particles of a comprehensive 'geography of the Netherworld'). If, in spite of all these differences, the inspiration for the new Greek usage did, after all, come from Egypt, the all-pervading diversity of inspiration and purpose would even so make this fact all but irrelevant.

(g) INTERPRETATION CONTINUED

With our perception of their characteristic features sharpened by the consideration of Egyptian analogies, we return to the interpretation of the Greek B-texts. The 'tree by the fountain' is a case in point. On the two larger plaques it is said to stand by that fountain which is to be avoided; on the Cretan, by the one at which the dead seeks to quench his thirst. Which of these alternatives is, intrinsically, the most appropriate? Even if the tree were no more than a picturesque detail suggested by the scenery around this or any spring[2] (but one is bound to feel that it has some greater significance . . .), or if it were mentioned merely as a landmark, ought it not to mark the spot sought, rather than the one to be avoided? If so, the shorter and more recent texts seem here to preserve a genuine trait, and this impression is reinforced by the Egyptian combination of tree and saving water; for although dependence of the Greek myth upon the Egyptian has proved uncertain, the typological analogy remains.

Therewith arises the question of the relation between the longer and shorter Greek texts. When the first Cretan leaves were found, and very

---

[1] This argument has been urged by S. Morenz (in 'Aus Antike und Orient', *Festschrift Wilhelm Schubart* (1950), pp. 65 ff. and *Zeitschrift für ägyptische Sprache*, lxxxii (1952), 67 ff.) on the basis of an evaluation of the Gold Leaves, which I cannot share (he would trace to Egypt also the preference for 'right' over 'left' and describes as the purpose of the 'Orphic passports for the dead', 'to enable the dead by magic means, that is, avoiding the judgement, to gain access to the places of salvation'). [2] Cf. above, pp. 372 f.

imperfectly published, the Petelia plaque had been known and studied for a long time; it is therefore understandable that their wording was regarded as a mere excerpt from that older and more extensive document; a 'verstümmelte Kopie desselben Originals', to cite E. Rohde;[1] and even though this extreme judgement was not generally accepted[2] (not explicitly, at any rate), they have to the best of my knowledge never been considered in their own right.[3] Now that their wording has appeared intrinsically superior in one significant detail, its general quality and coherence may be noted. Thirst to death and the request for a drink from the fountain 'on the right, by the cypress', countered by questioning,[4] and this, finally, overcome by the symbolic formula; this sequel not only contains (as previously noted) within the narrowest compass the essential points of the longer versions but gives them in an order perfectly logical, investing these few lines with the power of drama— impressive from the first word to the last, from the outcry of desolation to the certainty of salvation.

This organic and expressive whole did not come about by excerpting and rearranging pieces from a more circumstantial text; it is the reflection of one definitive inspiration.[5]

A consideration, on the same lines, of the longer texts is apt to confirm this impression. Far be it from us to disparage the imaginative beauty of verses which have impressed generations of sensitive readers with their adumbration of man's way through the Netherworld and its symbolism. Their main power, however, is in those passages which they have in common with the shorter version, and these passages occur in them in a different order, to the detriment of plausibility and emphasis. The short version gives with its first word, δίψαι, the cue for all that follows; in B1 and B2 the corresponding passage stands near the end and even after the formula through which the longed-for drink is secured. Until that late point it has not become clear that the soul on its way through Hades was plagued by thirst; it recites the 'saving formula' almost like someone handing in a visiting card. An unsympathetic listener could almost suspect the belated assertion of desperate thirst to be an after-thought;

---

[1] *Psyche*, ii. 390, n. 1.

[2] Not e.g. by J. Harrison, *Proleg.* p. 575 (the Cretan leaves a 'sequel' to Petelia).

[3] The exception, once more, is Wilamowitz; see his brief but suggestive remarks in *Der Glaube* . . . , ii². 200.

[4] 'Who art thou? Of what descent?': this twofold question counters the preceding request and elicits the subsequent answer with perfect precision. In the short version which defines neither of the speaking parties, this question was indispensable to motivate the uttering of the crucial 'saving formula'; it occurs in exactly the right place and its wording is as apt as it is concise—all this in marked contrast with the superficially similar question in B2, v. 5a which, therefore, cannot be regarded as its model.

[5] The formal shortcomings of the Cretan text (noted above, p. 363) will shortly be reconsidered against this background of perfection in substance.

a feint thought up in order to secure—why?—a drink from the fountain of Memory; the formula by which alone it could be secured having been pronounced previously and before the need of it has been made clear.

This—admittedly one-sided—interpretation has aimed to emphasize what seems—to me, at least,—a real weakness in these, still beautiful, verses; particularly in comparison with B3. The reason for this less effective and implausible arrangement is, obviously, in the presence of the opening verses 1–5 (or 5b) in B1 and B2, of which there is no trace in B3; that is, the introduction of the two springs and the guardians. The verse Δίψαι αὖος κτλ. apparently was traditional and could not be changed; nor could it be spoken before the soul had met the guardians. These in turn had to be at once propitiated by the 'saving formula', and hence the words δίψαι κτλ. could not be fitted in until later; but their proper place is where B3 has them.

If this analysis is correct, it follows that B1–2, vv. 1–5 (5b), were added to a pre-existing wording of the type B3. Support for this result is in the observation that the B3 text is transmitted in six copies almost identical, while the two copies containing the—on this analysis—additional verses are widely at variance, and, what is more, B1 as well as B2 exhibit indications of variation and addition each of them in its own wording. Fixity, coherence, and authority over against variability and incoherence: these appear indicative of an original kernel and subsequent expansion. And the two verses (Δίψαι αὖος . . . and Γῆς παῖς . . .),[1] which in B1 and B2 fit the context but imperfectly, are of the essence of B3.

If the section peculiar to B1 and B2 is less ancient than the rest, it is not therefore without significance. The imagery of the two fountains has been so fully considered by many students[2] that nobody is likely to say anything about it that has not been said by others before; but the progress of the present argument requires that we define our understanding of it. Since one of the fountains is said to flow from the Lake of Mnemosyne, the other must be Lethe; odd though it be that the name is not cited. This contrasting pair has a parallel in the 'Laughing' and 'Wailing' springs at Kelainai in Phrygia;[3] it is likely, besides, to have suggested to Theopompos[4] the invention of the rivers of 'Joy' and 'Sorrow' in the

---

[1] The variant παῖς:υἱός (on which below, p. 382, n. 2) may here be disregarded.

[2] e.g. E. Rohde, *Psyche*, i. 316 and ii. 390, n. 1; J. Harrison, *Prolog.* pp. 575 ff.; A. Gruppe, *Griech. Mythol.* ii (1906), p. 1039; S. Eitrem, P.–W. *R.E.* xv. 2, 2225 ff.; M. Ninck, 'Die Bedeutung des Wassers . . .', in *Philologus*, Suppl. xiv. 2 (1921), 106; M. P. Nilsson, *Opuscula*, iii (1960), p. 85 (from *Eranos*, xli (1943), 1 ff., summarized *G.G.R.* ii (1950), 225 f.); A. B. Cook, *Zeus*. iii. 1 (1940), p. 420.

[3] Plin. *N.H.* xxxi. 16; a piece of folk-lore transferred to the *Fortunatae Insulae* (Pomponius Mela iii. 10. 102), and other places; see E. Rohde, l.l. i. 316.

[4] Summarized by Aelian, *V.H.* iii. 18 (p. 48. 17 Hercher).

fable-land of his *Meropis*.[1] The closest analogy is supplied by Pausanias in his detailed report about the oracle of Trophonios at Lebadeia,[2] but it is a useless analogy; what profundity has been found in it has been put in by his readers. M. P. Nilsson[3] has characterized this cult with restrained but crushing realism. The visitor to that subterranean chasm was made, after a series of preparatory purifications, to drink from the water of Lethe 'so as to forget all that he knew before', and of Mnemosyne 'so as to remember what on his descent he was going to see';[4] how lucky that the waters had so specific an effect! And when he emerged again he was seated on 'the throne of Mnemosyne'.[5] Theseus had been tied, once, to the throne of Lethe in Hades;[6] how lucky that its counterpart was kept in that well-furnished Boeotian sanctuary! With the effect of the waters so powerfully reinforced, the adept could be confidently expected to remember, and tell the priests, what, in the bowels of the earth he had 'seen and heard'.

This is not myth, but allegory materialized and exploited; a device by smart priests aiming to refurbish the waning lustre of their patrimony in an age when traditional cults were faced with the alternative of 'progress or perish' (the oldest mention of the two springs at Lebadeia is in the elder Pliny).[7] A notable if unpleasant symptom of the state of Greek religion in Roman times, this priestly hocus-pocus cannot effectively illuminate the words on the Gold Leaves; on the contrary, it is likely that its originators allowed themselves to be inspired by a surviving tradition of that theology to which the Gold Leaves testify (a Pythagorean tradition, for short). Caecilia Secundina is not alone in providing evidence of its survival. Mneia and Lethe are among the very numerous mythological figures which were impersonated—or so it seems—when, in the age of Hadrian, Dionysiac mysteries were enacted at Ephesus.[8] Much later still, Mnemosyne is invoked in one of the Orphic Hymns;[9] this time her office is said to be in helping the celebrants to remember the 'sacred ceremony' (it must have been hard to memorize these dreary litanies). Much earlier, the name of Mnemosyne had been added to a long list of deities who were due, according to an inscription of *c.* 350 B.C., to receive sacrifice in the sanctuary of Asklepios at Munichia;[10] presumably she was expected, as at Lebadeia, to keep alive the recollection of the dreams in which the god appeared to his devotees.

[1] E. Rohde, *Rhein. Mus.* xlviii (1893), 123 ff.   [2] Paus. ix. 39. 6 ff.
[3] *G.G.R*, ii. 450.   [4] Paus. ix. 39. 8.   [5] Ib. 13.
[6] Apollod. Epitome 1. 24 (p. 182 Wagner).   [7] Plin. *N.H.* xxxi. 11.
[8] *Ancient Greek Inscriptions in the British Museum*, iii (1890), p. 221, no. DC., ll. 28 f.; W. Quandt, *De Baccho* . . . (1913), p. 265.
[9] *Orph. Hymn.* 77.
[10] *I.G.* ii. 1651 = *I.G.* ii². 4962 = Dittenberger, *Sylloge³*, 1040 = Ziehen, *Leges Sacrae*, 18; but E. and L. Edelstein, *Asclepius* (1945), T. 515 omit the addition.

Some or all of the instances quoted may well derive, in the last resort, from the ideology with which we are concerned (for Mnemosyne was not a conceit alive in popular belief), but their petty and lifeless rationalism is out of touch with that reality of myth which emerges from the verses on the two lamellae. They have to be interpreted in their own light.

Why, then, is the dead expected to long for a drink of 'Remembering' and is warned against 'Forgetting'? Death is Forgetting. The dead enter another world beyond our comprehension and beyond our reach; they forget—forget us, and all. This is true with Homer and Plato and a thousand others;[1] because, simply, it is true. Cutting the connection between us and them—wherever, howsoever, they may be; however much we may remember them—death is, in essence, forgetting; their forgetting. And not-forgetting would be not-death. To seek the drink of 'Memory' is to seek Life.

The fountain of Memory is the Fountain of Life; this was perceived by many readers of our text who felt themselves reminded of the wide-spread fairy-tale motif of the search for the 'Water of Life'. We shall return to this perennial motif; but have first to consider why in our texts the general concept of 'Life' and 'Death' is viewed under the meaningful specific aspect of 'Memory' and 'Forgetting'. Here, too, the answer has been given by many students, who pointed to the particular import in Pythagorean thought of these very concepts. To him that believes in repeated lives on earth, death is not the abandonment, for ever, of this world in entering an absolutely different form of existence; it involves, for him, not necessarily that absolute separation which the drink from Lethe symbolizes; to him it is conceivable that the departed returning to this earth may retain the memory of what he had seen in this world and the other. This is not given to all, but only to the perfected. Pythagoras brought back the revelation of the lot of the immortal soul and was able—so his followers asserted—to recall his own previous incarnations;[2] Empedokles was aware that he had been bush and bird and fish and knew the stations of the long peregrination which brings the fallen god back, in the end, to his lost home. They remembered; they had not drunk of Lethe—the fountain which all the departed meet first, at the entrance to the Netherworld, but which the knowing-one may avoid. A welcome confirmation of this interpretation is afforded by the last words preserved on B1: 'and then you will be a lord[3] (in Elysium) among the

---

[1] E. Rohde, *Psyche*, ii. 382, n. 1, and M. P. Nilsson, *Opusc*. iii. 88, n. 10, quote a number of epigrams illustrating the point; the dead has drunk of the water of Lethe.

[2] Diog. Laert. viii. 5; Ennius, *Ann*. proem.; cf. E. Rohde, ii. 186, n.

[3] Thus understood, correctly, e.g. by G. Murray (*apud* Harrison, pp. 574 and 661) (*contra* Nilsson, *Opusc*. iii. 87 and *G.G.R.* ii. 225). The verse is modelled on *Il*. 4. 61, cf. 14. 94 and 23. 471; the future ἀνάξω is attested *Il*. 20. 180; Hes. *Th*. 491). (Aisch. *Choeph*. 355–62, finally, may be pondered with reference to this passage as well as to Pindar and Empedokles.

heroes'; they who retain memory are those who are ripe for a higher form of existence.

The main motif, then, of the extended B-text is explicable on a basis of Pythagorean thought, and not easily on any other. Further Pythagorean elements have been noted in it long ago—the notion of a crucial parting of the roads; the insistence on the prerogative of 'right' over 'left'. B1 and B2 may thereafter be described, with fair confidence, as a Pythagorean development of the folk-tale motif (still to be investigated) of the 'Fountain of Life', reinterpreted as a 'Fountain of Remembering' on the basis of the Pythagorean metaphysical concept of Memory and of the current notion of the 'plain', and 'river', of Lethe in Hades. The well-known fact that the concept of a 'Fountain of Lethe' cannot be traced back beyond the Hellenistic age[1] may accont for the first fountain remaining nameless in our text and for the ambiguity regarding its location.

The Cretan Leaves, so we argued previously, convey what may be taken for the foundation of the expanded versions B1 and B2. We stressed the concentration and organic unity of their wording and have to ask now: can they be held, in spite of their comparatively recent date, actually to represent the original form of these Pythagorean poems? And, indeed, are they Pythagorean at all? As to the latter question, there would be little to quote in support of a positive answer, if the longer versions were not preserved; as it is, however, it would be an excess of scepticism to deny to the shorter text what may now be taken as established for the closely related longer versions. One suggestive detail can be quoted in support, even though by itself it would be far from cogent: namely, the presence, in this very condensed version, of the indication that the fountain is 'on the right'. This feature is, at any rate, in the Pythagorean line. Does it involve the notion of another fountain on the left? Did those who wrote and used this shorter text conceive of the 'fountain on the right' as that of Mnemosyne, and the other—if any—as that of Lethe? Did they identify the questioning voice as that of the 'guardians'? Or was their imagination satisfied with the unspecified but profound mythology which these words by themselves convey? I can put the questions; I cannot confidently answer them.

This much, though, can be said: as it stands, the Cretan text, however solid and primordial its substance, cannot be taken for the original of the expanded versions. First, because of its formal imperfections. This combination of perfect poetry with completely unmetrical prose cannot

[1] Nilsson, *Opusc.* iii. 88, n. 12 shows how rare and recent the specific notion of a 'Fountain of Lethe' is.

possibly represent the primitive form of conveying this eschatological vision;[1] nor, obviously, is it in the least likely to have been done, originally, in a local Cretan dialect. The obvious vehicle would have been the traditional epic *Kunstsprache*, retranslation into which indeed can afford a cure for the most striking irregularity: namely, the question in prose ('v. 3');[2] but not for all (unless indeed one were to rewrite the whole *ad lib.*). The unmetrical αἰειρόω in v. 2 may have taken the place of αἰενάω in the model, and the hiatus after the first word is easily removed by inserting δ', which the Cretan text fairly certainly did not have originally. Was it in its model, as it is in B1 and B2? If so, there must have been a verse preceding the first of B3[3] (e.g. 'I come from . . .'; cf. A1). The wording of the request (vv. 1–2) likewise suggests a model somewhat more extensive. The meaning indeed is perfectly clear, but the omission of the governing verb is unique and baffling;[4] it suggests an original which, like B1 and B2, contained the imperative δότε. And, finally, one would expect that original to have included the adjective λευκή, for the very strangeness of its application, in B1 and B2, to the cypress-tree suggests that, so far from being a mere stop-gap, it was an integral feature of this mythical imagery.

The upshot of the preceding analysis may be felt to be disappointing. A text which has been known, appreciated, and expounded for over a century has been presented as the product of expansion and interpolation; a second testimony to the same, happily discovered, has been laid under contribution, only to reinforce the assertion that, with these venerable relics, we are far from holding the original documents of a momentous religious revelation; and a third form, amply attested, which appeared to convey its original essence, has proved to be the reflection of an unattainable original. Thereafter, any attempt at establishing a direct interdependence between the longer version and the shorter becomes hopeless; their irrational relationship being indicative of a rich variety of thought and formulation at which we can only guess.

---

[1] The possibility of accounting for this feature by recurrence to a ritual, attempted with reference to A-texts, does not, to my mind, here apply.

[2] A possible cure was suggested above, p. 363; for other suggestions see Olivieri and Kern ad loc. and Wilamowitz, *Der Glaube* . . . , . ii². 184, n. 1 (the noun παῖς, or υἱός, in the 'sacred formula' is, as noted above, 'expendable' and becomes suspect in view of this very variation; none the less the wording seems jejune without either).

[3] The situation here is not the same as with Ἀλλ' ὁπόταν . . . in A4 or even with Εὑρήσεις (δ') in B1, where the superfluous connecting particle is at a pinch tolerable.

[4] The verb πιεῖν obviously is not here to be explained as an instance of the normal imperatival use of the infinitive; nobody is here ordered to drink! The grammars (Kühner–Gerth, ii. 23; Schwyzer, ii. 707) do indeed quote a few infinitives expressing a wish or prayer; but there is always either the optative εἴη nearby (Hes. *Op.* 592, cf. 589) or a vocative addressing the god at whom the prayer is directed (Aisch. *Choeph.* 303; Eur. *Suppl.* 3, cf. v. 1). Neither applies in the passage under discussion, and even the 'unparalleled' (Wilamowitz) infinitives in Aisch. *Choeph.* 366 f. cannot really legitimize it.

Once more the present writer is led to deplore that he was in the end
denied the chance of a search, at a promising spot, for further evidence
which, if successful, could have furthered the interpretation of problematical passages and clarified the development of doctrine and the interrelation of the extant pieces of evidence. Even the luckiest find, however,
could not be expected to reveal the very fountainhead of the tradition.
Failing this, the preceding analysis may perhaps help towards a better
appreciation of the documents actually extant. Each of them, whatever
its place in the evolution of the underlying religion, remains a witness to
a definite and profound perception of man's root and goal in the divine;
a perception realized in a myth which grew more elaborate in detail but
always centred on the truth Γῆϲ παῖϲ εἰμι καὶ Οὐρανοῦ ἀϲτερόεντοϲ.

If any reader should care to try and correlate the imperfect data and
uncertain results so far assembled, he might be willing to consider the
following hypothetical reconstruction of 'wie es etwa gewesen sein
könnte'.

Pythagoras, to convey his insight into the lot and task of the soul, made
use of a current folk-tale; a tale describing the way of the dead through
the Netherworld, parched by thirst, in search of the Water of Life which
flows by the gleaming Tree of Life and is guarded by demons; to overcome their enmity, a magic formula has to be recited. This tale he put
into verse, in the form of a short dialogue between the soul and the
guardians, leaving the speakers undefined and replacing the magic
formula by that beautiful line which summarizes his understanding of
man (and if this verse really was written by him, Pythagoras was a far
greater poet than one would expect on reading those pedestrian rules of
conduct traditionally ascribed to him). This little verse-dialogue was
spoken at the funerals of members of his order and thus became part of
its tradition; its essence was faithfully kept, although subordinate details
were adapted to local speech and custom. It may be, moreover, that the
Master himself occasionally enlarged upon the meaning of this poem;
hinting that the fountain by the mysterious tree flowed with the Water
of Memory, which was within reach of the perfected while the rest of men
turned to the Water of Lethe. An elaboration on these lines of the concise
original became current in the school but did not acquire the same
authority; its wording, in consequence, was altered and expanded at
various times and places.

Since the texts discussed in the present chapter come from the same
milieu—Pythagorean, so we hold—as the A-texts previously surveyed
("Ερχομαι ἐκ καθαρῶν . . .), the question of their interrelation poses itself.
The scenery of B is at, or near, the entrance of the Netherworld, while

A places the bearer face to face with its queen; one might, therefore, incline to regard them as fragments of a full vade-mecum for the soul on its way through Hades, similar to the Egyptian *Book of the Dead*, which gives guidance for all the stations (including the sycamore at the refreshing well) on the way to the judgement before Osiris. The existence, among Pythagoreans, of an elaborate eschatological myth is beyond doubt, and the ideal continuity of the B-series and the A-series is confirmed by the first lines of A4 and by A5. A further pointer at this ideal continuity could seem to be given with a small gold leaf (not previously mentioned) which comes from the same place as the bulk of the small Cretan Leaves B3–8, that is, from Eleutherna; it may even have been found in one of the graves containing some leaf from this series.[1] We may label it, for completeness' sake, 'B9'. It contains the inscription $Πλού]τωνι$ καὶ $Φ[ερο]πόνει$ χαῖρεν. The dead person, so it seems, was expected, after drinking from the fountain at the entrance of Hades, to proceed further, and, on meeting the divine rulers of the Netherworld, to greet them with these words. It may, however, be doubted whether this piece of evidence can be held to attest a concept shared by the bulk of those who buried their dead with either of the standard texts inscribed on the other Gold Leaves; for here, and only here, Pluton is mentioned, and that even before Persephone, who, on the texts of the A-series, eclipses 'Eukles, Eubuleus and the other gods' and is sole ruler of the dead in the related texts from Pindar and Plato. B9, by contrast, suggests a notion of the Netherworld such as is depicted e.g. on the Apulian vases; the generally current notion, that is, which was conveyed by poetry, lyric and dramatic, and formed the basis also of the Eleusinian celebrations. M. Guarducci may therefore well be right in suggesting that this small tablet is evidence of the 'creed of the Gold Leaves' conflated with a local (or, as I should prefer to say, general) tradition.

However, even if the various texts quoted are held to evince that those furnished with the Gold Leaves were expected to proceed from the fountain at the entrance of Hades to its rulers, the A- and B-texts cannot be taken for excerpts from one comprehensive poem. The arguments against this assumption are given with the following. (1) The prose passages in A; (2) the promise of heroization at the end of the Petelia tablet (with no hint of an encounter with Persephone); (3) the variations and elaborations of each type; (4) the fact that, so far, at least, A and B have nowhere been found together; and (5)—to my mind the most cogent argument—the self-sufficiency of either text.

---

[1] M. Guarducci, *Inscr. Cret.* ii, no. XII. 31 *bis*, p. 170; size 40 mm. × 11 mm.—It will suffice to say that the Cretan inscription which O. Kern, *Orphic. Fragm.* 32. iv (p. 106) joins to the Cretan Gold Leaves has nothing whatever to do with either Orpheus or the Gold Leaves. It is the advertisement of a sanctuary of the *Magna Mater*, comparable to that of a Cretan interpreter of dreams at the entrance of the Serapeion in Memphis.

It seems more in keeping with the evidence to assume that both A and B derive from verses and acclamations which were recited at Pythagorean funerals. Their combination into one comprehensive 'Guide through the Netherworld'—if such ever existed—is more likely to have been the end of a gradual development. Such indeed was, beyond doubt, the case of the *Book of the Dead*.

(h) EAST AND WEST

Some reader may feel inclined to inquire into the antecedents of that popular motif which, if the previous suggestion is considered, Pythagoras adopted; that concept of an elixir of life with which Scripture and fairy-tale have made us familiar since childhood. The main features of its Greek form, with which we are concerned, are these. There is a fountain from which the thirsting dead seeks to drink—not really a spring; it flows out of a lake (this though is not mentioned in the most concise text); it is guarded, and it flows by a tree. The tree is a cypress, and it must be more than a mere land-mark or picturesque detail—for which the shorter version certainly would not have had room; it appears to have some magic-mystic quality; and this its character is enhanced by the fact that it—the dark cypress—is described as λευκή, 'gleaming',[1] at least in the longer versions.

All of these features were anticipated in the ancient Near East; one of them in Egypt, as we saw; the rest in Mesopotamia and neighbouring countries. However—to quote an authority in the field[2]—'the subject is so vast and demands such linguistic knowledge as not to be mastered by one scholar'. This will be found true by anyone trying to get even a little beyond the most obvious; hence all that can here be aimed at is to reassemble a few well-known facts.[3]

---

[1] Cf. above, p. 373.—There are 'white' poplars and birches but no 'white' cypresses; the Greek λευκός therefore must here be taken in its wider, and basic, sense; cf. lat. *lux* and our 'light'. This point is going to prove important, so here are some proof texts: *Od.* 6. 45 λευκὴ αἴγλη (the sheen over the abode of the gods); *Il.* 14. 185 λευκόν (*v.l.* λαμπρόν) ἠέλιος ὥς; Soph. *Ai.* 708 λευκὸν φάος; Eur. *Andr.* 1228 λευκὸς αἰθήρ; Aisch. *Pers.* 301 λευκὸν ἦμαρ νυκτὸς ἐκ μελαγχίμου; λευκὸν ὕδωρ often in Homer and later; ξεϲτοὶ λίθοι, polished with oil, are called λευκοί *Od.* 3. 408; polished metal vessels likewise *Il.* 23. 268; from later literature cf. e.g. Kallimachos, *Hymn.* vi. 122 and Matt. 17: 2 and John 4: 35.

[2] G. Widengren, 'The King and the Tree of Life in Ancient Near Eastern Religion', in *Uppsala Universitets Arsskrift* (1951) 4, 57, n. 3.

[3] In addition to the authoritative but specialist essay quoted in the preceding note and biblical handbooks and commentaries, I have found the following titles useful: A. Wünsche, *Die Sagen vom Lebensbaum und Lebenswasser* (1905); E. Dhorme, *Recueil* (1951), pp. 557 ff. (from *Revue biblique* (1907)); E. Schrader, *Die Keilinschriften und das A. T.*[3] (1902), pp. 521 ff.; A. Jeremias, *Das A. T. im Lichte des Alten Orients*[3] (1930), pp. 92 ff.; J. B. Pritchard, (*a*) *Ancient Near Eastern Texts*[2] (1955) = '*ANET*'; (*b*) *The Ancient Near East in Pictures* (1954) = '*ANEP*'; Bolte–Polivka, *Anmerkungen zu den . . . Märchen der Brüder Grimm*, 3 vols. (1913–18). Of the special treatises on the Tree of Life by U. Holmberg and Bergema (on which Widengren,

We may begin with the Bible, from which the notions of a 'Tree of Life' and the 'Water' or 'Spring of Life' are familiar. The two occur together in the Apocalypse 22:1 ff.: the 'Tree of Life' grows by the 'River of the Water of Life'; besides, the 'Spring of the Water of Life' occurs ib. 7:17, 21:6, and 22:17. In the Book of Proverbs, 'Tree of Life' and 'Spring of Life' occur frequently; they are practically synonymous and serve as metaphors for 'life', i.e. 'salvation' or 'well-being',[1] intimating a mythical reality no longer felt. Some of this mythical reality is still felt in Ps. 36:9 'with you (God) is the Spring of Life'; it is fully present in the significance allotted to the Tree of Life in the story of Paradise Lost in Gen. 2:9 and 3:22 ff.; man would have gained immortality if he had been permitted to eat its fruit, but the access is barred by the 'flaming sword' and the cherubim.

This myth has long since been traced, together with the set of related concepts, to Mesopotamia.[2] Its pessimism agrees with a mental attitude prevailing among the peoples there. With them the word 'life' entails, beyond physical aliveness, well-being, abundance, preservation; in short, all 'man's desire'. It is his prime concern, but it is given him, at best, only for the short span of his being in the flesh, and even there requires every effort of labour, and, no less, ritual for the propitiation of the unaccountable divine powers who 'allotted Death to mankind, but retained Life in their own hands'.[3] There was, in consequence, an obsession with the terrors of death, and, correspondingly, an incessant concern and effort to secure 'life'. Among the symptoms of this attitude are those mythical concepts which we are reviewing. One recalls, first, Gilgameš realizing the power of Death and forcing his way to the 'Land of the Living'; he secures, from the bottom of a river, the Plant of Life—only

---

pp. 53, n. 2 and 57, n. 3, passes severe judgement), Bergema has been beyond my reach. Holmberg (*Ann. Acad. Fennicae*, xvi. 3 (1922–3)), presents interesting information, mainly about mythical notions among Mongol tribes in northern Asia; he identifies, however, the concepts of the 'Tree of Life' and the 'World-tree' which, to me, seem basically distinct. An article by K. von Spiess, 'Der Brunnen des ewigen Lebens' (in *Studien für F. Hommel, Mitteil. d. D. Vorderasiat. Ges.* xxii (1918), 328 ff.) centres on representations of this symbol in Byzantine miniatures but also points out the suggestive similarity between the castles in German fairy-tales, at whose gates lions guard the access to the 'Water of Life' inside, and the lay-out of Assurbanipal's palace at Khorsabad.

[1] Prov. 3:18; 11:30; 13:12; 15:4 and 10:11; 13:14; 14:27; 16:22.

[2] See e.g. H. Gunkel's commentary (4 Aufl. (1917), pp. 7 ff.). I cannot, with Gunkel and others, believe that the elaborate comparison, in Ezek. 31:1 ff., of Assur with a giant tree belongs in this category (however welcome a parallel its description as a cypress growing among rivers would afford); but it appears, rather, to be a development of the, equally ancient, concept of the world as a tree.

[3] *Gilgameš*, tablet x, column iii, line 4 of the Old Babylonian version (*ANET*, p. 90).— I am impressed by S. G. F. Brandon's outline of this ancient Mesopotamian attitude (*Man and his Destiny* . . . (1962), pp. 70 ff.). To him it appears as a 'more realistic estimate of the experience common to man' than is, for example, the eschatological hope of the Egyptians (ib., p. 104).

to be speedily deprived of it.[1] Similarly characteristic is the myth of Adapa who, deceived by a god, misses the chance of eating the Food of Life and drinking the Water of Life;[2] that water with which even the goddess Inanna-Ištar is revived on her disastrous descent into the Netherworld.[3]

Most significant to us is an often quoted text in Sumerian and Akkadian,[4] which I repeat in Widengren's translation:[5]

In Eridu there is a black (dark) *Kiškanu*-tree,
    it grows in a pure place;
Its appearance is lapis lazuli,
    it is erected (stands) on (over) the Apsū (the waters of the Depth).
Enki,[6] when walking there, fills Eridu with abundance.
    In its foundations (i.e. underneath) is the place of the nether world,
In the resting place is the chamber of Nammu.[7]
    In its holy temple there is a grove, casting its shadow,
Therein no man goes to enter.
    In the midst (of the grove) are the Sun-god and the Sovereign of Heaven,
In between the river with the two mouths.[8]

'That this Kiškanu-tree, in the Sumerian text giš-kin, is identical with the Tree of Life is perfectly clear': so Widengren comments,[9] quoting, in evidence, the almost identical description, in the Gilgameš epic, of the habitat of Utnapištim, to whom the hero turns in his search for 'Life' because he was the one mortal to gain immortality.[10] This magical tree, then, grows at and above rivers; it is 'black' and, at the same time,

---

[1] *Gilgameš*, Tablets ix ff.; esp. xi. 270 ff. (*ANET*, p. 96).—The earlier exploits of Gilgameš and Enkidu (Tabl. iii–v), in reaching the cedar wood and slaying its guardian, the monster Huwawa (Humbaba), can hardly, as P. Jensen held, likewise represent the hero's quest for 'Life'. However suggestive the description of 'the cedar' (? actually collective) on the 'Mountain, abode of the gods' (Tablet v. 1, *ANET*, p. 82; cf. H. Frankfort *Cylinder Seals* (1939), Pl. XVII. 1), those critics (e.g. Dhorme and Loisy) seem right who urge that this is a scene of outstanding but mundane heroism, while the quest, afterwards, for 'Life' is motivated by the impact upon Gilgameš of the death of his friend. Originally, though, it may have had this meaning. In the Sumerian version (*ANET*, p. 48) the cedar wood is located in the 'Land of the Living'; but even there the purpose is not the quest for 'Life'; Gilgameš fells its trees in order, so it seems, to bring them to his city. Cf. Widengren, l.l., p. 45.

[2] *ANET*, p. 101, esp. B 60 ff. (p. 102).

[3] Ib. 56, 1. 221 ff. (Sumerian); p. 108, reverse 1. 34 ff. (Akkadian).

[4] *Cuneiform Texts in the Brit. Mus.* xvi, Pl. 46. 183 ff.; quoted e.g. by A. Wünsche (above, p. 385, n. 3), p. 2.

[5] l.l. p. 6 (I have permitted myself some very slight stylistic retouches and, in brackets, a few elementary additions).

[6] The chief god of the city of Eridu: the god of the sweet waters and also of the earth.

[7] I do not understand this line (Nammu is the goddess of the primordial sea).

[8] This line, too, overtaxes my competence; the interpretation of the term pî nârâti, 'the mouth of the rivers', being a task for specialists (as I learn from W. F. Albright, *Am. Journ. of Sem. Languages*, xxxv (1919), 161 ff.).

[9] This is the traditional view; it was, however, opposed by Bergema.

[10] Tablet xi. 195 (*ANET*, p. 95); cf. the last line of the translation above.

shining with (or like) precious stones (v. 3). Gilgameš beheld it, shining with carnelian and lapis lazuli, at the end of his long way through the dark.[1] I am strongly tempted here to find the solution of the puzzle presented by the description, on the Gold Leaves, of the dark cypress tree as 'shining'.

With regard to the Mesopotamian sacred tree the explanation of this feature is given by an all-pervading characteristic of religious thought in those parts; namely, the identification of concrete and transcendental entities. As Dilmun, for example, is an identifiable place on earth and, at the same time, Paradise, so the Kiškanu tree stands in the realm of the gods, in a mythical place in, or above, the Netherworld called Eridu; but Eridu is, at the same time, the concrete city (now being excavated); the magic tree stands in its temple and indeed not there only. 'It seems possible . . . that every temple had its holy grove with its own "Tree of Life" as well as its *apsū*': so Widengren[2] argues, offering persuasive evidence. Thus, at any rate, it was at Eridu; its Kiškanu tree, gleaming with the sheen of its magic power, stood in, or near, its temple—a trunk studded with metal and precious stones;[3] in a technique for which the excavations of Sir Leonard Woolley at Ur, among others, have provided ample evidence.[4] And nearby was a pond, or basin—the apsū, symbolizing that subterranean ocean of sweet water from which come the springs and rivers upon whom all life depends;[5] the domain of Enki, the creator of man, who 'gives abundance to Eridu' when walking in the grove of the Kiškanu tree.[6]

Here then we seem to find the main elements which occur on the Gold Leaves: the shining, dark Tree of Life and the life-giving water; elixirs denied to man—unless he knew the right word, which Adapa missed; all this in a context of ideas and symbols recurring throughout the Ancient Near East and living on in folk-lore to our day. Three points, though, still require investigation: namely, the notion of the *soif des morts* (instanced so fully from Egypt—and elsewhere—but not, so far, from the Mesopotamian orbit); the guardians of the sources of life, and the description of the magical tree as a cypress.

The Mesopotamian attitude to death and after-life, so different in its pessimism[7] from the hopefulness which made the Egyptians furnish their

---

[1] End of Tabl. ix (*ANET*, p. 89).   [2] L.l. 9.

[3] For this conclusion, Widengren (p. 7) quotes an article by S. Smith in *Bull. School of Orient. Studies* (1926), 69 ff.

[4] *Ur Excavations*, i, p. 100 and Pl. 35. 7.

[5] The model of the so-called 'Sea' in the temple at Jerusalem.

[6] A representation, so it seems, of this replica, in sanctuaries, of Sacred Tree and Water is quoted below, p. 391, n. 3.

[7] The present subject does not require a rehearsal of the relevant texts which begin with Gilgameš (esp. Tabl. x, col. iii, *ANET*, p. 90) and go down to the '*Vision of the Netherworld*' (ib. 109).

dead with the detailed instructions collected in the 'Book of the Dead', makes it understandable that very few texts tell of the lot of man after death in a manner that could be compared with the eschatology of the Gold Leaves. They are not in fact entirely lacking. A judgement of the dead has been held to be described, in a strangely humorous manner, in one text;[1] in another one, found in Elam but based on an Akkadian original, the dead himself describes his way to the Judgement and actually thanks his god with the words: 'On the field of thirst you gave me water and oil (?) to drink.'[2] These texts are certainly exceptional, for the dead appear to have been regarded, in Mesopotamia, predominantly as potential enemies who had to be appeased by gifts and rites. Even so, the fact that vessels with liquid were in abundance placed in graves and libations poured over them shows that the notion of the *soif des morts* was as common there as elsewhere;[3] but a myth entailing this motif was bound, in view of so different a basic attitude, to be thoroughly different in Mesopotamia from any Greek or Egyptian counterpart. No such myth has as yet been found (apart from the hint just quoted), for man was not thought, after death, to walk towards a place of eternal and heightened life. Gilgameš and Adapa provide instances of heroes seeking it during their lives; seeking and failing.

The 'guardians' of tree and water—not further defined in the longer Greek texts, not even named in the shorter, while in Egypt a benign goddess takes their place—are well defined in the Near Eastern traditions. The unwillingness of the Sumerian and Akkadian gods to let man partake in the elixirs of Life is a general analogue; the cherubim of Gen. 3: 24 are its mythical concretization. Sphinx-like, or in the shape of winged humans, they guard the Tree of Life (as well as e.g. the entrances of royal palaces) on many a typical representation; e.g. on a relief from Tell Halaf,[4] and, very frequently, on ivory carvings from Assyria, Syria, and Phoenicia.[5]

The Tree of Life, being a mythical concept, is not necessarily identi-

---

[1] E. Ebeling, *Tod und Leben nach den Vorstellungen der Babylonier*, i (1931), no. 2, pp. 9 ff.

[2] Ib., no. 3, p. 21 (i. 14 f.). The text (which the editor describes as a 'vade-mecum for the dead' and compares with Ps. 23) is comparatively recent (vii–vi cent.) but not too recent for comparison with the Gold Leaves.

[3] A. Parrot elaborates this point (*Le Refrigerium*, pp. 3 ff.); I hesitate, however, to accept his further contention (pp. 39 ff.) that the frequent representations of persons—men as well as gods—drinking are evidence of a 'refrigerium dans l'au-delà' in the Babylonian religious imagination.

[4] *ANEP*, no. 654; many Assyrian instances are illustrated in W. H. Ward, *The Seal Cylinders of Western Asia* (1910), pp. 220 ff.

[5] R. D. Barnett, *A Catalogue of the Nimrud Ivories in the Brit. Mus.* (1957), e.g. Pls. XIX–XXI. The incisive discussion, ib. 85 ff., of the motif (and its impact upon the Temple of Solomon) deserves pondering. Everybody knows, besides, the mighty demons flanking the sacred tree on Assyrian reliefs (such as *ANEP*, no. 656; more in Strommenger–Hirmer, *Mesopotamien* (1962), pp. 191 ff.); these, though, are worshipping rather than guarding it.

fiable in terms of botany. We have already spoken of replicas, in sanctuaries, of the Kiškanū tree; it does not seem that they suggested any natural tree. Besides, there occur, on seal cylinders, reliefs, and ivory carvings, many representations which are commonly called 'sacred trees'. It is disputed whether they were regarded as varieties of the Kiškanū or not, but it is evident that they are not symbols and conveyors of Life Eternal. These trees, or plants, are seen in various stages of growth; they are nibbled at by goats, watered and tended by kings and demons;[1] even so they are certainly symbols;[2] conveyors of 'Life' here, and not beyond the grave.[3] This restriction is perfectly in keeping with the mental attitude previously outlined, and in this sense, I suppose, it is permissible to speak of these representations as of 'Trees,' or 'Plants, of Life'.[4] Their various forms have been the subject of exhaustive studies which provide answers also for our specific question. The best-known form, on Assyrian reliefs and seals,[5] is as far from representing any natural tree as is the original Kiškanū, and has indeed been held, like it, to stand for a kind of maypole,[6] while those guarded, on ivories, by sphinxes are palm trees. However, our search for cypresses in the same role does not go unrewarded. E. D. van Buren[7] shows, with full evidence, that on Elamite seals the 'sacred tree' is predominantly a cypress placed on a mound between two animals; the cypress is, likewise, one of the two standard types on Akkadian seals, where it often forms the centre of a scene of heroes contending with lions or bulls;[8] besides, the small tree (alternating with the 'plant') watered by kings or demons may perhaps, in view of its pyramidal shape, likewise be held to be a cypress. Finally, the Kiškanū tree has a counterpart in the 'black cedar' of Dilmun, the land of Paradise,[9] which is specified as the 'ḫašurru-tree', and I would ask my Semitic colleagues if possibly this word can be equated with Hebrew te-aššūr which denotes the cypress.

It seems not unreasonable to acknowledge one concept of the 'Tree of Life' embracing varying aspects; from the goal of immortality, unattainable for man, to the guarantor of Life Abundant on earth; the former

---

[1] Widengren, pp. 12 f., Figs. 1 and 2.—H. Danthine, *Le Palmier-dattier et les arbres sacrés* (1937), N. Perrot, *L'Arbre sacré sur les monuments* . . . (1937), and R. Bauerreis, *Arbor Vitae* (1938) were not within my reach; hence I have gratefully used the full summary of the archaeological evidence given by E. D. van Buren in *Symbols of the Gods* (1945), pp. 22 ff.

[2] On this point I venture to differ with the authority of H. Frankfort (*Cylinder Seals* (1939), p. 205), who regarded the representations of trees as merely decorative, excepting only the late Assyrian, which he traced to the Egyptian dejd-pillars.

[3] This point was urged by van Buren (l.l. 22 and 29) as, previously, by W. H. Ward (l.l. 222).

[4] Cf. Detached Note XIII, below p. 412.

[5] e.g. *ANEP*, nos. 88, 656, 706; and cf. above, p. 389, notes 4 and 5.

[6] Thus H. Frankfort, l.l.; possibly the Asherah of the O.T. is related.

[7] l.l. 22 f.   [8] Ib. 24.

[9] Here again I am following H. Widengren (l.l. 9 f.).

specifically symbolized by the Kiškanū tree which still, in its material replicas, stood for the fulfilment of mundane aspiration; the latter finding a final expression in the Assyrian 'sacred tree' and, earlier and among others, in the shape of a cypress.

In the same way there is, beside the apsū, a second symbol also of life-giving water: namely, the 'flowing vase' held[1] by gods and goddesses. There are instances of the two combined,[2] as there is reason for assuming the interrelation of the oldest Kiškanu and the recent Assyrian 'sacred tree'. And a sanctuary with the cypress, Tree of Life, and apsū, Water of Life, may be found reproduced in a charming small bronze model from Susa.[3]

Tree of Life and Water of Life, sought by mortals but guarded by gods, demons, or monsters; this proved to be a concept of infinite vitality. We may quote a few instances bearing, in one way or the other, upon our subject. 'In Zoroastrianism the Tree of Life is called "the white Hôm" ' (note the adjective; Greek λευκός); 'it grows by a spring . . . and from it come all waters on earth.'[4] In Greek lore it is the tree of the Hesperidae. Guarded by the dragon Ladon it grows, at the end of the Earth, in the Garden of the Gods, 'where ambrosian springs flow'.[5] No ship finds the way to it; Herakles alone obtained its golden apples, the fruits imparting the immortality which is the preserve of the gods. Celtic and Germanic mythology contains images strikingly similar to this; the former in particular an elysium in the far West, where 'the blessed-ones refresh themselves with apples from miraculous trees with silver-white (again!) branches and streams flowing with ale and wine'.[6]

The story of Gilgameš's way through darkness to Utnapištim, the immortal, and the water in which the Plant of Life grows re-emerges in an

---

[1] E. D. van Buren, *The Flowing Vase* . . . (1933); here again I had to use the summary given by the distinguished authoress (*Symbols* . . . , pp. 124 ff.).

[2] Van Buren, l.l. 129 ff.

[3] *ANEP*, no. 619; our Plate 30.—Another instance of the two combined may be found on one of the wall-paintings in the palace at Mari where, from 'flowing vases held by goddesses rise, with the water, plants which may be small cypresses' (A. Parrot, *Le Palais* . . . (1958/9), ii. 19, Pl. VI; Strommenger–Hirmer, l.l., Pl. 165 and p. 88; cf. *ANEP* 610).

[4] A.Wünsche, l.l. 3; relevant texts are collected in W. H. Ward, l.l. 335 f. The main source is the *Bundahish*, ch. 27. 4 (tr. E. W. West in *Sacred Books of the East*, v (1880), p. 100): '. . . the white Hôm, the healing and undefiled, has grown at the Source of the Water Arêdvîvsûr; everyone who eats (of it) becomes immortal. They call it the Gokard tree, as it is said that Hôm expells death.' For the Source here named cf. ib. 13. 3 (p. 42); it is 'the source of all pure water and all the creations of Auharmazd acquire health from it'.

[5] Euripides, *Hipp.* 748 (the sources for this myth are quoted e.g. in Preller–Robert, *Griech. Mythol.* i. 563). Wilamowitz *ad.* Eur. *H.F.* 339 (summarized in *Der Glaube* . . . , i. 262) shows that the Hesperidae were primitively demons, similar to the Sirenes, guarding the Tree of Life—thus enhancing the similarity with the oriental prototypes.

[6] A. Wünsche, l.l. 76 and 85 ff.; more recent literature in A. B. Cook, *Zeus*, ii. 1. 420 and ii. 2. 1136.

episode of the Alexander-novel,[1] which probably goes back to a time not long after the king's death;[2] he, too, penetrates through darkness to the 'Land of the Blessed', reaches the spring of the Water of Life, and misses the chance of immortality. It would lead too far to trace the ramifications and developments of this story in classical Persian poetry[3] and its echoes and analogies in mediaeval Western courtly literature and folk-lore; from knights errant who, in a dark wood, find a miraculous well (e.g. Erec) to countless localities claiming to possess the spring of Life or eternal youth.[4] We may instead, in conclusion, recall some of the Brothers Grimm's Fairy Tales: The 'Water of Life' which the young prince, to save his father's life, fetches from the well guarded by lions; the Tree of Life, guarded by wild beasts, from which 'The Prince who knew no Fear' gathers the golden apples; he, too, is served well by the Water of Life, while the golden apples recur in the story of the 'Golden Bird'. In these fairy-tales, the ancient Babylonian motifs are amalgamated with various others and serve a new context; even so, they are distinctly, and down to characteristic details, discernible in these German tales as well as in countless others.[5]

It will, I hope, be agreed that the mythology of the B-tablets fits and belongs in the frame of the tradition just sketched; it will surely be no less evident that here is no question of a 'taking-over', by Greeks, of a Babylonian myth. The basic motifs of that myth do indeed recur with them; but, re-shaped, they have become expressive of a new concept of man and his destiny. The same has already proved true of the Egyptian elements—if indeed these have been taken over; for they could have been recreated independently. Primarily, then, the Gold Leaves are evidence and product of this new concept; they are the expression of a new and unique inspiration and this is what essentially constitutes their character. The fact of their similarity to, or even derivation from, oriental proto-types still remains; here as in almost all Greek creation. In the present case this fact may be accounted for by various hypotheses.

A pragmatist might here argue about as follows. We have been led to infer that the Gold Leaves, in their original form, were devised by Pythagoras; we detect in them elements pointing to Egypt and Babylonia; and we accept, with K. von Fritz[6] and others, as reasonably credible the tradition that Pythagoras spent many years in Egypt, studying the 'wisdom' of the priests there, and that he visited Babylonia for the same

---

[1] ii. 39 ed. Müller; new edition by H. Engelmann (1963), pp. 306 f.

[2] This is the view of R. Merkelbach (*Die Quellen des griech. Alexanderromans* (1954), p. 47, cf. ib. 98).

[3] A. Wünsche, l.l. 77 ff. gives a summary.　　　　　　　　　　　　　　[4] Ib. 86 f.

[5] Bolte–Polivka (above, p. 385, n. 3) present a staggering wealth of parallels (i. 513; ii. 400; iii. 17).　　　　　　　　　　　　　　　　　　　　　　[6] P.–W., *R.E.* xiv. 186.

purpose. We conclude that Egypt gave him the idea of a vade-mecum for the dead and, moreover, certain mythical notions which he included in that vade-mecum: namely, the notion of the *soif des morts* and, perhaps, also that of a dialogue between the soul and infernal guardians. In Babylonia, Pythagoras found the pregnant concept of the Tree, and the Water, of Life; which lent itself for combination with the notion of the *soif des morts*. Pythagoras utilized these oriental motifs when drawing up an order of the funeral ceremonies for members of his school, and he—or, perhaps, one of his followers—had some main items of it reproduced on the Gold Leaves, which he devised on the analogy of the various Egyptian 'guides for the dead' and as a counterpart to the traditional Greek *defixionum tabellae*.

This hypothesis could claim to derive support from Herakleitos,[1] who accused Pythagoras of having scraped together his pretended 'wisdom' from all possible corners; even so, some students might well find it too simple to be true. They might hold that the Egyptian analogies can be accounted for without the assumption of any interdependence and that the Mesopotamian Tree-of-Life-imagery is likely to have sunk into Greek consciousness, or subconsciousness, many centuries before its re-emergence on the Gold Leaves. Anyhow, I like to imagine both the sceptic and the pragmatist agreeing that the study of the Gold Leaves themselves proves the question of their historical antecedents to be of slight relevance. Even if the oriental origin of all the details considered were established; and even if the 'doctrine', so-called, of the 'transmigration of souls'—which is basic to them in their entirety—had grown out of Indian roots, the resulting whole is infinitely more than the sum of its parts. It is a creation in its own right, determined, down to every element in its structure, by an ideology which is worlds apart from Indian yearning for Nirvana, from Egyptian striving after endless prolongation and heightening of the earthly life, and from Babylonian nihilism. It is Greek; one more monument of a national genius as different from the Babylonian, and all others, as Zeus is different from Marduk, and Ereškigal from Persephone.[2]

---

[1] Fr. 129 *DK*; cf. fr. 40.

[2] To end on a curiosity: in the great Magical Papyrus at Paris (*P.G.M.* i. 82, line 338) the two goddesses are invoked as one and the same: Κούρη Περcεφόνη 'Ερεcχιγάλ—an illustration of the blending, in the latest Roman period, of the religious traditions which we have endeavoured to trace.

DETACHED NOTES

I

THE CRETAN DOUBLE-AXE IN MALTA?

(above, p. 55)

THE hour-glass mark scratched on a sherd from Tarxien[1] cannot demonstrate the adoption, in Malta, of the Cretan double-axe. Wherever this sacred symbol is represented, from its early origins in Anatolia[2] and Upper Mesopotamia[3] to Crete, it is identified by the clear indication of the handle; which is never absent, either, where it is used as a sign in the Cretan Linear A script, as a perusal of W. C. Brice's *corpus* will show.[4] Where this distinctive indication is wanting, there remains the plain geometric pattern of two triangles set point to point; a pattern occurring frequently, and often together with other combinations of triangles, from neolithic Persia and Mesopotamia to the Balkans and further west; e.g. at Tepe Syalk I, Susa and Anau,[5] Arpachijah,[6] Nineveh, and Khafajah;[7] in Europe, on bell-beakers,[8] on Danubian corded and other ware,[9] and, again purely geometrical, in Crete at the end of the Early Minoan period.[10] Geometric figures served occasionally, with quite small additions, as representational ones; thus our pattern could represent bucks in Persia[11] as well as in Crete.[12] Similarly, the addition of a mere line to denote the handle could make the pattern into a double-axe; without it, this interpretation is unconvincing even where, besides, the complete rendering is attested. This applies to Mesopotamia[13] as well as to Crete, where the so-called 'butterfly pattern'[14] is anyhow thoroughly different from the shape of all Cretan double-axes as well as from the Maltese pattern under discussion. The latter has two near and striking parallels in the hour-glass décor on a bowl from Serraferlicchio near Agrigento[15] (oddly similar to the much older one from Tepe Syalk just mentioned) and in the pattern incised on a bowl from Moarda near Palermo;[16] neither of these is suggestive of double-axes. If in Malta the double-axe had had anything like the significance which it had in Minoan Crete, it would stand

---

[1] Pictured by Zammit, Fig. 34, cf. p. 118, and by Evans, Pl. 85, cf. p. 164.

[2] Çatal Hüyük, *Anat. Stud.* xiii (1963), 64, Fig. 10.

[3] See e.g. Schachermeyr, *Die minoische Kultur . . .* , p. 162; H. G. Buchholz, *Zur Herkunft der kretischen Doppelaxt* (1959), p. 29.

[4] *Inscriptions in the Minoan Linear Script of Class A* (1961); esp. Table 1, no. 52.

[5] Cf. R. Ghirshman, *Iran*, Penguin Book (1954), p. 30, Fig. 4, p. 34, Fig. 7. 4.

[6] *Iraq*, ii (1934), Figs. 33. 10, 64. 1, 78. 6–10 and 14.

[7] M. E. W. Mallowan, *Early Mesopotamia and Iran* (1965), pp. 21 and 24.

[8] Hoernes–Menghin, p. 333, Fig. 2. 1; cf. ib. 203. 7 for bronze work in the same style.

[9] Ib. 321. 5 and 343. 1.   [10] Hutchinson, *Prehistoric Crete* (1962), p. 158, Fig. 27.

[11] Ghirshman, pp. 34 and 38.

[12] According to Hutchinson, p. 125; cf. p. 158, Fig. 27, centre bottom.

[13] *Pace* A. Parrot, *Sumer* (1961), p. 50.

[14] Hutchinson, p. 124, Fig. 19; p. 130, Fig. 22, top; p. 167, Fig. 29, top.

[15] Bernabò Brea, p. 78, Fig. 11.   [16] Bernabò Brea, p. 92 and Pl. 26.

out in the sanctuaries in numerous and unequivocal representations; in the absence of these, the isolated and equivocal Tarxien sherd cannot evidence any relation with Crete.

Nor can the mark consisting of three vertical lines underneath a horizontal, which is engraved on a cylindrical bead (the dating of which seems open to question), and also on a potsherd and on a stone pendant, be traced to the Minoan Linear A script.[1] This elementary sign is indeed found all around the Mediterranean[2] and it is likely in Malta to have served as an amulet—but it does not occur in the Cretan script.[3]

II

THE END OF THE MALTESE 'TEMPLE FOLK'
(*above, p. 60*)

Were the 'temple-folk' suddenly exterminated—or did they die out, perhaps succumbing to a plague, to be succeeded by the 'Cemetery-people' after quite a long time? The answer to this open question depends on the interpretation of T. Zammit's excavations at Tarxien, and his reports about them are unfortunately not free from contradiction. He maintained the second alternative because he found, on top of the 'temple-' and below the 'cemetery'-layer, a stratum, about three feet thick, of 'sterile silt' which, so he maintained, had been blown across from Africa in the course of many centuries. It is, however, somewhat upsetting that, according to *Prehistoric Malta*, p. 5, the ashes making up the 'cemetery'-layer extended over an area *c.* 20 feet in diameter; according to ib. 46 the same area measured 'about 40 feet in diameter', and according to p. 47 'rain water subsequently diffused the black fine ash throughout the . . . earth that buried the ruins'. A more probable interpretation of these indications would be (or so it seems to me) that the temples were burned. If so, the layer of 'silt' is made up of the covering mound which fell down when the roof-beams gave way, and it is their ashes which were found covering most or all of the ruins. J. D. Evans (*Malta*, p. 168) emphatically favours the alternative that 'the peaceful temple-folk were ruthlessly exterminated by the . . . fierce invaders'. An argument in support of this view is in the fact that, according to Zammit–Singer, pp. 79 f., two of the figures found at Tarxien (nos. 2 and 3) 'bore marks of having been exposed to fire'; the priests' statues 'had been reduced to fragments by large stones falling on them' and the head of one of them 'had fallen near a fire that baked it' (ib. 94 and *Prehistoric Malta*, p. 96). How could this have happened, if these figures had lain peacefully, the sand rising over them throughout the centuries, and 'the Bronze Age people never saw' the temples themselves (*Prehist. Malta*, p. 47)?

Addendum: Since the foregoing was written, L. Bernabò Brea has discovered,

---

[1] Evans, p. 164 and Pl. 84; cf. Zammit, p. 92.

[2] As, once, I had occasion to observe: *Mus. Helv.* viii (1951), 20.

[3] See Brice, loc. laud.; the uncertain lines on the base of a cup from Tylissos, ib., Pl. XXV, no. ii. 19. iii, are insignificant.

on the tiny island off Ognina, south of Syracuse, a settlement of the Tarxien Cemetery-people—the first notable trace of them in Sicily—which may well have been their base for the conquest of Malta; see his exciting report in *Kokalos*, xii (1966), 40 ff.

III

ON THE RELATIVE DATE OF THE 'BOSSED BONE PLAQUES'

(above, p. 67)

The excellent workmanship of several among the Sicilian plaques, far superior to anything else left by the Castelluccio people, made Orsi suspect that they had been imported from the East, but it is now seen that 'no member of the Eastern group resembles them closely enough to warrant the import theory' (Evans, p. 89). Maltese stone-work *is* of comparable high quality, but the distribution of the evidence is strictly the opposite of what would be required to bear out the (otherwise tempting) assumption that the plaques had been made in Malta; it supports Evans's view that there is 'no reason for not treating the Sicilian plaques as an integral part of the Castelluccio culture'. Is this culture contemporary with the Maltese Bronze-Age ('Tarxien Cemetery') following upon that of the 'temple-folk'—with Bernabò Brea, *Antiquity*, xxxiv (1960), 137—or are the beginnings of Castelluccio to be synchronized—in agreement with Bernabò Brea, *Sicily*, p. 115 and J. D. Evans, p. 42—with the last 'temple-period' ('Tarxien')? And is the Maltese plaque evidence, as assumed in the text above, of contact between Sicily and the earlier of the two Maltese cultures? The overlapping of the 'Castelluccio' and 'Tarxien-temple' periods was accepted above, p. 64, in view of the dependence of the Sicilian upon the Maltese stone-spirals. The date of the Maltese plaque is not unambiguously established. T. Zammit, its finder, indeed stated (p. 93) that it was 'recovered from the neolithic layer', but J. D. Evans (p. 86) established from the excavation diary that this layer—a 'confused mass' according to Zammit—contained, in addition to the 'neolithic' (i.e. Temple-period) material, a few relics from the subsequent occupation. The plaque in consequence might come from the latter, and J. D. Evans (p. 91) inclined towards this alternative. I cannot help finding the earlier date vastly more probable. We have a fair number of symbolical representations of the goddess by the 'Cemetery-people' (Zammit, pp. 49–54 and Pl. XVI; Evans, Pl. 89); they are, in form and spirit, quite incompatible with the plaques. On the other hand, the particular symbolism of the plaques; the reduction of the body of the goddess to a number of oval (or, more rarely, circular) sections; the exclusive use of curved lines in the patterns engraved on these, contrasting with the equally exclusive use of rectilinear décor by the 'Cemetery-people': all this seems to make the plaques, to say the least, fully compatible with the mind and style of the 'temple-folk', and their comparison with pieces from Troy II and Lerna likewise suggests the earlier date.

IV

ON A SELINUNTINE COIN-TYPE

(above, p. 81, n. 4)

Conclusions which would cut right across much of the argument of the present book may be based upon a certain Selinuntine coin-type. I am far from convinced that they impose themselves, but feel bound to submit them for the reader to consider.

Certain didrachma of Selinus, traditionally ascribed to the late fifth or early fourth century, with a man-headed bull on the obverse, exhibit on the reverse a female seated (on a rock, so it seems), and, erect before her, a big snake which she touches with her outstretched right hand.[1] One such type is pictured by G. F. Hill, *Coins of Ancient Sicily*, Pl. VI. 5[2] (cf. p. 86); a somewhat different design by A. Holm, *Geschichte Siziliens*, iii (1898), Pl. IV. 8[3] (cf. p. 595). S. Haverkamp (1684–1742) interpreted the group as 'Dea Salus et Asclepius'. This interpretation may seem surprising to those familiar with authentic representations of Asklepios and Hygieia; none the less, it seems, to judge from the authors quoted, still to be basically accepted; even though a 'local nymph' is considered for the place of 'Dea Salus'. Haverkamp was prompted by the interpretation of the most outstanding set of coins, which H. Goltzius (1576) had connected with the legendary sanitation of Selinus by Empedokles (Diog. Laert. viii. 70)—a long-lived error, of which L. Lacroix[4] has recently disposed. On some of these (Hill, Pl. VI. 6) a snake twines around an altar. It was held to represent Asklepios; hence Haverkamp assumed the same with regard to the didrachma under discussion.

Haverkamp was opposed, in 1792, by the immensely learned J. Eckhel, who stated:[5] 'fingitur Juppiter serpentis specie cum Proserpina congressus; in aversa natus ex hoc commercio Bacchus tauriformis.'[6] The latter half of this statement can hardly survive the consideration that the man-headed bull represents a river-god on many coins from Sicily and elsewhere[7] and also at Selinus;[8] but Eckhel's interpretation of the reverse of the coin cannot but strike one as more appropriate than the one which finds on it 'the nymph Eurymedosa, well-pleased with the healing agency of the snake' (Holm). The character of the representation seems undoubtedly erotic, particularly so in the variant pictured by Holm; it may be compared with the rendering of similar subjects on Cretan coins.[9]

[1] Cf. B. Head, *Historia Nummorum* (1911), p. 169. The type was copied at Segesta (ib. 146).
[2] Our Plate 15c.   [3] Our Plate 15c.
[4] *Monnaies et colonisation dans l'Occident grec* (1965), pp. 26 ff. and 118 ff.
[5] *Doctrina nummorum veterum*, i. 240.
[6] This stems from Clem. Al. *Protrept.* ii. 16, p. 14 Potter.
[7] See lately L. Lacroix, l.l. 116 ff., with indication of literature.
[8] Lacroix, l.l. 121.
[9] B. Head, *Hist. Num.*², p. 476 (Priansos); *Brit. Mus. Cat. of Coins, Crete*, Pl. 18. 6 and 7; Nilsson, *G.G.R.* i², Pl. 27. 3–5 (Gortyn and Phaistos).

If Eckhel's explanation is accepted, breathtaking conclusions seem to offer themselves. The offspring of the union of Zeus and Persephone is the Dionysos Zagreus of Orphic theology (frs. 58 f. Kern; also 145 etc.) ;[1] if this myth can be found in fifth-century Selinus, Persephone's 'ancient grief'—the old enigma in Pindar, echoed in v. 23 of the Orphic *Argonautica*—could be due to her having been violated by her father and subsequently ceded to his brother, and the gift, likewise mentioned by Pindar, of Akragas, or all Sicily, to her would be painfully understandable as amends for all this violence . . .

On this basis, though, the duty of humans to 'pay amends' for Persephone's 'ancient grief' would be inexplicable. The Orphic theory on this point places it in a different context, and I have already stated[2] why I for one cannot visualize the rigmarole of Orphic speculation among the tendencies of Sicilian thought and religion in the fifth century; not, at any rate, of official and authoritative thought; and what appears on a city's coins must have enjoyed at least local authority.[3] In fact, this particular myth need not be supposed to have been confined to Orphic circles and poems. It may well have been adopted and adapted from some local tradition; for Ovid (*Met.* vi. 114) and Kallimachos (fr. 43. 117 ff.) are hardly likely to have drawn their references from Orphic poems; the same holds good for mimes of the imperial period (Lucian, *De salt.* 39) and for learned scholiasts on Pindar (*I.* vi (vii). 3), Euripides (*Or.* 964; *Tro.* 1230), and Aristophanes (*Ran.* 324; cf. Diodor. 3. 63). All these are likely, rather, to have drawn on learned mythographical works (such as Apollodoros' Περὶ θεῶν), in which also Christian apologists and other critics found the obscenities in which they revelled.

If, then, the coins in question are assumed to illustrate a local myth of Selinus, the snake on it may or may not be Zeus, nor is there anything to show that the female figure is Kore; she may be some other goddess or nymph.[4]

---

[1] See Lobeck, *Aglaophamus*, pp. 547 ff.

[2] Above, p. 86, n. 3.

[3] E. Gàbrici (*Problemi di numismatica greca* (1959), p. 106) based on the particular style of the man-headed bull and on the inscription ΣΕΛΙΝΟΕΣ the argument that this coin-type was issued by Campanian mercenaries settled at Selinus. If this is right, the scene on its obverse, unrelated to anything at Selinus and indeed in all Sicily, need not be assumed to represent any Sicilian tradition at all.

[4] The origin of that myth of Zeus and Kore which was finally embodied in the Orphic system may be sought in the ancient notion of the male chthonic power, embodied in a snake, fertilizing the earth goddess (cf. E. Küster, *Die Schlange in der griech. Kunst und Religion*, RVV, xiii. 2 (1913), 85 ff.). This may be illustrated by the Cretan statuettes of priestesses, or goddesses, with snakes; by the Argive relief showing the Eumenides holding snakes (J. Harrison, *Prolegomena*, p. 255, Fig. 57); by the representations of the *cista* of Demeter with snakes (e.g. on the Ny Carlsberg relief, Farnell, *Cults* . . . , iii (1907), Pl. XVa), and by the story of the giant snake which became the ancestor of the Mysian Ophiogeneis (Aelian, *De nat. an.* xii. 39; Strabo xiii. 588); and one may assume that the earth-snake came to be named Zeus, as it was in the case of Amphiaraos, Ktesios, Meilichios, and Trophonios (Rohde, *Psyche*, i. 120, n. 2, and 125). However, even if the Selinuntine coins, as well as their counterparts from Priansos, are supposed to represent this ancient myth, the specific form and context in which at the time it was realized remain unknown, and we are not free to guess at Meilichios, even though he was worshipped at the Gaggera, for no evidence and no intrinsic aptitude will permit us to identify him as the ravisher of Kore.

V

A FIGURINE OF THE 'LINDIA' TYPE ADAPTED TO REPRESENT ATHENA

(above, p. 117)

I owe to Mr. R. A. Higgins the reference to a figurine which I ought not to have overlooked when writing on the 'Lindia', and which he mentions in his recent book (*Greek Terracottas* (1967), p. 87) as 'adding substance' to Blinkenberg's theory. *Am. Journ. Arch.*, lxvi (1962), 401, Pl. 117, Fig. 18 shows a seated goddess, roughly of the type under discussion, 'wearing also the aegis' and thus characterized as Athena. Its finder, P. Orlandini, who published it in *Kokalos*, vii (1961), 139 with Pl. XIV. 5, declared that it proved Blinkenberg's thesis. I submit that in this instance the type has been adapted to represent Athena; in consequence, the type itself does not represent Athena. This figurine, found on the akropolis of Gela, is carefully worked. The beautiful head is quite different from those of all other specimens; the body, though apparently with no indication of arms but with feet fully modelled, is more realistically shaped than that of most figurines of the 'Lindia' type. Its shibboleth, the upper garment, is not indicated; but the characteristic décor covers the whole chest (as e.g. in Higgins, l.l., Pl. 37A). A gorgoneion has been put on top of its centre, apparently by a separate little mould applied to the already made figure. The result is a highly inorganic combination; in particular, it remains obscure how the gorgoneion is related to the body and to the original décor. This recent find thus seems ill suited to determine the original meaning of the type.

VI

DEMETER NOT A GODDESS OF THE NETHERWORLD

(above, p. 83)

All too much has been made, especially by S. Ferri, of Plutarch's report[1] that 'the Athenians called the dead Δημήτρειοι'. Having been initiated in the mysteries of Demeter and her daughter which conveyed the assurance of a 'better life yonder', the dead were felt to have been committed to Demeter's care, and the ever fresh growth of her corn was surely regarded as a comforting symbol; Cicero, *De leg.* ii. 63, after Demetrius of Phaleron, reports an ancient usage of sowing corn on fresh graves.[2] Hence an ear of grain was shown, according to Hippolytos,[3] at the supreme moment of the Eleusinian rites, and

---

[1] *De facie* . . . 943 b.   [2] Cf. M. P. Nilsson, *Opuscula*, ii. 592.
[3] *Refut.* v. 8. 39.

the beautiful golden ear found near Syracuse and profoundly interpreted by
P. Wolters[1] together with its counterpart, found in a Hellenistic grave near
Kertsch,[2] can still convey some of the emotion with which this symbol was
contemplated. We are, however, liable to overlook the ambivalence in the
notion of Greek χθών, which is the life-giving soil as well as, below, the infernal
region of death. Persephone is, on the Gold Leaves, χθονίων (or χθονία)
βασίλεια in the latter sense, but Δημήτηρ χθονία is the goddess of the fruit-giving
earth and not of the deep Hades. This ambivalence made it possible for both
goddesses to be comprised under the term χθόνιοι θεαί,[3] and for Pluton (who is
not attested before the fifth century) to become one with the ἄναξ ἐνέρων
Ἀϊδωνεύς; but all this does not make Demeter a goddess of the Netherworld;
the ἄλσεα Φερσεφονείας are not her domain.

VII

PERSEPHONE NOT RETURNING TO THE UPPER WORLD

(above, p. 165)

A form of the myth as particular as that attested by the Lokrian pinakes may be
expected to have left some traces elsewhere. That Persephone 'did not return'
is, after all, concordant with the essential character, previously sketched, of the
goddess; the Netherworld could not really, at recurrent intervals, be without
its queen. No beholder of one of the 'Underworld vases', surely, would be
expected to reflect and say to himself: 'Lo! Persephone happens, just now, to be
present', and no one of those buried with one of the 'Gold Leaves' was felt to
risk arriving in Hades while the 'Queen of those below' happened to be revisit-
ing her mother in the world above. Her permanent presence in Hades could
not be combined with the myth of the *raptus* of Demeter's daughter in any other
way; Persephone remained below: . . . *nec repetita sequi curet Proserpina matrem*,
Vergil, *Georg.* i. 39. Modern commentaries, as far as I have seen them, treat or,
rather, neglect this remarkable verse as though its content were obvious rather
than startling. Similarly, the so-called Probus ad loc.[4] briefly censures it as
contra historiam, and the implication that it was of Vergil's invention is made
explicit in Servius.[5] The anonymous *Brevis Expositio*[6] is better informed: *In
infernum descendit Ceres ut filiam reciperet; quae matrem sequi noluit.* A Κάθοδος of
Demeter is in the Orphic tradition,[7] but this cannot be Vergil's source, seeing
that, according to it, Persephone did in the end return. A second indication in
the *Brevis Expositio* leads further: *Item: Rex Molossorum Proserpinam rapuit et*

[1] *Festschrift J. Loeb* (1930), p. 122.
[2] A. A. Peredolskaja in 2. Beiheft of *Antike Kunst* (1964), frontispiece, Pl. 16. 4, and p. 22.
[3] Herodotus vi. 134; vii. 153.　　[4] Servius, ed. Thilo–Hagen, iii. 2 (1902), 354.
[5] Ad loc., ed. Thilo (1887), p. 142.　　　　　　[6] Ad loc., ib. iii. 2, 213.
[7] Orph. *Hymn.* 41. 5; cf. Hyginus, *Fab.* 251.

Ceres ostia cum cantatoribus multis pulsavit, nec veniebat ad eam filia pro eius loci amore.
The continuation of the story of Aidoneus, King of the Molossians and husband
of Persephone, is in Plutarch, *Theseus*, 31. 4–5 and 35. 1; it comes from the
second book of Philochoros' *Atthis*, and hence figures, with some parallel texts,
among the collected fragments of Greek historians.[1] If, in this matter, Philochoros was not following Euhemeros, at any rate his source resembled Euhemeros as one egg resembles another.

The whole topic has been admirably treated by R. Förster,[2] on whose work
the preceding account largely rests. One may hesitate, though, to follow him in
describing Philochoros (or, for that matter, Euhemeros) as Vergil's source.
A myth must exist, and have some currency, to qualify for euhemeristic treatment; a myth, and no doubt a poem, telling of Persephone's refusal to return
to the world of light must therefore have existed at, and before, the time of
Euhemeros and Philochoros. This poem, rather than its rationalistic perversion,
is likely to have inspired Vergil; and not him alone, but also Columella (x. 272)
and Lucan.[3] What poem this was I see no way of guessing.

This hypothesized poem, then, would appear to afford a parallel to the
Lokrian myth; yet with a difference; for the latter solved the problem given
with the identification of Kore, the Maiden abducted by Hades, and Persephone, the Queen of the Netherworld, in a different and more radical fashion.
The Roman poets just quoted make Persephone reject her mother's entreaties;
in the Lokrian myth—as Dr. Zancani-Montuoro recognized—Demeter does
not exist. For this extreme version I know of no explicit parallel. Suggestive
analogies, however, exist; they may be put under the heading 'Death and the
Maiden'. I am going to summarize a much discussed argument, which was
brilliantly initiated by K. O. Müller[4] and fully elaborated by L. Malten.[5]

The dead, according to the general Greek notion, 'go to Hades'; there are,
however, telling traces of an alternative concept: the Lord of the Dead
emerges on his chariot from the Netherworld and carries his victim off to his
realm. A hint at this concept was found by some scholars, even in Antiquity,[6]
in the Homeric description of Hades as κλυτόπωλος;[7] and, indeed, what other
use could he have made of his vehicle? The horse which, as a symbol of death,
appears on grave reliefs,[8] is likely to evoke this very idea. Associating it with
the ancient custom—traditional with Greeks as with many other peoples—of
the abduction of brides, popular imagination appears to have conceived of
young maidens as a favourite prey of the κλυτόπωλος; thus the Lord of the

---

[1] Vol. i, pp. 391 f., frs. 45–6 Müller; vol. iiib, p. 104, no. 328, fr. 18 Jacoby.

[2] *Der Raub . . . der Persephone* (1874), pp. 45, 59 ff.

[3] *Phars.* vi. 698 and 739; see Förster, p. 61.

[4] *Prolegomena zu e. wissensch. Mythologie* (1825), pp. 302 ff.

[5] *Arch. f. Rel.wiss.* xii (1909), 308 ff. Malten gives full indication of the relevant literature,
which I refrain from copying out; add however Wilamowitz, *Der Glaube* . . . , i². 172 and
M. P. Nilsson, *G.G.R.* i². 453.

[6] Schol. *Il.* 5. 654. The inferred reference of the Homeric epithet is to the abduction of
Demeter's daughter (of which there is no hint in Homer) and the same implication was
found in the epithet χρυσήνιος applied to Hades by Pindar in his hymn on Persephone (fr. 37;
Pausanias ix. 23. 4).

[7] *Il.* 5. 654; 11. 445; 16. 625.

[8] L. Malten, *Arch. Jahrb.* xxix (1914), 186 ff.

Netherworld won his queen. Four reliefs, Attic works of the fourth century but only one of them found in Attica itself, are convincingly held to illustrate this myth and its wide currency.[1] They show a woman—not Persephone—standing beside a bearded man on a fast-moving chariot, and two of them have the names of both inscribed: they are Zeuxippos or Echelos, with Basile or Basileia.[2] The 'Queen' with the 'Yoker of horses', who is none other than the Κλυτό-πωλος and identical with Echelos, the 'Holder of people', and Agesilaos, the 'Leader of people'—the leader in, and to, the realm of Death:[3] this is the common subject of these reliefs. Nothing suggests, or could even justify, the assumption that Basile is Demeter's daughter; she is a *kore*, but not ἡ Δήμητρος Κόρη; a maiden, abducted by Hades. Hence, those many laments, beginning with Antigone's, over 'brides of Hades'[4] need not altogether be held to assimilate them to Kore–Persephone, but may stem from that more general concept. The argument is completed by the gloss, in Hesychius, Ἀδμήτου κόρη· Ἑκάτη, τινὲς δὲ τὴν Βένδιν; for this Admetos is not the king of Pherai but (as K. O. Müller recognized) Ἀΐδης ἀμείλιχος ἠδ' ἀδάμαστος,[5] whom Apollo—in the original form of the Delphic myth—had to serve for a 'long year' to atone for the killing of the Python.[6] The Thessalian goddess of the Netherworld would not be styled 'his Kore', had she not—a human maiden—been abducted by him, to become his queen.

There is no evidence that a similar myth was current in mainland Lokris, but no other assumption could account—as far as I can see—for what the pinakes attest for its Italian colony; the ancient tale of 'Death and the Maiden' provided the frame for the revelation of the godhead of the new land. In the Lokrian version, the name of the 'Queen' was not Basilis but Persephone (Pēriphonā, so it appears, in local parlance[7]); before her elevation she was a 'maiden', a kore, but not 'Demeter's Kore'.[8] The mythology of the Gold Leaves may have grown out of a similar root. In them, too, the goddess is Persephone; she is addressed as 'queen' and, again, there is no trace of Demeter.

---

[1] R. Kekulé von Stradonitz, *Echelos und Basile* (*65. Berliner Winckelmannsprogramm*, 1905).

[2] The near-identity of the latter two names, and the meaningful implications of the former, make it impossible, to my mind, to accept the view of O. Walter (*Ephem. Arch.* (1937), 97 ff.— a very valuable discussion, with excellent pictures, of the whole find to which the Echelos relief belongs), according to which (ib. 114) the reliefs represent family ancestors rather than the god and goddess of the Netherworld; for the same reason, the alternative reading Ἰασίλη for Βασίλη remains unattractive. Echelos is the hero of the Echelidai but, like Admetos, he appears to retain the essence of an older myth. This interpretation became inescapable (so it seems to me) on comparison with the inscriptional evidence for a cult, at Athens, of the pair Neleus and Basile (Kekulé, l.l., after E. Meyer).

[3] *Aischylos*, fr. 406 N. (= 612 M.); Kallimachos, *H.* v. 130 etc.

[4] A full list of relevant passages was given by R. Förster, l.l. 73.   [5] *Il.* 9. 158.

[6] A. Lesky who, in a classic article (*Sitz. Ber. Akad. Wien*, 203. 2 (1925)), put an end to the attempts at finding the goddess of the Netherworld in the figure and story of Alkestis, none the less admits (l.l. 7) the original identity of Admetos and Hades.

[7] *I.G.* xiv. 631.

[8] L. Malten (*Arch. Jahrb.* xxix (1914), 229) interpreted the pinakes with representations of the *raptus* as 'Death carrying off various girls'. One may welcome his rejection of an interpretation on the lines of the Eleusinian tradition and still feel that he does insufficient justice to the fact that the whole series appears to illustrate successive phases of one myth.

VIII

THE SPEAKER OF THE 'REVELATION' IN *KATHARMOI* I

Reasons were given (above, p. 257) for assuming that the speaker was Persephone. Alternative possibilities deserve consideration. Empedokles, so one might argue, is unlikely to have allotted this most outstanding part to one of the traditional deities—seeing that elsewhere he either discounted these or profoundly altered the current notions of them. This would not in itself be a very strong argument, for no evidence survives to show if and how he introduced Persephone; it can, however, be reinforced by the consideration that, wherever Empedokles introduces active divinities, these tend to appear in forms previously unknown, or even with new names, expressive of his own concepts. Accordingly, the alternative may be pursued that this central speech was made by one of those deities in whom Empedokles visualized the essential forces of the universe as he conceived it. The possibility that the speaker was, like the deity of Parmenides, merely called 'Daimon' does not commend itself, seeing that the listeners were themselves 'daimons' and that, moreover, the action of 'clothing them with flesh' was carried out by a 'daimon' (fr. 11). The deity presiding over this scene must have been more significantly individualized. The speech was the revelation of what was inevitably ordained; the speaker accordingly is likely to have been some impersonation of inevitability. The daimons' exile was enforced by the Decree of Ananke; could it have been she who set forth their further destiny?

Ananke was mentioned as determining the world-process in *Phys.*; this much may be inferred from the doxographic reports which DK present as A 32 (p. 289. 9) and A 45 (p. 291. 35),[1] however much her image may have been distorted by its subjection to Aristotelian terminology. With Parmenides (B 8. 30 and 10. 6) she had assumed mythical near-personality, and Empedokles' inspiration derives from Parmenides more than from any other thinker except Pythagoras, especially with regard to (wrongly so-called) 'personifications'. Hence, and particularly in view of fr. 3 (115 DK) v. 1, a goddess Ananke uttering the 'revelation' in *Katharmoi* appears conceivable and suitable. A suggestive analogy at once springs to the mind: in Plato's *Republic* 616 c, the souls proceed from the 'field' to the world-column which is the 'spindle of Ananke' and the act of incarnation takes place in her domain.[2]

If this hypothesis is considered, our fr. 10 (116 DK) evidently could not be included in her speech; in fact, this very fragment, wherever placed, renders the attribution of the speech to Ananke unlikely. As opposed to the Parmenidean concept of a necessity embracing and determining the whole of Being, this fragment presents Ananke as one of the antithetic forces in the

---

[1] For further relevant evidence see Zeller–Nestle, *Philosophie der Griechen*, i (1920), 969, n. 2.
[2] Cf. also *Doxogr.* p. 321. 24 Πυθαγόρας ἀνάγκην ἔφη περικεῖσθαι τῶι κόϲμωι.

world-process, opposed by Charis as Neikos is countered by Philia. This concept of Ananke is perfectly in agreement with Greek thought of the time and of later times, for in tragedy as well as in sepulchral epigrams Ananke is often the equivalent of destruction and death. This 'Necessity', an aspect or agent of Neikos, could very well have laid down the decree sealing the daimon's banishment, but she could hardly, in person, expound the laws of his penance which, though enforced by Neikos, could lead to liberation from his power and, therewith, from this 'Necessity'. If accordingly we seek to attribute the speech to the embodiment of a 'Necessity' wider than the Empedoklean Ananke (equivalent, rather, to the Parmenidean), the name of this divinity, I suppose, could only have been Adrasteia.[1]

Having been led, by the course of the argument, to posit Adrasteia as the speaker of the 'revelation-speech' in *Katharmoi* I, one may, in confirmation, refer to the θεσμὸς Ἀδραστείας in Plato's *Phaedrus* 248 c 2[2]—and one will recall, moreover, certain passages in Orphic literature which yield notable analogies as well as new problems.

Ananke and Adrasteia were identified, according to Damascius, *De princ.* 123,[3] at the beginning of the Orphic 'Theogony according to Hieronymos and Hellanikos'. She was conjoint with Χρόνος ἀγήραος—whose figure and name so strongly recall the Iranian Zervan akarana that I, like many others, should hesitate to ascribe this poem to pre-Hellenistic times. In the 'Rhapsodic Theogony', on the other hand, these two, though close neighbours, were distinguished, and Adrasteia was the older and more comprehensive of them—as, according to the present tentative argument, she was with Empedokles.

Proclus, *In Tim.* 41e,[4] states that, in this 'Theogony', the demiurge (that is, Zeus, as the following citations confirm) 'is nursed by Adrasteia and is together with Ananke'; while Hermias, commenting on *Phaedrus* 248 c,[5] describes Adrasteia as one of the nymphs nursing the newly-born Zeus 'in the cave of Night'—as also Kallimachos and 'Apollodoros' do;[6] the same Adrasteia is said, both by Hermias and by Proclus elsewhere,[7] to be sitting in the porch of that cave 'proclaiming the divine laws to all the world'; for she 'comprises in herself all laws of the kosmos and yonder'.

It is very clear that different myths have here been blended together: the Trojan nymph Adrasteia[8] (wielding the tympana of the Asianic Kybele) has been drawn from the Trojan to the Cretan Mt. Ida—hence Amaltheia has become her mother—and has been pressed into identity with Adrasteia-'Necessity'; who is thus called 'because her ordinances are inescapable': so Hermias observes, and he is right there. When Aischylos and Plato wrote οἱ προσκυνοῦντες τὴν Ἀδράστειαν σοφοί and θεσμὸς Ἀδραστείας ὅδε, they were not

---

[1] Any one of the Moirai would have been unsuitable because of the specific and limited range of each and all of them. Lachesis takes the place of Ananke in Plato, *Rep.* 617 d merely to make possible the apologetic assertion 'God is not guilty'; a preoccupation from which, one trusts, Empedokles was free.

[2] Cf. Plut. *De sera* . . . 25, 564 e: Adrasteia, Ananke's daughter and highest of the 'avengers' in Hades. [3] DK 1 [66] B 13 (p. 12. 4) = *Orph. Fragm.* 54 Kern.

[4] Vol. i, 450. 20 Diehl = 162 Kern. [5] 105 Kern.

[6] Callim. *Hymn.* i. 47; Apollod. *Bibl.* i. 1. 6. [7] *Theol. Plat.* iv. 16 = 152 Kern.

[8] Plut. *Quaest. conviv.* 657 e; cf. Wilamowitz, *Der Glaube* . . . , i². 128, n. 1.

thinking of the Trojan or Cretan nymph nor of Kybele nor even of Nemesis of Rhamnus[1]—but of the 'Inescapable'.

The similarity between the Orphic scene—Adrasteia in the porch of the 'Cave of Night', proclaiming laws for all the world—and the one inferred for the *Katharmoi* is striking enough. It is not complete, for the Orphic Adrasteia is pictured speaking to 'all' outside, not inside the 'cave'; that is, she proclaims to all creation the laws which, issuing from transcendental reality ('night'), govern the world of the living; even so, if the suggested reconstruction of the *Katharmoi* is taken for granted, this similarity calls for an explanation. Has Empedokles borrowed an Orphic trait? Even more: could the two or three hundred verses of this speech—of which only eleven remain—have contained a summary of Orphic theology? Does this coincidence (always supposing that the tentative reconstruction here outlined is not an illusion) demonstrate the Orphic origin of Empedokles' theology?

Until, with luck, the Salonika papyrus, or some other fresh evidence, has shown how much or how little of the Neoplatonic evidence about the 'Rhapsodic Theogony' may be traced back to the time of Empedokles, one will here tread very warily. The far-reaching suspicions thrown out just now may in any case be discarded, for the Empedoklean mythology and theology are sufficiently clear to show, at any rate, that the monstrous phantasmagories of the Orphic 'Theogony' could not be fitted into it.[2] The specific conception of Adrasteia in the cave, revealing their destiny to the newly-incarnated, could, even so, have been suggested by the Orphic scene—if indeed at the time it existed. The inspiration might as well have worked in the opposite direction—if indeed the identification of the speaker posited in the present note is held to be preferable to the one previously advocated. The part played by Persephone in the analogous passages in Pindar and on the Gold Leaves is, I feel, a crucial argument against it.

IX

CΩMA XITΩN ΨYXHC

(above, p. 206)

Cῶμα χιτὼν ψυχῆc says the Italian sepulchral epigram *I.G.* xiv. 2241,[3] which is unlikely to antedate the second century A.D. and, as Kaibel noted, is likely to be Pythagorean. The same phrase recurs in the epic *Unterweltsbeschreibung*

---

[1] Identified with Adrasteia by Antimachos, fr. 54 Wyss.

[2] In an additional note in DK (p. 501) Plato is said in *Leg.* vi. 782 b (read 'c') to reproduce Empedokles' fr. 128, 'describing its character as orphic'. Of this assertion, the first half may be right (at least in so far as an echo of the Empedoklean verses seems discernible); the second is certainly wrong. Plato uses the term 'Ορφικοί τινες λεγόμενοι βίοι to summarize the vegetarianism of an idealized past age; he does not thereby indicate, nor even imply, an 'orphic character' (with all that this vague formulation insinuates) of Empedokles and his teaching. Hippolytos has been described as an 'orphic' on evidence not quite as flimsy as this (Eur. *Hipp.* 952 ff.) but equally fantastic. [3] 651 Kaibel, 1763 Peek.

published by Merkelbach,[1] who may be right in calling this text 'Orphic', since it contained a pedantic system of sins and their punishments in hell; for the same reason, it too is likely to belong to the Roman period. Porphyry finally uses the same term three times.[2] This is hardly a sufficient basis for calling this concept 'Orphic'—as even Wilamowitz[3] once did; but the question could only be considered together with all the other formulations of the notion of the body, as well as of human qualities, as 'garments' of man, or of the soul; a notion widely spread, and original, both with Greeks[4] and particularly in the Orient. This would require a book to itself.[5] Anyhow, the use of this concept by Empedokles does not make him an 'Orphic'; him as little as e.g. Epictetus or the bishop Sextus;[6] it may have been current among Pythagoreans. An argument in support of this assumption can be based upon a fragment of Kastor of Rhodes preserved by Plutarch;[7] I refrain from copying it out, because it has to be read in its context. W. Lameere[8] added another argument from the symbolism of Roman third-century sarcophagi (Pythagorean according to F. Cumont): namely, the representations of genii divesting the image of the dead person of a large veil; he suggested that the liberation of the soul from the body is intimated, quoting *inter alia* Seneca *Epist.* 92. 13 *hoc* (scil. *corpus*) *natura ut quandam vestem animo circumdedit* and referring, for further evidence, to V. Macchioro, *Zagreus* (1930), pp. 532 ff.

X

EMPEDOKLES, FR. 2, v. 8 DK

(*above, p. 218*)

Empedokles hinted at the divine essence of man at the very beginning of the *Physika*, (as well as in fr. 15 DK), for E. Rohde's[9] interpretation of cὺ δ' οὖν, ἐπεὶ ὧδε λιάσθης, 'da du hieher — auf die Erde — verschlagen bist', seems clearly right to me. H. Diels[10] indeed wanted this phrase to mean 'in secretum secessisti, ut Achilles νόςφι λιαςθείς'; but νόςφι—the operative word in his parallel from the *Iliad* (1. 348)—is by no means the same as ὧδε, and ὧδε does not mean 'in secretum'. Kranz, though, felt encouraged by H. Fraenkel's discussion of

---

[1] *Mus. Helv.* viii (1951), 10, fol. 3, v. 8.

[2] *Antr.* 14, p. 66. 13 Nauck; *Abstin.* i. 31, p. 109. 14 and ii. 46, p. 174. 22; cf. ib. i. 1, p. 85. 11.

[3] On Eur. *H.F.* 1269.

[4] e.g. Pind. *N.* xi. 15; Eur. *H.F.* 1269 and *Ba.* 746; Artemidor. iv. 30 ἱμάτιον ψυχῆς; Plato, *Rep.* x. 620 c, but not *Crat.* 400 c; hardly Arist. *De an.* i. 3, p. 407^{b}22; cf. Herodot. ii. 123. 2.

[5] An excellent *prolusio* is P. Wendland's posthumous article published in *Hermes*, li (1916), 481 ff.

[6] Epictetus i. 25. 21; Sextus, *Sententiae* 346 (Latin) and 449, ed. H. Chadwick (1959), pp. 51 and 62.

[7] Plut. *Quaest. Rom.* 10. 266 e; Jacoby, *F.Gr.Hist.* 250 F 15.

[8] *Bull. Corr. Hell.* lxiii (1939), 43 ff.; esp. 79 ff.   [9] *Psyche,* ii. 185, n. 2.

[10] *Sitz. Ber. Berlin. Akad.* (1898), 407.

the problematical verb λιάζομαι[1] similarly to translate 'da du dich hier ⟨von ihnen⟩ absondertest'. Again, though, λιάζομαι does not—without νόϲφι—mean 'absondern', and Kranz's supplement 'von ihnen', though indispensable with this translation, is inadmissible. This pronoun could, if anything, be related only to the 'men' mentioned in the preceding verse, and this is not possible, since the word is there used, generically, of 'men as they are', namely, endowed with sorely limited faculties; Pausanias is one of them.

On considering all the passages in which the verb λιάζομαι occurs, its basic meaning is found to be 'to move away from a place occupied, or expected to be occupied, to another'; specific nuances, such as 'to bend', 'fall', 'go aside', resulting from the context and the addition of adjectives (like πρηνήϲ) or adverbs (like ὕπαιθα, ἑτέρωϲε, also ἐϲ πνοάϲ, ἐκ ποταμοῖο). In the Empedoklean passage, the adverb ὧδε takes the place of δεῦρο in the nearest Homeric parallel, Il. 22. 12, where the implication of 'hither' is clear from the context; it is 'away from your goal, to this place'. In Empedokles nothing supports the assumption that Pausanias, relinquishing his customary station, has joined his master at some solitary place; on the contrary, this romantic inference must break the connection with the preceding verses which is stressed by the particle οὖν. 'Men can only grasp limited knowledge. Since you are man, you will hear no more than human understanding can stretch to.' The disciple has, by divine ordinance, exchanged his Olympian home for 'this place', on Earth—as Achilleus, in the Homeric model-verse, was drawn from his goal by Apollon; the daimon Pausanias is, at least for the time being, man.

XI

ON THE CHTHONIAN DIONYSOS

(above, p. 311)

When Herakleitos asserts the identity of Dionysos and Hades, he is not offering, for the benefit of historians of religion, a piece of plain information, but stating a paradox fraught with recondite meaning. Its basis is that Dionysos and Hades were generally held to be as different, and mutually exclusive, as life and death. Anyone to whom this is not immediately obvious may learn it from A. Lesky.[2] Here as with all of his paradoxes, the philosopher points at some

---

[1] Antidoron Wackernagel (1923), pp. 275 ff.

[2] A. Lesky, Wien. Stud. liv (1936), 24.—H. Metzger is wrong in asserting (Bull. Corr. Hell. lxviii–lxix (1944–5), 314 with n. 2) that—in addition to Herakleitos!—also the Etymologicum Magnum, p. 406. 46 'confirms the complete identity of Dionysos and Hades'. The words which he quotes, 'some say that he is the same as Pluto' refer—not to Dionysos, but—to Zagreus; for the statement: 'by Zagreus, some poets mean Dionysos, others Hades' indicates an alternative; it does not imply that Dionysos 'is the same as Hades'. And, finally, it is a tall assumption that the universal deity invoked in Euripides fr. 912 N. (. . . Ζεὺϲ εἴτ' Ἀίδηϲ . . .) is Dionysos; if it were so, he would be 'infernal' no more, nor less, than 'Olympian', but—universal. This is a facet of the religious thought—not of some nebulous 'Orphic', but—of Euripides (cf. Tro. 886, etc.).

profound unity underlying opposites. A profound unity of life and death—
unity in rapture—did underly the Dionysiac experience: this was beautifully
shown, after E. Rohde, by W. F. Otto (*Dionysos* (1934), pp. 104 ff.), even
though much of the evidence adduced by him is invalid. This unity found cult
expression in the Attic Anthesteria and also, so it seems, in the Agrionia
(Agr(i)ania) celebrated by Dorians as well as in Boeotia and Thessaly; feasts
of life and joy returning—and of the dead; and it made it possible for devotees
to expect that after death they would continue to rove in the train of their god.
The earliest evidence for this faith are the Cumaean inscriptions mentioned
above (p. 173, n. 3); it abounds from the fourth century onward and throughout the Hellenistic period; in the Roman age, finally, the Dionysiac mysteries
offered the main surety of immortality. Nothing could justify the assumption
that all those sharing this faith had themselves initiated by Orphic priests—one
could not imagine it, for example, of Plutarch[1]—although some presumably
did so, while many more may have found confirmation in reading the epic
poems circulating under Orpheus' name. The various and even contradictory
essence of their god is reflected in the variety of his cult and myth; a variety
which Hellenistic scholars studied and described[2] and which Orphic speculation exploited in constructing its systems of mythical genealogies.

A giver, to his followers, of eternal bliss, Dionysos by no means either was,
or became, identical with Hades (and where indeed is Hades considered
a giver of immortality?); and yet their identity—erroneously supposed to be
attested by Herakleitos—has been widely held to stand out palpably in the
figure of a 'chthonian Dionysos'. This figure has attained, among modern
archaeologists and historians of religion, a prestige disproportionate to the
extant evidence; which is scanty and late. I find no more than two relevant
texts.[3] One of the Orphic Hymns (53) is addressed to him. And, notably
indeed, he is in this hymn not, as in others (e.g. 29), addressed as Persephone's
offspring; still less, as taking the place of Hades; but as the god who returns to
the earth every other year and, in the meantime, 'sleeps by the house of
Persephone'.[4] The other text is the grammarians' observation, surviving in
several Byzantine lexica, that 'Zagreus, in poetry, is Dionysos, for Persephone
gave birth, from Zeus, to the χθόνιος Διόνυσος'; they illustrated this by Kallimachos fr. 43. 117 Pf.[5] In what sense this Dionysos is 'chthonian', the text does
not tell, nor does it emerge from his equation with the equally obscure Zagreus
(cf. above, p. 167, n. 4); it is, however, self-evident that he could not be
identified with the Lord of the Netherworld, who subsequently abducts the
same Persephone.

Faced with this scarcity of literary evidence, one turns to archaeology for
enlightenment. K. Schauenburg, in an instructive article entitled 'Pluton und
Dionysos',[6] presents interesting illustrations of Dionysiac eschatology, mainly

---

[1] *Consol. ad uxorem* 11, 611 d.
[2] See Diodorus 3. 62 ff. and the evidence quoted by Lobeck, *Aglaophamus*, pp. 656 f.
[3] Proclus *In Tim.* 40 b (Orph. Fr. 194 Kern) is not substantive evidence.
[4] Cf. above, p. 167, n. 5.
[5] See Pfeiffer on Kallimachos l.c.; add Harpocration, s.v. λεύκη.
[6] *Arch. Jahrb.* lxviii (1953), 38 ff.; cf. id. ib. lxxiii (1958), 48 ff.

from Italian vases, but arrives at the conclusion (p. 69) that a fusion of these two deities is not evidenced in Greek art.[1] H. Metzger has discussed 'Dionysos Chthonien' repeatedly and fruitfully.[2] He observed the distinction, inherent in the term 'chthonic',[3] between Dionysos as a 'divinity of Nature renascent' and 'infernal'. The evidence, once more, proves to be scanty for the former—apart from the ample illustration, from the fourth century, of Dionysos joining the deities of Eleusis—and non-existent (to my mind) for the latter.

On an Attic fourth-century crater, formerly in the Hope Collection (no. 163) and now in the British Museum, Dionysos, a satyr, and two maenads are seen watching, and hailing, a young god emerging from the earth, in the same manner as female deities are so often represented.[4] 'He can be none other than the child of Semele, the earth-Dionysos himself', asserted J. Harrison[5]—undaunted by the fact that Dionysos himself is represented witnessing the scene. She was followed by others and also by H. Metzger—originally;[6] subsequently, though,[7] on examining the vase in the original, he observed that the one solid argument for J. Harrison's interpretation rested on a mistake; for the deity arising is holding a normal sceptre and not, as had been thought, a thyrsos.[8] In return, he presented two earlier vases—there are no other, later representations—which are plausibly taken to picture a chthonian Dionysos: namely, a late black-figure Attic lekythos[9] and a middle-Korinthian alabastron.[10] On the former, two satyrs are busy about a large bearded head which has emerged from the ground; on the other, an apparently more youthful head

[1] This does not prevent him from asserting (1953, p. 62) that 'bekanntlich' the two gods were identified, quoting in evidence Herakleitos, and Lesky's article . . . I am not, in fact, convinced that the Heidelberg skyphos (S.'s central subject) qualifies, by showing a satyr in front of the seated Pluton, for the description as 'eine Darstellung des dionysischen Jenseits'. Satyrs in Hades are exceedingly improbable. The one in question is looking back at the pair, satyr and maenad, on the other side of the beaker (thus ib. 62); in fact, he is beating the rhythm, on his tympanon, for their dance. Which is to say that he has been placed in front of Pluton for no other reason but lack of space on the picture to which he belongs. On the other hand there is considerable temptation to find Dionysos, in the place of Hades, facing Persephone, on an Apulian crater (id., 1958, p. 66, fig. 11); without thyrsos, it is true, but seated on a panther's skin . . . One will, in the end, probably share S.'s hesitations with regard to this interpretation (1953, 57; 1958, 77 f. 'jugendlicher Hades'). He refers to some representations of—probably—Hades not bearded and of the—still unexplained—youthful person (not Hades) carrying off Kore on Lokrian pinakes. Like these, the vase-painting also may illustrate a myth unknown to us.

[2] (a) 'Dionysos Chthonien', in Bull. Corr. Hell. lxviii–lxix (1944–5), 296 ff.; (b) Les representations dans la céramique attique du IVe siècle (1951), esp. pp. 243 ff.; (c) Recherches sur l'imagerie athénienne (1965), pp. 49 ff.

[3] Cf. above, p. 400.   [4] Above, p. 82, n. 3.

[5] Prolegomena . . . , p. 406 (with Fig. 128). If evidence counted for anything, the 'earth-Dionysos' ought to have been described as 'son of Persephone' rather than 'of Semele' (cf. Pfeiffer ad Callim. fr. 643).

[6] Metzger (a), 304; cf. 297, Fig. 1.   [7] Id. (b), 262, with Pl. XXXV.

[8] One will then, here again, have to acknowledge the representation of an unknown, youthful deity or demon; cf. above, note 1.

[9] Metzger (a), p. 298, with Fig. 2 and Pl. XXV.

[10] Id. (c), p. 49 (with indication of literature) and Pl. XXV. 1.—The phallus oculatus on an Attic black-figure lekythos (Metzger (c), 49 with Pl. XXVI) may well stand in the place of Dionysos, but not of the 'chthonian' Dionysos; it is not seen rising through the ground but lying on it.

is sticking up between padded dancers and musicians of the grotesque, Korinthian type. Dionysos 'from the ground'; this is one more realization of the 'coming god'; coming, this time, not from the sea, nor from the mountains, nor awakened from sleep, but rising through the soil and thus χθόνιος in that particular sense which is implied by the scanty literary evidence.[1] He had 'gone away'; now he is coming back with 'nature re-awakening'. This 'coming' means very much more than an allegory on the renewal of vegetation;[2] but this 'Dionysos emerging' is not the infernal King of the Dead; nor does M. claim these vases to show him in this character. He does, however, claim just this for 'a whole series' of other monuments which, according to him, show the 'infernal Dionysos' 'gradually taking over the place of Hades'.[3] Here, to my mind, Metzger fails to carry conviction. When the most famous metope of the temple E at Selinus[4] is alleged—not by him only—to represent (not Zeus and Hera but) the infernal Dionysos and his spouse, Persephone, and when the same couple is said to be portrayed on the equally well-known relief from Chrysapha, the *probandum* is taken, against all appearance, for *probatum* (for, as previously urged,[5] there is no valid evidence for this association of Dionysos and Persephone—which in fact would mean that the god was held to have had his mother for his wife). Lokrian pinakes show Dionysos, the giver of the vine, before Persephone now a giver of fruitfulness (together, on one type, with Hades–Pluton);[6] this fact is far from making Dionysos a 'Lord of the Dead'. His (later) association with the deities of Eleusis does not imply this either; nor does his representation, together with a bearded god holding a cornucopia on a Hellenistic relief at Chalkis,[7] even if that second god were called Pluto rather than Agathos Daimon. I refrain from discussing the few remaining pieces of evidence by which Metzger aims to support his thesis;[8] they seem to me no more cogent than these.[9]

[1] The son of Demeter's daughter, from Zeus and prior to her entering the realm of Hades, could be 'chthonian' in the sense in which the word applies to Demeter; but he could not belong to the sphere of Hades; still less, be Hades.

[2] Cf. W. F. Otto, *Dionysos*, pp. 74 ff.   [3] l.l. (*a*) 314 ff.

[4] Langlotz–Hirmer, *Die Kunst der Westgriechen* (1963), Pls. 105–7.

[5] Above, p. 167, n. 5.

[6] Langlotz–Hirmer, Pl. 73; R. A. Higgins, *Greek Terracottas* (1967), Pl. 38D; cf. above, p. 167.

[7] *Bull. Corr. Hell.* lxviii–lxix (1944–5), 264, Fig. 13.

[8] For the Attic cup E 82 in the British Museum (Metzger (*a*), 318, Fig. 8), M. himself subsequently ((*c*), 26) withdrew the assertion that it shows Dionysos in the place of Hades. On the fresco in the Villa dei Misteri I find no representation of Persephone (*Proc. Br. Acad.* (1963), 177 ff.); for the Tarentine 'funeral banquet' terracottas see above, p. 167, n. 5. Two vases in the Louvre (F136 and F311) finally, which are quoted ib. (*a*), 311 as representatives of 'a whole series' showing the 'infernal couple', are ib. 300 said to represent Dionysos and Semele, or Ariadne; the latter interpretation is traditional and admissible; the former, gratuitous.

[9] The one type of monument which, to my mind, can reasonably be held to represent Dionysos as a deity of the Netherworld are the fourth-century terracotta busts from graves in Boeotia of a bearded man with, normally, a kantharos in one hand and an egg in the other (such as Louvre C87 and *Arch. Jahrb.* lxviii (1953), 61, Fig. 16). Even here, though, this interpretation meets with serious obstacles. On a Boeotian vase (G. Lullies, *Ath. Mitt.* lxv (1940), 21, Pl. 26) a person of the very same type is seen resting on a couch and feeding

Dionysos was, to many of his devotees, a giver of life after death; they expected to follow him in an eternal komos; perhaps on earth or perhaps in some other, mystic realm—but not in Hades. In religion and myth, Dionysos is not one with Hades. The evidence for a 'chthonian Dionysos' is extremely scanty; as far as it goes, it intimates the god 'coming', with his gifts, from out of the earth, as an alternative concretization of that periodic 'appearing' and 'disappearing' which is of his essence; it does not attest an infernal 'Lord of the Dead'.

No 'chthonian Dionysos', then, can be assumed to have met the bearers of the Gold Leaves in the realm of Persephone.

XII

APULIAN 'UNDERWORLD-VASES' AND THE GOLD LEAVES

(above, p. 298)

A specific similarity, or even identity, of the concepts underlying these vases and the Gold Leaves has been asserted by some scholars (A. Kuhnert—after F. Welcker—in *Arch. Jahrb.* viii (1893), 104 ff. and *Philologus*, liv (1895), 193 ff.; A. Dieterich, *Nekyia*, p. 128, and, before them, F. Lenormant, l.l. i. 410 ff.) and denied, rightly to my mind, by others (A. Milchhoefer, *Philol.* liii (1894), 386 ff.; ib. liv (1895), 750 f.; E. Rohde, *Psyche*, i. 318, n. 4). The vases represent typical figures of Attic mythology, adding to the traditional denizens and visitors of Hades (such as Tantalos, Sisyphos, and Herakles) the judges of the dead whom we know from Plato, and the Furies in the shape which Aischylos and Euripides had made canonical. Among them, Orpheus was as obvious a choice as were Herakles and Theseus, and indeed even more so—he, the singer who with his lyre moved the infernal powers. And as 'kitharode' he is depicted. His picture may, moreover, at the time, to some beholders have suggested the 'inventor of all mysteries and purifications'; even though the vases in no way characterize him as such. At any rate, his presence on these pictures suggests specific 'Orphic mysteries' no more than that of Hermes and Herakles suggests 'Hermetic' or 'Heraklean' ones; add that there is no trace of Dionysos, the main deity of Orphic theology, on any one of these vases (for it is wanton to find him in the figure of Pluton).

a huge snake from his kantharos; he cannot be Dionysos. Of the terracottas, some have not got the egg, while others lack the kantharos; some, finally, represent women not men. It therefore seems likely that these busts represent, as Lullies held, the exalted dead, rather than a 'chthonic Dionysos'. The cult of the dead, as heroes, was as outstandingly widespread in Boeotia as it was in Lakonia (for the evidence see W. Roscher, *Lexikon der . . . Mythologie*, i. 2, s.v. Heros, cols. 2458 ff., 2552, 2562 ff.). Everywhere they are represented holding a kantharos quite as often as a rhyton (ib. 2586); the acceptance, finally, of the egg as a symbol of life (on this see M. P. Nilsson, *Opuscula* i (1951), pp. 3 ff., from *Archiv f. Rel.wiss.* xi (1906)) is anything but confined to Dionysiac circles.

On the vase from Canosa in Munich (Furtwängler–Reichhold, *Griech.*
Vasenbilder, T. 10; Text i, p. 49) a man, woman, and child form a group (not
recurring on any other vase) on the left of Orpheus and below him. They
cannot be held to be initiates introduced by him, for no relation between them
and Orpheus is indicated; he stands isolated, in his singer's pose, as on most
of the vases (including the fragment from Ruvo published by M. Jatta in
Mon. Ant. xvi (1906), 517 with Pl. III), with no hint of any concern for this
group, such as he does show for Eurydike on a vase now in Leningrad (*Wiener*
Vorlegeblätter, Ser. E, T. 3, 2). It is true that no satisfactory explanation, from
mythology, of the group on the Canosa vase has so far been found and the
same holds good for some untypical figures on other vases. It may therefore be
that they represent human initiates, in contrast with the Danaides, the traditional (and by no means specifically 'Orphic') mythical representatives of the
uninitiated. Thus Polygnotos painted, on his Nekyia in Delphi (Paus. x. 28.
4 f.), a human parricide and a temple-robber among mythical persons. If this
interpretation (advocated by Welcker, Milchhoefer, and Furtwängler) is considered, the non-mythical figures on these vases would have to be taken for
initiates of the Eleusinian mysteries, for the mythology of these pictures, while
neither particularly mysterious nor specifically mystic, is popularly Attic and
Eleusinian. The same obviously cannot be maintained with regard to the texts
on the Gold Leaves. They contain no hint of the mythical figures which are
represented on the vases; the latter, on the other hand, offer no counterpart to
'Eukles, Eubouleus and the other gods' who are addressed on the Thurii
lamellae; which, moreover, allot to Persephone a prerogative which the
Apulian painters deny her. Nor, finally, do the latter depict the fountain and
the cypress tree which are so marked an element of the B-tablets; for the
gargoyle in the shape of a lion's head, on the Canosa vase only, does not—as
Lenormant, p. 416, held—represent that mystic fountain but is part of the
installations of the palaestra from which the sons of Herakles emerge.

More recently, a valuable contribution in this field has been made by K.
Schauenburg (*Arch. Jahrb.* lxxiii (1958), 48 ff.; esp. 57 ff.; instructive also by
the illustrations, e.g. p. 65, Fig. 10 showing Orpheus with Eurydike on
a Neapolitan vase). He rejects (p. 74) any relation to the Gold Leaves but
would admit a modicum of 'Orphic influence'. A comprehensive study of this
group of Apulian vases is still very much a *desideratum*. If it were undertaken on
the basis of a complete and reliable collection of the evidence, including also
those decorated with scenes from tragedy, it would probably enlighten us on
significant details of Greek religion, myth, and art—but hardly on the Gold
Leaves.

XIII

CONCERNING THE 'TREE OF LIFE'

(*above, pp. 386 ff.*)

Shortly before going to press I was at last able to read H. Danthine, *Le Palmier-*
dattier et les arbres sacrés (1937) (cf. above, p. 390, n. 1). The immense material

gathered in vol. ii and its careful discussion in i, have a bearing on the following points:

(*a*) It was asserted, above, p. 51, n. 2, that the 'potted-plant pattern' on a Maltese offering table represented a 'Tree of Life'. If so, its peculiar form must have had antecedents in the ancient Near East, and such may indeed be found on seal cylinders (Sumerian and later) illustrated by Danthine, Figs. 526–30; cf. 283, 1165 and, perhaps, 775.

(*b*) Miss Danthine, while regarding most of the various representations of the Tree of Life as developments of the date-palm, admits the composite and unrealistic character of the Assyrian standard form (as above, p. 390), and illustrates older representations (from Susa, Ur, and Akkadian ones) of 'conifères'—which have been presented as 'cypresses' above, (ib.)—by Figs. 670–3, 684 f., 690 ff.; cf. Fig. 614 (Iran) and vol. i, pp. 60–3, 67, 83, and 161. Besides, Fig. 955 presents an exception to a rule stressed above, p. 372; namely, the Egyptian 'Lady of the Sycamore' emerging—contrary to her name—from a date-palm. Miss Danthine herself stresses the rarity of this exception (vol. i, p. 176).

(*c*) Her Fig. 1125, a relief—previously unpublished—on an orthostat from Tel Halaf, appears strikingly similar to those from Castelluccio (our Pl. I) which are discussed in the first part of this book—and it is undoubtedly the highly-stylized representation of a date-palm and, therewith, a 'Tree of Life'. Consideration of the related representations pictured on Figs. 215, 218 f., 223, and 1126–32 will show that this particular coincidence argues no relation between these monuments; however similar in appearance, they are separate in origin, context, and association.

BIBLIOGRAPHY

N.B. For Empedokles see also p. 186, and for the Gold Leaves see pp. 277 f.

ANATI, E., *Camonica Valley*, 1961.
BACON, E. (ed.), *Vanished Civilisations*, 1963.
BECATTI, G., *Oreficerie antiche*, 1955.
BERNABÒ BREA, L., *Sicily before the Greeks*, 1957 (cited 'Bernabò Brea').
BLEGEN, C. W., *Troy*, i ff., 1950 ff.
—— *Troy and the Trojans*, 1963.
BLINKENBERG, C., *L'Image d'Athana Lindia*, 1917.
—— *Lindos*, i, 1931 (cited 'Blinkenberg').
BOSSERT, H. T., *Alt Kreta*, 1921.
—— *Altanatolien*, 1942.
—— *Altsyrien*, 1951.
BOYANCÉ, P., *Le Culte des Muses*, 1937.
BRAIDWOOD, R. J., *The Near East and the Foundations for Civilisation*, 1952.
BRANDON, S. G. F., *Man and his destiny*, 1962.
—— *Creation Legends*, 1963.
—— *History, Time and Deity*, 1965.
BRICE, W. C., *Inscriptions in the Minoan Linear Script of Class A*, 1961.
BRITISH MUSEUM, *Catalogue of the Terracottas*, by R. Higgins, 1954.
—— *Catalogue of the Jewellery, Greek, Etruscan and Roman*, by F. H. Marshall, 1911.
BUCHHOLZ, H.-G., *Zur Herkunft der kretischen Doppelaxt*, 1959.
BUSCHOR, E., *Alt-Samische Standbilder*, 1934 ff.
CHANTRAINE, P., *Grammaire Homérique*, i³, *Phonétique et Morphologie*, 1958; ii, *Syntaxe*, 1953.
CHILDE, V. G., *The Dawn of European Civilisation*, 4th edition, 1947.
—— *The Danube in Prehistory*, 1929.
—— *Skara Brae*, 1931.
CIACERI, E., *Culti e miti nella storia della Sicilia antica*, 1911 (cited 'Ciaceri').
—— *Storia della Magna Grecia*, 1928.
CLES-REDEN, S. VON, *The Realm of the Great Goddess*, 1961 (a bad translation of *Die Spur der Zyklopen*, 1960).
COMPARETTI, D., *Laminette orfiche*, 1910.
CRAWFORD, O. G. S., *The Eye Goddess*, 1957.
DANIEL, GLYN, *The Megalith Builders of Western Europe*, 1958.
—— *The Prehistoric Chamber Tombs of France*, 1960.
—— *see* ÓRíordáin.
DAWKINS, R. M., *The Sanctuary of Artemis Orthia* . . . , 1929.
Dawn of Civilization, The, ed. S. Piggott, 1961.
DELATTE, A., *Études sur la littérature pythagoricienne*, 1915.
DEMARGNE, P., *Aegean Art*, 1964.
DIETERICH, A., *Nekyia²*, 1913.
—— *Mutter Erde³*, 1925.
DODDS, E. R., *The Greeks and the Irrational*, 1951.
DUHN, F. VON, *Italische Gräberkunde*, i, 1924; ii (ed. F. Messerschmidt), 1939.
DUMITRESCU, V., *L'Art préhistorique en Roumanie*, 1937.
DUNBABIN, T. J., *The Western Greeks*, 1948.

ÉLIADE M., *Traité d'histoire des religions*, 1949.
EVANS, A., *The Palace of Minos*, 1921 ff.
EVANS, J. D., *Malta*, 1959 (cited 'Evans').
FARNELL, L. R., *Cults of the Greek States*, 5 vols., 1896 ff.
—— *Greek Hero Cults*, 1921.
FERRI, S., *Divinità ignote*, 1929.
FOERSTER, R., *Der Raub und die Rückkehr der Persephone*, 1874.
FRANKFORT, H., *Studies in Early Pottery of the Near East*, ii, 1927.
—— *The Art and Architecture of the Ancient Orient*, 1954.
FREEMAN, E. A., *The History of Sicily*, i, ii, 1891.
FRITZ, K. VON, *Pythagorean Politics in South Italy*, 1940.
GÀBRICI, E., *Il Santuario della Malophoros a Selinunte* (*Mon. Ant.* xxxii, 1927).
GIEDION, S., *The Eternal Present*, i, 1962; ii, 1964.
GOETZE, A., *Kleinasien*, in *Handbuch der Altertumswissenschaft*, 2. Aufl., 1950.
GRUPPE, O., *Griechische Mythologie und Religionsgeschichte*, 2 vols., 1906.
GUARDUCCI, M. (ed.), *Inscriptiones Creticae*, ii, 1937.
GUIDO, M., *Sardinia*, 1963.
GUTHRIE, W. K. C., *Orpheus and Greek Religion*[2], 1952.
HANELL, K., *Megarische Studien*, 1934.
HARDEN, D., *The Phoenicians*, 1962.
HARRISON, J., *Prolegomena to the Study of Greek Religion*[2], 1908.
HAWKES, C. F. C., *The Prehistoric Foundations of Europe*, 1940 (cited 'Hawkes').
HAWKES, J., *Prehistory*, 1963 (in *History of Mankind*, i).
HEPDING, H., *Attis*, 1903.
HIGGINS, R.A. *Greek and Roman Jewellery*, 1961 (cited 'Higgins, *Jewellery*').
—— *Greek Terracotta Figures*, 1963.
—— *Greek Terracottas*, 1967.
—— (see British Museum, *Terracottas*).
HILL, G. F., *Coins of Ancient Sicily*, 1903.
HOERNES, M., and MENGHIN, O., *Urgeschichte der bildenden Kunst in Europa*, 3. Aufl., 1925.
HOLM, A., *Geschichte Siziliens*, i–iii, 1870 ff.
HOLME, C. (ed.), *Peasant Art in Austria*, 1911 (special number of *The Studio*).
HUTCHINSON, R. W., *Prehistoric Crete* (Penguin Book), 1962.
JEFFERY, L. H., *The Local Scripts of Archaic Greece*, 1961.
JOHNSTONE, P., *Greek Island Embroidery*, 1961.
KASCHNITZ-WEINBERG, G. VON, *Die Grundlagen der antiken Kunst: i. Die mittelmeerischen Grundlagen* . . . , 1944; ii. *Die eurasischen Grundlagen* . . . , 1961.
KEKULÉ VON STRADONITZ, R., *Die Terrakotten von Sizilien*, 1884.
KERÉNYI, K., *Labyrinth-Studien*[2], 1950.
KÜHN, H., *Kunst und Kultur der Vorzeit Europas*, i, 1929.
—— *Vorgeschichtliche Kunst Deutschlands*, 1935.
LANGLOTZ, E., and HIRMER, M., *Die Kunst der Westgriechen*, 1963.
LENORMANT, F., *La Grande Grèce*, 3 vols., 1881.
LEVI, A., *Le terracotte . . . di Napoli*, 1926.
LOBECK, C. A., *Aglaophamus*, i–ii, 1829.
LORIMER, H. L., *Homer and the Monuments*, 1950.
LOUVRE, MUSÉE NAT. DU, *Catalogue . . . des figurines et reliefs*, by S. Mollard-Besques, 1954.
MACCHIORO, V., *Zagreus*, 1929.
MALLOWAN, M. E. L., *Twenty-five years of Mesopotamian Discovery*, 1956.

MALLOWAN, M. E. L., *Early Mesopotamia and Iran*, 1965.

MARCONI, P., *Agrigento*, 1929.

—— *Agrigento arcaica*, 1933.

MARSHALL, F. H. (*see* British Museum, *Jewellery*).

MATT, L. VON, and PARETI–GRIFFO, *Das antike Sizilien*, 1960(?) (cited 'von Matt').

MATT, L. VON, and U. ZANOTTI-BIANCO, *Großgriechenland*, 1961 (cited 'von Matt²').

MATZ, F., *Die Ägäis*, 1954, in *Handbuch der Archaeologie*, ii.

—— *Kreta-Mykene-Troja*, 1956.

MAYER, M., *Molfetta und Matera*, 1924.

MELLAART, J., *Earliest Civilisations of the Near East*, 1965.

METZGER, H., *Les représentations dans la céramique attique du IVe siècle*, 1951.

—— *Recherches sur l'imagerie athénienne*, 1965.

MOLLARD-BESQUES, S. (*see* Louvre, Musée Nat. du).

MONTELIUS, O., *Der Orient und Europa*, 1899.

MÜLLER, V. K., *Der Polos, die griechische Götterkrone*, 1915.

—— *Frühe Plastik in Griechenland und Vorderasien*, 1929.

MYLONAS, G. E., *Eleusis and the Eleusinian Mysteries*, 1961.

NARR, K. J. (and others), *Abriß der Vorgeschichte*, 1957.

NEUMANN, E., *The Great Mother*, 1955.

NILSSON, M. P., *Geschichte der griechischen Religion*, i², 1955; ii¹, 1950 (quoted '*G.G.R*').

—— *The Minoan-Mycenaean Religion*², 1950.

OPRESCU, G., *Peasant Art in Roumania*, 1929 (special number of *The Studio*).

ÓRÍORDÁIN, S. P., and DANIEL, G., *New Grange and the Bend of the Boyne*, 1964.

ORSI, P., *Gela* (*Mon. Ant.*, xvii, 1906).

PACE, B., *Arte e civiltà della Sicilia antica*, 4 vols., 1935 ff.

PARROT, A., *Le 'Refrigerium' dans l'au-delà*, 1937.

—— *Tello*, 1948.

—— *Sumer* (English edition), 1960.

PAYNE, H. (and others), *Perachora*, i, 1940.

PEET, T. E., *The Stone and Bronze Ages in Italy*, 1909.

PENDLEBURY, J. D. S., *The Archaeology of Crete*, 1939.

PIGGOTT, S. (ed.), *The Dawn of Civilization*, 1961.

PRELLER, L., *Demeter und Persephone*, 1837.

—— *Griechische Mythologie*, i, *Theogonie und Götter*, 4. Aufl., by C. Robert, 1894 (cited 'Preller–Robert').

PRZYLUSKI, J., *La Grande Déesse*, 1950.

QUARLES VAN UFFORD, L., *Les Terres-cuites siciliennes*, 1949.

ROHDE, E., *Psyche*², 1902; 5. and 6. Aufl., 1910 (*reprint*).

RUHL, L., *De mortuorum iudicio*, 1903.

RUMPF, A., *Die Religion der Griechen* (H. Haas, *Bilderatlas* . . . , 13/14, 1928).

SCHACHERMEYR, F., *Dimini und die Bandkeramik*, 1954.

—— *Die ältesten Kulturen Griechenlands*, 1955.

—— *Die minoische Kultur des alten Kreta*, 1964.

SCHLIEMANN, H., *Atlas Trojanischer Altertümer*, 1874.

—— *Ilios*, 1880.

SCHMIDT, H., *H. Schliemanns Sammlung Trojanischer Altertümer*, 1902.

STAUFFENBERG, A. SCHENK VON, *Trinakria*, 1963.

THIERSCH, H., *Ependytes und Ephod*, 1936 (cited 'Thiersch').

TSOUNTAS, C., *Dimini and Sesklo*, 1908 (in Greek).

UFFORD, *see* Quarles.

Vanished Civilisations, ed. E. Bacon, 1963.

Viski, C. (and others) (ed.), *L'Art populaire Hongrois*, 1928.
Wace, A. J. B., *Mediterranean and Near Eastern Embroideries*, 1935.
Wieten, J. H., *De tribus laminis aureis . . .*, 1915.
Wilamowitz-Moellendorff, U. von, *Der Glaube der Hellenen*, 2. Aufl., 1955. (I regret that, *faute de mieux*, I have to refer to this scandalously faulty reprint, published by the Wissenschaftliche Buchgesellschaft, Darmstadt, of the original edition of 1931–2).
Wilke, G., *Die Religion der Indogermanen*, 1923.
Winter, F., *Die Typen der figürlichen Terrakotten*, 1903.
—— (and others), *Kunstgeschichte in Bildern, Neue Bearbeitung;* i. *Das Altertum*, n.d.
Wölfel, D. J., *Die Religionen des vorindogermanischen Europa*, in *Christus und die Religionen der Erde*, i, 1951.
Yavis, C. G., *Greek Altars*, 1949.
Zammit, T., *Prehistoric Malta*, 1930.

(*Note: Eranos-Jahrbuch*, 1938: *Vorträge über Gestalt und Kult der 'Großen Mutter'*, 1939. Contributions not originally German to this volume are given in 'translations', which have made it impossible for me to grasp the meaning intended by their distinguished authors.)

Articles in periodicals have not been listed in this bibliography, even though some of them are of greater importance to the argument of this essay than many books. In the following, some of the most outstanding are gratefully recorded:

Adamasteanu, D., and Orlandini, P., 'Gela', *Not. Scav.* lxxxi (1956), 203 ff.
Ashby, T., Bradley, R. N., and others, 'Excavations in 1908–11 in the various Megalithic Buildings in Malta and Gozo', *BSR*, vi (1913), 1 ff.
Dumitrescu, V., 'Les statuettes de l'âge du bronze découvertes dans la nécropole de Cîrna (Roumanie)', *Ipek*, xix (1954–9), 16 ff.
Kahn, C. H., 'Religion and Natural Philosophy in Empedocles' Doctrine of the Soul', *Archiv für Geschichte der Philosophie*, xlii (1960), 3 ff.
Mallowan, M. E. L., 'Tell Brak', *Iraq*, ix (1947).
Mellaart, J., 'Excavations at Çatal Hüyük, First Preliminary Report, 1961', *Anatolian Studies*, xii (1962), 41 ff.
—— 'Excavations at Çatal Hüyük, 1962, Second Preliminary Report', ibid., xiii (1963), 43 ff.
—— 'Excavations at Çatal Hüyük, 1963, Third Preliminary Report', ibid., xiv (1964), 39 ff.
Orlandini, P., 'Gela: la stipe votiva arcaica del predio Sola', *Mon. Ant.* xlvi (1963), 1 ff.
Orsi, P., 'Locri Epizefiri, Resoconto sulla terza campagna di scavi locresi', *Boll. d'arte*, 1908 (1909), 406 ff. and 463 ff..
—— 'Locri Epizephyrii', *Not. Scav.*, 1913 suppl. (1914), 3 ff.
—— 'Daedalica Siciliae', *Monuments Piot*, xxii (1916), 131 ff.
Otto, W. F., 'Der Sinn der eleusinischen Mysterien', *Eranos-Jahrbuch* (1939), 88 ff. (repr. in *Die Gestalt und das Sein* (1969), pp. 313 ff.).
Quagliati, Q., 'Rilievi votivi arcaici in terracotta di Lokroi Epizephyrioi', *Ausonia*, iii (1908), 136 ff.
Zammit, T., and Singer, T., 'Neolithic Representations of the Human Form', *Journal of the Royal Anthropological Institute*, liv (1924), 67 ff.

SELECT INDEX OF PASSAGES QUOTED

INDEX OF GREEK WORDS

ἀγνός, 307 n. 5, 317 n. 1
αἰδοῖος, 188
ἀλύω, 229
ἀϲτεροβλῆτα, 314 f.
ἀϲτεροπῆτα, 314 f.
ἀϲτραπή- ἀϲτήρ, 315

βαϲίλεια, 308 n. 6

γεύομαι, 231

δαίμων, 270 f., 312
δειλός, 230 n. 3
δύϲζηλος, 193
δυϲηχής, 219 n. 7

ἐμπεδόκαρπος, 210
ἐμπεδόφυλλος, 210
ἐνδέξια, 369
ἔοικα, 189 f.
ἐπιβαίνω, 219 n. 1
εὐαγής, 317 n. 3
ἐφήμερος, (-ιος), 212

θύϲανοι, 134 n. 1, 139 n. 1
θύω (ῡ), 223 n. 1

καθαρός, 306 ff., 317
κακότης, 188, 229 f.
κόλπος, 219
κύκλος, 320 ff.

λειμών, 253 f., 332
λευκός, 385 n. 1, 391

μᾶλον/μῆλον, 100
μειλίχιος, 101 n. 8
μελάγκο(υ)ρος, 217 n. 1
μίτρα, 134
μύριοι, 197 n. 3

νήκουϲτος, 220
νηϲτεύω, 231

ξανθός, 186

ὁμαρτέω, 195
ὅϲιος, 307 n. 5, 317

πεπαρμένος, 192 n. 2
πίϲτις, 193
πραπίδες, 208 n. 5
πρόϲλημμα, 134
προϲτηθίδια, 139 n. 1
πρόφρων, 317 n. 2
πρωτόγονος, 349

τορός, 225 f.

φυλάϲϲω, 330
φύομαι, 197 n. 5, 206

χαλεπός, 229 f.
χθών, 153, 400, 410 n. 1

ψυχή, 227 n. 2, 270 n. 5

ὥρα, ὧρος, 196 f.

GENERAL INDEX

ACCOUNT AND ACKNOWLEDGMENT

THIS book would not have been written but for help and inspiration from many quarters, for which I wish here to express my gratitude. Like other writings of mine, it originated in my seminar. Theological colleagues suggested, for the two years 1958–60, a study of the Greek texts basic to what is commonly called 'Early Orphism', and I want to thank them, and particularly Professor S. G. F. Brandon, for their stimulating collaboration. The literary upshot was a detailed commentary on Empedokles' *Katharmoi* and a sketch of one on the 'Gold Leaves'. Thereafter this study had to be laid aside for two years, so as to gain time for the completion of a book on the transmission of the plays of Euripides; besides I felt that I could not carry on without having seen the lands where these texts had originated. This long-cherished desire was fulfilled, early in 1963, thanks to the generosity of the University of Manchester and of the British Academy. On my Sicilian journey I met with the most helpful and kind reception, in particular, by the soprintendenti alle antichità at Naples, Reggio, Siracusa, Agrigento, Palermo, and Trapani (their names are household words among scholars). At Naples I was able to examine the Gold Leaves from Thurii, letter by letter, with the help of a special lens kindly lent by our Department of Metallurgy. I also elaborated a plan to seek, at Thurii, for further evidence which might elucidate the remaining difficult questions posed by these unique relics. This plan met with friendly encouragement by the local authorities and also by the venerable U. Zanotti-Bianco; but when all was set for its realization, it was finally foiled by the refusal of a permit by the central authorities.

For one whose opportunity for serious writing was practically confined to the months of the summer vacations, it would have been difficult, or even impossible, to elaborate the results of this journey within a reasonable time. An invitation, at this juncture, to the Institute for Advanced Studies was a godsend. I spent the winter 1963–4 in its stimulating atmosphere, benefiting from the company and advice of many scholars, among whom I may mention, with particular gratitude, A. Alföldi, G. Becatti, H. Cherniss, U. Holmberg, E. Sjøquist, Homer A. Thompson, and Dorothy Burr-Thompson. At Princeton, the chapter on Empedokles was revised and the 'Goddess of Sicily' drafted. During this work the need to see the prehistoric remains in Malta became imperative. It was satisfied with the help of the same authorities that had helped me in 1963. I visited Malta at Easter 1965. The helpfulness of the authorities there was beyond praise. Thus I was enabled, during the same year, to complete the first, prehistorical section. In 1966, that haven of classical studies, the Fondation Hardt, gave me the opportunity to elaborate the commentary on the Gold Leaves in the serene atmosphere of Kurt Hardt's foundation at Vandœuvres. The following year saw the completion of Book One (Professor Donald White, of the University of Michigan, read it in manuscript and gave me valuable suggestions and criticism). Much of the summer 1968, finally, went in revising and polishing the completed manuscript until, at the end of July, it was sent to the Press.

This gradual growth may account for some of the imperfections of the present book. It means, among other things, that many publications which were not available at the time of writing, like the second volume of W. K. C. Guthrie's monumental *History of Greek Philosophy*, are not referred to (readers, no doubt, will anyhow compare his results with mine). This shortcoming will be most notable in my first part. In the field of prehistoric archaeology, progress is so rapid, and changes even of basic assumptions so unpredictable, that the attempt at working-in the results of subsequent investigations (which in some other sections I did make) would have been futile. Besides, I must here express my thanks to our libraries at Manchester which made every effort to supply my needs, but I have to add that nobody will be able to appreciate the remaining difficulties who is himself privileged to work within reach of well-stocked and specialized institutes. Such readers will be slow to believe that, for example, the chapter on the Sicilian terracottas had to be completed without a possibility of reference to the basic *corpora* by Kekulé and Winter.

Professor E. R. Dodds read the whole book in manuscript and favoured me with a long series of observations. He thereby saved me from many slips small and great, provided me with additional evidence on some points, and induced me to specify or reformulate others. I cannot thank him enough for his help.

The printing—difficult in places—has been carried out with those resources of expertise and goodwill for which the O.U.P. is famous. I have been told that it is not the convention to thank members of the Press by name; but I must break this convention in, at least, two instances, to thank Mr. B. G. Gosling for the care he devoted to the illustrations, and Mr. J. K. Cordy who, time and again, settled intricate problems with infinite patience and wisdom. The task of proof-reading finally was lightened, and its efficiency doubled, by the kind assistance of Herr and Frau Dr. H. Cancik, Tübingen.

My thanks go to these and all helpers, named and unnamed. A particular debt of gratitude is owed to the authors of the books listed in the *Bibliography*—and also to many not listed, though known to every student, because their works were not to hand at the time of writing. I am thinking of F. Cumont and W. Jaeger, O. Gigon, Isidore Lévy, I. M. Linforth, and many others, whose writings have become basic to every endeavour in the field of Greek religion and philosophy. Not listed are, besides, some books which I did read but found unhelpful, as well as some others which, for dietetic reasons, I refrained from reading. In conclusion, here is my thanks and praise for the classical works of E. A. Freeman and A. Holm, which nurtured my old love of Sicily.

*

GUARDAVI IL CIEL E INTORNO VI SI GIRA
MOSTRANDOVI LE SUE BELLEZZE ETERNE
E L'OCCHIO VESTRO PUO A TERRA MIRA
ONDE VI BATTE CHI TUTTO DISCERNE

*

PLATES

For List of Plates see above, p. xi.

PLATE 1

Castelluccio, Slabs 1 and 2 (p. 3)

PLATE 2

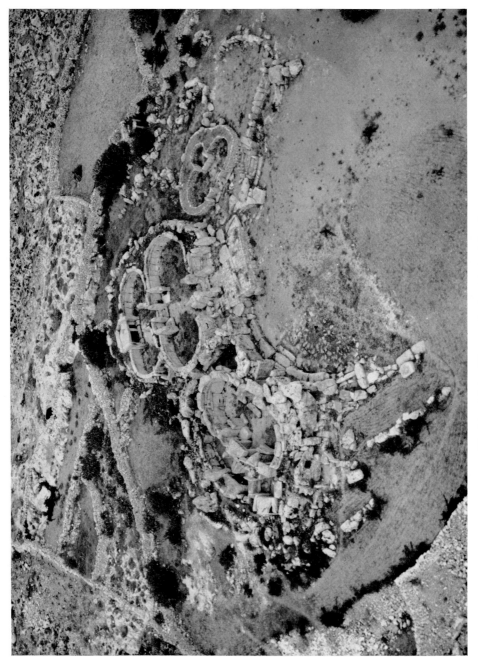

Mnajdra, Malta: The temples (aerial view) (p. 5)

PLATE 3

c. The 'worshipper' from Tello, Sumer (p. 12)

b. The 'shaven priest' from Tel Asmar, Sumer (p. 12)

a. Statuette of priest from Tarxien, Malta. Height originally *ca.* 24 in. (p. 11)

PLATE 4

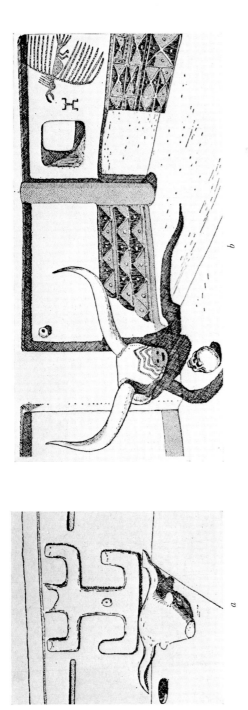

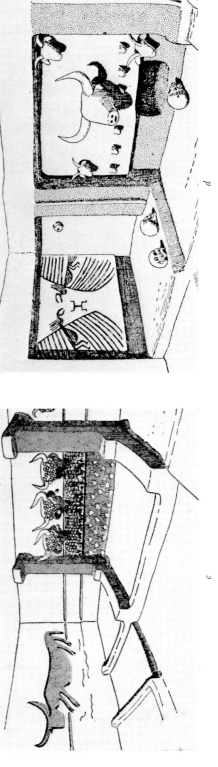

Çatal Hüyük, Shrines VI. B8 (*a* and *c*) and VII. 21 (*b* and *d*) (p. 14)

PLATE 5

b. Slab inside (p. 43)

a. Slab at the entrance (p. 27)

Tarxien: Middle temple

PLATE 6

a. Sesklo Kurotrophos (p. 29) *b.* The 'Goddess of Philippopel' (p. 29)

c. New Grange, Kerbstone 'b' (p. 29)

PLATE 7

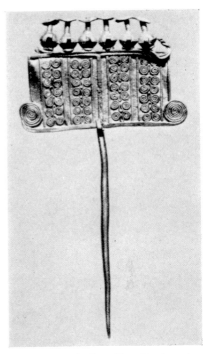

b. Golden pin from Troy ii g (p. 32)

a. Statuette of Syrian goddess with spiral
décor (Louvre). (p. 32)

c. Face-urn from Troy ii (p. 32)

PLATE 8

Cîrna, Figs. 2 and 10 (Dumitrescu, Ipek XIX) (pp. 33 ff.)

b

a

PLATE 9

b

a

Cîrna, Figs. 1 and 5 (Dumitrescu, Ipek XIX) (pp. 33 ff.)

PLATE 10

b

a

Hallstadt funerary vases from (*a*) Gemeinlebarn and (*b*) Langenlebarn nr. Vienna (p. 39)

PLATE 11

a. 18th century dowry chest, Upper Austria (p. 40)

b. Dowry chest, Carinthia (p. 40)

PLATE 12

Statuettes from Haġar Qim and Hal Saflieni, Malta (pp. 49 ff.)

PLATE 13

a. Spirals on the ceiling of the 'Hypogeum' of Hal Saflieni (p. 47)

b

c

d

e

f

b–f. Spirals on pottery from Butmir (p. 57)

PLATE 14

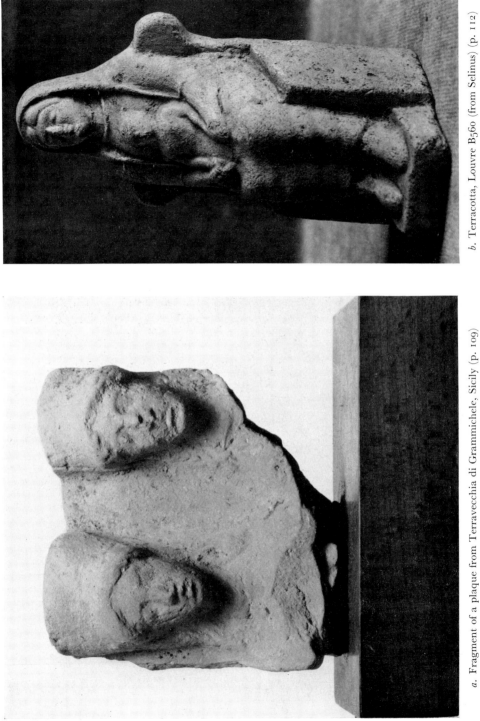

b. Terracotta, Louvre B560 (from Selinus) (p. 112)

a. Fragment of a plaque from Terravecchia di Grammichele, Sicily (p. 109)

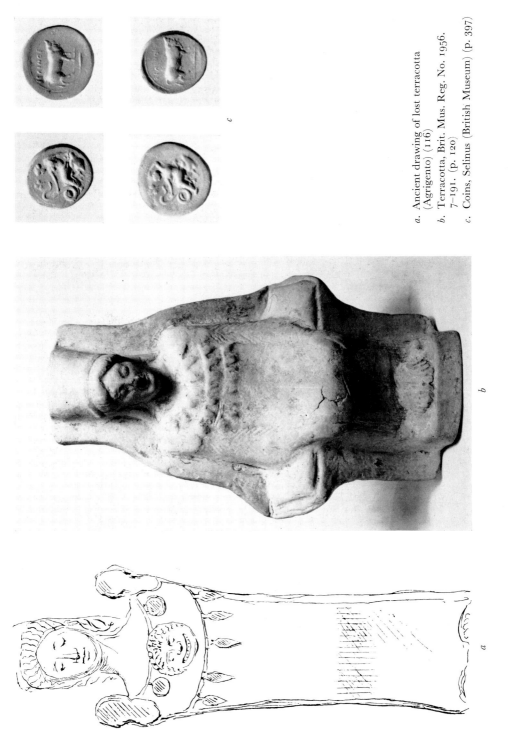

PLATE 15

a. Ancient drawing of lost terracotta (Agrigento) (116)

b. Terracotta, Brit. Mus. Reg. No. 1956. 7–191. (p. 120)

c. Coins, Selinus (British Museum) (p. 397)

PLATE 16

PLATE 17

JUPITER HELIOPOLITAIN
DIT -BRONZE SUR SOCK...
II^ IIP S AP. J.C.
Aq 700
AO 19 534

b. Jupiter Dolichenus (Paris, Louvre) (p. 128)

a. Aphrodite of Aphrodisias, from Ephesus (Vienna) (p. 128)

PLATE 18

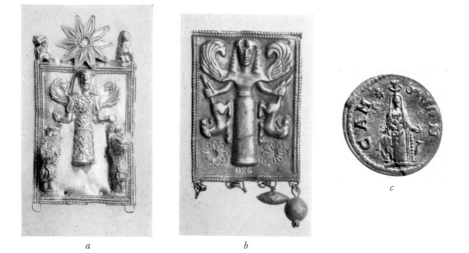

a   *b*   *c*

d

a and *b*. Gold plaques from Samos (pp. 133 f.) *c*. Coin, Samos (p. 132) *d*. 'Zeus Stratios'
(British Museum) (p. 140)

PLATE 19

'Maschere' from Predio Sola (*a* and *b*) and Bitalemi (*c*), Gela (pp. 144 f.)

PLATE 20

a

b

c

'Maschere' from Bitalemi, Gela (pp. 148 f.)

PLATE 21

a and *b*. 'Maschere' from the Gaggera, Selinus (p. 148). *c*. Terracotta from the Gaggera. *d*. Terracotta from Monte Bubbonia (both p. 151)

PLATE 22

a. The double-bust from Agrigento (p. 154)

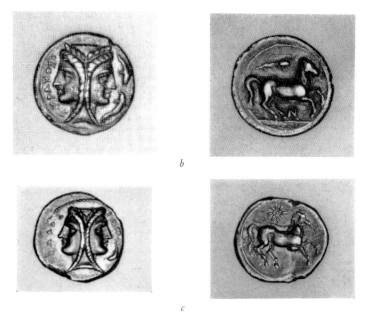

b

c

b and *c.* Coins of Timoleon (British Museum) (p. 154)

PLATE 23

a. 'Maschera' from La Mannella, Lokri (p. 161). *b* and *c*. Fragments of two Aphrodite statuettes from
Medma (p. 163)

PLATE 24

c. Persephone from Megara Hyblaia (p. 177)

b. Persephone from Kamarina (p. 175)

a. Nude figurine from Ruvo di Puglia (p. 169)

PLATE 25

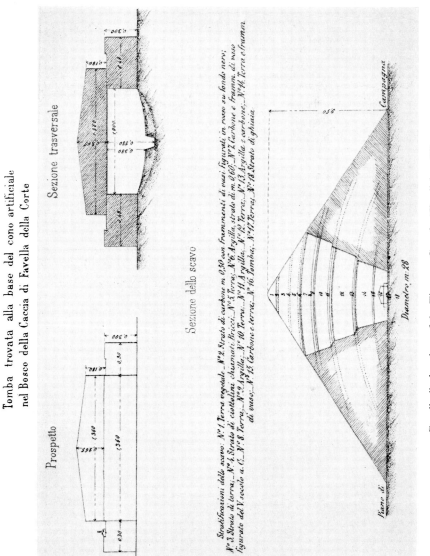

Tomba trovata alla base del cono artificiale
nel Bosco della Caccia di Favella della Corte

Sezione trasversale

Prospetto

Sezione dello scavo

Stratificazioni dello scavo:_ N.° 1. Terra vegetale._ N.° 2. Strato di carbone m. 0,50 con frammenti di vasi figurati in rosso su fondo nero;
N.° 3. Strato di terra._ N.° 4. Strato di ciotolini; chiamati bricci._ N.° 5. Terra; N.° 6. Argilla, strato di m. 0,02._ N.° 7. Carbone e fram.a di vaso
figurato del V secolo a. C._ N.° 8. Terra._ N.° 9. Argilla._ N.° 10. Terra._ N.° 11. Argilla._ N.° 12. Terra._ N.° 13. Argilla e carbone._ N.° 14. Terra e fram.n.
di vasi._ N.° 15. Carbone e terra._ N.° 16. Tomba._ N.° 17. Terra._ N.° 18. Strato di ghiaia.

Diametro m. 28

Campagna

Piano di

Cavallari's drawings of the Timpone Grande, Thurii (p. 288)

PLATE 26

a. Gold Leaf A1 (Napoli). 51 × 36 mm (p. 300)

b. Gold Leaf A2 (Napoli). 47 × 28 mm (p. 302)

PLATE 27

a. Gold Leaf A3, verso (Napoli). 46 × 25 mm (p. 304)

b. Gold Leaf A4 (Napoli). 54 × 29 mm (p. 328)

PLATE 28

a. Gold Leaf A5 (British Museum). 65 × 24 mm (p. 333)

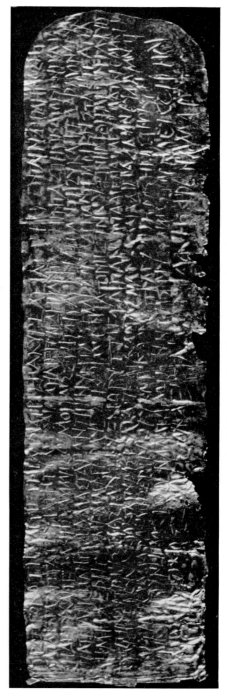

b. Gold Leaf C (Napoli). 81 × 23 mm (p. 346)

PLATE 29

Gold Leaf B1 (British Museum). 45 × 27 mm (p. 358)

PLATE 30

Bronze model of a sanctuary. From Susa. (Louvre) (p. 391)